The Crimson Letter

ALSO BY DOUGLASS SHAND-TUCCI

The Gothic Churches of Dorchester

The Second Settlement

Church Building in Boston

Ralph Adams Cram: American Medievalist

An Eliot House Miscellany

Ashmont: An Architectural Tour

Built in Boston: City and Suburb, 1800–2000

Boston Bohemia: Life and Architecture: Ralph Adams Cram

The Art of Scandal: The Life and Times of Isabella Stewart Gardner

Harvard University: An Architectural Tour

The Passions of Copley Square (forthcoming)

Gothic Modernist: Life and Architecture: Ralph Adams Cram, II (forthcoming)

THE
CRIMSON
LETTER

Harvard, Homosexuality, and
the Shaping of American Culture

DOUGLASS
SHAND-TUCCI

ST. MARTIN'S PRESS ❧ NEW YORK

Library of Congress Cataloging-in-Publication Data
Shand-Tucci, Douglass
    The crimson letter : Harvard, homosexuality, and the shaping of American culture /
Douglass Shand-Tucci.
        p. cm.
    Includes index (p. 391).
    ISBN 0-312-19896-5
    1. Gays—United States. 2. Gays—Education (Higher)—United States. 3. Harvard
University—Alumni and alumnae. 4. Harvard University—Faculty. 5. Homosexuality and
education—United States. 6. Gay college students—United States. 7. Gay college
teachers—United States. 8. United States—Civilization—20th century. 9. United
States—Intellectual life. I. Title.
HQ76.3.U5 S49 2003
305.9'0664'0973—dc21

                                                                            2002036751

First Edition: May 2003

10   9   8   7   6   5   4   3   2   1

To one only will I tell it.

Thrice happy and more are
they whom an unbroken bond
unites and whom no sundering
of love by wretched quarrels
shall separate before life's dying day.
                    —*Horace,* ODES: I, 13

The confusion that there are two teams—one
good, straight; one bad, gay—is not helped
by reversing the adjectives. . . . There is only
one team, the human, and the rest is politics.
                    —*Gore Vidal*

Contents

The Crimson Letter

Prologue

HARVARD YARD, 4 September 1960: the old halls were dark, the night
quiet enough. But that night, as Lord Byron might have said, the storms
were in men's souls.

Fall Term had not yet begun. Even Harvard Square appeared to move at
a slower pace; the surrounding professorial streets of the Old Cambridge
neighborhood seemed almost asleep. In fact, under this serene surface, all
Hell was breaking loose. Not just telephone lines were humming. "Safe
houses" (safe houses, for god's sake!) would soon be in operation, something
like the Underground Railway that had run through these old buildings in
the days of slavery, and a cloak-and-dagger scenario altogether more fitting
to Berlin than to Boston began to unfold. First *The Boston Globe*, then *The
New York Times*, had reported the arrest in the town of Northampton, Massachusetts, of two professors at Smith College, Newton Arvin and Edward
Spofford, on charges of possession and trafficking in homosexual pornography. A wider ring of "perverts," highly placed in academic circles and
dangerous, was hinted at; *The Boston Globe*, ever attentive to all things Harvardian, the *Times* hardly less so, was developing the story. It developed
quickly.

Soon it was reported that a third member of Smith's faculty, Joel Dorius,
would be charged. In Provincetown, the Boston area's legendary gay play-
ground, where he had gone for the weekend, Dorius had seen the *Globe* and
was frantically trying to get on the air shuttle back to town and thence back
to Northampton, only too aware of the contents of his own closets.

Dorius's close friend Roy Fisher was also alarmed. He too had seen the
Globe story that Sunday morning, in his case on one of those leafy, quiet
streets of Old Cambridge. Fisher, who was finishing his Ph.D. at Harvard
(Dorius was also a Harvard graduate), was rooming that summer with Harvard professor Arthur M. Schlesinger Jr. Barry Werth, Arvin's biographer,
takes up the tale:

> Fisher knew about Dorius's pictures and that he was in Provincetown.
> After reading the story in the *Globe*, Fisher sped by car to Northamp-
> ton . . . but he was too late. He found Dorius's apartment ransacked. . . .

1

Schlesinger gave him the name of a lawyer, William P. Homans, Jr., a tenth-generation Massachusetts Yankee and Harvard Law School graduate. . . . Homans . . . agreed to take the case; he told Fisher to try to keep Dorius from returning to Northampton. . . .

Fisher knew Dorius had flown to Provincetown and planned to return through Boston's Logan Airport. He consulted the plane schedule . . . and drove to the airport access road. . . .

It was already dark, in heavy traffic, when Fisher spotted the dim headlights of Dorius's Volkswagen and flagged him down. At the side of the road, Fisher explained Homans's instructions. Dorius was dazed, unbelieving. . . . Dutifully, Dorius followed Fisher to a leafy street with big houses near Cambridge Common, where a sympathetic family named Sprague agreed to hide him until Homans's return.

There, in sight of Harvard Yard, which overlooks Cambridge Common, Dorius waited. Meanwhile, back at Smith the growing scandal threatened also to engulf America's preeminent architectural historian, Henry-Russell Hitchcock, another Harvard luminary. Hitchcock, in Werth's words, was "a high-toned WASP with Rabelaisian appetites . . . [who] openly entertained a large circle of young homosexual faculty members from area colleges who idolized him." Traveling in Europe that summer as he always did, Hitchcock, whose house turned out to be a time bomb filled with letters and photographs, was not there to defend himself. Instead, when the police telephoned seeking Hitchcock, they got a friend who was house-sitting and—fearing a raid—the friend began a desperate search through the house. As it turned out, Hitchcock's papers included explicitly homosexual correspondence from the noted American composer and *New York Herald-Tribune* music critic Virgil Thomson, and might just as easily have contained similar letters from Hitchcock's other close friends, architect Philip Johnson and Lincoln Kirstein, founder of the New York City Ballet. There was also copious erotica. The house sitter filled a laundry bag with it, Werth reports, and forthwith drove twenty miles into dense forest; there he "dumped the magazines into the Westfield River, making sure not to be seen. . . . [The letters] he took into an open field and burned."

Back in sight of Harvard Yard, Dorius still waited, alarmed by one report after another, nearly all of which dwelt on the devastating news at the heart of the scandal, that one of the two original suspects, Arvin, had implicated others. The Mary Augusta Jordan Professor at Smith, a preeminent literary critic admired by Edmund Wilson and Lillian Hellman, and the mentor (and onetime lover) of Truman Capote, Arvin had won the National Book Award in 1951 for a biography of Herman Melville. The other suspect arrested, Spofford, just due to start his graduate studies at Harvard, was Arvin's dearest friend, possibly his lover.

Dorius, Fisher, Schlesinger, Homans, Hitchcock, Kirstein, Johnson, Thomson, Arvin, Spofford—gay or straight, this field or that—wherever you look in Werth's cast of players in his biography of Arvin, *The Scarlet Professor*, the players in this stunning homosexual scandal, which included figures of more than a little importance in American culture and intellectual life, were all Harvard men.

ANOTHER LINE OF sight, another vector, a little later, more personal—in fact, my own—into the subject of this book: my old Harvard mentor, John. That's not his real name, though I've chosen a false name that rhymes with it. He's dead now, still closeted. But in my own undergraduate years between 1968 and 1972 he was my best mentor. A very senior administrator—at varying times dean of this and director of that (we're talking whole schools here, not committees or institutes)—John was also the master of one of Harvard's famous residential colleges, or Houses, when there were only ten, and he was a Korean war veteran who, if gossip is to be credited, was also a long-standing CIA recruiter at Harvard.

I never guessed he was homosexual; never was looking for it, I guess. I never saw past the second wife or the son by the first. Years later, when he told me he was gay, I also learned why he remained so closeted. He was afraid, even in retirement, that if he came out he'd never be allowed to see his grandchildren again. He told the truth to only a very few, he said, and as I knew how much his grandkids meant to him, I eventually stopped arguing with him about it and tacitly joined in the conspiracy—always the easy way out and a mistake. I could not (thus compromised) complain when I was shut up on the subject after his death. Invited to speak at his memorial service, I was uninvited when I refused to perpetuate the lie—in history, for God's sake, and under the auspices of those two august institutions, the family and the university, both of which I believe in, yet so often liars both.

I thought of all this recently, fingering yet again David Leavitt's *The Lost Language of Cranes* (1986), which John gave me many years after my graduation. Under his inscription of 1993 is one of my own:

> [John] gave me this after lunch at the Faculty Club. My old [mentor] is, in fact, gay! So, too, his eldest son. Asking about it, he [gave me] this book, of which I had heard but not read. We walked back to Hawthorne Street via a wonderful secret path behind the Loeb I never knew of. Shangri-La!

I remember the path so well. I walk it still: so circuitous, so hidden, so beautiful—and in a sense, I suppose, somewhat dangerous. It was a fitting metaphor for John in his Harvard, for me in mine, and, as it turned out, for the Harvard of my best friend (and great love, too; tell anyone you like, he used to say, but not me—please) who was yet a third generation thus situated. Call him Will. Leafing through the book on the subway after that lunch with John, I highlighted a passage apt enough to all of us:

> At Philip's graduation, he stood with Rose and watched as his son, full-grown and handsome now, took his diploma and with what seemed to Owen uncharacteristic exuberance threw an overblown, Eva-Peron style kiss to the world at large. He hoped that someday Philip would recognize how he had loved him—quietly, and from a distance—and appreciate all the unspoken ways in which his father, from behind the scenes and without ever making overt claims, had watched and sympathized and protected him, and perhaps made his life better. But the love of a silent father, he knew from experience, was hard to appreciate, even for the most empathetic son. The truth was, he was afraid that if he got too close to his son, things might rub off on Philip—things he preferred not to name. Thus the distance between them grew rather than shrank, as Philip got older, until sitting across from each other at breakfast, Owen reading the paper, Philip whispering French verbs to himself in preparation for an exam, it was as if the white kitchen table were an Arctic tundra stretching between them, vast and insurmountable. There was no tension, no suppressed anxiety; there was just miles and miles of nothing. And that was as it should be. For if they had been closer, then, if Philip ever found out the truth about Owen, he'd have interpreted his father's affection as something sick, something perverse. But if there was no overt affection,—if he stayed at a distance—well—, then what could Philip accuse him of? Only of staying at a distance. And there was nothing ignoble in that.

I know better, learned better. A silent father, a silent friend, is something I know something about, too. Silence. Silencing. I got no closer to my father than the Harvard Club he was a member of so many years before me; he and my mother separated when I was seven; divorced when I was nine. And like so many gays, though it was my mother I thankfully depended on, I fantasized often about my father's sexuality (am doing so as I write this) and all the more for his absence. Which was, of course, an important aspect of what John was all about to me as an undergraduate: a superb father figure, as later Will, the other Harvard man, would prove a superb friend or younger brother (or even son) figure. I can see John now, in his big armchair in the bay window of his office, a student facing him across the coffee table, the student usually talking, John most often listening, his hand cupped over his pipe, seeming always to be looking pensively into some middle distance, where often I wondered what he was looking for, and whether or not there might be something to be found there for a young man like me. Surely John had his issues with his own son—what father and son haven't—and he probably had felt more than once the discomfort of the father in the book he'd given me. Talk about risks. The ancient taboo brought up to me by my own best friend (so much younger, Will, and we as much father and son as brothers, friends, soulmates, not lovers, though we love). Incest. Dread the word; the feeling that my own friend said too close intimacy with me aroused. John ran all those risks. And not just with his son. That he did so well—CIA recruiter or no, gays must make good spies—says so much about him. And about the Harvard for which ultimately he ran those risks: his Harvard—by no means everyone's, Harvard College, the oldest Harvard, the one each generation, gay or straight, has to fight for anew amid the ever-growing university, so magnificent but so forgetful of its collegiate roots.

Nor did it end with John's own work. He appointed as his Allston Burr Senior Tutor, or the dean of his college, another homosexual (I did know he was gay; he was my generation, and he also loved an undergraduate, even lived with him), a dean who survived John to become himself a great legend at Harvard. Indeed, both he and John, I can see now, were two keepers of the flame, in my generation at Harvard, of a long and venerable tradition reaching back through John's own Harvard mentors to legendary deans—gay or straight, it's hard to say now—enshrined in Harvard's history.

TWO VECTORS. TWO of many. A third, more general, is well put by Martin Smith, the Australian writer on spiritual life and the onetime superior of the Cowley Monastery in Old Cambridge, which has ministered to Harvardians for so many generations. Telling the truth—"coming out" from whatever closet (we all have them)—while beneficial to both teller and listener, is most beneficial, Smith declares, to the teller, the point being that it is hardly ever a matter of imparting or receiving information—already known or suspected—but, rather, of trying "to bring the truth out of our hearts," to extract the facts from "the safe realm of the unspoken and deal with them in the open." It is supremely good for the soul, Smith insists, "to stop trying to deal with the oppressor, as it were, as when gay students home from Harvard for the holidays, to cite an example, are told they are," in Smith's words about this scene generally, "welcome at [their] parents' home, even with their companions, only on the condition that complete silence is maintained on the subject of homosexuality." Only then, Smith concludes, does one begin to realize that "what goes unsaid has enormous power. An iceberg moves not because the wind blows upon its surface, but because its vast bulk hidden beneath the water is moved by the currents of the depths."

Charting those currents, difficult to locate and sometimes thankless to detect, powerful as they are, because they are so deeply hidden, is for me the most worthy task of any historian alert to his calling.

*　　　*　　　*

FINALLY, THE CHILD sexual-abuse scandal that erupted so explosively in the Boston Roman Catholic Archdiocese, of which Harvard is a part, has subsequently raised our national consciousness of this matter so forcefully that it will have an impact on certain parts of this book.

In the first place, a key misunderstanding is bound to arise, one that is well cleared up by the Ernst Freund Distinguished Service Professor of Law and Ethics at the University of Chicago, Martha Nussbaum. Also an authority on ancient Greece, Nussbaum writes of a "verbal confusion":

> Scholars have often used the word "paederasty" to describe the Greek relationship, but those who do that are usually British, and British usage of that term makes a strong distinction between paederasty and paedophilia. The former doesn't mean a relationship with a young child but rather with a young man of roughly university undergraduate age.... Young men who were just on their military training and were about to take their place as full adult citizens.... Very often, the two partners are rather similar in age.... You might be, let's say if you're 18, the erastês of a 17-year-old and at the same time the eromenos of a 25-year-old. But the idea that it's a 50-year-old who's hanging around the gym waiting to pick up a 12-year-old, that's not the case.

However, in *The Crimson Letter*, more than one fifty-year-old will be found to be involved with more than one fourteen-year-old, if not twelve-year-old, at least initially. And that's not pederasty; if acted upon physically, that's pedophilia.

I will treat pederasty with the respect it deserves, at least insofar as that ancient institution has survived in some form in once all-male institutions. It is important to pay attention to historical context. In modern times not the least change in the traditional brotherhood is that the age spread in this kind of same-sex relationship—as between undergraduates and graduate students and both with professors—has widened somewhat. Moreover, women's higher education has resulted in a new parallel kind of same-sex relationship, a sisterhood that is a kind of "women's pederasty" which, like the male original, may or may not be physically as well as intellectually and emotionally intimate. At the same time, coeducation has for both men and women added a mixed-sex variant to the same-sex original that raises its own issues, now usually grouped under the heading of "sexual harassment." In whatever form, pederasty thrives in academe still.

As may it always. As Christina Nehring wrote so persuasively in "The Higher Yearning" in the September 2001 *Harper's*, it is "the best students who fall in love with teachers; the most engaged teachers [who] respond strongly"—Socrates and Alcibiades (and Agathon, with whom Socrates was sleeping while Alcibiades courted him) come to mind—and "the university campus on which the erotic impulse between teachers and students is criminalized is the campus on which the pedagogical enterprise is deflated. It is the campus on which pedagogy is gutted and gored."

However, while pederasty is dealt with here in a manner only the terminally narrow-minded could find offensive, pedophilia is another thing entirely. Defined as it has generally been in the West as a pattern of sexual abuse of prepubescent children, pedophilia remains as baffling to psychologists as it is horrific to society generally; though it is also the case that despite its much ballyhooed focus on family and children, American society has in years past profited from child labor and today is more and more fixated on children's sexuality, as suggested by the increasing erotization of children's advertising. (Equally puzzling, research on pedophilia has not been as extensive as the importance of the subject would suggest, society being at once more squeamish and sensationalistic than it is truly reformist.)

Statistically, homosexuals are much less of a danger to our children than heterosexuals, probably reflecting the small percentage of gays in the general population. But to the extent that sexual perverts of all kinds are not thought of as being in their own special category—neither heterosexual nor homosexual nor bisexual—the gay community has always had its share of such predators and must bear its share of the opprobrium attached to such behavior. So, too, must Harvard—as will become clear in this book, which has some sordid pages. However, I will not run away from such material. I have never been, nor do I intend to become, the sort of historian who tries to sweep dirt under the rug, all the more so in connection with an institution I esteem. Nor would I be drawn to write about any institution that could not withstand truth-telling; enough for me that Harvard's gay experience has helped to shape the national culture in ways mostly very healthy and fructifying.

P. D. S-T.

March 2002
Hotel Vendôme—Boston Athenaeum,
Boston Public Library—Cafe Iruña

WARRIOR AND AESTHETE

Charting the Continuum

1.

The Warrior Archetype: Walt Whitman's Harvard

You want to be brothers-in-arms, to have him to yourself ... to be ship-wrecked together, [to] perform valiant deeds to earn his admiration, to save him from certain death, to die for him—to die in his arms, like a Spartan, kissed once on the lips.

—Tom Stoppard,
THE INVENTION OF LOVE

ARTS AND SCIENCES, the age-old academic way of seeing the world. Compare and contrast, the examiner's perennial question. The artistic personality and the scientific? It is a good typology for the cast of characters in any play about Harvard, and thus for Harvard's gay experience I propose somewhat of a variant: the archetype, on the one hand, of the warrior (this chapter) and, on the other, of the aesthete (next chapter)—each an actual, indeed personal, presence in Harvard Yard in historical time, each a key vector, as scholars of Proust might put it, in psychological time ever since (and even in the very different Yard of today). Behold, then, Walt Whitman and Oscar Wilde, the second of whom, of course, it would be easy enough to cast as representing the artistic personality. But the leading homosexual examples of the scientific personality that have been most tellingly advanced—Austro-British philosopher Ludwig Wittgenstein and British mathematician and coinventor of the computer Alan Turing—disclose at once why it would be more than a little forced to cast Whitman in like profile. He was a poet, after all. Like Homer, however, Whitman sang of epic days; lived them, too. And perhaps because Harvard, whatever lens you look at it through, is above all an American story, its gay experience, historically, is not chiefly of Wilde's influence—though (like the Beatles later) Wilde certainly took America by storm. But it was Whitman whose influence took deepest root in Harvard Yard, decades before Wilde was seen cruising Harvard's fine new gymnasium: Whitman, as Homer might have said, of the fierce days, or, as Emerson did say, of the bold words.

Never bolder than on Boston Common, where on a sharp late-winter's day early in 1860 America's Plato, Ralph Waldo Emerson, perhaps Harvard's most illustrious graduate still, walked the Beacon Street path the better part of several hours with the poet most would agree is America's greatest. Back and forth, up and down, Whitman confronted Emerson's misgivings and foreboding about the 1860 edition of *Leaves of Grass* with deep feeling that day: the end of it all, what Whitman called "a bully dinner"[1]—and the publication of perhaps the most famous homosexual poetry ever written.

Of their dialogue that afternoon Robert K. Martin, a literary critic and professor of English at the University of Montreal, has declared that its great import lay in the fact that it was the keystone in Whitman's overarching, lifelong vocation: to name same-sex love in the modern era. He called it "adhesive," as opposed to "amative," borrowing from the language of phrenology a term Whitman applied to a love that, in Martin's words, had "been recognized for thousands of years . . . [and been] implied in the Bible"— David and Jonathan's "love passing that of woman"—but was otherwise nameless. There was, Martin reiterates, "no word for this love . . . Whitman was indeed Emerson's 'poet as namer.' " Martin concludes: "He gave that love the first name it had of its own, albeit a poor and borrowed one."[2]

Now the greatest Bostonian came in from Concord to see the visiting poet (so recounts Whitman's most recent biographer, Jerome Loving), calling at Whitman's humble boardinghouse (rooms two dollars a week), off run-down Bowdoin Street behind the domed State House on the crowded north slope of old Beacon Hill. Emerson, too, was the host at dinner, at the American House, a posh hotel nearby. Boston did not disdain Brooklyn. Harvard's philosopher king took the rough, uneducated poet very seriously. And although what we know of their discussion suggests they focused on the "Children of Adam" section about heterosexual love, it was Whitman's overall attitude to sexuality in *Leaves of Grass,* of which the "Calamus" section on homosexual love (new to this 1860 edition) was the most radical expression, that drove the debate so vigorously.[3]

They had argued long and hard, and it was a conversation Whitman cherished—"more precious than gold to me," he later wrote of their afternoon walk. Emerson, Whitman wrote later, was "in his prime, keen physically and morally magnetic, arm'd at every point, and when he chose, wielding the emotional just as well as the intellectual. . . . It was an argument-statement, reconnoitering, review, attack, and pressing home (like an army corps in order, artillery, cavalry, infantry). . . ."[4] After all, Emerson was keen: in his biographer Justin Kaplan's words, *Leaves of Grass* was a book he had "stood grandfather to."[5] Altered, would there be as good a book left? Whitman asked. Emerson, considering, said he thought not. Even in aid of his own view he would not bend his truth: "I did not say as good a book, I said a good book." Whitman, confirmed in his opinion, changed nothing. "The dirtiest book in all the world is the expurgated book," he said later. "Expurgation is apology," Whitman declared, "an admission that something or other was wrong." Though he would also write that "I have not lived to regret my Emerson no," he also affirmed, "Read all the Emerson you can." He was "not conclusive on all points, but no man more helps to a conclusion."[6]

MASCULINE. SOCRATIC. WHITMANIC. But, however enduring the poetry, Whitman's name for this nameless love hardly stuck. Nor his style. Both were virtually dead a century later when, in the 1950s and '60s, the dramatic change in "gay," as it was beginning to be called, from the androgyny and effeminacy that in the intervening century had become fashionable to the "new clone" look of the 1970s and '80s was explained by Felice Picano. Picano, among the foremost members of the seminal early 1980s New York literary coterie, the Violet Quill, whose other members included Edmund White and Andrew Holleran, pointed out that by the 1950s the most visible homosexuals had come to accept the medical and legal establishments' view that homosexuals constituted a "third sex." As such, for example, they "dressed not recognizably as men, not as women, but midway in between," in a style Picano called "fluffy sweater queens." Similarly, "their walk could be characterized as mincing."

Protesting that he did "not mean to belittle or demean these people," whom he called "courageous and defiant" in the face of a "conformist, xenophobic, lockstep society," Picano, though he admitted they were the "only homosexual role models extant," pointed out that "for most gay men they were inappropriate either as models or as sex objects." Indeed, Picano concluded, the masculine clone style "had nothing at all to do with '*not* being female.' Rather, it had to do with *taking back from The Man a masculine gay identity* [emphasis added]. Gay men came to see they were not some third sex . . . but instead male-sexed men who had sex with other such men."[7]

To this history lesson out of his own life, Picano made a point of adding his own memory of why so many—particularly "macho" heterosexual men and ardently feminist women—found what was really a revival of Whitmanic style in the 1970s so threatening: "Gay clones were men without women or children. . . . Possessing no weak links that could be used against them as blackmail or held against them as hostages, clones could not be controlled or corralled. They could only be gotten at by direct, physical force, and in a one-on-one fight, they had a pretty good chance of winning."

Now Picano's purpose remains contemporary and controversial, intended then as now to protest the 1990s fashion of reinventing "lesbigay history to suit current politically correct attitudes," particularly about the historic 1969 Stonewall Riots; "not . . . achieved," he wrote, "by those super heroes: dykes and drag queens. The truth is quite different. . . . Of those actually there, and thus those responsible for early gay politics having taken off, it was not in the racially balanced, ethnic-and-gender-correct proportions that the lesbigay media paraded in 1994, but was instead comprised of about 95 percent middle-class whites, mostly college-educated males."

In a larger sense, however, Picano was also recapitulating in our own time what I see as the two chief polarities of gay history, a reflection of the two great homosexual archetypes: that of the warrior, and that of the aesthete; in other words, in the modern period, Walt Whitman and Oscar Wilde.

Leonard Bernstein, who will figure importantly in this study, is a good example of the tensions between the Whitmanic and the Wildean. Himself a powerful man in every sense—a giant of a conductor in a profession few gays had then mastered—Bernstein was yet a child of his era and at a party in San Francisco where he met Tom Waddell, he showed it clearly enough. Waddell, a hero of the traditional Olympics (in fact, an Olympic decathlete in 1968), sought to create a gay equivalent to the Olympic Games he had so excelled in.[8] Before he was forbidden to use the term (for what are now called the Gay Games), he had planned to call them the Gay Olympics. Bernstein's response? "My god—who needs Gay Olympics?" But as Waddell turned on his heels and walked away, seething, Bernstein, himself provoked, gave his own game away; his voice pursued Waddell: "Who's *that* fucking queen?" "If he hadn't been drunk, I think I'd have punched him," Waddell told Paul Moor. Added Moor: "One dares hardly even to think of the resultant headlines."[9] As we will see, there was more than a little Wilde in Whitman, and no little Whitman in Wilde. But the archetypes they exemplify are nonetheless profoundly different.

Whitman first, or—because this book is about Harvard—Ralph Waldo Emerson.

Emerson's Story

THE SAGE OF Concord showed his hand clearly enough with respect to homosexuality when in *Representative Men* (1850) he declared: "Let none presume to measure the irregularities of Michel Angelo and Socrates by village scales."[10] Ouch: it can still be a salutary prick to our conscience in our own time. I am reminded of George Washington's judgment against slavery. Both pricks—both judgments—are decisive answers to the so-called presentism defense, which "can be useful for almost any era and almost any misdeed," in the words of historian and author Henry Wiencek. He recently responded to an attempt to defend Yale University from its entanglement with slavery by a University of California linguist intent on presentism's key assertion that "it's downright inappropriate to render a moral judgment . . . based on moral standards which didn't exist at the time." Noting that even Jefferson, himself racist, nonetheless saw slavery in its true colors, Wieneck returned fire briskly:

> George Washington was an enthusiastic slaveholder in his early decades; . . . but by the end of his life he found slavery repugnant. In his will Washington freed his slaves and specified that the children be educated. . . . If

we accept the statement "it's downright inappropriate to render a moral judgment" on slavery, we are more willing to accept slavery than George Washington was.

If the founders had such misgivings over slavery, how is it that they allowed slavery to continue? The answer is not that they didn't know any better, but that they kept slavery so the Southern states would join the union. . . . [11]

And just as Wieneck concludes we "compound" the sin by "draping a veil of innocence over the transaction" (he sees, of course, that "the true beneficiary of the presentism defense is not the past but the present"), so we note the implied criticism of Emerson's dismissive "village scales."

It is perhaps not surprising, therefore, that Robert K. Martin has written:

> The Transcendentalists were the first group in America to explore the relations between persons of the same sex, and they did so through their understanding of Platonic philosophy and German Romanticism. Ralph Waldo Emerson . . . had been infatuated with a classmate, Martin Gay, at Harvard. . . . His concept of friendship was gendered male and seen as superior to heterosexual love. . . . Thoreau also had difficulty reconciling an abstract commitment to friendship with an aversion to the physical. . . .
>
> Margaret Fuller also participated in the discourses of friendship . . . [and she insisted on] a fundamental androgyny: "There is no wholly masculine man, no purely feminine woman."[12]

Indeed, Emerson's infatuation with Gay (later a respected Boston doctor) is a much overlooked but key aspect of his life.

It was in the fall of 1819 at Harvard that young Waldo, in the words of his latest biographer, Robert D. Richardson, "found himself strangely and powerfully attracted by a new freshman named Martin Gay," at whom he found himself looking and looking, and Gay, it would seem, looking back. "The disturbing power of the glances"[13] troubled Emerson, wrote Richardson, while Justin Kaplan reported that forthwith Emerson "wrote ardent poetry about [Gay] as well as a fantasy laced with sexual symbolism."[14] Nor did it end there. According to Richardson, Emerson "remain[ed] susceptible to such crushes, expressed at first through glances, all his life," and though Richardson is careful to observe that "*most* of them would involve women [emphasis added]," leaving it at that and dropping the subject, he added that Emerson, at least in the case of Martin Gay, took pains to cover his tracks. Though the original journal entries were in Latin in the first place, at some later point Richardson agrees with Kaplan that Emerson deliberately defaced them, "heavily cross[ing] out the Martin Gay journal notes."[15] Other scholars attribute the deed to Emerson's son Edward.

Biographer Graham Robb has put both sides of the issue very well:

According to one view, it is crudely anachronistic to see friendships of two centuries ago as evidence of homosexuality. Michel Foucault suggested in 1976 that the homosexual . . . was invented by doctors in the mid-19th-century. . . . The effect has been to cordon off all gay experience that predates the advent of psychology. . . .

Only the most literal-minded poststructuralist would claim, however, that there was no such thing as homosexual passion until the word "homosexual" was coined in the second half of the 19th century. The apparent lack of references to what we now call homosexuality is misleading. It was "the crime not to be named among Christians," which, of course, was a convenient way of referring to it.[16]

This was, naturally, decades before Whitman. In addition to his infatuation with Gay, there are many other wonders in Emerson's life and work to account for, as well as a good deal of literary and philosophical material. Perhaps because of his own unhappy experience of heterosexual marriage, in his essay "Love" Emerson very deliberately allowed a safe refuge for all in opposite-sex *or* same-sex harbors.[17] Never mind that he filled a 250-page notebook with translations from the Persian, mostly of the work of the fourteenth-century poet Hafez, famously homoerotic—"almost all . . . poems of love, wine, fire and desire" in Richardson's words—or that some of Emerson's own best poetry ("Bacchus," for instance) was written under what his biographer calls "the intoxicating spell of Hafez," it is significant that Emerson made no attempt in his translations to change the gender of poems addressed by Hafez to a youth he liked: "Take my heart in thy hand, O beautiful boy of Shiraz! / I would give for the mole on thy cheek Samarcand and Buchara."[18]

Then there is what has been called a "sensuous daydream about intimacy with a man" from Emerson's journal entry of 7 June 1838: He imagines being "shut up in a little schooner bound on a voyage of three or four weeks with a man—an entire stranger—of a great and regular mind of vast resources of his nature." Nothing would be forced: "I would not speak to him, I would not look at him; [. . .] so sure should I be of him, so luxuriously should I husband my joys that I should steadily hold back all the time, make no advances, leaving altogether to Fortune for hours, for days, for weeks even, the manner and degrees of intercourse." Emerson went on to describe the man as one with whom he could "bathe and dilute . . . my greater self; he is me, and I am him."[19] How similar all this sounds to Emerson's diary entries about his and Gay's everyday life in Harvard Yard: "I, observing him, just before we met turned another corner and most strangely avoided him. This morning I went out to meet him in a different direction and stopped to speak with a lounger in order to be directly in [Gay's] way, but [he] turned into the first gate and went towards Stoughton [Hall]."[20]

The deliberate avoidances piqued rather than quashed Emerson's interest. Similarly, Emerson, hearing of a report that Gay was "dissolute," was disappointed he could still not shake free of his feelings. In April 1821, after a year of what today we'd call "cruising," the two had yet to exchange "above a dozen words."[21] As Emerson would bluntly write in later years, "Men cease to interest us when we find their limitations."[22] But not Gay. Not with Emerson. And this despite the fact—if "dissolute" has some relation with "vileness"—that Emerson may more and more have sensed what was at issue; in the years following his crush on Gay several entries on friendship in Emerson's journal degenerate almost to rants, rants on the dangers of "vileness."[23]

Views differ on the various meanings of all this fugitive data. Richardson feels Emerson's candor about his feelings for Gay is evidence that Emerson was "rather innocent and essentially unembarrassed."[24] Caleb Crain, on the other hand, in his superb study, *American Sympathy: Men, Friendship, and Literature in the New Nation*, suggests Emerson's attitudes, so contradictory to posterity's impression of him, are explained by nothing more complicated than the fact that "homosexuality was taboo in Victorian America": "This simple explanation has no high theoretical glamour to recommend it," writes Crain, "but it clears up a number of long-standing paradoxes about Emerson's heart."[25]

He does not argue Emerson was gay. He knows, and says clearly, that "gay love as we know it is modern," and as Thoreau wrote, "the *past* cannot be *presented*." But Crain also knows how misleading it has proved to be to dismiss the history of romantic same-sex love. He writes:

> [T]hough the terms and words and social categories have changed, I suspect that *because such people exist now, they existed then*. As Emerson put it, "One nature wrote and the same reads." . . . I am afraid that post-structuralist gay critics have outwitted themselves. . . . "There is no event but sprung somewhere from the soul of man," [Emerson] wrote in "Literary Ethics," "and therefore there is none but the soul of man can interpret."[26]

Crain, as a matter of fact, is distinctly in a position to know, for when he notes that the words and the social categories may have changed, but not the facts of the matter, he does so from the perspective of the time of his own study, the late eighteenth and early nineteenth centuries, so many words and terms and categories of which are unrecognizable to us today. Of that era, moreover, Crain has this to say of what he calls the reign of "sympathy," also called sentiment or sensibility, which he notes for a century and a half "had the force of a biological fact. . . . Well into the nineteenth century, undergraduates at Harvard and Princeton studied it. . . . Not until Darwin observed that competition, not cooperation, was the law of nature did its scientific prestige falter." And, according to Crain, two of his case studies in *American Sympathy*—the relationship of John André (the British officer in the American War of Independence hanged as a spy after negotiating the surrender of West Point) with a Philadelphia youth, John Cope, and that of a late-eighteenth-century Princeton undergraduate, James Gibson, with a Philadelphia businessman, John F. Mifflin—were just such intense examples of "sympathy," so much so he feels compelled to ask: "Did it mean they had sex?" He answers, "In antebellum America, men said little about sex between men. About their romantic feelings for one another, on the other hand, men were garrulous and subtle." Moreover, of the relationships between Gibson and Mifflin, Crain says more: not only that his study of the diaries of both offers "ample evidence that at the height of sympathy's reign, American men could express emotions to each other with a fervor and openness that could not have been detached from religious enthusiasm a generation earlier and would have to be consigned to sexual perversion a few generations later," but that whether or not they actually had sex, "they held each other in a regard that we would call sexual." Indeed, Crain seems to anticipate somewhat the provocative subtitle of Jonathan Ned Katz's *Love Stories* of 2001: *Sex Between Men Before Homosexuality*.[27]

It is in the context of this historical evolution of categories and terms (indeed, "the shape of sympathy had changed" between André's era and Emerson's later) that Emerson's crush at Harvard needs to be considered. This Crain does, pointing out that though it has been many years since Katz first collected some of Emerson's more provocative themes in his *Gay American History* (1976), scholars generally have yet to face the fact that "the feelings that came to Emerson during his crush on Gay provoked metaphors, ideas, and psychological compromises that became crucial to [Emerson's] mature philosophy and writing." Again, Crain does not say Emerson was homosexual but offers a far more important analysis:

> Homosexual eros is the motive and structuring metaphor of his work, and at times it is his explicit type. To most ears, this assertion may sound likely for Whitman but novel as a claim for Emerson. The expression of love for men was not Emerson's exclusive literary motive, and he probably never realized a love affair with a man. But this brand of eros was a crucial force in Emerson's life and writing.[28]

Crain instances two moments in Emerson's career when this was the case, neither of which, interestingly, is his friendship with Thoreau.

Emerson is not generally an entry in gay and lesbian literary anthologies. Thoreau, however, who never married (he did propose to a woman friend but was rejected) and wrote a famously homoerotic poem, "Sympathy"—always included in the gay canon—is often accorded a substantial entry in such books. In the end, though, the data amounts to as much or as little as one wants to make of it. Wrote Marylynne Diggs in *The Gay and Lesbian Literary Heritage*: "Biographers remain undecided about Thoreau's sexuality. . . . Some believe he was a 'repressed' homosexual and others that he was asexual. . . . But his *Journals*, his essay 'Chastity and Sensuality,' and the long discourse on 'Friendship' in *A Week* are prolific expressions of the beauty, and the agony, of love between men."[29] Some of his passions may indeed refer to Emerson, and there are certainly distinguished Thoreau scholars, such as Walter Harding, who argue for a gay reading of Thoreau's work, but the whole subject remains highly speculative; no authoritative consensus has yet emerged.

Interestingly, however, Crain, though he does not ignore Thoreau, focuses his discussion of Emerson's sexuality instead on just two matters: the Gay crush of 1819–1821, which he explicates through a poem by Emerson, "Dedication," and his essay "Friendship," which Crain links as intimately to Emerson's relationship with Samuel Ward. In each case, Crain argues, Emerson transformed first Gay, then Ward, from flesh, as it were, to literature, "channel[ing] his feelings into a work of literature, imbuing that work with a special energy and asking it to justify his renunciation." Crain calls this "a technique of separating one's feelings for a man from the man himself, in order to free them for literary use":

> From [Plato's] *Phaedrus*, Emerson had learned that he could preserve the sense of energy and purpose that love for a man gave him if, rather than simply kill this love as forbidden and sinful, he cut the love from the man, like a flower from its roots. If he kept Martin Gay or Samuel Gray Ward at a fond distance, Emerson could enjoy the feelings they inspired and transform the feelings into a literary ecstasy, which was presented in his prose as if it were abstract.

It was a technique of Emerson's that Herman Melville noticed in *The Confidence Man*, where, as was often the case, hierotomy, as Crain calls it, protected Emerson only too well. Concludes Crain: "It protected him from the men he thought he loved." Thus, "resolv[ing] his erotic attractions by Platonic abnegation" served very well the purposes of Emerson, "who instead of firing it," Crain perceives in a brilliant insight, "made it a principle to live his lie as a loaded gun."[30]

Yet Emerson, in fact, compromised to this extent: "Dedication" he never sent to Gay; "Friendship" he *did* send to Ward. What a present!

There is a sense in which Emerson, whom Oscar Wilde called "New England's Plato" (and, by extension, Richardson uses the term "American Plato"[31]), certainly equals and for moderns may surpass Plato in this matter. Observes Richardson: "In the end Emerson would prove more than the American Plato, since he would reject Plato's politics and struggle to reconcile Platonism with democratic idealism." Meanwhile, "there is nothing like Emerson's essay in the literature of friendship," Crain asserts. "Its closest relative is the work of Plato," who deals with "the question of eros in friendship." In fact, in Plato "the audience is never certain of the nature of the relationship discussed," Crain continues. "The same drama exists in Emerson's text." One wonders if it was as clear to Ward then as to Crain now that it was of Ward that Emerson wrote in "Friendship" when he reproduced in that essay a letter from his journals, which ends: "Thou art to me a delicious torment. Thine ever, or never." Certainly Ward can hardly have misunderstood Thoreau's "Sympathy," which Emerson is known to have sent him, nor *Leaves of Grass*, which, even before he found time to write back to Walt Whitman, Emerson forwarded to Samuel Ward.[32]

Walt Whitman's Story

IN LATER YEARS, surrounded by haters of Whitman among both family and friends, Emerson grew quiet about him, excluding the poet from his widely read poetic anthology, *Parnassus*, and solacing thereby those who were dismayed to ever have found Harvard's great luminary and America's most notorious poet on the same page. Similarly, Whitman, feeling himself ill used by Emerson's friends and family (though never by Emerson himself), grew restive, like Thoreau, with the burdens of discipleship ("Who wants to be any man's mere follower?" Whitman scoffed). It was "Emerson-on-the-brain" that explained his saluting the great man as "Master" in the second edition of *Leaves of Grass*, Whitman protested.[33] But Emerson hardly minded any of it, not just because as he grew old he lost his memory, but because if the master did remember, he remembered surely that his philosophy of Man Thinking (Thinking, not Learning) had not much use for the idea of disciples in the first place.

Nor has any of this led posterity to misread either man's view of the other. "Nearly all scholars now agree," wrote Allen in *The New Walt Whitman Handbook*, "that Emerson himself was the one single greatest influence on Whitman during the years when he was planning and writing the first two or three editions of *Leaves of Grass*."[34] Indeed, the Brooklyn poet had said too much over the years to ever unsay his debt. "I never get tired of talking to him," Whitman wrote once of Emerson. "I think everyone was fascinated by his personality." He wrote, too, of the "wonderful heart and soul of the man." Nor did he leave it at that. "Never a face more gifted with power to express, fascinate, maintain," Whitman wrote of his mentor, hero almost, whose mind he liked best of all, thinking it at one and the same time "penetrating and sweet." Not only Emerson got crushes. "They never could hold him; no province, no clique, no church," avowed Whitman. "I always go back to Emerson. He was the one man to do a particular job wholly on his own account." Even that was not enough. "Emerson never fails; he can't be rejected; even when he falls on strong ground he somehow eventuates a harvest." Finally, the accolade: "My ideas were simmering and simmering," Whitman told a friend, "and Emerson brought them to a boil."[35]

Nor was Emerson shy, either, of singing Whitman's praises, though in more literary guise, famously describing *Leaves of Grass* as "the most extraordinary piece of wit and wisdom that America has yet contributed." Nor of bluntly telling Whitman, as Richardson says, "You have a great pack howling at your heels always, Mr. Whitman; I hope you show them all a proper contempt; they deserve no more than your heels."[36] A passage well worth parsing. After their 1860 dialogue on Boston Common, Emerson had wanted to introduce Whitman to the Saturday Club (as he did, in fact, to the Boston Athenaeum)[37] but no less a triumvirate than Longfellow, Holmes Senior, and Lowell disparaged the idea, according to G. W. Allen, and disparaged it so intently Emerson desisted. Nor was that the worst of it. Thomas Bailey Aldrich, another Boston literary light then, now obscure, would call Whitman "a charlatan"; his poetry, Aldrich felt, belonged in a "quart of spirits in an anatomical museum!" And Lowell, not content with excluding Whitman from Boston's leading intellectual dining club, made a point of keeping all his students at Harvard from reading the poet. As Justin Kaplan writes, it was Lowell who was probably responsible for the fact that "*Leaves of Grass* was removed from the open shelves of [Harvard's] college library and kept under lock and key with other tabooed books."[38]

It cannot be overemphasized how far Emerson went way out on a limb for Whitman. Indeed, in a sense he stayed there—as Richardson attests: though Emerson said something once to Henry Wadsworth Longfellow's brother about "Whitman's rudeness in printing the [personal, not public] letter of praise Emerson had sent in later editions of *Leaves of Grass*], Whitman's impulsiveness had no effect on Emerson's enthusiasm for his work." And this despite the fact that almost everyone in Boston and elsewhere "recoiled" from the strong sexuality in Whitman's work. "For years," adds Richardson, "Emerson was nearly alone in his admiration for Whitman."[39] Indeed, Emerson surely sought to convince Whitman to pull back on the sexuality because he so admired the poet's work and worried Whitman would be destroyed in an era when—such was the virulence Whitman's treatment of sexuality aroused—even Emerson's most jubilant imprimaturs could not ensure his poetry the hearing it deserved. Polite society would just have none of it.

Of Boston generally, Whitman had mostly only good to say, and though it is unclear what neighborhoods he lingered longest in—he was sighted downtown, on Beacon Hill, along the waterfront, and in both Cambridge and Somerville—his own notations and diary entries make it clear Harvard Yard was well known to him. In August 1881 he noted, "The horse-cars form one of the great institutions and puzzles of Boston. I ride in them every day—of course get in the open ones—go out to Harvard Square often." He even notes his route—"through Cambridge Street across the Back Bay"— and although the locales of his socializing were mostly downtown Boston hotels and clubs and taverns, he specifically mentions "the fine old mansions of Cambridge" and also, specifically, "the College buildings,"[40] in which, I do not doubt, the maverick poet on each of his sojourns in Boston came into contact with less grand but perhaps more welcoming circles than Emerson's persnickety Olympians. Among Boston's demimonde generally, and particularly the denizens of Harvard Yard where, despite Lowell's efforts, several students stood out as ardent supporters of the radical poet, quite a number of the poet's strongest supporters were to be found over the years. These included the novelist John Trowbridge, with whom Whitman is known to have spent a day at his house on Prospect Hill in Somerville, just beyond Cambridge, and, most notably, William D. O'Connor, who was to become the leader nationally of a "Whitman movement."[41] At the time, in 1860, O'Connor was himself at work on a book for the Boston publishing house of Thayer and Eldridge, Whitman's own publishers for the 1860 *Leaves of Grass* and the reason Whitman was himself in town that year, composing and reading proof. ("We are young men," Thayer and Eldridge challenged Whitman; "try us.")

Others in other years who would draw Whitman back to Boston included two Harvard students, Charles Sempers and William Sloane Kennedy. Sempers, an undergraduate, actually once wrote quite a fine essay for the *Harvard Monthly* on Whitman, an essay Whitman biographer Jerome Loving calls "one of the earliest attempts by someone outside Whitman's various circles of support to identify what is most admirable about *Leaves of Grass*."[42] We also know, because Sempers once tried to get the poet to come and give a talk at Harvard by invoking the already famous philosopher and psychologist as host, that William James was not averse to Whitman. No surprise, really; James would quote one of Whitman's "fine and moving" poems, "To You," in the last chapter of his book *Pragmatism*. Kennedy, the other Harvard student, a friend of Sempers's at the Divinity School and later a *Boston Herald* reporter, would write a popular book, *Reminiscences of Walt Whitman*,[43] and help raise funds in 1886 to buy Whitman a summer cottage, the project of yet another small group of Whitmanic Bostonians led by the Irish-American poet John Boyle O'Reilly. By then Whitman had again made another visit to the New England capital, and O'Reilly, a leader of Boston's bohemia and a founder of several of its (once!) bohemian clubs, arranged with George Parsons Lathrop, Hawthorne's son-in-law, for Whitman to give a talk in 1881 at the St. Botolph Club. As the Botolph was not so stuffy in its brilliant early decades of bohemianism as the Saturday Club was, Whitman's appearance was a great success. Moreover, those attending included such literati as publisher James R. Osgood, who as a result of the evening shocked everyone in 1881 by proposing to issue yet another—the definitive— edition of *Leaves of Grass*.[44]

For Whitman, for everyone, Osgood's decision was full of Harvard resonances. Osgood himself was a Bowdoin man. But James R. Osgood & Co.

was the "in-house" successor (Houghton, Mifflin the outsider successor) to Ticknor & Fields, perhaps the greatest nineteenth-century American publisher, and one of Osgood's two partners when he approached Whitman was Thomas F. Ticknor, scion of the leading Boston family whose patriarch was Professor George Ticknor, one of Harvard's star professors, a founder of the Boston Public Library, the man sometimes called the father of American graduate education. There was no Harvard University Press then, and this was as close to Harvard's imprimatur as the era offered. It was also true, however, that in 1881 Osgood had just withdrawn from the first firm that succeeded Ticknor & Fields and was trying to reestablish himself. Thus the lure of Whitman, whose *Leaves of Grass* in its final, definitive edition (appendices aside) he published despite Whitman's refusal to expurgate anything.

> That spring all hell broke loose . . . [and]—in the words of Edwin Haviland Miller—the censorship and the ensuing debate in the newspapers immortalized Boston's "dubious morality by making it a national joke." The label, "Banned in Boston," was dramatically bestowed [by the district attorney at the behest of the Society for the Suppression of Vice, predecessor to the infamous Watch and Ward Society] on one of America's national literary treasures, *Leaves of Grass*.[45]

Osgood withdrew the book from sale; in 1882 it was reissued in Philadelphia. What had changed? Twenty years earlier it had been a Boston publisher that first dared to put out the "sex poems"! But it was always a tense business, Whitman's poetry, and Whitman himself was no stranger to equivocation. His own public attitude to the subject of homosexuality vacillated widely according to the position he found himself in—or, rather, was put in; witness, when pressed by John Addington Symonds, how boldly Whitman famously, and surely falsely, declared himself the father of six children! Andrew Delbanco, in a penetrating review in *The New York Times* of Loving's biography of Whitman, gives two little-known examples of Whitman's ways in this or that circumstance. On the one hand, in assembling reviews for advertisement in his books, he had, in Delbanco's words, "the prescience to grasp the first axiom of modern celebrity culture—that there is no such thing as bad publicity." Indeed, Whitman mixed in "just enough negative criticism" to titillate, "including one shocked review that alluded, discreetly in Latin, to his homosexuality: *Peccatum illud horribile, inter Christianos non nominandum* [that horrible sin not to be named among Christians]." On the other hand, in 1883, with the poet's close cooperation, Richard Maurice Bucke published a second laudatory biography in which Whitman himself made revisions, added passages of his own, and let stand Bucke's patently prudish description of the homoerotic "Calamus" poems, though, of course, these were named for a flower that resembles the shape of an erect penis.[46]

How did Harvard Yard view such things? Kennedy, a lifelong and devoted admirer of Whitman, in his 1896 book about the poet argued vigorously against any suggestion Whitman was homosexual.[47] Which, of course, may have been to protest too much. Especially interesting, however, somewhat on the other side, is the reaction from the Jameses—soon to move from Beacon Hill's Ashburton Place to their more famous abode on Quincy Street, overlooking Harvard Yard—and particularly from young Henry, to Whitman's Civil War poetry, *Drum-Taps*.[48] Sheldon Novick notes the book was "making a stir in Boston" and that it was "much admired" by James's father and by Emerson. But young Henry "dismissed [it] almost with anger." Whitman, Novick adds, "was on a course that diverged widely from his own." In more than one way. The effect on him of Whitman's verses, wrote Henry, was of "the effort of an essentially prosaic mind to lift itself by a prolonged muscular strain, into poetry."[49] All James's biographers have to address his initial reaction because in later years Whitman became virtually James's favorite American poet. And all react as one might expect. Kaplan suggests James for a long time tried "to pretend that this early review never existed."[50] Leon Edel, James's preeminent biographer, wondered if it was "Whitman's homo-eroticism" that led James to make his peace with Whitman.[51] Sheldon Novick gets it just right, telling very well the tale of how Edith Wharton recalled James reading *Leaves of Grass* by her fireplace in Lennox; "his voice filled the hushed room like an organ adagio." Adds Novick: "Wharton was delighted to discover that he thought Whitman, as she did, 'the greatest of American poets.' She was unaware of Henry James's hostile review of *Drum-Taps* years before and of the long process of sexual self-acceptance that had allowed yet another Harvard man to become a lover of Whitman."[52]

Henry James's Story

HENRY JAMES FIRST appeared in Harvard Yard, in 1862, seventeen years old, part New Yorker, part New Englander, soon to be in the same equal parts an American (expatriate) Britisher. James enrolled as a law student at Harvard somewhat out of the blue, with no prior college level work at all to his credit. It was, however, "purely a pretext," journalist Ariel Swartley has written, because "what [James] wanted was the freedom to pursue the literary life," and after a period in a university dormitory young Henry settled into his own rooms in a picturesque old eighteenth-century house facing Winthrop Square, a small parklike enclave just off of Harvard Square and the adjoining college yard.[53] This last was a place of some romance to James, a place he would describe as "brooding on sublime and exquisite heresies to come." The plainspoken Yankee elegance of its boxy brick precincts, the design by Charles Bulfinch (like Beacon Hill, which James also liked; "Oh, the wide benignity of brick," he wrote once of the hill, "the goodly, friendly, ruddy fronts, the felicity of scale, the solid *seat* of everything"), moved James. So did Winthrop Square. James reveled in its "dignified decay," and in the view from his sitting room. There was "a windowed alcove, large enough for a desk, that overlooked the Brighton hills," wrote Swartley, "and in this satisfyingly artistic setting, between languid strolls along the river, evening excursions to the brightly lit Boston theaters and the occasional class, James began to write." His first published work of criticism duly appeared: a theater review in *The Boston Traveler*. However, "a little more than a year after James entered Harvard," Swartley observed, "his parents moved [from Rhode Island] to Beacon Hill and James would never find Boston . . . so mysterious or romantic again."

It was an insightful remark. Though in later years James would set several novels and short stories in and around Boston and at the end of his life decide to be buried in Cambridge Cemetery with pretty much the same river view as his old rooms in Winthrop Square, during his lifetime he more and more resisted any identification with Boston generally and Harvard specifically, even as he increasingly obsessed (even at the height of his fame in London) about "superstitious terror" lest the Puritan capital stretch out "strange inevitable tentacles to draw me back and destroy me." It was the scrutiny of his family, of course—finally, of his brother William, whom Henry so greatly loved—that the "perpetual non-Bostonian," as Swartley calls Henry, so studiously tried to distance himself from. Indeed, Henry's much-dwelt-on negative reaction to most of late nineteenth-century Back Bay Boston, which he disliked as much as he liked eighteenth-century Beacon Hill and Harvard Yard, resonates with images not just of scrutiny, but of outright spying. Why was it that Back Bay's Marlborough Street, James wrote, "for imperturbable reasons of its own, used particularly to break my heart"? Perhaps it was because, being the area's most intimate and narrowest street, it was more true there than anywhere what James observed of Back Bay windows generally, that they seemed "almost terrible"; they were to James "like candid inevitable eyes"; their function, he wrote, to "watch each other, all hopelessly, for revelations, indiscretions . . . *or* explosive breakages of the pane from within."[54]

Actually, Isabella Gardner, also Julia Ward Howe (as we will observe later, in her invitation to Oscar Wilde especially), would oblige, so to speak. But James himself, in fact, might also have raised a few window shades—if, that is, any knew or suspected what Sheldon Novick, his most recent biographer, has surmised: that in the spring of 1865 young Henry performed his "first acts of love" within sight of, if not actually in, the Back Bay and not with a woman, but with a man, a fellow Harvard student, no less than young Oliver Wendell Holmes Jr.[55]

The liaison would seem improbable. All his life Holmes Jr. had the repute of a formidable flirt and notorious womanizer, and Novick admits his is only "a guess." But of James's homosexuality itself there remains little doubt. Without getting mired in the subject—or in the ruminations of various scholars on James's suppressed anality[56]—perhaps the range of possibilities can be indicated by noting the work of one scholar, Wendy Graham. I think particularly of Graham's *Henry James: Thwarted Love*, in which she makes a specific claim. She aims, in *The Gay and Lesbian Review*'s words, to "bridge our two perspectives of James as either coyly evasive or sexually tormented"[57] by arguing that "for James fantasy really was the medium of excitement. Thwarting passion, he spun out pleasure in his fiction and letters, using narrative for flirtation and intellect for a strangely disembodied form of seduction. Sublimation, Graham suggests, gave James a productive career with erotic compensation for missed experience. . . . The critic A. J. L. Busst has called this attitude 'cerebral lechery . . .' "[58] Well, then again if anyone is entitled to a secret life, of soul and/or body, it is surely James, whose subject is famously what can't be seen.[59]

Drum-Taps

WAR, HISTORICALLY, ALL too easy to see, is the most masculine of themes, very much at the heart of the poems by Whitman that so viscerally disturbed James at first and that he condemned so strongly; not surprising— although some still argue about Whitman's homosexuality, no one has ever argued about his masculinity.[60]

Not that the poet was warlike. Even more than Emerson, Whitman believed in the full equality of the sexes. But whether in war or peacetime, it was men, not women, that Whitman was interested in. And the result, as the poet's sexuality came more and more to the fore, was, in Robert K. Martin's words, the "identification of the gay man with the masculine," in a distinctively *American* way. Whitman, declares Martin, "creat[ed] a figure of masculinity that could free him [the American] from association with the European aesthete [such as Wilde]."[61]

To say this is, however, not altogether fair. Walter Pater, for instance, in his *Plato and Platonism* (1893), when he imagines (more as a British Victorian than an ancient Greek, but never mind) an Athenian visiting Lacedaemon and approving of the youths' cold baths, is extolling a more manly European tradition than the word *aesthete* usually connotes. And he does so quite tellingly when he writes: "The beauty of these most beautiful of all people was a male beauty, far remote from feminine tenderness; it had the expression of a certain *ascêis* in it, like unsweetened wine. In comparison with it, beauty of another type might seem to be wanting in edge or accent."[62] (I am reminded of Gore Vidal's observation in our own era that "a homosexualist like [Christopher] Isherwood cannot with any ease enjoy a satisfactory sexual relationship with a woman because he himself is so entirely masculine that the woman presents no challenge, no masculine hardness, no exciting *agon*. . . . Isherwood is a good deal less 'feminine' (in the pre–women's lib sense of the word) than . . . our own paralyzingly butch Ernest Hemingway."[63])

An emphasis on the masculine with homoerotic resonance is also by no means wanting in American literature before Whitman. As Martin observes, Herman Melville was in this respect quite like Whitman.

> Melville clearly disliked effeminate men; like Whitman his literary sexual ideal involves a love between two men, and not . . . a man and a pseudo-woman. The effeminate man was the over-civilized man, who had adopted the values of civilization (i.e., woman) over the primitive (i.e., man). The ideal therefore becomes an androgyny that represents the integration of the values of civilization and the primitive, or of female and male. This androgyny should not be confused with effeminacy; for Melville, androgyny indicates self-sufficiency and wholeness, whereas effeminacy indicates weakness, indulgence and partialness.

Whitman and Melville both, Martin declares, were interested in "dynamic masculinity, expressed and fulfilled in physical action." In *Billy Budd*: "Billy's graceful physique is endowed with enormous strength, *active* strength. While his beauty is a homosexual trap, his strength is a potential murder weapon."[64]

But Whitman was in every sense a whole new world. Not only was he unequivocal in response to Emerson's call for a national, for a truly *American* poet—Whitman was a rebel "against a European heritage that was still strong seventy years after the [American R]evolution," but even so small a thing as his flowing not very closely trimmed beard signals his rugged masculinity. Confident and aggressive, Whitman's determination in the "Calamus" poems "To tell the secret of my nights and days / To celebrate the need of comrades" similarly expresses a clear homosexual identity. Though, as Martin points out, "the 'Calamus' poems lack much of the frank sexuality of 'Song of Myself,' " what is remarkable about them is that "they insist, not on homosexual *acts*, but on homosexual being." Which points to why Whitman took up the task of naming what had been unnamed and thus, in a sense, incomplete.[65] Wrote Martin: "He was an American flaneur, sauntering around 'mast-hemm'd Manhattan' at about the same time that Baudelaire—who, not long after the first publication of *Leaves of Grass*, defined modernity as 'the ephemeral, the fugitive, the contingent'—was prowling Paris."[66]

It is a view (we now tend to forget) relatively recent. Writes Gregory Bredbeck, "Whitman's democratic visions of 'calamitic love' inspired the work in large part of Edward Carpenter, the British sexual theorist, whose "concept of democratic male bonding derived from Whitman's writings." Although it may be enthusiastic to a degree to link homosexuality inevitably with the abolition of class and sexual hierarchies, some affinity does suggest itself.[67] Thus today in *The Social Organization of Gay Males*, Joseph Harry and William B. DeVall conclude that among upper- and upper-middle-class (not working-class) American gays "rather than utilizing the conventional heterosexual marriage as a model for relationships, it seems that [gay] relationships are patterned after the nonexclusive conventional best friends model." In the bedroom, too: "Gay couples tended to exchange in reciprocal manner the various erotic positions," they report.[68]

We have again got somewhat ahead of ourselves; but if we turn around, so to speak, and backtrack again to "manly attachment," our base in this chapter, Whitman's own hypermasculine image can easily be seen as an important historical foundation for the particularly American gay image Whitman "named." This can be seen, for instance, as a key vector in the Whitman "movement," if one can call it that. In a short biographical sketch intended as a rejoinder to a highly bigoted Secretary of the Interior who fired Whitman from his government clerkship over his authorship of *Leaves of Grass*, William D. O'Connor introduces Whitman as familiar to "thousands of people in New York, in Brooklyn, in Boston, in New Orleans, and latterly in Washington." He is, says O'Connor, "a man of striking masculine beauty—a poet—powerful and venerable in appearance; large, calm, superbly formed; oftenest clad in the careless, rough and always picturesque costume of the common people . . . [his] head, majestic, large, Homeric, and set upon his strong shoulders with the grandeur of ancient sculpture." O'Connor's hero worship—there is nothing else to call it—spills over in every word. Even Whitman's clothes come into it, O'Connor extolling "the simplicity and purity of his dress, cheap and plain, but spotless, from snowy falling collar to burnished boot, and exhaling faint fragrance; the whole form surrounded with manliness, as with a nimbus, and breathing, in its perfect health and vigor, the august charm of the strong."[69] Every other word in this description—"powerful," "large," "calm," "majestic," "strong"—tells readers that, in physique as in dress, this is no sissy, no dandy. Manly attachment is expressed by manly dress and deportment. Indeed, as G. W. Allen points out, "Almost everyone who knew Walt Whitman intimately was conquered by his magnetic presence, and there is no reason whatever to doubt the sincerity of O'Connor's enthusiastic description; nevertheless, we have here the first of the superman legends,"[70] legends that lost nothing and, in fact, gained much in power: During and after the Civil War Whitman was linked more and more closely to Abraham Lincoln himself.

One sees this already in O'Connor's affecting—though entirely undocumented and, indeed, highly unlikely—vignette of Lincoln's spying Whitman from a White House window, and remarking, "Well, *he* looks like a man."[71] This almost surely apocryphal story gains weight, however, because it is known that for his part Lincoln appreciated *Leaves of Grass*, while in Whitman's case his hero worship of the president was hardly less fulsome than O'Connor's of Whitman. Writes G. W. Allen of Whitman in the year of his historic Boston Common dialogue:

The 1860 edition [of *Leaves of Grass*] contains not only the record of the great spiritual crisis of Whitman's life—in which he seems to have contemplated suicide—but it also reveals the means by which he saved himself. . . . Though torn and racked by conflicts within, he was struggling for both a personal and a literary unity. Conflicts within himself would be conquered. . . . For Whitman the great democratic fiasco of those years came to correspond to the fateful character of his love in the "Calamus" poems.

What saved him, above all else, was the unifying effect of the Civil War—not only through his own patriotic and devoted services in the army hospitals but also because the war gave Whitman and the nation Abraham Lincoln.[72]

Written after Lincoln's death, Whitman's "When Lilacs Last in the Dooryard Bloom'd" is the most affecting of all the elegies of Western literature in the modern period. Whether the brow was Homeric or not, the words certainly were.

College Friends

MASCULINITY—THE AESTHETIC of manliness, its style, so to speak—was in some sense what Harvard Yard in this era was all about. The College was a boys' school in many respects (though let us not be condescending; those boys would fight and win the Civil War). Many tales of the Yard then are extant, and one is of particular importance to us: the first in a series of Harvard novels that open windows onto the landscape of our inquiry.

Entitled *Two College Friends*, this Civil War novel is also the earliest of a significant genre, the Harvard gay novel, and is in fact one of the earliest gay-themed novels in American literary history. First brought to my attention years ago by a bookdealer who wishes to remain anonymous—a reader of my book *Boston Bohemia*, which seems to have sparked his memory of the obscure novel that had always puzzled him—*Two College Friends* is the work of Fred W. Loring, and while hardly Whitmanic in literary quality it is overwhelmingly Whitmanic in content. Published in 1871, only one year after another book usually described as the first American "gay novel"—Bayard Taylor's *Joseph and His Friend*[73]—the novel recounts a stormy but steadfast relationship between Ned and Tom, two undergraduates who fall in love at Harvard and enlist in the Union Army.[74] The two young men and their unnamed older mentor, a professor, are first encountered in Harvard Yard before the war. And the tale is immediately unusual in the frankly homoerotic quality of the author's descriptions of the two younger men, and in the way they meet. Tom is described as having "soft, curly brown hair, deep blue eyes and dazzling complexion"; with Ned "the complexion is of olive, the eyes brown, the lips strangely cut [and he has] a curious grace and fascination of manner." They meet in their mentor's professorial study in Harvard Yard in a scene that is surely the closest thing to a classic gay pickup that 1871 could handle.

Tom has sought out the professor's counsel, in the course of which both are rather taken aback by the unexpected arrival of Ned, who, having invited himself, belies rather a dull reputation by exhibiting a newfound wit and charm. Its stimulant, clearly, is Tom, who is soon "radiant with enjoyment." As for the professor, it is not long before he is uncorking his best Madeira.

It is only at the conclusion of this jolly session that the older man, detaining Ned at the head of the stairs as Tom exits below, asks earnestly: "Why have you never shown me what you really are?" This rather coded query is understood at once by Ned: "It wasn't for you, sir," said Ned, with a certain frankness that was not discourteous. "It was for Tom, sir, though I like you and hope we shall be friends. But the moment I saw him come up here I felt that here was a chance to get acquainted."

No persiflage there. This is very much a young man's book. Its author wrote it at the age of twenty-one.

Though frank, Loring was not foolhardy. He disarmingly deflects any objection that Ned was "morbid on the subject of Tom" by making the former an orphan. Equally adroitly, and in more treacherous waters, the author has it, so to speak, both ways with the professor, a bachelor with whom Ned and Tom remain close throughout the book. On the one hand, the professor is affirmed as a man of "tender sympathy, . . . exquisite delicacy of thought and life and [of] wit and scholarship." On the other hand, one of the young men allows that for all his affection for the older man, the professor's "liking for us boys is very queer to me."

"What you really are," "morbid" young men, "very queer"—this is not a tough code to break. But modern readers should be wary of being lulled into reading our own values and attitudes into those of a century ago. Both Tom and Ned, for instance, plan to marry women and have children and take their place in the conventional society of their day.

Though both Tom and Ned show a due appreciation of the possibilities offered by the opposite sex, any such interest expressed by one invariably provokes the other man to a furious jealousy, suggesting that much more is at issue. Ned, for instance, fancies one young lady sufficiently to produce some verses for her and send them to Harvard's magazine. But when they meet up and she inquires about the initials on a locket of Ned's, asking coyly, "Is she pretty?" Ned's reply is devastating to her *amour propre*: " 'She!' he answered; "it isn't any girl; it's my chum Tom, you know."

Nor do advancing maturity and the rigors of the battlefield—both men, who are depicted as ardent patriots, leave Harvard to enlist—alter this attitude. *Two College Friends* depicts no schoolboy crush. At one point during their time together in the army, Ned writes in his battlefield journal: "When this war is over, I suppose Tom will marry and forget me. I never will go near his wife—I shall hate her. Now, that is a very silly thing for a lieutenant-colonel to write. I don't care; it is true."

One possible reason for his outburst is that, just as the attitude toward heterosexual marriage of the author and his protagonists is distinctly at odds with that of most gays today, who would find such a union problematic for the homosexual, so too is what seems (at first glance, at least) their approach toward same-sex relationships, which somewhat mimic heterosexual ones of the era. Certainly Tom is depicted as noticeably more like a woman than Ned. Shown a photograph of Tom in drag for a student theatrical production while still at Harvard, the professor opines: " 'What a mistake nature made about your sex, Tom.' " Later, in the army, a grizzled old soldier says to Ned of Tom—all but abandoning the code of the closet—"You care for him as you would for a gal, don't you?" He goes on to describe Tom as " 'pootier than any gal I ever see anywhar.' "

While it is Ned who courts Tom, making the first approach, and Ned who enlists first, expecting Tom to follow, the fact is that through the book both are always fighting for dominance, Tom declaring at one point that he "will not accept dictation" from his friend despite liking him more than anyone else. In fact, their relationship in this respect hardly accords with the Mediterranean same-sex model, in which one man invariably plays the aggressive and penetrating role, which is *not* seen as homosexual, while the other man, who *is* seen as such, plays the receptive and passive role.

The extent of their belligerence is clear in this account from Ned's journal:

> Quarreled with Tom! How we have fought, to be sure! I don't know what this quarrel was about, but I know how it ended. We didn't speak for two days, and then came another attack from that restless creature, Stonewall Jackson. . . . I didn't see Tom, but I knew he was near,—we always kept close together at such times;—still, if I had seen him, I wouldn't have spoken to him. My horse had been shot from under me, and I had cut open the head of the man who did it; it seems strange, now that it is all over, that I could do such a thing. Suddenly I saw the barrel of a rifle pointed at me. The face of the man who was pointing it peered from behind a tree with a malicious grin. I felt that death was near, and the feeling was not pleasant. However, the situation had an element of absurdity in it, and that made me laugh a little. The man who was going to kill me laughed too. I heard a little click, a report, and his gun went up, and he went down. Tom had shot him.
>
> "Tom," said I, with some feeling, "you have saved my life."
>
> "There!" said he, triumphantly, "you spoke first."
>
> I saw that I had, and I was dreadfully provoked. However, he admitted that he was wrong; and so, under the circumstances, I decided that a reconciliation was advisable.

Such stubborn masculinity on each side surely implies a rough equality and, upon closer consideration, it would seem that the comparisons of Tom to a woman are not meant to imply Tom is *less masculine* than Ned, but rather that he is *more beautiful.* Certainly Ned is pronounced "not as handsome" as Tom, and much is made throughout the book of "Tom's beauty." But nowhere is it suggested that either is effeminate.

Two College Friends is rooted firmly in what is often called "muscular Christianity," to see the homosexual aspect of which one must recall that many if not most men then of whatever sexuality (clearly including Fred Loring) took the view—certainly the prevailing one today—that men who behaved in an unmanly way were problematic, and that it was gender-inappropriate behavior, not homosexuality as such, that affronted masculine values, heterosexual and homosexual. One can hardly avoid noticing that neither Tom nor Ned—despite a relationship open enough that the grizzled old soldier recognizes it at once as comparable to one between a man and a woman—seems, in today's terms, to have troubled unit cohesion at all. One is reminded instead of the battalions of lovers in the Theban army of ancient Greece.

Nor should any of this in the American Civil War come as a surprise, for Ned's journal is striking literary corroboration of the historical findings of Yale professor Peter Gay, whose study of the real-life nineteenth-century diary of a Yale student disclosed

> a capacious gift for erotic investment [in] men and women indiscriminately without undue self-laceration, without visible guilt or degrading shame . . . inclinations [that] seemed innocent to [him] and apparently to others, because his bearing and behavior, including his emotional attachments to others of his own sex, did not affront current codes of conduct. He preserved the appearances; it never occurred to him, in fact, to do anything else.[75]

We have entered here, of course, what has been called by Brian Pronger in his book of that title, "the arena of masculinity": *Two College Friends* deals finally and most importantly with men at war, and in this connection gays always, I believe, do well to consider the brilliant observation of A. L. Rowse, the legendary Oxford historian, who noted that both the Japanese samurai warrior tradition and the Greek homosexual warrior tradition "do not see manliness as instinctive, but, rather, as something to be gained by moral effort."[76] The mustering of that effort, on several levels, is really Fred Loring's fundamental theme in this book.

Later in the novel, when Ned is a prisoner of war, he is confronted by Stonewall Jackson's assertion—"I love war for itself, I glory in it"—and he stalwartly responds, "I hate war." Here he is making—and exemplifying—a moral effort not all men would be capable of. He will only fight, Ned insists, "when there is a cause at stake." Similarly, when he finds himself at odds with a much larger man, a civilian troublemaker whose antics are distracting his men during drill, Ned finally concludes:

> [R]emonstrance would be in vain; so I knocked him down, seeing my opportunity to do so effectively. My men laughed. The giant raised himself in astonishment.
> "You can't do that again," said he. Another laugh from the chorus.
> "I know it," said I. Still another laugh.
> "I could just walk through you in two minutes," he growled with an oath.
> "I believe you," said I; "and I shall give you a chance to, if you don't keep quiet."

After this sterling exchange it is hardly surprising that Ned shows yet more pluck by quickly seeing the man's underlying ability and convincing him to enlist; whereupon Ned makes him his first lieutenant.

The climax of Loring's book may seem curious to the modern reader. Not that it is not passionate enough. Ned, Loring recounts, visiting his wounded friend in a field hospital, directed his orderly to "let no one enter [the room] under any pretext whatever," and then "threw himself down [on the bed] beside Tom—kissed his hot face" and, still lying in bed next to his chum, who is described as "sleeping restlessly under the influence of some opiate," delivered rather a scorcher for 1871. For all its cloying tone it is still oddly moving:

> O Tom, my darling! Don't forget it. If you know how I love you, how I have loved you in all my jealous, morbid moods. . . . Don't you remember when we were examined for college together? . . . I saw you there; and I wanted to go over and help you. And your picture, Tom . . . it was the night when I determined to go to war that you gave me that picture; it was just before we enlisted. . . . You won't forget Ned, darling; he was something to you.

There is an age-old and honorable romantic heterosexual tradition of finding passionate love and even erotic fulfillment in relationships that, because of religious prejudice, age asymmetry, social custom, or whatever, are nonphysical in nature. Of an affair of Henry Adams's, for instance, a biographer writes: "Some lovers found it nobler—and perhaps even erotic—not to act on their physical impulses."[77] But though homosexual love, with its ancient heritage of Platonic self-mastery, has historically evinced an even greater affinity for such relationships (as in *Maurice*, for instance, where E. M. Forster writes about Clive and Maurice, "It had been understood between them that their love, though including the body, should not gratify it"[78]), for the modern reader the idea founders on the fact that even if men are no longer seen as necessarily lust-crazed sexual outlaws, gay men are still seen today as sexual predators, if only because genital sex now seems for us a necessary validator of passionate homosexual romantic love. Heterosexuals, after all, are married even if they never have sex; gays often still cannot envision a same-sex union without sex. It has been argued that Bayard Taylor's 1870 novel *Joseph and His Friend* is not a gay novel (even though the deepest and most fulfilling relationship is between the male protagonists) because one of the protagonists finally marries a woman, and the same can be argued of *Two College Friends*, where, of course, the same thing happens. But how could it not? It has ever been the classic solution whenever a permanent union is not possible between two lovers: one has to die and the survivor, happily wed, can almost be depended upon to name the first child after the lost love; in this case, Ned dies, shot for violating his parole to save the life of Tom, who is depicted at book's end as looking lovingly and tearfully into Ned's—his son's—face.

Is *Two College Friends* a gay novel? Is a same-sex union a union when sex ceases or if it never started? Are failed gay relationships (for whatever reasons) any the less homosexual? If gay people enter opposite-sex marriages, do they cease to be gay when they do? How many homosexual "acts" make a homosexual anyway (assuming one accepts that definition)? One? Two? Three dozen? Three thousand? What is a homosexual act? Will desire alone suffice? How about masturbation? Better yet, consider Robert K. Martin's sage remark of what a tip-off it is when someone is prepared to "assume that anyone is heterosexual until there is proof, not of homosexual feelings, but of homosexual (i.e., genital) acts."[79] Is *Maurice* a gay novel? If so, then so is *Joseph and His Friend*, as well as *Two College Friends*, whose author, like his protagonist, died young (he was killed in an Indian attack on a stagecoach out west, in the very year he wrote the book, 1871, at age twenty-one), thus foreclosing further inquiry. Who was it who said most gay history lies buried in bachelor graves?

If Fred Loring's early death defeats additional investigation, something further can still be ventured. His Harvard class notes do hint, for example, at a certain discomfort about *Two College Friends*—the not-inconsiderable achievement of a first book at age twenty-one is dismissed in a phrase without even noting the novel's title—and what little survives of Loring's remaining published work suggests he quickly turned to more conventional heterosexual subjects: a slim book of verses, for instance, which takes its title from the "Boston Dip," a popular dance of the period—"One way to dance it thoroughly / Is Much champagne to sip; / Or,—rub your boots with orange peel / Till they are sure to slip." Which Loring didn't do in *The Boston Dip*: one of his poems in the book, more in the nature of a "save" entitled "Tom to Ned," announces the former's forthcoming wedding in a tone of somewhat defensive false heartiness.[80] Taken in conjunction with Loring's departure, after graduation, for the western frontier, a dangerous enough place in the 1870s, this possibly hints at the sort of real-life situation that gay literature of the late nineteenth and early twentieth centuries (Forster's *Maurice*, for instance) depicted: the breakup of a same-sex relationship under the weight of society's pressure on a man to enter into an opposite-sex marriage, in aid not only of his social but also his professional or business success.

Some element of autobiography about *Two College Friends* is suggested by Loring's dedication of the book to a classmate, William Chamberlain.[81] Certainly, the tone of Loring's dedication seems to echo more than a little of Tom and Ned's quarrelsome relationship when he writes, in the book's preface and dedication:

> Indignation at my dedicating this book to you will be useless, since I am at present three thousand miles out of your reach. Moreover, this dedication is not intended as a public monument to our friendship;—I know too much for that. If that were the case we should manage to quarrel even at this distance. . . . But I can dedicate it to you alone of all my college friends, because you and I were brought so especially into the atmosphere of [the professor] who inspired me to undertake it.[82]

Loring's reason for the dedication, however, rings as false—dedicating it to the professor was hardly an unexampled proceeding among teachers and students—as his address to his absent friend about his quarrelsomeness rings true. Indeed, its testy tone is that of all of us when we feel betrayed by someone we still care for, and is reminiscent of Maurice's tone with Clive in Forster's novel when Maurice comes out (as we would say today) and Clive does not, electing instead to contract a conventional heterosexual marriage. This is, of course, all very speculative, but the Harvard class notes on Chamberlain also support such possibilities. Loring and Chamberlain went very different ways upon graduation—Loring to his death out west, Chamberlain within a year back to his rural Massachusetts hometown to marriage and a son, who was not named after Loring, though he had been dead over a year. Yet later class reports hint that Chamberlain, who outlived Loring by forty years, had a much less conventional history than one might expect. He is noted as having "lived abroad a considerable portion of [his life]"—always suggestive in the coded discourse of the day—and seems also to have quickly abandoned the family business for journalism and—even more suggestive— the theater. In fact, at one point he formed a very successful partnership with a leading figure of Boston's bohemian gay circles of the 1880s and 1890s, the playwright Thomas Russell Sullivan, with whom Chamberlain wrote a comedy that in 1880 enjoyed wide popularity in Boston. Entitled *A Midsum-*

mer Madness, it sounds a very different type of tale from *Two College Friends*, more the game of reveal-and-conceal that gays were forced to play then (and well enough to still amuse today: witness *The Importance of Being Earnest*).[83]

About one thing, however, there seems to have been no dissembling. Just as Tom and Ned were described as ardent patriots for the Union cause, so are both portrayed as, above all else, Harvard men. In one of his letters, Ned evokes the mood of his generation well enough:

> I can see the Yard, with Holworthy and Stoughton and Hollis beaming away from their windows at each other. . . . I can see fellows sitting around the tables in their rooms, studying and not studying; . . . The bell for morning prayers, which I still hate, begins to clang upon my memory. . . . If you ever want to think of me, and to feel I am near, walk through the Yard. . . . I wonder how many visions of its elm-trees have swayed before dying eyes here in Virginia battlefields.

There is everything Whitmanic about this early gay novel; there is hardly anything Wildean about *Two College Friends*. The subject is manhood—American manhood and manliness—the Whitmanic archetype of the warrior, and the masculine aesthetic that expresses it.

The Archetype

WHEN AN ENRAGED Norman Mailer once head-butted Gore Vidal in an altercation the two antagonists always seemed to be angling for, Vidal returned fire by punching Mailer's stomach. Writing about it later, Mailer confessed: "To my surprise, he hit me back."[84] Why on earth was he surprised? Hit a man and that's the likely response, certainly when the man is as aggressive as Vidal famously is. Perhaps Mailer's well-advertised macho disdain for homosexuality explains his reaction. Yet as Yale historian John Boswell—himself by most accounts somewhat effeminate in rather a boyish sort of way—pointed out, "an equation of homosexuality with effeminacy in men would hardly have occurred to people [like the ancient Greeks] whose history, art, popular literature, and religious myths were all filled with the homosexual exploits of such archetypically masculine figures as Zeus, Hercules, Achilles, et al.," adding that in the *Symposium* Plato has Aristophanes describe homosexuals as "naturally the most manly."[85] In *Boston Bohemia*, I wrote that "what the gymnasium was to the ancient [Greek] classical expression of male ardor, the English school chapel . . . became to the modern Anglo-American expression" and that in such schools generally only the fact that "the lavatories stood doorless" was more important than that the choir stalls face each other, in aid of what Sir John Betjeman called "ravenous glances." Most shocking of all, however, was the underlying design concept of what I called in that book "Gay Gothic," which Bishop William Lawrence of Massachusetts dubbed "chaste, strong and uplifting."[86]

Chaste? Although it would be wrong to argue that actual chasteness in and of itself was ever or is now more characteristic of the Whitmanic archetype of the warrior than of the Wildean archetype of the aesthete, as we will see in the next chapter, Bishop Lawrence's phraseology, so very Phillips Brooks–like in its "muscular Christianity," *is* distinctly Whitmanic. And Hellenist. As Jonathan Gathorne-Hardy pointed out in *The Old School Tie*: "During the last quarter of the nineteenth-century there developed a form of aesthetic, chaste homosexuality—a product of manliness crossed with the classical curriculum,"[87] the background, in fact, of the institution in that era of the modern Olympics and the Anglo-American sports culture of the twentieth century. It was the sort of culture that would produce Lawrence of Arabia, kin only once removed, culturally, from Tom and Ned of *Two College Friends*, and would lead their sort especially to join

> schoolboy secret societies like the Order of Chaeronea, which took its name from the great battle won by Philip of Macedon, a battle famous for the valor of the "sacred band" of homosexual soldiers, and school heroes (Rupert Brooke is the classic case) forever reading classical authors in the original Greek on their way to practice, for it was expected that they would throw javelins as well as they would compose sonnets—in each case in no small measure for the edification of the beloved.[88]

Typically, all things homosexual were more muted in America. But in the realm of higher education such things could not be entirely ignored, even at Harvard. As "Alligator" (librarian) of the now-venerable but then-outrageous Hasty Pudding Club in 1857, for instance, it was part of the education of Henry Adams to compose club minutes that amused, scandalized, and in the event were highly priapic and open to all sorts of constructions:[89] "A giant oak," for example, is said by Adams to grow—don't they all?—in "love's garden." The narrator is a woman, to be sure, but given the time-honored fashion of switching genders in such doggerel, the thing hymned is perhaps what's most significant. Furthermore, Adams attributes the poem to Lord Byron, notorious then for his homosexual affairs, and—in case the point should be missed—introduces it by a long peroration on the recent adventures in Greece of Harvard Greek professor Cornelius Felton, who was traveling with various young men as enthusiastic about same-sex gymnastics as he was. Nor was it only in salacious jest and in club minutes that the issue arose. In a letter of 1877 Alice Stone Blackwell, a leading feminist, supported but nonetheless complained about professors who found it necessary to explain Greek pederasty to their classes: "Harvard, where there are no women to restrain them," seemed to her particularly worrisome.[90] In fact, then as now, so much controversy surrounds the all-important subject of Things Greek, whether gay-positive or gay-negative, it will be useful here to consider authoritative sources not, on the one hand, issued by gay apologists but recent enough, on the other, to be free of antigay rhetoric: the *Oxford Classical Dictionary* (entries cited are by Andrew S. Brown, David M. Halperin, A. W. Price, and C. J. Tuplin); *A Dictionary of the Ancient Greek World*, by David Sacks; and *Cambridge Illustrated History: Ancient Greece* by Paul Cartledge, an array of varying schools of thought.

A good example of the confusion that bedevils this subject is the matter of Achilles and Patroclus, who are variously declared to be the most ardent of lovers or no lovers at all.[91] What is important is that they were best friends, soul mates, very close comrades, each other's surest confidant and sounding board. They loved each other whether or not they were *in* love. David Sacks supplies the historical context, observing that the Mycenaean world (ca. 1200 B.C.) in which the *Iliad* is set, as well as Homer's era (ca. 750 B.C.), may or may not have sanctioned such male couplings, but by the fifth century B.C. they were definitely fostered. Thus Aeschylus, in Andrew S. Brown's words, "portray[ed] Achilles and Patroclus as lovers."[92] Classical Athenians like Aeschylus, being considerably closer to their sources than we are more than two millennia later, may well have known something about the earlier period we don't. David M. Halperin sums up: "Homer did not portray Achilles and Patroclus as lovers (although some [later] Classical Athenians thought he implied as much. . . .) but he also did little to rule out such an interpretation."[93] Furthermore, Sacks declares, there were definite ground rules:

> Love between males was seen as harmonious with other Greek social values, such as athletic skill, military courage, and the idealization of male youth and beauty. . . . The Greeks tended to associate homosexuality with manliness and soldiering.
>
> [For males] there was only one kind of publicly approved romance available for people of the citizen classes—namely, the romance that might arise between a mature man and a younger male.
>
> Youths around ages 16 and 17 were considered particularly desirable. . . . The older male . . . might be in his 20's, 30's, or possibly 40's, anywhere from about five to 25 years older than his partner. . . . Probably at around age 20 a young Athenian would feel social pressure to relinquish his junior sex role. He might maintain a close friendship with his former lover(s), but he would now be ready to take on the adult role, as the active pursuer of a younger male.[94]

There is inevitably the issue of power in male-to-male sex. In our own era, for instance, I am reminded of Gore Vidal's observation that a preference for lower-class sexual partners is often accounted for because a sexual commitment between "strongly willed males" of the same class could lead to "a psychic defeat for one of the partners."[95] For the Greeks, it was not so much class as the type of intercourse that determined power relations: in classic Mediterranean mode, power is seen as belonging to the penetrator. Thus the preferred (because more equal) sex act, especially in Athens, between male lovers, was what is today called intercrural intercourse—two men standing or lying face-to-face with the older man moving his penis between the younger's clamped thighs.

Moreover, close friendship with former lovers was not the only adult model, says Sacks: ". . . where love relationships often continued after the younger male reached adulthood, it was customary to station lovers side-by-side in battle, on the theory that each would fight more fiercely if observed by his partner."[96] Thus the so-called Sacred Band, referred to above.[97] C. J. Tuplin calls it "an elite infantry unit formed by Gorgidas, after the liberation of Thebes from Spartan occupation (379 B.C.), perhaps as a symbolic counterpart to elite Spartan units, and consisting of 150 pairs of lovers maintained at state expense."[98] More explicitly, Paul Cartledge calls it a "band of 300 specially picked Theban hoplite [heavy infantrymen] warriors—reputedly a unit of 150 homosexual couples, who made war as well as love together."[99] Originally the idea was, in Tuplin's words, "to use them as a unit only in limited operations requiring rapid deployment while distributing them through the front infantry ranks in formal battle,"[100] presumably to inspire the troops. But the unit's crucial role in the Battle of Leuctra changed all that. Tuplin calls the details controversial, but John F. Lazenby states that while it is not clear if the Sacred Band formed the front ranks of the Thebans, it was this unit that, at a crucial point in the battle, charged the Spartans and carried the day, "ending two centuries of Spartan domination."[101]

Their undoing came at the Battle of Chaeronea where, in 338 B.C., Philip of Macedon, aided by his son, Alexander, who may have led the crucial charge, won a great victory over a Greek alliance led by Athens and Thebes, in the course of which the Sacred Band was all but annihilated. They so covered themselves with glory, however, that the ancient lion monument of Chaeronea, now restored from fragments and still presiding over this battlefield, "possibly marks," in Lazenby's words, "the resting place of the Theban elite Sacred Band." A moving story, however it is detailed. (Sacks writes of this battle that the disaster occurred because of Philip's brilliantly successful tactics: in the movement of battle he succeeded in isolating the Sacred Band from the rest of the Theban army, and so left it exposed to the full force of Alexander's cavalry, which "surrounded and overr[an]" them.)[102]

That the historical discussion has shifted two millennia forward is significant. For we are not just talking ancient history. Modern Hellenism is our subject here, the picture plane, so to speak, through which Victorians saw ancient history. It is best studied in Linda Dowling's *Hellenism and Homosexuality in Victorian Oxford*, where the issues are more literary though still philosophical. Dowling points out that "the Plato of Benjamin Jowett and the Oxford Reformers" was largely the Plato of John Stuart Mill's *On Liberty*: "the philosopher of a healthy and productive skepticism and a fearless determination" that, as a student, one must "follow one's intellect to whatever conclusions it may lead." Dowling continues: "Yet the same Plato could then at the same moment and by an identical logic be taken as the tutelary spirit of a movement never foreseen by Jowett, . . . in which such writers as Walter Pater and John Addington Symonds would deduce from Plato's own writings an apology for male love as something not only noble but infinitely more ennobling than an exploded Christianity and those sexual taboos and legal proscriptions inspired by its dogmas."[103]

Symonds repeatedly proclaimed, in *A Problem in Greek Ethics,* that Greek love was "in its origin and essence, military . . . nor had Malachia, effeminacy, a place in its vocabulary." Symonds's "manly" Greek lovers with their erotic "chivalry" and martial "comrade love" were to reappear constantly in the homosexual apologist writings of the years to come. Indeed, continues Dowling, Symonds dedicated himself to what she calls "the ideal of Dorian comradeship, the ideal that so powerfully contested the ancient slur of 'effeminacy' invariably raised in England and America against men who loved men." Which is to arrive here at the intersection of Whitmanic masculinity and Oxford Hellenism—Harvard Hellenism, too: by "Dorian comradeship" Dowling, a British scholar, means, an "ideal . . . unconsciously but completely realized by Whitman in the 'Calamus' poems of *Leaves of Grass*."[104]

Many and various roads lead from this intersection. The Oxford tutorial tradition, for instance, which Harvard would revive in the early 1900s, is full of "the Socratic Eros," as Dowling calls it; not for nothing, after all, was Socrates called a "corrupter of youth." Symonds himself found tutorial a very brisk experience of masculinity, and Dowling describes the "racking silences, penetrating queries, [and] quenching utterances. Whatever were the pains inflicted by this experience, its pleasures seemed to the young men to be unexampled. Symonds, paralyzed by the conviction of his own complete inadequacy, nonetheless left the tutor's room feeling 'obscurely yet vividly' that 'my soul [had] grown by his contact, as it had never grown before.' . . . [It was] a moral counsel so capacious in its scope that it became a 'pastoral supervision,' of an intellectual stimulus."[105] A Harvard example, from the period before formal tutorial was revived but when its values were still very clearly understood by this as well as that side of the Anglo-American collegiate world, is told by a biographer of Oliver Wendell Holmes Jr. It seems Holmes (in his student days) asked Emerson once to read a paper on Plato that Holmes thought to submit for a prize, seeking Emerson in particular because he had the repute, even with mere undergraduates, of dealing "man to man." And in good tutorial fashion, Emerson pulled no punches—the Socratic Eros defined—handing it back to Holmes with what would become a famous judgment indeed: "I have read your piece. When you strike at a king, you must *kill* him." Holmes hadn't. Equally Socratic was Emerson's advice: in essence, respect Plato more, but say to him: you've impressed so many; now impress me.[106]

Symonds's first encounter with the Socratic Eros occurred at Oxford, where in his studies he first confronted Plato's teaching (in *Symposium* 209) that "the highest level of masculine love [was] procreating ideas—generating the creative arts, philosophy,"[107] and so on. It was in that light that both Pater and he saw "the ideal education of the Platonic or Socratic doctrine of Eros," specifically in the "model of love . . . by which an older man, moved to love by the visible beauty of the younger man, and desirous of winning immortality through that love, undertakes the younger man's education in virtue and wisdom."[108] It was a model that would be recaptured at Harvard, just as it had been "recaptured within the existing structures of Oxford homosociality—the intense friendship, the tutorial." Utterly besotted by the lifestyle, Symonds at Oxford spoke for all: "I wept, as I remembered how often you and I / Had tired the sun with talking and sent him down the sky."[109]

A parallel to all this was the growing athleticism of the Harvard experience in the mid-nineteenth century. As Charles P. Pierce has noted, Walt Whitman never stopped talking about "how baseball embodies the robust new national character that was brawny . . . and full-blooded." And Ronald Story has pointed out in his fascinating study on *Harvard and the Boston Upper Class*:

> The quest for "refinement and beauty always had boundaries conforming to the prevailing patterns of nineteenth-century sexual assertiveness and competitive fitness. Just as young men should not drink to excess, so they should not become "gloved and lisping dandies" or possess the "perfumed curls," the "slender waists," and the "tiny legs" of "D'Israeili" and the Young Englanders. If they could not be exactly "robust as a farmer's son," neither should they be "whey-faced and feeble, effeminate and fearful."
>
> One attitude to these extremes lay, of course, in physical exercise and sporting events. . . . By 1840 many students rode. . . . By 1850 cricket, baseball, and a crude version of rugby were familiar Cambridge pastimes [and in] the 1850's [Harvard] built a new gymnasium and also welcomed the adoption of crew as a suitably vigorous and masculine student activity.[110]

Here the concern with gender-appropriate deportment is apparently not confused with homosexuality—Disraeli was never thought to be homosexual. And this may help to bring into focus here what one scholar has called "George Santayana's somewhat paradoxical promulgation of Whitman worship at Harvard during the [eighteen-nineties]."[111] Often overlooked because less provocative stylistically than the Wilde worship of the same era, Whitman worship is well charted by critic James Gifford, who cites Whitman worship as evidence that

> at the end of the nineteenth century in America, what the homosexual might be(come) was very much in flux; there was no single workable paradigm of homosexuality. The medical establishment was creating a pathological portrait at the same time that the effeminized aesthete (à la Oscar Wilde) presented an obvious—and notorious—representation of homosexuality to late Victorian America. Recent studies have suggested that *another* sort of homosexual, Walt Whitman's blue-collar democratized man-loving man, coexisted with the willowy Bunthorne (the Wildean aesthete satirized in Gilbert and Sullivan's *Patience*).[112]

An example. The Whitmanic, rather than the later Wildean, archetype is the context of a leading Harvard figure of the mid- to late nineteenth century, Thomas Wentworth Higginson, most notable as the commanding officer in the Civil War of the First South Carolina volunteers, the first African-American regiment in the Union Army. Not only something of a war hero, throughout his life Higginson was an illustrious American reformer and a progressive, abolitionist above all, also keen for women's rights, and conspicuous not least for his zeal and devotion to American athleticism, which he argued for in a series of highly influential articles in *The Atlantic* in the late 1850s and 1860s, a literary landmark of the rise of sports in America in which Harvard played a major role.

This history, too, is often overlooked. Today's famous Head of the Charles regatta is a twentieth-century revival of a Fourth of July regatta sponsored first by Boston's aldermen in 1854 (it drew forty thousand viewers), two years after Harvard and Yale raced against each other in America's first intercollegiate sports event. By 1858 there was a Harvard University Boating Club, which rowed in the earliest racing shell built in America, and whose captain, when he bought six red handkerchiefs for headbands, inaugurated college colors generally and Harvard's own crimson in particular. Boston cheered all this mightily, supportive not only of newly minted professional civic baseball teams but also of Harvard's new amateur baseball, football, track-and-field, and tennis teams. When the Olympic Games were revived in Athens in 1896, "Boston athletes," according to journalist Stephen Hardy, "were the heart of the American team which dominated the games" and on their triumphant return were greeted with such enthusiasm that the *Boston Herald* compared the event to the way the ancient Greek city-states had welcomed home their heroes.[113]

It was, in fact, "the Greek ideal of the sound mind in the sound body," according to Harvard historian Bainbridge Bunting, that undergirded Harvard's magnificent new gymnasium of 1878, which Bunting calls "the most advanced building of its type and style in America." It was the domain of

Dr. Dudley Sargent (he held a medical degree from Yale), who had been inspired to make physical education his career after reading Higginson's *Atlantic* articles. Athletics, Sargent believed, yielded "bodily health and beauty" and "the manly virtues of energy, strength, courage, alertness, persistence, stamina and endurance." And it was Sargent, Bunting writes, who was "responsible for achieving a scientific rationale, long-range curricular continuity, and eventual acceptance for college athletics in America." Indeed, Harvard's gym became "the cradle of physical education in America," in Bunting's words; one of Sargent's assistants, George Meylon, director of the Boston YMCA in the 1890s, would obtain the first academic appointment in physical education in America at Columbia in 1903.[114]

Higginson's *Atlantic* articles, in which he urged the office worker, "his head a mere furnace of red-hot brains and his body a pile of burnt-out cinders," to "come with me to the Gymnasium," also had a wider effect on the American public generally and in Boston in particular. Higginson was a spokesman for a point of view, writes Stephen Hardy, that

> signaled the beginning of a new current of thought [about] . . . social life in the city . . . [including] sedentary and enfeebling work routines among clerks and shopkeepers. The call for public action laid the groundwork for the first major civic response to the problem . . . a public park system . . . [and] the development before the Civil War of organized sports clubs in rowing, cricket and baseball.[115]

Although Higginson's own lifestyle was as physically vigorous as one might have expected—he once helped batter down a courthouse door to free a slave—he was a man of brain as well as brawn. He was, for instance, the discoverer of Emily Dickinson, and people are too quick to seize on his stodginess and presumption in "correcting" Dickinson's grammar, and too slow to acknowledge that Dickinson's poetry only surfaced at all because she was cajoled into print by another *Atlantic* article by Higginson, this one urging women poets to send their work to him. Nor was Higginson always stodgy: when the enthusiasm for war with Spain was at its highest pitch at century's end, Higginson opposed Theodore Roosevelt, taking instead the side of the anti-imperialists, urging that taking the antiwar position "might often require more courage than the winning of battles; and [that] it was the glory of a great university to produce alike leaders in action and in thought."[116]

Roger Austen's *Genteel Pagan*, a study of the life and work of the gay novelist Charles Warren Stoddard, is in another vein altogether, but one ought not to be surprised that in that work, too, Thomas Wentworth Higginson comes up: as it turns out, he was a correspondent of Stoddard, the author of famously homoerotic travel stories set in the South Pacific, experiences with natives which were manly in another sense, a homoerotic sense.[117] As were some of Higginson's own experiences in the Civil War; he wrote of the "splendid muscular development" of his "Young Sambos" and how they delighted him. "I always liked to observe them when bathing," he admitted. Indeed, one is not surprised either that Higginson was just as keen on his own physique. At seventeen, he had been a tall, thin six-footer until he determined to do something about it; in 1876, when he was in his mid-fifties (in an era when that was considered old), he was still regularly working out on the parallel bars and with ropes and weights. Higginson quite unself-consciously delighted in his physique, and it would be strange indeed if that did not include sexuality. Certainly, he confessed in his diary how susceptible he was to feminine charms. Married twice, he had two children by his second wife. Wives and children took second place, however, to masculine charms—in particular, those of his Harvard classmate William H. Hurlbut: "a young man so handsome in his dark beauty," wrote Higginson, "slender, keen-eyed, raven-haired" and so on. But he did not stop there, insisting on his passionate love for Hurlbut:

> I never loved but one male friend with a passion—and for him my love had no bounds—all that my natural fastidiousness and cautious reserve kept from others I poured on him; to say that I would have died for him was nothing. I lived for him; it was easy to do it, for there never was but one such person. . . . To me, moreover, he was always noble and sweet, he loved me truly and generously.[118]

In life as in novels many Victorian same-sex relationships were, however, rather ill-fated. Sufficient here to see Higginson in the context Gifford sets up between the "democratized man-loving" Whitmanic ideal and the "willowy Bunthorne" of the Wildean ideal. Indeed, connect "democratized" with "bourgeois" (leaving "willowy" to the declining aristocracy) and the analysis of Eve Kosofsky Sedgwick seems to explain the matter fully: "Whitman—visiting Whitman, liking Whitman, giving gifts of 'Whitman'—was of course a Victorian homosexual shibboleth, and much more than that, a step in the consciousness and self-formation of many members of that new Victorian class, the bourgeois homosexual." It was a class, Sedgwick notes, which saw male-male love as "virilizing them more than . . . feminizing them," a class which, as opposed to aristocratic and more effeminate (Catholic) gays, "looked to classical Sparta and Athens for models of virilizing male bonds."[119]

All this shades almost imperceptibly into a consideration of the Civil War era's new concern with masculinity, a subject ably studied by Kim Townsend (overwhelmingly, however, from a heterosexual perspective) in his recent book, *Manhood at Harvard*. "After the Civil War," he writes, "men felt pressure to be masculine. The word itself took on new meaning. By the end of the century 'masculine' . . . had become useful to men looking for ways to describe and explain the authority they sought to establish. By 1890 the noun 'masculinity' was in the *Century Dictionary*."[120] Fascinating to find that *masculinity*, the noun, entered prominently into the language under entirely mainline heterosexual auspices in 1890, just one year before the word *homosexual* first appeared in English, in John Addington Symonds's *A Problem in Modern Ethics* of 1891, the same year fixed on by Sedgwick in *Epistemology of the Closet* as "a good moment to look for a cross-section of inaugural discourses of modern homosexuality."[121] Moreover, when one recalls that Foucault's famous assertion of a new concept of homosexuals—of homosexual *persons* as opposed to acts, which begat "their antitwins, heterosexual persons"[122]—(necessarily) derives from this same period, it becomes startlingly clear that some of the basic categories of a study such as this— "masculinity" as an idea, "homosexual" as a person (and "heterosexual," too)—are hardly one hundred years old. Notice, just as it is the homosexual *person*, not homosexuality, that is new, so masculine dress or masculine occupations were not new, only masculine *persons*, with masculinity as some quality of manhood. Men have always done masculine things, indeed, homosexual things. But they have not always erected doing such things into a master identity or aspect of some sort.

At Harvard as well, all this changed during Santayana's lifetime: "The way Santayana responded to the pressure to be masculine is especially illuminating," Townsend writes, citing the many clubs and organizations to which he was elected by Santayana's peers (all male, of course). Indeed, especially when he returned as a professor, it was observed that Santayana "preferr[ed] to pass his leisure in the company of handsome athletes rather than with colleagues or Boston matrons," and this despite the fact he himself was more intellectual than sportsman.[123] But Santayana *was* interested in sports; in 1894 he wrote a most interesting piece for the *Harvard Monthly* entitled "Philosophy on the Bleachers." He was especially insightful about football: "The whole soul," he wrote, "is stirred by a spectacle that represents the basis of its life." Masculine enough. Yet he later wrote: "I . . . was sure of [William James's] good will and kindness, of which I had many proofs; but I was also sure that he never understood me, and that when he talked to me there was a mannequin in his head, called [George Santayana] and entirely fantastic. . . . No doubt I profited materially by this illusion, because he would have liked me less if he had understood me better."[124] Indeed, Santayana was never in any danger of being allowed William James's "masculine directness" at Harvard, where President Eliot deeply disliked Santayana and thought him "abnormal."[125] Santayana would not only have been liked less, he would have been fired. And this despite the fact that Santayana was masculine enough—Whitmanic enough—that in his contending with James's philosophy in favor of his own, Santayana exemplifies a chief "masculine" vector of Whitman's: "He most honors my style who learns under it to destroy the teacher."[126] Of course, Santayana did this in his own manner, not James's. But a man is his own man, no? Indeed, there is a sense in which

Santayana could be seen as more thoroughly Whitmanic than James, a distinction Townsend observes:

> Both [Whitman and James] evoke a common figure, that of beautiful manhood ... but James put it to more modest use—as a metaphor for his ideal students, the ones with independent minds. ... But his ideal men were ... unambiguously masculine. ... Whereas Whitman challenged his readers to set out on their own journeys of self-discovery, and warned them that reading his poems could do them as much harm as good—perhaps involve actually touching another man, in fact—James carefully fashioned a particular image of manhood ... that stretched but did not burst the limits.[127]

For all his greatness, William James, adds Townsend, was in the view of one contemporary, "a Puritan." And Santayana was wise to be wary: in his *Principles of Psychology* James reacts with horror to homosexuality.[128]

Not surprisingly, Santayana was more in accord with James's brother's view of things. In Henry James's *The Portrait of a Lady* the two men who contend—the "managing man," Caspar Goodwood, he of a "strong push [and] a kind of hardness of presence," and Ralph Touchett, "inclined to adventure and irony"—are *both* Harvard men.[129] Yet Henry James ultimately fell under suspicion, just as Santayana did. Theodore Roosevelt, for example, criticized the "man of letters who flees his country because he, with his delicate, effeminate sensitiveness, ... finds he cannot play a man's part among men." Townsend observes: "Like Santayana, [Henry] James clearly did not fit the image [of a Harvard man]. They were not manly presences."[130]

South Sea Idylls

IF WALT WHITMAN was the great herald, to repeat Eve Kosofsky Sedgwick's words, of the "self-formation of many members of that new Victorian class, the bourgeois homosexual,"[131] another was Charles Warren Stoddard, whose *South Sea Idylls* Higginson so admired. Stoddard, in turn, much admired Whitman, writing once, "It means everything that Walt Whitman has ever said or sung," affirming that the poet (who, like Higginson, responded positively to Stoddard in correspondence, though they never met) "breathed life into me."[132]

Stoddard was the master of the exotic travel tale, bestsellers in the late nineteenth century, particularly *South-Sea Idylls* (1873), which depicted his travels to Hawaii and Tahiti in the 1860s, when he was in his late twenties. *South-Sea Idylls* abounds with veiled references to Stoddard's sexual initiation by Polynesian young men and boys. This reflected an aspect of Stoddard's homosexuality that approached pedophilia but does not translate, any more than does ancient Greek pederasty, into American mores today. It did much more so a century and more ago, however, and it is important to realize it was then seen as the reverse of problematic. In that premodern era, people like Stoddard, "pre-homosexuality 'homosexuals,' " entered the conventional family structure, if not married themselves, by being uncles, mentors, "daddies"—adoption was a common explication—and often at the behest of widows attempting to provide fatherless sons with male role models. Thus it was that Stoddard "fathered" one of Harvard's leading Whitmanic luminaries of the era, Santayana's faculty colleague William McMichael Woodworth.

"Both mentorial and erotic, Stoddard's relationship to Woodworth bears some resemblance to 'Greek love,' as it was (re)understood by John Addington Symonds." But as Roger Austen noted, Stoddard "never invoked the idea of 'Greek love' to describe his desire for youths"; the dominant narrative, thought Austen, "derived less from the Greeks than from American domesticity," and Woodworth, like other "kids" in Stoddard's life, was "a fatherless boy for whom Stoddard saw himself to be filling a personal need." For the wealthy San Francisco widow whose husband had just died, Stoddard fulfilled her son's need for "older male companionship and guidance." Stoddard, in Austen's words, began taking Willie, fourteen in the summer of 1878, "sailing off Monterey and botanizing in the Redwoods." Stoddard's account of these expeditions of "swimming and hunting and chasing dragonflies" was indeed idyllic:

> One night, the kid set out for the stubble-field and lay in wait for wild rabbits; when he came in with his hands full of ears, the glow of moonlight was in his eye, the flush of sunset on his cheek, the riotous blood's best scarlet in his lips, and his laugh was triumphant; with a discarded hat recalled for camp-duty, a blue shirt open at the throat, hair very much tumbled, and no thoughts of self to detract from the absolute grace of his pose.[133]

One feels so strongly the truth of John Crowley's observation that Stoddard, whose recollection of all this was published posthumously in 1911, was writing of a life lived in the context of what we now see as "the crisis of gender and culture at the American *fin-de-siècle*." Remembered years later, Stoddard's feelings for the fourteen-year-old boy in 1878 continued when the same young man entered Harvard College six years later, in 1884, after schooling in Europe, and carried over to the grown man who stayed on at Harvard to get his doctorate in zoology under Louis Agassiz. Indeed, they were thriving still in the summer of 1903, when Austen reports:

> By this time Dr. William McMichael Woodworth had become something of a minor legend at Harvard. His home on Brattle Street was famous

for its splendid array of exotic furnishings. As the keeper of the Museum of Comparative Zoology, Woodworth had accompanied Louis Agassiz on collecting trips to Samoa, Australia, Africa and South America, bringing back curios for his house as well as for the museum. Woodworth also collected a wide variety of seemingly disparate people. In his library on Sunday afternoons, one might find the colonel of marines from the Charlestown Navy Yard and an English army captain rubbing elbows with Charles Macomb Flandrau, author of *Harvard Episodes*, and Pierre La Rose, author of *Harvard Celebrities*.[134]

Flandrau and LaRose, who, as we will see in the next chapter, were leading lights more of Oscar Wilde's Harvard than of Walt Whitman's, must have been bowled over by Woodworth and his domicile if a contemporary report in the *Boston Evening Transcript* is to be relied on:

> It would take a Dickens or a Balzac really to picture the contents of that house—on its walls excellent paintings jostled by Fiji war shields, or photographs of elephants on which their owner had ridden, or portraits of Cingalese beauties, whose apparel caught the eye of the anthropologist as well as the artist. Samoan war clubs, spears and shields of Central African hunters, the garments and musical instruments of savage tribes in a dozen outlying quarters, were mingled with hammered silver bowls or boxes fashioned in India, with old sixteenth-century pewter shooting trophies from Germany. The book shelves groaned with ancient tomes bound by Elxivir and others equally famous, filled with Latin text about the Cosmos as savants of three hundred years ago understood it. The jeweled eyes of a Buddha stared weirdly from a corner. You picked your cigarette from a box lacquered by some Japanese wizard. Your matches lay in a great green cloisonné bowl on the desk.[135]

Woodworth himself exuded generally a great "personal fascination," according to Burton Kline, who added that he was also "perverse, exasperating, high tempered and over-whelmingly generous." Indeed, wrote Kline, Woodworth "offended his dearest friends whenever he pleased, safe in his infinite resource in winning them back, for there was no resisting his fascination when he chose to exert it." At the same time, Burton continued, while Woodworth lived a life "glittering with picturesque incident"—"liv[ed] books of travel and adventure"—there was what some would see as a problem: "There were two men in Woodworth, and a candid friend would have to say that they were enemies. Woodworth the scientist was always overshadowed by Woodworth, the man of the world. . . . He was as favorably known in Uganda as he was in London and Honolulu. . . . He was proud of the star before his name in *American Men of Science*," wrote Kline, "but equally proud of the gift of a hippopotamus tooth cane head from a native tribesman of Africa. And one Woodworth always took it as a joke that the other Woodworth was a world's authority on flatworms." No wonder Stoddard spent so much time in Boston, where Woodworth, like Santayana, was a key figure in a very exotic Harvard circle Stoddard too was drawn into.[136]

The people Stoddard kept company with illustrate very well the truism that he who travels farthest often travels least. Take William Sturgis Bigelow, for instance. A doctor and scion of a famous medical family, Bigelow traveled widely and was as much at home in Japan as in Boston. Unhappy in his practice after Harvard Medical School, he went to Japan in 1881 and at once engaged that civilization intensely, becoming a Buddhist and a collector of art the Japanese themselves were discarding in their rush to modernization. He endowed Boston's Museum of Fine Arts with some twenty-six thousand works—paintings, sculpture, ceramics, and manuscripts—"the heart," in Curtis Prout's words, "of one of the world's greatest museum collections." And hardly less important, he gave the Japanese a renewed appreciation of their own culture, which earned him the Imperial Order of the Rising Sun with the rank of commander. About all this he lectured at Harvard. He was also a trustee of the Museum of Fine Arts. Probably he was the model for Dr. Alden in Santayana's *The Last Puritan*. In fact, he was so much a Buddhist that when he died his ashes were not only scattered at that Boston Brahmin Valhalla, Mount Auburn Cemetery in Cambridge; some were sent to enrich the soil of a Buddhist temple in Japan. Yet Bigelow may never have traveled further than when he repaired every summer to Tuckernuck, his own more or less private island off Nantucket.[137]

A very gay blade who never married, Bigelow captured the attention of Thomas Russell Sullivan, himself a key player (and good friend of Isabella Stewart Gardner) in Boston's bohemia. Sullivan once reported to Gardner: "Sturgis Bigelow, MD, has come in with hypnotic influence and carries me off to dine with him tonight, seductively, with the resident literati and tutti fruiti."[138] Bigelow entertained extensively and stylishly at his Beacon Street town house, but it was at Tuckernuck where he came into his own. "A scene of medieval splendor," in Henry Adams's words, Tuckernuck was a large country house in an island paradise off Nantucket "where men," in John Crowley's words, "took their ease, often naked, in an untamed natural setting."[139] The rule was no clothes at all until dinner, when, of course, one was expected to appear in formal dress. The guest list included not only Sullivan and, whenever he was visiting the East, Stoddard, but also vigorous young men like the Harvard poet George Cabot Lodge, son of Senator Henry Cabot Lodge, and perhaps Stoddard's closest friend in Boston, Theodore Dwight.

Tuckernuck might not be quite the South Seas. But the South Seas were far from the only locale in the homoerotic travel novel. Xavier Mayne cited Boston in 1908 as the second of eight "homosexual capitals"[140] in the U.S., and Harvard and Princeton as the leading colleges where such activities thrived.

Mayne was the author of *Imre: A Memorandum*, which recounts the adventures of a thirty-something Britisher who, in a café in Budapest, meets a handsome twenty-something lieutenant in the Hungarian army. To describe Imre goes a long way toward describing the book.

> Imre is a hero: handsome, strong, athletic, a constant victor at military games and contests: He had been a singularly sensitive, warm-hearted boy, indeed too high-strung.... [noted for] his engaging manners and his peculiarly striking boyish beauty.
>
> Of middle height, he possessed a slender figure, faultless in proportions, a wonder of muscular development of strength, lightness and elegance. His athletic powers were renowned in his regiment. He was among the crack gymnasts, vaulters and swimmers.... He could hold out a heavy garden-chair perfectly straight, with one hand.... He could jump on and off a running horse, like a vaquero.... Not until he was nude, and one could trace the ripple of muscle and sinew under the fine, hairless skin, did one realize the machinery of such strength.[141]

It is key to add that Mayne's hero "is not vain of his looks, detests jewelry and adornment, and always dresses plainly." Yet Imre, Gifford adds, though very "masculine" in these ways, is also "emotional and introspective as well as cultured." No aesthete, no effete poseur, he is not a boorish lout, either.[142]

It is perhaps not surprising that Xavier Mayne was a pseudonym, used by Edward Irenaeus Prime-Stevenson, a well-known writer of this period, when he wrote overtly homosexual books. Under his own name, Stevenson published "boys' lit," in the mode of Horatio Alger—himself a Harvard man who all but invented the genre—in magazines like *Harper's* and in his own books. His "boys' lit" was much less flagrantly homoerotic, directed toward mainstream society and thus more homosocial than homoerotic. But such work invited, perhaps even demanded, a homosexual reading even when newly published, as is made clear by the author's own opinion of it when he had occasion (elsewhere, under his gay pseudonym) to critique it. And scholars today would not disagree.

James Gifford, for example, in his chapter on the "Athletic Model," traces that model's development, with all due deference first to Whitman, through the work of a number of authors like Stevenson and on to Owen Wister. Wister is of particular importance to us because he was virtually Stoddard's peer in this more mainstream homosocial variant, as well as being one of the most influential Harvard men of his generation: a member of the Porcellian Club as an undergraduate, the author of a famous Harvard novel, *Philosophy 4*, and after he graduated a member of Harvard's Board of Overseers. Wister was, moreover, a lifelong friend and Harvard ally of Theodore Roosevelt; Stoddard's friend William Sturgis Bigelow was also a close friend of Roosevelt. In fact, "TR" made Bigelow's Beacon Street town house opposite Boston Common his headquarters whenever he was in town. And Wister as a writer and Roosevelt as a public figure were very much at the center of what masculinity is, presumably, all about—the style of, the aesthetic of, manliness.[143]

Somewhat neurasthenic as a youngster, Wister, like Roosevelt, took up every sport, including big-game hunting, and, also like Roosevelt, he worked out strenuously in Harvard's Hemenway Gymnasium. Both were eager acolytes of Dr. Dudley Allen Sargent, whose key role in any discussion of manliness at Harvard has already been touched on here. Sargent's underlying philosophy, the Greek ideal of the sound mind in the sound body, is central to "manliness," a difficult subject even in the twenty-first century. On this topic, conservative Harvard professor Harvey Mansfield, in an article in *The Times Literary Supplement*, has defined manliness as the "individual quality that causes a human being to come forth, to stand up for something, and make an issue of it. . . . Manly types defend their *turf*. . . . Perhaps manliness is capable of being . . . refashioned into something sexually neutral, such as strength of soul. . . . Many women have admirable strength of soul. But . . . do they have it in the same way as men? It seems that women have more steadiness and endurance, men more alacrity and ambition." Adds Mansfield, "There are other words, such as courage, frankness, confidence, that convey the good side of manliness, at least, without naming a sex. But to use them, to drop 'manliness,' begs the question whether moral or psychological qualities specific to sex exist." His opinion? He cites Aristotle to the effect that "men find it easier to be courageous—and, likewise, women find it easier to be moderate."[144]

As we will see, it was Oscar Wilde, not Walt Whitman, who made a point of visiting Harvard's gym, but in the country of Dr. Sargent we are also inevitably in the country of the Whitmanic, not the Wildean, archetype (at least in an American context), for just as it is the Wildean archetype of the aesthete that yields usually the artist, so it is the Whitmanic archetype of the warrior—such close kin to Things Greek and to the growing sports culture of the late nineteenth century—that yields the athlete.

Warrior Becomes Athlete

WHEN THE LONDON Steelers, a gay rugby team, were given full membership in the English Rugby Football Union in 1999 there was quite a stir.[145] When starting linebacker and cocaptain Corey Johnson of the Masconomet High School football team in one of Boston's suburbs—a young man who also wrestles and plays lacrosse and baseball and has earned three varsity letters—announced in 2000 he was gay, there was another stir: it was front-page news in *The Boston Globe*.[146] The captain of any football team is an American icon in the way an artist, dramatist, or painter hardly ever is. Indeed, unless Corey Johnson goes to Harvard or a similar school, he is unlikely to find himself in a milieu welcoming to both drama or music, on the one hand, and sports, on the other. I'm struck, though, with how similarly in both cases one underlying issue frames itself. "It's not like we're playing gay hockey," says a member of the Boston Lobsters, winners of the gold medal at the 1998 Gay Games in Amsterdam and members of the otherwise entirely heterosexual (so far as is known) New England Senior Hockey League. Gay hockey? "There's no such thing. It's just hockey."[147] Well, substitute "music" for "hockey" and it's a point made about Aaron Copland's symphonies all the time. Schubert's, too. And as valid about Johnson's blocking. Or Greg Louganis's dives. Writes Robert Lipsyte (in "The Emasculation of Sports"):

> So who's a sissy now? Certainly not Greg Louganis, a homosexual ("toughest sissy on the planet," quips Eric Marcus, the co-writer of Louganis' best-selling autobiography) whose 10th dive in the 1988 Seoul Olympics' springboard preliminaries was the nerviest act I ever covered in sports. On the previous dive, he had banged his head against the board; the wound needed several quick stitches, no time for anesthetic. A few minutes later, he came back to nail the dive, perhaps the best of the Games. It was a textbook example of traditional manly heroism. The recent debate over whether Louganis should have told Olympic officials that he was H.I.V.-positive at the time has obscured the pure courage of his act, to say nothing of the fact that he went on to win two gold medals in those Games.[148]

Louganis, in fact, could have been either of those fast friends of the Union Army, Ned or Tom; certainly Ned or Tom—or Whitman—would have been proud to be Louganis. I think of the *New York Times* review of Norman Maclean's *Young Men and Fire*, in which James Kincaid writes: "With the fire pounding their backs, [the two young forest fire fighters] squeezed through a crevice, whereupon [one] fell exhausted into a juniper bush and would have stayed there and died had not [his friend] stopped and stared at him so coldly he was shamed into motion. The two, roommates at the jumpers' camp, then out-scrambled the fire."[149] Now the two men's sexual orientation does not arise. But this anecdote, like the Louganis dive, discloses the masculine aesthetic of Whitmanic manliness: the effectiveness of stopping to stare coldly, a kindness that probably saved his friend's life, was perhaps all the kinder, all the more effective, for being the father's classic lesson: do it yourself and you'll be stronger for it. I think of the Socratic Eros or the Sacred Band; of Walter Pater's *ascêis,* or unsweetened wine; of Gore Vidal on Christopher Isherwood's *agon,* or masculine hardness; above all, I think of A. L. Rowse's point that neither the ancient Greeks nor the Japanese samurai "see manliness as instinctive, but, rather, as something to be gained by moral effort." It is a view very much in sympathy with the

Harvard Puritan tradition. Certainly one of its greatest scholars, Perry Miller, wrote in *Nature's Nation* that "being American is not something to be inherited so much as something to be achieved,"[150] a point of view by no means dissimilar. Masculine *or* American, a style or an aesthetic—a role it surely is. But a performance can be authentic, the action can be real; and the masculine aesthetic of manliness is, at its most authentic, the outward sign of inner effort—the moral effort Rowse speaks of.

If it is hard for the mainstream heterosexual culture to see the Whitmanic archetype of the warrior as a gay polarity, it is even harder to see this of the warrior's derivative, the athlete. Indeed, there is a long history, in part Harvard's own, that explains why the Wildean archetype of the aesthete and its derivative, the artist, has been so much more readily acknowledged as gay by the heterosexual majority. It is a history rooted in the majority's persistent need to be able to identify and recognize the homosexual, although such stereotypes are misleading, as has been shown over and over again, most recently, for instance, in journalist John Leland's portrayal of spousal abuse in *The New York Times*: "Stereotypes of meek, overpowered women and rampaging abusive men are of little help to officers responding to a battle between two men or two women. *Often, the abuser is the smaller gay man*, or the more feminine lesbian [emphasis added]."[151] But stereotypes tempt us all. Gay men are artistic and effeminate for the same reason terrorists are dark-skinned and stony-faced. (There is a gay complicity in this stereotyping, too. One common response at least in the early stages of the American gay rights movement is reported by John D'Emilio: "We don't want people to know we [look like] everybody else. As long as they think everyone's a screaming queen with eyelashes, we're safe. . . . We don't want publicity.")[152]

This family of attitudes has endured the century and finds still its strongest focus in sports, which is indeed where (absent warriors) the Whitmanic gay archetype appears in its purest form. Witness another recent front-page story from *The New York Times*:

> [H]andsome, thoughtful and a celebrated "babe magnet," Billy Bean was the golden child. . . . Yet he was nagged by the feeling that something was missing. . . . Bean long suspected he was homosexual despite being heterosexually active since high school. He was married for three years. . . .
>
> "I've had good sex with women and good relationships, but something was missing, even with my wife. I wasn't fulfilled."
>
> [He experienced success] but also midnight walks on road trips to get away from his tomcatting teammates, to work off the stress of being a spy in his own life. . . .
>
> "He was right to keep it a secret. The guys would have been brutal." [This remark from an old college teammate, Jim Bruske.] Billy could have been a great player, but he tried too hard . . . he put too much pressure on himself.[153]

Characteristic of the Whitmanic gay, here is the problematic side of manliness's aesthetic—whose "design concept" was formulated in America's twentieth century, by the old Rough Rider himself, Theodore Roosevelt.

But in more than one way it was Roosevelt's sidekick, Owen Wister (Harvard class of 1882), who wrote the book. Long and strenuous expeditions out west, about which Wister wrote lovingly, yielded what is still manliness's textbook in twenty-first-century America: *The Virginian*, a huge bestseller ever since it was published in 1902, whose influence endured throughout the twentieth century in no less than three movies and a television show. In pointing out that "aside from the West the hypermasculine model of homosexuality owed a great deal to Walt Whitman," James Gifford takes note of perhaps *the* homoerotic locale for Americans: "*The Virginian* is not about cowboys so much as it is about a particular kind of manhood, the kind that Harvard had had in mind for years," and he concludes, "What is most significant about *The Virginian* [is] the stylishness with which an exemplary man faces violence and death, faces women, faces others, faces any threat to his manhood." Which is to say, of course, with "as few words as possible."[154] Clint Eastwood isn't new, either.

Wister, an anti-Semite who was not overfond either of women (he ridicules higher education for them), found his god in the Anglo-Saxon man. Like Dudley Sargent of Harvard's fabled gymnasium, Wister held little back. "The Virginian is, of course, glorious to behold," recounts Gifford: "He is 'a slim young giant, more beautiful than pictures, his thumb hooked in a cartridge belt that falls across his hips, his complexion glowing the way ripe peaches look upon their trees in a dry season.' " And there is more. The (male) narrator at one point imagines what it would be like to be married to his friend and later even fantasizes: "Had I been a woman, [his smile] would have made me his to do what he pleased with on the spot."

No wonder Gifford concludes that in *The Virginian* "several examples of male courtship [are] in evidence, and the book unites a hypermasculine dynamic with an underlying homoerotic." Which Henry James saw at once. So did Townsend, from a very different perspective. Townsend writes of how James found in it a "rejuvenating fantasy. How much better it would have been if the reader [James?] could have had the Virginian all to himself." Yet Wister "could no more do that than he could let Molly [the Virginian's fiancée] continue teaching."[155] Women's roles were as clear to him as men's roles. And if Wister dealt in stereotypes, we must not let that blind us to the archetypes that William James, for example, was so swift to tend: James's continual effort, in Townsend's words, "to discover in the social realm . . . 'the moral equivalent of war' [was the result of the fact] men would always love to fight."[156] And now that women box, too, there turns out to be a womanly way as well as a manly way. Performance it may be, but performance again can be authentic. And need not be limiting. Tom Waddell, the

American Olympic decathlete who founded the Gay Games in 1982, did not seem to mind cheerleaders in drag.

Kinsey's Story

IT MAY BE useful at this point to put a more personal and a more American face on all this literary and social history; its effect, for instance, on one boy—and future Harvard man—growing up in the 1900s, Alfred C. Kinsey, the celebrated scientist who would later revolutionize America's attitude to sex.

A sufferer in childhood from rheumatic fever, which doctors feared had damaged his heart, Kinsey, though a tall, strapping boy of athletic build and the usual competitive spirit, was forbidden rigorously to play all team sports. This made his boyhood difficult in an era Kinsey's biographer, James H. Jones, goes so far as to typify by reference to Kinsey's boyhood hero, Theodore Roosevelt, and to Wister's novel. Jones notes the importance of books like *The Virginian* in this context and that the *South Orange Bulletin*, Kinsey's boyhood home's newspaper, praised the play that evolved from the book, which enjoyed an eight-year run. Yet the American middle class had no need to read books to recognize they were, in Jones's words, "experiencing a crisis in masculinity. . . . By the turn of the century, new epithets, such as 'sissy' . . . gained currency. . . ."[157] Fascinating, the testimony of language: first *homosexual,* then *masculinity,* now *sissy*—all these words (and according to very different sources) are words of the 1890s—no older.

The last epithet is particularly interesting in this context. Both the homosexual and the heterosexual worlds produce sissies, and of more than one type: the (more Wildean) "fairy" or "pansy" of street lore, for example, and also the Whitmanic bully, the type I suspect Gore Vidal had in mind when, lamenting the seemingly unsporting overkill of Theodore Roosevelt's big-game hunting (which reputedly filled whole halls at Harvard with whole herds of stuffed heads), Vidal declared, "Give a sissy a gun and he will kill everything in sight."[158] That there are different varieties of sissy is especially key to bear in mind when the idea of sissy meets the idea of gay. Heterosexuals don't register or easily understand this, in no small measure because they register only the Wildean classic gay stereotype, whereas all distortions and extremes—the hypermasculine male no less than the effeminate male—should arouse suspicion. Evelyn Waugh knew this well, even as a schoolboy, noting about his headmaster:

> J. F. did not approve of Mr. Crease. . . . He would not allow boys in his House to go to Mr. Crease's. Mr. Crease, as I have said, was effeminate in appearance and manner; J. F. was markedly virile, *but it was he who was the homosexual* [emphasis added]. . . . Most good schoolmasters—

and, I suppose, schoolmistresses also—are homosexual by inclination. . . .
J. F.'s passions ran deep. I do not think he ever gave them physical release
with any of his pupils, but as distinct from the general, romantic pleasure
of association with the young . . . he certainly fell in love with individual
boys. . . . [He was] ardently attached to a golden-haired Hyacinthus. He
gave this boy a motorcycle from which he was immediately thrown and
much disfigured, but J. F.'s love remained constant until the friend's death
in early middle age.[159]

Indeed, the heterosexual sissy (Bernard Berenson was another) is not unknown in literature. A hit play and movie that comes to mind is Robert
Anderson's *Tea and Sympathy* (1953), in which "the sissy is heterosexual and
the macho man is a latent homosexual. [His] wife confronts her husband,"
John M. Clum writes, "with his latent homosexuality and, at the final curtain, offers herself to the sensitive young man, who has been accused of
being the unspeakable [i.e., gay], to affirm his heterosexuality."[160] Similarly,
these words and concepts—homosexual, masculine, sissy—pervade even
standard reference works such as *The New Princeton Encyclopedia of Poetry
and Poetics*, in which contributor Earl Miner notes that although lesbian
poetry "prefers tender committed relationships," it seems to him indisputably the case that "gay male poetry is about energy, adventure, quest, danger," certainly the reverse of the sissified.[161] Indeed, to take one final pass at
the young Kinsey example, it becomes clear the extent to which this crisis
in manhood—with its new words: *homosexual, masculinity, sissy*—has pervaded twentieth-century discourse. As a boy, Kinsey found his answer in the
Boy Scouts, with its goal of building "real men," and

> attacked scouting with all the fervor of a boy determined to demonstrate
> his mettle. . . . Scouting gave Kinsey the opportunity to succeed in the
> masculine world of athletics, since the Boy Scouts awarded merit badges
> in both hiking and mountain climbing. . . . By the time he finished high
> school, Kinsey was the embodiment of the all-American boy.[162]

All-American, but not to himself. It is important to acknowledge here,
because we now know Kinsey was sadomasochistic in his practices as well
as homosexual, which is the highly problematic extreme risked by the war-
rior/athlete archetype, often expressed through gay bashing. (As we'll see in
the next chapter, the extreme risked by the aesthete/artist archetype is that
of the drag queen, a type of the gay basher's victim.)

It is equally important to observe that, in his youth in the 1900s and for
some years thereafter, Kinsey probably did not think of himself as homosexual; that would have required, in the words of his biographer, James H.
Jones, "a level of self-understanding he did not possess" at that time. "Two
powerful defense mechanisms—denial and repression—may have shielded

him from the truth." The question of how such a thing may dawn on one, however, goes past Owen Wister and back to Walt Whitman, an artist, of course, of much greater, indeed, transformative, power whose continuing force is well illustrated by a reminiscence of a gay writer of our own time, Bruce Bawer, who one summer night at age fifteen at a summer cottage took from the bookshelves "a volume that mesmerized me." It was *Leaves of Grass*. Wrote Bawer:

> I sat there transfixed by Whitman's long, lusty lines, which washed over me as powerfully and sensuously as the high ocean waves had in the hot sun of the day.
>   I knew the moment I began reading Whitman's muscular, nature-ridden verses that something in them touched me deepdown. . . . Not having identified myself yet as homosexual, I didn't yet realize what that something was.[163]

When he did, Bawer recalled that early messenger, rather as one might an Old Testament angel. The thinker and writer Bawer became was naturally more than a little affronted when he encountered those who deny Whitman's homosexuality:

> There are those—and I'm one of them—who have cautioned about the danger of reducing writers to their race, gender or sexual orientation. Yet when it comes to sexual orientation there's another danger which is still far more commonly fallen into . . . the danger of minimizing its impor-tance. With Whitman . . . the habit of soft-pedaling his homosexuality—or pretending that he was heterosexual or bisexual or that his sexual orientation cannot really be known or that, if gay, he never actually acted on his impulses or that, even if he did, he'd have preferred for us to keep quiet about such things—has been widespread. . . . What is a nation to do, after all, when the National Poet—a man for whom high schools and shopping malls have been named—was gay?[164]

The list of the critics and literary historians, some gay, who have per-petuated this denial is long, still current, and would include some very fine scholars: witness Van Wyck Brooks, Paul Zweig, Harold Bloom, and David Reynolds. Yet even here there is something to learn, as Gary Schmidgall points out in his *Walt Whitman: A Gay Life*, from scholarly denial of Whit-man's homosexuality. Such homophobic responses "are precisely the sort that Whitman sought and expected from heterosexual readers in an age when total openness about such matters was impossible." At the same time, Schmidgall makes clear, Whitman sought to convey fuller truths, with a wink and a nod, to homosexual readers conversant in the elliptical language of the closet. Borrowing a term from Whitman, Schmidgall calls the poet's straight readers "civilians," and proposes that he, as a gay man who has lived many years in Whitman's "Manhatta," which for him as for Whitman has been a "city of eros," can read Whitman—or at least his gay references—better than they can.[165]

I object as strenuously as Bawer to the tendency, "all too familiar in queer cultural and political circles," Bawer writes, "to reduce gay life and identity to gay sex, and to equate openness about sexual orientation with explicitness about the details of sexual behavior." And I am also reluctant, as he is, to do anything that does "not primarily [deal with Whitman] as an artist who speaks to all readers, male and female, straight and gay." And I sympathize, too, with Bawer's concerns that Schmidgall's "exclusivity above universality" risks emphasizing "gay marginality and segregation." But whether or not gay people understand Whitman "better," they will understand him differently from heterosexuals. And the difference can mean a good deal, there being what Heidegger calls *Vorverstandnis*, or preunderstanding,[166] the lack of which, for example, Richard Hall complains of when he notes that Henry James's principal biographer, Leon Edel, though he recognized the evidence for the novelist's sexuality, "was not empowered by his own life and experience to see an erotic component in the relationship between [Henry and William James]." By contrast, Bawer, at age fifteen, came to Whitman with a great deal of *Vorverstandnis*.

Ned and Tom, those Whitmanic warriors of *Two College Friends*, were teenagers, too, and came out of a culture in Harvard Yard that also understood that the warrior/athlete archetype is well defined (by a Victorian-era Harvard rowing coach) as standing for "strength without aggression, confidence without self-assertion, cheerfulness without ostentation, and endurance to the end."[167] Yes, there were aberrations. But S/M is no more the essence of the warrior archetype than drag queens are the essence of the aesthete archetype; the gay basher is no more characteristic of the athlete than his victim of the artist.

Walt Whitman, wrote Symonds, was "more truly Greek than any other man of Modern times." Oscar Wilde did not disagree. When Robert Ross and Wilde first slept together, wrote Dowling, "Wilde understood their intercourse as proceeding along the Platonic ladder of love, passing from pandemic physical delight to Uranian intellectual friendship. With Ross, the Platonic ideal of an erotic procreancy of the spirit generating thought and art, as well as the frank Greek practice of 'embracing to wrestle and wrestling to embrace,' seemed to issue in a perfect fulfillment of Hellenism."[168]

2.

The Aesthete Archetype: Oscar Wilde's Harvard

I have been guileless long: angels and you
And beauty in my dreams together played....
What mystic love is this?
What ghostly mistress? What angelic friend?

—George Santayana,

SONNET 39

APRIL 1895: MORE than a generation has passed since Emerson's and Whitman's dialogue on Boston Common—thirty-five years—and a world away, or so it must seem, from Boston's Beacon Street Mall. In London, at the Old Bailey: charged with acts "against the peace of our said Lady the Queen her Crown and dignity," acts judged to be "gross[ly] indecent," the foremost British playwright is in the prisoner's dock; Oscar Wilde answers the court's charge with what has been called by the noted British scholar Linda Dowling "a speech of sudden and eloquent energy [in which he] passionately defends male love as the noblest of the attachments, a love 'such as Plato made the very basis of his philosophy, and such as you find in the sonnets of Michaelangelo and Shakespeare . . . ,' his superb self-possession and ringing peroration so electrifying that the courtroom bursts into applause." Wilde, who once told Whitman that at Oxford the American poet's verse was heard all the time among his friends (who brought books by Whitman on long poetry-reading walks), carried the matter much further and much more explicitly in just the few moments of his famous courtroom speech: "The applause of Wilde's listeners," Dowling notes in her study of Oxford Hellenism, "marks the sudden emergence into the public sphere of a modern discourse of male love."

Dowling's further reading of Wilde's apparently damning trials is equally penetrating. As opposed to the crown prosecutor's reliance on "a legal language conceiving sodomy in what Alan Bray calls 'directly physical terms,'" a language deriving from the English common law, so medieval in its roots, Wilde, she writes, "deploys a new and powerful vocabulary of personal identity, a language of mind, sensibility, and emotion, of inward and intellectual emotions, . . . [of] deep spiritual affection between an older and a younger man seen as so global in its reference to the full individuality of each as to involve the underlying and invariable substratum of personality traditionally regarded as constituting identity." Though Wilde is master of this "new and powerful vocabulary," that is only half his achievement as Dowling sees it: "Wilde's triumph," she writes, "was to have equated this thoroughly modern notion of personal identity with the ideal of male love surviving in the writings of ancient Greece . . . [and] to have outlined in irresistible terms an idea of male love as a mode of inward erotic orientation and sensibility wholly distinct from mere genital activity." Who would disparage the joys and trials and rituals of sex? Not I. But Dowling does not mean that. And she is right on the mark: Wilde's speech was "a crucial moment in the modern emergence of homosexuality as a positive social identity."[1]

Boston Common, the Old Bailey, and finally the Stonewall Inn: the New York bar where the gay civil-rights movement would erupt in 1969. Each is a scene, and each unlikely perhaps, in a three-act play, as I see it. There would of course be other and significant interludes elsewhere, and much important action offstage, and intermissions, too, of more than a little interest in the century or so between the 1860s and the 1960s. But these three acts in my reading of events are the hinges of the history of homosexuality in the modern era: Boston, London, New York. Whitman and Wilde, the fathers of the modern gay male experience.

Art and Identity

BOTH WHITMAN AND Wilde—indeed, both archetypes—have, in our time at least, been inevitably dogged by the stereotypes to which we are all too prone. And it is as well to try to clear away this underbrush. Whitman, for all his rough-hewn masculinity, was no redneck—he loved opera, for instance—Italian opera. "But for the opera," he insisted, "I could not have written *Leaves of Grass*." Nor is this unimportant: "It is because of Italian opera that *Leaves of Grass* must be read aloud to appreciate its full power," Whitman biographer Jerome Loving writes.[2] Verdi was Whitman's particular delight. Paul Berman has written eloquently on the matter:

> Either gradually or in a flash of insight, Whitman realized that he could convert those vigorous and extravagant Italian sounds back into verse.
>
> You can hear the results as soon as you compare *Leaves of Grass* to poetry by Longfellow or Emerson. The music in Longfellow's ear could have been sung by a clear, untrained voice over the simplest of guitar strums—a music you can sway to. The music in Emerson's ear was austere and Protestant, the melody of hymns. . . . But the sound in Whitman's ear was infinitely more flexible and sensuous.[3]

Similarly, just as Whitman gives warriors and athletes leave to go in search, say, of Tebaldi at La Scala, so too Oscar Wilde was not quite the frail flower of legend. Nor was his lifelong and most faithful friend, who brought Wilde out—Robert Ross, a young Canadian who rowed in the second college boat at King's College, Cambridge. Nor was Wilde's later and more famous lover, Lord Alfred Douglas: as Christopher Hitchens has pointed out in a recent essay in *The New York Review of Books*, "One says 'epicene' because [Douglas's] portraits and photographs of the period seem to require the word; however, he excelled as an athlete into the bargain. Wilde was no drooping pansy either; when challenge or affront demanded it he was good with his fists and—as Bosie's father was to discover—hard to intimidate."[4] In fact, Richard Ellmann, in his excellent biography of Wilde, cheerfully relates the following account:

> According to [Sir Francis] Benson, himself an athlete, Wilde was "far from being a flabby aesthete" and "only one man in the college, and he rowed seven in the Varsity Eight [J. T. Wharton] . . . had a ghost of a chance in a tussle with Wilde." To prove his point Benson quotes Wharton's respectful comment about Wilde's muscularity and goes on to tell how the Junior Common Room at Magdalen decided one evening to beat up Wilde and break up his furniture. Four undergraduates were deputed to burst into his rooms while the rest watched from the stairs. The result was unexpected: Wilde booted out the first, doubled up the second with a punch, threw out the third through the air, and, taking hold of the fourth—a man as big as himself—carried him down to his rooms and buried him beneath his own furniture. He then invited the spectators to sample the would-be persecutor's wines and spirits, and they accepted.[5]

No wonder Wilde had seemed to Whitman "so frank and outspoken and manly" when the British playwright called upon him in America in 1882. It was then the high priest of aestheticism assured Whitman that he and his friends during their Oxford years had regularly carried *Leaves of Grass* about with them on walks. True enough. It was Whitman's subject, his gospel, not his style, that so intrigued them. Whitman's verse Wilde disliked actually; for his taste it was *all* subject, no form. In other words, awful form. But Whitman himself, Wilde declared, was "the simplest, most natural, and strongest character I have ever met in my life. . . . The closest approach to the Greek we have yet had in modern times."[6] And with Whitman, Wilde seems to have let down his guard and dropped his pose. Certainly that's just what his lily waving seemed to be to Whitman. "Wilde was a big, strong man. His effeminacy was part pose, part media myth," in Gregory Woods's words, and "he evidently satisfied those high standards of manliness which the great democratic connoisseur [that Whitman was] had been establishing over the previous three decades."[7]

In fact, Wilde, his genius aside, was in every way a far more considerable figure than the Gilbert and Sullivan caricature so widely accepted today. Of Irish descent and gentry stock, he was superbly well educated—at Trinity College, Dublin, and Magdalen College, Oxford, where at one and the same time he feasted on the teachings of both Ruskin and Pater, men of very differing views that Wilde was sufficiently intellectual and individualist to compass. Moreover, it is too often forgotten that Wilde was as much social critic and essayist as playwright, advocating libertarian socialism, for example, in *The Soul of Man Under Socialism* (1891). Even as a wit he was best known for deflating the pompousness of his era. Though he liked the good life and cultivated the aristocracy, he spared not them nor anyone in his attack on philistinism, even after emerging as a kind of high priest of aestheticism and the Decadence. Wilde was also happily married, in 1884, to Constance Lloyd, a union that yielded two children. Even his ill-fated affair with Lord Alfred Douglas was by no means only a disaster. Douglas, who introduced Wilde to London's homosexual underground of hustlers and brothels—dissipations that Wilde would pay dearly for later in his trials— was distinctly *not* a faithful friend or lover. But Claude J. Summers is surely also correct in asserting that "the tumultuous affair may have inspired Wilde to some of his best work," even that "unquestionably, the self-discovery of his homosexuality liberated [Wilde's] art and marks a major breakthrough in his artistic maturity." Certainly, the 1890s yielded *The Picture of Dorian Gray* (1890–1891), *Lady Windermere's Fan* (1892), *Salomé* (1893), *An Ideal Husband* (1895) and, also in 1895, *The Importance of Being Earnest*, this last play so endlessly popular it is still widely performed in the twenty-first century. Of it Summers observes that out of the homosexual's need then to live a double life—"Bunburying," Wilde calls it—the playwright conceived "a complex parody of both himself and his society and thereby create[d] a masterpiece, perhaps the greatest comedy in the language. Without ever mentioning homosexuality, Wilde in *Importance* creates the quintessentially gay play. He turns Victorian values on their heads and discovers . . . a means of covertly attacking his society's prejudices and discreetly defending his own nonconformity. The farce brilliantly depicts the liminal position that Wilde occupied in relation to his homophobic society, *in* it, yet not *of* it."[8]

Hardly less significant from our point of view is Wilde's "The Portrait of Mr. W. H." (original version 1889), the reference being to the hero of the *Sonnets* of Shakespeare, with whom Wilde identified strongly. And Summers is again surely right to point to the "emphasis on the continuity of homosexual feeling from the past to the present," as the work's chief feature, disclosing an affinity between Wilde and Shakespeare not unlike that I will propose later in this book between Tchaikovsky and Leonard Bernstein.

If Wilde's coming out and his subsequent problematic relationship with Douglas spurred his best work, so his trial and imprisonment—when Douglas deserted him—may also be said to have yielded even more of the same—*De*

Profundis, which, though some have found it self-pitying and resentful, is, in gay terms, "a work that creatively transmutes the disaster of his prosecution and imprisonment into a ludic triumph," in Summers's words. "The most daring aspect of *De Profundis*," Summers writes, "is Wilde's simultaneous depictions of Christ in his image and himself in Christ's image. . . . The embodiment of *agape*, Christ understands the sufferings of others. . . . The portrait of Christ as the romantic artist martyred by a philistine society functions for Wilde . . . as a means of attacking the religious base of philistine morality."[9] Thus Wilde the martyr, the final incarnation of this remarkable man.

Like so much about Wilde, there is much ambiguity to his martyr's aspect. It was, of course, his own doing. But true martyrdom always is. And while that may mean that to many Wilde can seem a fool, his tormentors *must* be seen as hypocrites—worse, as losers—hypocrites who tried several times to avoid having to prosecute and imprison Wilde—sensing, doubtless, that history's verdict on them would be merciless. For Wilde (and his cause, as it became) it was a great victory, perhaps the only (or at least the greatest) victory he could achieve. Thus it was Wilde who repeatedly forced their hand, refusing clear suggestions he take the easy way out and flee to France. Martyrdom is easily misunderstood, whatever the cause. The slightly tasteless self-dramatization, even the need, perhaps unconscious (even masochistic), for punishment is present. Indeed, it is a matter T. S. Eliot deals with brilliantly in *Murder in the Cathedral* insofar as Christian martyrdom is concerned, and I have often thought the annexation by gays of St. Sebastian as cult saint or household god has as much to do with the arrows (traditionally shown piercing him) as the body—naked, of course, and usually beautiful. All this reflects in Wilde's case not only the effect on a supremely successful man in the modern era of alienation from an oppressive society, but it is a necessary part of martyrdom's purposes: to flush out and expose the oppressor's true nature, and to make him face himself as well as the world—and, ultimately, because he will not be able to survive that—to defeat him. It is, in a sense, to turn his own power against him, to use his own weight to throw him. Wilde's fame today is in no small sense testimony to his victory. As Richard Ellmann observed, even his detractors saw that ultimately Wilde had "made of infamy a new Thermopylae."[10] Similarly, it will not do to try to undermine Wilde's victory by attacking his courtroom defense of spiritual male love by pointing out that it was meant to mislead and to cloak his dissipations. The ambiguity and incongruity between the spiritual and the physical can hardly be limited to Wilde. Sex makes fools of us all.

Harvard Yard

BOTH WHITMAN AND Wilde visited Harvard Yard and left behind there, as we will see time and again in this book, more than a little of themselves. However, though it is pretty well known that, in Gregory Woods's words, "the most influential modern homosexual writer *in late nineteenth-century Britain* [emphasis added] was no Greek scholar, and no Anglo- or Roman Catholic; but the Good Gray Poet himself, Walt Whitman,"[11] it would seem that in America, Wilde's influence would rival that of Whitman insofar as the role of homosexuality in helping to shape the broader culture is concerned. Whitman, as we've seen, by no means went unnoticed when he was in Boston. But Wilde created a furor. We know only the bald fact, and that from his own notes, that Whitman visited Harvard Yard. In Wilde's case there are columns of newspaper print about just the effect he had on Harvard at firsthand, never mind at second or third.

Wilde spent 1882 in America, lecturing from coast to coast, and when in Boston always arranged to stay at the Hotel Vendôme in the Back Bay. (What does it say of history's continuities that I write these words today also in the Vendôme, where I live?) Indeed, Wilde was Boston-based, in fact, for different legs of his American year. In January and then again in June of that year he made highly publicized appearances in Boston, lecturing in large downtown theaters to enthusiastic audiences. Some of his Boston stays seem to have been primarily social respites during which he tried to engage a culture he admired—in particular its presiding genius, Emerson. When asked by a reporter upon docking in New York who were the greatest American literary figures, Wilde at once answered Whitman, but in the same breath insisted also on Emerson—"New England's Plato," Wilde called him, whose "Attic genius"[12] he thought so highly of that when he was in prison and allowed to choose only a few books, one was Emerson's essays. He quoted from Emerson twice in *De Profundis*—and very significant quotes they were: "Nothing is more rare in any man than an act of his own"; "all martyrdoms seemed mean to the lookers on."[13]

Emerson would always be with Wilde in the tight places of his life—he was, like Aeschylus or Balzac, a part of the furniture of his mind. He was also a sunny part of these happier days of Wilde's 1882 American sojourn. Though they never met (Emerson was fast fading and died while Wilde was in America), Wilde could not help but quip to Julia Ward Howe: "What would Thoreau have said to my hat box?" And, a little more shamefacedly, because Wilde's wardrobe was an extensive one, what would have been the response of "Emerson to the size of my trunk"?[14]

As was the case with Whitman, Wilde's intellectual kinship with Boston was reflected in his publishing and business relationships. Most of the American premieres of Wilde's plays took place in New York (except for *Lady Windermere's Fan*, which premiered in the United States in Boston in January 1893). But Wilde's American publishers were Boston firms (except for Dodd, Mead & Company of New York, which issued Wilde's *Intentions, A House of Pomegranates*, and *Lord Arthur Savile's Crime* in 1891–1892). In fact, simultaneously with his first publication in Britain, Wilde made his American debut at the very dawn of his career in 1876 in *The Boston Pilot*.[15] Similarly, in 1910, after Wilde's tragedy and death and in the wake of his great scandal, it was a Boston publishing house, John W. Luce & Company, which brought out the first authorized edition of his complete works, authorized by Wilde's executor, the ever faithful Robert Ross. This edition also restored Wilde's American copyright for the benefit of his children, a fact I know well because it is a proud boast of my family history; my mother brought me up with the help of a live-in uncle and eventual mentor, Harrison Hale Schaff, who was the editorial director at Luce's, responsible for the Wilde edition.[16] Boston always had a special regard for Oscar Wilde, whose publishers in 1882 were Robert Brothers, who had brought out Wilde's poems in 1881 and would publish his *Happy Prince* in 1888.

These early publishing relationships in turn informed Wilde's social activities in Boston. The man responsible for publishing him in the *Pilot*, for example, was its editor, the poet John Boyle O'Reilly ("In Bohemia," his best-known verse), and Wilde surfaces with O'Reilly several times during his Boston stays. O'Reilly, wrote Wilde in a letter to the writer Douglas Sladen, was "a delightful fellow," so it is not perhaps surprising they are known to have kept company both at the theater and in the clubs. When Wilde was fleeced by a confidence trickster in New York, it was to O'Reilly that he at once wrote, asking for a loan.[17]

O'Reilly, who had introduced Whitman into the St. Botolph Club in 1881 with a lecture appearance, also introduced Wilde into that bohemian quarter the next year, in a much more private and intimate way: at a time when that prince of effete narcissism, Bunthorne (a character in Gilbert and Sullivan's *Patience*, which Wilde was promoting in America), was everywhere celebrated and denounced, his sexuality hardly in doubt, O'Reilly dropped a note to his friend, the gay playwright Thomas Sullivan, that is highly suggestive indeed: "Tonight at about ten, I shall take Oscar Wilde to the St. Botolph. Please mention it to a few fellows so that we may have a welcoming smile for Narcissus."[18] Even more suggestive was Wilde's phraseology in O'Reilly's autograph book, signed after Wilde had called on Whitman. According to Ellmann, Wilde (who after his visit to Whitman answered not one but *all* questions about the American poet's sexuality for years to come by repeating, "The kiss of Walt Whitman is still on my lips") expanded on the matter significantly: under an inscription by Whitman, Wilde (quoting himself about Wordsworth; it was nothing if not a literary age) wrote of Whitman: "The spirit who living blamelessly but dared to kiss the smitten mouth of his own century."[19]

But Wilde by no means allowed the bohemian undertone of his stays in Boston to interfere with the rather grander court society, as it were, of the literary elite. No sooner had he arrived in town (for the first time in late January 1882) than he was enmeshed in the higher reaches of America's reigning literati. On his first morning in Boston, after breakfast at the Vendôme with producer Dion Boucicault, whom he was trying to interest in producing one of his plays, Wilde, who had written ahead to more than one luminary (to Harvard law professor Oliver Wendell Holmes for example, on 27 January: "I arrive at the Vendôme on Saturday"), dispatched signals on arrival to any he had yet to be in touch with. To Charles Eliot Norton, for instance, Harvard's (and America's) first professor of fine arts, Ruskin's friend, and himself the leading art arbiter in America of his time: "I am in Boston for a few days and hope you will allow me the pleasure of calling on you." Doubtless Wilde enclosed his letter of recommendation to Norton from the Pre-Raphaelite master Edward Burne-Jones ("any kindness shown to him is shown to me"). Within the day, moreover—Boston's literati were a very tight circle, and servants often delivered notes by hand—Wilde seems to have booked the week; Holmes's town house was just a few blocks from the Vendôme, and he dispatched a reply that very morning, to which that afternoon Wilde responded with a promise to call at once. Another day and Holmes had introduced Wilde to the Saturday Club, which met at the Parker House, where Wilde's London elegance made him at once more welcome than Whitman had been twenty years previously, even with Emerson's sponsorship. That first week Wilde was in Boston Holmes himself even extended to a dinner party for the aesthete visitor from London, to which (it being January in Boston) Wilde doubtless traversed the length of Commonwealth Avenue in a closed carriage, depriving his critics of a view of the knee breeches he habitually wore with evening dress. "That bright party I met at Dr. Holmes'," as Wilde recalled it, was but the first of many; another was described in more detail (not omitting the knee breeches) by Alice Cary Williams in her autobiography: "The two large [Beacon Street] drawing rooms were . . . a brilliant scene. . . . Beneath the twinkling chandeliers ladies in brocaded gowns . . . milled about . . . their diamond tiaras and necklaces glinting. . . . I saw coming down the stairs . . . a pair of patent leather shoes with silver buckles, then black stockings and above them green velvet breeches [and] a matching green doublet, a ruffle running down its length [and] . . . a pale white hand which held a lily."

Breakfast on Brattle Street with another Harvard professor, poet Henry Wadsworth Longfellow—through a heavy snow—was rather more sober, but not, Wilde insisted, less artistic: "When I remember Boston I think only of that lovely old man, who is himself a poem," Wilde said later. And so it went. So pressed was the "professor of aesthetery" he had to apologize to Nathaniel Hawthorne's daughter-in-law that he'd not even had time during his first Boston stay to call on her, and hoped on his return to visit not only with them but also with the Alcotts.[20]

Boston's anticipations of his lecture can only be imagined. The wily machinations of one Colonel Morse, Wilde's press agent, abetted as it turned out by Harvard student bravado, didn't hurt, either. The night of Wilde's first lecture, though marked by so heavy a snowstorm that horse-trolleys were halted in their tracks throughout the city, Boston's Music Hall was packed (admission fifty cents to a dollar). And not only with literati. No one could fail to notice that fifty or sixty seats down front had been left vacant. Most could surmise why. Press reports all week suggested Harvard's best and brightest were planning *something*, God only knew what! Soon enough matters became clear: before Wilde made his appearance, a large group of Harvard undergraduates were heard and then seen as, sixty strong, they made their way down the aisles, entering *en masse* and seizing the vacant seats. All were conspicuously attired in various modes of aesthetic dress (knee breeches and such), waving lilies or sunflowers (accounts differ; perhaps both), and striking various languid poses. It was a good "rag," much appreciated by all, but when Wilde (surely forewarned) emerged on stage at 8:30, he was observed to have left his breeches and ruffles and lilies somewhere else. Instead, he was in conventional evening dress, including trousers. Very Boston. Glancing about, moreover, he was as pointed in his riposte as were the students in their challenge. "As a college man, I greet you," he began. "I am very glad to address an audience in Boston, the only city in America which has influenced thought in Europe, and which has given to Europe a new and great school of philosophy." Stroke—then strike—seamlessly he went on, smiling, glancing slyly, one imagines, at the Harvard contingent before him: "I see about me certain signs of an aesthetic movement. I see certain young men, who are no doubt sincere, but I can assure them that they are no more than caricatures." One imagines he must have paused. "As I look around me, I am impelled for the first time to breathe a fervent prayer, 'Save me from my disciples.' " Laughter, doubtless on all sides. "But rather let me, as Wordsworth says, turn me back from those bold, bad men." And so Wilde did, having routed them utterly.

Actually, though, Harvard men were made of sterner stuff, and according to Ellmann, "The students tried to recover their advantage by applauding heartily every time [during his talk that Wilde] drank a glass of water." But soon enough this seemed "small revenge." Besides, having scored decisively— the larger audience, the *Transcript* later agreed, was with Wilde—the speaker was prudent enough not to press his advantage too hard on the Harvard men's own home ground, going on to graciously enlarge on his visit that very day to Harvard Yard: "I beg to assure the students before me that there is more to the movement of aestheticism than knee-breeches and sunflowers." He had particularly liked visiting Harvard's gymnasium and had urged the college authorities, Ellmann reports, "to combine athletics and aesthetics by placing a statue of a Greek athlete in that building." General good feeling, of course, broke out throughout the hall. Wilde later said he thought it was at that point that "the young men lapsed into acquiescence at last," adding in a cheerful and sporting manner: "I could sympathize with them, because I thought to myself that when I was in my first year at Oxford I would have been apt to do the same [as they did]. But as they put their head in the lion's mouth," he chuckled, "I thought they deserved a little bite."[21]

Tracking more specifically Wilde's actual contacts with any of those undergraduates that night in 1882 is, of course, difficult, though at the end of this chapter an exploration of the life and work of one such student, Ned Warren, may well be example enough of the importance of Wilde's Boston appearances. Still, the temptation is great to try to discover Wilde's effect on the life and careers of other Harvard students—not generally, but specifically. However, such data surfaces only by accident usually, and only registers when a scholar (as distinct from a researcher) working on one subject is alert to other subjects. One such is Joan Navarre. At work at the Harvard Theatre Collection, this independent scholar stumbled across one of those stiff old sepia photographs of Oscar Wilde, and, turning it over, encountered the great man's autograph. Above it, furthermore, Wilde had inscribed "To J. Wendell," with the date 31 January 1882. It was the date of Wilde's first Boston lecture, when he was notoriously heckled by Evert J. Wendell's classmates, and the photograph all but proved Wendell to have been there, heckler or no. Here was the end of a strand: when I followed it, I was certainly not surprised to learn it led to no reminiscence of Oscar Wilde. That would undoubtedly have been too dangerous for Wendell to indulge in, given Wilde's eventual disgrace and the profile that emerges of young Evert in his periodic alumni reports to his classmates over the years, and in their final assessment of him in his obituary.

These all disclose that Evert, whose brother Barrett was a legendary Harvard don, was a classmate of Owen Wister, whose strenuous life Evert certainly matched (loving as he did rough travel, whether it was his expeditions up the Nile or to the wildlands of Texas). Described in his obituary as "one of the prominent men of the Class" (at Commencement, for instance, he was chair of the Class Day Committee), Evert was eventually elected to Harvard's senior governing board, the Overseers. In college yet another child, with Wister and Roosevelt, of Hemenway Gymnasium, and a varsity athlete of considerable renown, Evert was at least as Whitmanic as he was Wildean, the catalyst for what has been called the "Golden Age" of track at Harvard, notable for his victories in the 100-, 220-, and 440-yard dashes and in the one-fifth mile hurdles. Active generally—A. D. Club, *Crimson,* Glee Club, and Hasty Pudding—Evert Wendell also sang and acted a good deal in college theatricals. He carried both interests into adult life, furthermore, accompanying Harvard teams in later years to Oxford and Cambridge, for instance, and amassing a theater collection that was one of the largest in the country, which he left to Harvard (the very same in which the Wilde photograph turned up). But though he was a gregarious, sociable man, he never married. His passion as an adult (he was independently wealthy) was his work "among the Boys' clubs" in the poorer quarters of New York, where he was a long-time trustee, for example, of the Society for the Reformation of Juvenile Delinquents. (His chief interest, according to a later obituary, was in "finding good homes for thousands of them in other parts of the country . . . ever the good angel who befriended them.")[22] Athletic, theatrical, charitable, social, unmarried, dedicated to boys' clubs—to realize why Wendell's profile was not such as to encourage him in many reminiscences of Oscar Wilde, one has only to add the names of Phillips Brooks—and Wagner. Specifically, *Parsifal*. That "shadowy center of a world of male homosexual attractions," as Richard Mohr has called that opera,[23] was the reason Wendell went to see the Wagner Festival at Bayreuth just after his graduation from Harvard in 1882. *Parsifal's* "erotic religiosity" also was noticed by Peter Gay, who reported that many even then saw in *Parsifal* a kind of "orgy," and were not, moreover, "too genteel to call it by its right name."[24] ("Pornography" was what D. H. Lawrence called *Tannhäuser*).[25] Eve Kosofsky Sedgwick, noting that Wagner was actively heterosexual, has written that he, nonetheless, "like Nietzsche crystallized a hypersaturated solution of . . . homosexual signifiers. . . . The Wagnerian lodestar for what Max Nordau . . . refers to as 'the abnormals.' "[26] Done with Wagner, Wendell forthwith departed for Berlin, where he hooked up with Phillips Brooks, whom he almost certainly knew at Harvard. Then rector of Trinity Church in Boston, the future Episcopal bishop of Massachusetts was Harvard's most influential religious leader in this period. He was also very shy of women and very drawn to young men, to whom it is not too much to say he was a charismatic figure.

Meanwhile, Wendell did not linger with Brooks in the German capital. Instead, Brooks, according to Wendell, said he was alone and would like Wendell to come with him to India, which the young man, a friend of Brooks's brother Arthur, agreed to do. They sailed from Venice for Bombay in December 1882, and there ensued a three-month odyssey, not just to the great cities of India but to the Himalayas and the caves of Ellora.[27]

It is almost anticlimactic to report that, according to his class photograph, the man Oscar Wilde handed his autograph to that night of his first Boston lecture and whom Phillips Brooks carried off to India was as a young man both brilliant and handsome.

If Wendell left no account of Wilde's lecture, others there are aplenty. The most authoritative reports, those of the *Boston Evening Transcript*, declared the lecture a triumph. But not everyone agreed. A report that appeared in the *London Daily News* put a very different construction on events: "After [Wilde] had spoken for fifteen minutes many went out. Whenever he paused to drink water the audience [not just the Harvard students] broke into uproarious applause lasting several minutes . . . so often Mr. Wilde paused and glared upon the audience." Wilde's own reports home were, however, more along the line of the *Transcript's*: "I live like a young sybarite, travel like a young god. At Boston I had an immense success," he wrote Mrs. George Lewis. But he certainly did not dwell on his lectures—widely thought less than exciting—but on his social life: "Nothing could exceed the entertaining at New York," Wilde wrote. "At Boston I dined with Oliver Wendell Holmes, breakfasted with Longfellow, lunched with Wendell Phillips, and was treated glorious." So much so that when later in the year he was complaining to his agent of "small towns" and how "depressing and useless" such lecture dates were, Wilde urged advice on Morse that certainly would have made no sense if the great Eastern capitals had not seemed welcoming to the speaker: "I hope you are reserving time for my return lectures at Boston, New York and Philadelphia," Wilde wrote from Bloomington, Indiana, "where I am sure to draw large audiences, instead of wearing my voice and body to death over the wretched houses here." Indeed, his confidence was growing: "When Yale students foolishly tried to repeat the same jape [as the Harvard students in Boston] a week later . . . Wilde could afford to ignore them entirely," according to Davis Coakley. Indeed, he entered into the spirit of the Harvard rag so fully, working it for all it was worth, that one suspects Colonel Morse was not the only one conspiring to make the Boston evening memorable.[28] One of the student leaders of the demonstration had been Winthrop Chandler, favorite grand-nephew of Julia Ward Howe no less, she of "Battle Hymn of the Republic," who became Wilde's principal supporter in Boston. Indeed, that this great lady received Wilde in the first place was quite the talk of the town and for more than a week, a tale worth retelling.

As it happens, Wilde's Boston debut in 1882 coincided with the early stages of the biggest romantic scandal of the day in Boston, the affair between the young novelist F. Marion Crawford and Isabella Stewart Gardner. Wilde was certainly drawn to Crawford—whom he once called "the young robust transcendentalist from Boston"[29]—and, perhaps in part out of a desire to cultivate him, made strenuous efforts to cultivate Julia Ward Howe herself, with whom Crawford was then living in her Beacon Street town house, only a few short blocks from Wilde's rooms at the Vendôme. The elder Howe, despite her repute as America's Queen Victoria, was actually a lively and sophisticated lady, the chief mentor, for instance, of Isabella Gardner, who was one of the guests at an impromptu Sunday luncheon Howe gave for Wilde. "We had," Howe confided to her diary later, "what I would call 'a lovely toss-up,' i.e., a social dish quickly compounded and tossed up like an omelet."[30] One can almost hear the laughter.

Others heard something else. Any kind of "toss-up" between so sacred a figure as Howe—as much Virgin Mary as Queen Victoria in Boston—and anyone so notorious as Wilde was bound to get tongues clacking and pens scratching. Many in Boston of the highest stature—Thomas Bailey Aldrich, editor of the *Atlantic Monthly*, for instance—disapproved of Wilde and conspicuously shunned him, expecting the likes of Howe to follow suit. But far from cutting Wilde, Howe went to the first at least of his Boston lectures and received him in her home more than once. Once was enough, fumed many—including that muscular Whitmanic progressive first met here in Chapter 1—Thomas Wentworth Higginson.

Given the antagonism often evident between the Whitmanic and the Wildean—the reader will recall we first studied Higginson as an example of what James Gifford called the "democratizing man-loving" bourgeois Whit-manic ideal, as opposed to the "billowy Bunthorne" of the Wildean ideal—one might expect Higginson to see Wilde, the English aesthete, from the American muscular Christian perspective, and react with hostility. But Higginson's protests to Howe were very much broader. He did attack Wilde for writing "prurient poems" and Howe for receiving the "pornographic" aesthete. But he went much further, writing in *The Women's Journal* in February 1882, a month or so after Wilde's first sortie in Boston but probably knowing he was expected back at midyear: "Women of high social position receive [Wilde] in their homes and invite guests to meet [him], in spite of the fact if they were to read aloud to the company [Wilde's] poem of 'Charmides,' not a woman would remain in the room until the end. We have perhaps rashly claimed that the influence of woman has purified English literature. When the poems of Wilde *and Whitman* [emphasis added] lie in ladies' boudoirs, I see no evidence of that."[31]

Notwithstanding Howe's haughty and studiously injured reply, in a letter to *The Boston Evening Transcript* ("I, as one of the entertainers alluded to, desire to say that I am very glad of receiving Mr. Wilde at my house. . . . To cut off even an offensive member of society from its best influences . . . is scarcely Christian. . . ."),[32] and Wilde's own letter of thanks (a "noble and beautiful" letter, he wrote to her), it is more than interesting that Higginson should have linked Wilde and Whitman in just this way. Equally arresting is the fact that though in London "the *Pall Mall Gazette*," according to Ellmann, "ironically endorsed Mrs. Howe's courage in trying to improve Wilde,"[33] her diary entry indulges in none of that. Howe, with Isabella Gardner at her side, clearly thought beside the point what Higginson thought not just a literary but a moral crisis, and of dimensions far greater than Howe imagined or, indeed, understood. In fact, in his article, Higginson took refuge not in Whitman, but in his Greek ideal, where he found the moral high ground as he saw it. He needed such a distant safety, moreover, surrounded on all sides as he must have felt, not to say betrayed and humiliated, or so we are entitled to believe in view of another volume with yet another perspective on Higginson—most contradictory of men—Mary Blanchard's *Oscar Wilde's America*. In her book Blanchard frankly surmises that Higginson seemed "unsure of [his] gender orientation," and that "in fact his outburst [about Howe's receiving Wilde] betrayed his own strong homoerotic inclination."[34] But she puts forward explanations never before advanced. It seems that Higginson's situation was rather more complicated than has been previously understood; in fact, he was embroiled with Wilde in a competition for the attention of another Harvard man.

Higginson's relationship with William Hurlbut, a relationship quite intense, began at Harvard in the 1840s and endured throughout the two men's lives. Its very intensity seems to have led them both into very troubled waters; Blanchard calls their friendship for each other "long and anguished,"[35] and by 1853 matters had reached a point where Hurlbut definitely was trying to discourage Higginson's attentions. Higginson, on the other hand—his first wife was an early invalid and denied children—seemed more and more needful. It was something of an impasse, and since the two men had always been strongly drawn to each other, something too of a tragedy. Eventually Hurlbut refused even to reply to the monthly letters Higginson would not stop writing him.

In his diary, though, he faced the facts of the matter: Higginson loved Hurlbut utterly; never perhaps was Carson McCullers's observation clearer that the lover and the beloved come from different countries:[36] "Give too much love to the dearest and fairest and oh! What sad dissatisfactions," confided Higginson to his journal, feeling only slightly less trapped, one imagines, than his friend.[37] Higginson doubtless failed in other ways and was too demanding and insistent, not giving Hurlbut enough space, but in one way he never failed—in loyalty to his beloved (which he would have seen as the manly virtue above all, being an aspect of courage). Though one of Higginson's biographers does assert he sent no note of congratulation when Hurlbut married (equally virile as Higginson, it would seem, Hurlbut married at nearly sixty), Higginson, though long estranged from Hurlbut, never spoke ill of his friend and remained, in one scholar's view, "ever hopeful," though so many years later it is hard to know the details.

Hurlbut, though clearly a gifted man (he became the editor of a New York newspaper as well as a successful playwright), seemed to attract no defenders, certainly not among Higginson's biographers. One such, James W. Tuttleton, calls Hurlbut "a breaker of many female hearts and the disappointer of many high hopes" generally, his life in the end "destroyed by personal licentiousness and social scandal."[38] Tilden Edelstein calls his life "scandalous."[39] But both affirm the unusualness of Hurlbut and Higginson's friendship. Tuttleton says, "Their relationship had been a curious one. . . . Higginson was half in love with him,"[40] while Edelstein reports one observer as saying the letters that passed between Higginson and Hurlbut were "more like those between man and woman than between two men."[41] After the era's fashion, Higginson wrote a book about it, but thinly veiled, and Tuttleton goes so far as to assert "the genesis of [Higginson's only] novel [*Malbone*] was Higginson's youthful disillusionment with a divinity school friend of the 1840's, William Hurlbut."[42] As he wrote the book, however, Higginson's positive rapture, confided to his diary, would certainly seem to argue against such an interpretation. Though not perhaps against Edelstein's contention that "the disloyalty with which [Hurlbut] had returned Higginson's affections was reflected in the novel by Malbone's evolution into an unfaithful lover of the faithful and pure [woman], Hope."[43] Hurlbut does seem, however, to have been a heartbreaker, the inspirer of such a character not just in Higginson's novel but in two others of the same era: Charles Kingsley's *Two Years Ago* and Theodore Winthrop's *Cecil Dreeme*. One critic described the

Hurlbut character in Winthrop's novel as the object of "a love passing the love of woman." Indeed, *Cecil Dreeme* has been called "a transvestite romance between two men."[44]

This was the setting—surely one of the most intense Harvard gay romances of the nineteenth century—into which Oscar Wilde unwittingly burst during his year in America. Wilde and Hurlbut in New York and later in Washington were mutually attracted to each other as intensely as Wilde and Higginson in Boston were *not*, and all the intensity that made Higginson so formidable an abolitionist burst out in jealous rage against Wilde. Writes Mary Blanchard:

> Wilde was, however, contemptuous of this rival for Hurlbut's attention, castigating Higginson after the *Women's Journal* article as "this scribbling anonymuncule in grand old Massachusetts who scrawls and screams so glibly about what he cannot understand." Newspapers reported on Hurlbut's attendance at receptions for Wilde. At a stag dinner honoring Wilde hosted by Hurlbut at the Merchants' Club in New York, "the first homeward-bound carriage left the portals long after midnight." Higginson was, of course, excluded from these festive evenings, as he was not privy to more intimate outings between Samuel Ward [Julia Ward Howe's brother], his beloved Hurlbut, and the "unmanly" Wilde. "My dear Oscar," wrote "Uncle Sam" Ward to Wilde on 2 February 1882, "I enclose a letter from Hurlbut . . . and suggest nay urge that you surprise him by joining him at the Hot Springs by 3 p.m." By July, Ward was still arranging expeditions with Wilde and Hurlbut, evidence of Hurlbut's defection to an aesthetic crowd.
>
> Thus, Higginson's attack on Wilde's aesthetic style may have been a more personal and complicated reaction, a jealousy bound up with Higginson's own homoerotic and suppressed identity. For Higginson, aesthetic style was connected to a vision of moral decadence. And, to the anguished Higginson, this sense of moral decadence and Wildean aestheticism infiltrated Victorian society at large, claiming his life-long passion, Hurlbut.[45]

Thus it was that Oscar Wilde came and went from Harvard's most immediate orbit neither quietly nor, perhaps, even tactfully, leaving behind much talk (that continues to this day) and rather a grand present. Having in mind his suggestion that Harvard endow its gym with a statue of a Greek athlete, Wilde, according to Ellmann, "presented a plaster cast of the Hermes of Praxiteles to [Harvard]," which was certainly "by way of casting coals of fire on the Harvard students," said Robert Ross gleefully. An athlete himself, Ross reported the statue was still there a decade later when next he was in Boston in 1892. "It has since vanished," notes Ellmann.[46] (A project for the Harvard Gay and Lesbian Caucus?)

Nor did Wilde neglect contemporary sculpture. Among the handsome young men Wilde fell for in America, for instance, was a Chicago sculptor, John Donoghue, who quickly became (in Wilde's letters to friends) "my very dear friend, young Donoghue." Donoghue's artistic gifts did indeed excite Wilde, but so did the sculptor's "very handsome Roman face but with Irish blue eyes." And at once the Harvard gymnasium—in those days quite the center of physical culture, the first at any American college with separate facilities for each sport—was on Wilde's mind again. And so he wrote to Charles Eliot Norton midway in his American year: "I send you the young Greek: a photograph of him: I hope you will admire him. I think it very strong and right, the statue: and the slight asceticism of it is to me very delightful. The young sculptor's name is John Donoghue, pure Celt is he ... [and] I feel sure he could do any one of your young athletes, and what an era in art that would be to have the sculptor brick in the palaestra."[47]

I know of no reply from Norton. Well, a plaster cast in the Harvard gym was close enough.

Like St. Paul's various peregrinations through the Mediterranean world, the real significance of Wilde's American speaking tour was that he left disciples all over the place, nowhere more so than in Harvard Yard. Although the most immediate purpose of Wilde's tour was to promote the D'Oyly Carte production of *Patience*, a work in which Wilde himself and his ideas were mercilessly lampooned, Wilde was determined to use the publicity for *Patience* for his own purpose. Beyond his financial interest (Wilde reported home that in major cities like Boston and Chicago he got two hundred pounds [one thousand dollars] a lecture, and never less than forty pounds even in the smallest place) he had other motives, aptly described by Richard Ellmann: "The United States had a subculture which was dissatisfied with money and power, but this had no single and famed exponent. Neither the shirt-sleeved Whitman nor the bearded Longfellow, nor the tense Emerson could remotely be thought of as Gilbert's model [for the aesthetes in *Patience*]."[48] Wilde, of course, in real life, found reasons to admire all three Americans. But one must distinguish between those reasons. Certainly his visit with Longfellow—whose poetic style was not Wilde's cup of tea—was more sentimental than anything else. Indeed, in a different way, Wilde's approach to Whitman was not dissimilar; as we saw in the last chapter it was the man, not the verse, Wilde admired. Whitman's poetry, Wilde said, was really "neither prose nor poetry, but something of his own ... grand, original and unique."[49] And even in the case of Emerson, though Wilde was known to quote him (the most Wildean Emersonianism? Surely that Emerson insisted: "I am always insincere as knowing that there are other moods"), it was as a thinker that Emerson impressed; Wilde likened him to Plato.[50] He therefore stinted nothing in his attempt to address this American vacuum of leadership, hoping as Ellmann noted he "might gather the strands together [to] give them the force of a program" in the New World as in the Old.[51]

In this purpose Boston, and Harvard in particular, was key to Wilde's plan: note that two of the three figures we have been discussing were respectively Harvard's best-known professor and most famous graduate. And Wilde succeeded to an extent we hardly yet quite admit or understand, wary perhaps of what such an admission might mean. Yet Wilde's efforts were nowhere more fruitful than in Boston, perhaps because nowhere else was he taken so seriously, by a community that prides itself, then as now, on being dedicated above all things to ideas.

Already, by the time of Wilde's coming in the early 1880s, as Mary Blanchard has observed, Boston was becoming strongly identified with the aesthetic movement. Blanchard cites two stories in *Peterson's Magazine* in 1882 and 1884, in which "Boston's aesthetic circles" were depicted as "subversive and decadent." One narrative, "The Utterly Utter Boston Browns," concludes with the triumph of "sensible country values" over aesthetic ones; another traces the seduction of a certain Cousin Tilly by the Bostonians who "belonged ter them estheticks." Indeed, in this and in the following decade it was increasingly the case that while "to many Americans, Boston was a city that symbolized older standards that stood in opposition to the commercialism and modernity of a cosmopolitan New York, . . . it was also the seat of the new 'gospel,' aestheticism, a gospel that attacked those very standards."[52] By the mid-1890s, when Wilde's career was coming to its tragic, devastating climax, the way Boston's Museum of Fine Arts, Trinity Church, and the Boston Public Library coalesced in Copley Square seemed to Martin Green to have established Boston as "the world capital of the aesthetic movement." Just in time. And *sotto voce.*[53]

Queer Young Men

AS MUCH AS *Two College Friends*, the Civil War novel discussed in the last chapter, exemplified the mores and roles of the Whitmanic archetype of the warrior at Harvard, so did another Harvard book published in the 1890s exemplify the very different parameters of the Wildean archetype of the aesthete: *Harvard Episodes*, by Charles Flandrau.

Its publication caused shockwaves throughout college circles for many reasons, not least because of its pervasive Wildeanisms; one character is described as having been "such a nice little boy at St. Timothy's—piping liquidly in an angelic 'nighty' at Chapel—that when the inevitable rumors reached there, the rector and masters were deeply pained to learn that still another butterfly had burst at Harvard from the godly chrysalis. They assumed lank, Pre-Raphaelite expressions, and murmured, 'Oh, Harvard—Harvard.'" One whole chapter was about Santayana: though in real life he somewhat blurred the two traditions, he hardly did so in the pages of *Harvard Episodes*. In real life he had accepted election as "pope" of Harvard's Lacadocian Club, the members of which were sworn to be neither too hot nor too cold, and also membership in something called the Stylus, where he and his friends stocked the club's library with aesthete literature by Wilde and his French opposite number, Joris-Karl Huysmans, so no exception could really be taken by him to Flandrau's reading of the situation. Furthermore, it was the students who most interested Flandrau, himself an undergraduate in the 1890s. One particularly telling scene portrays a mother visiting her son. Shown Max Simon Nordau's *Degeneration*, a popular book of the era, she says to her boy, "They're queer young men," and asks him if he likes them. "Oh, yes," comes the reply—and the Wildean pose.[54] Well might the *Harvard Graduates' Magazine* protest that "Harvard men are not habitually . . . unmanly."[55] Yet *Harvard Episodes* was one of two books Santayana regularly recommended to those eager to absorb the Harvard ambience in the 1890s.[56] At first glance that is to make too much of the book, but there is a sense in which *Harvard Episodes*—though Flandrau's satirical gifts may not quite equal Max Beerbohm's—is very much Harvard's *Zuleika Dobson*.

Today, perhaps the most visible reminders of those days are the magnificent theatrical posters of turn-of-the-century musicals, arrayed throughout the Hasty Pudding clubhouse near Harvard Square[57] or, a block away at Adams House, the splendid murals by Edward Penfield—probably the only remaining Penfield murals by the artist of so many 1890s *Harper's* magazine covers—in the original breakfast room of Randolph Hall.[58] But the whole of Harvard's fabled Gold Coast of private clubs and once-exclusive dormitories—dormitories with swimming pools!—is still resonant with the feeling of Wildean Harvard.

Charles Flandrau's club was the Delphic, whose history is about as blue-chip as imaginable. Its clubhouse on Linden Street, off Mount Auburn, is very much the *other* house that Morgan built—that's J. P. Morgan, the New York financier and Harvard graduate. Rejected, so the story goes, by the most prestigious of these final clubs, the Porcellian, Morgan founded his own, together with several other similarly spirited young men. Morgan's pockets being deep indeed, the original clubhouse was reputedly the first building in the area illuminated by electricity, a feature that early members evidently flaunted. Explains historian Joel Porte: "So novel and striking a method of illumination did not pass unnoticed, and inspired Harvard wits, resorting to the classically approved principle of *lucus a non lucendo*, soon dubbed Delta Phi [as the Delphic was first known] the 'Gas House'—quite simply because there was a glaring lack of gas." Brightness from the not very bright indeed—a wit so harsh it makes plain the jokes Morgan and his "rejects" had to deal with, though their flash in investing in the new technology so conspicuously showed a commendable spirit in riposte.[59]

Nothing very gay in all that? But Porte also points out that the Delphic was unique also in being "illuminated" by a certain honorary faculty member, that "abnormal" professor, as President Eliot called Santayana. If rumor was true, Santayana was more apt to be found with his students at the

Delphic than with his colleagues at the Tavern, Boston's adult bohemian club for musicians, academics, painters, actors, and like-minded professional and business types. Both the Tavern and the Delphic were for men only, of course, and in his history of the Delphic, Porte noted the same-sex association of those days, certainly homosocial, frequently homoerotic, and—one may be sure when Santayana was around—fully homosexual. It was at the Delphic that the "brilliant and elegant young instructor" was able "to enjoy convivial dinners surrounded by the gifted young men whose sprightly conversation evidently pleased him much more than that of his colleagues. And . . . at the Gas House, moreover, Santayana was to form friendships of lasting importance: [in particular] with Warwick Potter, the 'WP' of [Santayana's] sonnets, whose premature death in 1893 contributed substantially to the 'metanoia' [of] Santayana." Indeed, rather touchingly, in the dedicatory poem he wrote for the present clubhouse of 1902, Santayana wrote of his Harvard social club: "Half the soul clutches what the world can give, and remains where youth and beauty live."[60] Amen.

To understand such clubs, it is necessary to understand the adult Boston clubs that set the tone for the Harvard youth clubs. Not just Santayana, but most well-born Harvard students would join such adult clubs after graduation. Though some were very grand, oriented like similar New York clubs toward business and finance—Beacon Hill's august Somerset Club, for instance—several were very bohemian indeed—the Papyrus, the Tavern, and the St. Botolph. These were the only clubs Xavier Mayne could have had in mind when in his 1908 book, *The Intersexes*, he wrote, "Certain smart clubs [in Boston] are well known for their homosexual atmosphere."[61] Bohemian? In his history of American bohemianism, Albert Parry noted that Boston's "Bohemia was smuggled in by an adventurous Irishman . . . John Boyle O'Reilly," first in his "bachelor's den in Staniford Street," later in the Papyrus Club. "The dangerous word 'Bohemia' was not passed too widely," however, Parry observed: "Certainly, when Thomas Bailey Aldrich and William Dean Howells were elected to the club they did not know its scarlet lining." Adds Parry, "O'Reilly waited until 1885 [by which time he'd helped found the Tavern and the St. Botolph, too] to come out openly with his grand declaration of Bohemianism."[62]

As it happened, the Tavern became the most Harvard-identified of these three clubs. Also the most bohemian. As Francis Watson wrote, the first one hundred members, "for the most part young men," had often studied in Europe—art, medicine, architecture, or science—and had "more or less Bohemian habits of living." Indeed, Watson added, "most of them were either artistic in temperament or in close sympathy with those having this temperament."[63]

At this point it ought not to startle the reader to note a Tavern founder using words like *Bohemian*, *artistic*, and *comradeship* in connection with the club, words then widely understood, as scholars have long since documented, as euphemisms or code words for *homosexual*. Usage varied, of course. Yet whether the use is in a more positive or more negative sense (i.e., associated in this case with homosexuality) is often the key to decoding a word's meaning then. For example, another Harvardian among the Tavern's founders was Owen Wister, author of *The Virginian*, and he used the word *bohemianism* in rather a telling way, surely, when in a club speech years later he assured his listeners that the Tavern "never *sank* into Bohemianism [emphasis added]"—which leaves little doubt that this now somewhat benign-sounding word once had more bite. Interestingly, Wister also appealed to his fellow twentieth-century Taverners to recall "the vanished world of 1884" by way of explaining the club's origins, in the twentieth century a more and more embarrassing burden that led to such nervously defensive explanations as Wister's: "The Boston of 1884, and the little assemblage of young men who formed the Tavern Club, seem in retrospect of a naïveté almost Arcadian."[64] As with Arlo Bates's novel about the St. Botolph Club, the Tavern was soon "found out." In the Tavern's post-Freudian club history, all reference to bohemianism is eschewed. Yet there are all sorts of reasons in Harvard lore that the Tavern is cherished. It was there, for example, that perhaps the college's most exacting major, history and literature, first came into being as an academic field; there, too, that Santayana introduced the second Earl Russell (brother of Bertrand Russell), one of the great loves of Santayana's life, with whom he had an "intensely physical affair."[65]

In the case of the St. Botolph Club, not so strongly Harvard-identified as the Tavern, but still important in this context, there is perhaps less anecdotal evidence as to its homosexual aspect. However, Bates's novel of 1884, *The Pagans*, trumps all such reminiscences in every sense, for it offers virtually a portrait of the club, according to Joseph Chamberlain in an 1898 article in *The Chap-Book* on the Botolph under the guise of the "St. Filipe Club." It was "a name which is so thin a mask that one wonders why it was put on at all," wrote Chamberlain, who went on to answer his own question when he reported how prone the club membership was to what he called "epigrammatic talk—consciously and very intentionally epigrammatic—and some philosophy of life which quite out-Verlaines Verlaine." *The Chap-Book*'s avant-garde readers, Chamberlain knew, would be quite familiar with the attitudes of that notorious French homosexual poet of fin-de-siècle Decadence and would not misunderstand such snatches of club talk as one character's pronouncement that "Emerson lacked the loftiness of vice. He knew only half of life. He never had any conception of the passionate longing for vice per se; the thrill, the glow, which comes to some men at the splendid caress of Sin in its most horrible shape."[66] This is just about as explicit as one got in 1898, and Bates, a member of both the Tavern and the Botolph, was in a position to know. Moreover, it was significant that, as Doris Birmingham has observed, the Botolph's gallery in the 1880s and 1890s "showed some of the most advanced art available in the United States" and therefore played a significant role in the development of American art (the club's 1892 Monet exhibit, for example, was one of the first one-man shows of that artist in America).[67]

We know something more of these clubs from the more intimate memories of some of their leading members. Theodore Dwight, for instance. He was appointed director of the Boston Public Library on the eve of the opening of its palatial new building in Copley Square, and his lifestyle sheds much light on these circles in the 1890s. "Dwight's private library was well stocked with pictures of naked young men [including] some Neapolitan photographs he had purchased from Pluschow," according to historian Roger Austen, who notes that in 1892 Dwight procured such material while touring Europe with Isabella Stewart Gardner. Dwight was also known to make a habit of "taking pictures of naked young men in Boston—and, if possible, going to bed with them."[68] This at a time when *Leaves of Grass*, locked up at Harvard's library, was also double-starred at the Boston Public Library— lent only on application to adult students. Dwight was close to Henry Adams as well as to Isabella Stewart Gardner, and also knew well the Harvard scientist mentioned in Chapter 1, William Woodworth. The nature of these intimacies? Consider Dwight's correspondence with Gardner "of a nature 'in his words' quite too confidential to have been written with propriety." For example, in one letter Dwight sighs: "I never cease thinking and talking of Angelo and Tito [the two gondolier boys at the palazzo in Venice where the Gardners stayed]"; in another he was even more daring, confiding to Gardner that at lunch one day with the La Farges "the aesthetic John appeared. (Under breath—*entre nous*—I like Bancel very much—very much—the other—well, there is an infinite question involved.) (Again—*sotto voce*—I like Mabel in the same way.)"[69] Of course, this is somewhat cryptic, but Dwight was right about lack of propriety in his correspondence, for it is unlikely these references to John and Bancel, and Mabel, too, had to do with his or their tastes in, say, politics. Moreover, it is significant that though Dwight was one of Gardner's most intimate friends—his signature appears in her guest book more than fifty times, and she kept his photograph (and only his) on her writing desk—he is nowhere mentioned in the two earliest biographies of Gardner.[70]

Homosexuality in Boston, particularly in this era, is itself very *sotto voce*. But, like the figure in the carpet, if one listens and looks hard, it can be pretty evident. Another place to look is the literature of the period. Behold, yet another Harvard gay novel.

Cultists and Visionists

IF *HARVARD EPISODES* records Wildean gay Harvard as aptly as *Two College Friends* does Whitmanic gay Harvard, a third book of the turn of the nineteenth and twentieth centuries records a much more fantastical homosexual Harvard, a book with the highly improbable title of *The Cult of the Purple Rose*. It is the work of a man named Shirley Everton Johnson, published in 1903.

The two real and most popular cults of this time and place, critic Van Wyck Brooks recalled, were the highly serious cult of Dante, led by Charles Eliot Norton, and that of the White Rose, led by Ralph Adams Cram. Isabella Stewart Gardner was involved with both, but was particularly intrigued by "the picturesque fanaticism of the Order of the White Rose," Gardner's friend Morris Carter wrote, and known to host occasionally "a little supper for a few enthusiasts and an intimate, romantic service" in her private chapel, Isabella Stewart Gardner all the while costumed (Stuart that she was) as Mary Stuart of Scotland.[71] The Cult of the Purple Rose may not, however, have been real, existing only perhaps in Johnson's book, where it is certainly picturesque enough. Johnson spins an altogether unlikely tale of purple this and purple that—Theosophist rallies on Boston Common under purple banners, meetings called by putting a pale purple light in a window of Harvard Yard, convivial "purple teas"—all in aid of combating the meaninglessness of modern life (the book's climax is the suicide of one of the members). Though purple is the color of choice, in one characteristic scene there is a discussion of Robert Hichens's book, *The Green Carnation*, itself an echo of the same flower, worn as what Beckson calls "the unnatural flower of decadence" by Wilde at the premiere, for instance, of *The Importance of Being Earnest*, and by Aubrey Beardsley, the famous designer, as a "symbol of homosexuality,"[72] which it certainly was in the 1890s in London and Paris, and evidently in Boston, too. Declaims one of the Harvard aesthetes present in the college rooms of a character in the novel: "It [*The Green Carnation*] is verily the most modern of modern books; so modern, indeed, that its very modernity makes one regret one is modern."[73]

One might as well be back at Wilde's Boston lecture. But all this happens in a student room that itself has a tale to tell:

> Eddie DeLancy belonged to the most original set at Harvard, and his study [reflected this]. . . . On the wall were pictures hung with incongruity, for beside a large photograph of St. John's Cathedral was a nude from the Salon; and there was a group of college editors hanging between a pen imitation of one of Mr. Aubrey Beardsley's drawings and a picture of Phillips Brooks.
>
> In a cozy nook, made by a fish net and some ribbons, was a small wood carving, and on the mantel stood a statuette of Apollo Belvedere, surrounded by queerly-shaped pipes, daily themes and glasses which alternately held beer and dust.[74]

It is a tale that purposely fuses (confuses?) Wildean signifiers—Beardsley, for instance—with Whitmanic ones, some frankly religious—Phillips

Brooks, for example—and nudes both of men (the Apollo) and women. Never very serious, the tale is always deadly serious. And perhaps real after all. "Many of the episodes here recorded," Johnson writes, "actually occurred," and there seems little doubt some of the personalities of *The Cult of the Purple Rose* did exist in some form, if only for a season. Certainly it reflects the circle around Santayana, most resonantly one of his closest associates at the time, Pierre Chaignon de La Rose (né Peter Ross, according to Lincoln Kirstein[75]), whom we first encountered at Woodworth's Sunday open house. Assuredly the aesthete at Harvard in the 1890s and 1900s who distinctly caught *everyone*'s eye, La Rose was an early interior decorator; his is the décor of University Hall's Faculty Room in Harvard Yard and the Signet Society clubhouse. Ultimately, he designed the coats of arms of all Harvard's graduate schools and residential colleges. A graduate of Exeter, an editor of the *Harvard Monthly* in college, after graduation in 1895 he became an instructor in the English department. Dubbed "the aesthete of Apley Court" (the reference is to a fashionable Gold Coast private luxury dormitory of the time), La Rose's general impression has been wonderfully preserved in a bit of versification by Henry Ware Eliot Jr., in a third Harvard volume of this era, one of caricatures and verses celebrating the Harvard scene in general titled *Harvard Celebrities*. Wrote Eliot of La Rose:

> Mon Dieu! What is it that it is!
> A-walking on the Square?
> We'll brush away the smoke—Voilà!
> Il est le bon Pierre!
> He has the figure—is it not?
> Petit et débonnaire!
> At morn he punctures daily themes
> With aphorisms neat,
> At noon he "bubbles" with the sports
> Upon Mount Auburn Street;
> At eve he does the nobby stunt
> With Mrs. Jack's elite.
> See how the Radcliffe maidens turn
> To rubber at his clothes;
> He has a truly high-life way
> Of turning out his toes.
> The nifty Prince of Apley Court
> Our dainty, home-grown rose.[76]

La Rose's set, whose life centered on rooms in Matthews Hall that he shared with Daniel Gregory Mason,[77] the future composer, could hardly have escaped notice as boldly bohemian, and it included a wide range of types that showed the same diversity of the Wildean and Whitmanic observable in *The Cult of the Purple Rose* itself. They might be seen as a loosely stitched-together "waiting club" of sorts for other groups in the adult downtown world, groups more fantastical and (because more risky in the adult context) more secretive than the newly forming bohemian clubs. Behold, above all, the Visionists, as they called themselves, not captained by Harvard men, though they comprised a majority of the club's ranks.

We may get glimpses of this group in *The Pagans*—where it is possible (though not at all certain) that the Pagans are, or at least herald, the Visionists. Bates describes a group of "earnest and sometimes fiery young men . . . anti-Philistine . . . [and] anti-women" who were fixated on the ancient Egyptian cat-headed deity, Pasht, "patron saint of pagans," whose statue at Boston's Museum of Fine Arts they admired.[78] Similarly, the nature of the Visionists, which was founded by Ralph Adams Cram, Fred Holland Day, and six or seven others (including four Harvard students), will be clear in the colorful and highly coded memory of the Visionists' clubhouse interior bequeathed to us by Cram:

> On the walls, the painter-members had wrought strange and wonderful things: the Lady Isis in her Egyptian glory, symbolic devices of various sorts, mostly Oriental and esoteric. There were pictures, oddments of varied types, rugs. . . . In some indefinable way its place had a mildly profligate connotation, which misrepresented it utterly. . . . When from time to time a light shone in its windows at a late hour . . . the police force would make investigation, . . . [but there was present] no beverage more potent than beer; while the smoke, which was indeed dense, was innocent of any aroma other than that of pipes and cigarettes, or, on occasion, the lingering perfume of incense when Herbert Copeland officiated as Exarch and High Priest of Isis, clothed garishly in some plunder from Jack Abbott's trunks of theatrical costumes.[79]

Fantastic. Intimate. Secretive. But serious? About that there is more than one view. One scholar, Nancy Finlay, concludes the Visionists were young men (with occasional women visitors such as poet Louise Imogen Guiney and various actresses of the gaslight era) who "played at being wicked."[80] And there is contemporary evidence, certainly, that bohemia did not always take them seriously. Witness Gelett Burgess's verse (Bates's "Pagans" have become Burgess's "Orchids"):

> The "Orchids" were as tough a crowd
> As Boston anywhere allowed;
> It was a club of wicked men—
> The oldest, twelve, the youngest, ten;
> They drank their soda colored green,
> They talked of "Art" and "Philistine,"

They wore buff "wescoats" and their hair
It used to make the waiters stare!
They were so shockingly behaved
And Boston thought them so depraved.[81]

But bohemia often threw inquirers off the scent that way. Note the code: "They drank their soda colored green." Absinthe. More likely, Finlay is wrong and another scholar, Estelle Jussim, is right to characterize, not all of Boston bohemia, but certainly the Visionists as "an eccentric and sometimes notorious group of young poets and artists who combined worship of the occult and the supernatural with aestheticism, ritual and drugs."[82] And it is only when one takes Jussim's view (read "homosexuality" for "aestheticism," "opium and hashish" for "drugs," and for "ritual" the famous British occult society, the Hermetic Order of the Golden Dawn) that the Visionists make much sense. Indeed, Jussim, Fred Holland Day's biographer, suggests a link between the controversial British society and the Visionists through Day, who was introduced in 1890 by Guiney in London to William Butler Yeats, a Golden Dawn member who Jussim thinks it likely proposed Day for membership.

The Visionists were very much involved in perpetuating, not bad magic, but good art, particularly collaborative art, art by various members. A fine example is the publication by the Visionists of Harvard poet (and Visionist founder) Bliss Carman's *Ballad of St. Kavin*, enshrined in an exquisite design by architect Bertram Goodhue, not a Harvard man, but whose cover showed not only the Visionists at supper but the tower of Harvard's Memorial Hall. Above all, there was Carman and Richard Hovey's poetry, published together under the title *Songs from Vagabondia*. Carman's biographer has written that Carman's

> particular friend was Hovey, and they reacted violently upon each other, to the advantage of both. They both had high opinions of each other's verses, [both] published in *Harvard Monthly* [a journal founded by Barrett Wendell and others in 1885, which published some of the earliest American studies of Verlaine].... They were earnest and young, both around twenty-five, and considered themselves quite unique; after all, poets were rare in America at that time. Together they turned away from things academic ... and became practicing poets instead.... They complemented each other both in looks and attitude. Hovey was dark and muscular, Carman was fair and lanky.... The aesthetic Carman, the pale youth, became a counterpart for Richard Hovey.[83]

The resonance of all this is very clear. But how seriously all this was taken at the most learned level of the Harvard community, both by faculty and students, is evident in the fact that in 1914 Carman was commissioned to write and deliver the Harvard Phi Beta Kappa poem. Sample: "One scholar band of gypsies I have known, / Whose purpose all unworldly was to find/ An answer to the riddle of the earth. . . . / Ah, softly, brothers! Have we not the key / Whose first fine luminous use Plotinus gave, / Teaching that ecstasy must lead the man."[84]

It's all more than a bit too much for us now. The year 1914 is the great dividing line, after all. But for all the likely (artistic) idealism of the Visionists, we cannot lose sight of what does appear to have been a darker side. Cram's architectural partner, Charles Wentworth, was very concerned when, as early as in 1895, he wrote to Cram and Goodhue: "I hope you boys have given up the Visionists; certain questionable characters belonging to the society are likely to give it an extreme black eye." And it was also Wentworth who pointed out to Cram and Goodhue how risky to their careers their bohemian activities were in the wake of Wilde's trial and downfall. "You are both queer," he wrote his partners, "and queer things are looked at askance since Oscar's exposé." "Poor Oscar," added Wentworth, "what horrid privations he will have to endure."[85]

Closing the Circle

IN THE LAST heady years before his fall, Oscar Wilde and the Boston bohemians he sparked—led by Charles Copeland and Fred Holland Day—rendezvoused in a way that surely constitutes one of the crests of gay history at Harvard. Thus while Santayana's own circle always retained a special cachet, it was one of several, and the chapter of greatest importance to all of Boston's bohemians was the Pinckney Street group on Beacon Hill, led by architect Cram, photographer-publisher Day, and poet Guiney. None were actually associated with Harvard. But each group was heavily seeded with Harvard students—Thomas Buford Meteyard, for instance, who brilliantly illustrated Carman and Hovey's *Songs from Vagabondia*.[86]

A winsome and beguiling young man, Meteyard knew Wilde personally. Indeed, Meteyard could count the high priest of the aesthetic movement himself as an admirer; there is even more explicit documentation in this case than there is in the case of Evert Wendell, of whom there is only the autographed and dated photo. Meteyard, later a minor painter, was the son of a Bostonian mother and a Chicago father, and in 1882 he and his widowed mother, Marion, who held a vigorous intellectual salon, first in Chicago, later in Boston, met Wilde during his American tour. Tom, then sixteen, registered on the distinguished visitor with particular force. Writing to the boy's mother in Chicago that year, Wilde was at once effusive in his admiration of young Tom and respectful in his advances: "I thank you so much for the flowers, they take these winds of March with beauty. I am glad that there is something in the world that the world cannot harm, nor the reporter interview." Added Wilde: "To your boy with the solemn thoughtful eyes pray give the enclosed, one is written by the Venus of the little Melian Farm, the other by the Velasquez *de nos jours*."[87]

"A friendship" was established, that according to Nicholas Kilmer, the author of a biographical sketch of Meteyard, "would be renewed later." Although on Wilde's side there is only the one early letter to mother and son in Chicago, there is abundant other evidence to suggest that Kilmer is correct. A decade and more later, in the 1890s, it was through the Meteyards, for example, that Wilde, in London, met the actress Elizabeth Robins, who became a member of one of Wilde's own interlocking circles. Another such circle, including the producer Herbert Beerbohm Tree and the painter William Holman Hunt, seems to have centered on the Meteyards' friend Louise Chandler Moulton.[88] Poet, author, and journalist, as well as a schoolmate and lifelong friend of Whistler, Moulton lived alternately in Boston and London, and Wilde thought highly enough of her to ask her to write for a magazine he briefly edited. ("Do Boston for me," he pleaded: " 'Boston Literary Society' . . . with anecdotes of men like Longfellow and Emerson." On another occasion: "Your pen drops honey, my dear.")[89] A mentor of Guiney, Moulton was a godmother to the Pinckney Street circle, and it was perhaps for that reason that, in the late 1880s and early 1890s, Meteyard found something of a home in that circle when, after finishing Andover, he entered Harvard. Actually, however, after 1888 Meteyard was as often to be found in Paris as in Boston; in the French capital he was probably a student of Puvis de Chavannes. He was also a regular at Mallarmé's Tuesday evening gatherings (attended by Degas, Gauguin, and Whistler as well as by younger painters like Toulouse-Lautrec). His entrée to that superior Parisian circle was either through the Norwegian painter Edvard Munch or Wilde himself, whose own good friend, the painter William Rothenstein, was a close friend of the Meteyards. Around and around the circles went—Boston, London, Paris. And Giverny, too. There it was, at the feet of Monet, that Meteyard helped issue the first number of a famous little magazine, *Le Courrier Innocent* (Dawson Dawson-Watson, another painter, was editor), a magazine that was brought to America in the mid-1890s and based at the Meteyards' seaside refuge in Scituate, on Boston's South Shore.[90]

Meteyard's closest friend of these years (aside, perhaps, from Bliss Carman)—a lifelong relationship as it turned out—was Morton Fullerton, a classmate first at Phillips Academy at Andover, Massachusetts, then at Harvard, where the two worked together on the *Harvard Monthly*. Fullerton launched himself on a heady life indeed. At Harvard he studied with both Santayana and Charles Eliot Norton (Bernard Berenson was a classmate in Norton's course). After graduation, while working as a journalist in London and Paris, Fullerton, scion of an old Puritan family, became a friend of Wilde's, had an affair with the model for Lord Henry in *The Picture of Dorian Gray*, and later all but supplanted Proust's friend, Walter Berry, as Edith Wharton's lover. Dark, dapper, handsome, something of a "bounder"

in the slang of the day, with what his biographer Marion Mainwaring
has called "an agile, Catholic penis,"[91] Fullerton suavely juggled "multiple
lives . . . multiple secrets," his claim to fame really that he deeply moved two
authors of genius with whom he was intimate: Henry James, who used
Fullerton as a model for the character of Merton Densher in *The Wings of
the Dove* and wrote of "something—ah, so tender!—in *me* that was quite
yearningly ready for you," and Wharton, whose long passionate poem, "Ter-
minum," described a sexual encounter with Fullerton. So did her novel *The
Reef*, a full-length treatment of the affair after it foundered. Coolly, she asked
Fullerton to critique the work!

Fullerton himself was cool enough, friendly with both James and Wilde, for
instance, who were decidedly not friends in the classic Whitmanic-Wildean polarity. When in 1882 Wilde announced to James, "I am going to *Bossston;* there I
have a letter to the dearest friend of my dearest friend—Charles Eliot Norton
from Burne-Jones," James was not only offended at the name-dropping but, in
Ellmann's words, "revolted by Wilde's knee breeches, contemptuous at the self-
advertising . . . and nervous about the sensuality. . . . James's homosexuality
was latent, Wilde's patent."[92] (The same dynamic seems also to have been at
work with Sargent, a Tite Street neighbor of Wilde's in London, who seemed
to have kept his distance from Wilde.)

At Harvard the younger Meteyard's role in Boston's bohemia also took
a highly literary form; *Le Courrier Innocent*[93] was actually only one of a
number of "little magazines" launched in Boston in this era, several of which
were Harvard-based. One of the most famous, founded in Harvard Yard in
1894, was *The Chap-Book*, already touched on here as the journal which in
1898 exposed the St. Felipe Club of Bates's *The Pagans* as really the St.
Botolph Club. *The Chap-Book* was a journal as peripatetic as the *Innocent*,
though in *The Chap-Book*'s case it moved not to Boston (from Giverny) but
away from the Puritan capital to Chicago, the home of its founders, Herbert
S. Stone and Ingalls Kimball, two Harvard undergraduates at the heart of the
Pinckney Street circle who returned to Chicago after graduation in 1894. *The
Chap-Book*, in which Meteyard was also involved (a woodcut by him appeared
in the second issue), became as notable in its time as London's *Yellow Book*.
Stone went on to be the editor from 1897 to 1913 of *House Beautiful*.[94]

Less celebrated than *The Chap-Book*, but godfather to even more famous
progeny, was *The Mahogany Tree*, which started in January 1892 and folded
that July, largely the work of Harvard undergraduates ("Little care we / Little
we fear / Weather without / Sheltered about / The Mahogany Tree") and
resonant of all sorts of Wildean things: "We have tried, of course, to reform
the world,—to induce mankind to turn now and then from the mad chase
after the Almighty Dollar, and smoke cigarettes and read Oscar Wilde. . . .
We have sung the praises of cigarettes and coffee, not for themselves alone,
but because they stand for a mood." Like so many things of those days
(Harvard's still-extant Fox Club, for instance, founded in 1898 at the Café

Marliave near Beacon Hill), *The Mahogany Tree*, according to Cram, was founded in a downtown Boston bar, at a "not altogether sober party at the Bell-in-Hand" in Pi Alley. (This alley off old "Newspaper Row" was so raffishly bohemian and full of youthful memories among Bostonians that a hundred years later, in the late-twentieth-century era of urban renewal, it was carefully preserved in the middle of a block mostly of skyscrapers.) "The idea originated with Herbert Small and Phil Winn," reports Cram, recalling the party years later: "Winn, as I remember, was unable to keep sober long enough to become a contributor and most of the editorial work fell on Herbert Copeland as Editor-in-Chief. Phil Savage contributed each week. . . . Herbert Small [wrote] many of the book reviews"—Harvard classmates all of them, and all went on to some accomplishment of a literary sort. Small eventually became the Small of Small, Maynard & Co. (founded 1897), a significant turn-of-the-century Boston publishing house; Savage became a fin-de-siècle minor poet of note; Copeland one-half of one of the most famous of American publishers, Copeland & Day, which would become, so to speak, the flagship enterprise of this whole bohemian cohort. It was this partnership that may be said to have closed the circle in a very real sense because, at the height of Wilde's career, Copeland & Day became his American publisher.[95]

Vagabondia

COPELAND & DAY was an outgrowth of yet another of bohemia's little magazines, *Knight Errant*, praised by distinguished British designer Walter Crane during his 1891–1892 American tour; the publication was founded in 1892 by Cram and Goodhue and the Pinckney Street group. It was Copeland & Day that introduced the full-fledged Wildean aesthetic in its most highly developed (indeed, highly decadent, Beardsley-esque) form into the United States. Wilde and Beardsley's scandalous *Salomé*, and their equally notorious *Yellow Book*, to take two examples, both bore Copeland & Day's imprint.

Nor did the Boston firm only import talent; Day, wrote Louise Guiney, had "the lofty taste of the true Emersonian, not of a sybaritic dilettante." He was inspired, wrote his biographer, Estelle Jussim, by "the Keatsian romanticism that pervaded not only Pre-Raphaelite ideology, but the aestheticism of Oscar Wilde."[96] The firm's native authors and designers did not disappoint, either; Copeland & Day's designers included Bertram Goodhue and Will Bradley, whose work is rivaled only by Louis Tiffany's, and Ethel Reed, who succeeded Beardsley at *The Yellow Book* in London. Copeland in a more conventional way (his Harvard contacts ensured a constant stream of young and promising authors) and Day in a more unconventional, even outré way (his contacts were with the London literary world and Wilde himself, and Day in his own right became a pioneering pictorialist photographer, famous for his imaginative nude males) kept Copeland & Day at the forefront, leading the aesthetic movement in America. Not quite what Wilde had intended in 1882, but when you tell someone what to aim for and what the destination should be, but not how to get there, what transpires is often an amazing journey. Copeland & Day turned out to be as American as Harvardian, as Whitmanic as Wildean. Publishers of the highly Wildean *Harvard Episodes*, the firm also launched the Vagabondia series of books, which led to a Copeland & Day bestseller of the 1890s, the influential *Songs from Vagabondia* (which quickly begot *More Songs from Vagabondia*, followed by *Last Songs* and so on), perpetrated by those two Harvard students, Meteyard and Carman, and by Hovey, their mutual friend from Dartmouth.

Does Vagabondia seem somewhat at odds with *Salomé* and *The Yellow Book*? In fact, bohemian aesthetes of this period were characteristically one thing in the winter, another in the summer; Wildean in town, as it were, Whitmanic in the country. These are roles, if not altogether poses, in both cases very much acting out conviction. And there was definitely a larger context in which both styles fit, one most clearly set out by Gelett Burgess, who went on after Boston and MIT to become something of a bohemian missionary to an increasingly lively San Francisco. Burgess in 1902 essayed a quite extensive guide to America's 1890s bohemia. Admittedly highly idealized, never mind impossibly romantic, it was not naive, however ("in Bohemia one may find almost every sin except Hypocrisy"), and he very much caught the spirit of the thing: bohemia encouraged "generosity, love and charity," Burgess insisted, "for it is not enough to be oneself in Bohemia; one must allow others to be themselves as well." Which may be life's hardest lesson. Bohemia, as Burgess saw it, was significantly countrified in aspect. In fact, it is a very Arcadian image Burgess conjures: there are "no roads in all Bohemia," he writes, "only signs in the wilderness"—and the gay subtext comes into focus at once to the alert eye:

> Within Bohemia are many lesser states. . . . On the shore of the Magic Sea of Dreams lies the country of Youth and Romance, . . . free from care or caution. To the eastward lie the pleasant groves of Arcady, the dreamland, home of love and poetry. . . . To the south, over the long procession of the hills lies Vagabondia, [for those who claim] . . . a wilder freedom . . . outlawed or voluntary exile from all restraint. . . .
>
> One other district lies hidden and remote, locked in the central fastness of Bohemia. Here is the Forest of Arden, whose greenwood holds a noble fellowship. . . . It is a little golden world apart, and though it is the most secret, it is the most accessible of refuges, so that there are never too many there, and never too few. Men go and come from this bright country, but once having been free of the wood, you are of the Brotherhood, and recognize your fellows by instinct, and know them, and they know you, for what you are. . . . Happy indeed is he who, in his journey of life . . . has found his way to the happy forest.[97]

Tuckernuck?—William Sturgis Bigelow's island off Nantucket, where the rule was naked by day, formal dress for dinner. Perhaps. Certainly it seems the sort of place where one would always "recognize your fellows by instinct, and know them, and they know you, for what you are"—as much indeed, as in some Copeland & Day books or literary dreams generally or in sexual fantasies, either. Tuckernuck was just the peak. Day himself rejoiced in a summer retreat in Little Good Harbor, Maine, where he offered young men—always handsome but always poor and always very much needing the push Day gave them—not just the chance to pose for plein-air nudes but an entire Whitmanic experience of "comradeship." Similarly, there was Tom's Meteyard's summer retreat, Testudo, on the Scituate marshes along Boston's South Shore.

Carman, so highly thought of that he was published even in *The Atlantic Monthly*, as ever Boston's most august magazine (of which, indeed, Carman later became an editor), was Canadian by birth, and beyond doubt the leading Harvard poet of the '90s. He first joined the dance at Harvard as a graduate student in 1886 at age twenty-five, and was—of course—linked to Santayana. Tall and handsome, blond, and given to heavy tweeds, he was also apparently highly flamboyant. "Carman wore his hair long and favored full flowing cravats," reports Roger Austen, and also affected "sandals and jewelry"—herald of Edward Gorey. He, too, was as convincingly summer as winter, vagabond in the country, fop in town.[98]

Several figures held circles both Wildean and Whitmanic together, above all Santayana and Gardner. The latter, for instance, is always pictured in elegant urban settings, and yet usually spent much of her year on Boston's North Shore or on an island in Maine just about as "primitive" as Tuckernuck. Even in town Gardner—who was *not* the childless/thwarted grande dame socialite and eccentric dumbed-down artist chaser, flower arranger, and society hostess she is often presented as today, but a brilliant maverick reformer of many things and a visionary art patron, designer, and mentor—was often quite as happily to be found at Harvard Stadium or rooting for the Red Sox at Fenway Park—or at her nephews' hockey practice—outdoors at dawn on cold winter days. But perhaps the most startling example that bridged discourses both Whitmanic and Wildean was Edward Perry Warren.

Madonnas versus Athletes

NED, AS HE was universally known and not known—in the sense that he was a man as detested as well as loved—was born into one of Boston's grandest families; new money, to be sure (his father was the founder of S. D. Warren and Co., in Maine, today a division of Scott Paper), but there was a very great deal of it. And no little culture, either: his father was also a trustee of Boston's Museum of Fine Arts; Ned's mother a well-known collector (her *Holy Family* by Filippino Lippi is a great treasure today of the Cleveland Museum). Ned's brother Sam, whom Ned followed to Harvard College in 1879, would become the president of Boston's museum. Ned's Harvard years were crowded. He was enraptured by Oscar Wilde's Boston lecture of 1882, and though brother Sam talked him out of a tête-à-tête with Wilde, Warren met him later in New York. Back in Boston, Warren began to emerge as something of a mentor to younger men often not from Warren's sort of privileged background. Among these was perhaps his most brilliant protégé, Bernard Berenson, then an obscure if charming Boston University freshman. It was Warren who discovered "B.B.,"⁹⁹ helping him transfer into Harvard and introducing him not just to Boston society, but to the great world, where Berenson would encounter, among others, his great patron, Isabella Stewart Gardner. It was Warren who (with Gardner and others) funded Berenson's first study trip to Europe in 1887, a journey from which in a very real sense the young man— soon to become the world's leading authority on the attribution of Italian Renaissance painting—never returned. Warren also subsidized Berenson when others withdrew, enabling him to remain in Europe. But Berenson, despite his effete, effeminate ways—he walked across Harvard Yard, someone once said, as might a faun (were a faun to dance!)—was "aggressively, competitively heterosexual," in the words of the anonymous author of a lengthy article on Warren which appeared in the Bowdoin College Magazine in 1987, and which is in many ways more informative than the two biographies Warren has inspired. And in fact Warren settled on his Oxford classmate, the classicist John Marshall. He was not easily won, but after an 1889 buying trip to Rome and the discovery of an English country house he liked south of London at Lewes, Marshall accepted Warren's proposal and they embarked on a relationship as personal as it was artistic, dedicating themselves to the acquisition of what the author of the Bowdoin article aptly calls "works of a school of art whose highest ideal of beauty was found in the nude body of the young male athlete." Success followed rapidly. Soon, Warren and Marshall were "competing with the Tsar."¹⁰⁰

And winning. Indeed, his victories are to be seen today not in St. Petersburg or Moscow but in Boston; they were also, it should be noted, Marshall's victories; though it was Warren's funds and Warren's taste, it was often Marshall's eye and Marshall's tactics, for the junior partner proved the more skillful man in negotiation and intrigue.

Ultimately Warren and Marshall came to share not only their great task but their own joint protégés, among them John Davidson Beazley, very much the golden youth, an Oxford undergraduate who would later virtually invent the study of ancient Greek Attic pottery. The "Grecian urn" had long been celebrated, of course, but it was Beazley, later an Oxford professor and knighted, who in the 1900s charted its stylistic development historically and identified its masters, applying to ancient pottery, in fact, the same technique Berenson applied to Renaissance painting, based on the new theories of visual perception of the Italian writer and political figure Giovanni Morelli, which in the age of Freud focused more on the artist's unconscious habit (the syntax of his fingernails, for instance) than on his artistic power or subject matter. Even today, when the study of the ancient world is less concerned with aesthetics and patrician politics than with anthropology and broad social history, Beazley's work cannot be dismissed in the face of images like that of the Pan Painter vase—one of Warren's treasures now in Boston's Museum of Fine Arts—depicting the death of Actaeon and widely thought to be one of the great images in Western art.[101]

Warren's country refuge was a big, plain eighteenth-century country house set in the English countryside. And though the experience was in one sense luxurious (at every turn, in every room, were notable art treasures, and in the stables the horses that Warren and his cohort rode daily were Arabian stallions), it was also spartan. Warren's *taste*, in fact, was very Whitmanic, a distinctly masculine elegance, deliberately austere and unfeminine. (If there was a word that Warren hated it was *refined*.) At Lewes, where Warren spent most of his life, and also at the Boston-area refuge he always maintained, an 1807 house called Fewacres near the family's paper mill in Maine, his taste was invariable. He loved porcelain, for example, but ever the spartan New Englander, he always maintained "old porcelain['s] color was best when seen against snow." It was a reflection of a lifelong conflict of taste with his mother; Warren, according to biographer Martin Green, "blamed the luxurious furnishings and art work [of their Beacon Hill town house] for the effeminate sensuality [he felt] it developed in him"; even as a boy he had struggled with her "to install men in the place of women [in the house's decor], Greek athletes instead of medieval Madonnas."

Taste and deportment were, however, in Warren's case, two different things. The trouble was "his refusal to be boyish—and later, manly. . . . He had bitter experiences as a sissy," in Green's words; his behavior was in no sense gender-appropriate *by his own standards*,[102] which, ultimately, of course, became erotic standards. Warren was as Wildean in his deportment as he was Whitmanic in his tastes. Deeply ashamed of his effeminacy, Warren yearned to be more manly and to attract the sort of lover who would, as he put it, "shout to him at football." By no means frail—he was a fearless rider of horses, for instance, and always stood up for himself—Ned was also far too intelligent not to have realized how highly privileged his upbringing was. Nor was he by any means a victim. His Harvard years (he was class of 1883) were by his own account quite successful, and if he didn't quite "come out" in today's sense, he certainly described very well something close to it when he wrote, "My life at Harvard was beginning to be fruitful in love and melancholy. I was not yet aware of myself. I was searching for something, but did not know what, or whether I should find it. Friendship with me passed very naturally into love."[103] All the easier was the flowering, at Oxford, where he seems to have given himself over to nothing less than enthrallment. Consider this from his hand:

The peculiar damp twilight of Oxford, settling over spires and towers, and turning one's thoughts inward, was invading the Broad as I left the bookshop, with a dear little vellum book just purchased, one November afternoon. The sturdy bells of the college were clambering up. . . . The chapel lights showed through the stained windows. There would soon be a sound of chanting. The sense of mysterious peace, and of the still more mysterious lesson which Oxford had to teach me, not only through books and lectures, but through the subtle influence of its venerable traditions and beauties; the feeling that Oxford alone had a region of arcana and delight, which the world at large neither knew nor cared to know, filled my mind as I passed up the staircase where the damp drifted in and trickled from the walls, and along through the dark lobby to my room. Here Plato and my notebook lay open; and the lamp stood ready to light. As I struck a match, however, I saw the long legs of Byngham stretched from the easy-chair to the glowing coals.[104]

A member of Corpus Christi College, then noted for its strong classicist tradition (and also for its equally strong homosexual sensibility), Warren went on in later life to become an honorary fellow and rather a luminary of its senior common room, no small achievement for a man who was neither an academic nor a public figure, and who was an American, too. Indeed, the expatriate Bostonian (though he never lost his forward ways; perpetrating among other things a three-volume *Defense of Uranian Love*; not what Corpus expects of even its honorary fellows) flew quite high at Oxford. Green argues that if "the crucial imaginative experience for [Evelyn] Waugh and . . . John Betjeman and others . . . was Oxford in the 1920's" out of which came *Brideshead Revisited*, it was Ned Warren in important ways who "was shaping that experience for them," so pervasive was Warren's influence on that generation of English aesthetes.[105]

Literary history aside, however, Warren's greatest significance was his bringing to America, chiefly for Boston's Museum of Fine Arts, but also for Harvard's new Fogg Art Museum of 1895, one of the greatest collections of Greek and Roman art in the world. It was an achievement, moreover, positively Freudian in its dimensions, for, as one critic writes, Warren "made no secret of his loathing for Boston."[106] Indeed, it was as if "by sending his native city the vestiges of an earlier and, to his way of thinking, much superior civilization, he could both express his contempt and try to improve the place." Very Boston. Very Wildean. Very Whitmanic. Very Harvard.

How to study all this? If the discourse here is seen as between the Whitmanic archetype, on the one hand, and the Wildean, on the other, the organizing principle is home and away—not just Whitman the one and Wilde the other—but the traditional back and forth, not only of the varsity, but of the collegiate year.

First: Home.

[II]

HOME AND AWAY

Rules of the Road

3.

Home: Old Cambridge, Beacon Hill, Back Bay, North Shore

We are what we pretend to be.
—Kurt Vonnegut Jr.

HOME FOR HARVARD is Boston, but by no means invariably the Old Cambridge neighborhood where Harvard Yard, the university's centerpiece, famously stands witness to nearly four centuries of Harvard's history. Indeed, the varsity has played "home" games for over a hundred years now in Harvard Stadium in quite another neighborhood of Greater Boston, Allston. Harvard medical students, meanwhile, are never found far from the Longwood neighborhood. As for gays at Harvard, they have historically been most visible in the dozen or so of Boston's downtown gay bars.

Leaving aside for a moment the bohemian men's clubs, the earliest incarnation of this scene was the milieu in downtown Boston of the bohemian cafés of the 1880s and 1890s so much frequented by Isabella Stewart Gardner and John Singer Sargent, cafés like Vercelli's and Marliave, in both of which exclusive men's clubs were founded—the Tavern in the case of Vercelli's and Harvard's own Fox Club at Marliave. Then there were the early-twentieth-century tearooms—Joy Barn, the Pen and Pencil, and the Brick Oven, mostly on Beacon Hill—some of which evolved into Prohibition-era speakeasies. One of those, the Napoleon Club, in the theater district (its "Josephine" dining room the design of a leading Harvard gay figure), survived as a full-fledged gay bar, an institution by the post–World War II period. By then several other downtown watering holes of some elegance—the Monarch Club, the Chess Room, the Lincolnshire Bar, and the Café Amalfi—were in competition with more populist and increasingly raucous gay bars of the 1940s and '50s—Playland, the Punch Bowl, Jacques, Mario's, Sporters, the Silver Dollar, and Harvard Gardens.[1] One bar, however, even more legendary than the Napoleon Club, has long thrived hardly five minutes from the Old Cambridge Yard of Harvard—the Casablanca.

A part of Harvard Square's Brattle Theatre, which takes its name from the elegant early-eighteenth-century Tory Row mansion the theater was built next to in the late nineteenth century, the bar is a direct outgrowth of this theater's storied history. The locale of several productions of Harvard's famous "47 Workshop" of the early twentieth century (a seminal course in playwriting of which Eugene O'Neill was the most notable graduate), everyone from T. S. Eliot (as a student in the 1912–1913 season) to Paul Robeson (as the star in the American premiere of Margaret Webster's 1942 production of *Othello*) has appeared on the Brattle's stage. It was also the home, after World War II, of a still-celebrated resident repertory company, and during the McCarthy era the Brattle became a haven for blacklisted Hollywood stars.

In the 1950s, Bryant Haliday, a Harvard graduate student who knew a thing or two about gay bars and who had been intrigued while a student in Paris with the intense interest the French took in film history, transformed the Brattle into one of the early American art-film theaters. His Janus Films, founded with Cyrus Harvey Jr., became the U.S. outlet for a whole series of the era's most important work by Ingmar Bergman, François Truffaut, and Federico Fellini. Together with the classics—Sergei Eisenstein and so on—the Brattle challenged old Puritan blue laws, for instance, in defense of August Strindberg's *Miss Julie*.

The sardonic Humphrey Bogart of the 1942 film *Casablanca* was ever the favorite, however, growing so popular it may well be true, as is so oft claimed, that the "Bogie" cult began at the Brattle, where at its height late-night audiences were sometimes said to have chanted aloud the lines with the actors on the screen. "Bogie décor" was not long in following, and off the theater lobby "the Blue Parrot" soon offered cappuccino and the "Club Casablanca" stronger stuff, all to the soundtrack of an authentic juke box.

The place was ventilated romantically by slowly revolving ceiling fans and evocative murals by illustrator David Omar White of Boston's Museum of Fine Arts School. In the words of critic John Engstrom, the Brattle has been "a springboard for several major talents in the American theater, the setting for one of America's first regional theaters . . . an early home for art films, a shrine to a neglected movie star, and a battleground for the First Amendment." That it also housed a famous bar was just the sort of thing one expected in Harvard Square.

The picturesque history of Harvard's own "gay local"—eschewed for that reason by many collegiate gays who preferred the anonymity of downtown Boston—has only been recounted in literary odd corners of books primarily about other things. But the cast of characters that had emerged at the Casa-B by the post–World War II era opens as wide a window on the gay experience at Harvard, historically, as any of the Victorian college novels already touched on here.[2]

Consider, for instance, socialite and 1960s icon and Andy Warhol protégée Edie Sedgwick, a daily regular at the Casablanca. Patricia Sullivan, another habitué of the bar, wrote that Sedgwick allowed herself to be used by an older gay as a decoy to attract heterosexual freshmen to his parties, Edie being, to say the least, a great beauty and great fun, too. "What did Edie find in that scene?" Sullivan asked. "Well, adoration," she thought, "and a great deal of safety. . . . And it was heightened by the scene being decadent and probably dangerous . . . it was exciting. This is the big world. This is the wicked world."[3] And so Edie missed not a night; bartender Jack Reilly recalled she was always pleading to get in, even before she was twenty-one, a fact Reilly found very disturbing; nobody, he felt, should attach so much importance to a bar.

Then there was Cloke Dosset, in Patricia Sullivan's words, "the fabled Cloke Dosset":

> A very brilliant man, very promising scholar who had come to Harvard
> . . . older, balding, but with a kind of ageless quality . . . a graduate student teaching a section. . . . [His] seduction of beautiful boys had reached the point at which the University could not tolerate it, and he was, I'm told, not allowed to enter Harvard Yard. . . . Dosset did have a fine mind. He'd draw these men in. . . .
>
> The walls of his apartment were decorated with something like black satin.[4]

Less fatal a character was Ed Hennessy, who, as the distinguished Harvard professor and playwright William Alfred remembered, was "an outrageous dandy at a time Harvard was not producing many." A Casablanca regular, Hennessy has recounted a classic Harvard gay story:

> I was in the Lamont Library reading room pretending to study, and this incredibly attractive boy walked through. I *just* about fell apart . . . Robert Taft Hollingsworth the Third. Virginia. St. Mark's. . . . We found out that [he] occasionally went to the Casablanca bar. . . . introductions were finally arranged . . . [and] I introduced him, my love object, to Edie. He fell in love with her! *Aggghhh!* Started calling her up every five seconds. . . .

There ensued what Hennessy aptly called an eighteenth-century comedy: "Edie couldn't bear him. I was in love with him. She wanted to be with me. I wanted to be with him. He would put up with me just to be near her."[5]

The Casablanca was like that. Hennessy also remembered "a sophomore, a very nice Porcellian boy—they seem to be the *most* fragile—whom Cloke saw across the room at the Casablanca and apparently liked." Apparently? You could still start a movie with the unfolding scene. Cloke, in Hennessy's words, got the young man's attention "just by focusing on him, and then he walked across the room very slowly, snapping his fingers, click, click, click, and finally he got right up to him, and the boy fainted! He was on the crew and a big jock."[6]

Part of the Casa-B's mystique—the reason it was such a good place for a decoy like Edie Sedgwick—was that it was always deliberately a "mixed bar," postmodern decades ahead of postmodernism. Nothing if not sophisticated, and all the more effective for gays for that reason; you could go to the Casa-B (in fact, be seen there frequently) and not be "typed." Yet many a Harvard gay found his future lover on its barstools, where only men foregathered. Women, however, were not far away, and not just socialites like Edie Sedgwick. Beginning in 1943 and with increasing momentum in the 1950s and '60s, all levels of women's education were gradually absorbed by Harvard from Radcliffe. And though full coeducation would not begin until the 1970s, no one doubted the direction of events when in the 1950s one encountered women students at the Casablanca; Dorothy Dean, for instance, studying first for her undergraduate degree (in philosophy) at Radcliffe and then as one of the first significant generation of Harvard women graduate students working toward her graduate degree (in fine arts). Dean typified, moreover, what might be called the Casablanca gay style in her capacity as virtually the den mother (fag hag, some said) in the mid- and late 1950s of perhaps gay Harvard's most conspicuous circle.

The theme was definitely Wildean. In Hilton Als's full-scale *New Yorker* profile of Dean—itself a measure of what an iconic figure she became— there is a wonderful portrait of the Casablanca in the 1950s:

> [a] loosely formed clique of mostly white gay men who shared a number of attributes that Dean admired: wealth, intelligence, wit, beauty, social standing. She dubbed them, unforgettably, the Lavender Brotherhood, and she served as confessor, thesis advisor, and "cruise" director.
>
> She would meet the Brotherhood for Daiquiris. . . . "The Casa B was an atmospheric place, and the sentimental music . . . the darkness of the place all helped the milieu," the late writer John Anthony Walker once recalled. "It was like being in a theater; someone would make an entrance. . . . "Dean, with her skill as a verbal caricaturist, regaled the Brotherhood. . . . She was known as Nurse Dean. . . . Upon being introduced to a man who had rented an apartment below a friend she was angry at, Dean said, "I hear you're beneath contempt. . . . "[Dean and her friends created] a brittle aesthetic [evident in the portrait of Dean by Robert Mapplethorpe that symbolized] the twin recourses of flamboyant display and closeted furtiveness. . . . [Dean] constructed her role through language—language that took the form of punitive humor, "unladylike" opinions, and a fearful resistance to the exigencies of romantic love. If her gay male companions established "nice," careful, and remote public personas, especially in straight society, Dorothy gave voice to the ultimately self-punishing anger they had learned to repress.[7]

In fact, if Dorothy Dean seemed well attuned to privileged and yet relentlessly self-loathing gay white men of her era, it was just because she was herself a black woman who no more identified with being black than some gays with being gay. That she *was* black in the first place, critic John Simon once said, would have probably seemed an "astonishing revelation" to Dean, who once described herself as "a white faggot trapped in a black woman's body"—which is surely transfiguring if not quite transgendered. Thus it was, just as so many of her gay friends seemed to despise the gay rights movement then just gathering momentum, that Dean refused, according to Als, to take "even a perfunctory interest in the politics of civil rights." She called blacks "niggers" (and rhythm and blues "screaming nigger fuck music") and was vicious in ridiculing progressives: Bob Dylan was "Fifi Zimmerman," James Baldwin "Martin Luther Queen," and so on. The picture does darken, especially after 1965, the year Dean performed in Andy Warhol's film classic *My Hustler*. Transferring her activities to Manhattan, she became the first woman fact-checker at *The New Yorker*, where for another decade or so she cultivated a similar gay circle in Manhattan. But the low camp of her wit fueled by too many martinis grew tired. There were, she reported, fewer and fewer calls to her "Central Swishboard." Her circle dissolved. Als's article ended: "The Witty Repartee Peters Out."[8]

But the Casablanca in its day was very cutting-edge. When the elites more or less swallowed Susan Sontag's celebrated "Notes on Camp" in the 1960s— with Tiffany lamps, Bellini operas, Noel Coward plays, Wilde, Beardsley, and all the rest—who noticed, as Paul Varnell did in an excellent rebuttal years later, that what it had swallowed was not just Sontag's view that camp was a "sensibility that evaluates the world strictly in aesthetic terms . . . characterized by a love of the theatrical, the artificial or the exaggerated . . . a victory of style over content, aesthetics over morality"? They had also swallowed Sontag's allied view that camp was offensive. In fact, she felt "revulsion," she wrote. Her "analysis of camp seemed rooted," Varnell writes, "in many then-current, condescending stereotypes about gays," whom she hardly praised either when she wrote: "Camp is the solvent of morality. It neutralizes moral indignation."[9]

For me and my friends in the Harvard class of 1972, the Casa-B had indeed become a tired scene by then, distinctly so in an era that was itself becoming so bohemian as to abolish bohemia itself. I do not recall if ever I had a drink there with my dearest gay friend and mentor at Harvard— the dean and master I called John in the Prologue. But I doubt it. Mostly we would have a drink in one of the college common rooms, called Senior Common Rooms (SCRs) because they were for faculty (senior members) as opposed to student or junior members. (The Junior Common Room did not have a bar.) And if the Casablanca's Lavender Brothers seemed the Wildean Cult of the Purple Rose of the 1900s all over again, the SCR seemed much more, as I see now, Whitmanic—at least in the sense that John stood in a long tradition of college deans and teachers. Ned and Tom, the two Civil War officers of *Two College Friends*, would not have recognized Cloke

Dosset, much less Edie Sedgwick. But both would have recognized John immediately. Of course, not all deans or all dons have been gay. But John was not the first. A hundred years before, in the 1870s, perhaps Harvard's foremost dean ever was, never mind homosexual, a pioneering advocate of what can only be called gay rights.

Professor X

IN HIS SPLENDID and widely read book *The Metaphysical Club*, historian Louis Menand dwells admiringly on the American pragmatist thinker Charles Sanders Peirce. The son of Harvard professor Benjamin Peirce, perhaps the first world-class American mathematician, and a member of Boston's famous Saturday Club (along with Emerson and Nathaniel Hawthorne and Louis Agassiz), Charles grew up in a house frequented by luminaries such as Henry Wadsworth Longfellow, Daniel Webster, and Charles Eliot Norton. Charles himself became one of three Bostonians in the post–Civil War era (the others were William James and Oliver Wendell Holmes) whom Menand calls, along with their disciple John Dewey, "the first modern thinkers in the U.S." Indeed, in a memorable phrase, Menand goes so far as to assert that "William James invented pragmatism as a favor to Charles Peirce."[10]

Charles's brother, James Mills Peirce, was no slouch, either. A much esteemed colleague and friend of modern Harvard's great founding president, Charles Eliot, James Mills Peirce was the president's chief collaborator and sounding board and, indeed, coparent of Eliot's dearest progeny, the newly established Graduate School of Arts and Sciences of 1872, the early development of which under Eliot and Peirce was to be of profound importance to the history of American higher education, and marked Harvard's ascent in the last decades of the nineteenth century from venerable New England college with not-yet-fully-realized university aspiration to an international seat of learning. And James Mills Peirce seems also to have been, though publicly discreet, as he would have to have been as the first dean of Harvard's Graduate School of Arts and Sciences, a militant, even a fierce, homosexual prophet, and one of wide influence. Did Eliot suspect? Peirce was as conspicuously unmarried as Santayana. Why did Eliot, who called Santayana abnormal and also banned Charles Peirce, distinctly a womanizer, from any Harvard position, call James Peirce a close and valued friend?

An economics and government major, my own mentor, John, would have had much in common with Peirce, an expert on analytic geometry. I, on the other hand, would have probably had much more in common with the man Peirce loved best, so far as we can tell at this great distance of so discreet a relationship, one of his undergraduate students, Thomas Sargent Perry. Later in life a notable late-nineteenth-century Boston littérateur, ultimately chief critic for *The Nation* for foreign work, Perry was a man of broad and liberal sympathies, among the first Harvard figures, for instance, to agree to teach women at the "Harvard Annex" of his day that would later become Radcliffe College. An intimate of Henry James, Perry also adopted as a protégé the young Bernard Berenson, who allowed grandly enough that Perry was the "one person in the world" whose views on literature he admired.[11] When Berenson fell afoul of Charles Eliot Norton (who was perhaps anti-Semitic in his attitude toward his precocious student), Perry, in Ned Warren's wake (how well did they know each other?), also came to Berenson's rescue, helping with the grant Harvard had denied Berenson for study abroad.[12]

Peirce and Perry were in some sense a couple. Whether or not they were ever lovers cannot be said. But they were certainly intimate with each other. Perry, an eighteen-year-old sophomore in 1863, is known to have taken a math course taught by Peirce, then nearly thirty. The nature of their relationship we can but guess at, though a surviving letter the older man wrote to the younger a decade later, when Perry told him of his engagement to marry, is suggestive. Wrote Peirce in part:

> I am so glad you are so happy. It makes life seem less cruel to me, even if it has no mercy for me, that you have found its only joy.
>
> I had a charming call the other day. I was received so sincerely & feelingly & in a way that seemed to make me really a sharer in your joy. Our friendship is among the things I value most in life, & I like to think that now its pleasure is to be heightened for all coming time. I am apt to dread my friends' friends, for you know how few people there are who can like or understand me. But here I feel that I have already a strength which you have given me.[13]

Perry did well what in most lives is done badly. The customs of the day, of course, led many (if not most) homosexuals to marry, not a member of the same, but of the opposite, sex. But they also, in ways admittedly rather warped and repressive sometimes, allowed those in such desperate throes as those men often got themselves into to continue specially intimate male relationships in the context of the heterosexual marriage. Peirce, for instance, though he seems to have often visited socially with Perry and his wife, especially abroad, was surely the person who persuaded Perry to stand for election to the St. Botolph Club, so bohemian then, which became for both men a second home. Indeed, it was evidently at the St. Botolph that their relationship continued to flourish at least into Perry's late forties (and Peirce's early sixties) in the 1890s. Wrote the younger man to a friend in 1892 of his club life with Peirce: "I have nothing more to do with my own happy home, it is deserted; the fire is never lit in my library; I scarcely know my children by sight. I spend all my time here wildly reveling. . . . We are a wild set; J. M. Peirce & I especially sit up to midnt. &, as it were, personally lead the dance."

Peirce, be it said, by no means confined his attentions solely to Perry; the relationship to which he seems to have given precedence was not exclusive. According to mathematician Hubert Kennedy, this Harvard dean can also be linked to another young man: "Mr. Clifford, a young friend (a bright young physicist from the [Massachusetts] Institute of Technology) who is going out with me (to Europe) for the summer," as Peirce described him to his brother in 1889.[14]

In a letter Peirce wrote to Perry in 1891, the smoking gun, so to speak, is first discerned: the first mention of a famous name indeed in the history of homosexuality, John Addington Symonds: "Clifford & I had a charming day walking in the New Forest. We are on the Isle for a day or two. But I don't much care for it. Then we head for Switzerland. We do not go to Bayreuth. [Wagner again.] I had a pleasant letter from Symonds just before sailing, asking me to go to see him. I mean to accomplish that, if possible. I have just been writing him."[15]

A distinguished and widely respected historian of the Italian Renaissance,[16] Symonds chiefly knew Perry, with whom he had initiated a correspondence on literary matters in 1883. Certainly the relationship between them was a frank one, clear especially in the fact that Perry visited Symonds in England during the summer of 1887, four years after the publication of Symonds's first privately printed book on homosexuality, *A Problem in Greek Ethics* (1883), a copy of which at Perry's request Symonds sent him, along with his later *A Problem in Modern Ethics* (1891). Symonds, moreover, was impressed, writing Edmund Gosse in 1891 that Perry was "quite one of the most learned & clearest-headed men in the USA."

Kennedy surmises, altogether logically, that "Perry must have shown Symonds's essays to Peirce and it was probably this that initiated their correspondence," as well as a historic relationship, quite unsuspected until Jonathan Ned Katz, in his *Gay American History* (1976), identified the author of Appendix D in Symonds and Havelock Ellis's *Sexual Inversion*, the first of six volumes of Ellis's monumental *Studies in the Psychology of Sex* (1896–1910), a book Symonds suggested in mid-1892 that he and Ellis collaborate on.[17] The appendix is titled "Letter from Professor X." Symonds identified the letter's author only as "an American of eminence, who holds a scientific professorship in one of the first universities of the world." As the article was dispatched to Symonds in mid-1891, the year after Peirce became the first dean of Harvard's new Graduate School of Arts and Sciences, it may very well have been written in his private office—the dean's office—in Harvard Yard. The "ideas expressed in this letter establish Peirce as one of the most progressive advocates of homosexuality in the nineteenth century. That Peirce was unwilling to publicly state these views is entirely understandable. Even in the second half of the twentieth century what Peirce wrote is controversial." Indeed, Symonds himself seemed more than a little bit nonplussed by this missive from America: "I have found a fierce & Quixotic ally, who goes far beyond my expectations," he wrote to Gosse in 1891, "in hopes of regenerating opinion on these topics." In this private letter he named his ally: "a Prof. Peirce of Cambridge, Mass. . . . I hear he professes mathematics."[18] Peirce also professed homosexuality, writing that he believed Greek morality was "Far higher than ours, and truer to the spiritual nature of man," and, as Katz has written in his most recent work, Peirce argued

> against four of the theories then in use to explain homosexual passion. First, we should not "think and speak of homosexual love . . . as 'inverted' or 'abnormal'"—the condemnatory medical theory. Second, homosexual love was not a sort of color-blindness of the genital sense"—the most liberal medical theory. Third, homosexual love was not "a lamentable mark of inferior development"—the theory of evolutionary degeneracy, one version of which appeared in Freud's analysis of homosexuality as a "fixation" of sexual development. And, fourth, homosexual love was not "an unhappy fault, a 'masculine body with a feminine soul'"—Karl Heinrich Ulrich's theory of Urnings.

Peirce concluded instead that homosexual desire should be thought of as "being itself a natural, pure and sound passion, as worthy of the reverence of all fine natures as the honourable devotion of husband and wife, or the ardour of bride and groom."

Peirce's ideas would probably be of more interest today for his further view that as sexual passion may be aroused by either a man *or* a woman, "the *abnormal* form of love is that which has lost the power of excitability in either one or the other of these directions. It is *unisexual* love (a love for [only?] one sexuality) which is a perversion." But Peirce's view that homosexuality was "a natural, pure and sound passion" comparable to heterosexual marriage was hardly less startling. Indeed, Peirce's was a penetrating mind: "There is an error in the view that feminine love is that which is directed to a man, and masculine love that which is directed to a woman"; that was to beg the question, he thought, and to assume what ought to be questioned.[19] Moreover, as Jonathan Katz has pointed out, Peirce's teaching that there was no particular love proper to a particular sex was "a rare, major innovative insight into his age's conception of sex, sexuality and love," and in holding that passion is not characterized by the nature of its object, but by its own nature, Katz, very much a "Foucaultian," feels that "Peirce anticipated Sigmund Freud's theory of an originally roaming libido that, only gradually, through a child's interactions with the world, becomes focused on a particular object or specific sex." Katz has certainly discerned just how radical Harvard's senior dean was in the 1890s.[20]

Either idea would have astounded President Eliot and most of Peirce's colleagues. Even Peirce felt constrained, publishing under a pseudonym. But historian Bert Hansen, author of the marvelously titled "Has the Laboratory

Been a Closet? Gay and Lesbian Lives in the History of Science and Medicine," a lecture given in 1996 at Wesleyan University, speculates that Peirce was "not an isolated thinker, but was rather part of an intellectually challenging and supportive circle of homosexuals, who self-consciously discussed their lives and their place in society." Hansen adds, "I have not yet been able to discover the other members of his circle, though it seems possible that it overlapped with that surrounding the Harvard naturalist, Willie Woodworth."[21] Although Hansen reaches this conclusion based solely on internal evidence, I suspect he is right; one tends to lose track of relationships *between* faculty because they are usually so much less adventuresome (and sexy) than those between faculty and students. Still, Peirce and Perry introduce the characteristic pattern of the gay experience at Harvard, as elsewhere in academia, at least at "home"—that between the teacher and the student.

"Love and Friendship"

SUCH WAS THE title of a book of 1993 by Allan Bloom, a key mentor of Saul Bellow (though Bellow was some fifteen years older); both men taught a famous course at the University of Chicago on that much misunderstood category of life—the romantic friendship. And in Bloom's book, he discoursed at length on one key aspect, "the close relationship between the male teacher and his younger male pupil, which formed the ideal in [Plato's] 'symposium,'" remarking particularly that "the teacher-pupil relationship is as mysterious as the lover-beloved relationship" and that the underlying "justification" of pederasty derived from that fact; indeed, in his fine chapter on "The Ladder of Love" he pronounces "the lover and beloved in the highest sense are the teacher and student," adding significantly that "although a certain bodily attraction might occur, it is not the essence of the relation," that, indeed, the whole point of the Socratic ideal is that "souls and what they contain are more beautiful than the body."[22] Today that will seem controversial in circles both heterosexual and homosexual. A digression.

In a fascinating article of 2001 in *Harper's*, already alluded to in the Prologue, Christina Nehring observes, "Teacher-student chemistry is what sparks much of the best work that goes on at universities," adding: "It must not be criminalized." It is fine, she writes, to

> disarm a certain type of old-school professor who thought that his students' bodies (as well as their research . . .) were his birthright. It is one thing to discourage gross sexist speech and to counsel caution in the initiation of student-teacher relationships. . . . It is quite another . . . to try to ban professor-student relationships altogether. Knowledge is unremittingly personal; the best students fall in love with teachers, the most engaged teachers respond strongly. The campus on which the chance

of ... sexual "impropriety" between teachers and students is eliminated is the campus on which ... pedagogy is dead.

Is there a more quintessential pedagogic model in the history of Western civilization than Socrates and his pupils? ... One can't legislate against pain or against mistakes.[23]

Not only Socrates comes to mind, of course. According to Nehring, in Harvard's own orbit in the mid-nineteenth century, students exposed to Margaret Fuller sent her love letters. In the Victorian Boston example it was the students' initiative, as was the case in ancient Athens: in Plato's *Symposium* there is hardly any length the handsome young Alcibiades will not go to in an effort to seduce his teacher; not content with cajoling Socrates to the gymnasium and challenging him to wrestle, he contrives as well an intimate supper in his efforts, which Socrates resists only because of faithfulness to another young man. Indeed, Nehring argues that her own affair as a freshman with a college professor

did not reinforce my student sense of inferiority; it eliminated it. As much as I admired my teacher, I also found I could talk with him; I had something to offer him that had nothing to do with the old clichés of youth and beauty. Or if it had to do with them, then long live mixed motives, for they certainly were not the most important or lasting causes of our understanding. . . . The relationship enfranchised me intellectually; it gave me a voice, and faith in it.[24]

Citing a whole litany of teacher-student intimates—"Camille Claudel and Rodin, Hannah Arendt and Martin Heidegger? Paul Verlaine and Arthur Rimbaud, Allan Bloom and his student lovers ... Heloise and Abelard?"— Nehring admits that as with Socrates himself, there was some pain, surely ("Not one of these relationships," she writes, "was perfect [which is?] ... but all were spectacularly productive, revelatory, heated, and formative for both parties—in several cases, formative for Western culture and philosophy.")[25] It is not a road one should block, nor a door one should nail shut by any means.

Peirce, in love with Perry when first they were professor and student, knew that well, nurtured as he was in the Anglo-American collegiate tradition. Peirce's biographer, R. C. Archibald, wrote of him:

His interests and gifts were varied. Widely read in literature, he was in particular a lifelong student of the plays of Shakespeare and an enthusiastic admirer of the work of Shelley [and surely of the rather bohemian man as well]. He was fond of travel, a lover of the best in art, and a devotee of music; but the stage and whist were his passions. [In college he was a member of the Hasty Pudding Club.] He saw most of the best actors and plays for half a century, and he himself was no ordinary dramatic reader. . . . His colleague and intimate friend, Professor Byerly, has made the following characterization: "Careful in dress, dignified in bearing, scrupulously polite to everyone, courteous and kindly, he will be remembered . . . for his friendly greeting, his earnest speech, at once measured and impetuous, his quick indignation at any suggestion of injustice, and his scorn of everything narrow or crooked or mean. . . . His ready interest in everything human, and his keen enjoyment of life made him the most charming of companions."[26]

Finally, his relationship with his students attracted particular notice: in addition to being "patient and helpful," it seemed to many that Peirce's outstanding characteristic was his "understanding and sympathizing with [his students'] tastes, their aspirations, and their struggles, as if he were still one of them." (Where have we heard that before? Santayana, of course.)[27]

Very many superb deans and tutors and professors have been/are heterosexual; one must be careful—as with the whole question of gays in the arts—to remember that any seeming disproportion of gays in any particular field may well reflect the fact that some fields have been, historically, more welcoming to homosexuals (for whatever reason is another subject) than other fields, not that gays, for instance, find the arts generally more congenial than the sciences, any more than women are drawn more to nursing than to doctoring. Peirce, after all, was both an ardent homosexual and a mathematician. And no more do gays than mathematicians or men generally have a lock on being good deans, which is distinctly a vocation. But given the historically same-sex character of higher education, the homosexual traditions of dons and schoolmasters are long-standing and nearly always most noticeable in just such an identification on the professor's part with his students, more than with any faculty colleagues, as Peirce showed. Such relationships between professors and students, as opposed to among faculty, are inevitably age-asymmetrical, and those who see sexuality in only its physical expression will always find such relationships troubling. But looked at from a broader perspective, they have seemed to many over the years as more enabling than troubling. Parents discover soon enough that a somewhat adversarial "us-as-distinct-from-them" parent/child relationship is an almost necessary part of child-rearing. Professors, on the other hand, engage young people in a less adversarial, more Socratic way, relying on a real identification with students. Of course it can be abused; so can the relationship of a birth parent with a child. Thus Jung himself conceded that:

Homosexual relations between students and teachers may serve a valuable function: when such a friendship exists between an older man and a younger its educational significance is undeniable. . . . [It] can be of advantage to both sides and have lasting value. An indispensable condition for the value of such a relation is the steadfastness of the friendship and their loyalty to it.[28]

Personalities of the Yard

PEIRCE WAS NOT the only homosexual professor, nor is the student-teacher relationship the only discernable pattern characteristic of the gay experience at Harvard. Another pattern which sheds light on how Harvard's gay history has thrived, really, in the face of widespread animosity over the years, is the way the most patrician families, long identified with the college and university even in the nineteenth century, have led the way; Trojan horses of particular importance because homosexuals have always been difficult to identify. Almost pathetic, for example, is the way would-be moral guardians (never stopping to consider or take seriously the great archetypes) hunt down effeminacy relentlessly, as if it were not only a crime, but even a reliable signifier. Yet gay seeps in, as it were, as a sort of fifth column. The perennial way subversives breach the highest walls is through family. To take an historical Harvard example—in this case, women—the university gained a prize for its faculty with the great Swiss naturalist Louis Agassiz in the mid-nineteenth century. His wife, Elizabeth, neither bonus nor burden so far as anyone knew, ended up, however, according to one's point of view, playing a pivotal role in Harvard's history—some would say more pivotal than her husband: Elizabeth Agassiz would become a pioneer in women's education as the founding president of Radcliffe College, established to ensure that women could gain access to the Harvard faculty—not by any stretch of the imagination one of President Eliot's goals but today seen as one of the great achievements of his reign because Agassiz so effectively forced his hand in the founding of Radcliffe.[29] Had Agassiz tried to forthrightly apply to enter Harvard she would have been rebuffed unequivocally, as would any woman.

Similarly with homosexuals, and above all with the galaxy of bachelor dons who have always perhaps more than anyone else fueled any college on a day-to-day basis. Under cover of their pedigree (as Agassiz under cover of her husband) they created a thriving gay subculture that in time would surface boldly. Two outstanding such dons, for example, were the nephews (sons, really, as they were all but adopted) of Isabella Stewart Gardner and her husband, John L. Gardner, who served as Harvard's treasurer in the latter part of President Eliot's reign. Each of the two Harvard men is a remarkable case study of the two great archetypes I've proposed here.

William Amory Gardner, or WAG, as he was called, though he was certainly a sportsman—he was a keen sailor and a good rider—was very artistic, and after a brilliant career at Harvard as a classicist ended up the resident aesthete at Groton School, a place very much in need of same. WAG did not in this respect disappoint. To the large house he built for himself on the school grounds, he added, for instance, nothing less than what he called the "Pleasure Dome," presumably after Kubla Khan's, and such amenities as an indoor swimming pool, a small theater, squash courts, and an attached maze. All of this sustained a pretty exotic lifestyle by Boston Brahmin standards.

Consider the well-known minister who called on WAG with his student guide one morning after school chapel. Summoned upstairs, the visitors soon found themselves in Gardner's bedroom: WAG, breakfast porridge in hand, stark naked (except for a pair of outrageous slippers), was with a student, similarly naked, who was reclining on WAG's sofa, the don all the while exclaiming, "It makes not the slightest difference that you won the first rubber, my dear boy.... That is la courtoisie de la maison." Teacher and student, in a state of nature, were attended by a butler in morning coat, holding more porridge! Furthermore, by no means taken aback at visitors, WAG, according to Groton historian Frank Ashburn, promptly "dropp[ed] an elaborate curtsy." He didn't spill the porridge, either. What Wildean would? Certainly not Gardner, one of Groton's three founders, who had a stereotypically Wildean childhood and youth.[30] A close friend of Ned Warren, his Harvard classmate, Gardner went on to be an excellent master and also a generous donor for Groton.

His elder brother, Joseph Peabody Gardner, according to Colin Simpson in *Artful Partners* (where he depends for this intelligence upon a rumored unpublished biography of Bernard Berenson by his wife, Mary), reputedly fell in love with one Logan Pearsall Smith, not a nice guy, it seems safe to say, who is said to have "broken Joe Gardner's heart," and precipitated his suicide.[31] Without a doubt WAG gave to Groton its magnificent chapel in Joe's memory and presumably chose the architect, Henry Vaughan. Given by one gay man in memory of another and designed by a third, I have called Groton Chapel well and truly Gay Gothic.

If WAG personified the Wildean archetype, Archibald Carey Coolidge can well stand for the Whitmanic here. Also a lifelong bachelor in an era when, given the pressure to marry, it meant nothing in terms of sexuality to do so but everything not to, Coolidge is best known today as the founder of Apthorp College, the predecessor to Adams House, significantly always the most bohemian of Harvard's seven original residential colleges established by President Lowell in 1930. An excellent student and athlete in his undergraduate years, Coolidge as a don built Apthorp College around Randolph Hall, a dormitory he had erected and named after himself on Harvard's Gold Coast in 1897. It forms still a quad with a splendid eighteenth-century mansion, Apthorp House, which is today the Master's Lodgings of Adams House. Coolidge himself resided in Randolph Hall, to which over time he attached not only squash courts but an indoor swimming pool—the minds of dons seem to run in the same direction. It was Coolidge, who had wrestled at Harvard as a freshman, who commissioned Edward Penfield, he of the stylish, asexual females and languid male Adonis types of his 1890s *Harper's* magazine covers, to paint the still surviving and unique murals for Randolph Hall's breakfast room. They depict college scenes, none more memorably than Penfield's series of sensuous, muscular athletes—polo players, rowers, footballers, and so on—in very homoerotic poses. It is high style and high sex; discreet, to be sure, but artistically pretty much the outstanding homoerotic architectural art at Harvard since Oscar Wilde's statue was quietly lost, stolen, or dumped in the Charles.[32]

Coolidge and WAG were hardly unique as representatives of this pattern of old patrician families. An even older Harvard legacy than the Coolidge family are the Saltonstalls—Cleveland Amory reported in *The Proper Bostonians* they and the Winthrops were the only Brahmin families entitled to coats of arms continuously since royalist Boston days in the seventeenth century when Sir Richard Saltonstall came over with John Winthrop in 1630. The Saltonstalls, who never did lose their habit of leadership (one of Sir Richard's descendants, Leverett Saltonstall, was elected governor of Massachusetts in 1938 and in subsequent years became a U.S. senator), contributed a notable homosexual to the class of 1928, Nathaniel Saltonstall. A graduate of the MIT School of Architecture, who after serving in the Army Air Corps in World War II went on to become a prominent Boston architect and interior designer (it was Saltonstall who designed the interiors of the Napoleon Club), he was also an ardent modernist. Though a principal of Putnam, Cox, and Saltonstall, he became best known as founder of—and sometime president of—Boston's Institute of Contemporary Art. Often a thankless-seeming task in the ultra-conservative Boston of those days, posterity pays him more and more attention as that institution waxes more important in the twenty-first century.[33] His own sort of gay blade, Nat moved in lively circles; a friend of the composer Cole Porter, he once threw at the Boston Ritz one of Porter's famous "boy parties"—Harvard boys almost certainly—parties the composer encouraged his friends to mount for him, in this case to celebrate the premiere of Porter's new musical of 1935, *Jubilee*.[34]

By far the most conspicuous example, however, in the early twentieth century, of an old-family gay "Trojan horse" at Harvard was Amy Lowell, sister of Eliot's successor as Harvard's twenty-fourth president, Abbott Lawrence Lowell. Now this book is about Harvard in its mostly all-male years—Radcliffe's history is another book. But as mothers, wives, sisters, patrons, mentors, collaborators, muses, and so on, it goes without saying that women like Isabella Stewart Gardner and Amy Lowell (the two did know and influence each other, by the way) have always figured in Harvard's history even before women were able to do so in their own right as faculty, students, deans, and such. And just as Elizabeth Agassiz brought the subject of women's education at Harvard to a head in the 1880s, so Amy Lowell brought homosexuality its highest profile to date at Harvard in the 1910s.

How high? There is the story, fully documented, of the commencement ceremony of 1915: E. E. Cummings, the future poet, then a rising senior, in his student commencement oration, included a reading of Amy Lowell's "The Letter," occasioned by the absence of her great love, Ada Dwyer Russell. One lady in Harvard's Memorial Hall was heard protesting that day that the poem was "lascivious." (It's all in the eye of the beholder, of course. Seems mild enough today.) Cummings did not help himself in describing Amy Lowell's poetry as "a development from the normal to the abnormal," and this in the very presence of her enthroned and presidential brother. The next day the *Boston Transcript* trumpeted: 'Harvard Orator Calls President Lowell's Sister Abnormal." That high.[35] And it was, of course, a journalist's dream come true.

"Harvard's Class of 1900 began their undergraduate careers," Stephen Watson has pointed out, "at a time when Boston was suffering from grandfather on the brain." Thus in Watson's *Strange Bedfellows: The First American Avant-Garde*, though Boston is one of the six places he notes as "cradles" of twentieth-century modernism (London, Paris, Florence, New York, Boston, and Chicago), it is also the only case in which he substitutes a particular institution for a city—Harvard, not Boston, keeps company with New York and Chicago, the other two American modernist cradles, an indication of the importance of Harvard's role as the earliest spearhead of modernism in Boston. But about the Boston Brahmin who most rigorously rocked that cradle there is no confusion in Watson's mind at all—it was Amy Lowell. In the first period of modernism in the twentieth century, 1914 to 1922, "the prime minister," in Van Wyck Brooks's words, "of the Republic of Poetry"— whether writing her own, sending off a typewriter to an impoverished D. H. Lawrence, or writing letters of recommendation for young Cummings—was the sister of Harvard's president.[36]

The daughter of perhaps Boston's preeminent family, Lowell at first felt drawn—of all things—to the stage. And, indeed, she founded in 1911 in an old carriage house at the foot of Beacon Hill the Toy Theater, which critic Eliot Norton described as the first "little theater" of America. There her "Amateur Professionals," as she called them, not only pursued the little theater ideal but suggested other associations as well, conspicuously producing Oscar Wilde's *An Ideal Husband*, for instance, in 1907, a brave enough thing to do only a few years after Wilde's death in exile and disgrace.[37] Lowell also was a pioneer in the introduction of modernist music to the U.S. In the music room of her Brookline estate, known as Sevenels, she confronted American musical circles in the 1910s with Debussy and Bartók, Fauré and Stravinsky, even Eric Satie and George Antheil. Antheil, who set to music one of Lowell's poems, thus gave her a certain status even in Paris, where the composer, an American expatriate and extreme modernist, was seen as every bit as cutting-edge, as we would say today, as that capital's experimental poet, Gertrude Stein.

Another sister of a Harvard man of the era, Stein had studied at Radcliffe in the mid-1890s and was also virtually the discoverer of Picasso.[38] "In Stein's case," maintained Amy Lowell's biographer, Jean Gould, the story was "Cubism and the new art; in Lowell's, Imagism and the new music."³⁹ It was a much more intelligent comparison to make between the two modernist women poets than the more usual and more sensational pairing of them as both huge and masculine and lesbian, and it underlines as well the difference in this period between Paris and Boston; for just as the French capital had emerged as the progressive art center of the Western world, so Boston was increasingly a major music center, even as it was declining by the 1900s into an artistic and even literary backwater.

But it was Lowell's poetry that became her primary pursuit after 1914. That year marked the publication of her first widely read and influential book, *Sword Blades and Poppy Seed*, after which she rapidly displaced Ezra Pound (who soon moved on to espouse vorticism) as the leader of what was called Imagism; indeed, Van Wyck Brooks did not say too much when he affirmed that "in poetry Miss Lowell was all that in other fields Elizabeth Peabody and Susan B. Anthony had been."⁴⁰

Lowell's interest in music helped give her poetry a quite distinctive tone, more like musical rhythm than traditional poetic meter, though here again it was a very modernist taste. As Robert Crunden observes, she was "fascinated by . . . the Ballets Russes and the experiments of Debussy and Satie. She even wrote poems consciously evocative of Bartók and Stravinsky."⁴¹ Her goal, however, was to inject new vitality into verse, which she wanted to be experimental and modern but not after the manner of Aesthetes and Decadents. She wanted a poetry in the American idiom, American in the way Whitman was American. A guiding force in the first phase of the modernist movement, from Pound's *Des Imagistes* of 1914 to Eliot's "Waste Land" of 1922, Lowell was a major transatlantic cultural force.⁴²

Although Lowell couldn't attend Harvard (even as its president's sister) because she was a woman, she came ultimately to play an even greater role than the president's notorious and "abnormal" sister: "She lectured and read . . . with a verve and brilliancy particularly her own before audiences at Harvard, Yale and Columbia." According to Jean Gould, "Some Musical Analogies to Modern Poetry," given 3 March 1919 at Harvard's Paine Hall, was "the first [lecture] by a woman ever presented under the sponsorship of the university."⁴³

In 1926, the year after her early death, one of her books won the Pulitzer Prize for poetry, Lowell being among the first women to win that accolade. She was outstanding in her healthy, well-adjusted, and relatively open attitude, not only toward her lesbianism, but toward sexuality and the body generally. This was all the more remarkable because she became hugely obese and was not physically healthy at all; hence her early death. Yet so sensual was she that she could feminize in the most erotic way even her trademark cigars; biographer Jean Gould writes that Lowell compared once the slow unwrapping of one of those cigars to the undressing of a lady—and then finished off the simile with a seductive suck. Indeed, Lowell's poetry could be quite candid and openly lesbian, doubtless reflecting the fact that much of it was inspired by her two great muses, Ada Russell, Lowell's partner of many years, and Eleonora Duse, an actress with whom Lowell was deeply in love, though they met only twice. It was Russell, however, Lowell's life partner for her last decade, who inspired the poet's best love poems, including the impassioned forty-three-poem sequence, "Two Speak Together" in *Pictures of the Floating World* (1919). No wonder a young poet of the 1920s, John Wheelwright, in "Gestures to the Dead," once wrote: "What a pity Amy was not president of Harvard."[44]

This was a reflection—so the poem explicitly notes elsewhere—of the colossal embarrassment (shame even) among many Harvard men caused by President Lowell—who, truth to tell, was in the main a brilliant president—when he, in common with two others appointed as judges by the governor of Massachusetts, validated the highly controversial death sentences of two anarchists (convicted but in a very flawed process, laced with bigotry), Sacco and Vanzetti, the cause célèbre of progressives in the 1920s in America and Europe.[45] Nor, as we will see soon enough, was this President Lowell's only fall from grace.

Nothing is so short-lived as modernism—there is always another revolution coming, the staying power of which can hardly at first be known, and thus it was that one evening after World War I, at the end of a meeting of the Harvard Poetry Society at which Amy Lowell was the speaker, a younger poet, E. E. Cummings, asked Lowell if she liked Gertrude Stein's work. Lowell turned the question back on Cummings. When he said he did like it, Lowell replied determinedly, "Well, I don't."[46] Perhaps Winnfield Scott was right, that both women exercised such "compellant dominance" in their respective circles (though each circle included figures far more renowned than their founders; in Stein's case, Picasso; in Lowell's, D. H. Lawrence) that "we should be grateful they set up shop on separate continents."[47] But Lowell's task was harder in America, a place only too willing to ridicule and trivialize her because of her gender, even more because of her widely known lesbianism, a problem we now know existed even in the privacy of her own family thanks to the candid memory of another and later modernist poet of the 1950s, Robert Lowell, who in his fascinating autobiographical essay, "91 Revere Street," recalled, "Amy Lowell was never a welcome subject in our household. . . . though irreproachably decent herself apparently, like Mae West she seemed to provoke indecorum in others. There was an anecdote which I was too young to understand; it was about Amy's getting migraine headaches from being kept awake by the exercises of honeymooners in an adjacent New York hotel room."[48]

Does one have to point out the sexual innuendo here? It remains only to say that Robert Lowell himself, whether deliberately or not, brought some clarity to all this by the way he remembered such after-dinner family talk, particularly comments about President Lowell's new "Georgian Houses for Boston quee-eers with British accents."[49]

One such probably meant was Wheelwright, yet another scion of an old patrician family who, though a radical enough poet to bait Amy, and Marxist enough to despair of her brother, nonetheless was sufficiently a Boston Brahmin to want her as Harvard's president. He was, in fact, a bundle of contradictions and paradoxes. Expelled from Harvard for one prank too many, Wheelwright was nonetheless a splendid example of what critic Austin Warren called the "two strains" of the Boston character: the "Yankee trader and the Yankee Saint (often a combination of scholar, priest and poet)."[50] Money and ideas, usually quite revolutionary ideas, and usually of a "moralizing" nature, have always kept close company in Boston, above all in Harvard Yard, never closer than in Wheelwright, in whose case the representative ancestors were—on his mother's side—Peter Chardon Brooks, richest of colonial Boston's merchant princes, and—on his father's—the seventeenth-century John Wheelwright, nonconformist Anne Hutchinson's chief ally in leading the Antinomian Rebellion in Boston in 1636–1638. Nor could anyone have been more conscious of this lineage than the twentieth-century John Wheelwright, who saw Boston's history as a whole parade of righteous rebels—not only the colonial and Revolutionary heroes, but then the intellectual heroes, Emerson and Thoreau and Fuller, and the abolitionists Wendell Phillips and William Lloyd Garrison. To which he would have added figures in the arts in his own era, such as Amy Lowell or even, later, Robert Lowell: in fact, critics like Austin Warren compared Lowell's poetry with that of Wheelwright, calling Wheelwright the "apostolic successor to Mrs. Jack Gardner and Amy Lowell."[51]

Wheelwright's poetry, not much known today, can now seem pallid. But listen to the critic Alan Wald:

> Radical poetry of the Great Depression . . . was an authentic response to conditions that polarized many Americans. . . . Tutored by the experimental masters of the 1920's, the new voices of the 1930's did not forget their lessons in the forms and sensibilities generated by Pound and Eliot. . . .
>
> One of the most exciting examples of this phenomenon—a true burst of literary light that has been extinguished in all extant literary histories—took place in Boston. An experiment in "rebel verse" was conducted there under the tutelage of several Harvard graduates [led by] John Wheelwright and Sherry Mangan. . . . The price paid by these writers for such a heresy against conventional perceptions . . . has been a neglect that borders on total invisibility.[52]

Wheelwright was controversial, no doubt about it. President Eliot thought the Mormons latter-day Puritans; not Wheelwright. He often said it was "the Communists [who] were the modern Puritans." Indeed, Wheelwright's determination to see all sides of a thing was positively cubist.

The young poet was, however, carrying on the rebel tradition from his own father, Edmund, a distinguished architect who was rambunctiously and aggressively antiphilistine; the *Lampoon,* of which he was a founder and for which he drew the first cover, was a result. So, too, his *Rollo* parodies.[53] The son's biographer observed that "there is evidence [Edmund, who was very high-strung,] had some difficulty in finding a suitable wife. . . . He remained a bachelor . . . [until] at the age of thirty-three. . . . [Then he married] Elizabeth Bott Brooks," a union that, though it yielded two sons, seems related to the "long term stress" and "melancholia" and extreme depression cited in connection with Edmund's "nervous breakdown" in 1910, and his subsequent suicide in 1912. The Lampoon building, among his last works, was called by his friend Barrett Wendell an example of "freakish gayety and beauty."[54]

The effect on young John, who was at St. George's School, in Newport, Rhode Island, when his father committed suicide, was traumatic. Already known for his high-strung aesthetic sense and deep personal, religious emotions, John was an ardent Anglo-Catholic whose faith was also fueled by his strong attachments to several other men, including sculptor Joseph Coletti and Father Spence Burton. There is much more evidence of the son's homosexuality than of the father's:

> Elroy Webber remembers that the precise sexual orientation of [John Wheelwright] "was a constant mystery" to his friends. "He didn't speak much of girls nor did he seem to know many." Yet Webber also recalls a party at which Jack was accused of making improper advances toward a female guest. Matthew Josephson and Malcolm Cowley thought there were homosexual liaisons. . . .
>
> Howard Nemerov recalls that Jack "once tried timidly to kiss me" and conjectures that he was probably "a touch homoerotic rather than homosexual, and equally timid with women." Jack's only explicit statement about his sexual views in later life [was his bitter attack on] "those who split the monism of love into the dismal triad of heterosexuality, bisexuality and homosexuality."[55]

Wheelwright's first solo volume of poems, *Rock and Shell,* was published in 1933; *Mirrors of Venus* followed in 1938; his third, in 1940, was *Political Self-Portraits,* and he seemed poised to become a leading American poet. One too many one night in a Back Bay bar and a speeding driver, however, and Wheelwright's life was ended in 1940, at only age forty-three.[56] My favorite of his poems is "Boston Public Library," in which he damns both of Copley Square's great landmarks for not living up to their high aspirations, which he yearns to enable: the library he calls "most beautiful, most Tuscan, most useless,"[57] Trinity "mauve and inquisitorial . . . [a] great horned toad." He reserves his greatest bitterness for the library—the first in the world, in the founding of which Harvard played a conspicuous part. Here Wheelwright expresses equal parts fierce pride and furious shame. One sees what Austin Warren meant when he wrote that, of all Wheelwright's rebellions, none was so important to him as his "rebellion . . . against verse merely refined. . . . He wanted a prophetic and menacing poetry. With Emerson, whom, both as revolutionary and poet, he respected, he loathed the 'tinkling of piano strings,' would have the Kingly bard 'smite the chords rough and hard.' [He took] the ancient and primitive view of the poet as maker, seer, and sayer."[58]

And he could be as tough on people as on institutions. As a young man he wrote about Isabella Stewart Gardner in a poem by turns harsh and respecting, but not unsympathetic. He was cruel, writing of her "magentaed hair and ostrich-plumed / money face" and of the sort of society events she attended where "Men crossed and uncrossed their legs all evening, / like bees who cluster round a honeycluster." But he saw, too, that she was "fed by her [museum's] interior court's interior life." This pointed rejoinder to Gardner is also useful evidence here that the den mother of bohemian, artistic, and homosexual Boston was not the cup of tea of every gay blade. Then again, consider what great style he had, like Gardner. Those Marxist speeches on Boston Common were given in what A. Hyatt Mayor called his "devastatingly flat Harvard accent" and with more than "a touch of Dada," with the speaker always attired in his raccoon coat. No wonder *Time* magazine likened Wheelwright's crusading to "the antics of an annunciatory angel dancing on top of a Harvard education."[59]

Lowell and Wheelwright, poets both, after the dons, WAG, Coolidge, and architect decorator Saltonstall, may seem a highly selective example of patricians—very ivory-tower and arty—who set rather a gay tone at late-nineteenth- and early-twentieth-century Harvard. The same pattern is discernable, however, in the life and work of their opposite, if ever there was one, the financier, A. P. Andrew.

A DON AT Harvard between 1893, when he graduated from Princeton, and 1900, when he earned his Ph.D. from Harvard in economics, Andrew stayed on as a professor on the Harvard faculty until 1909. The year before, on the recommendation of President Eliot, Senator Nelson Aldrich took Andrew with him on his trip to study European banking systems, and thereafter Andrew became more and more important as an adviser to Aldrich, ending up as director of the mint, and assistant secretary of the treasury, where he laid the foundations of today's Federal Reserve System. At the same time, he served during World War I as treasurer of the American Red Cross and proved an inspiring leader. Determined to serve the Allied cause, Andrew was the organizing force behind the famous American Ambulance Field Service, an emergency ambulance system for the wounded made up of American college volunteers attached to the French army. After the U.S. entered the war in 1917 the service was transferred to the American forces, in which Andrew was commissioned, first as a major, then as lieutenant colonel. By the time America entered the war, Andrew's force numbered over one thousand ambulances manned by over twelve hundred volunteers, men who confronted on the Western Front "challenges of endurance, psychological stability, patience, physical strength, mechanical deftness, courage, and will," wrote A. J. Hansen in *Gentlemen Volunteers*, and whose saga has been immortalized by Ernest Hemingway in *A Farewell to Arms* and E. E. Cummings in *The Enormous Room*. Nearly all were volunteers from American colleges, Ivy League dominated, all male, of course, "the very pick and flower of American youth," as John Masefield called them. And in Andrew's leadership of these men there were shades of the ancient Theban Sacred Band, particularly in his underlying concept. Significantly, Andrew's Gloucester home was full of Roman war relics. Andrew earned a Princeton honorary degree and the Croix de Guerre and the Distinguished Service medal; both he and his cofounder, Henry Sleeper, received the Legion of Honor.[60]

Chief recruiter and fund-raiser, mostly back in Boston, Sleeper was Andrew's dearest friend and confidant who himself was aided by two other young friends, also likely lovers, John Hays Hammond and Leslie Buswell. Even after the war, when Andrew took up politics and ran for the U.S. Congress (to which he was repeatedly elected from 1921 to 1936), he was the animating spirit of a mad dance indeed, engaged in by both couples in an era when "private lives" were often safe harbors for gays in a censorious society.

Andrew had been the leading light of a clearly homosexual circle since his graduate student days at Harvard in the 1890s, when he first caught the eye of Isabella Stewart Gardner, soon to become his close friend and adviser. Settling in Gloucester on Boston's North Shore in 1900, he and a small but scintillating group of gay men and their lady friends—the latter including most notably Gardner and also portraitist Cecilia Beaux—created a discreet but intense bohemian enclave on Eastern Point. It was called Dabsville, a cryptogram of Sleeper's for New York intellectual Joanna Davidge, Andrew, Beaux, the Philadelphia art patron Caroline Sinkler, and Sleeper, all of whom built adjoining houses on the point. At its heart were four men and another cryptogram. ("What acronymic antics they engaged in, those four," wrote Joseph Garland of the male foursome: "Buswell, Andrew, Sleeper, Hammond—what BASHes!") Author Andrew Gray described Dabsville this way:

> Sleeper, Beaux and Andrew ran the show. . . . Andrew [was] the king pin. The nucleus they formed . . . expanded to absorb people according to their wit, good looks, vivacity and capacity for self-dramatization. . . . They all drank very little—most worked rather hard, even when playing. . . . They were very hospitable to outsiders—Leslie Buswell and Jack Hammond among others—but surely rather snobbish toward people less verbally adept than they. They were very private people. The key . . . was

the absence of children. No sailing, no nonsense, no preoccupation with childish things.[61]

Of course the absence of children wasn't the key at all; that was obviously secondary to the central aspect of Dabsville. Joseph Garland fairly exhausts himself with explanations: "Dabsville," he writes, "was dubbed by some sharp-tongued neighbor the 'Sheshore' of Eastern Point. Yet it was from the queer cubbyholes of 'Red Roof' and the quaint closets of 'Beauport' that [the] American Ambulance Field Service emerged." Although the gatherings were ostensibly a matter of Roman feasts and costume parties and musical evenings, all in imaginatively designed "stage set" seaside houses, it is not surprising Garland calls the scene "slightly spooky."[62] Yet E. P. Hayden Jr. and Andrew Gray do not exaggerate when in their *Beauport Chronicle* they describe Andrew thus: "a brilliant lecturer at Harvard, a first rate intellect . . . an urbane and rambunctious temperament, cuts a wide, social swath, entertains prodigiously, and is spectacularly handsome. . . . The combination [was] magnetic." Add "Andrew's proclivity for hard sport in the company of younger men" and you have something of a fusion of the Whitmanic and the Wildean that was irresistible. Especially to Sleeper, who, as Garland discreetly remarks, was the "same age, same non-marital status" when the two met. They grew very close indeed. So, too, did Hammond and Buswell.[63]

Actually, it was more complicated than that. Although Sleeper, partial to Buswell, was himself always passionately loyal to Andrew, there are hints that Sleeper's dogged devotion sometimes seemed suffocating to Andrew. Equally, according to Sleeper's letters to Andrew, Hammond was "spellbound" by Buswell, while Buswell is described as "fond" of Hammond—though "fascinated by his genius." Buswell, it seems, if he tried to hide his attraction to Andrew (at whose house he had met Hammond), did not entirely succeed. Hammond was "jealous of [Andrew's] lure—& *fears* it," Sleeper once wrote to Andrew, thereby doubtless hinting at fears of his own as well. At least he and Andrew never married anyone else. Both Hammond and Buswell did.[64]

A most fascinating aspect of this Edwardian foursome is that each gave (in several cases very revealing) architectural expression to himself, touching importantly on sexuality. So, too, did a nonresident member of this circle, so to speak, a mutual friend of Sleeper's and Andrew's, Henry Chapman Mercer, the celebrated American tile designer, himself Harvard educated, whose famous house in Doylestown, Pennsylvania, much resembled Sleeper's in Gloucester.[65] Both in turn had not a little in common with Fenway Court in Boston, the spectacular domain of another honorary member of this cohort, Gardner, who one suspects inspired them to more than architecture, but certainly in that respect at least set the tone and begat variation after variation (Sleeper, incidentally, was one of the first trustees of Fenway Court named to take over in Gardner's will after her death).

Of the foursome's houses in Gloucester the most dramatic homage to Fenway Court was Jack Hammond's. A scientist of legendary gifts, Hammond was an engineer-inventor whose work is still seen today as an important forerunner of rocket science and the space program. Most notable in his day for his development of a radio-controlled torpedo and for his design of Mussolini's communication network, he was an early associate of David Sarnoff in the Radio Corporation of America, of which Hammond was a director. After his controversial marriage to artist-editor Irene Fenton in 1925 he began to erect, across Gloucester Harbor from Eastern Point, a Hollywood-style extravaganza of a castle, Aba Mair: Hammond's Castle, everyone else called it, noting its towered stone silhouette and the medieval details on the interior, including whole façades that Hammond bought in Europe and had shipped to this country.

In the end more like San Simeon, the famous Hearst castle in California, than Fenway Court, which it certainly does not rival either in brilliance or imagination, Hammond's keep seems more like a movie than real life, nowhere more so than its dark and mysterious great hall and huge organ, in its "secret passages and bedrooms, peepholes, peekaboos and such naughty niceties and narcissistic knicknacks first favored by his friends Doc Andrew and Harry Sleeper," and in the way its courtyard emerges almost as if seen underwater, through a moist green scrim.[66]

Hammond's landmark quite eclipsed Stillington, the English manor house built nearby by Buswell, a Winchester- and Cambridge-educated Britisher, as well as an actor who, on his first American tour in 1914, had caught Gardner's eye (and Andrew's, too) and was a Bostonian forever after. (He and Hammond met in the fall of 1914; by early 1915 Buswell gave up the stage to join Hammond.) But even Hammond's Castle could not compare with Sleeper's earlier house—Beauport, legendary then as today for its design by Sleeper, one of the first great interior designers of the twentieth century. His work at Beauport stimulated a generation of scholars, collectors, museum directors, and Americanists generally. It was both an inspiration and a source for places like the American wing of New York's Metropolitan Museum of Art and the Winterthur Museum.

Still maintained today as a work of art in and of itself in its interior design and installation of exhibits, Beauport is, however, more than an American masterpiece. Even mainstream scholars like Nancy Curtis and Richard Nylander have noticed that the house's "maze-like shape has always suggested secrets," that "its crooked passages, doors leading into nowhere, secret staircases, dramatic surprises and shadowy recesses is Sleeper's most revealing statement about himself." It is key to note that Beauport, built in 1907, is a kind of homage (become masterpiece) to an earlier house (by no means a masterwork) of 1902 next door—Red Roof, built for himself by Andrew.[67] Red Roof was the pivot Dabsville revolved upon. Andrew, to be sure, did not possess Sleeper's artistic genius, but Andrew's own reputation as an economist (the Federal Reserve System is no small thing) was far more widely known when they first met. And it speaks so well of Sleeper that he made of what was a secondary strand in Andrew's life—architecture—his main avocation, playing the disciple's role in this as in fund-raising for Andrew's work in France while yet developing his own genius. Indeed, out of his admiration for Andrew, Sleeper was able to find the agency to excel at something—which Andrew appreciated more and more as Sleeper developed it. Central to it all, furthermore, was the fact that Andrew's house—clearly Sleeper's inspiration for Beauport ("Nothing ever was more dear to me than Red Roof," Sleeper wrote to Andrew just before the former's death, decades later, in 1934)—arose as much out of Sleeper's feelings for Andrew as out of Sleeper's own reaction to Andrew's creativity. Friend and house fused as I read their relationship—for if Beauport was so masterful because of Sleeper's genius, it was so revealing because of Andrew's. Garland again spoke in tongues, writing of Red Roof as Andrew's "strangely dark and Gothic cottage, honeycombed with secret rooms, hidden passages, bedchamber peepholes and unsuspected mirrors." Even more picturesque was Louise Hall Tharp's description of Red Roof in her biography of Isabella Stewart Gardner; written in 1965, it is hard to take in its cloying snideness today; nonetheless it tells the story:

> Andrew had an organ installed in the passage between the living room and a recently added study. Here, Isabella sat on the couch . . . to listen to his music. She was probably unaware of a hidden space above the books—too low to stand up in but equipped with mattress and covers where . . . guests could listen in still greater comfort. She had seen the Brittany bed in the living room but that there was a small hole over it [opening out from an alcove amounting to a sort of built-in bunk bed accessible from another room], perhaps no one had told her. The sound of organ music [from an adjoining passage] could be heard the better through the hole—and was it just a coincidence that a person in the hidden alcove above could look down through it? Gossip had it that often [at Red Roof] all the guests were men, their pastimes peculiar. Yet all the ladies on Eastern Point were fascinated by Piatt. . . .[68]

Nor was Gardner so naïve as Tharp thought her. Added Joseph Garland:

> Was there anyone to whom Piatt Andrew was not a deepening riddle . . . his brilliant, probing intellect, his sunbathing in the nude and physical culturism and fear of growing old (he kept gymnastic equipment in his attic quarters, and a steel-spring hand exerciser on the desk), his narcissism, his full length portrait of himself on the wall of his secret mirrored

bedchamber . . . his acoustic battles with Jack Hammond across the Harbor when they directed their phonographs vis-à-vis full blast on calm evenings in a curious quiz of musical sophistication.

Mysterious, marbled, magnetic . . . unfulfilled . . . restless . . . what on earth, people wondered, made Piatt tick?[69]

The ellipses are Garland's. So, too, the puzzle. Who today would not recognize this profile? Suffice it to say Andrew's full-length portrait in the mirrored bedroom spoke clearly enough to Hammond's full-length outdoor nude statue of himself across the harbor.[70]

Andrew's fashionable enclave on Boston's North Shore was very gay—whatever it was then called. And this is the third part (after the student-teacher and old-family "Trojan horse" part) of the characteristic pattern we've been trying to discern here of Harvard's gay experience. Very closeted, it was a home game strategy, of course; away, as we will see in the next chapter—in Paris or even New York—Harvard gays were much less discreet.

They learned the home game as young men, in Harvard Yard, where on this subject (E. E. Cummings on Amy Lowell being a very conspicuous exception) a spade was hardly ever called a spade. An example of that is the contortions developed over the years to describe the life and work of a now obviously homosexual and highly beloved Harvard luminary, Charles Townsend Copeland, the don-in-chief of Harvard Yard from whom his disciples—Andrew and students like him—learned very well what I have called the rules of the road.

So deep and so pervasive was the Copeland legend in its day that in his later years this Harvard don actually made the cover of *Time* magazine in 1927. And he was not (as any of his sort would have to be today) either a serial killer or a winner of the Nobel Prize. In fact, Copeland had barely been given a tenured professorship, and only after President Eliot (who viewed Copeland with the same wariness he had Santayana) had been succeeded by President Lowell. *Time*'s explanation for the Copeland cover? "Every year for 21 years the Harvard Club of New York has had a 'Copey' evening, a dinner in which a fortunate company, the Copeland Associates (by invitation only) sit down, followed by a reading. Here Theodore Roosevelt used to come. Here now come J. P. Morgan . . . publisher George Palmer Putnam . . . and many a plain John Smith and Tom Jones . . . [of] one of 'Copey's' courses."[71] The occasion that year marked the publication by Scribner's of *The Copeland Reader*, a literary anthology that was really a script for Copeland's celebrated Boston readings, exported not just to New York (where Copeland would appear at the Harvard Club every year until 1937, when he was nearing eighty), but to the nation at large.

A Maine native, Copeland entered Harvard College in 1878 and did the usual literary things—including *The Harvard Advocate*, the college's oldest journal for "creative" writing—graduating in 1882 to become the drama critic of the *Boston Post*, where throughout the 1880s and 1890s he reviewed both plays and books in an especially lively era; indeed, Copeland reviewed Wilde in his own lifetime as well as performances by Edwin Booth and Sarah Bernhardt. In 1893 he began teaching at Harvard. One of the reasons he waited so long was explained by his biographer, J. Donald Adams, who observed, "Sometimes the outstanding teacher and scholar are combined in the same person—as they were *not* [emphasis added] in Copeland," from which plusses and minuses Adams contrived a profile of the qualities that make a great teacher, none extraordinary in themselves but very much so in combination: "human sympathy with and interest in others, especially the young; the gift for clarification and simplification of subtle matters; a strong desire to communicate what he knows, and the capacity to create enthusiasm in others; and lastly, the power to project his own personality, even to the point of being a showman, as Copeland unquestionably was." Adams added, "The great teacher, as distinct from the great scholar—the contributor to knowledge—acts as a kind of catalyst";[72] all the more effective because Copeland was the only senior don—after Santayana left Harvard in 1912—to live in the Yard among his students. Settling ultimately in Hollis Hall, where he held court between 1904 and 1932 in Ralph Waldo Emerson's old room—Hollis 15—Copeland had a study that was as much a stage as any lecture platform, and his weekly open houses became as celebrated as his public readings. If Copeland himself did not read, he was apt to have a guest who did. And what guests he had. They included, over the years, John Barrymore, Ernest Hemingway, and Christopher Morley.

John Reed, later a journalist of wide repute for his reporting from Russia during its 1917–1918 revolution (the author of *Ten Days That Shook the World*), has left a vivid description of Copey's student open houses:

> On a Saturday evening only a swimming meet could keep Reed away from Hollis 15.
>
> He liked the room with its walls solidly lined with books, the fireplace, the autographed pictures, and Copey sitting in an armchair under the single light, smoking and talking. He liked the crowd, the boys sitting close-packed on the floor, athletes, scholars, aristocrats, radicals, editors, and the obscure, the unknown. He liked the talk: "Everybody talks of the thing nearest his heart; everybody finds himself alert, quick, almost brilliant." This was romance, drama, greatness, life. "There are two men," Reed wrote in 1917, "who give me confidence in myself, who make me want to work, and to do nothing unworthy." One of them was Copeland.[73]

In perspective, Copeland emerges more as tutor than professor, in the classic Oxbridge and Harvard tutorial tradition of one-on-one teaching; indeed, that it was in President Lowell's reign that Copey finally achieved tenure eighteen years after he joined Harvard's faculty reminds one that Santayana once said Lowell's more collegiate style tempted him to stay at Harvard, but came too late. Indeed, Copeland produced more readers than writers, more journalists than authors. But that is no small thing, for they were of the highest class, including not least Brooks Atkinson, who from his lofty perch at *The New York Times* (where he was chief drama critic) wrote:

> Copey was certainly the most effective teacher of English composition in my experience. . . . He had the most profound influence on me. To this day—forty years after I studied with him—I imagine that I adhere to some of his maxims. For instance, the use of the periodic sentence: he explained its value and also cautioned me against over-using it. He explained to me the value of carrying over one thought into a new paragraph, and thus pulling together the whole structure of an article. "Good old A," he used to say acidly, or "Good old The," when I began several sentences with those colorless words. He was death on over-use of the definite or indefinite article.[74]

In his own person Copeland was not prepossessing; the impression he created, wrote Adams, was of "a serious little man with cropped dark mustache and magnificent forehead . . . small and shrunken, [in] a checked suit, a collar of material that had a figure in it, and a black derby hat that seemed larger than his head. . . . No one ever saw a professor who looked like this. He might have been an actor."[75] But, of course, that's what he was, and very fast on his feet too, though Santayana called him "an 'elocutionist' who, by 'declaiming,' provided a 'spiritual debauch' for many of the well-disposed waifs at Harvard." T. S. Eliot, who took Copeland's English Composition 12, was another detractor. So was John Dos Passos, who remembered his relationship with Copeland as one of "armed neutrality." Conrad Aiken did admit he found Copeland "stimulating," but added, "To be candid I never really could take to him; the vanity, and the insistence on adulation, was too much for me."[76] Truly, Copeland did once explain to a graduate who had not written or dedicated anything but had just married, that he, Copeland, had had six children named after him: "So if you can't qualify in one respect," he observed, "perhaps you can in another." Furthermore, when an admirer deferred in writing a biography of him to someone he thought had the idea first, Copeland was bewildered. Was there a law, he inquired, against having *two* biographies?[77] He hoped not. Of course, Copeland is easy to poke fun at. But how many professors anywhere have their own alumni association, one that gets them a *Time* cover story? And he did have a generous side to him; Adams attests he was often known for slipping money into young graduates' palms with his handshake, "never caus[ing] the slightest twinge of embarrassment."

Was Copeland gay? Certainly his profile is hard to miss today. His triumphs as a teacher, for instance, were invariably same-sex, and stand out from his repeated failures with women students. There were exceptions— one was Helen Keller, the blind Radcliffe student—but Adams admits that Copeland generally "was not—and this is understandable—quite the same catalytic force among women students that he was among the men." Just why that was understandable Adams does not say, but buried in the memories of a Radcliffe student, Constance Bridges Fitzgibbon, a woman more alert to men's sexual signals than most men would be, is the more likely reason, whether Adams suspected it or not: trying to explain why she responded so much more to another, perhaps even more legendary professor, George Pierce Baker, Fitzgibbon recalled, "Unlike Copey, Baker was neither unaware of nor displeased by youthful feminine admiration from the front row. It always seemed to me that Copey could not get out of Radcliffe Yard fast enough." Indeed, had Fitzgibbon but known it, Copeland was equally averse to women even as *subject matter* for his male students, many of whom judged him to be a woman hater because one of only "two subjects taboo in the daily themes," Adams wrote, were "the squirrels in the Yard, which were one of his pet aversions—and what he described as 'the female element.' "[78]

By contrast, Copeland was anything but shy of young men. A recognizable character in *The Diary of a Freshman*, a somewhat less Wildean sequel to *Harvard Episodes* written by the same author, Charles Macomb Flandrau, Copeland was known to love "din[ing] in [downtown] Boston, at Marliave's or the Parker House, or other favorite haunts, with his young student friends, for a mildly bibulous evening." It is a contrast more conspicuous to us than it was to Adams, the way Copeland was hardly aware of feminine ardor directed his way as opposed to his ardent search for young male company, but his biographer still finds explanations necessary— and more than one. Noting that there were occasions when Copeland, "after a night on the town, was ready to accept a helping hand in mounting the stairs to his room," Adams protested, "Copeland was never an alcoholic." Similarly, that "there was no question, ever, of any sexual deviation in Copeland; his attitude toward the young men who flocked about him was always that of a father, uncle, or older friend. He could be bawdy with them on occasion, but never was there a hint of any homosexual relationship. He admired good looks in men as well as in women, but that was the sum of his physical attraction to those of his own sex." But it was just such "tales of indecorous proceedings [that] no doubt came to President Eliot's ears," admits Adams, and that "unquestionably played their part in the tardiness of [Copeland's] academic advancement"—also the case with Santayana.

In fact, Adams mounts another of those labored and rather forced explanations for Copeland's bachelorhood that seem so implausible to us today:

The basic facts about Copeland's amatory life would seem to be these: He never, from childhood on, had any excess vitality, and it was necessary for him always to husband carefully his physical resources. He had the genes requisite to long life, but never an abundance of animal spirits. Then too, he had strong convictions regarding the responsibilities of marriage; having finally chosen a career in which the monetary rewards were small, he felt that he had no right to ask a woman to share his meager resources.[79]

There were also the usual stories of lost loves and secret affairs intended to turn aside questions, though in Copeland's case the tales are thin enough. In the end, Copeland survived it all because his methods anticipated the revival of Oxbridge-type tutorial at Harvard by President Lowell, who appreciated Copeland's gifts, one of the few things he would have found himself agreeing about with Walter Lippman, the celebrated columnist who was once Copeland's student: "Copey was not a professor teaching a crowd in a classroom," Lippman wrote in the special issue of the *Crimson* that marked Copey's ninetieth birthday: "He was a very distinct person in a unique relationship with each individual who interested him." Furthermore, his teaching methods were a hyper form of classically male-oriented Socratic technique.[80] On this subject Adams quotes no less than Lowell's successor as Harvard's president, James Bryant Conant, who saw that Copeland's method had "its analogy in the world of sports. . . . Selecting the best material he can, the coach badgers [his] men, often mercilessly, out of too easy satisfaction with themselves . . . in the same way the teacher [like Copeland put] his students on their mettle . . . draw[ing] out from them the best they have to give."[81]

Santayana was right. So was T. S. Eliot. It was not a technique for the brilliant and the self-assured, but for the shy. Not like swimming pools and squash courts.

Three figures in the pattern stand out: the student-teacher relationship; the leading role of several old patrician Harvard families; and the very closeted, secret-society nature of the Harvard gay experience. But running like a thread through much delight and fructification and downright happiness, not forgetting conspicuous achievement, is more than a little angst. Discernable in virtually all of these men and women, it is an angst that, while perhaps productive enough in its effects, extracted a huge price, an angst that when it surfaced was both humanly revealing and extremely costly, not excluding any of the usual crimes, including rape and prostitution, even pedophilia, often turning on scandal, blackmail, disgrace, and—for more than one in Harvard's gay experience—suicide, all set to a characteristic soundtrack that ranged from sordid to heroic. Witness a half dozen men, all of whom knew each other, many of whom were friends, whose lives were importantly rooted, however global the reach of their career, in the discreet gay scene of Brattle Street and Beacon Hill.

Full of Sex

ONE WONDERS IF Havelock Ellis, the pioneering English sexologist we first met up with here in the 1890s in company with Dean James Mills Peirce and who again in the 1920s surfaced in Harvard's gay history, was ever tempted to visit the New England university whose faculty he involved himself with, not once, but twice, in an effort to heal the wounds of homosexual angst and sexual repression. Indeed, any of the cast of characters we've focused in on in Harvard Yard, from the Gay Nineties to the Roaring Twenties, would doubtless have intrigued Ellis: Peirce or Santayana, Amy Lowell or John Wheelwright or A. P. Andrew or Charles Townsend Copeland, all would have fascinated the famed sexologist Ellis. In the event the second Harvard professor who we know collaborated with Ellis was Arthur Kingsley Porter.

At only age twenty-five, when he was a student at the Columbia School of Architecture in New York, Porter published *Medieval Architecture: Its Origins and Development*. Like his book, Porter was a knockout. As M. C. Ross, in his biographical sketch of Porter, has observed, the book's impact was huge because he relied solely on firsthand study of documents and dated landmarks. "At that time this was the most important contribution made by an American scholar to the history of medieval architecture and one that was to revolutionize the whole method of writing on the subject."[82] Harvard, of course, came calling. Appointed to the faculty in 1920, Porter became the first William Dorr Boardman Professor of Fine Arts five years later; still in his thirties when he assumed this chair, he was already the greatest medievalist of his day. His best-known book, still important, was published in 1923: *Romanesque Sculpture of the Pilgrimage Roads*, and in 1928 came *Spanish Romanesque Sculpture*, before which no such thing had ever been heard of. It was Porter who discovered it, who showed conclusively the independent development of that sculpture from the French school. No one else had documented it before.

A Yale man (fourth in his class in 1904), Porter was from a privileged and quite wealthy background, also happily married (to Lucy Bryant Wallace in 1912), and once ensconced at Harvard became not only a scholarly luminary but a key figure in Boston society. He and his wife lived at Elmwood, today the residence of Harvard's president, and the Porters made that splendid mansion of Old Cambridge's Tory Row—the seat and state in so many ways of Boston's vice-regal court in the eighteenth century—a centerpiece in Boston's intellectual and social life, where family and guests rejoiced in the ministrations of four superbly trained Italian servants who, Walter Muir

Whitehill remembered, "cooked admirably," and—hardly less important—"made wine that relieved the draught of Prohibition."[83]

Of Harvard's Boardman Professor no one could say enough, Marvin Chauncey Ross, Porter's biographer, included: "Tall and slender and fond of the out-of-doors from his youth when he had hunted great game in Canada, he was yet shy and retiring, with the look of the poet. These traits are found equally in his researches—the boldness of the great game hunter combined with the sense of beauty of the poet."[84] Porter, Whitehill also recalled, was "immensely thoughtful and considerate," and he became "an almost legendary figure at Harvard."[85] John Coolidge went further, describing Porter as "almost saintly."[86] A rewarding and supportive family life, a superb education, a splendid professorship in a great university, physical attractiveness, a highly civilized lifestyle sustained by independent wealth—it is almost too much to add scholarship of genius and personal saintliness. Yet, as Ross affirmed, "such were [Porter's] accomplishments that he is generally considered as probably the greatest American medieval archaeologist of his day."[87] Seemingly, Porter had it all. But he lived on a perpetual precipice, risking scandal at every turn because he was homosexual. He recognized it fully though and acted upon it regularly, though he worried it would be his undoing; his sexuality was perhaps not unrelated to his genius as a teacher-scholar. "A lecture was never given twice," recorded Whitehill; Porter "used to try out as yet uncrystalized ideas . . . [and] was always open to the questioning of the student. . . . His library . . . and his own time were more than generously placed at the disposition of his students." Indeed, Porter's last book bore the dedication: "To my teachers—my Harvard students."[88] All of which can be illustrated by a single case study: Joseph Coletti.

A gifted and personable young man of modest background from a working-class Boston suburb, Coletti found himself in Porter's medieval sculpture class at Harvard because, in time-honored fashion, he had become the protégé of two eminent gay elders. The first was John Singer Sargent, the foremost portraitist of his day, one of whose assistants Coletti had been in Sargent's Boston Public Library mural project, prompting the master to sponsor preparatory work by Coletti at Northeastern University prior to getting him into Harvard, where he paid the young man's tuition. The second elder was Ralph Adams Cram, who in 1916 gave the teenage Coletti his very first commission—for a funeral monument in the form of an elaborately carved Celtic cross.[89] Cram and Porter were good friends; Sargent apparently knew (and didn't care for) Cram; all three probably knew each other—and all three certainly knew young Coletti as well as another young man, from quite a different background, who was also in Porter's class, John Nicholas Brown, famously described at birth by the American press as "the richest baby in the world." John Wheelwright was also in Porter's class. Alan Priest, Coletti's biographer, puts it all together very nicely:

A fortuitous thing that John Nicholas Brown and Joseph Coletti were both students in A. Kingsley Porter's class in medieval sculpture. . . . The surprised students did not hear lectures—they were introduced to piles of photographs and asked their opinions. Very quickly they began to have opinions. Expected as a matter of course to have some knowledge of medieval Latin, they soon acquired it. For Coletti, of all the pupils, this worked as does the nourishing of a seed or plant. . . . And there was John Nicholas Brown, surely with plans in his head for St. George's Chapel and surely appreciative of his fellow student.[90]

That magnificent chapel, built for Brown's old prep school of that name in Newport, is full of some of Coletti's finest work. The occasion of the crush the young John Wheelwright developed, as already noted, for Coletti, the chapel is the design of Cram. Nor did the matter end with a landmark built or a sculptor launched. There was also an academic field finally consolidated, for in the 1920s Cram, Porter, and Brown spearheaded the founding of the Medieval Academy of America, still located today in Harvard Square; its founding marked a turning point for medieval studies in America.[91]

All this the world saw admiringly—and something else, too, for those who were alert in Porter's works to the contemporary and personal aspects of his scholarly writing. Indeed, he could be in his way as fierce an advocate as James Mills Peirce had been.

Witness one of Porter's best books, *Beyond Architecture*, in which a work of Cram's of similar stature to St. George's Chapel—the Swedenborgian Cathedral in Bryn Athyn, outside Philadelphia—was the frontispiece. Here is Porter's discussion of Greek art, which he insists is fully "red-blooded" (code: not effeminate) and which he pronounces bluntly is

> full of sex. The emotion it conveys is the emotion of sex, the beauty it interprets is the beauty of sex! This fact has very largely been misunderstood or ignored because the type of sex which appealed with especial power to the Greeks is considered perverse and repulsive by the modern age. Not being willing to grant that an art obviously of the highest type could have been inspired by ideals which seem to us depraved, we have willed not to understand. Yet delight in the nude, and especially in the nude male, is the keynote of Greek art. Where else has the vigor of youth, the play of muscles, the glory of manhood found a like expression? It is the ideal of masculine sex which the Greeks eternally glorified; this is the beauty they never wearied of interpreting. . . . The[ir] sculptures were the idealization of male sex, that and that only.[92]

Reading this, the tragedy that befell Porter is the more easily understood, although in typically Harvardian fashion all the approved texts and formal obituaries and biographical sketches utterly obscure the truth, which we know only because in 1932 Havelock Ellis told an intern at Bellevue Psychiatric Hospital in New York, Joseph Wortis, about Porter's homosexuality! Ellis was proposing Wortis undertake research on the subject, to be funded by an anonymous donor on Ellis's behalf, research so intense it would lead Wortis to undergo analysis by Freud himself. Ellis's biographer, Phyllis Grosskurth, tells the story in her biography of Ellis, published in 1980, forty-seven years after Porter's death: a strange enough tale, how in the summer of 1932 Porter and his wife called on Ellis, confiding that Porter was homosexual and suffering from depression, concerned over the

> danger of losing his job because of scandal. His wife was very sympathetic. What advice had Ellis to proffer? There is no way of knowing exactly what Ellis actually said, but in a letter of July 31st, 1932, Porter told Ellis: "I feel a deep sense of gratitude to you, deeper than I know how to express, for having put me in touch with Alan." Alan Campbell was a young aspiring American novelist, a homosexual also, who moved into the Porters' beautiful home in Cambridge, Massachusetts, a few months later, and there apparently a *ménage à trois* was established. With Ellis's views on the impossibility of "curing" homosexuality and with his own experience of accepting [his wife] Edith's lovers (the Porters were among the few people in whom he ever confided the truth about his own marriage), one can only assume that this was the solution Ellis proposed for their difficulties. In October Porter wrote to him: "You have made over my life. You know it. I do not need to tell you. . . ." However, during the following months Porter's letters indicate that Campbell was restless and did not settle easily into the Cambridge scene. . . . Eventually Campbell left for a trip to California. On January 3rd, 1933, Porter wrote: "We are sailing on the 14th, not without misgivings on my part, for depression has been gaining again since Alan went to California." . . . He and Mrs. Porter then crossed the Atlantic to their castle in County Donegal, Ireland, and in June they paid Ellis a visit in London. On July 11 Alan Campbell wrote that Porter had thrown himself off a cliff near his home.[93]

Back in Cambridge, as in many other places on both sides of the Atlantic, condolences were, of course, legion. Doubtless they included those of just-retired President Lowell, who had appointed Porter and must have been sorry to lose him. Or maybe not. We do know Lowell's mind generally on the subject. A historian of Harvard, Richard Norton Smith, tells the story (confirmed by sometime Senior Fellow Francis Burr and seconded by the Boston jurist Charles Wyzanski) in his *The Harvard Century* of what happened "when an elderly professor was revealed to the president as homosexual": Lowell, Smith reports, "summoned the man to University Hall (where the president's habitual pacing often cowed visitors into the far corners of the room) and demanded his resignation on the spot. He had devoted his life to Harvard, replied the professor. What was he expected to do now? What would President Lowell himself do, if he were in his shoes? 'I would get a gun and destroy myself,' said Lowell."[94]

In a sense, Porter had only done what many at Harvard then would have expected of him.

Even Porter's suicide for years remained a secret (and like many secrets begat endless rumors, like the one reported to me by Richard Newman that it was a faked death which allowed Porter to begin a new life). Even the evidence of Ellis's biography is at second hand. But Porter's story is not really very unlikely. Witness the fact that during the period another great eighteenth-century mansion on Tory Row was presided over by yet another Harvard homosexual (whose surviving correspondence shows that he was a friend of the Porters) about whose inner life we know much more—Henry Wadsworth Longfellow Dana. It was up Brattle Street at the Longfellow House, not at Elmwood, that the scandal erupted.

Pal Hal

ON 11 JUNE 1936—three years after Porter's suicide—Harry Dana, as his friends all called him, had a tea party. Grandson of America's poet laureate, Dana presided over the Longfellow House, by then Dana's own home, the most famous home in America—aside from the White House and perhaps Mount Vernon or Monticello. Not only Longfellow but also George Washington had lived there, in the eighteenth century (in 1775–1776, at the start of the American Revolution). And so that patriotic citizens of the twentieth century could build their very own copy of the house ("Listen, my children, and you shall hear . . ."), architectural plans were regularly for sale in the Sears catalogue. Tea at Castle Craigie, as Longfellow's house is called in honor of the American patriot who succeeded its eighteenth-century Tory builder as owner, was always a special occasion.

And a very proper Boston tea party it was; State Street lawyers set the tone. Dana's guest list consisted entirely of trustees, one from the Longfellow Trust, which administered the property as a house museum, open to the public but with continued family occupancy, all the rest trustees of Radcliffe College. It was, Dana said later, a "Mad Tea Party," though "like the Mad Tea Party in *Alice in Wonderland* it was only mad in the sense that it was crazy." How crazy? The trustees—bankers and lawyers, all—were really trying to oust the poet's grandson from his family home and, "having tried vinegar," wrote Dana, and failed, they were now "trying molasses": their plan was to embarrass Dana into ending the trust and the house's family occupancy by turning it over to Radcliffe as a residence for that college's president. "High-minded men" they were, Dana allowed, adding somewhat sarcastically: "I don't know just what 'high-minded' means, but apparently it gives them the right to look upon those who disagree with them as 'low minded.' "[95]

Just how low-minded *was* the poet's grandson? This was the trustees' constant preoccupation of this time. It was the issue everyone was thinking about and nobody was talking about as their host moved genially among them. The police—unthinkable—had actually come to the Longfellow House, shrine that it was, and arrested Dana on a morals charge. Trustees, of course, are often more prudent than honest, characteristically more defensive than forthright. Never mind that Dana had been acquitted of all charges. No one could acquit him of the scandal; and the boy in question seemed to remove any and all doubt that Henry Wadsworth Longfellow Dana, as they used to say, was as queer as a three-dollar bill.[96] Was Hiawatha shuddering in the afterlife? Certainly the poet's trustees were. Selling the house to Harvard and dissolving the trust was the only solution anyone could think of. But Dana would have none of it. He was sometimes called a dandy, even a wit. E. E. Cummings, whom Dana befriended, once said Dana seemed to him "quite a character." He reminded Cummings of Jack Benny, the comedian. (Dana appears as a character in Cummings's earliest prose work, *Eimi* of 1933.) Dana had also been called worse things: "in his fussy, effeminate way (some . . . called him 'Mrs. Dana' behind his back), he mothered Cummings at every turn," wrote Robert S. Kennedy, the biographer of the poet.[97] But Dana was also a fighter. Some photographs show him plausibly dressed as a Cossack!

Born in 1881 to Longfellow's daughter, Edith (subject of "The Children's Hour"), and Richard Henry Dana III (the son of the author of *Two Years Before the Mast*), Harry Dana was raised on Brattle Street in another and later family mansion adjoining Castle Craigie itself. After Browne and Nichols School in Cambridge, he entered Harvard College, where his grandfather, the poet, had been a professor; young Harry graduated with the class of 1903. He then taught for several years at St. Paul's School, in Concord, New Hampshire, perhaps the most prestigious of the exclusive Anglican New England boarding schools, then at another school in California—the first sign of his adventurousness—before returning to Harvard in 1906 as a graduate student in the English department. Teaching assistant to that legendary grandee of the English department Barrett Wendell, whose brother Evert we've already encountered in the Oscar Wilde chapter, Dana taught at Harvard for several years, taking his Ph.D. in 1910.[98] Thereafter he studied in Paris. He taught briefly at the Sorbonne and actually founded the Harvard Club of Paris. In 1912 he took up what he had every reason to think was a career teaching appointment at Columbia. A traveler, in 1914 he found himself in Europe at the start of World War I: "I was in the crowd under the Kaiser's balcony when he declared war," he reported in his Harvard class notes; and then "in Paris I stood with the people in the streets watching the

German aeroplanes flying over the city just before the Battle of the Marne."⁹⁹ Both experiences were evidently powerful ones. Perhaps these and other wartime events converted him, or just confirmed Dana in longstanding convictions, but by 1916 the will of the previous year of his uncle Ernest contains this very clear codicil: "Owing to the socialist and pacifist opinions of my nephews Harry L. Dana and Allston Dana I strike out their names from my Will as legatees thereunder."¹⁰⁰ Harry Dana's uncle certainly thought him no patriot and perhaps a coward, no gentleman by the standards of Ernest Longfellow, and this may explain why Dana was called (despite the Cossack attire) effeminate. Certainly it explains another trauma of Harry Dana's life, which he shared with his Harvard classmates: "In June, 1917, at the end of my fifth year as instructor in English at Columbia University, I was promoted to the position of assistant professor of comparative literature. In October, however, at the beginning of the next academic year," Dana was dismissed "on account of my activities for 'international peace [with the People's Council of America for Democracy and Peace, an organization opposed to American entrance into the war]."¹⁰¹

It was a devastating, life-changing blow that only a man with Dana's strength of character—and private means—as well as gathering professional achievement, could have survived. Yet he hardly taught again in any sustained way—except at New York's prestigious New School for Social Research in the 1920s. But Dana, who by then had taken up residence in Longfellow House with his Aunt Alice, continued his work as a scholar in his field, work that dovetailed with his increasingly socialist—indeed, communist—politics. In that sense that E. E. Cummings was not wrong to call Dana not only a "New England idealist" but an outright "justifier" of the new Soviet regime that so shocked most of his friends and colleagues. More exhilarated than alarmed by the Russian Revolution, Dana, along with many others in those days, saw fascism as a far greater danger. Thus he could write to his classmates in 1938 how he identified with Harvard's tradition in *his* way: "During the last three hundred years of our country (and of our College) novel experimenters—explorers, settlers, pioneers, Sons of Liberty, builders of democracy, abolitionists of slavery, inventors, free-thinkers, scholars—have triumphed over the forces of conservatism that tried to block their progress."¹⁰²

He was certainly an activist. In the years between the two World Wars Dana lectured at the Progressive Labor School of Boston and the Rand School in New York, was the founder of the Boston Central Labor Union's Trade Union College and also of Young Democracy of America, as well as second vice president of the Intercollegiate Socialist Society, editor of the *Socialist Review*, and an active member of the Harvard Teachers' Union—all while still applying himself to his special field, Soviet drama, of which he became a leading authority. He spent year-long periods in the Soviet Union between 1927 and 1935, not only in Moscow and Leningrad but in Armenia and the Ukraine. He was in touch with such major cultural figures of the era as film director Sergei Eisenstein, and with Gorky and Stanislavsky, as well as in this country with Theodore Dreiser and Sinclair Lewis. By his own estimate Dana had seen over six hundred Soviet plays. He remained an adviser to the Harvard Dramatic Club and also wrote both books and magazine articles. Among his books, still useful today, are *Handbook on Soviet Drama* (1938), *Drama in Wartime Russia* (1943), and *History of the Modern Drama* (1947).

One of the most singular aspects of Dana's life is that, though he maintained a highly productive career in his field, and was very active in (not unrelated) social and political causes, this radical and indeed subversive (as it seemed to many) side of him was balanced by an equally strong commitment on Dana's part to New England's traditional religion—historic preservation and family history. He virtually turned himself into the live-in curator of the Longfellow House, wrote widely on the subject (*Longfellow and Dickens*, for instance, published in 1943), and established the Longfellow Archives, today administered by the National Park Service, which took over the house when it was given to the nation in 1970.

It was another dimension of Dana's breadth of experience and deft balance of apparently competing interests. Of course it was also an example of how provoking he was: that the resident authority on Longfellow family history and the archives and collection of so famous a house-shrine not only to Longfellow but also to George Washington should have been what the *Boston Herald* called, on the occasion of his arrest, a "Communistic lecturer!"[103] Well. No doubt it also scandalized many when the black actor, Paul Robeson, appearing nearby at the Brattle Theatre, was feted by Dana at the Longfellow House.[104] Indeed, the whole situation there must have kept tongues wagging. After all, in the decade before Aunt Alice's death in 1928, Dana lived with her in the Longfellow House; they did so apparently in perfect comity, despite the fact that Alice was a member of the infamous Watch and Ward Society of "Banned in Boston" fame, and Harry all the while was cheerfully participating in what most of the society would have called the worst possible vice.

Of course, it would be very easy to play up the differences between Alice's activities and Harry's, and the sordid secrecy imposed on someone of Dana's sexuality in those days would only heighten the contrasts. This is all the more the case because Dana's sex life was as active as his scholarly and political life; one can never really assess such things with any degree of confidence, but he certainly seems to have had a healthy libido. That said, however, one must also be attentive to context. In the first place, in society generally and among his social peers (particularly when young, male, and attractive), Dana was a welcoming host and guide, and without any strings attached, according to Robert Creeley. Creeley remembers that for him and three or four of his mostly heterosexual friends, Dana's apartment in the Longfellow House was a cherished refuge for freshmen at Harvard, where at ten or eleven at night the group could ring the doorbell in search of drink and talk and always be sure of good company. Creeley, today a leading American poet, recalls Dana as witty and droll, usually in his smoking jacket, drink in hand, often memorably wise in the way he eased youth's often anxious moments in their first-year talk at college.[105] Hardly less significant, moreover, was the testimony of others about the efficacious part Dana, like other men his age, played in easing youth's passage through the highly repressed gay subculture of the period, a part documented by historian John Loughery. From the 1920s to the late 1950s, many young gays in their teens and twenties, Loughery finds, had

> their first [gay sexual] experiences . . . with men one, two, or even three decades older. . . . High-school or college peers were apt to be confused about their sexual interests or uninformed about how same-sex desires might be made the basis of a workable life. Older men . . . were the key . . . on park benches in New York, San Francisco, and Los Angeles; on street corners in New Orleans, Detroit, and Kansas City; on Florida's beaches; at subway stops in Boston and Chicago; and at the public library in Fort Worth, Texas—the restroom of which . . . was in the 30's "a hangout that was more like a truck stop."[106]

It was a contradictory business. Recalls Loughery: often "pick-ups . . . with older tearoom [restroom] regulars in New York in the 30s . . . began with sex and ended with trips to Carnegie Hall." There was, to be sure, a dark side, and this was evident to Loughery: "A not surprising undercurrent of pain and anger that sometimes took the form of withering sarcasm and cynicism." For every "supportive mentor one might happen upon, there was a bitter, middle-aged man who had no interest in helping the young," and their effect could be corrosive, Loughery reported. "A sourness permeated . . . gay conversation," he continues; and when he cites "the bitchy queen on her barstool" he could just as easily be talking of Dorothy Dean at the Casablanca.[107]

The overall picture that emerges from this research, however, in the course of which the documentation intersects quite specifically with Harvard several times, is more complex:

> Not only strangers, but any adult male identified as queer by the grapevine or public exposure was a potential sex partner and/or shoulder to lean on for a younger gay man. . . . When Bertram Schaffner, a Harvard freshman (today a prominent New York psychiatrist in his eighties), turned up [at Dana's doorstep], he wasn't taking much of a risk. . . .

At Harvard as elsewhere young Schaffner and other gay freshmen needed Dana and figures like him, one of whose functions in life was "introduc[ing to] their juniors," in Loughery's words, "the argot, history, and contours of a society previously hidden."[108]

With Harvard freshmen and family friends—or with youths of all classes run into and picked up here or there—the line in pederastic relations between supportive and exploitative has always been a thin one. But one way to better understand the ideal in modern times (there is no need to understand the degeneration only too well known from the daily news) is to recall our discussion of ancient Greek mores and morals, so often appealed to by homosexuals.

A more intimate discussion of all this has been mounted by Bernard F. Dick, a literary scholar who studied the Hellenism of the modern homosexual author Mary Renault.[109] Writing of "the Hellenic referent against which the contemporary action will be measured," Dick explains the dilemma that Dana poses to us:

> Socrates distinguished between homosexual lovers pursuing the ideal of *philia* and those who merely lusted after youths. . . . [A] father [in Renault's work] explains the phenomenon of the courtship to his son as if it were a fact of life; he tells his son that he must first *deserve* [emphasis added] his suitors but under no circumstances should he succumb to gifts and flattery. . . . His double standard was essentially Socratic; Socrates felt it was prostitution to offer one's beauty indiscriminately, but a mark of virtue to become the lover of a man of honor.
>
> Socrates, in fact, represents the mean between homosexual friendship and loveless sodomy. . . .
>
> The Greek ideal of *philia* or mutual love [is distinguishable from] sexual gratification; the latter was merely a manifestation of the former and not the end or *telos* of love between males.[110]

Was Dana "a man of honor" or merely "lust[ing] after youths"? Charting his sex life may place us more in lust's land than love's, but as we'll see more than once in this book, the sexual dynamic has ever operated in each realm not dissimilarly. Consider, for example, Dick's observation that "admirers of Plato's *Phaedo* with its exalted view of the soul might shudder at the thought that the innocent youth whose hair Socrates loved to stroke was really a male whore."[111] Or consider Socrates' own famous image of "the tripartite soul" in the *Phaedrus*: the soul is like a charioteer who drives two horses, one white (who loves honor and temperance and needs no prodding from the driver), the other black (insolent, stubborn, and prideful, indifferent to goad or whip, much less honor); the charioteer symbolizes reason; the white steed emotion, the black one appetite, especially sexual. Dana may have struggled. Or he may not have. Dick again: "There can be *no* cheerful predictions, for even Plato recognized the recalcitrant nature of the black steed in all of us,"[112]—not least a man given to mad tea parties. And Dana certainly approached it all coolly enough, carefully saving and filing for posterity everything from thank-you notes to hate mail, as well as opening a window onto the most shadowy of Harvard's homosexual worlds then, as well as onto a human situation usually beyond recovery because kept so secret and also onto a literary genre that is consequently hard to study—the blackmail letter. Those sent to Dana cannot have been very different from those that may have been sent to Porter or to any other Harvard luminary of the period who was homosexual.[113]

Ironically, in a book so much concerned with silencing, because predators of all kinds—whether blackmailers or pedophiles or neither or both (however you judge)—are protected by intellectual property laws as much as you and I, legal concerns argue against the publication of the full and complete text of any of these letters, even without names or dates and even three quarters of a century later. It would be possible to summarize or paraphrase them, quoting some of their contents, but to weigh evidence without being able to present it is as problematic for a historian as for counsel in a courtroom. My *opinion* is protected speech, but that is as irrelevant as a prosecutor's would be to a juror not allowed to hear the evidence for himself or herself. Reluctantly, therefore, all I can do is point the reader to this treasure trove of early-twentieth-century homosexual blackmail letters (a literary genre in and of itself long overlooked by scholars, who have perhaps neglected it because sufficient documentation so seldom survives to study the genre) in the archives of the Longfellow House National Historic Site.

They make fascinating reading, not least because Dana, who by the 1930s had traveled widely, had long since mastered the skills of the double life, which we know he had already absorbed by his student years because of all those diaries and papers he also preserved, and these can be presented.

Yet the young man of the 1890s and 1900s that emerges from these papers seems fairly healthy in mind and body. For example, from a journal of about 1897: "A good day of sport ... This is the first day of this year that I have devoted my time so much to athletic sport ... an exciting game of baseball. Played wonderfully well, which put me in good spirits. After a brilliant and scoreless game ... got ready for lecture this evening at the Fogg Museum." Clearly he was culturally alert, too, recording at the same time, for example, a concert of the Kneisel Quartet of Brahms's music given just a few days after that composer's death. Then the Tuesday following he "went to Copley Hall ... and studied with great interest the wonderful collection of pictures. ... There was an exhibition of the so-called 'Arts and Crafts'—the idea being useful things beautifully made." Not many days later and he is exulting about Wagner, whose operas, he wrote, "have opened a new door to me of great interest and beauty."[114]

By the time Dana was a graduate student in Paris he was part of the gay underground of the period, a genial and popular figure evidently, and for the first time can be linked as a student to Morton Fullerton, who first arose here in Chapter 2 as a friend of Tom Meteyard, he of the soulful eyes Wilde himself admired. A letter of Fullerton's to Dana in Paris in 1911 refers to one Chafee as "a peculiarly winsome youth" and counts on Dana to join them both at "a rendezvous to which I am looking forward with delight."[115] If his acquaintance with Fullerton proves that, as a young man, Dana was no stranger to the fast lane, to understand Dana's character fully, one must take account of an early love that was to become a lifelong relationship, albeit at a distance, with a man his own age, Karl Young, who became a professor at Yale.

Letters from as early as 1908 survive, documenting the men's intimacy. On September 1 Young wrote to Dana: "The days with you in Europe were lovely. . . . I was not disappointed. They were far dearer even than I had hoped." On September 13: "I don't suppose I could make you realize how happy I was with you and how deeply I was comforted by the strengthening of the bonds between us. I feel that we've never meant so much to each other before." The complimentary close of 1908—"affectionately your friend"—had by 1910 become "Lovingly your Karl"; and by 1911, "Ever your loving Karl." A long letter, undated, aptly discloses the troubled but long-lived nature of Dana and Young's relationship, so characteristic of the time:

> Can't you decide, dear Harry, that I am, perchance, as sincere and straightforward as most people, and can't it occur to you that your companionship can help me very much.
>
> Honestly, Harry, it's time for us to get down to business, for I can't believe that you'll deny me all that I want from you.
>
> Please don't call it "patronizing" when I take a little interest in your work and do try to see something beside egotism in my telling you about my work. . . . [116]

In the end it was Castle Craigie Dana loved most. And always had. Here is his diary entry of 26 January 1902, the night he came of age: The evening before, he wrote, he'd had

> my 21 best friends to dinner at home. Towards midnight I wandered outside into the garden. I seemed to see there the years as a whole clearly and resolves came, though I made none. I walked out in front of the Craigie House, which is dearer to me than anything else. I knelt on the door step and tried to pray. It was very misty, but I could just see the branches of the elm trees swinging slowly across the sky. . . . I heard the clock on the stairs [inside the house] strike twelve. . . . A little later I heard the clock in [Harvard Square] and in Memorial Hall [tower].[117]

He died in that house, its curator, a half century later.

Fight Fiercely Harvard

"I WONDER IF they would attempt to dislodge you if you were a good Republican and a pillar of the Episcopalian Church?" a relative wrote to a beleaguered Harry Dana in 1936,[118] probably not knowing that though Dana was an announced Communist and presumed atheist he could (and, discreetly, may) have called on a future bishop of that church to vouch for him: Bishop Spence Burton, Harvard class of 1903, who was a classmate of Dana's in Harvard College. Both were in the English department, and that may explain what brought them together. We do not know how they met, and, as his career unfolded, "Spence" Burton, as one might have expected, was more and more careful of the company he kept. It is only in what would then have been called his private life, and in faraway Haiti, of which he would later become the Anglican bishop, that any documentation survives as to his sexuality.[119] Although presumably he never physically acted upon his impulses (Burton was a monk and remained all his adult life under the vow of celibacy), his lifestyle nonetheless was unmistakable. Burton was a very worldly priest; not surprising, really, as his order, the Society of St. John the Evangelist, or the Cowley Fathers, had by then long had the repute of being "the Anglican Jesuits." (Its nickname comes from the small village of Cowley, outside Oxford, where the society was founded.) Both a wit and a charmer, he was, however, for those reasons, often underestimated and misunderstood; so many saw *only* the wit and the charm.

Scion of an old and wealthy Cincinnati family, Burton first came in contact with the Cowley Fathers at Harvard. The American branch, started in Boston because it was hoped that Harvard would play the same role in staffing the American work of the society that Oxford long had in the British work, never attracted a more willing recruit than young Burton. "No oppressed immigrant sailing up New York harbor ever beheld the Statue of Liberty," wrote Burton, of his return from years of study with the British Cowleys, "with more emotion than I," adding, "to make [one] work in a foreign country under foreigners and by foreign methods was a sure-fire way to Americanize an American utterly." The British fathers really didn't seem so impressive after all to Burton with his worldly ways and breezy Americanisms. Right after graduation from Harvard, Burton, with his accustomed gumption, had got a job as a cub reporter for the *New York Daily News*—a tabloid that was more than worldly. (Burton's only complaint about the job was that his salary never rose above his bar bill at the Harvard Club of New York.) It was only some years later that Burton found his way to New York's General Theological Seminary: ordained an Episcopal priest in 1908, he joined the Cowley Fathers, rising ultimately over the next sixteen years to Suffragan Bishop of Haiti and in 1942 Lord Bishop of Nassau.

His greatest achievement, in aid of his vigorous Americanism, was establishing close ties with Harvard, close to which he built (and largely funded himself) the magnificent monastery church that is still today the order's home on the banks of Boston's Charles River. But to all his work for Cowley Burton brought the same verve and flair and imagination he brought to everything else he did. Assigned in the early 1920s, for instance, to a parish in San Francisco, he began an active ministry in San Quentin State Prison, forthwith reporting: "One of my first 'reforms' was to found the San Quentin Harvard Club . . . a select organization of only four members. . . . We [had] meetings and Harvard Club dinners. I challenge any other [Harvard class of 1903] man to produce, as I did, Harvard Club dinners 'on the inside.' We were honored in having a Ph.D. as the president of the San Quentin Harvard Club." Sounds so flip! But he added, "I have been most useful as a priest when I have been in prison; I know I have been happiest there."[120] And, indeed, he was by repute "a pastor of individuals in trouble" ("managing church organizations did not seem to be my line," he wrote), and perhaps for that reason was elected Superior of a by then independent American congregation of Cowley in 1924. He proved a very successful leader. Indeed, like Dana (the founders of the Harvard Club of Paris and San Quentin had much in common), Burton was interested in aesthetics and history and architecture.[121] Also like Dana, he was progressive in his social thinking.

How close were they? Witness part of a letter from the young novice, as Burton then was, to his friend at Harvard:

> I will not start another [argument?]. Your reference to the defective logic in my letter reminds me of "Grays 18" [Professor Barrett Wendell's study then in Grays Hall in Harvard Yard]. I remember Barrett Wendell swinging out of his chair there across the room to the fireplace, and wheeling around upon me saying at a high pitch, "Mr. Burton, I beg of you, never attempt to be logical." That was his criticism of an Eng. 22 "argument" I had handed in. . . .
>
> How surprised you will be someday either before or after death, to find what a good Christian you have been all along! Now you are like Absalom with your head caught in the oak. I know it is an uncomfortable fix to be in, but all the rest of you is healthy and Christian as can be.[122]

Such intimacy speaks words. Also revealing was the way Burton closed another letter to Dana in the same year: "Thank you beyond words for your friendship, your confidence, for yourself. Affectionately, Spence."[123] Nor was Dana the only such confidant of Burton's. There is some reason to think that he was, if not clearly the center, certainly the common link between a widening Harvard homosexual circle of the era. He was friends not only with Dana, for example, but also with a circle of men and women, most of them residents in and around Brattle Street who were worshipers at the Cowley Monastery or parishioners at the Cowley mission church of St. John's on Beacon Hill, a circle that included Thomas Whittemore, Catherine Huntington, Stewart Mitchell, and Ralph Adams Cram and, through Cram, Fletcher Steele. Most had Harvard associations.[124]

St. John's, run by Cowley on the run-down back slope of Beacon Hill since 1871, was a very sophisticated place. Eldridge Pendleton, writing of one of its leading lights, Father Hamilton Johnson, once observed that Johnson served as spiritual director and confessor not only for Cram, but for British author Rose Macaulay and a generation of strippers from the Old Howard burlesque theater in downtown Boston's Scollay Square.[125] Furthermore, only a block or two away, on bohemian Pinckney Street, the always fascinating (because opaque) boundary between the hill's run-down back slope and its fashionable front slope, lived another St. John's regular, beloved I'm sure of Father Johnson—Catherine Huntington, a Marxist who put Burton in the 1920s up to one of his more drastic enterprises: sheltering at St. John's a large (and, to many, villainous) band of anarchists. Indeed, it was a veritable vigil of Sacco and Vanzetti's supporters, who were picketing the statehouse the night before the men's execution. The Boston police asked Burton to throw them out. He refused. An astonishing event—word even spread abroad. In London the *Church Times,* citing Burton's determination to em- phasize Cowley's ministry to "that section of the people which is most shunned and hated in these days—the Radicals," reported that the superior's actions were prompted by the fact that, though Boston was full of sympa- thizers of the two condemned men, "they were not allowed to hold meetings in halls or congregate in the streets." Burton agreed with Huntington: "A place of safety and refuge for the radicals" was necessary.[126]

Johnson and Burton disclose two very different aspects of Cowley's un- conventional ministry in Boston. In Johnson's case, we have recourse not only to the oral tradition, but also to his correspondence with Macaulay, which documents his focus on counseling homosexuals as fully as Stewart Mitchell's diaries document Burton's intimacy with the Dana gay scene. Moreover, once Johnson had raised the issue, Macaulay's response, though edited (*Letters to a Friend* was published in the 1950s), suggests they shared a fairly liberal attitude on the matter: "As to ... [homosexuality], who does know the answer?" wrote Macaulay. "I am sure it grows commoner all the time. I suppose there was a good deal of it in the M[iddle] A[ges] among the Religious Houses; all the contemporary social satirists spoke of it; and, of course, it was one of the counts against them at the Dissolu- tion—not that they say much, when so much was pure fabrication for a purpose."[127]

If the cast of characters at Cowley, either in Cambridge or on Beacon Hill, was always interesting, the continuum was also diverse. At one end at either place was Burton, very masculine and "hail fellow well met"—and, according to Dr. Richard P. Wunder, very drawn to black athletes[128]—and at the other end of the continuum on Bowdoin Street was Thomas Whittemore, something of a Quentin Crisp type. An ardent Anglo-Catholic, keen aesthete, and lifelong bachelor, Whittemore was also a man of wide-ranging tastes.[129] A friend of Henri Matisse and Isabella Stewart Gardner, Whittemore was the one who in 1912 gave Gardner the first Matisse to enter an American museum.[130] A friend of Cram and Whittemore, Gardner, in turn, also in 1912, almost certainly gave to St. John's, Bowdoin Street (to which Whittemore was devoted), the superb high-altar reredos that Cram—another friend of Whittemore—had designed for Cowley; its altarpiece was by Martin Mower, another Harvard graduate who subsequently taught there, and was sufficiently representative of our bachelor cohort to have been called by Lincoln Kirstein distinctly "high-bohemian."[131] One is sometimes breathless at the density of the connections—and the commissions—which were, of course, very much a part of this scene.

It seems equally likely it was Cram who recommended landscape architect Fletcher Steele to Cowley to do their garden when the Cowley Fathers were finally in a position to commission from Cram their Cambridge monastery. Like Burton's, the pattern of life of Steele, a very close friend and artist collaborator of Cram, strongly suggests Steele was homosexual. A brilliant landscape architect (indeed, one of the greatest America produced in the last century), Steele suffered from lifelong bouts of depression and attempted suicide in college. He was a lifelong bachelor, and though there is the usual tale of a lost lady love who turned him down, Steele's biographer, Robin Karson, notes that as to "evidence that Steele felt deep, romantic attachments to other woman during his lifetime, there is none," there being only "flirtatious involvements with many female clients"—almost, of course, as much a business prerequisite for a designer of gardens as for an interior decorator. Moreover, on at least one occasion, the issue surfaced explicitly: the time Steele's office manager, George Campbell, "traveled to Europe with Steele, which raised subtle questions in the office about the nature of their relationship," according to Steele's biographer.[132] So too, I suspect, did his several trips to Haiti with Cram, when Burton was the Anglican bishop there, in the late 1930s.

Running Away

THERE IS SOMETHING more to learn of Burton, and of Dana too, in the life and work of a mutual friend of both, another Harvard man—Stewart Mitchell—who, while not any more devout than Dana, was close to Burton in particular. From this distance he appears to have been something of a failure in life, but that failure—if that's what it was—reveals considerable information about Harvard gays in those years. One thing, certainly, is that although a decade and more separated Mitchell, class of 1915, from Dana and Burton, both 1903, seen as a threesome these men seem (in part because

Mitchell was as meticulous in preserving his papers for posterity as Dana was) to begin to outline yet another developing Harvard gay circle of the years just before and after World War I.

Like Burton, Mitchell was from an old Cincinnati family; unlike Burton, there was no money left. Born in 1892, Mitchell, who entered Harvard in 1911, distinguished himself particularly in literary circles; he was the editor, for instance, of the prestigious *Harvard Monthly*. A good student, he graduated cum laude; an ardent supporter of the Allied cause, he soon enlisted in the army and saw active service in France as a field artilleryman. At war's end he hooked up with some of his college literary chums in New York, somehow fumbled the editorship of *The Dial*, and, returning to Europe, took up graduate studies at the University of Montpellier, and then at Jesus College, Oxford.

In 1925 he transferred his studies back to Harvard and became a tutor; that he so immersed himself in this so highly demanding form of teaching probably explains why it was not until 1933, at age forty-one, that he achieved his doctoral degree. One not very inspiring book later he was an editor again, this time of the *New England Quarterly*, then of the publication program of the prestigious but very staid Massachusetts Historical Society, of which he later became the director. In that office he was a much thwarted advocate of change and an indifferent author; only as an editor did he succeed: "His naturally keen memory and sharp eye," Malcolm Freiberg said of him, "coupled with a sure ear for words and an occasionally brilliant wit, permitted him to excel." It was the best that posterity had to say of him. More interesting, though, was the worst that was said—of all places, in an obituary, a literary genre not conspicuous even today for candor: Mitchell, one writer opined, had "serious personal failings, which were a trial to his friends, who never ceased to regard him with exasperated affection." It was a pronouncement that suggests the opposite was also the case, and it pointed to how often the homosexual, perhaps especially in Harvard's orbit, was at war, not only with the world, but with himself.[133]

Mitchell's youth was immediately compromised by his decision (the best solution in sight, he thought, to his family's rapid impoverishment, but in retrospect seriously Faustian in the view of several friends) to indebt himself to a much older, wealthier woman—Georgine Holmes Thomas—whom John Dos Passos once (doubtless in passing anger, but perhaps insightfully) called "a vampire." She agreed to pay for Mitchell's postgraduate education if he would "forgo marriage" and live with her as her "companion";[134] in other words, to serve as what is sometimes called a "walker," that sad (and humiliating) office into which gay men in those days were frequently tempted by forceful, thwarted (and in consequence often embittered, even man-hating) women made by society to live pretty much through the achievements of the men in their lives, men often absent from the marriage in any emotional sense, nearly always in any cultural or literary sense, never mind in a sexual sense. The only plausible stand-in, of course, was the gay man, "morally" unthreatening to society because sexually unthreatening to the husband. Convenient for both husband and wife, the bargain had also its appeal for gays. Quite beyond the universal lure of wealth and high living, homosexuals, always socially vulnerable, were offered a role, respectable and somewhat protected, like wives then. But for gays it was not a good alternative. Most gays seem to have themselves married, and raised families; a better alternative, and one which had its joys.

The allure of the walker was frequently fatal for homosexuals. The gay man, especially vulnerable in his youth, wrestling then with society's strictures that he was not quite a man—not only sick but a sinner and a criminal as well—risked as a "walker" being utterly emasculated before he even got out of the starting gate, turned into a kind of "poseur," really, blocked by society from any aboveboard homosexual relationship even as he was forced into a phony heterosexual one as an escort. A wink and a nod and any sense of one's dignity was gone; all this in one's twenties; it was too much. Mitchell, whose relationship with Mrs. Thomas seems not to have had much intellectual content, and to have been more draining than stimulating, was very conflicted, and at one and the same time he succumbed and rebelled. On the one hand, he bore the burdens of a servant-filled seaside mansion on Boston's North Shore as easily as any of us would; ditto on Fifth Avenue in New York and in various European capitals. On the other hand, he postponed his ambitions, drank too much, and led an extremely full, but largely episodic and fugitive, sex life with other men, a life at once clandestine and promiscuous.

At intervals, however, he did bestir himself and pursue his graduate studies and doggedly kept alive the possibility of a career that, truth to tell, was always waning more than it was waxing throughout his twenties, thirties, and even forties, as Mitchell became more and more conscious he was not looking forward to it, but having it. All the while, he was too smart not to see what was happening. Writing to a friend, he said, "As far as my own life, it is still something of an unused pencil: it needs cutting off and sharpening to its point." In the same letter he confessed the underlying conflict: by nature no compromiser, he had nonetheless compromised utterly: "I hope some day to be at ease in Zion—for it's Zion or bust—like Conrad's 'Judea,' " he wrote, disclosing too his determination and perseverance, which must have seen him through many a dark night and been mostly what kept him going. That and sex and alcohol. To another friend he confided, "For years I have lived under an almost intolerable burden of despair, which has practically paralyzed my brain, my two sole outlets have been getting drunk and you know what." (I am reminded of Richard Newman's observation that the largest contingents in early gay pride marches walked under the banner of "Recovering Alcoholics.") In the very next sentence, however, Mitchell went on to write: "Now I find to my amazed relief, that I can live with myself at last," while to another at the same time he wrote of having "at last got the habit of happiness."[135]

Consolidating that happiness would seem to have had most to do with Richard Cowan, a young man whom Mitchell, in middle age, fell deeply in love with. And this points us right back to the work of John Loughery, who dealt not only with Dana's sex life but with Mitchell's, too, this time in more of a context of a partnership at once self-serving and self-sacrificing:

> Every gay man knew what his younger friends confronted in adolescence: either a wall of silence or soul-destroying stereotypes about freakishness and loneliness. Alleviating these burdens was a mission for some. . . . Harry Hay has spoken . . . of a night spent on the beach in California in 1926 with a merchant seaman . . . [who] fired his imagination about the "secret brotherhood" that they were a part of, a world of men who loved men and recognized one another by a look or signal unnoticed by others. Many gay men in their seventies and eighties have similar stories of being "set right" in their thinking by a buddy or lover who took them under his wing . . . [and attempted] to create a fresh perspective, a counter-mythology to mainstream images of perverts, predators or hopeless misfits. . . .
>
> Early in my research I encountered the diaries of Richard Cowan (1909–1939). . . . As a student at Cornell in the 20s, Cowan had plenty of gay sex, but it doesn't appear (to read between the lines of the diaries) that he had a clear sense of "a gay life" until forming a relationship with Stewart Mitchell, ten years his senior, in Boston in the 30's.[136]

From the point of view of the narrow, dry, scholarly world Mitchell worked in, the world that found his failings "a trial"—how sustaining it could be to be taken up by a brilliant older man was, of course, beside the point: "aggressively homosexual"[137] (the words are from the Massachusetts Historical Society's official history) was that world's judgment, and it is hard to see how Mitchell stood a chance against that sort of consensus.

Mitchell's response was to suffer no fools and take no prisoners, no matter how ill-tempered this made him. He resolved once, he wrote to a friend, "no more to suppress or restrain my semen than I do my piss and my etcetera, but on the other hand I shall not for ever be lurking about urinals and water closets. In these cases promotion were as fatuous and dangerous as suppression."[138] This from the guardian of Jefferson's own copy of the Declaration of Independence (with corrections in Jefferson's own hand), the greatest of many treasures the director of the Massachusetts Historical Society has charge of. The words disclose so acutely the sort of problems a man in Mitchell's position had to contend with unless he chose to pretend he was something he was not, thus ceding to his critics, of course, the moral high ground, confirming that they were right to think him duplicitous, mitigating any guilt they might have felt, and yielding to them the dubious satisfactions of the self-righteous—some of them closeted hypocrites themselves. It was a recipe for at least alcoholism.

If such was Mitchell's position, imagine Cowan's. A gifted young man, a landscape architect, handsome, charming, just out of college, hormones raging. Cowan's diaries, extracts of which appear in an excellent compendium of gay oral history (though titled, rather disappointingly, *Improper Bostonians*), are interesting in that they give the younger man's perspective on this type of older man/younger man relationship as it existed between the World Wars:

> It was not until last June that Stewart and I had any physical relations. . . .
> Met a Dartmouth boy on the Common one night after the Symphony.
> Made a date with him. . . . [In the evenings] Stewart and I would walk
> for an hour or so. Then dine with Mrs. T[homas] and I'd talk to her
> and play the victrola 'til about eleven while Stewart worked on his thesis.
> They were very pleasant evenings. . . . Met George. . . . Stayed with me in
> Plympton Street [off Harvard Square] quite often and we walked with
> Stewart one evening. S[tewart] didn't like him and I'm sure was very
> jealous. I love S very much but am incapable of being true to any one
> person. . . . George was an intimate friend of Abram Piatt Andrew, con-
> gressman from Gloucester. . . . One night at the Monarch club I met a
> boy. . . . I was very drunk and foolishly told him I loved him . . . slept
> with him. . . . [At the theater one night] in the lobby a boy and I eyed
> one another. After the show he followed me up the street and we went
> to the Public Garden & talked . . . slept together. . . . He's a fine kid but
> melancholy and has the falling-in-love-with-me-sickness.[139]

The result of all this we now know. First there was Cowan's suicide, in 1939, naturally devastating to Mitchell, who, made of sterner stuff perhaps, or just older and more mature, stayed the course much longer. But the official record—written by that same establishment so out of sympathy with him— tells a hardly less dismal story: he resigned as the director of the Massachusetts Historical Society the year of Cowan's death, "not a voluntary action" in Louis L. Tucker's words (in the society's history). Mitchell, forced out by officials concerned with his "excessive drinking," agreed all the more readily because of Cowan's death, which he referred to as a "personal misfortune which has caused me a lot of trouble." It was not Cowan's suicide, but the relationship itself, however, which seems to trouble Tucker. Doubtless reflecting the attitude of officials then, he writes, "The 'personal misfortune' cited by Mitchell *was a relationship* [emphasis added], well known among Mitchell's friends and associates." Tucker then quotes Melvin Landsberg, John Dos Passos's biographer, about the relationship: "Mitchell's private life was unfortunate. Aggressively homosexual, he was strongly attached to a young man named Richard Cowan," and so on.[140]

So many "unfortunates," so many "misfortunes." It was all intended, surely, as a moral tale. Of course, it will now seem to many to point to a different moral. "There is no running away from a broken heart," a usually acerbic Mitchell wrote to Spence Burton.¹⁴¹

What happened to "the Great Auk," as Mitchell was called at Harvard because of his long, narrow face? Whence the "charming witty young man" that Robert S. Kennedy, the biographer of E. E. Cummings, evoked when describing Mitchell in his undergraduate days?¹⁴² Cummings was the most notable figure in Mitchell's sparkling undergraduate circle, a circle Mitchell himself shone in. His debut had been rather brilliant: one of the *Eight Harvard Poets* (Cummings and Dos Passos and John Wheelwright were three others; "it was the beginning of my style," Cummings wrote later), Mitchell conceived the idea of publishing that book, to which he was a contributor, as well as a founder of the Harvard Poetry Club.

Mitchell's homosexuality stood out (according to Kennedy) even then: "consider[ing] the sexual coloration of the *Harvard Monthly* group and the friends they had gathered around them . . . [also, later, in New York, at] *The Dial*," Kennedy concludes that "only one of them, Stewart Mitchell, was an overt homosexual. Nevertheless, an innocent homoeroticism marked their devotion to each other."¹⁴³ Innocent? Kennedy goes on to say he feels that devotion reflected the fact these men were "outgrowing a sexual immaturity brought about, to a great extent, by the repressions of the American home and church and by the ethos of the boys' school and men's college, where the friendship of young fellows together is the basis of life and any attention to women is a secondary matter, even a diversion."

That this ethos—basically Greek (even Whitmanic) in the Anglo-American/Victorian understanding of the word—was and is in any way innocent or in any way immature is, of course, a matter of (mostly long since repudiated) opinion. And if there *was* a predominance of heterosexuals in this circle, it was—like the Casablanca, in fact—sexually ambiguous with a point being, surely, the conspicuous welcome it gave to gays. Mitchell was both creator-editor and contributor to *Eight Harvard Poets*, his sexuality notwithstanding. It was after Harvard that things changed for Mitchell. He and Cummings, for instance, remained lifelong close friends. Early on Mitchell functioned virtually as Cummings's agent, was a confidant of the poet in his divorce, and as late as 1949 gave the never-very-prosperous Cummings a thousand dollars, a large sum at the time. Throughout his life Mitchell continued to find acceptance from Harvard bohemians, straight (like Cummings) or gay. It was in the "outside" world that he ran into trouble, and that it was his world of choice never made it easier; in that world an open homosexual, if he was not effeminate or retiring and was instead overt and aggressive, was unacceptable. And Mitchell's private papers allow a revealing glimpse into the background of the life of the slowly coming-out gay Harvard undergraduate of the 1910s. Not just Mitchell's life is discussed, either; perhaps also the lives of other Harvard men of his time whose diaries haven't survived.

The ordinariness of Mitchell's undergraduate journals stands out: he joined a fraternity (Alpha Phi Sigma), skated on the Charles, rowed, spent an evening at the Old Howard burlesque theater, shopped in Harvard Square, engaged in table talk at Memorial Hall, watched Olympic tryouts at Harvard Stadium, dined at Marliave's (where else?), attended football games. And, of course, his take on contemporary events is fascinating, in an age of quite a few very important ones: he attended one of the first airplane meets in 1910; was devastated by the sinking of the *Titanic*; was delighted by the opening of the Harvard-to-Downtown-Boston subway; scorned the Armory Show ("trash and idiocy"); drank his first martini; saw Woodrow Wilson (at Sanders Theater), Pavlova and Caruso (at the Boston Opera House), the English suffragist Emmeline Pankhurst (at Brattle Hall), the French philosopher Henri Bergson (at Sanders again), the new Sargent murals at the Boston Public Library (he wrote a poem sparked by the "Astarte" mural).

But very soon, as early as his freshman year, telltale signs begin to appear. The expected names arise: Wilde (Mitchell knew an older man who had known him), Leonardo, Michelangelo, J. A. Symonds, Walter Pater, Plato, Wagner, Bliss Carman; also the expected books: *Dorian Gray* ("fascinating but dangerous"); the expected poems: "The Hound of Heaven"; the expected music (Tchaikovsky's Fifth Symphony, Wagner's *Tristan*, Debussy's *Prelude to the Afternoon of a Faun*); the expected plays: *The Mikado*; and so on. Soon more explicit signposts are evident: wrestling matches with his roommate, "fooling around," nights out downtown, roughhousing again and again, a medical school lecture on sex, pickups, doubts about the manliness of his deportment and the morality of his "base passions." Finally there are unmistakable entries. He is sympathetic to Wilde: "It is as unjust to crush the pervert as it would be to crush the normal man whose trans-sexual passions are no more genuine to himself." He discusses "sex inversion and Havelock Ellis," concludes he himself is "abnormal," and "not as I should be." His only explanation that he is "a spiritual hermaphrodite . . . my way of thinking . . . as much a woman as a man, even more feminine than masculine."[144]

Mitchell survived all this angst well enough, as his later letters show. Where else is one likely to learn (letter of 23 January 1944 to his friend and confidant, Richard Beatty) that a boy "had been bounced from Harvard last March for participating in a homosexual black mass"—whatever that is— or (to Cuthbert Wright, undated) "there is a night club in Boston the most uninhibited place I have seen outside of pre-Hitler Berlin." Letters to Mitchell himself also illuminate. One of the most amusing, from Wright, one of the other "Eight Harvard Poets," refers to an eighteen-year-old Andover boy he had just met:

You know that in the course of half-a-dozen years I have met an astonishing aggregation of morons, harvies, pimps and pansies at Wellesley,
but to meet there an Andover School boy of fascinating appearance and
manners was a new experience. He is a dark Lithuanian, v. Well built,
with a charming brown face and really green eyes. At Andover they have
just taken away his cherished life of *Hart Crane*. . . . [I] murmured within
me: "My God, I must tell Mitchell this!" Anyway, an enchanting youngster, and I am seeing him again soon. One writes to him in care of his
mother at Lawrence, as the school authorities don't know he is queer,
but his mother does.[145]

Later, in the same missive he complains to Mitchell about "the whole gang
of average phoneys and pederasts who collect [in Wellesley] of a Sunday
afternoon," but plans to go anyway else he will miss this new young man
("I've been hit hard"). He concludes by wishing Mitchell were at hand to
"counsel" him, and asks to borrow Mitchell's *Hart Crane* by mail. Finally:
"I shall win the trick."

What a delightful letter! I bet he did land the trick. Certainly, this Harvard cohort was made up of men who were nothing if not risk takers. And
perhaps the only finale to their life stories is one by another young man who
will turn up in this book more than once, a man who became more famous
than any of this circle—the future novelist John Cheever. After high school
and Europe, Cheever was, according to his biographer, "befriended by members of an intellectual group, including Hazel Hawthorne and Henry Longfellow Dana," both of whom subsidized the young writer. Of this era in his
life Cheever himself used to tell a tale I cherish about a call he once made
on Dana. It seems that in the house where the creator of Hiawatha and of
Evangeline and the Village Blacksmith is reverently invoked by so many
tourists to this day, Cheever recalled the poet's grandson was more than a
little "interested in his person." In fact, so Cheever in later years recalled,
Dana "pursued him through the halls of Castle Craigie demanding, 'How
can you be so cruel?' "[146]

Cheever, like Gore Vidal, was a member of a club even more interesting
than those who dropped out—or were thrown out—of Harvard. He and
Vidal were both *supposed* to go to Harvard but frustrated their families'
plans. Vidal was very direct about it: "My father gave me the bonds that he
had set aside to send me to Harvard. I cashed them in, to his horror."[147] If
Vidal had missed his Harvard moment, Cheever may have had a better one
in Castle Craigie. Though, of course, it's always complicated with Cheever,
whose ruminations about all the issues Harvard raised for him appear in a
short story he once wrote for *The Atlantic*—"The President of the Argentine"—which I read (rearranging the sequences of its "scenes" somewhat)
as a three- or perhaps four-act play.[148]

In the first act his father takes possession of the family dining room one day and amidst much to-ing and fro-ing and poking of the fire and so on ends up downing the contents of the sherry decanter on the sideboard. And, presumably to mislead (however briefly!) any passersby, "as a precaution— merely a precaution," writes Cheever—"he pissed the decanter full. The color was exactly right." Act Two, father long gone: "Enter the rector [of Boston's venerable Church of the Advent, Father Frisbee] then . . . Mother, taking off her apron." The rest of Act Two is mostly predictable. So the rector, according to Cheever, sat contentedly in his mother's parlor and "ate moldy pilot crackers and sipped piss. No wonder"—and here is the sur- prise—"none of us ever wanted to go to Harvard."

Act Three is longer. As I stage this story in my mind, I recall Cheever's assertion that he was "not a Bostonian," remembering as he did the city's aristocracy in his youth as "tragic and cranky," as, for example, when John Wheelwright, who had invited Cheever to tea one day, tossed all the sand- wiches into the fire because "they were unsuitable." The maid, a pretty Irish girl, cried. And though the painting over the mantelpiece was a Tintoretto and Wheelwright had been talking about Henry Adams, his favorite uncle, all Cheever could recall as he walked home was that "the night was dark and cold" and that "having already read Proust . . . nothing in his accounts of the fall of Paris . . . seemed to me so horrible as the smoking sandwiches and the weeping maid." Thus Act Three, another macabre story of violating the rules of hospitality.

It is likely Wheelwright, like Dana, was not uninterested "in Cheever's person." But it is unlikely that Wheelwright, a far shyer man than Dana, pursued Dana through the rooms of his Beacon Street domicile. But in Act Four of the play I am constructing out of Cheever's short story there *is* pursuit. Cheever again, "bang [ing] down Commonwealth Avenue":

> Statues in parks, I've always thought, have a therapeutic effect on one's posture. Walking among gods and heroes one always keeps one's head up. . . .
>
> Ahead of me I could see the statue of the President of the Argen- tine. . . . I decided to put my hat on his head. Why should I. . . . my life is impetuous and unorthodox, and I cannot distinguish persiflage from profundity, which may be my undoing. . . . I decided to make my as- cent. . . .
>
> The President is difficult to climb. . . . I was struggling up the bronze surface when a man said: "Ciao, bello."
>
> He was a good-looking young man who wore a serge middy blouse with three crimson chevrons sewn to the sleeve. No navy in the world, I knew, had ever issued such a costume. . . . "Desiderai tu un' amico?" he asked.
>
> "You've got a terrible accent," I said. "Where did you learn Italian . . . ?"
>
> "From a friend," he said.

"Break it up," shouted a policeman. "You boys break it up." He came running down the block. . . . You spoil everything.

The two young men split up—the narrator (Cheever, of course) to the Exeter Street Theater to see a film by Bergman (big help that probably was) and then back to the President of the Argentine—where this time he tries to pick up *a girl.*

Why do I suddenly think of Dana's youths? No wonder Cheever didn't go to Harvard, though in the end it didn't matter either way. (Eventually, "as Cheever became more accepting of his sexual orientation," Carmine Esposito writes, "it was reflected in his work. In his breakthrough novel, *Falconer,* Cheever invests homosexuality with redemptive and transforming powers. [His protagonist] . . . acquires the ability to love only after [a homosexual] affair [in prison].")[149]

As befits their queer profiles, Dana (who died in 1950) and Mitchell (who died in 1957) both did rather a bizarre thing. By no prearrangement we know of, in the full knowledge of what they were doing—each being, after all, a scholar and an archivist, not likely to be casual in the manner and style of preserving for posterity their private papers—they left as a part of their collection photographs of themselves stark naked: full frontal nudity, no apologies, in your face. Gay rage?

Indeed, Mitchell's bookplate is of a frontally nude man, genitals prominent against the rising sun.[150]

That Hard, Clear Shape

THE HOME GAME, tough to play anywhere, was either more or less so at Harvard, according to your point of view. Relatively easy-seeming for Thomas Sargent Perry and Archibald Carey Coolidge and Burton, perhaps even for Peirce, for WAG, for Amy Lowell, and for Copeland (about Nat Saltonstall we hardly know enough to guess), it was more difficult for Dorothy Dean as for Wheelwright and for Andrew, and finally too much for Porter. For Dana and Mitchell, too. The angst, moreover, was toughest on the best. Witness F. O. Matthiessen.[151] Though he was a very aggressive man (who volunteered for the U.S. Marines in World War II, not the army), Matthiessen was never called aggressively homosexual. Indeed, it was said that "for most of his students and younger colleagues Matthiessen's homosexuality was suggested, if at all, only by the fact that his circle was more predominantly heterosexual than was usual in Harvard literary groups of the time and that he was unusually hostile to homosexual colleagues who mixed their academic and sexual relations."[152] Matthiessen *was* called enough other things. Today, though, I think above all of Dartmouth professor Donald E. Pease's assertion that "the scholarship already accumulated on the subject of F. O. Matthiessen may be larger than that on any other American scholar born in the twentieth century."[153] It is, Pease asserts, the result of "the remarkable authority Matthiessen exercised in his various cultural duties as scholar, critic, political activist, and professor of literature at Harvard." Once processed—for Pease's assertion is astounding on its face—most will find themselves agreeing. All the more so if one adds to his catalogue of Matthiessen's roles in the history of his time—as Pease carefully doesn't, altogether ignoring the subject—that Matthiessen has surely become, of all Harvard's professors of the modern era, the most famously homosexual.[154]

A native of California, raised in Illinois, the child of divorced parents, Matthiessen came east to go to Yale, was thereafter a Rhodes Scholar at Oxford, and then earned his Ph.D. in 1927 at Harvard. He returned two years later to join the Harvard faculty, attracted to Eliot House, one of the seven residential colleges Harvard College was subdivided into at the end of President Lowell's tenure as a result of a visionary educational reform. Matthiessen, a tutor born, heartily agreed that education flourished best in small residential colleges (traditionally called houses at Harvard; later, at Yale, colleges), a system established uniquely by those two schools in the 1930s. Matthiessen was also drawn to the field of "History and Literature, [which] had served as pioneer and pilot of the tutorial system at Harvard," in the words of his fellow tutor in English, Harry Levin.[155] The houses were the capping stone of the tutorial system—and since its founding at a small dinner at Boston's Bohemian Tavern Club in 1906, the field of History and Literature had been one of the most elite at Harvard. Matthiessen became head tutor of Eliot House, and chair of the Board of Tutors of History and Literature, thus dedicating himself to what he thought the best teaching. Though he could be an effective lecturer, it was tutorial he thought pivotal. He thrived on "the one-to-one conditions of the study," in Levin's words, "trying to throw out sparks," as he put it, and getting an immediate reward when minds were ignited."[156]

As both scholar and teacher he was brilliantly successful. T. S. Eliot himself, then the Norton Professor, lived in Eliot House Matthiessen's first year, serving as head tutor, and one result of this was Matthiessen's *The Achievement of T. S. Eliot*, the first full-length study of Eliot's work. Inevitably, however, it was overshadowed by Matthiessen's most famous book, *American Renaissance*, published in 1941, of which it is not too much to say it really created the field of American literature, until then a footnote to English literature, and the allied field of American Studies generally. Written on the eve of World War II, Matthiessen's book remains magisterial even sixty years later, and "produced the cultural capital America needed," wrote Pease, "to take its place as a great nation among the other great nations of the world."[157]

Matthiessen met the love of his life, the painter Russell Cheney, on a transatlantic ocean liner in 1924. Theirs was a very full, complete union—emotionally, intellectually, and physically. It was also a long relationship, over twenty years, and it had many ups and downs; both spent time in McLean's,

Boston's prestigious mental hospital (Cheney for alcoholism, Matthiessen for depression). Through it all, however, each remained devoted to the other to the end, sustained when apart by an extensive correspondence (itself now historically important in detailing their union), and passing every summer in person at their cottage on the Maine coast. Writes Louis Hyde, editor of *Rat and the Devil*, a published compendium of their remarkable letters:

> The nature of their life together gradually appears—opening with the first spellbound wonder, through sentimentality and shy uncertainty, changing interpretation of their joint life, happy combining and mingling of their friends, shared impact of triumph and disappointment in their careers, emerging problems of illness and strain, the onset of older years—through all this to maturity and durability.

Adds Hyde: "The sex element in this correspondence should be emphasized no more and no less than if the two protagonists had been man and wife."[158]

As might be expected, each much influenced the other's work. As a result of Matthiessen, writes Hyde, "Cheney overcame a dilettantism . . . and became a well known American artist, while Matthiessen's first book, on the writer Sarah Orne Jewett, was suggested and illustrated by Cheney."[159] Just below the surface of this happy alliance—as happy professionally as personally—trouble, however, always simmered. Cheney and Matthiessen had much in common; both were Yale graduates and both were upper-middle-class men who'd enjoyed privileged youths. Cheney was forty-two when Matthiessen, only twenty-two, first met him, however, and although the fact that a generation separated them had many aspects that were fructifying, it had also its share of unfortunate effects, not least that Cheney, born in 1881, was more Victorian in his repressions—particularly about sexual intercourse—than Matthiessen, born in 1901.

The most serious repercussion of Cheney's attitude was his alcoholism, all the more troubling because, for obvious reasons, Cheney was better able to control it away from Matthiessen and the immediate possibility of sexual interaction. Yet Cheney's attitude did have this positive effect on his lover: it forced Matthiessen to think hard about what it meant to be homosexual. Previous to meeting his beloved, Matthiessen had confessed to a close friend, Russell Davenport, he could only see three outcomes for him: "morbidity" (complete sexual repression), "self-abuse" (masturbation), or "the old business with men" (anonymous sex). But post-Cheney, there opened before Matthiessen the wonderful new perspective of "love between men."[160] And although Cheney's own repressions stood in the way, these only forced Matthiessen to a greater intensity on the subject. His approach was always more Socratic than Talmudic, and was, in David Bergman's words, "spurred by opposition" to a more furious processing, so to speak. Just as had been, for instance, the case with Irving Babbitt, from whom Matthiessen claimed he learned the most because, disagreeing at nearly every point, he was forced "to fight for [his] tastes, which," in Bergman's words, "grew stronger by the exercise," so with Cheney. Matthiessen preferred strong minds and vigorous exchange, which was why he preferred the marines to the army, and the tutorial to the lecture hall.[161] When Cheney's Victorian attitudes toward homosexuality surfaced and he asked Matthiessen (who, after reading Ellis's *Sexual Inversion* in 1924, could write: "Then for the first time it was completely brought home to me that I was what I was by *nature*") to try to give up sex, Matthiessen, for all his love for Cheney, fought back vigorously against the older man. According to Bergman:

> Matthiessen refutes Cheney's notions that they should abstain from sex and keep their relationship secret from their dearest friends. At the heart of Matthiessen's argument is the importance of human "completeness" and integrity, two conditions that cannot be achieved unless the individual not only integrates the various parts of his own self, but joins his integrated self to the society at large. Sixteen years later these values, as Jonathan Arac has pointed out, will be among the most important aesthetic criteria used in *American Renaissance*.[162]

Thus did Matthiessen's sexuality and his scholarship intersect at a very fundamental level. And the debate Cheney provoked jump-started *American Renaissance*, perhaps most effectively in the matter of Matthiessen's overall structure in that book and his selection of authors. "*American Renaissance*," in Bergman's words, "is Matthiessen's ultimate expression of his love for Cheney and a covert celebration of the homosexual artist," focusing on five authors: two essayists, Emerson and Thoreau; two novelists, Hawthorne and Melville; and a poet, Whitman. Of the first Matthiessen prefers Thoreau; between the novelists, he chooses Melville; the poet is Whitman. "In each case," notes Bergman, "the homosexual writer (or the one whose words reveal the strongest homoerotic tendencies) is preferred."[163] Moreover, Whitman's preeminent role in *American Renaissance* in a sense reflects the influence of Cheney, for as in the case of Matthiessen's first book, Cheney's influence was very specific: Matthiessen's muse as well as his dearest friend and lover, Cheney introduced Matthiessen to Whitman, who became "not only the first American author Matthiessen grew to love, but the touchstone for all his notions of homosexuality," in Bergman's words.[164]

This was all the more true because, as Bergman also observes, "for Matthiessen as for Freud, the creative process is directly related to specific psychic conditions which allow the individual access or propel the artist into the creative act." Without the muse, one could almost say, the genius is stilled.[165]

Whitman, it is also clear, is utterly key to Matthiessen's thinking in *American Renaissance*, having to do with the integrity with which the individual integrates the various parts of his soul and his soul to other souls. Thus Matthiessen maintains that in his best work Whitman returned to that primordial relationship of psychic and social wholeness in which "poetic rhythm was an organic response to the centers of experience—to the internal pulsations of the body, to its external movements in work and in making love, to such sounds as the wind and the sea." No artist, Matthiessen knew, could sustain such moments; Whitman himself, Bergman continued, "was reared in a culture that imposed division. Nor can there be a society in which Evil does not force such division on the psyche." Yet one can hardly overstate the importance of what Whitman did: it being "through art and in moments of spiritual grace," Matthiessen felt, that "we gain glimpses of the wholeness that ordinarily eludes us," and in those glimpses that convince us of "the constancy of wholeness" find what persuades us that "the soul endures beyond all natural phenomena." At the same time, Matthiessen recognized that such a vision had to achieve concrete, focused, artistic form to register; "the conception of art as inspiration . . . is in sharp opposition to that of craftsmanship," he wrote. But Matthiessen knew the tension between "form and liberation" out of which came the artistic form—and that "the hard, clear shape that Matthiessen so admired," in Bergman's words— could not occur without the artist's fundamental "primal perception."[166]

Matthiessen approached politics hardly less seriously. Distinctly leftist (and very much the activist), Matthiessen was as committed to Christianity—he was a lifelong and ardent High Church Anglican—as to socialism. He was, for example, a founder of the Harvard/MIT Teachers' Union in 1935 and president of the Boston Central Labor Union. "Considering himself not a liberal but a radical," in Levin's words, he was certainly libertarian and very controversial. John Finley, the great Harvard classicist and master of Eliot House, wrote: "Moral sensitiveness is not an easy matter. The very qualities which lead to insight, devotion, and generosity, all of which Professor Matthiessen had as a teacher, are subject to doubt and strain. They do not grow from contentment and security, but from search and perhaps from insecurity. . . . But from the same nature as sprang his political intensity and his last fearful decision grew also gentleness, vision, and sympathy."[167]

That last decision was to kill himself. During World War II the justness of the cause as he saw it led to his effective abandonment of pacifism; similarly, Stalin's reign of terror much lessened his faith in Soviet communism. But even after the war Matthiessen still regarded himself as a radical, and it is hardly surprising his many libertarian crusades "incurr[ed] the jaundiced surveillance," in Levin's words, "of the [U.S.] House Committee on Un-American Activities." In the 1940s, for instance, he had become a sponsor of the Marxist journal *Monthly Review*, and in his last major book, *From the Heart of Europe* (1948), he still argued his view of the Russian Revolution of 1918 as the fulfillment, whatever its issue, of the French and American revolutions, a highly controversial view to have made so much of as the Iron Curtain was descending across Europe. It gave his enemies the chance to identify Matthiessen's leftist politics in that dangerous era with the worst excesses of Stalinism.

Harvard also seemed to fail him. In 1939 his decision, in aid of a greater intimacy and privacy for him and Cheney, to set up housekeeping together off-campus on Beacon Hill, also underlined even as it exacerbated his increasing dissatisfaction with the university in the era of James Bryant Conant, a chemist like President Eliot, and like Eliot more at home in the graduate school. (Matthiessen was not being prejudiced. Chemistry had been the one department to reject the tutorial system.)

If Harvard seemed increasingly to disappoint, Cheney's death in late middle age (he was only sixty-three) in 1945 was devastating. Matthiessen, just entering early middle age, was only forty-three, and thus bereft at the likelihood of thirty or more years alone. As Louis Hyde points out of the suicidal depression that came to bedevil Matthiessen:

> World politics and, in particular, Matthiessen's leftist leanings led to the tragedy. . . . but the root cause lay elsewhere. . . .
>
> [A] few months before Matthiessen died he wrote me about "the problems of living alone for one who has known love and companionship. There is no real solution that I can expect for that kind of incompletion. . . ." His last letter to me, which I found on his apartment desk the day he died, continued, ". . . I can't seem to find my way out of this desperate depression. I'd try to stick it out, if I didn't think it would recur. . . . I have fought it until I'm worn out. I can no longer bear the loneliness with which I am faced."[168]

Matthiessen had never tried to obscure his homosexuality. Neither, however, had he made an issue of it, a terrible conflict for so honest and forthright a person: "Damn it. I hate to have to hide when what I thrive on is absolute directness," he wrote Cheney, adding that he knew that "the falseness [elsewhere he calls it 'the falseness of my position in the world'] seems to sap my confidence of power." But a homophobic society left him little choice if he was to be the intellectual (indeed, political) activist he determined to be. Such as he attract enemies, to whom one does not freely give ammunition that can be used, however unfairly, to discredit one. Cheney was the safety valve, and as Levin would say so many decades later, "the loneliness of the single life [was] more precarious than what had been, for him, the strain of leading a double life."

Christianity, finally, was not enough; Matthiessen, great fighter that he was, surrendered. His suicide, moreover, in 1950 by no means devastated or even displeased everyone, foremost among them his tormentors in the Boston press in its worst era: "vile and venal," Bernard Carman, one of Matthiessen's students called them, singling out a *Herald* columnist particularly, whose "rabid pursuit of Matthiessen continued beyond the grave" in a "valedictory column [which] set a standard of viciousness" Carman thought "remarkable even in that vicious time and place."[169] It was the same column Harry Levin remembered as so "scurrilous" thirty-two years later ("hard to forget," said Levin, "painful to recollect") when Matthiessen's old tutorial room at Eliot House, filled anew with all his books, was finally dedicated as a permanent memorial to one of the greatest scholars in Harvard's history.

Somewhat, at least, this memorial counteracts Matthiessen's dreadful end, which, as Levin also said, "haunted" a whole generation of his friends and students, some of whom may not have been surprised Matthiessen on his last night eschewed the fashionable hotel closest to where he dined on Beacon Hill—the very literary Lincolnshire, its bar very friendly to liberals and homosexuals and such like—and headed instead for a much more grimy hotel, farther away, and very unfashionable. But it was the right place for how he must have felt without Cheney and, as he saw it, without Harvard, too. Homeless, he jumped; the title of May Sarton's thinly disguised novel seems perfect: *Faithful Are the Wounds.*

4.

A Stoic's Perspective: Ohio Hellenist

There is a chastity of the mind, just as there is a chastity of the body. There are certain creative processes which a sincere thinker would no more reveal to casual eyes than he would strip in a public place. A rule of mental chastity: Do not hold promiscuous mental intercourse. The shallow would intrude into these austere places like picnickers in a sanctuary, littering it with their luncheon refuse.

—Lucien Price

PEDERASTY, ARISTOCRACY, SECRECY, and guilt—that was the overall pattern, the home game, historically, for homosexuals at Harvard. Let us now step back from that larger picture and focus on a less theoretical and more personal discourse; individual lives naturally disclosed varying emphasis as between one facet of the pattern and another, the result of many different perspectives. One such was Lucien Price: the Stoic's perspective.

It is sometimes said of politicians what used to be said of English parsons: individuality is fine, but only to a point. The rule is, you can only be eccentric politically if you are highly acceptable personally and, conversely, you can only be eccentric personally if you are very acceptable politically. By all means keep a lion as a pet, but at the same time be a very traditional Republican; by all means favor colonizing Mars, but be an exemplary family man.

Ditto homosexuals. Especially at Harvard. If you're gay, it's wise to be "good"—and doubly unwise to be "bad" in any sense; which in mainstream American society might include being black, being a socialist or pacifist, a civil libertarian, or an activist of any sort, much less say a spy. Or being prominent—in anything. A conspicuous target is at much greater risk. Noticing this, critic Michael Berthold refers to a kind of continuum of marginality, for example, when he declares that to be both homosexual and a socialist in America has always been to suffer from a "double marginality."[1]

Price added to his homosexual orientation the hardly less dangerous fact that in World War I he was a pacifist; he preferred to hazard jail, with which he was threatened, rather than answer the army's call. He was also a dedicated socialist. On top of all that, he was (depending on your reading of him) certainly non-Christian and probably anti-Christian—in fact, a convinced pagan.[2] Nor was all this kept under wraps; rather, it was evident day in and day out, discreetly in some ways; not, however, in other ways—in Price's editorials for one of Boston's leading newspapers. A pariah Lucien Price should have been—pacifist, socialist, pagan, homosexual, un-American, and unchristian that he was. However, he became one of Harvard's leading graduates and, amazingly, preacher-in-chief to New England and beyond from the 1920s through to the 1950s. Price, Berthold might have said, had to deal with a "quadruple marginality." But deal with it he did. Lucien Price never found himself at that terrible moment Matthiessen did.

Yet he was stoic enough to meet such an event, if he thought suicide the just outcome. Just? Price was a convinced Stoic, though with a strong dash of romanticism. Can one be a romantic Stoic? It would seem so. Certainly Price early mastered himself in his own service, as it were. On the desk in his Beacon Hill sitting room/study stood two statues of those two lovers Aristogiton and Harmodius. Intent on overthrowing the Athenian tyrants of ancient times, the advances of one of whom had been spurned by Harmodius, they slew only that one before themselves being killed. But when the tyranny was overthrown four years later, the two became heroes of democracy, associating male lovers with the upholding of self-government even to the point of tyrannicide.[3] These two Price took as his inspiration; these and Prometheus. Dominating the room—in fact, over his sofa—was a full-length, highly homoerotic male nude of a friend in the character of that hero, not smoldering behind a closed door in Price's bedroom (as was the case years later, in the apartment of a more timid Beacon Hill bachelor, where the now famous black male nude of John Singer Sargent was rediscovered) but right out in the open, in the room in which Price received his friends. Price, though no disturber of the peace, indulged in no cover-ups, either. Indeed, before his life wound down he would become prominently associated with Gore Vidal, the author of the first explicitly homosexual American novel published in the U.S., *The City and the Pillar*. Later, *Julian*, Vidal's bestselling "comeback book" after years of persecution, was dedicated to Lucien Price.[4]

A Message for the Middle Class

PRICE'S FATHER, GRANDFATHER, and great-grandfather were Ohio country doctors. After some years at Western Reserve Academy, in Hudson, Ohio, by all accounts an exacting experience in a school Price observed later was "first-rate" but "poor as Job's turkey" (and in a community where hard country work and a devotion to classical education went hand in hand),

Price came east to Exeter, entering Harvard College in 1903. Chiefly he studied philosophy. Yet another product of the Yard in its "Great Age" (Price's
own words), a student particularly of William James and George Santayana,
he was also active in the glee club and was elected both to the Signet Society,
the leading undergraduate literary club, and the more raucous and theatrical
Hasty Pudding Club. "At the Signet Society dinner table," he wrote later, "I
first heard young men talk well." He seems generally to have been well liked.
Socially, he was a modest success. Among his classmates was the young
Boston Brahmin Samuel Eliot Morison, later an eminent historian (they
remained lifelong friends), and Price's best friend at Harvard, Fred Middleton, who was the scion of a prominent Back Bay mercantile family. Academically, Price was an even greater success and was elected to Phi Beta
Kappa, for instance. Furthermore, though this was the era just after President Eliot's assault on the classical curriculum, Price, who loved the civilization of ancient Greece he'd been introduced to at school back home,
remained an unrepentant classicist; decades later he would recall the thrill
he felt when, in 1906, amid the columned pomps of Harvard Stadium, *Agamemnon* was performed in ancient Greek—that "most sonorous of languages," he always felt. He saw the production three times.

Graduating magna cum laude in 1907, he resisted the lure of teaching at
Harvard, and rather than becoming a don—no more apt candidate could
have been imagined—Price took a job as a newspaper reporter at the prestigious *Boston Transcript*, evidence of a certain independence of mind. The
spartan lifestyle he adopted whilst he was a cub reporter, living at a seaman's
hostel near the East Boston docks, suggests, too, that Price kept his feet
firmly on the ground while embracing fully the new opportunities presented
to him by Harvard and the whole Boston scene. In seven years he rose
through the ranks to become an assistant music and drama critic and, finally,
an editorial writer; all the while he continued to live very frugally so as to
pay his father back the cost of his Harvard tuition. It says as much perhaps
of his and his family's values as of their economic situation that this was
agreed to by all quite cheerfully so as to allow Price's younger brother his
turn at a college education.

Yet all was not well in Zion! Price's mind was ever in motion. In fact,
within five years the classicist had become a socialist as well: his social conscience was awakened by the bitter and violent textile workers' strike of 1912
in the Boston satellite city of Lawrence. The mill workers' conditions that
precipitated the strike shocked Price. "But that was not the story the *Transcript* wanted,"[5] reported Louis Lyons, later curator of the Nieman Foundation at Harvard, in a consideration of Price's early career published decades
later. Lyons's story rings true. Although the *Transcript* was in some ways a
progressive journal, its bread-and-butter readership was Boston's mercantile
ruling class, increasingly troubled in the years before World War I by labor
unrest generally, both in Europe and America, and by the potential for social

instability, to say nothing of disruption of profits. Price's story on the Lawrence strike was rejected by the *Transcript*. "They didn't use it," wrote Lyons, observing that if the mill workers' conditions had been Price's "first awakening," the *Transcript's* decision about not running his story was his second—to the conditions of his own situation.[6] Years later Price wrote bluntly: "I was booted out . . . for having written for *The Atlantic Monthly*, in July, 1914, 'A Message to the Middle Class,' a performance which was considered quite hot then." Using the pen name Seymour Deming, Price had declared: "You are not getting the news. Editors see no demand for news of the rumblings of the industrial revolution. Colleges don't teach it. Ministers don't preach it. . . . A reformer is a dangerous person. The middle class does not understand. It will not listen. It can only intensely resent."[7] Price's article was the making of him, the hinge of his career, according to Lyons: "In 1914 Lucien Price joined the [*Boston*] *Globe*, which for the next 50 years published the work of the most superb essayist and penetrating social philosopher in New England journalism . . . [one of four men who] constituted the editorial staff of the *Globe* . . . [for] just under 50 years. . . . It was one of the most extraordinary teams in the history of journalism."[8] Lyons calls Price "the *Globe's* leading editorial writer"; more accurately, Museum of Fine Arts, Boston, curator W. G. Constable declared that he was "mentor to New England." Yet Lyons hardly would have disagreed, observing once that Price, in his years at the *Globe*, ultimately "made pulpit and classroom of a newspaper page," a page on which his work was read far beyond Boston.

It was all very unlikely and at first Price's foothold at the *Globe* can only have been precarious. The *Globe's* publisher during Price's time there, William O. Taylor, was an "inbred conservative," wrote Lyons, adding, "amazing that so orthodox a publisher presided on the whole so amicably over a liberal newspaper." But Taylor was a shrewd as well as a conservative man, once querying the paper's editor, "Price is about the best writer we have, isn't he?" He was, and if he was more liberal, he was no less shrewd. Though he always made clear the differences between what he called the "owning class" and the "working class" and of both with the "thinking class" (his own, of course, and elite; but open to all), Price had learned a thing or two from his altercation with the powers-that-be at the *Transcript*. One senses well-thought-through tactics in Price's attitude at the *Globe*. A crusader on social issues at first, "later, perhaps in reaction to the communist revolution in Russia, he applied his social conscience less ideologically," wrote Lyons; his primary concern was with the intellectual growth of the individual as the first requisite for a good society." (The *Globe* editorial page was quiescent enough throughout the worldwide furor caused by the Sacco-Vanzetti trial in the late 1920s, for example.) Thus did the socialist become a classicist all over again—though he never ceased to be a socialist in the first place. Perhaps because Price realized early on that he had so much going against him—by his own account he missed "going to jail as a conscientious objector by about twenty days," no idle threat in an era when the conductor of the Boston Symphony was arrested for not playing "The Star-Spangled Banner"— he forged in his own mind a strategy not only of how to be true to himself and his beliefs in a hostile environment, but how to bring the environment around to his way of thinking.[9]

The sources of his inner life were never mysterious or obscured. In his fiftieth Harvard class report he wrote of "Greek, which, with music, was to form the twin preoccupations of my existence"; his "guiding stars" were "Greek poetry and German music." Samuel Eliot Morison put it more largely: "First, the ancient world. [Price] never tired of bringing the writings of Thucydides and dramatists like Aeschylus, Sophocles, and Euripides, to bear on modern problems"—but also "a second source: German Romanticism, especially Goethe's *Faust* and the music-dramas of Wagner."[10] And, not surprisingly, these two predominant inner sources were the subjects of Price's two most characteristic books, for he charged ahead on that front, too. In *Winged Sandals* of 1928, a superb collection of his travel writing for the *Globe*, he went in search of the Greece of Homer's "wine-dark sea." But his first love in no sense blinded him to his second, celebrated in 1936 in *We Northmen*, in which Price probed with equal wit the North European mind—traveling from Oxford and Cambridge to Weimar, touching on Bach and Wagner and Sibelius, the last of whom he came to know and spent some little time with in Finland.[11] Chapters of his book appeared in *The Atlantic Monthly, The Yale Review*, even *The Times* of London.

From these sources, the ancient ones especially, came models of excellence he thought would serve his personal and editorial purposes. Though generally they were not always brought close to home, Price seldom missed a target. Of the much-vaunted legacy of conservative Boston, he made his point in a way calculated to register especially in the monied, conservative halls of the city's State Street banks and trust companies: "An historic past is a credit balance," he admitted, but only "so long as it is not dipped into as principal." On yet another tack to the same place: "Boston Tea Party, anti-Slavery, Hawthorne in *The Scarlet Letter* . . . Unitarians revolting against orthodoxy, and Transcendentalists, headed by Emerson, revolting against dead dogma." These were all examples of how Boston's *tradition* had always "nursed revolution." As he grew older and more eminent, his statements grew, perhaps, more pointed. From the McCarthyite 1950s, for another example, in an editorial mostly about Anne Hutchinson and Mary Dyer (both seventeenth-century dissenters, the one banished, the second hanged on Boston Common), and on the Abolitionists Wendell Phillips, William Lloyd Garrison, and Robert Gould Shaw—Price wrote, risking cliché until the last line: "Not one of these men or women would have gone unscathed from the squalid witch-hunts of the 1949–1955 era. Things don't stay won. . . . And how prone we are to honor dead revolutionists not because they were revolutionists, but because they are dead. . . . [Liberty] has to be earned anew not only by each generation but by each individual . . . for in the end, nobody can liberate me but myself."[12]

Price was infinitely cosmopolitan, very well traveled. Perhaps because of that he was able to catch hold of truths both subtle and elusive about Harvard's own values: Mr. Jameson, for instance, a character Price created for his editorials, was described by Price's biographer, Raymond McClure, in 1965 as

> that curious (since now it is rarely seen in the ever-diminishing numbers of Boston's Anglo-Saxon minority group) reminder of the Yankee gentleman, gentleman not by virtue of possession of exclusive habits of a class with wealth or family tree, but by virtue of personal integrity, an individuality which the Yahoos elect to call eccentricity, and a strong concern for the common welfare. Under the pseudonym "Fabian Forge," Mr. Jameson *fought the prejudices of his own class* [emphasis added] toward the less privileged, fought for the dissenters, the non-conformists, the conscientious objectors. He had what those of an aristocratic class may not always have in sufficient quantity, for the lack of which they eventually go down in defeat: imagination.[13]

Imagination was supremely what Price had, as his editorials showed time and again. Of creativity Price wrote often, for example, warning that talent was not enough, nor even "willingness to drudge," but, above all, "willingness to place . . . talent at the disposal of a mysterious force," acknowledging humbly that "creative force, even in genius, will not be commanded. It will only be obeyed." Not what one expects an editorial to be about. Nor Stendhal. But Price frequently urged writers or thinkers on his readers, and Stendhal he urged with particular force: "One of humanity's rare pieces of good luck, a man not afraid of himself," wrote Price, Stendhal was "highly disconcerting, and therefore all the more worth knowing because to know oneself is to know the world." In a similar way he sought to engage his readers with Goethe. "Most people are young only once; others live a new lifetime each decade. Goethe's eight decades are a succession of adolescences (as he himself said): 'Perish, and become!' . . . That is the key signature of his life. We die continually in order to be born again: it is painful, but it gets results." This, in an *editorial*! No less incredible is the fact of the three other works he urged on his readers in the same editorial as necessary to their understanding: the *Agamemnon* of Aeschylus, Shakespeare's *Hamlet*, and Michelangelo's frescoes on the Sistine Chapel ceiling![14]

It was, truly, his art form, the editorial—or if you prefer, the essay. Yet, as Lyons pointed out, "Price never wrote down. He brought his readers up," and in a "rushing century he pointed," said the great Harvard classicist John H. Finley, "to the longer directions."[15] And often in the most practical of ways. Too few school teachers, or doctors of education, have understood the truth of Price's straightforward educational theory, for example, about the training of boys. But Price knew both sides of the matter, and connected them:

> Youths' articles of faith are two. One is athletics. . . . the other is [the] passionate delight of the awakened mind.
>
> What a stupid superstition it is that boys naturally detest study! What they do detest is a bore. . . . Give me a hero schoolmaster and I will guarantee that the intellectual passion gets kindled in any mind that is combustible. . . .
>
> Reticent, self-contained, a shade taciturn—[the master Homer O. Sluss had] the mind of a stoic housed in the body of an Olympian athlete. His classroom discipline . . . [was] a look. Yet his power [was] not intimidation. Besides, he [kept] us too interested to think of misbehaving.[16]

Is a school of dance any different? In this case Price had an immediate and practical effect, as attested by the American dance pioneer Ted Shawn: "Without [Price's] constant help for seven years the most important chapter of my own career would never have happened," Shawn wrote. "The prodigious athleticism of dancers like Vaslav Nijinsky notwithstanding, dance remained associated in the public's mind with 'feminine' grace and sensitivity. . . . [Dancers were looked upon] as 'pansies.' " And the earliest attempt to attack this stereotype head-on was the All-Male Dancers Group, established by Shawn in the U.S. in 1933. Shawn and his wife, Ruth St. Denis, founded the Denishawn schools, today credited with establishing modern dance as an important American art form. Dedicated as he was, in Julia Foulkes's words, to "re-cast[ing] the effeminate image of the sissy into a hardened, heroic, dancing American athlete," Shawn won Price's wholehearted support, based, Foulkes writes, on Price's agreement with Shawn's idea "to re-create a Greek ideal in his group of male dancers, combining athletic grace, philosophical import and the quest for beauty through the male body."[17]

Does the nature—and scope—of Price's life grow clearer here? I find it easy to miss; recounting his story carries you along in the telling—just as it did in his lifetime in the doing—to what were obviously his interests, but does not always disclose fully some of the deeper strata. Notice that while Price's need to live frugally was not in doubt, nor his insights into boys' education, seamen's hostels, boys' schools, and male dance suggest another interest of Price's as much as did his nude Prometheus. Yet New England saw all and saw nothing. Listen to his biographer, Raymond McClure, in respect to one of Price's most conspicuous burdens—not being Christian in, of all places, Boston, city of the Puritans, by Price's day also a bastion of Roman Catholicism. And when a Jewish center, Brandeis University, was established in Boston after World War II, the best McClure can muster is this from Price in 1922: "What . . . have we from Israel except a religion which we mostly don't use?" In *Winged Sandals* he mitigated that harsh judgment only to the extent of adding: "Hebrewism and Hellenism: I suppose the world needs both." It was not exactly a ringing endorsement, no more of Judaism than of Christianity. "Lucien felt," his biographer explained, "that there was something missing in the Christian ethos."[18] Did his readers notice how labored McClure's explanation sounded when he wrote that Price "didn't consider himself to be a Christian in the historical—and to him—narrow sense"? Or how pagan or Hellenist Price was? "Since popular [i.e., Christian] concepts of sin, guilt, hell and salvation were somewhat alien to Lucien's austere thought and his stoic attitude toward life and death, he reverted to certain Hellenic concepts . . . *hamartia* (the missed shot—try again, and discipline yourself not to repeat the error); *hubris* (overweening pride, arrogance—failure to overcome which surely brings *nemesis* or retribution); *areté* (that excellence in virtue which should be the aim of living)."[19] Price beyond question identified with Socrates' repeated complaints of people's "ignorance of how to achieve one's excellence or *areté* . . . a highly complex word," as Bernard Dick explains, "that means, among other things, being good at one's craft." But as Dick shows in his reading of an early novel by Mary Renault that plays into her later *The King Must Die*, there is much more to *areté*. In that novel "Vivien and Mic [the two protagonists] achieve their *areté*, but in another sense of this remarkable word—self-knowledge as well as professional perfection. Their self-knowledge, however, was attained only through the death of Jan [Vivien's look-alike brother], and the love they find at the end of the novel is a sober, asexual kind . . . The author allows *each of them* [emphasis added] to experience the consequences of a sacrificial offering." Indeed, writes Dick, Renault's novel ascends to explore "the ultimate stage of Platonic love, mutual affection (*philia*)."[20]

Price was gifted with but then denied that mutual experience, and while the gift can sustain one for many years, its repercussions so fine that even its withdrawal (temporary or permanent; how can one ever know) seems bearable, the events do not leave the soul unwounded. The man in Price's life—his great love—was Fred Middleton, who, after graduating from Boston Latin School, entered Harvard in Price's class. Whether on walking tours through New England, Nova Scotia, and across Central Europe, or sailing along the coast of Maine, Lucien and Fred, who gave up State Street finance for farming (surely one of the few Harvard graduates besides Thoreau, perhaps, to become an orchardist), formed the deepest of relationships—soul mates forever—though what Price saw in Middleton, a man of hardly comparable worldly endowment, it is hard to say. McClure speaks of "Fred's integrity, his honesty with himself . . . the warmth of his spirit . . . his rare and sensitive nature," and—unusually bluntly for the era—how he had always "to be exercising his mind earnestly—painfully, he sometimes confessed—in an effort to come up with something that was a little out of reach." McClure also observes that, in running what became a big farm, Fred, more conservative, was "a healthful foil to Lucien, who was somewhat of a visionary idealist in matters involving the 'common man' that Fred had to deal with in the field of labor relations."[21]

Soul mates or no, the idyll did not last. Whether there was an estrangement I cannot be sure. McClure says little, but that little is telling: "The David-Jonathan friendship was interrupted" by Fred's marriage to Evelyn Stowe. The wording is key. Though Price, in classic fashion, was best man, McClure suggests a fundamental difficulty in his résumé of the storyline of a novel by Price, a novel known to be based on him and Fred: the Price and Middleton characters, McClure notes, "were finally reunited . . . in the autumn of their years. *In real life this was not to be* [emphasis added]." Yet Lucien never ceased to love Fred, whatever happened on the other side. So much so that he told McClure he could not bring himself to attend Fred's funeral. Price himself, moreover, was dead within three months of Fred's death.[22]

Heartache? Probably. Yet there was also that astonishing boon of the gods (as Price might have said) offering yet another Fred—Fred Demmler, a Boston artist, evidence perhaps of another dictum of Price's: "The more you love, the more love you are given to love with." This relationship is much more accessible to us because Price wrote of it at length in a biographical sketch of Demmler, *Immortal Youth* (1919), in which one sometimes has the feeling that Price is conflating both Freds in his memories—idealized memories—of one. Just as *College Friends*, which we discussed in Chapter 1, details a Harvard man in love with another man in Harvard Yard and then in the Union Army during the Civil War, and *Harvard Episodes* and *The Cult of the Purple Rose* disclose the more Wildean lifestyle of late-Victorian Harvardians, so does *Immortal Youth* describe a Harvard man in love with another on Beacon Hill on the verge of World War I.

Immortal Youth

PRICE'S BOOK BEGINS frankly enough, like *College Friends*, with a pickup—in this case, too, of one young man by another:

> There was a humble restaurant on Charles Street. . . . Across the table one evening in the spring of that year [1912] sat a young man about twenty-four years old. Anyone would have taken a second look at him; also a third, a fourth, and as many more. . . . The dark eyes . . . the rugged features . . . The hands; very large and finely muscled. (I have never seen a more beautiful pair of hands on a human being.) It was all of these things and none of them. Rather it was the look of one with immense forces in reserve, bound on an errand. . . .
>
> Was this stranger conversible? He was. Presently he was speaking of

the colonial doorways on Chestnut Street with a discrimination that suggested the architect. No. It appeared that he was studying . . . at the Boston Museum School. . . .

He climbed Beacon Hill with me to the house where I lived. . . .

He promptly took off his coat, displaying in the rays of a green-shaded student lamp a pair of forearms worthy of the hands that went with them. . . . He stretched out his long legs on a cot which did duty by the fireplace as a sofa. . . .

Was he talkative? Not much! . . . He would and he would not. Shy, reserved, proud, devoured with ambition, savagely determined, a prey to some misgivings, genuinely modest, and anxious to talk it over with the right person, but by no means sure who the right person was.

On sped the ambrosial hours of the spring evening. . . .

He had rowed [in college] in his class eight. . . . hence that physical self-respect which betokens the young man accustomed unconcernedly to strip in a college boathouse or gymnasium. But to eyes grown impatient with the college athlete's all too customary intellectual torpor and social complacency it was a holiday to find this well-made body, tall, broad in the shoulder, narrow at hips, lean and muscular, housing also the brain of a thinker and the spirit of the pioneer.[23]

The talk that night was on "the conflict between the artist and the trader," a theme invariable among young men, "and which for Fred it was to be." Lucien, only twenty-nine and himself an athlete—he rowed regularly into his late sixties—was described once as a "handsome youth . . . blond, [with] blue eyes, very bright." So perhaps Fred was as keen as Lucien, whose emphasis, significantly, in his account, is as much on Fred's body as his mind, the former a theme announced by an illustration on the title page; facing a frontispiece of the (fully clothed) Fred, the title-page sketch is of Michelangelo's (quite unclothed) David.[24]

It is a subject—Fred's body—that Price does not drop. Here is the coda of a day's hike along Cape Anne, on Boston's North Shore, as the two men made their way back to their base at Gloucester. The ellipses are Price's: "Past midnight, stumping dog-tired into the inn; cold meat and bread, ravenously devoured; bed, and the sleep of the just. . . . Morning; and such a morning as never was. Quite forgetting to dress, Fred lost himself staring out of the open window at the quaint harbor, the fishing fleet, the blue bay and the gaunt headlands until it was suggested to him that passersby might be enjoying him as much as he was enjoying the morning." The suggestion, presumably, was Price's. "Morning; and such a morning as never was." Similarly, Price is surely recalling the best of fantasies another time (or was he there?) when Fred was one with nature: "And withal he was half pagan. . . . The ugliness of modern clothes disgusted him. He was alert for chances to take off his own: impromptu baths in cold brooks on walking trips. . . . There was some place among the mountains . . . where he used to go. . . . When the moon had risen he loved to steal away for a plunge in the river, then lie out naked in the moonlight on these great slabs of warm rock, alone with the magic night." Magic indeed and almost—though not quite— pornographic, though it goes against the grain to suggest that even now of Price's feelings, which are conveyed with real delicacy.[25]

Also conveyed in *Immortal Youth* is a sense of rough masculinity. Here is his description—also a splendid example of Price's style generally—of the Beacon Hill locale of *Immortal Youth*:

> A once aristocratic residential street now reduced to a teeming thoroughfare; pedestal to Beacon Hill; narrow, ill-paved, spattered with mud to the second story, double row of tall, brick houses, where Thackeray and Dickens were once guests, now placarding "rooms to let"; assorted antique shops and restaurants,—"the long unlovely street." . . . yet with a certain wistful charm in its decayed gentility: that is Charles Street.
>
> Number 94 . . . the art colony [was on] the fifth-floor-back. . . . The young barbarians were usually out.
>
> It was a colony of three. . . . Their room was a first act stage-set for an American version of *La Bohème*. There was an iron bed and a cot . . . a writing table strewn with pipes, unanswered letters . . . drawing pens . . . jars holding bouquets of paint brushes . . . the place reeked with that heavenly odor of paint tubes. . . .
>
> Their windows looked into a deep courtyard formed by a triangle of tall brick houses,—the rears of houses on Charles and Brimmer Streets . . . all enclosing a tiny greensward. . . . In the farthest corner of this court rise the walls of mullioned windows of the Church of the Advent. . . . But I was never able to observe that it produced any pietistic tone in Number 94. On the contrary they affected to take a lively interest in the upper windows of the houses opposite and threatened to keep a pair of field glasses. . . .
>
> One always [looked up in passing to see if the windows] were lighted, . . . [and if so] it was impossible not to go up; for in that room there was always some form of what is technically known as "trouble."

It is all, notice, the reverse of "arty" in any sense. Asked why the spartan decor, Fred made perhaps an unexpected reply: "I keep it bare on purpose," he confided, "to frighten away loafers." It was a response with more than one meaning, as Price explains: there was the conviction that one should "not hold promiscuous mental intercourse," for "the shallow [are] . . . like picnickers, littering," and to be avoided at all costs. "It appeared," wrote Price, "that certain amiable slayers of their own and others' time, envisaging a studio of divans, Russian cigarettes, tea and twaddle, paid one visit, and only one."[26] Whitmanic, not Wildean, even among artists.

Price might have written the party scene in Mary Renault's *The Chari-*

oteer, in which the author makes what Bernard Dick calls a "valuable distinction" between homosexual men who "strive to be males and achieve a certain measure of *andreia* [Greek for manliness or courage]; and men who strive to be women and only succeed in acquiring the worst qualities of the female. [The two males] are noticeably uncomfortable in the presence of dancing couples and bitchy queens. The entire sequence is a kind of anti-*Symposium* where soggy erudition (an outrageous synopsis of the *Odyssey*) and witless repartee ('What's he got that I haven't?') prevail over rational discourse."[27] I think again of A. L. Rowse's conviction that manliness is something to be gained by "moral effort." Price would certainly have agreed.[28]

Comes World War I, of course, and the windows go dark on this school for men; but before Fred ships out to France there are the (not very) fraught farewells, the occasion for the old all-male prep school ritual: the asking for a photograph (the closest one gets to saying anything aloud) and the gruff assent (the closest one comes to reciprocating). In Price's story, the dialogue goes like this:

> I asked him for a picture of himself. . . . "What size would you like?"
> "Small enough so that it can go wherever I go."
> He made no promises. His way was to wait until the time came and
> then let the performance speak.
> Not three weeks later it came. . . .
> Strangers seeing it remark "What a striking face!"
> His friends view it and say, "He was much finer looking than that."[29]

Fred, of course, never came home; he was killed in action in Belgium—of which Price says neither too much nor too little, working and grieving his way through something more than love as most of us know it, accepting not the blame but the responsibility, as the older man must, making the loss of both Freds into something more than good. Not only would there be *Immortal Youth*, and a later opus, *All Souls*, but forty years of editorials published each year on the second of November, from 1918 to the 1950s. Not even one verged on morbid, though his subjects were ever grave enough, and even by Price's standards these editorials are extraordinary literature, soon enough recognized as such. Beacon Press eventually brought them out in book form under the title *Litany for All Souls*.

Price's annual All Souls essay began in the melancholy induced by reflection on Fred's death, but it was a melancholy always informed by the author's Hellenist perspective, as was the joy of Fred in life, a perspective just dissonant enough in so determinedly Judeo-Christian a culture to arrest the tired mind at day's end:

> On such nights as these of clear skies and bustling winds which set leaves
> swirling and surf resounding on the granite shores of the seagirt head-

land, those glittering stars are eyes that as they peer and sparkle, say ever more clearly on this Feast Day of the Dead: "Eternal beings that we are, we ask you, mortal: What do you make of your mortality?[30]

Fred was seen as a part of "a mysterious coming and going between the quick and the dead." ("Those who know most about it say the least . . . fearful lest revealing it in speech should break the contact," wrote Price.) *Not* a spiritualist, but a Hellenist, Price forthwith opines: "What could we wish for [our dead] better but another life," he asks, especially for those like Fred, dead when hardly thirty. "Then how if that life be our own?" Price does not fail to add: "Has the body a soul? No. The soul has a body."[31]

After the Hellenist custom, Price, a dedicated and lifelong athlete, was hardly the man to disparage the body. He wasn't doing that. Though for him the body is the soul's and not vice versa, Price urges the virtue of the ancient way he saw in the young Fred (both of them), and took as model and held up in turn to others, by using the mode of the body as his continuing reference point. This was not unwise in an increasingly sports-minded Anglo-American culture—popular sports being then almost entirely male and more amateur and collegiate than professional—a culture in which the almost universal-seeming folk traditions of manly behavior was a continuing alternative Price knew he could count on in lieu of the more specifically Christian moral teaching he wished to avoid. In Price's belief system (what we would now call, in an era when non-Christian sermons are welcome even in Harvard's Memorial Church, "faith tradition"), Fred's behavior, manly behavior, spoke to the dialogue or tension between body and soul he made so much of. Witness this from his 1929 All Souls entry: "To put more into [life] than we take out; to give without asking too narrowly what or even whether we shall receive; this is the sportsmanship of the soul, as high and fine—higher and finer—than the sportsmanship of the body which we call courage."[32]—Far from disparaging the body, Price finds it beautiful in every sense. Furthermore, he tweaks the worthy but seemingly commonplace idea that it matters less whether one wins or loses but how one plays: "The answer to despair is hope, the retort to misfortune is generosity. Does the grim Poker Player seem to hold a winning hand? Raise the ante! The very willingness to accept the discipline of failure constitutes a victory. Did I lose on a lower field? On a higher I won."[33]

In this vein Price essayed his best sustained writing; at once he asks, and the reader is really driven to answer:

Were there not certain exquisite moments during the journey . . . an instant of two hearts beating each to each? . . . When the fingers of your first baby closed round your own; or it might have been a forward movement of troops in battle, such strange creatures we are! delighting to destroy as well as to create—which made all the rest worthwhile. . . . The drama had great moments which I felt and understood, and in them I have already tasted eternal life.[34]

One glimpses Fred Middleton's loss as much as Fred Demmler's in these editorials, in Price's counsel that "when our lives lie in ruins, our loves in ashes," there is a duty to be sympathetic: "Give sympathy like the cool touch of blessing hands to those who suffer," he admonishes, "but save your sorrow for those to whom such ordeals never come, for those souls are dead, and there is no death like their death." He was apt to contrast that situation with another: to cling to anything "in selfish desperation" is to lose it; "he only may possess who has the strength to renounce." Those who don't know their Aeschylus will find only loss in suffering; one can really hear Price talking to himself. "Life," he wrote, "seems lent to us to see how we will use it. The pressure of pain seems put on us to see how we will behave. Is not suffering sent in order that from it we may learn? Does not evil exist in order that by us it may be turned to good? What if evil and good should prove to have been parts of the same thing.... Looking back on the bitterest of our days ... If they were borne bravely, even sweetly, then by now they have begun turning to good.... Hardship is for growth, happiness for recuperation."

New England did well to listen. Above all to what was, I think, his culminating sermon: "To fight well in confident expectation of victory is the proper valor of youth; the virtue of mature years is to fight equally in the face of a strong prospect of frustration.... Not until one is willing to lose is he worthy to win. Sportsmanship is all." In old age, too: then virtue was to muster "the determination to keep working after the future has lost its sanguine hue, working as valiantly as when prizes still gleamed ... to keep putting forth the same effort, not on faith (since faith so naïve is no longer possible) but on principle, even from sheer force of habit; this, while still in the fray, is to be above the battle."[35]

No wonder *The Harvard Crimson* once called Price a "Periclean Hellene." Although the source of the tribute is not unimportant (Price's following at Harvard was always considerable: Samuel Eliot Morison, one of the foremost American historians of the mid-twentieth century, not given to exaggerating others' influence, went so far as to thank Price in one book for having shaped decisively his style of writing; and in another book for having "first opened to me the beauty of the Pilgrim story"; quite an acknowledgment for a New England scholar), Price's own mentors were both near and far away. He knew and was much influenced by two renowned modern British classical scholars, Sir Richard Livingstone and Gilbert Murray, and was particularly close to the French writer and mystic Romain Rolland, whose *Jean-Christophe* won the Nobel Prize for literature in 1915. But the most vital influence on Price was indeed to be found at Harvard, the British philosopher and mathematician Alfred North Whitehead. A celebrated figure, whose students at Cambridge included Bertrand Russell and John Maynard Keynes, when he took up his chair at Harvard in 1924, in his early sixties and at the start of a decade of considerable achievement, Whitehead found Price—by then a member of Harvard's senior governing board, the Overseers—to be his Boswell. Price's *Dialogues of Alfred North Whitehead* became his best-known book, and Price the most important popularizer of Whitehead's philosophy: the prohibition against treating half-truths as whole truths; the dictum "all generalizations are false, including this one"; above all, the postulate "the process is the reality"—these Price himself conveyed to the world far more accessibly than ever did Whitehead. As to the last postulate, Price put it this way: "Nothing stays put; not objects, ideas, philosophies, religions, cosmologies, sticks, stones, trees. . . . Nothing is except as it is becoming, the universe is all process, and the process is itself the actuality."[36]

Gore Vidal, Golden Eagles

PRICE'S LAST ACT was as good as his first or even his second; he survived betrayal, the form tragedy took in his life, and which was ever his deepest subject: "What we can do," as he put it, "about what we can do nothing about." Is *betrayal* the right word, either for Fred I's marriage or Fred II's death?[37] David Hare's play *The Judas Kiss* comes to mind, with its assertion that life is inevitably "a series of betrayals." (Says Hare: "I've betrayed as many people as I've been betrayed by. . . . Treachery is just deep human life."[38]) And betrayal can be as simple (depending on your point of view) as parents who decide to have a second child, or as complicated as the traitor in John le Carré's *Tinker, Tailor, Soldier, Spy* whose betrayal of King and Country is the result in large part of too deep a love to survive disillusion-ment.[39] All of which accords very well with the underlying thesis of *The Judas Kiss*, which explores two incidents in Oscar Wilde's life. Never mind the negativity of always killing the thing you love; Wilde's enduring thesis is that "you only see the true person when you love." And that "love is not the illusion, life is." Hare sees what Wilde saw (and Price, too): "Honesty is not as simple as saying what you're feeling. It's [also] the effect of what you say. It's how the other person receives what you say. . . . It isn't honest to recriminate. Wilde comes to us," Hare concludes, "so wise about the idea that honesty is almost always as much of a pose as hypocrisy. You can never really be honest. All you can be is generous. All you can be is giving."[40]

Price exactly. After all, it was, in a sense, his religion, explained aptly by the distinguished classicist Edward Salmon:

> Plato discusses friendship (philia) most fully as an aspect of erotic desire (eros). In the *Symposium*, Plato extends the Socratic psychology by mak-ing the ultimate goal of all desire . . . being happy forever. Within this world, this may be achieved . . . through passing on one's physical life to

a child, or one's mental life to a beloved. . . . The ladder of love then advances the lover's attention from persons, through practices, laws, and sciences, to the Form of Beauty, until his goal becomes to beautify his (and arguably also a beloved's) soul by the light of Form.[41]

Is it any surprise then to learn—it was the strategy of Price's survival of betrayal—that he all but made a profession of mentoring young men (everything from advice and a good dinner to concert tickets, or money for books, or travel, or even tuition, and no thanks asked). As his biographer detailed:

> Some had meager backgrounds and they needed guidance. . . . Some were troubled, uncertain of what step to take, and they were reassured. . . . The prime value . . . [was] the revelation to [all] of them of what constitutes the good life, the exhortation to live the self-examined, the self-criticized life, the posting of the ideal of creative living. . . . The young man was expected to be ambitious, not afraid of work, somewhat of an idealist, and possessed of enough gray matter. . . . It helped, immeasurably, of course, if, besides sharing Lucien's interest in literature and music, he was curious about Ancient Greece.[42]

It also helped if the young man's sound mind resided in the classical sound body, as I can attest, having been one of Price's young men (introduced to him by my publisher uncle, the American publisher of Wilde touched on in Chapter 1). McClure, of course, did not dare to say that; nor that this was a classic pattern, one that William Cobb, for example, a classicist at the College of William and Mary, elucidates very well in his translation of Plato's erotic dialogues, entitled *The Symposium and the Phaedrus:*

> That eros is initially understood to be sexual desire is obvious. . . . Moreover, the possibility is also raised that eros has much greater significance than the more sexual desire, so that sexual desire is only a limited manifestation of something more profound. . . . [In Socrates's views] eros is seen as the means of actualizing the highest potentialities of human being through achieving an understanding of the ultimate principle of beauty, which is the ultimate object of eros. Here is found the life that human beings are truly fit for.[43]

For Price, of course, a born don, it was very right, this vocation of his, the practical acting out of the philosophical views we've seen in his All Souls editorials—his "Fred" editorials. Those he mentored were interesting to him not only in themselves (that, too, I can attest) but in honor of, in memory of, in lieu of—take your pick—Fred reluctant or Fred dead. Enter Gore

Vidal, himself not a Harvard man, though as we saw earlier a member of that select club who deliberately evaded that fate.

Price, nearly seventy-one, and Vidal, only twenty-nine, met in 1954, when the older man was at his height (it was the very year, in fact, of his big book on Whitehead) and the younger man at perhaps the lowest point in his career, dark days for the now-celebrated essayist, playwright, novelist, and historian, then hoping for some success for his novel of that year, *Messiah*. A brilliant work, highly controversial, it doubtless appealed to Price just because it was very anti-Christian. Price spied the book's genius at once and—the dream of every author—dedicated himself to seeing that the reviews in at least one major American city would be laudatory. Not only that: in 1955 Price made Vidal's book the subject of a lead *Globe* editorial, a fascinating example of the way he seemed, even in the '50s, quite unrepressed at the *Globe*.

Nor was Vidal's book just a case of a little harmless, titillating literary paganism. There was in Vidal's situation a very conspicuous and widely known homosexual dimension. And no subtext, either. Since the publication of his blatantly homosexual novel only six years previously, *The City and the Pillar* (1948), Vidal had been blackballed by the literary powers that be in more than one way. Though his seminal novel later would become a *New York Times* bestseller, Vidal recalls in *Palimpsest*, his autobiography: "For twenty years—and more—I was regularly attacked. . . . Orville Prescott, the daily reviewer for *The New York Times*, told my editor that he would never read much less review another book by me. *Time* and *Newsweek* followed suit. Seven novels went unnoticed in their pages. I was also carefully erased from the glittering history of American Literature. . . . In order to make a living, I was forced into television, movies, theater, and the essay." (Admitted Vidal in a later interview, "I was practically destroyed. My friend John Horne Burns *was* destroyed.")[44] Price's decision to editorialize on Vidal's behalf in a major American metropolitan newspaper must have meant a good deal. Vidal's biographer, Fred Kaplan, describes Price as becoming Vidal's "old mentoring friend and admirer," a friend, moreover, Kaplan notes, who was "supportive when Gore's literary career in the 1950's had looked grim."[45] Vidal himself wrote of Price in the mid-1960s: "In the dark days [he] was a most bright companion."[46]

The relationship endured. Six years later Price's letters confirm his continued interest in Vidal: "While Gore is here (another week), I am spending available time with him," Price wrote a friend in 1960, "and at the performances [of the Boston tryout of Vidal's play, *The Best Man*]."[47] Vidal was often in Boston in those years, drawn to friends from Exeter who were then at Harvard, and later his publishers were in Boston; indeed, he thought through *The Best Man* during three weeks in Provincetown in 1959, doubtless sometimes in company with Price, who, Vidal later disclosed, had an influence on *Julian*, "at least half of [which he read in manuscript]," Vidal wrote.[48]

And surely enjoyed every word of that novel about the emperor who tried to roll back the Christian tide and restore Hellensim. ("When the rough going came," Price said, in one of his few entirely personal allusions, "it was Plato, not Jesus, who saw me through.")[49] And, in this case, the context of Price's shared thoughts with Vidal on *Julian* has been well discerned by Robert F. Kiernan, who caught also what Price and Vidal shared with the novel's protagonist:

> Ever since the New Hellenism of the late-nineteenth century, the historical Julian has been respected both as the legislator of a religious tolerance the world was not to see again until many centuries after his death and as the lonely defender of a culture more noble in its decline than upstart Christianity. He has come to symbolize, in effect, a kind of doomed political intelligence too refined for this world. Vidal permits Julian a measured amount of this appeal because he shares Julian's liberality and anti-Christian sentiment.[50]

Years later Vidal himself allowed that the great comeback book of his career "would not have been written without [Lucien Price's] bright example and sly maneuverings."[51] A bit mysterious, that, but many a bright evening's companionship is surely to be imagined between Price and Vidal in the older man's modest Beacon Hill lodgings: two rooms, third floor back, a small bedroom and a larger study/sitting room—in the larger room a wall of books, a big writing table piled with manuscripts and journals, a lowboy, a sink in the corner for washing up (bathroom down the hall), an upholstered wing chair facing the wood-burning fireplace, a sofa, and above the sofa the glory of the room—the vivid oil of the chained Prometheus, at once creative force and masculine beauty: the work of Arthur Spear, the model one of Price's young men, Neil Stewart. At seventy-one, and just having given up his daily row (though not his regular swim at the Y), Price still "reveled in the beauty of form and action of athletes," in McClure's words, and he delighted in studying his Prometheus in the season's changing light.[52] Doubtless, too, the young Gore Vidal, who, if not quite Prometheus, probably seemed to Price not out of place on his sofa under it. I never pass his old door on Hancock Street without thinking of him. Price, who had lived for years in the bohemian quarter of Beacon Hill, but on Pinckney Street, moved to the third floor of 75 Hancock Street three years before meeting Vidal— and memories of his room there evoke for me Vidal's about his travels in Greece.

From *Palimpsest*:

Over the years, I have made several pilgrimages to Delphi. Today, the place is ruined for me—everything fenced in, so one cannot wander through the Sacred Enclosure at night and brood on the eagle-shaped mountain that rises above the Castalian Spring. During the day golden eagles used to be a common sight in the sky above the theater of Apollo, where, the year before my first visit, a famous actor played Prometheus in the ancient theater. At the play's end, Prometheus is bound to his rock, liver gnawed at by a vulture. Then, just as Prometheus curses Zeus and pronounces an anathema upon the gods, three golden eagles suddenly appeared in the sky above the actor's head and circled him slowly as he shouted to heaven, "I am wronged!"[53]

Sad to report, so was Price at the end, in the matter of his major work, a novel entitled *All Souls*. "The paramount achievement of his life," his biographer calls it, a work that "consum[ed] forty years of [Price's] available time and incalculable amounts of his energy, thought, and writing skill," even I have never read it through completely. Indeed, it never found a publisher. Finally Price found it necessary to print the novel at his own expense, distributing a few hundred copies, a stinging rejection for a much-published literary figure of Price's stature. It was another betrayal. Nor is the reason hard to find. After the fashion of the early twentieth century, *All Souls* was a *roman fleuve*, or novel cycle, in eight volumes. Moreover, McClure is right to describe it as a "most imposing edifice to fraternal love and creative activity." Hellenistic religious tradition as well as homosexuality are at the work's heart, as McClure allows in all but words, admitting, too, that "some may have found in *All Souls* a negative force tearing at the fabric of the Christian ethic." Nor was Price's socialism scanted. Indeed, the "three central issues" personified in Price's novel of ideas are "religion, property and sex"— or paganism, socialism and homosexuality, the last most problematic of all, as McClure makes plain in his defensive attitude toward how Price "relegate[s] boy-girl love affairs to a minor position in his work." McClure insists that in *All Souls* there is "neither the intent to denigrate, in the slightest degree, love between man and woman, nor the desire to exalt, for its own sake, affection between men."[54] Yet it reminds one that not a few of the most powerful arguments of antiquity *for* homosexuality were hardly very positive to women. As far back as the third or fourth century, *Erôtes*, by pseudo-Lucian advocates male-male love on the following basis, in classicist M. Morgan Holmes's words:

Marriage to women was invented out of reproductive necessity, whereas love for men was cultivated for its beauty . . . ; though animals do not engage in homosexual love neither do they know anything of philosophy or friendship. . . . Callicratidas [in so arguing] departs from normative hierarchical pederasty by envisioning an Aristotelian friendship between equals that also includes sexual relations.[55]

It is all very well today, when the Western world's marketplace of ideas is so much bigger and freer, but it was quite otherwise in the 1950s and '60s. To the repeated rejection of Price's life's work McClure allowed himself in 1965 only the mild remonstrance: "Lucien's views on these central issues [paganism, socialism, and homosexuality] were more startling when he first began to express them forty years ago," he writes, clearly indicating that as early as the 1920s Price—like James Mills Peirce before him—was a very early riser insofar as matters gay are concerned.

The centerpiece—hardly a surprise—of *All Souls* is Price's Harvard chum and best friend and life's great love, Fred Middleton, after whom, McClure recounts, one of the two chief characters in *All Souls* is "rough modeled."[56] The other, of course, is Price. Both, moreover, are cast as members of the Sacred Band of homosexual lovers of the ancient Theban army. Almost, but not quite, McClure abandons denial: "The shortcomings and problems to be found in the conduct of some individuals in both relationships have been documented under the names of Freud, Kinsey, and Wolfenden. Examples of male friendship involving such historical figures as Plato, Michelangelo, and Leonardo down to humble G.I.'s in Korea have been well publicized. . . . *All Souls* depicts dedicated male friendships as one of the central themes in its presentation of the joys and sorrows, and mysteries of life and death." Wolfenden? That's the Wolfenden Report, or, more properly, the British Parliament's Report of the Committee on Homosexual Offenses and Prostitution, of 1957, prompted by the Church of England; the report advised the decriminalization of private homosexual relations. And it is the closest McClure gets to the H-word in his biography of Price.[57] No one else got that far. In his *Globe* obituary—Lucien Price died on 30 March 1964—the story appeared on the front page, but made no mention at all of his major literary work; only *The Harvard Crimson*, to its everlasting credit, noted *All Souls*.[58] A nice contrast not only to the *Globe*, but to Price's old school, in Ohio, to which he left (along with his books) his cherished *Prometheus*, which is no longer anywhere to be found. That Price was among the school's most beloved and honored alumni doubtless only made it more necessary to lie about him and to obscure his homosexuality.

Price would not have let any of this get him down; insistently, he urged his readers that "to have given more than one took, to have produced more than one consumed . . . that is to leave the world in our debt. . . . At the end of such a career death collects no dues."[59] I am reminded of Mary Renault's image at the end of *Fire from Heaven* of a golden eagle clutching a snake in its talons. "The powerful vision is Homeric," writes Bernard Dick, "the eagle, the sacred bird of Zeus, was a symbol of masculinity."[60]

5.

Away: Left Bank, Red Square, Harlem, Greenwich Village

Heterosexuals, especially Christian heterosexuals, are expert at calling upon homosexuals to deny themselves the consolations they themselves could not live without.

—Bishop Richard Holloway,
Primus of Scotland

HOME AND AWAY—the invariable rhythm of the collegiate year: Boston and its orbit—Harvard's home base—is hardly half the picture for an institution that over the years has projected its life into every state of the union and every country of the world, determined not to decline any engagement with what one eighteenth-century trustee of another old college (Princeton, determined to be religiously and culturally purer than Harvard) called "a promiscuous converse with the world, that theater of folly and dissipation." And if the home game for homosexuals at Harvard, as we've seen, disclosed a distinctive pattern—pederasty, aristocracy, secrecy, and guilt—the marks of the away game in the Harvard gay experience are just as discoverable. They are also four: politics, repression, rage, and prophecy, to which—though whether this is a change in fact or just in being more candid about it is scarcely knowable—a possible fifth mark of the away game is an observably greater emphasis on sex; say, four plus one.

Away? How away? Furthest, perhaps, and the most exotic possible introduction to this side of things, is the example of Thomas Whittemore, whose Boston life we touched on in Chapter 3, but who spent most of his career overseas. A character so amazing authors took him as inspiration more than once—most notably Graham Greene in "Convoy to West Africa" (1946), in which Whittemore is the basis of "X"; and Evelyn Waugh in *When the Going Was Good*, in which Whittemore figures as "Professor W"—Whittemore was also an early mentor of Gertrude Stein,[1] and a friend of Matisse, one of whose portraits of Whittemore is now in the Fogg Art Museum.

A memorable figure of 1890s Harvard—although he took his A.B., in 1894, at Tufts, where he went on to teach—it was as a graduate student at

Harvard in 1895–1898 that Whittemore bloomed. Though an aesthete, he later distinguished himself by prodigious relief work for the French Red Cross during World War I and by similar efforts thereafter in Russia, all the while becoming so notable a Byzantine scholar that Turkey's founder, Kemal Atatürk, gave his imprimatur to Whittemore's appointment in 1931 to begin the restoration of Hagia Sophia in Istanbul; once the greatest church in Christendom, by then a mosque, it was then slated to become (as it is now) a museum. Whittemore, "at once abstemious, mysterious, elegant, pensive and positive ... an aesthete with an iron will," in the words of William MacDonald, his biographer in the *Dictionary of American Biography,* was a man as much at home in Istanbul as in Boston, though it was notable how well Harvard Yard shaped this short, slight, and very sharp Quentin Crisp character, who never married, of course, and spent the rest of his life on the banks of the Bosporus, except when he came home to the banks of the Charles to his beloved Cowley Fathers.

Home and away is never static. The conversation—the traffic in general—goes both ways, of course. It was from St. Louis, Missouri, that T. S. Eliot came to Harvard in 1906; it was to London ultimately that he sailed away in 1914 to his fame. And it was in Paris in just that fateful year of the start of World War I that Eliot had an experience some scholars have made much of and some nothing at all, but which may be central to arguably the most notable poetry in English in the twentieth century. Yet the Harvard roots of *The Waste Land* are not widely known. Nor their homosexual resonances.

As always with Eliot, the tale is complicated but worth the trouble to try to sort out, though in this case the matter covers a period of over thirty years, only reaching its climax in the 1950s when "possibly the most influential American writer of the twentieth century," as Eliot scholar Lyndall Gordon has asserted, invoked, in a violent and embarrassing spasm, the laws of libel to suppress in Britain (and in effect the U.S., the First Amendment notwithstanding) an article about his famous poem by a young Canadian scholar, John Peter. Troubled by Peter's reading of *The Waste Land* (that "at some previous time [its] speaker has fallen completely—perhaps the right word is 'irretrievably'—in love"), Eliot was especially perturbed by Peter's conclusion that "the object of this love was a young man [who] it would seem afterward met his death by drowning. Enough time has now elapsed since his death for the speaker to have realized that the focus for affection that he once provided is irreplaceable. The monologue which, in effect, the poem presents is a meditation upon this deprivation, upon the speaker's stunned and horrified reactions to it, and on the picture which, as seen through its all but insupportable bleakness, the world presents."[2] At once suppressed, Peter's article was not published widely until seventeen years later—after Eliot's death—and the second time around it suffered from some further speculation many thought weakened Peter's original thesis. The article attracted the attention, however, of James E. Miller Jr., professor of English at the University of Chicago, a distinguished Eliot scholar who, amazed at what he called the "conspiracy of silence" that Peter's essay had met in the field of Eliot studies, pronounced Peter's revolutionary analysis "breathtaking in its simplicity and almost defiant in its specificity," addressing as it did so well many aspects of *The Waste Land* Miller had long found puzzling. The outcome was Miller's seminal book, *T. S. Eliot's Personal Waste Land*, and the saga is hardly yet over; Professor Miller promises a full-fledged biography, forthcoming in the 2000s.

His first book, brash enough in 1977, was itself immediately and violently attacked, despite the author's clear declaration that a solely "homosexual interpretation" of *The Waste Land* would be absurdly reductionist, as one-dimensional as a solely "heterosexual interpretation." Yet one can see why—especially in the late 1970s—Miller's book alarmed so many. His analysis, for instance, of the twenty-seven lines of the poet's response to "What the Thunder Said" in Part V of *The Waste Land* (the heart perhaps of the whole poem) is stunning:

> The meaning of the passage appears to me lucid, and the tone not ironic but deeply moved, deeply moving. It is a confrontation that is also a confession. The poet and his friend have experienced the "awful daring of a moment's surrender." An age, or lifetime, of "prudence" cannot "retract" that moment, cannot replace it: it exists, it endures in the memory. Moreover, this moment has been the essence of their existence, this memory shaping their very selves, giving them their essential, their emotional identity. When they die, this shaping event will not even be listed in their obituaries, nor will it be found in "memories" (mementoes, "treasures") that the spiders will take over, nor in the documents, "under seal," opened after their death by their lawyers (solicitors) going through their "empty rooms." Clearly this passage is clarification for the self, and an affirmation, a confrontation with the truth that the poet-protagonist must learn to live with, not evade, not suppress, not deny, not duplicate.[3]

Proven or not proven, that there *was* a homosexual dimension to *The Waste Land* should not really startle; long evident have been the all-but-disabling sexual repressions of Eliot's "The Love Song of J. Alfred Prufrock" as well as the distinct homoeroticism of two other poems from Eliot's early oeuvre, "The Death of St. Narcissus" and "The Love Song of St. Sebastian." Both were written during Eliot's Harvard period, eight years (1906–1914) that were formative in some measure because his coming from St. Louis to Boston—to Milton Academy and then to Harvard—was for the young poet-in-training (he was actually majoring in philosophy) something of a (fatal?) homecoming, as the Eliots were an old Boston family who continued to return every summer, to Gloucester, on Boston's North Shore. Indeed, Eliot's original draft of *The Waste Land* began with a group of (in Miller's words) "young college men"—surely Harvard men—"out on the town in Boston," whose chief luminary when Eliot first arrived was his cousin Charles—Harvard's then president, the son of a famous Boston mayor.[4] Young Eliot, by the way, when not carousing, showed commendable literary ambition (he was elected to the editorial board of *The Harvard Advocate*), and it was also during his Harvard years that he fell in love with Emily Hale, the daughter of a Boston Unitarian clergyman. That was just after (and perhaps on the rebound from) the same-sex relationship Peter and Miller find so significant in Eliot's life, a relationship with Jean Verdenal.

From the fall of 1910 to the spring of 1911 Eliot was in Paris, as Harvard's traveling fellow to the Sorbonne, and his year there was more than splendid, in no small measure due to his Harvard connections. Kakuzo Okakura, curator of Japanese art at Boston's Museum of Fine Arts and a friend of Isabella Stewart Gardner, one of Eliot's Boston backers, took Eliot to meet Henri Matisse, for instance, one of whose friends, Matthew Prichard (who gave Gardner Matisse's portrait of him), was to become a part of Eliot's circle in Paris. But the closest of his friends in Paris was Verdenal; Eliot's friendship with him seems to suggest a homosexual aspect of his Harvard years, an aspect since lost sight of because of the burning of so much of his correspondence of that period. The other aspects? One thinks not just of the early poems already cited but of the reactions to Eliot, for instance (documented by Valerie Eliot in her selection of her husband's letters), of several of his colleagues and teachers at Harvard. One accused him of "a certain softness of moral fibre"—perhaps anti-homosexual code. Another saw Eliot as "a sort of attenuated Santayana"—almost certainly code, and telling code, given Santayana's very problematic repute in this era.[5]

Verdenal, the son of a doctor, was a medical student the year Eliot met him at the pension at which they would live throughout their stay in Paris. Twenty years old, Verdenal was on all accounts a young man of great charm, and of evident artistic and literary as well as scientific interests; also, as wartime dispatches would shortly disclose, a very kind man of strong dedication and great courage. He renounced his medical deferment on the outbreak of war in 1914 and joined the Eighteenth Infantry of the French army, serving first on the Western Front and then in the Dardanelles campaign; at the Gallipoli landings he was killed, cited in dispatches for his bravery treating the wounded under fire. Only one fugitive sentence in all Eliot's writings of half a century describes him. But what a memorial. In a review in *Criterion* in 1934, Henri Massis's *Evocations*, a book about Paris in Eliot's and Verdenal's time before the war, stirred in Eliot what were obviously important memories: "I am willing to admit," he wrote, "that my own retrospect is touched by a sentimental sunset, the memory of a friend coming across the Luxembourg Gardens in the late afternoon, waving a branch of lilac, a friend who was later (so far as I can tell) to be mixed with the mud of Gallipoli."[6]

It is an almost jarringly personal comment in a review for the invariably so impersonal Mr. Eliot, who all his life avoided personal matters in public discourse. Perhaps one should notice that just as it was immediately after leaving Paris and Verdenal in 1911 that Eliot fell in love with Emily Hale, so also after Verdenal's death he made his sudden and, as it quickly turned out, catastrophic marriage, to Vivienne Haigh-Wood, of which Eliot himself admitted later that any explanation "would require a good many words, and yet the explanation would probably remain unintelligible." Furthermore, that one fugitive sentence is not all Eliot ever *implied* about Verdenal—and implications, when they take the form of book dedications, speak loudly: Eliot's first published collection of poems was dedicated to Verdenal in 1917 (*Prufrock and Other Observations*).[7] So was his second book. Although *Ara Vos Prec* had no formal dedication, its title was drawn from Dante's *Purgatorio* ("The Reign of Lust," Canto XXVI), and the epigraph is from the *Purgatorio*, Canto XXI: "*Or puoi la quantitate / comprender dell'amor ch'a te mi scalda, / quando dismento nostra vanitate, / trattando l'ombre come cosa salda*," which Miller translates as "Now you are able to comprehend the quantity of love that warms me toward you, / When I forget our emptiness / Treating shades as if they were solid." Surely, a dedicatory epigraph; that it was in fact a dedication to Verdenal is made clear in the American edition of *Ara Vos Prec*, which, while it omitted the Dantean epigraph, was frankly dedicated "to Jean Verdenal / 1889–1915."[8]

It is in *Ara Vos Prec*, moreover, that was published one of Eliot's most obscure but important poems, "Ode," which Eliot never permitted to be republished. Miller again:

> We might describe the speaker in the poem as a poet who has somehow found his gift of poetic inspiration turned to poison, who has turned away from a misunderstood kind of poetry [called in the poem "profession of the calamus"] he wrote in the past and has been unable to find a new poetic voice, and who remains in a state of paralysis caught between the painful reality of a destructive, loveless marriage and the poignant memory of a dead friend, the loss of whose love has left a deep psychic wound of bitterness and anguish. We *might* posit such a speaker, but we know that the outline pretty much fits Eliot's own situation at the time [1918] the poem was written.[9]

Finally, in a 1925 volume of Eliot's poetry, that direct dedication to Verdenal (with the additional line: *Mort aux Dardanelles*) was combined by Eliot with the Dantean epigraph at the head of the Prufrock section of poems (the whole 1925 book itself was dedicated to Eliot's father). Certainly T. S. Eliot never forgot Jean Verdenal.

Facts are facts and speculations are not. But these facts are very suggestive. And I, of course, am of the school of Richard Ellmann, who I think is

CENTRAL TO ANY HARVARD SCRAPBOOK IS THE SEVENTEENTH- AND eighteenth-century College Yard *(above)* and burying ground in the Old Cambridge neighborhood, some of its landmarks unchanged for centuries. History and romance—it was between Hollis and Stoughton Halls (*above left and right, respectively*) that Emerson and the object of his desire (another undergraduate) reconnoitered each other endlessly in 1821—combine here with mind and body, flesh and blood, to evoke the most intensely erotic land-scape of all Boston's many collegiate neighborhoods, more and more so as the life of the Yard has played more and more intimately into the increasingly faster pace of the urban Boston scene around it.

(*Above*) THE BEACON STREET PATH AT DOWNTOWN BOSTON COMMON. Famously the scene in March of 1860 of Emerson's and Whitman's hours-long dialogue about *Leaves of Grass*, Boston Common was thus the first, as London's Old Bailey (site of the Wilde trial) was the second, and New York's riotous Stonewall bar the third, of the critical hinges on which the history of the modern gay rights movement turns. (*Below*) The Hermes of Praxiteles bearing the infant Dionysus was unearthed in the ruins of the Temple of Hera at Olympia. Oscar Wilde, while visiting Harvard's gymnasium, presented the college with a life-size plaster cast of Hermes, shown here as pictured in a turn-of-the-century catalogue of the Wilde cast's probable maker, P. P. Caproni.[1]

THE PART OF THE OLD CAMBRIDGE NEIGHBORHOOD WHERE BY THE 1900S
Harvard's gay experience was chiefly enacted: the so-called Gold Coast on
Mount Auburn Street *(below)*, where clustered elegant private dormitories
(to the left, Claverly and Randolph Halls) and exclusive college social clubs
(on the right, the Iroquois and Phoenix and Fly clubhouses). The domed
Lampoon castle is in the center of this most picturesque of all Boston's collegiate cityscapes, crowned by the St. Paul's Church campanile. *(Above)* The
distinctly homoerotic murals of Randolph Hall, Adams House, the work of
Edward Penfield, he of so many notable *Harper's* covers of the 1900s.

SONNETS
AND·OTHER·VERSES·BY
GEORGE·SANTAYANA

THE WHITMANIC ARCHETYPE. *(Above)* THE TITLE PAGE OF SANTAYANA'S first book of 1894, which famously contains sonnets dedicated to one of his students, his great love of the 1890s, Warwick Potter. *(Below)* Professor F. O. Matthiessen, first Senior Tutor of Eliot House, a leading exponent at Harvard of the Oxford-Cambridge-Harvard tradition of Socratic homoerotic tutorial.

THE WILDEAN ARCHETYPE NO MORE THAN THE WHITMANIC SHOULD be confused with reductionist stereotypes: Whitman loved Italian opera; Wilde was a good boxer. Yet the continuities of both archetypes are evident in the contrasting sensibilities of *(above)* T. B. Meteyard's cover art for *Songs from Vagabondia* (1894), showing Meteyard, Harvard poet Bliss Carman, Dartmouth poet Richard Hovey, and *(below)* F. H. Sturgis's sketch of two Harvard men in a time-honored exchange in a Boston club.[2]

SOMETHING OF A FUSION OF THE WHITMANIC ARCHETYPE OF THE
warrior (and by extension, the athlete) and the Wildean archetype of the aesthete (and by extension, the artist) is suggested in this 1907 *Saturday Evening
Post* cover by J. C. Leyendecker, who usually used a long-standing lover as a
model. The somewhat provocative *contrapposto* of the Harvard athlete the
artist depicts certainly does not detract from the young man's evident com-
petence to row a boat.

LONG RUMINATIVE WALKS OR BRISK RUNS OR ROWS MAY BE THE CHIEF use Harvardians, gay or straight, put the riverfront to, but gay men especially have played sexual hide-and-seek—and often something more—here for generations. *(Above)* The Weeks pedestrian bridge connecting Cambridge and Allston sides of the Charles. On the Cambridge side is Dunster House and Peabody Terrace, in the background the Downtown Boston skyline. *(Below)* The Weld Boathouse with the towers of Eliot and Lowell Houses in the background.

HOMOSEXUAL STYLE, FLAMBOYANT AND MINIMALIST, GOTHIC AND Baroque and several kinds of modern: *(above)* Bertram Goodhue's cover art for Bliss Carman's *Saint Kavin*, superbly detailed and very droll. Note Harvard's Memorial Hall in the upper part of the third niche up on the left.[3] *(Below)* The gayest exterior décor on Harvard's Gold Coast, the exuberant Baroque frontispiece (1902) of the Signet Society clubhouse, also Goodhue's work, this time in collaboration with the wildly picturesque decorator, Pierre LaRose.

(Above) PHILIP JOHNSON'S SUPERB HOUSE OFF HARVARD SQUARE, built in 1942 when he was an architecture student at Harvard, heralds his famous Glass House. A particularly intriguing example of form expressing function was the bricolage-type architecture of Boston Brahmin Prescott Townsend, who imaginatively deployed found objects—everything from submarine doors to beachfront driftwood—to design and build a quite charming summer residence in Province-town, which to the outrage of his neighbors he operated as a shelter for young gay runaways. He called his compound "Province-towns-end." *(Below)* His study.

THE HARVARD GAY EXPERIENCE particularly in the 1940s and '50s was often amusingly—sometimes dangerously—schizoid. *(Above)* Frank O'Hara used to play Satie for John Ashbery on the piano in the Eliot House tower's music room beloved in a prior generation by Leonard Bernstein and Aaron Copland. *(Below)* The favorite bar of O'Hara and many of his classmates was the most raucous in Downtown Boston's grimiest quarter. Wrote O'Hara of the Silver Dollar's clientele: "Powerful in their evil or cheapness, atypical, stoic in hidden suffering, knowing their own meaning and not denying it, not licked yet."

THE MORE PRIVATE LOCALES OF HARVARD GAY LIFE INCLUDED STATIONS on the old Underground Railroad used to rescue slaves, stations where by the twentieth century older queers sheltered and helped younger ones or, according to your point of view, exploited and perhaps seduced them, and in turn might be themselves blackmailed. Many a confused freshman in the 1930s sought the mentoring of Henry Wadsworth Longfellow's gay grandson, Harry Dana, at Castle Craigie on Brattle Street *(above)*, built when Boston had a royal governor and a vice-regal court and later occupied by George Washington and later still by Longfellow. Others sought out Prescott Townsend, who lived in much seedier gentility *(below)* in Lindall Place on Beacon Hill.

GAY SENSIBILITY, VARIOUSLY PASSIVE OR AGGRESSIVE, EVIDENT IN these two male nudes appropriated as an intimate expression of self by two Harvard gay men. One fights, one suffers, both endure, though neither may win. *(Above)* Lucien Price's *Prometheus* by Arthur Spear, which hung for years in Price's Beacon Hill sitting room over his sofa.[4] *(Below)* Stewart Mitchell's bookplate.

GAY SENSIBILITY AS SEEN BY HOMOPHOBIC VICTORIANS: PRESIDENT
Eliot, the visionary who created modern Harvard, though generally progressive and an inspiration in particular to Jewish students, had his blind spots;
for example, women's education and people like philosopher George
Santayana, whom he called "abnormal," and architect Ralph Adams Cram,
whom he thought "peculiar." Both words were code. One result is that opposite Harvard's main gate today Cram's splendid church design illustrated
above is nowhere to be seen; instead, the bare, wooden church it was to have
virtually replaced in 1899 is still there. According to Cram's daughter, Mary
Nicholas, when Eliot saw the design and learned who the architect was, "he
had a fit."

IN HIS EARLY TEENS LINCOLN KIRSTEIN, A
young man of nearly Proustian imagination, con-
jured his own erotic landscape on Commonwealth
Avenue *(above)*, the street that the Kirsteins lived on,
especially just before dawn, when Kirstein would slip
out for "Tom Kittenish" prowls. Years later John
Cheever also haunted the mall, though when
Cheever, an interloper from working-class Quincy,
tried to scale a statue he was warned off by a policeman. *(Below)* The Lincoln Kirstein Tower, designed
in 1985 by Philip Johnson on his Connecticut estate
near the Glass House, itself a descendant of his
Harvard Square house. One has to scale the Kirstein
Tower to discover its meaning (disclosed in an
inscription at the very top), and no more than
Commonwealth Avenue for young Kirstein is it an
easy passage.[5]

(*Above*) In 1909 THE ARCHITECTURAL FIRM OF WHEELWRIGHT AND HAVEN
(E. M. Wheelwright was the father of Lincoln Kirstein's Harvard friend
John Wheelwright) designed the Boston Opera House, where Kirstein
said he had his "first brush" with the art of the body when the Ballet
Russe—its principal dancer the notorious Nijinsky—appeared there in
1916. An erotic as well as an artistic vector in Kirstein's life, the ballet no
more than the opera, however, thrived in Kirstein's youth in Boston,
which allowed the Boston Opera Company to go bankrupt and eventually tore down and did not replace its opera house. None of which surprised
Kirstein. Jewish, gay, modernist, unappeased in his love-hate relationship
with the Puritan capital in the era of the Sacco-Vanzetti trial, Kirstein
ended up repudiating Boston generally and Harvard particularly.[6]

KIRSTEIN'S FIRST PROTEST AGAINST BOSTON'S ARTISTIC CONSER-
vatism was to rent a gallery with three friends (above the columned
entrance to the left of the sculpture in Harvard Square), where in historian John Coolidge's words the idea was "to pick up the torch lit by the
Armory Show of 1913" in New York, Boston, and Chicago and to relight
it in the 1920s. This time it did not fizzle. Today, Kirstein's ultimate victory in his hometown is signaled by Dimitri Hadzi's "omphalos" in Harvard
Square. Anciently the landmark of a spiritual center such as Delphi,
Hadzi's "world navel," though it has many aspects (a multidirectional sign
as a crossroads, even shifting weathervanes), fundamentally stands, in the
words of critic Joseph Maschek, for "Boston itself, that 'Hub' or omphalos of the Universe" and, be it noted, in strikingly modernist terms.[7]

correct to hope that "biographies will continue to be archival, but the best ones will offer speculations, conjectures, hypotheses." And a good thing, too, as this data illustrates so well. Eliot's own observation in his lecture on "Virgil and the Christian World" is also pertinent: "A poet may believe that he is expressing only his private experience; his lines may be for him only a means of talking about himself without giving himself away; yet for his readers what he has written may come to be the expression both of their own secret feelings and of the exultation or despair of a generation. . . . A prophet need not understand the meaning of his prophetic utterance."[10] Miller, like Peter before him, may have found Eliot out, that the poet's friendship with Verdenal was one, as Eliot described Dante's love for Beatrice, that "no subsequent experience abolished or exceeded," and one that depended not just on the original experience but on a very Dantean reflection on that experience—*The Waste Land*. Of course. April was the cruelest month; it was the month the Gallipoli landings began, the landings that killed Verdenal that May. Of course, too, it bred lilacs "out of the dead land"—remember the memory, sacred for Eliot I'm sure, of the young man striding toward him through the Luxembourg Gardens, a branch of lilacs in his hand. We all have such memories. So do we all mix memory with desire.

Verdenal's own testimony? There is a little more than Eliot's, but that little contradicts none of Miller's reading. The half dozen letters from Verdenal to Eliot that survive are certainly not conventional love letters. But then they wouldn't be. And some facts are suggestive. Two of the three Bostonians Verdenal refers to in his letters, both clearly friends primarily of Eliot—were Henry Wadsworth Longfellow Dana (another resident of Eliot's and Verdenal's old pension, a visiting professor at the Sorbonne where Eliot was studying) and another New Englander, Matthew Prichard, then a student at the Sorbonne—both luminaries of Boston's homosexual community. Prichard particularly was evidently a close mutual friend of Verdenal's, and he is known not to have had many friends in Paris. "A fine, strong nature," writes Verdenal in one letter, where he sings Prichard's praises, impressed by his "sincerity, his instinct for vital truths, and his good sense." That they were all in some sense confidants is also implied when Verdenal writes how in some matter "Prichard . . . seems to me to be on the wrong course—an 'artificial' course, I should say, in relation to morality." He complains that his friendship with Prichard "is not progressing." But then again, he complains, too, that he has no friends anymore, nor even acquaintances: his "best friend," he says, is "away."[11]

Generally, Verdenal's letters are mostly quite matter of fact, even chatty. He writes at one point of returning from "an intentionally athletic and health-giving holiday, well-showered and with muscles in trim"; another time he is lively in a different way, reporting on Shrove Tuesday in Paris: "The evening is filled with an ever-mounting sensual excitement . . . lottery wheels spin; a merry-go-round . . . a shapely leg can be glimpsed through the slit of a 'fashionably split skirt'; a heavy, sensuous gust flows warmly by." There is some wit ("Incidentally, Cubism has been destroyed by Futurism") and more than a little intellectuality ("positivism [materialism poorly disguised] spreads downward through society"). But Verdenal's letters also disclose a very passionate, artistic nature: "I went the other day to the *Götterdämmerung*, conducted by Nikisch," Verdenal reports; "the end must be one of the highest points ever reached by man." (Wagner was yet another passion he shared with Eliot, who first heard *Tristan und Isolde* at the Boston Opera House in 1909, an event Igor Stravinsky thought was for Eliot one of the seminal events of his life).[12]

There is also a good deal of a young man's musing in Verdenal's letters: "The Will to live is evil, a source of desires and sufferings, but beer is not to be despised—and so we carry on. O Reason!" And again: "I am not sure of ever having had an idea that really belonged to me." However, Verdenal's love of Wagner is also explained: "I feel vague surges of melancholy," he repines, which only music helps; "still mainly Wagner," he adds. But invariably he apologizes for such down moments, at one point pleading that, after all, in their old Paris days, "I was in the habit of sometimes coming down to your room in an old jacket, collarless and in slippers." And when he worries, out loud, that their intimacy is fading, notwithstanding these are not conventional love letters, a surmise begins to form, and the relationship comes suddenly more into focus: "My dear friend, we are not very far, you and I," writes Verdenal, "from that point beyond which people lose that indefinable influence and emotive power over each other, which is reborn when they come together again." He blames himself; should write more, and so on. But though one assumes Eliot replied, it is not really clear who is more the pursuer, as only one side of the correspondence survives.[13]

This now all-but-lost but very important friendship between Eliot and Verdenal is the more moving for its brief duration and sudden end and now stubborn obscurity. Nor was Eliot's memory of Verdenal striding toward him in a Paris springtime with a branch of lilac the only poignant moment left to us. Verdenal, too, though it would be too much to call this the dominant theme of his letters, had his memories of Eliot, some of which he wrote to his distant friend in America. Once, for example, Verdenal made an outing to Saint-Cloud and, reporting on his trip to Eliot, he wrote: "I thought of writing to you, because *you* were especially called to mind by the contact with a landscape we appreciated together." Verdenal added: "However, the landscape only faintly recalled the worthy [Bostonians] Prichard and your great friend Child." Even more arresting is the close of one of Verdenal's last known letters to Eliot. The Frenchman was still in Paris, studying intently for his medical exams, spending night after long night at his books in the old pension where he and Eliot had passed their year together. Suddenly it is ten o'clock and all the bells are ringing "(. . . soon blotted out by the measured pealing of a deeper bell, do you remember?) suddenly I think of you as ten o'clock is striking. And your image is there in front of me."[14]

Night and Day

SEX WAS NEVER actually banned in Boston, but as London has always had Paris so Boston has always had New York, while for both Americans and Europeans there was in Eliot's day what the Victorian explorer Sir Richard Burton called in 1886 the "Sotadic Zone" where homosexual romance, or at least sex, was rampant: basically—and this is, of course, a racist view—the Mediterranean coasts, narrowing through the Middle East and Kashmir, and then widening to include China, Turkistan, and Japan; beyond, the South Sea islands.

On the good theory that in all ages one's sex life, like one's prayer life, is entirely private—because the value of either proceeds exactly from the fact that it is shared with only one other person—it is never really the case, nor should be, that the historian can other than guess about these aspects of a person's life. But my guess would be that, in Eliot's case, the emphasis was on romance, whereas, in Cole Porter's, it was on sex. This character trait was already well developed by 1913, when Porter arrived at Harvard Law School, just as Eliot was coming to the end of his doctoral studies in the Graduate School of Arts and Sciences. Different discourses. Different leagues. Yet the audacious, subtle, sophisticated, psychologically complex, sometimes devastating songs Porter would go on to write remain still "the top." Porter, in critic Alexander Chancellor's words, "possibly the greatest popular song writer of the twentieth century," was a poet, too; a master not only of melody but light verse.[15]

He was, of course, famously a Yale man, composer, indeed, of several Yale football songs, not least "Bulldog." And though his time at Harvard was brief (the better part of two years), it was very significant; it was the dean of the law school, in fact, who suggested Porter take up songwriting—or so Porter contended, saying to a reporter once: "I'm used to being sat on in Boston. If Dean Thayer of Harvard hadn't been so thorough in refusing to admit that I could ever become a lawyer I might have never become a song writer. . . . As a matter of fact he suggested I try song writing. So I took up music with a swell recommendation from the Dean of Harvard's Law School."[16]

Actually, "considerable apocrypha have been generated around Porter's Harvard years, some of it seemingly by Porter himself," according to his most recent biographer, William McBrien. What is clear is that Porter roomed at Harvard in Craigie Hall (one of his roommates was Dean Acheson, later U.S. secretary of state) and that Porter and T. Lawrason Riggs, an old classmate from Yale who was a graduate student in English at Harvard at the same time, collaborated in the fall of 1915 at Harvard on his first professional musical, *See America First*, which opened in New York the next year (it closed after only fifteen performances). There is also a wonderful souvenir of Porter's Harvard years, "Craigie 404," about their "crazy Craigie crowd. They play all day, all night they play" and so on.

By *See America First* Porter had bid good-bye to the law school and had indeed enrolled in Harvard's music department, and that's what the Porter apocrypha at Harvard was mostly about. One version has Porter, while still a law student, the center of a disciplinary ruckus (a loud party); afterward, when the dean threatened expulsion, Porter is said to have offered to withdraw if the dean would let Acheson and Riggs remain. Another version, less heroic but more likely in view of Porter's own testimony, has the dean, no fool, saying to Porter after hearing a song he had written, "Porter—don't waste your time—get busy and study music." A classmate of Porter's used to tell the most dramatic version: it appeared that Professor "Bull" Warren called on a quite-unprepared Porter in class one day, and when he fumbled, Warren got very angry, leaning over the desk and declaring very superciliously, "Mr. Porter, why don't you learn to play the fiddle?" Porter, according to his classmate, got up and walked out of the class, never to return.

It was Dean Thayer, though, who according to McBrien arranged for Porter's transfer to the music department. Together with Porter's other musical studies, that department greatly shaped his musicianship, according to critic Alan Rich, who in examining Porter's famous song "Night and Day," explains how. McBrien points, above all, to the song's "harmonic richness . . . resulting from (and here he is quoting Rich) "a constant fluctuation between major and minor (phrases that begin in one mode and end in another) . . . [and to] the beautiful, clean, gradual rise-and-fall of the melodic line, [and] the fascinating way the bass line descends over a repeated-note tune in the introduction. . . . So," concludes McBrien, "Porter's music studies at Yale, Harvard, and the Schola Cantorum were not missteps."[17]

The Schola Cantorum was in Paris, where Porter moved after Harvard. After military service in World War I he married Linda Lee Thomas in 1919, returning to Paris, where he began in the 1920s the lavish social life there (and in New York and in Hollywood) for which he and his wife were so widely known for the rest of their lives, the romance and high style of which was famously celebrated in *Night and Day* with Cary Grant. "None of it, of course," Porter said contentedly once, "is true." Actually, his courageous, even heroic response to the lifelong acute pain that followed a nearly fatal horseback-riding accident, and the gallant way he insisted, for example, on climbing Machu Picchu *on crutches*, was real enough. Porter's physical courage was legendary. But the romance of the movie was what he meant. His feelings for his wife were tender but not passionate; it was "a mother-son relationship," his biographer wrote, and while Porter was dutiful and attentive to his wife, he also engaged in a secret homosexual party scene wherever he was, including back in Harvard's orbit, where, for instance, his great friend Nat Saltonstall (he of Chapter 3) threw a "boy party" after the Boston opening of Porter's musical *Jubilee*, in 1935. According to McBrien, this was "the same 'wild party' at the Boston Ritz that writer Schuyler Parsons alluded to in his book, *Untold Friendships*."[18]

Porter did have, however, a series of long-standing very serious relationships with boyfriends who were as well close friends and muses, most notably perhaps with Eddy Tauch—an architect, a Cornell graduate, and probably the inspiration for "Night and Day"—who was perhaps the love of his life. Fascinatingly, it is in no small measure Porter's sincerity, as much as his wit, that endowed his songs (he was his own lyricist) with their genius: they shine all the more if one knows the deceit and hypocrisy of his life. One suspects how Porter dealt with that. The same way, no doubt, he dealt with another problematic aspect of his life—the fact that "he failed," in his biographer's words, "to find an enduring romantic attachment." He learned to fulfill the better part, perhaps, of all those yearnings by "giv[ing] artful shape to his feelings even though these would only be read by one other person." The world heard one thing, his beloved another. In 1942, for instance, it was dancer and choreographer Nelson Barclift, a graduate of Ted Shawn's dance school (the one Lucien Price got so involved in), at that time in the army, stationed at West Point. Porter's "You'd Be So Nice to Come Home To," the only song from Porter's film *Something to Shout About* still heard today, was "our song," Barclift recalled years later, the more happily so, he said, because it knocked Irving Berlin's "White Christmas" off the hit parade that year.[19]

Porter did once address the question of sensibility in his work, and he thought there *was* one—but it wasn't gay. Writes Alexander Chancellor: "Porter once claimed to Richard Rodgers that his most successful songs, with their constant shifting from the major to the minor key, were 'Jewish tunes.' Rodgers agreed . . . [and] added, 'It is surely one of the ironies of the musical theatre that despite the abundance of Jewish composers, the one who has written the most enduring 'Jewish' music should be an Episcopalian millionaire who was born on a farm in Peru, Indiana." "[20] Indisputably, in the American political landscape of eros, to be openly Jewish was possible, if difficult. To be openly homosexual was not. Openly black? Therein lies, perhaps, a more complicated tale.

The Harlem Renaissance

NOT SO FAR away as Peru, Indiana, no place, however, was more "away" from Harvard than Harlem. But the New Negro Movement, as it was originally called, which emerged in New York after World War I, was in several ways very Harvard—and very homosexual. Indeed, the movement as a whole seems sometimes as gay as black. For instance: it was in the pages of the important African-American art quarterly *Fire!!*, created by a group around Langston Hughes which included John P. Davis, who studied at Harvard Law School, that in 1926 Richard Bruce Nugent's "Smoke, Lilies and Jade" first appeared. It was among the first American literary productions that was explicitly homosexual, and it was way ahead of its time, even ahead of the New Negro Movement generally. According to critic Thomas S. Wirth, the "Niggerati," as the youngest and most rebellious artists and writers associated with the movement were called, were not adverse to *Fire!!* being banned in Boston, which might have generated enough publicity to rescue the fledgling quarterly from the financial difficulties that ended its run with the first issue; one example of the way the dynamic of "home" and "away" could play out. Another was that their mentor—the godfather of the Harlem Renaissance, as he is often called—Howard University professor Alain LeRoy Locke, was a Harvard man. He was also gay.[21]

A native of Philadelphia, Locke entered Harvard College in 1904, graduating three years later after a career of so many honors and prizes it would be tedious to enumerate the half of them. Sufficient to recount that Locke won several highly competitive scholarships, was elected Phi Beta Kappa in his second year, won the coveted Bowdoin Prize in English Literature, and was the first African-American to be chosen a Rhodes scholar to Oxford— the *only* one until 1963. At Harvard, Locke's experience, furthermore, was successful both academically and socially; he not only thrived as a student of philosophy—a disciple of William James and Santayana—but also coxed the Weld Boat Club crew. After graduating from Harvard College, Locke pursued his education not only at Oxford but at both the universities of Berlin and Vienna, returning to Harvard to take his doctorate—only the third black to do so—in 1918. He went on to distinguish himself as a professor of philosophy at Howard University, where he became the head of the philosophy department and helped establish there the first Phi Beta Kappa chapter in a historically black university.[22]

The other side to all this, however, is that at Harvard Locke's success had *only* been with whites. He had, in critic J. C. Stewart's words, "distanced himself from fellow black students. . . . In letters to his mother, he articulated his belief that prejudice existed largely in the eyes of the beholders, that blacks interpreted nonracial situations in terms of race, and that blacks complained of race prejudice mainly to cover up fears of inferiority. . . . When black Americans had written him . . . celebrat[ing] his achievement as a victory for the race, he had not been happy. . . . 'I am not a race problem. I am Alain LeRoy Locke.' " It was a classic strategy. Relatively enlightened Boston whites hardly prepared Locke, however, for the huge opposition his winning the Rhodes would arouse among Southern whites. It was a mistake in the first place, from the point of view of the Pennsylvania selection committee, which had acted on glowing reports from Harvard before meeting him; though shocked to discover he was black, they concluded it would be too embarrassing to reverse themselves. Yet his selection was protested by a delegation sent to the Rhodes trustees to try to overturn the selection. And when that didn't work, Locke was dogged at Oxford itself by what Stewart calls "a virulent group of Southerners who were committed to challenging his right to be there."

To be sure, he enjoyed at Oxford the same social success among whites that he had had at Harvard, but naturally anyone so keen as Locke must have seen that a good deal of it was the result of British outrage and sympathy for him in the face of his American persecutors. It made Locke into a liberal cause, so to speak, taken up for that reason perhaps more than for strictly personal reasons, and it also placed him very much in the middle as an American when Locke began to realize that British anti-Americanism (so often keenly felt by Americans at Oxford) accounted for no small amount of his support, rather a mixed blessing. He never took any degree at Oxford, doubtless because of all this stress.

But if he would not be "de-Americanized" by Englishmen, neither would he be "Negroized" by Americans or "liberalized" by anyone else. He held to his own vision of himself, which always seemed to be all that mattered to Locke, especially as he did find support in a circle of Indian, Egyptian, and South African intellectuals who "helped him," in Stewart's words, "recast himself in terms of the international movement against imperialism and colonialism. It was in that community that he began to find his own Afro-American identity."[23] And here is his genius—while Locke faced *down* all these day-to-day problematic aspects, refusing at every turn to be a victim, at the same time he by no means took refuge in denial, facing up to the demand that must have been clearer and clearer to him, and upon which he acted urgently when he returned to America in 1911, not abandoning taking his ease among whites, but newly insisting black Americans accept their "Afro-American" identity.

Indisputably a patrician, Locke had predictably patrician—and very Eurocentric—tastes. But again he fused opposing ideas without difficulty. More attuned to Hegel and Mozart than to spirituals or jazz, Locke understood, however, the necessity for a more diverse cultural experience in America (and not just for blacks) and was in fact already an adherent of cultural relativism when he arrived at Oxford. The idea—indeed, the term—had already emerged in his undergraduate experience. As Russell J. Linnemann has explained, Locke not only "utilize[d] the intellectual scaffold of [William] James and [John] Dewey," but at Harvard he "gain[ed] a first-hand account of pluralism from Horace Kallen, who coined the term 'cultural pluralism.' Kallen had first used the term in 1906 or 1907 when he worked as an assistant in a class taught by George Santayana." Linnemann goes on to say that while Kallen "was particularly interested in pluralism as it related to the variegated forms of Jewish particularisms, Locke's interest was focused on Afro-American particularisms." A counterweight to the idea of "melting pot," cultural pluralism gives parity to all cultures, and it is interesting that Kallen's teaching of the idea at Harvard has remained controversial. Kallen was Jewish. Santayana was homosexual. Locke was black—and homosexual.[24]

Locke's involvement with the leading lights of the Harlem Renaissance took many forms. He took a particular interest in mentoring Zora Neale Hurston, his student at Harvard, whom Cornel West and Henry Louis Gates Jr. have called, in *The African-American Century*, "the most widely taught black woman writer in the canon of American literature." Gates and West also point out Locke's importance to another important contemporary writer, Ralph Ellison, as well as to painter Jacob Lawrence. Locke's sexuality, moreover, was at the heart of these connections. Though Locke was a believer in the then very popular theory of the "open secret" and was concerned that the black cause might suffer through any association with homosexuality, his erotic interests were entirely directed toward his own sex, and the very secretive and exclusive—and brilliant—circle of handsome young black men he kept company with and mentored reflected this fact.

Although Locke seems to have enjoyed matchmaking as much as scoring himself—putting together younger colleagues, he seemed to realize, would normally yield more physical mutuality than was possible with him as he aged—there is evidence that some of Locke's tutees felt taken advantage of sexually, a specter that haunts such relationships. Indeed, Locke was not universally loved: Hurston once called him "a malicious little snit," accusing him of being a misogynist, and Locke was caricatured as more than pompous in Wallace Thurman's *Infants of the Spring*. Certainly he was very aggressive in pursuit of his favorites. And, according to historian and critic Richard Newman, Locke amassed a collection of semen samples of his conquests, a collection thrown away by an overzealous "Keeper of the Flame." It suggests to me what Mitchell's and Dana's self-nudes and Hammond's nude statue suggest—"gay rage." After all, he paralleled his more private work as teacher, muse, and mentor with an equally important public role as literary critic and public spokesman for the movement, his major contribution *The New Negro: An Interpretation*, which elucidated both the social and literary thought of the Harlem Renaissance. He would have felt more than repressed. And not easily appeased. For instance, Locke was concerned more with racial and ethnic than gay sensibility. Of one aspect of an African-American sensibility in literature, he wrote: "It is not enough to sprinkle 'dis's and dat's' to be a Negro folk-poet, or to jingle rhymes and juggle popularized clichés traditional to sentimental minor poetry.... One must study the intimate thought of the people who can only state it on ejaculation, or a metaphor, or at best a proverb, and translate that into an articulate attitude ... with Aesopian clarity and simplicity—and above all, with Aesopian candor."[25]

*   *   *

IN THIS CONTEXT the work of another major figure of the New Negro Movement who was both gay and Harvard-educated—Countee Cullen—comes to mind. As Darwin Turner has pointed out, Cullen was "one of the few black writers to appear in American literature anthologies published before 1960." A widely celebrated poet in his day, Cullen, though undeniably gifted, was rigidly antimodernist and was perhaps for posterity's tastes too enamored of Keats: and many black writers have been concerned not to repeat Cullen's neo-Romanticism and to insist that literature is at the heart of such a discourse, not race.

In his day, however, Cullen was much admired. Though his origins were obscure, he was raised in the cultivated family of a Methodist minister and educated at New York University, performing outstandingly and graduating Phi Beta Kappa in 1925 (one of only nine students to receive this honor out of a class of 102). He was much influenced there by Hyder Rollins, who received a Ph.D. from Harvard and accepted a Harvard professorship. Cullen followed his mentor to Harvard, where he earned a master's degree. He was a student of poet Robert Hillyer. His Harvard year was in fact quite a triumph. Though, according to H. R. Wintz, there is some evidence that despite the fact that he was a published writer he had difficulty getting into Charles Copeland's famous class (his publisher, Knopf, had to intervene) during Countee's time in Cambridge his first volume of poems, *Color*, was published to wide acclaim (a flurry of nationwide raves was led off by *The Harvard Crimson*), and in his second term he entered the celebrity world of leading writers in his first "appearances," arranged by Knopf that spring at Jordan Marsh's bookstore in Boston. Furthermore, Cullen married the daughter of W. E. B. Du Bois, undoubtedly the leading black intellectual of the era (the first African-American to earn a doctorate at Harvard), in whose honor the W. E. B. Du Bois Institute for Afro-American Research at Harvard is now named. After the fashion of the era, the marriage's failure was referred to only in code. According to the *Dictionary of American Biography:* "Temperamental differences between Cullen and his wife appeared almost immediately."[26] It is reliably reported the bride begged off the honeymoon, which Countee, however, enjoyed greatly—with his best man.

Cullen spent much time in the 1920s abroad, mostly in Paris, and when he returned to America he refused several invitations to teach at the college level at Southern black schools and took a position instead teaching French, English, and creative writing at Frederick Douglass Junior High School in New York. He became well known for his devotion to teaching. Today his name has been given to a school in Harlem and to the Harlem branch of the New York Public Library. One of his students at Douglass was James Baldwin.[27]

On the Left

HAVE WE SUDDENLY turned left? Certainly not only politics but repression—rage, too—come now to the fore. It is not surprising, however, that one of the first times Harvard fields important players, so to speak, on the African-American side of twentieth-century culture, these facets are so noticeable. Speaking of James Baldwin, I am reminded of something he once said: "There is no need for racial understanding since we [blacks and whites] already understand each other all too well, because we have in fact invented each other." This is surely akin to Foucault's contention that we have just in the last hundred or so years invented not only homosexual persons, but "their anti-twins, heterosexual persons."[28] That's too easy by far. But, all things considered, what may be emerging here is the fundamental affinity of the Harvard gay experience not just with bohemia, but with the Left generally, which has generally been the most effective in driving a whole family of issues—especially civil rights and freedom of expression. Without the success of the Left's "progressive" view, there would hardly be, certainly politically, a homosexual discourse in the first place. Witness the life and work of the center of that notorious Smith College scandal, the brilliant literary critic, Newton Arvin, who earned his Harvard degree in 1921, five years before Countee Cullen earned his.

Indiana born and raised, Arvin was an undergraduate at Harvard, where, according to his biographer Barry Werth, he quickly set himself apart as a progressive with communist leanings, and this within three years of the Bolshevik revolution itself. He also found his first love in Harvard College in his Thayer Hall roommate, Bud Ehrensperger, though nothing much seems to have come of it; Arvin could be bold—in politics, for instance—but he could be timid, too, and usually was as a young man in matters romantic. He distinguished himself, however, in his studies, graduating summa cum laude (one of only six students to do so in a class of 442), and began his ascent up the academic ladder, in Arvin's case to a tenured chair at Smith.

There his contradictory nature stood out even more. As a boy "timid, shrinking, weak and unadventuresome" (his own words), and by many accounts equally shy and introverted as an adult, Arvin grew up to be a distinctly shrinking violet; more than once at Smith he attempted suicide. On the other hand, faced with Arvin's forceful criticism and scholarship, Van Wyck Brooks, himself a notable critic, concluded that Arvin was truly "a quiet man with a violent mind"; a man, Brooks insisted, who "would gladly have stood against a wall and faced a fusillade for his convictions."[29] Certainly Daniel Aaron, who taught at Smith (indeed was drawn there because of Arvin), is on record as seeing "that indomitability in Arvin's handwriting; slashing and extroverted, it was fiery 'like Savanarola's. " Arvin considered himself a coward, but he was often braver and more resilient than many of those he envied as 'normal.' " In his Harvard College class notes, for instance, he declared his "shame" at Harvard's role (through President Lowell) in what Arvin called Sacco and Vanzetti's "judicial murder." In 1932, moreover, he publicly pledged (with John Dos Passos, Sherwood Anderson, Lincoln Steffens, and Theodore Dreiser) to vote communist in the U.S. presidential election—all the braver a decision, in Michael Berthold's words, because of "the relation of [Arvin's] Marxism and his homosexuality—a double marginality—to the institutions of literature and academics."[30]

Everywhere, contradictions. If it was true that Arvin was "unmanly in appearance, [but] a bold thinker with a masculine mind," it was equally true, as his biographer Werth put it, that Arvin, however timid about his homosexuality, "wasn't just homosexual but a sexual adventurer" as he got older. Although he "understood the grave risks he was taking," Arvin not only aggressively sought out young gays on the faculty at Smith for sex and socializing; he went regularly to Springfield, Massachusetts, a regional transportation hub near Smith, to cruise, and as often as he could, he traveled to New York, where the Everard Baths were for him, in Werth's words, a kind of "sodomist's paradise." Repression now, added to politics. And rage. And sex, which came very much to the fore.

The composer Ned Rorem, in his *New York Diary*, described the Everard's dim and grimy interior memorably. Natural light never penetrated at any time. It was, Rorem wrote, "a brothel lit like Guernica by one nude bulb"; to go there was to "penetrate an obscure world [of] . . . gray wanderers so often compared to the lost souls of Dante." It was a world where, in one cubicle after another on all four levels, one continually glimpsed male "couplings," sometimes "of beauty with horror." Hell for Rorem, the Everard Baths were an astonishingly cathartic and even purifying experience for Arvin. Writes Werth: "Arvin liked to wander—'hunt,' as Ned [Spofford, his friend,] said. . . . [And Arvin often was] the initiator [in sex]. He reveled in Everard's variety. . . . Arvin loved the starkness, the abandon. Far from feeling ashamed or degraded . . . he was seldom so exhilarated. Sylvan Schendler, who was heterosexual . . . remembered picking [Arvin] up after a few nights at the baths and asking how it went. 'Oh, Sylvan,' he said, 'I feel so clean.' " It was a contradiction that seemed only to disclose deeper ones in Arvin's case. He was extremely self-loathing: "Arvin verged on a constant panic. It fell to Aaron . . . to try to stop the slide"—and more than once. Psychiatry hardly helped. Arvin also tried marrying a woman, one of his students at Smith, Mary Garrison. Although they cared for each other and appear to have had adequate sexual relations, their overall situation deteriorated within a few years into what Arvin's biographer calls a "nightmare," and after eight years the marriage ended in divorce.[31]

Against this disastrous personal backdrop Arvin's professional and scholarly life unfolded in striking relief. Edmund Wilson once declared that among American writers and critics of the period, only Van Wyck Brooks and Arvin "can themselves be called first-rate writers." Certainly Arvin was a formidable literary historian and critic, in no small measure because, in Werth's words, "for Arvin more than most biographers, subjects were surrogates. . . . Solving 'the problem' of another writer was an act of transubstantiation," which Arvin's great mentor, Van Wyck Brooks, seemed to know. Wrote Arvin's own biographer:

> A literary biographer must share an essential bond with his subject. Brooks was convinced that [Arvin] was one of the few people knowledgeable about American literature who was capable of discerning the true Hawthorne, whom Brooks called "this most deeply planted of American writers, who indicates more than any other the subterranean history of the American character."[32]

Indeed, if Arvin "discovered himself in Hawthorne, even as he recoiled from what he found," the greatness of Arvin's book still lies in how he illuminated Hawthorne:

> Reading Hawthorne [Arvin] identified dark strains in Puritan America, which perhaps only someone who had spent much of his life in hiding could detect as fully. Like Arvin, Hawthorne had withdrawn from the world, substituting literature for life; yet that retreat had led him to discover the great theme that would pervade his most important books— what Arvin called "the dark connection between guilt and secrecy." In Hawthorne's Calvinist America—the colonial America of *The Scarlet Letter* and *The House of the Seven Gables*—people were punished most harshly not for their acts but for their secrets.[33]

Arvin, who had many, thus made his own secrets in a sense his friends, strengths almost, a kind of steel framework, so to speak, of his best work.

In my view Michael Berthold has mounted the most convincing analysis of Arvin's work in relation to his sexuality, in fact detailing Werth's idea. Although he notes that it was "to Arvin's credit that he could even begin to address Whitman's homosexuality as openly as he did in the 1930's," Berthold's is an analysis that is itself highly critical, suggesting, in fact, a gay sensibility that is distinctly problematic in effect. Witness his observation that "Arvin's sexual orientation skews his relationships with his subjects; in his treatment of the homosexuality of Whitman and Melville, for example, detachment and vicariousness meet. Arvin may have regarded his biographies as indirect and protective ways of writing about himself; he seemed unaware of how revealing his books sometimes are." However, if Berthold sees in a more negative light what to Werth's eye is more positive, it is Berthold who picks up more obviously on Arvin's evident conflictedness with respect to his sexuality: "An inadvertent pathos results from [Arvin's] gestures of identification and recoil from his biographical subjects." Finally, Berthold is penetrating on what really underlay Arvin's work:

> Arvin's biographies provide an almost empyreal contrast to the pain and disappointment that constituted the reality of his life. His oeuvre tends to center on the ways in which his subjects affirm their autonomy in the face of sorrow. Arvin particularly admired his subjects' brave attempts at throwing off despondence and purposelessness. . . . Arvin's was no facile idealism. As Arnold Goldman has suggested, Arvin's "tragic sense" was rooted in the conflict between "personal wholeness" and the social environment, or conflict whose tragic issue was laid as much to the door of the individual as social failure.[34]

Indeed, Arvin found in Hawthorne's life, for instance, the same "affectional impotence"—telling phrase—as he found in his own. And when Berthold suggests "Arvin's *Moby-Dick* chapter . . . is animated by [his] shock of recognition in reading Melville and finding a version of the courageous American writer he needs," it is no wonder it leads him to declare that in the first place, and for just these reasons doubtless, "Arvin [was] a pioneer in recognizing Melville's homosexuality and the psychic price he paid for his repressions." This was all the more so, moreover, because Arvin, a careful scholar, himself "doubt[ed] whether Melville recognized the 'sexual undercurrent' of his feelings for men." The Melville biography won the National Book Award in 1951.[35]

One must also factor into Arvin's life and work two transforming events, one ecstatic, the other catastrophic. The ecstasy was prompted by his great love—a man who "seemed to evoke a passion and ebullience in Arvin that he rarely displayed," a man who Gerald Clarke believed made Arvin feel "younger, no doubt, than he had felt when he actually was young"—his lifelong friend and sometime lover, Truman Capote. They met at the Yaddo artists' colony in New York State in 1946. Only a year or two younger than Capote's father, Arvin was an odd choice for Capote and—somewhat in explanation, though it was hardly the whole truth—Capote explained once: "Newton was my Harvard." He paid his debt by dedicating his first novel, *Other Voices, Other Rooms* (1948), to Arvin. According to Werth, Capote was "dazzled by Arvin's learnedness, erudition, experience with language, and passion for books. Arvin, who had so recently feared he was incapable of love . . . melted irresistibly. . . . The phenomenon was well-known. Oscar Wilde had famously described it as 'that deep physical affection that is as pure as it is perfect . . . [which] repeatedly exists between an elder and a younger man, when the elder man has intellect, and the younger has all the joy, hope and glamour.' "

Capote, of course, could be off-putting, in the sense that many were offended by what they saw as gender-inappropriate behavior. Daniel Aaron recalled that when he first met Capote the young man kissed him, and it was like "a blow to the face," which embarrassed Arvin.[36]

And that social confidence was just what Arvin needed all along the spectrum. For example, when Capote protested that Arvin should be at Harvard, but that "he wouldn't lift a finger to do anything for himself," Arvin did not seem to respond, perhaps because he was so happy in a small New England college town with Capote, who made the long train journey from New York to the Berkshires every weekend for what seems to have been a sort of country-house idyll with Arvin. But it is also true that "Arvin's shame about his sexuality . . . quickly dissolved" and that his few years with Capote comprised "the happiest and most productive period of Arvin's life," according to Werth. To be sure, Capote and the anemic, balding, mousy professor made an odd enough pair. Yet whoever it was who opined that the chief sexual organ of man is, after all, the brain, was friend to Capote, who once said that Arvin's was "a wonderfully subtle mind. He was like a lozenge that you could keep turning to the light, one way or another, and the most beautiful colors would come out."[37]

The union did not endure, however; it evolved ultimately into occasional friendship. And, again, it was Arvin's doing more than Capote's. Many reasons there were for the breakup, not least Arvin's refusal to leave Smith. As Werth points out, in Capote's New York or Arvin's Boston—"where Harvard's Matthiessen," writes Werth, "lived with his lover, Russell Cheney, in a magnificent apartment in Louisburg Square, on Beacon Hill"—it might have been possible. But Arvin was nearing fifty, high middle age, was a recluse (more so than even a scholar must be) "encysted" (Aaron's word) in the Berkshires, and, in truth, though Arvin loved Capote deeply, he loved his solitude more. It was for Arvin, says Werth, like oxygen. Too late he realized that in the long run solitude changes shape as one ages, and not always for the better.

Nearly a decade of loneliness and personal unhappiness descended upon Arvin after the end of his two-year affair with Capote, not really brightened by his National Book Award in 1951 and only made more complicated in 1957 when he met his last love, Ned Spofford, a young classics instructor at Smith. Though the two became intimate friends ("He fills my spirit too full for me to feel any other need"), Arvin, still sexually highly needful, was now older, and Spofford, unlike Capote, did not reciprocate physically, leaving Arvin (as he saw it) no recourse but those big-city excursions to bus stations and gay baths. As Werth put it, with unusual fairness: "In the prevailing view of the time [Arvin] had reached that reckoning, supposedly peculiar to the conspiratorial world of the homosexual, when debasement replaces mutuality, and desperation trumps precaution. The fact is, though, Arvin was the commonest of sufferers: an aging, single man looking for a young lover to rekindle his spirits."[38] Arvin's way of dealing with this situation was lethal, and culminated in a lifestyle in those days highly reckless, a lifestyle that brought two unmarked patrol cars and a federal postal inspector, three state troopers, and a local policeman to his front door and precipitated the dramatic events recounted in the prologue to this book.

Again, as always on the personal side, Arvin failed—his arrest and the ensuing scandal hardly brought out the best in him. Capable of being "remorsefully selfish," in Aaron's words, "in his dependency on others, Arvin was a survivor," Werth concludes. "Whenever he tried to kill himself, he had always managed to be discovered." Arvin was quite different from the "more manly and combative" Matthiessen. Writes Werth: "[Arvin] was not the type to risk success by leaping, like Matthiessen, from a twelfth-floor window." Thus Arvin, when accused by the state police of being part of a gay pornographic network, not only confessed, but informed on his friends, including Joel Dorius and even Ned Spofford. Eventually, of course, the U.S. Supreme Court struck down the legal basis for the prosecution, and the Massachusetts Supreme Judicial Court also in the end reversed the convictions of both Spofford and Dorius. But at the time, for Spofford particularly, there were hardly words to frame such a betrayal. Though Arvin did find the words—telling words—confessing in his characteristically weak and timid way to Spofford that "I couldn't go through this alone"—it ruined their relationship; Spofford was so angry he refused Arvin's deathbed offer of reconciliation. Nor can one entirely blame him. Arvin, whom Carson McCullers thought so comforting, could also be intensely manipulative, deeply unattractive, something Sylvia Plath caught in her journals. "Arvin: dry, fingering his key-ring compulsively, . . . bright hard eyes red-rimmed, turned cruel, lecherous, hypnotic." Eventually, though, Spofford, like all of us, grew up: "Newton and I," he later allowed, "were each other's closest friend."[39] It was the best that could be said of the man whose biography is entitled *The Scarlet Professor*.

Right Turn, Left Turn

NEWSPAPERS IN BOSTON and New York headlined Newton Arvin's disgrace, and the Left was sure it was exactly Arvin's politics that had got him into trouble in the first place, even spurred the police raid. Certainly more than a few of their opposite number on the Right in the 1950s thought the words *communist* and *homosexual* invariably two sides of the same despicable coin. The Right, however—at Harvard especially—would surely have been considerably less pleased with Arvin's downfall had they known what we know now: that one of their own, one of the Right's foremost champions and Cold War warriors—another Harvard man and as much a luminary of the Right as was Arvin of the Left—was in those years also violently entrapped and threatened with the blare of a similar scandal. The headlines would have been even bolder, moreover, because in America the political always trumps the literary, Left *or* Right. Just three years, in fact, separate the police raid on Arvin's apartment from another raid, equally brutal—this time not west of Boston but in the heart of Moscow. There, in 1960, waiting for word about a possible interview with Soviet premier Nikita Khrushchev, Joe Alsop, the most famous American journalist of his generation, one of the staunchest Cold Warriors and a most influential Harvardian, fell afoul— not of the Massachusetts State Police, but of the K.G.B.—for exactly the same reason. "Moscow-trained thugs barged into [Alsop's hotel] room," recounts his biographer, Robert Merry, and wasn't it odd the way it was a scenario at once so similar to Arvin's and yet so different. Alsop had no pornography; the K.G.B. brought their own. They had wired Alsop's room and caught the journalist deeply engaged with a young man whom the K.G.B., of course, had arranged for Alsop to meet in the first place. In Alsop's case, of course, the aim was blackmail and espionage.[40]

Am I exaggerating the significance of all this? Consider George Stephanopoulos's description of the situation (so traditional in the 1950s and '60s) faced by Lyndon Johnson only four years later, on 14 October 1964:

> With only three weeks left in his race against Barry Goldwater, his personal lawyer, Abe Fortas, calls to report that the president's longest-serving aide, Walter Jenkins, has been arrested for performing oral sex on another man in the basement pay toilet of a Washington YMCA. An incredulous Johnson immediately takes charge of damage control. He directs Fortas to force Jenkins's resignation and to spirit damaging files from Jenkins's White House safe; orders the FBI to produce an official report declaring that Jenkins is not a national security threat; asks the Pentagon to scour Jenkins's military reserve file for positive comments from his commanding officer, Barry Goldwater; urges the attorney general to intensify a bribery investigation of Goldwater's running mate, William Miller; coaches the first lady on how to secretly assure the Jenkins family that its financial future will be secure; and commissions a poll on the scandal's impact from his private pollster. Johnson . . . fears the Jenkins arrest will cost him the presidency. . . . He tells Fortas, "It could mean . . . the ballgame."[41]

Other events—a Chinese nuclear test, the fall of Nikita Khrushchev, Goldwater's decency (no homophobe he, as many conservatives were later amazed to discover)—intervened. But in the 1950s and '60s Johnson's fears were not fanciful. Nor were Alsop's in the same period. The stakes were very high, even for the columnist. But Alsop, if he was not Johnson, was not Arvin, either. Though the renowned journalist was just as queer as the distinguished professor, Alsop was much surer of himself. The blue-blooded columnist, thoughtful and sensitive and amusing though he was to friends and colleagues, was otherwise generally a bit of a bully, temperamentally mercurial, highly arrogant, and distinctly a snob; a graduate of Groton School as well as of Harvard College, Alsop was a relative of one president

(Theodore Roosevelt) and the confidant of another. A war correspondent notable for his battlefield reporting from both Korea and Vietnam, Joe wrote a column with his brother Stewart in the *New York Herald-Tribune*, a column that was read the world over; the men were a dominant force in the Washington press corps in the post–World War II period and have been aptly called the "guardians of the American century."

All the greater, of course, Alsop's humiliation in Moscow. But whereas Arvin went to pieces, Alsop, made of sterner stuff, went on the offensive at once. Himself a former intelligence officer who knew well the mores of a subculture that, while it targeted gays as inevitably vulnerable to blackmail, understood what good spies they made because of their lifelong training in leading the double life, Alsop complimented the agents on their work, doing so as one "pro" to another. And he made no efforts at denial. But he did not seem concerned, either: to flattery he added disdain, "dismiss[ing] the agents with contempt." According to Merry, "he . . . inquired sarcastically as to whether he could get extra copies of the photos for his personal collection." No, thank you, it was "a fool's errand" to think he was about to become a Soviet spy, he declared, and in the end it was the K.G.B. that retreated. Their superiors doubtless learned quickly that Alsop's confidence was not misplaced; he went immediately to the American ambassador and on his advice promptly left Russia, following up with a full and forthright report to U.S. intelligence. And here is the essence in Harvard history of the away game: what the masters of Soviet spydom may not have known (but surely should have) was that the ambassador, Chip Bohlen, was a close friend of Alsop's; not only had they been at Harvard together—where Alsop, who entered Harvard College in 1928, had shown himself a good student and a social success, too—but he and Ambassador Bohlen were fellow members (in an era when it meant almost everything) of the college's most elite club, the Porcellian.[42] Whereas the raid to the west of Boston effectively ended Arvin's career, the one in Moscow had no discernable effect at all on Alsop's career or life generally.

The celebrated journalist, it should be emphasized, though as strong a man as Arvin was weak (gays, like any group, come in all sizes, so to speak), was as tortured as Arvin about his homosexuality, which, indeed, in Merry's words, forced him to lead "a secret life, a life apart and veiled, yet central and fundamental." In fact, Alsop's friend Isaiah Berlin recalled the famously arrogant columnist's palpable hesitation—a station, certainly, of the same continuum on which Arvin was pronounced timorous—when, late one night, after many drinks, Alsop declared: "Isaiah, there's . . . uh . . . something . . . I . . . uh . . . I am . . . uh . . . I am a homosexual."[43]

Yet in the case of Arvin and Alsop it is not just a matter either of Left and Right, strong and weak, great confidence and not nearly enough: Arvin, particularly in his relationship with Capote, had—if only for a few years— a great advantage over Alsop, whose biographer recounts how "near the end of his life [Alsop] confided to a friend that his greatest regret was that he had never settled down or developed a long-time, meaningful relationship with a man. An open homosexual affiliation for someone in Joe's position in those days wasn't possible," especially for Alsop, who was an influential member of Harvard's senior governing board. The result, of course, was another bad marriage to a woman; while it was a loving and honest relationship (Alsop told Susan Jay Patten he was gay before the nuptials), it ended as so many such marriages did, in divorce. Ultimately, Alsop came to feel, as he put it, "trapped by marriage."

He had had, to be sure, an extended affair in the 1940s with Frank Merlo, a sailor later beloved as well of Tennessee Williams, but the difficulties of sustaining the relationship only underline how difficult Alsop's position made such a thing. It is not surprising, accordingly, that the Moscow incident was not the only one. There was another in Germany. Worst of all was one in San Francisco, where the police once picked up Alsop cruising in a well-known homosexual haunt.[44] Alsop, powerful, also had powerful enemies; above all, the Eisenhower White House, which once debated lifting Alsop's press pass. ("He's a fag, and we know he is," said White House press secretary Jim Hagerty.) Nor was Alsop a man to take much notice of any of them, for any reason. Whether it was one of the weaknesses of his strength or one of the strengths of his weakness, Alsop, according to Merry, was not just a born fighter who thrived on outrage—to his "zest for controversy" was added an "instinct for the jugular" and positively "a need to court danger," so evident in his battlefield reporting from Vietnam. Admittedly the best sort of bully[45] and the best sort of snob (focused, as Arthur Curley used to say, on rigorous standards, rejoicing in high expectations fulfilled, and willing to be the enforcer), he *was* nonetheless not very likable, or even tolerable. Typically, he won any fight he took on. But the effort was often seen to be disproportionate, nearly always more denunciatory, more violent, than was probably necessary, perhaps doing as much harm on one front as good on another.

In fact, rage has now come very much to the fore in these pages. It might sharpen any truth to observe that any point of view urged by a self-aware and scrupulous but necessarily closeted homosexual, whether of the Right or of the Left in this era, was bound to be subversive. And in that discourse Alsop was a winner, even as Arvin was a loser. Also holding a losing hand was novelist John Horne Burns (Harvard College, 1937), who in the three years between the two police raids discussed in this chapter, quietly became yet another statistic in that roll of notable literary or academic figures and gay sons of Harvard who saw but one way out and killed themselves. It is a long list.

"AN AWFUL MAN. Monster. Envious, bitchy, drunk, bitter," Gore Vidal writes of Burns, "which was why *The Gallery* was so marvelous. It was his explosion into humanity at a fairly late date."[46] *The Gallery* was Burns's great book, the one success of this highly controversial author; Vidal pronounced it "the best book of the Second World War." Only Burns's book, he thought, was "authentic and felt."[47]

A closely observed peregrination through American social and political mores of the time as these revealed themselves in various escapades in Naples by American military personnel, *The Gallery* was sometimes deeply moving. As in all Burns's novels, the characters and situations were mostly hetero-sexual but included homosexuals as well. Yet another literary marker of the liberating effect Mediterranean civilization so often has on Northern Euro-peans, *The Gallery* celebrates Italian mores above all: "Unlike the Irish, who stayed hurt all their lives," wrote the Boston-Irish Burns, "the Italians had a bounce-back in them," a bounce-back he thrived on.[48] And as for its gay aspect, John Loughery has called Burns's "treatment of a gay bar the first, and still the best, in American literature."[49]

Burns himself, however, was another matter, as Vidal's memory suggests. With a "receding hairline above a face striking in its asymmetry, one ear flat against the head, the other stuck out," Burns was the reverse of cute, ac-cording to Vidal, and absurd as well, he thought, in insisting that "to be a good writer it was necessary to be homosexual." It was the sort of remark calculated to get a rise out of Vidal, and it did. He at once instanced Faulk-ner. Burns's response, to be "disdainful" of that master, was not an attractive one for a young man.[50] But in a defense of Burns's point of view, Mark A. Graves suggests that if on the one hand Burns's "war service provoked in Burns a skepticism about America's class-coded, heterosexist morality, as well as its ethnocentrism and marketplace mentality," on the other hand it led Burns to feel that the homosexual's "marginalized status provid[ed an author with] an objectivity not attainable within mainstream culture. Certainly the type of critique that such marginalization can engender is apparent in Burns's novels." Graves cites Burns's second book in particular, *Lucifer with a Book*, in which "Burns reveals the coterie of young homosexuals who form the underground social structure of the [private] school whose other secrets he lays bare."

As *Lucifer* is "autobiographical"—Graves's word—the school is perhaps Andover, near Boston, or perhaps Loomis School, Windsor, Connecticut, where Burns taught, but whichever New England school it focused on, the novel was savaged. Indeed, Burns left the country when *Lucifer* was not well received, returning to the Italy he had grown to love so during the war.[51] All Vidal, who thought Burns a "brilliant satirist," would say was that *Lucifer* was "perhaps the most savagely and unjustly attacked book of its day. . . . With good reason, Burns exchanged America for Italy," where he died seven years later, in 1958, after other failures, literary and romantic, a ru-mored suicide at thirty-seven.[52] Responding to Burns's protest against America's "loathsome values of a civilization in which everything is mea-

sured in terms of commercial success," Vidal declared many years later that
Burns's indictment, "now a cliché," had in 1947 "struck a nerve."[53] So also—
though more prophetically—in January of the very next year, did the publication of another book by another homosexual—another Harvard misfit, if
we agree on that word—a scientist rather than a novelist, but a scientist
whose work would begin to answer, really, both Arvin's problem and Alsop's,
if not Burns's, a scientist whose impact on the twentieth century would be
compared by W. C. Pomeroy to Darwin's on the nineteenth century—Alfred
C. Kinsey.

Kinsey Again: Prophecy

WHEN FIRST WE touched on Kinsey in Chapter 1, it was the boy—veritably
the "embodiment of the all-American boy"—that was of interest. By 1948
the model Boy Scout had become the model scientist. But it had not at all
proceeded with untroubled mien. "While he had managed to satisfy nearly
all the cultural requirements for passage from boyhood to manhood, one
part of the formula had eluded him," in James Howard Jones's words, as
was already evident during Kinsey's student years at Harvard, from 1916 to
1919: "at Harvard, as before, he did not date. This was by choice. Had he
desired female companionship, however, Kinsey would have had plenty of
takers. . . . Everyone agreed that he came across well."[54] Most important of
all Clara McMillen agreed. An undergraduate chemistry major at Indiana
University in Bloomington, where after Harvard Kinsey accepted a teaching
position, McMillen was much attracted by the young entomologist from
Harvard who, like her, loved nature. After her graduation (Phi Beta Kappa),
they married, in 1921, and it should be stressed there was nothing either
unusual or wrong in their doing so. And, for Kinsey, nothing difficult: "Out-
wardly, he did not arouse suspicions, since he did not fit any of the stereotypes of homosexual males," wrote his biographer, adding, "To Kinsey,
Clara was someone who shared his interests and might be willing to share
his life. . . . Nor is it difficult to understand what Clara saw in Kinsey. Handsome and athletic looking . . . Kinsey was obviously brilliant." Sex? How easily we forget the cultural mores of the era:

> Both were virgins . . . and their chastity remained intact throughout
> their courtship. Nor were they unusual in this regard. . . . Society expected
> young people (especially women) to remain sexually naive before mar-
> riage. . . . Clara matched the profile of contemporary women who marry
> homosexuals. . . .
>   It seems doubtful that Kinsey and Clara discussed their sexual his-
> tories. . . . An exchange of such intimacy would have been extraordinary
> for people of their generation and class. . . . He would have risked driving

her away [and] candor of this degree would have required a level of self-understanding he did not possess.

Social pressures to wed were so great that many men who did not know what to make of their homoerotic urges (and many who did) elected to marry. Studies some half a century later estimated that from 10 to 25 percent of all male homosexuals . . . either are or have been married.[55]

Eventually they had four children. (As Vidal once famously opined: what is in the mind in sex is not necessarily who is in the bed.) Meanwhile, he and Clara spent twenty years hiking all over Guatemala and Mexico hunting gall wasps—Kinsey's specialty—before he turned his focus onto human sexuality, with the result, of course, that he and the world collided fiercely in 1948 when *Sexual Behavior in the Human Male* was published. His findings were revolutionary—that at least 95 percent of men masturbated, for instance, and without going blind. But none were more revolutionary than those about homosexuality.

For Kinsey, labels such as *homosexual* made no sense as his data took shape before him. There were heterosexual acts and homosexual acts, not homosexuals or, indeed, heterosexuals. The word *homosexual* was, like the word *heterosexual,* an adjective, not a noun. Everyone, or almost everyone, was bisexual; human sexual behavior he found to be a continuum, which he brilliantly organized on a seven-point scale. At one end were persons entirely homosexual in sexuality, at the other persons entirely heterosexual; in between, however, *nearly everyone else was either bisexual but mostly heterosexual* or *bisexual but mostly homosexual.* Thus he satisfied humankind's love of categorization while subtly nuancing it. Most important, he pronounced homosexuality entirely normal within this scheme, not an "identity," more biological than either hormonal or psychological. "Homosexual Outlet" was only one chapter in Part III of his book. But it was one of the longest, and of many bombshells it was the most sensational.[56]

The publication of his biography in 1997 was somewhat of another. It now appeared, wrote Jones, that Kinsey loathed Victorian morality as only a person does who has been really maimed by the guilt and repression it encouraged. Kinsey's "stupendous gift," writes Jones, "had combined with his puritan work ethic to produce his spring-coil vitality," itself fueled by his secret life. For Kinsey was not only homosexual; he was SM. Writes Jones:

It was no accident that his emotional problems and compulsive behavior manifested themselves most graphically in sexual dysfunction. . . . His great accomplishment was to take his pain and suffering and use it to transform himself into an instrument of social reform. . . .[57]

Detractors there are. The objective scientist turned out to have been an ardent reformer. But supporters have also appeared. In *The New York Times*, Richard Rhodes criticized Kinsey's biographer because

> Jones questions Kinsey's motives for studying sexuality . . . appear[ing] to cherish the quaint notion that good science is disinterested science, that a scientist must somehow contrive to avoid emotional investment in his work. . . . Unable to distinguish between the personal values that motivated Kinsey and the careful protocols that guided his scientific project, Jones concludes that Kinsey was promoting a hidden agenda of sexual liberation and tries to use that conclusion to impeach his work.[58]

Kinsey's was a very different homosexual "scandal" from Arvin's or Burns's; the publication of his great work meant that the sort of jittery dance Arvin and Alsop performed with the vice squad would soon be over. And even as we try to grasp the past as the present it once was, overcoming our knowledge of the outcome, even recapturing past generations' ignorance of their future—these worthy admonitions are those of Harvard historian Bernard Bailyn—it is possible (without telescoping past and present, or surrendering to some progressive theory of history) to affirm that Kinsey's work was a watershed that heralded a whole new world. Indeed, Kinsey's study was prophetic, reflected in the high point of Harvard's mid-twentieth-century gay experience, which occurred in, of all things, poetry. Enter romance again; and sex.

Beat, Beat, Beat . . .

NOT EVERY HARVARD man settled in New York, Boston, or Washington, as Kinsey's life in Indiana showed. But increasingly in the twentieth century those three cities became Harvard's megalopolis—with air shuttles for trolley cars and subway trains. To be honest, though, it all started quite a long time ago; it is a development whose beginnings one can trace as far back as the late nineteenth century. Henry Adams, though he deliberately moved from Boston to Washington in the 1880s, remained so much a Bostonian as to commission as the architect of his new Washington house Boston's leading designer, H. H. Richardson. The architect had himself just moved to Boston from New York. On the other hand, Charles McKim, though he became the other fashionable architect in Boston (and in Washington, too), remained all his life in New York. Another example a few decades later: John Reed, previously mentioned, one of the first Harvard bohemians who, rather than sail away to Paris, instead settled in New York after graduation and was a founder of Greenwich Village, that most famous, as it would become, of all America's bohemias. Reed's biographer calls this, unthinkingly perhaps, "Boston influence in New York."[59] Conversely, was J. P. Morgan, the lead donor of Harvard Medical School in the 1900s, a case of New York influence in Boston? I don't think so. What really was going on, and had already become far advanced by Alsop's day, is that all these men—Adams, Richardson, McKim, Reed, Morgan—were graduates of a university becoming a dominant influence in all three cities: New York, the country's cultural and commercial capital; Boston, its intellectual center; Washington, its political nexus. Chicago, and later Los Angeles/San Francisco and Atlanta, would, in turn, evolve into the capitals of almost other countries. Meanwhile, the well-rounded Harvard graduate increasingly spent some part of his life in all three parts of his "extended" orbit. What is the American dream, after all, at the top? Harvard, Wall Street, and the Cabinet/Boston, New York, and Washington.

The division of labor, the assigned roles, in the three Northeast metropolises would not be, and is not today, exact. New York has always boasted of a considerable university in Columbia; Boston's State Street, not Wall Street, became the nation's mutual fund center; Washington would lay claim to a vital new cultural life. But the fundamental niche of each city in the national consciousness became clear, as did the network that laces them together for Harvard graduates. The characteristics of each city—what draws a John F. Kennedy or Joe Alsop to Washington or a John Updike or a Yo-Yo Ma to Boston, a Lincoln Kirstein or a Leonard Bernstein to New York (again, all Harvard men)—are very clear, never more so than in the small but highly influential world of American poetry, very much in transition in the post–World War II period. From the point of view of Harvard's most immediate orbit, poet Peter Davison explains: "Young poets in the mid-1950's, still overshadowed by the sequoias of Frost, Pound, Eliot, Stevens, Cummings, Marianne Moore, and William Carlos Williams, had taken refuge in a formal elegance that they were beginning to want to outgrow. The Beat Generation had urged stripping off those costumes altogether, but in Boston the transformation suggested a change in clothes rather than walking naked."[60]

Doesn't it always? And if Harvard was very much the centerpiece of what turned out to be Boston's "second poetic renaissance," as Davison calls it in *The Fading Smile*, "one of the most vital milieux for poetry in the history of the country"[61]—Robert Lowell, Sylvia Plath, Stanley Kunitz, Adrienne Rich, W. S. Merwin, Richard Wilbur, Anne Sexton—it is a measure of the school's range that it would also play a key role in the wider circle Davison rather condescends to, that of the New York School of poets of the 1950s. They were not quite so "Beat" as the San Francisco School (truly another country then), but consider the perspective, so very different from Davison's, of Allen Ginsberg:

From 1955 on there was somewhat of a breakthrough in American poetry known variously as San Francisco Renaissance or New York School or Beat Generation or Open Form or whatever, but antiacademic, anti-formalist style. I don't think people nowadays realize what a strong hold the notion of stress and accent and stanza had on poetry in what were con-sidered the serious literary magazines. . . . [In the 1950s] there seemed to be some sort of alliance between the San Francisco Open Form people . . . and the New York group of O'Hara, Schuyler, Ashbery. The common ground seemed to be building on William Carlos Williams' American vernacular idiomatic diction and rhythm and the spontaneous writing of Gertrude Stein.[62]

Ginsberg, who clearly took his turn to be condescending toward the Boston poets of the 1950s, as Davison had toward New York's, dedicated "My Sad Self" of 1958 to Frank O'Hara,[63] whom he met in Boston in 1956. O'Hara, who would go on to settle in New York after Harvard and become, really, the epitome of the New York School, which, with the abstract expressionist movement also centered there, helped make New York the rival of Paris as the major cultural capital of the West in the post–World War II era. Here too, though, Harvard pulled many of the strings. It was for a revised version of his Museum of Modern Art catalogue on Picasso that Alfred Barr fulfilled his requirements for his doctorate in 1949—from Harvard.[64] Indeed, ac-cording to University of Washington historian Meredith Clausen, it was a fact of life for all concerned in this era that, in general, "Boston . . . was [in the 1950s] the architectural capital of the country, with even MOMA in New York in effect being run from there." Harvard in particular pulled not just many but the most important strings.[65] And "the chain of friendships that turned into the New York School began [in 1946 when] Auden read . . . in the Yard."[66]

A native of small-town Massachusetts—today the outer rim of the Boston suburbs, then very rural—O'Hara was born in 1926 into a prosperous but conservative middle-class Irish-Catholic family. He grew up a feisty loner. Though not gregarious, O'Hara as a teenager was likely to dominate any social situation, according to his friends then (he was the editor of his high school paper). The self-discovery of his homosexuality in what was a very repressive milieu seems to have isolated him in a really fundamental way, though as a teenager he was careful not to reveal his sexuality. Spunky and pugnacious, he had his nose early broken in some adolescent scuffle; as a boy he loved swimming and, less typically, also reading, but mostly was sustained by a growing passion for movies and, above all, music. These passions also expressed his often contradictory nature; he loved Tchaikov-sky's somber Symphony no. 6 (Pathétique), for instance (the first concert he ever attended was a performance by the Boston Symphony Orchestra, under Serge Koussevitzky, of Tchaikovsky's Symphony no. 5),[67] but reveled in the pyrotechnics of Igor Stravinsky's The Firebird. Among composers, Stravinsky was O'Hara's favorite, and it was a characteristic choice. Even as a boy

O'Hara was an ardent, rebellious modernist in a very unfriendly rural quarter. It was while viewing an exhibition of Assyrian sculpture in Boston that
he decided to become an artist. Picasso, Kandinsky, Stravinsky, Gertrude
Stein, James Joyce—particularly Joyce's *A Portrait of the Artist as a Young
Man*[68]—these are what got him through the moronic hellfire sermons at his
Roman Catholic high school in Worcester, Massachusetts, run by the Xav-
erian Brothers, and all the harder to endure, I'm sure, for his burgeoning
youthful sexuality. One senses relief as well as wartime necessity when
O'Hara went directly from high school into the navy, enlisting in 1944.

A sonarman in the Pacific War, in the last stage of MacArthur's triumphant campaign of island warfare as the U.S. Navy fought its way toward
Japan, O'Hara was posted to the U.S.S. *Nicholas*, a destroyer of the Seventh
Fleet. He saw action in the closing phase of the Okinawa Campaign, as severe
an assault as any of the Pacific War. In between the rigors of kamikaze attacks
and nightly barrages, however, he began to find himself more surely, not
only as a man but as a gay man. The "shadowed homoeroticism" of his
ship, which was very queer but never admitted to be, was distinctly a new
experience for him. What this kind of situational homosexuality, akin to that
of schools and prisons, may finally mean is endlessly debated. But for a gay
man the experience can often be telling. "The shower room," O'Hara's biographer, Brad Gooch, writes, "was the scene of some of O'Hara's loosening
up—he wrote home: 'about four of us take them [showers] together each
night and have lots of fun, our chief amusement is throwing each other into
an all-cold, icy shower.' " It was a kind of roughhousing O'Hara obviously
much enjoyed, and for more than one reason: it took the mind off war,
compensating somewhat for the pervasive tension of shipboard life in a war
zone, and relieved, too, the overall homesickness that he and his fellow
sailors experienced. "Don't think I'm a sissy," O'Hara wrote about his homesickness in another letter home, "as all the kids here are worse."[69] A less
healthy response to navy life was his drinking, which began to be noticeable
at this time, when nerves necessarily were on edge. Yet the excitement was
also hard to beat, clearly disclosed in O'Hara's very early work, "Ode to
Michael Goldberg," characterized, in Gooch's words, by a "mixture of the
military with the erotic, the constant threat of sudden death with the romantic."[70]

Eliot House

AT WAR'S END, O'Hara, who had taken a course for one semester at the
New England Conservatory in his last year of high school, was still more
interested in the musical than in the literary scene. Indeed, the highlights of
his early years at Harvard, which he entered in 1946 after his discharge from
the navy, were more often in Boston's Symphony Hall than in Harvard Yard:
present when the modernist composer Darius Milhaud conducted his own

work, O'Hara also attended Koussevitzky's premiere in 1946 of Aaron Copland's Third Symphony.[71] Meanwhile, however, Harvard was transformed by
O'Hara and his fellow veterans, energized as they were by the GI Bill. However, the effect was all very brief: "I went into the Harvard of Norman Mailer,
and the Harvard I left was John Updike's," a friend of O'Hara's remembered.[72] But while it lasted O'Hara warmed to it well enough, such as the
course on Joyce and Proust given by young Harry Levin, who had already
written a brilliant book on Joyce, which O'Hara had doubtless read.[73]

The milestone of O'Hara's Harvard years was his movement, impercep-
tible at first, decisive in the end, the result of experiences like Levin's course,
from music to poetry. Key to consolidating that experience was his meeting,
in his last year at Harvard, John Ashbery, an English concentrator but a
musician, too. They shared much else. Both came from alcoholic homes: in
O'Hara's case it was his mother, in Ashbery's his father, who was also abusive, so often "walloping" his son (the word is Ashbery's) without apparent
reason, the poet later recalled home life was "like living in a volcano."[74] Both
men were also homosexual in a predominantly heterosexual and rather
tricky community, though each was rather differently gay: O'Hara had always
been deeply closeted; Ashbery, more confident, came out to his mother at
sixteen when he left home for boarding school—itself another difference.
Ashbery's school was Deerfield Academy, an elite world unknown to O'Hara
until Harvard. Ironically, the two ended up in just the opposite of the residential colleges from what one might have expected: O'Hara, not Ashbery,
was in the "preppy" Eliot House, very grand; Ashbery was in distant middle-
class Dunster, though thereby hangs a characteristic tale of the atmosphere
of those days:

> Just as an issue [of the *Harvard Advocate*] was closing, the editors noticed
> a half-page gap in the magazine, room for one last-minute poem. Ash-
> bery said he thought he might have one. Leaving the office he walked to
> his rooms in Dunster House—the most geographically distant of the
> Harvard houses and therefore sometimes called the "Sphinx on the
> Charles"—and returned thirty minutes later with the requested work, a
> poem beginning with the phrase "Fortunate Alphonse, the shy homosex-
> ual." It was clear that he had written the poem on the spot. Reminded
> of the incident forty years later . . . "Admit it, John, you wrote the poem
> in twenty minutes." . . . Ashbery replied, "Yes, I took longer then."[75]

Both men were indifferent students (though Ashbery enjoyed his studies
with Theodore Spencer, he preferred reading Elizabeth Bishop's poetry to
doing his course work, and managed to graduate cum laude only because
his senior thesis—on Auden—was so good) and spent much of their time
walking and talking along the Charles or high up in the music room of Eliot
House's tower,[76] with its grand piano and breathtaking views of Boston

(where Ashbery often played Satie or Sessions or Schoenberg for O'Hara) or, indeed, at the *Advocate*, in many ways the heart and soul of their undergraduate years. Just as the Porter-Cram-Sargent-Coletti-Wheelwright-John Nicholas Brown circle at the Fogg in the 1920s (discussed here in Chapter 3) was a classic case study of scholarly and artistic Harvard networking (as we'd say today)—in and of all the members' causes, public and private, present and future—so, too, the situation at the *Harvard Advocate* in O'Hara's and Ashbery's day discloses how extracurricular activities (literary as well as artistic pursuits) could serve that same purpose as well as classroom activities. Gooch describes the scene:

> *Advocate* editors, for example, had direct dealings with the school's straightlaced Boston legacy. . . . the magazine had actually been disbanded in the early 1940s because of indications that its editorial board had turned into an exclusively homosexual club.[77]

Accordingly, when the *Advocate* was started up again in 1947, gays were not encouraged. Never anything but scoffed at, the alumini threat to disband the magazine again was nonetheless always present and very nearly kept John Ashbery out. He was saved by Kenneth Koch.

As David Lehman makes clear in his superb history of New York poets, *The Last Avant-Garde*, the *Advocate*'s conservative angels were even more demanding than O'Hara remembered; the exclusionary stipulation was not just gays, but also Jews—and alcoholics. Then editor Kenneth Koch protested: "Maybe at Brigham Young. Everyone on the *Advocate* was either a Jew or a drunkard or a gay. . . . I was merely a Jew, the least objectionable of the three things."[78] What a meal one could make of all that. Ashbery's aversion to being read as a gay poet may date from all this. It was an interesting time. In the March 1948 issue of the *Advocate*, in which O'Hara made his debut, there was also a review of Vidal's *The City and the Pillar*.

Meanwhile, however, lives all around O'Hara were still storm-tossed; in Eliot House alone, one of his classmates, Donald Hall, recalled more than one scandal. There were the two men caught necking by a maid "in one of the nooks of the Eliot House library." One of them (the black one) was expelled! Another student, this time a "rather wealthy Eliot House resident," was also expelled for the same sort of thing, Hall recalled. Another friend of O'Hara's, Frederick English, never forgot the two very good friends who were "thrown out of Eliot House for a [homosexual] scandal that deserved nothing more than a yawn," but turned out to be "a horrible tragedy because one of them eventually killed himself." One House, four years; English declared that it left "a cloud over Harvard that I never really recovered from."[79]

Then again, being in a metropolitan rather than in a provincial center meant there were always alternatives to House libraries, and the Casablanca was far from the only gay watering hole popular among Harvard men in

O'Hara's day. These ranged from the chic jacket-and-tie Napoleon Club near the Back Bay to the raucous Silver Dollar, "a mixed bar with heavy gay overtones," in what came to be called Boston's "Combat Zone," to which O'Hara's biographer does no more than justice when he writes: "There a woman in a crazy gown played the organ nightly above a din of drunken soldiers and sailors and their girlfriends, sleazy drifters, homosexual hustlers, and Harvard boys." Besides O'Hara, of course, whose favorite bar it long was, the clientele, he wrote (in his unpublished novel "The 4th of July," which included a description of a thinly disguised Silver Dollar), was "powerful in their evil or cheapness, atypical, stoic in hidden suffering, knowing their own meaning and not denying it, not licked yet."[80] Nor was Eliot House itself altogether as repressive as Hall remembered. Certainly no one at Harvard since those days has ever quite topped the flamboyant Edward Gorey, O'Hara's sometime roommate there, of whom much more later. They went everywhere together; Boston's oddest duo became a fixture at such places as the avant-garde Kenmore Theater, near Boston University, and Harvard Square's Grolier Poetry Book Shop. They also had the repute of giving the best parties at Harvard in Eliot F-13. But O'Hara deserted Gorey his senior year, moving into O-22 with another roommate.[81]

O'Hara's evolving persona is a fascinating one: the whole continuum of entirely gender-appropriate to entirely gender-*in*appropriate behavior—seen as instinctive or as performance art at either end of the continuum—can be charted at some depth in this excerpt from *City Poet*, in which Gooch quotes O'Hara's former roommate, Fondren, and another friend of O'Hara's, Jerome Rubenstein:

> Some observers were struck by [O'Hara's] obvious effeminate gestures, while others failed to observe any such signs at all. [Recalled Fondren:] "He was quiet, not aggressive. . . ." Such indecipherability sometimes led to problems. Having double-dated with O'Hara and Elsa Ekblow at Harvard football games, Jerome Rubenstein was caught by surprise. "I wasn't aware of his homosexuality. . . . But once I repeated to him a comment I heard from a mutual friend of ours about someone else we knew . . . 'that dreary fag.' Although Frank didn't say anything, I think I could see immediately I was wrong. [J]ust before we graduated he came up to my room, slightly drunk, and told me I had hurt his feelings with that remark. . . . But he forgave me [dedicating to me 'Morgenmusik']."

"Practice a falsetto lilt / that's only partly keen" are the lines of O'Hara's "Morgenmusik"[82] that strike me today, when that line of defense has long since lost its bite. But it was surely a battlecry for a football game. And O'Hara just the man to make it.

Not that depression did not also dog him at Harvard. In his junior year he would sit for hours listening to Schumann and contemplating suicide, a line of thought invariably continued over coffee at Harvard Square's white-tiled Waldorf cafeteria; and then as well along the Charles River—"good and cold and raw"—arguing, arguing, arguing ("simply to exist doesn't justify existence)." Writes Gooch:

> O'Hara's father died while he was at Harvard, and his journals of the period show him in a soul-searching mood. Already he had developed his nervous "loophole for life" as a way of talking himself out of suicide. . . . "Something wonderful may happen. It is not optimism, it is a rejection of self-pity (I hope) which leaves a loophole for life." He added: "I merely choose to remain living out of respect for possibility." O'Hara's poetry is well described as the noble "possibility" justifying the pains of existence. The poems he wrote in his senior year at Harvard already contain the note of gently self-lacerating irony that makes his work so distinctive and so unprecedented in American poetry.[83]

Yet it is also not too much to say O'Hara and his cohort invented the Eliot House cocktail party of the 1950s, which became not just one of the notable sights and sounds of the whole Boston-area university scene but became for cocktail parties generally the gold standard for years of Western Christendom (i.e., New York, Boston, or Washington): "Having survived Kamikaze attacks on a perimeter ship in Okinawa, and the swift and absurd death of his father, [O'Hara] had developed a taste for games of life," Gooch writes, verbal games for which the cocktail party was the vehicle—both stage and play. So memorable did this manic liturgy of killer wit become that the poet John Ciardi famously celebrated the genre in a poem that appeared in *The New Yorker*. "Psychoanalysis by bourbon," Ciardi called it,[84] and certainly there was no dispute about O'Hara's wit: "You're ruining American poetry, O'Hara," a bellicose Jack Kerouac once shouted at him at a reading. O'Hara instantly and witheringly returned fire: "That's more than you ever did for it, Kerouac."[85]

Ideas as well as egos fueled Eliot House scuffles. Hall and O'Hara fought constantly, respectively the champions of two rival camps, the one favoring Yeats, the other Auden. Hall did his thesis on the former, Ashbery in 1949 wrote his on Auden. Meanwhile, the more traditionalist Yeatsians rejoiced in Robert Lowell, whose *Lord Weary's Castle* earned a Pulitzer in 1947; those favoring Auden were much uplifted by his presence at Harvard in December 1947, when, following a reading, a party was given for him at Eliot House.[86]

Heady days. So much so that one evening when Ashbery and Koch, two close allies of O'Hara at the time, were playing pinball, probably at Tommy's, a Mt. Auburn Street dive (still there today), and Auden himself, in town for some reason, stopped by for a cup of coffee and left, "Ashbery said he was miffed that the poet had not greeted them. 'But we don't even know him and we haven't published anything,' Koch said. 'Well, you'd think that he would know,' Ashbery replied glumly."[87]

Both O'Hara and Ashbery clearly thrived at Harvard. Ashbery hoped to stay, applying to graduate school there, but he was rejected and decamped for New York and Columbia. O'Hara also enjoyed Harvard, and he seems equally to have liked Boston generally: if Cambridge was "not crowded enough, there's not enough asphalt, and you can see over buildings too easily," as he wrote to Grace Harrington, an old friend, Beacon Hill did appeal; the north slope, he wrote another friend, "was the dirtiest place in the world and the best."[88] But even Beacon Hill's appeal did not last. Perhaps he had not yet figured it out, but just as Robert Lowell was a Boston poet wherever he was, so Frank O'Hara, wherever he was, was a New York poet. Thus the well-worn but insightful tale of O'Hara and a friend out walking in Manhattan, O'Hara's companion complaining about the disappearance of yet another landmark: "Oh, no, that's the way New York is," O'Hara replied. "You have to just keep tearing it down and building it up."[89] Higher and higher, of course, so there's less and less chance of seeing over the buildings. Washington was never going to attract O'Hara. Boston only for so long. It was New York, after a brief stint of graduate study at the University of Michigan at Ann Arbor—which O'Hara attended, as it were, incognito— that O'Hara would give his heart to. Like the neighborhoods of cities, so the cities of megalopolis, find their lovers out in the end.

New York, New York

SOME OF O'HARA'S circle lamented this, thinking he was making a mistake: "New York has brutalized Frank," protested Bunny Lang, the poet who, along with Ashbery, most immediately influenced O'Hara.[90] Indeed, at first, New York hardly lived up to O'Hara's own expectations. There *was* another Waldorf (many!), but for Frank O'Hara there was never going to be a Waldorf to beat Harvard Square's. New Yorkers themselves yearned for more. Recounts Gooch: "A bit desperate for the café-life of Paris, for their own version of Picasso's *Au Lapin Agile*, [New York's] painters gathered during most of the 1940's at the Waldorf Cafeteria at Sixth Avenue and Eighth Street," where the likes of Willem de Kooning and Robert Motherwell, leaders along with others like Mark Rothko of the emerging abstract expressionist school, "drank coffee and talked leftist politics and modern art." Ultimately they did contrive more: out of that scene emerged "the Club" all these painters famously founded.[91]

Painters? Although John Shoptaw is probably right in feeling that the New York school of painting never equaled the New York school of poetry, the visual arts of modernism, more even than its music, turned out to be O'Hara's other side, so to speak. Ashbery, too, would later perpetrate art

criticism for various journals, including *Newsweek*, while O'Hara, no sooner
had he arrived in New York, was at once transfixed by its art scene, something that had by then ceased to exist in any but the most boring way in
Boston. O'Hara's "curiosity was aroused in a way that it had never been in
the art history lectures at Harvard," Gooch writes. "It was," O'Hara wrote
in 1965, "a liberal education on top of an academic one."⁹² And O'Hara took
full advantage of it, rising through the ranks to become a leading curator at
the Museum of Modern Art, even as he became better and better known as
a poet, famous above all for *Lunch Poems* (1964). A kind of lyrical diary of
daily life in Manhattan, it was published four years after Grove Press brought
out a very important anthology edited by Donald Allen, *The New American
Poetry, 1945–1960*, which prominently featured O'Hara's work. That same
year Braziller published O'Hara's monograph on Jackson Pollock. O'Hara
and New York in the end hit it off very well.

There were many New Yorks, of course, and O'Hara seemed to thrive on
them all—not just the elegant world of MOMA⁹³ but the brawling, boozing
Cedar Tavern (Boston's Silver Dollar in excelsis), where when Jackson Pollock ripped the men's room door off its hinges O'Hara defended it all as
"interesting, not an annoyance," protesting "you couldn't see into it anyway."⁹⁴ Which is to hint at yet another world beloved of the poet perhaps
most of all—that of gay New Yorkers: the parks, the subway stations, even
the docks, O'Hara hunted them all with some regularity, alive and excited
by the danger. This was no new thing, of course. O'Hara's tastes had early
been formed at Harvard by Boston's infamous mid-twentieth-century ten-
derloin, Scollay Square, centering on the world-famous (certainly to the U.S.
Navy) Old Howard burlesque theater of bump-and-grind fame, and, too, by
the lower Washington Street "Combat Zone."⁹⁵ But Manhattan was bigger
and boozier yet, and in its sleaziest quarters, as, indeed, at MOMA, O'Hara
found old friends. On Eighth Avenue, for instance: "A Harvard friend who
had preceded us by one year, taught us the ropes," recalled Hal Fondren,
O'Hara's old Eliot House roommate: "He said: 'There's a special train. After
you've done the Third Avenue bars, you take it at Fifty-third and Third and
it goes right to West Eighth Street. And then you have all of Eighth
Street' "⁹⁶—and, behold, for O'Hara in action the E Train was hardly enough,
for he lusted not just after life but especially after straight men, black men.

Indeed, in his usual pugnacious, high-spirited way, O'Hara dared all com-
ers. His broken nose "gave him the look of a scrappy boxer," writes David
Lehman; O'Hara's walk, a friend used to say, was "a beautiful walk; confident"; "his face," according to Harold Brodkey "maintained a deadpan that
yet sparked and buzzed with signals—a form of wit."⁹⁷ As James Schuyler
wrote in his elegy, "To Frank O'Hara," taking chances was a key part of
O'Hara's personality; he loved to swim recklessly, diving into the ocean *during electrical storms*. Nor did New York faze him. Walking back to his apartment once, laden with groceries, O'Hara was, in Gooch's words, "accosted

in the dark doorway of his building by at least one young hoodlum, who demanded his wallet and keys. O'Hara casually brushed off his assailant. 'Go rob someone else,' he said. But as he started to go upstairs, he felt the impact on the first few steps of a sharp pain in his right buttock that he registered as a knife wound. He kept going." As he always did. (Actually he'd been shot.)[98] No wonder Larry Rivers painted O'Hara full length, stark naked but with his boots on. "You just go on your nerves," O'Hara once said, talking of life generally; and was it any surprise he said, too: "You just start writing."[99]

O'Hara had three major romantic relationships, including Rivers, the love of his life. It was a stormy and not entirely mutual relationship in every dimension: at O'Hara's funeral Rivers, though he had slept often with O'Hara, called him, not his lover, but—what may be more—his "best friend."[100] Always somewhat on the rebound from Rivers, O'Hara also had affairs with Vincent Warren and Bill Berkson. Warren, a handsome but rather flighty Metropolitan Opera dancer—not O'Hara's usual type—became O'Hara's love object and chief muse in his early thirties; the result a cycle of no less than fifty poems. Warren, however, was only twenty; "the whole tragedy about Frank and me . . . is that he loved me," Warren later admitted, "and I didn't know how to love at that age. It scared me. He gave the poems to me and I never could know what to say." Warren, writes Gooch, found O'Hara's "intense confrontations a bit over his head."[101] Berkson, on the other hand, a Brown dropout, also twenty-something (though O'Hara was by then approaching forty), was, in Gooch's words, full of "patrician reserve, bohemian curiosity, intelligence and politeness and brash rudeness"—much more in O'Hara's league. In Berkson's case, the demon was not age but sex; though the relationship was an intimate one—friend, confidant, sounding board, collaborator, soul mate—it was not physical enough for Berkson, who did not find O'Hara physically attractive, perhaps the deciding factor in their breakup. It was "like being friends in the eighth grade," Berkson complained.[102]

The effect of all this on O'Hara's work? Larry Rivers inspired poems of "expressionist pain and dazzling surface." Otherwise, it is interesting to contrast the "open" style of O'Hara's love poems to Warren with the "closed" style of the "experimental poems, parody, reportage, dialogue and such to, or in collaboration with, Berkson."[103] The words are Gooch's, who knew that the "sharpest satire in [O'Hara's] verse is reserved for effete homosexuals" (known, O'Hara wrote to a friend, "as dishing to some of our acquaintances. . . . Not that there aren't a lot of heterosexuals of similar persuasion, but they usually have to be drunk to talk that way. . . . They don't seem to make quite so much of a professional attitude of it)." O'Hara, for all his wit and camp, showed no such colors. His was always, Gooch insists, "a tough resolve to salvage his pain poetically."[104]

Edward Gorey's Haunted House

QUITE A CONTRAST was an illustrated limerick from the same period by one of O'Hara's college roommates, the soon-to-be-famous Edward Gorey. First published in *The Listing Attic*, it is one of the drawings and verses that Gorey scholar Karen Wilkin concludes were written in Boston just after Gorey's graduation: in it "some Harvard men, stalwart and hairy" are described as "shrieking with glee" at "burning a fairy."[105]

Now no one—even verbally—ever burned Frank O'Hara. Though many tried. But Gorey, though also a veteran, was somewhat of a different story (though it is always hard to tell with Gorey, who would certainly have admitted to no self-loathing). He once said, "There is almost no heartless work around, so I feel I am filling a small but necessary gap." To another interviewer he expanded, I think, the same point: "My mission in life is to make everybody as uneasy as possible. I think we should *all* be as uneasy as possible, because that's what the world is like."[106]

The son of a Chicago newspaperman, Gorey, if he did nothing else at Harvard, liberated O'Hara; suffice to say that their coffee table in Eliot F-13 was a slate tombstone itself liberated from Mount Auburn Cemetery. Even then Gorey, a handsome enough lad, was beginning to construct his flamboyant, spooky aura. A classmate in Eliot House, George Montgomery, later a photographer, remembers: "The first day Ted Gorey came into the [Eliot House] dining hall I thought he was the oddest person I'd ever seen . . . his hair plastered down across the front like bangs. . . . He was wearing rings on his *fingers*. It was very, very faggoty." Perhaps that's why O'Hara in the fall of 1949 changed roommates (Gorey would later remark, "I have to admit I did feel mildly abandoned").[107] Though to say, by the way, Gorey was "very faggoty" may be to suggest style more than anything else—beyond that one limerick he never said much at all about being gay. "I've never said that I was gay and I've never said that I wasn't," he told an interviewer once, adding that when a friend said to him "his creative life and his homosexuality were one and the same," all Gorey thought was 'Hogwash.' " He admitted immediately that he was being "unfair, I suppose, because maybe for him the two are linked." Never, however, did he see any evidence of that in his own work. He portrayed himself to be amazed, moreover, that anyone (as more than one critic did) should find that his books were "seething with repressed sexuality." Yet so they are, and in the oddest possible ways. Gorey's *The Curious Sofa* is subtitled, for instance, "a pornographic work," and is full of oddly contrived sexual innuendo (men described as genitally very well endowed are only depicted from behind, and so on). Gorey protested, "It's not pornographic in the standard sense. It's all in the style."[108] So perhaps he himself wasn't gay in the standard sense, either.

That Gorey's idea of gay may have been more physical than not is evident not only in the limerick, however, or in *The Curious Sofa*. "A lot of people would say I wasn't [gay] because I never do anything about it," he asserted once, denying identity on the same grounds he denied that his sexuality influenced his work. But neither assertion holds up. He did once, apparently, "do something about it." Or so at least one is entitled to construe from other of his observations. Illustrating his view of the distinction between choices and alternatives in life, Gorey admitted to Richard Dyer in *The Boston Globe Magazine* that he'd had "emotional entanglements," but that "whole stretches of your life go kerplunk when that happens." And to Stephen Schiff in *The New Yorker* he used the word *infatuation*, confessing to being "accident prone in that direction." He added, "O God, I hope I don't get infatuated with anyone ever again." He also insisted he was "reasonably undersexed." When pressed by Dyer about his solitary life, he declared: "Sometimes I ask myself why I never ended up with somebody for the rest of my life, and then I realize that I obviously don't want to, or I would have."[109]

Gorey always refused to say much more than that. One always sensed, however, that in interviews very little of a carefully constructed persona was allowed to emerge, and that Gorey, in Karen Wilkin's words, was "essentially guarded and self-protective" as opposed to "forthright." However, he was "a voluble talker once he got going," even "seems to have enjoyed, or at least, to have been interested in the process." In fact, he said too much. He once admitted, in rather a flash of insight, however fundamentally illusory, "I don't think I do anything I don't want to." Did not Gorey also say once that he thought "a creative piece of art is only interesting if it purports to be about something and is really about something else." The Harvard limerick? Gorey "took no prisoners," and as a critic he could be "vicious," in Richard Dyer's view.[110] (That was one reason perhaps he did not remain close with O'Hara, whose poetry he declined to take very seriously. Said Gorey: "I don't think anyone has done anything new since the First World War." And about O'Hara: "If Rimbaud did it all that long ago, why do it now?")

Gorey set no easy problems, admitting, "Part of me is genuinely eccentric, part of me is a bit of a put-on. But, I know what I'm doing."[111] It was certainly never in doubt at Cambridge's Poets Theatre, which, in Dyer's words,

> concentrated the aesthetic energy of the [Boston] area and the [1950s] era in a way not seen again until the advent of Peter Sellars at the Boston Shakespeare Company. In that heady art—and self-infatuated atmosphere, Gorey drew posters, designed sets, wrote, and directed a little. "It was the most fun I had in the early days," Dyer quoted Gorey as saying, "because of the variety of people who were involved—faculty, faculty children, graduates, undergraduates, and strange people" [including, Dyer adds] one of the strangest, the poet V. R. (Bunny) Lang, a great Boston eccentric and *monstre sacré*, [who] became a particularly close friend [of Gorey's and of O'Hara's].[112]

Indeed, one of Gorey's greatest triumphs, for which he won a Tony, was designing the sets for *Dracula*, at the height of his fame in New York, where he too migrated, though never so happily as O'Hara and never to O'Hara's circle and only for so long. Ultimately he was drawn back to Boston's orbit and was much seen about Cambridge and Cape Cod. He had first visited the latter while at Harvard, and he settled there for half a year in 1963, full-time in 1983 after the death of George Balanchine, whose every performance at the New York City Ballet Gorey had attended for years. Not the least mysterious thing about Gorey, all his adult life, was his dress, which was far more than just "faggoty" as it evolved. It was a case, wrote Schiff, of "half bongo-drum beatnik, half fin-de-siècle dandy." On the one hand, there were the ever-present sneakers. On the other, the always abundant jewelry—rings all over his fingers and African necklaces of beads and shells so that when the author of *The Haunted House* walked by, he was forever jingling and jangling. Invariably, too, the tall, bearded, be-sneakered and bejeweled Gorey was in a long fur coat.

It was at Harvard, whether or not he initiated this drag there, that he consolidated what we'd call today his "look." Indeed, it's possible to see Gorey's Eliot House entrance in the light of Oscar Wilde's on the Boston Music Hall stage in 1882. The response of most Harvard students had hardly changed ("it was so faggoty"). But in that the aesthete was a fellow student this time, there is just a glimpse here that along the way to the triumph of the more Whitmanic image (more middle class, more American, and in that context more masculine), the Wildean image had hardly yet exhausted itself at Harvard.

In fact, it is possible to name just the link between Wilde and Gorey, disclosed in their signature fur coat.[113]

Why Must You Know?

IN *THE LAST AVANT-GARDE*, David Lehman has written of "the predominantly masculine identity of the New York school":

> Masculine the poets were, but they deviated boldly from the prevailing masculinity. . . . While I would not want to overemphasize their homosexuality as an element of their aesthetic practice, it does seem to me that one question some of these poets are asking some of the time is whether the American pursuit of happiness may be consistent with a poetics of gaiety in both the traditional and modern senses of the world.[114]

Putting aside at this point whatever answer there may be, but keeping that large question hanging there, so to speak, there is a smaller, apparently more prosaic question to address at this point: why is there, behind Ashbery par-

ticularly but also behind O'Hara, so often clearly discernable—of all people—
a certain poet, long obscure now, whom we discussed in Chapter 3—John
Wheelwright?

Ashbery, as Brad Gooch points out, once responded to two of O'Hara's
poems ("Quiet Poem" and "Today") by sending his friend Wheelwright's
"Why Must You Know?" Ashbery told O'Hara that Wheelwright had been
"somewhat like you, though not much." A guarded insight, to be sure, but
obviously key to Ashbery's opinion of his friend's work. In fact, after
O'Hara's absurd and horrific death at age forty (Wheelwright, too, died
young, at forty-three)—as a result of injuries inflicted after a night of revels
by a dune buggy on a Fire Island beach—Ashbery remarked that his friend's
passing was "the biggest secret loss to American poetry since John Wheelwright was killed by a car in Boston in 1940."[115] And, indeed, the two deaths
were in more than one way startlingly similar—Wheelwright, also returning
from revels one night, was run down (by a driver himself drunk) on Massachusetts Avenue near Beacon Street in the Back Bay. Which may be all
there is to say.

But how different the development of the New York school and the history of American poetry itself might have been had O'Hara lived out his
expected span of life is still a commonplace of literary criticism. A far less
common question is how different Peter Davison's tale of Boston's poets and
their impact on American poetry might have been had Wheelwright, too,
lived on and developed fully. Davison doesn't bring the matter up in his
consideration of the poetry of the 1950s; nor does Allen Ginsberg (there was
less reason) in his. Yet it is a measure of Wheelwright's genius that something
like his ghost has persisted even down to our own day, words I choose
carefully. Who is that spook in the fur coat stalking through all the rooms
of all the world? Edward Gorey. But it is also John Wheelwright, of course.
And behind Wheelwright, Wilde. Certainly O'Hara's biographer makes no
bones about it: "Gorey dressed . . . in the same sort of long fur coats trailing
behind him as the Boston Brahmin poet John Wheelwright (class of '20 [at
Harvard])."[116] What *is* going on here? (Especially as it is only a little bit more
of a stretch to see in Gorey's abundant jewelry another and much earlier
Harvard Wildean, Bliss Carman.)

Gooch ventures the rather tame suggestion that Wheelwright was already
in the 1950s a "legend" at Harvard, and leaves it at that—though there are
too many legends at Harvard already (and were then) and no obvious reason
why Wheelwright should stand out. Why not John Reed, he of the jaunty
fedora and the Kremlin wall? One possible answer is that Reed wasn't
homosexual; Wheelwright probably was. Perhaps Lehman's question—
"whether the American pursuit of happiness may be consistent with a poetics
of gaiety"—must come up now after all.

Lehman himself supplies one context, concluding that the New York school of poets "favored a tradition of literary outsiders," the stranger the better:

> They admired the deliberate "derangements" of Arthur Rimbaud, the artificial continuances of Raymond Roussel, the peripatetic musings of Guillaume Apollinaire; they learned from . . . Gertrude Stein and Laura Riding as well as such neglected homespun originals as David Schubert, Delmore Schwartz, and John Wheelwright. . . . By adopting unconventional methods and models, they were able to reject the academic orthodoxies of the New Criticism . . . which seemed to have a stranglehold on mid-century verse. Enlarging the sphere of the poetic, they revitalized poetry at a moment when it seemed that everything that could be done had been done. . . . They took Pound's old dictum to heart: They made it new.[117]

Yet, in Ashbery's mind particularly, Wheelwright seems the most pointed presence; year after year, decade after decade, he seems to wax not wane in this theater, in the forefront of not only Ashbery's mind but, in some way, of Gorey's, too—every time he puts on his damn coat. In *The New York Times Book Review* in 1979, nearly three decades after first comparing Wheelwright's work with O'Hara's, Ashbery listed Wheelwright's collected poems as among the one hundred greatest post–World War II American books. A decade later, Ashbery dedicated the fourth of his Charles Eliot Norton lectures at Harvard to Wheelwright. By then his *Self-Portrait in a Convex Mirror* had won the Triple Crown (the Pulitzer Prize, the National Book Award, and the National Book Critics Circle Award), and Ashbery significantly emphasized in his Wheelwright lecture the very poem he had sent O'Hara so many lives before, "Why Must You Know?"[118]

Actually, Wheelwright's question, in a very real sense, may be the best answer to Lehman's; all the answer there is to the question of the American pursuit of happiness and gay poetics. "Why Must You Know?" *What* Must You Know? It is a question trapped in history, in some sort of homosexual collective unconscious. Why or what or when . . . Wheelwright's own exact meaning seems long past knowing now, even for Ashbery, though he does introduce his exegesis of Wheelwright's poem in his Norton lecture with two pages on the poet's "ambiguous sexuality," concluding, "The poem seems to be a highly circuitous return from the contemplation of death to the possibility of embracing life, a kind of *valse hésitation* whose rhythms recall what we know of Wheelwright's affective life," which sounds I think a little bit like O'Hara's fighting toward his "loophole for living."[119]

It is, to be sure, Ashbery's conclusion, another very guarded insight, a very circumspect exegesis, itself reminiscent of his comparison of the work of O'Hara and Wheelwright so many years earlier. But that is somewhat the point: "guarded" is characteristic of Ashbery. "Affective life" is actually pretty clear and specific in his terms. So, too, is Ashbery's intelligence that Wheelwright is still one of a half dozen or so writers he often reads "in order to get started," or for a "jump start."[120]

Ashbery, who came out to his mother at sixteen, has lived ever since quite evidently the life of an out gay man in a long-term relationship, but as a poet he has resisted labeling, like Auden and those who, in Gregory Woods's words, are "quite open about being homosexual but do not wish to be read as gay writers."[121] Yet since critic John Shoptaw's brilliant *On the Outside Looking Out,* a study of Ashbery's work, it is "incontestable," in Gooch's words, "that aspects of Ashbery's poetry, and in particular his irony and evasiveness, owe something to the culture of homosexuality, in which concealment and disguise—and their opposite, the occasional histrionic display—play a vital part." Indeed, another critic, Helen Vendler, has called Ashbery's poetry a form of "disguised autobiography."[122] What a continuum of being gay at Harvard in the 1950s these literary landmarks stand for— O'Hara's "Morgenmusik," Gorey's limerick, Ashbery's "Some Trees." One begins to understand more than only John Ashbery or John Wheelwright, or any of their friends, in Ashbery's telling lines—written at the continuum's center—"A face looks out from the mirror / As if to say, / Be supple, young man, / Since you can't be gay."[123]

Heralds, prophets even, of something larger that we all still participate in, O'Hara and Ashbery and Gorey were strikingly alike in one thing above all. When Karen Wilkin remarks on "the complicated relationship of Gorey's work to literary tradition, both high and low," she touches on something that Gooch found was also key to the work of the two poets:

> O'Hara's and Ashbery's innovation was to be able to pass with each other from the high to the low, to gather in their net such disparate fascinations as French Surrealist poetry, Hollywood's "guilty pleasures," Japanese Kabuki and Noh, Schoenberg's twelve-tone compositions. . . . Ashbery credits O'Hara with having been the leader in instilling such an original, and almost impossibly inclusive, esthetic into his group at Harvard. [Their] pluralism became a striking trait of American culture in later decades. . . . thanks in part to the range of tones in Ashbery's and O'Hara's poems. . . . Their springtime chats on the banks of the Charles . . . contributed to what later became thought of as the "postmodern" attitude.[124]

Finally, the New York school shows very well the effect on each other's game of "home" and "away." It had as much to do with Harvard as with Manhattan, with Boston Brahmin strengths as well as weaknesses and New Yorkers' more open and thus more gay-welcoming attitude. Writing in *The Boston Globe* of "the appropriateness of selecting a Boston newspaper to herald the glory of the New York School," David Lehman pointed out that poet James Schuyler—along with O'Hara, Ashbery, and Kenneth Koch, one of the school's core poets—thought of the other three

> as "the Harvard wits." Harvard in those years was charged with intellectual ferment and artistic possibility. It was there in June 1947 that George Marshall unveiled the European Recovery Plan. . . . It was another landmark piece of legislation, the GI Bill, that enabled O'Hara (a Navy veteran) and Koch . . . to attend Harvard. As Jewish and working-class veterans arrived in unprecedented numbers, the conception of Harvard as a gentleman's club with restricted access gave way rapidly to a model of the university as an intellectual center doubling as the site of advanced social change.[125]

Beat Trinity

PROPHECY THERE WAS. And acted out in the New York school, a part (mostly O'Hara's) of which heralded "gay liberation." But another herald was much bleaker, its explanation more rage than prophecy. Certainly the Harvard gay experience was never bleaker—blacker—than in the astonishing work of William S. Burroughs, which in that decade of rich literary ferment arrested and shocked the whole country.

Burroughs's first and most conventional literary niche was having been the mentor and guide in mid-1940s New York to both Jack Kerouac and Allen Ginsberg, with whom he became the nucleus of the Beat movement in America—a more violent and much raunchier version of the pre–World War I, Harvard-centered Vagabondia movement of Richard Hovey and Bliss Carman and Tom Meteyard. In fact, after World War II, Kerouac, Ginsberg, and Burroughs soon constituted what has been called "Beat's Unholy Trinity."

Of these 1950s vagabonds, one was sort of attractive—Kerouac—something of a Whitmanic gay in denial. Born north of Boston in the industrial city of Lowell, of French-Canadian background, winner of a football scholarship to Columbia, Kerouac was a bohemian born: freewheeling, almost unmeaning, but able to tellingly distill meaning from an episodic and random life and transform that meaning in turn into poetry. Never mind that he was also irresponsible, predatory, misogynistic, guilt-ridden, and given to short-term marriages with women he abandoned and one-night stands with men (including, famously, Gore Vidal) he always "forgot." He was also handsome of face and body.

The second person of this trio, Ginsberg, neither in personality nor form anything so attractive, was, however, equally a bohemian, with a libido as large as his ego. Although also more disreputable (to the point of defending so-called man-boy love), Ginsberg became probably the best-known American poet of the post–World War II period, always confessional, frequently homoerotic, relentlessly revolutionary.[126]

Burroughs, the third member of this gang of outlaws, was a novelist. And his work was no prettier than that of the two poets, which was the point, of course. It expressed the zeitgeist of an age of profound, even seismic, change: Kerouac's *On the Road* of 1957, Ginsberg's *Howl* of 1956 (dedicated to Burroughs), and Burroughs's *Naked Lunch* of 1959–1962 (the earlier date its Paris publication, the second the U.S. debut) were literary landmarks of an era of conspicuous transition in American literary history. Whether seen as obscene or liberating, they defined the age for many. And Burroughs, the *least* attractive by far, was the Harvard man (class of 1936).

Born in 1914, the scion of one of America's great fortunes—his grandfather invented the adding machine—Burroughs was raised, if not in want of money, then in want of what most would have expected; his father having been swindled out of most of his inheritance, the Burroughses of St. Louis, though they lived comfortably enough right through the Great Depression, had the peculiar problem of "bear[ing] the name of a famous company that [they] didn't own a part of."[127] So writes Ted Morgan, Burroughs's biographer; it was "rather like a Potemkin Village made out of cardboard." Burroughs's early education was not obviously lacking but vaguely unsettling. He was sent as a youngster to Los Alamos School in Santa Fe, New Mexico, a very rugged outdoorsman's school founded by one of Theodore Roosevelt's Rough Riders, a school that seemed to young Burroughs something of a prison, and was certainly a very anti-intellectual place to send a young man before Harvard. Yet Burroughs didn't like Harvard any better. Indeed, there seemed little enough happiness in his youth, unless it was duck hunting with his father, and that legacy—he became a good shot and a lifelong gun enthusiast—would in later life come back to haunt him. He came out sexually at Los Alamos (told his mother, left school, returned home) but still felt very sexually frustrated at Harvard, where he resorted to prostitutes, from whom he caught syphilis. Burroughs was no happier academically—only Shakespeare and Chaucer seemed at all to register, and they not much. The controlling factor of his college years seems clearly to have been his even more dismal social experience. His only sport seems to have been rowing. Nor did he do anything of any literary significance. "Billy wasn't rebellious at Harvard," Ted Morgan observes; "but he soon began to hate the place. There was an 'in' crowd made up of boys from Eastern prep schools and they never accepted him. . . . No club wanted him."[128]

In truth, many of his habits were problematic, to say the least. Adams House was his house at Harvard, and in his room there he kept a ferret named Sredni Vashtar after a story by Saki in which a ten-year-old trains the ferret to kill his bossy guardian. Some of his friends were equally strange. Among them was William P. Frere von Blomberg, the adopted son of a sister of Hitler's first minister of defense. According to Morgan, moreover, "Members of the Porcellian Club . . . all but crossed the sidewalk when they saw him coming." And no wonder. It would be hard to paint a more un-alluring picture. Nor does it become more attractive when one considers the building blocks of his future literary distinction Burroughs was putting into place. Seeing himself more and more as an outsider, and concerned above all with debunking what he saw as control systems, Burroughs, writes Morgan, was increasingly "fascinated by low life and by the behavior of crimi-nals." Perhaps that explains his postgraduate study there and abroad of anthropology and medicine. But neither interest was pursued professionally after Harvard, where though he got his degree, his social isolation was such that according to Morgan, he felt that "he had flunked out as a member of the WASP elite."[129] He had no better luck with the U.S. Army, failing as he did the psychological test.

Talk about a self-fulfilling prophecy, the same pattern of rejection is not hard to see in his homosexuality:[130] as an example of his deep self-loathing, one need only dip into *Junkie*:

> In the French Quarter there are several queer bars so full every night the fags spill out on to the sidewalk. A room full of fags gives me the horrors. They jerk around like puppets on invisible strings, galvanized into hid-eous activity that is the negation of everything living and spontaneous. The live human being has moved out of these bodies long ago. But some-thing moved in when the original tenant moved out. Fags are ventrilo-quists' dummies who have moved in and taken over the ventriloquist. The dummy sits in a queer bar nursing his beer, and uncontrollably yapping out of a rigid doll face.[131]

No wonder Burroughs's work reaches a certain climax in visions of homo-sexual youth as violent, tough, heartless terrorists.

It did not help that by the time he met Ginsberg and Kerouac in New York in the mid-1940s he was a drug addict, his demons equally heroin and morphine, the crest of this scene coming in 1951 in Mexico City, where Burroughs and his then-wife, Joan Vollmer, had taken refuge from drug possession charges, and where—in the mother of all William Tell stunts—he turned out not to be a good enough shot after all, killing Vollmer. It was an accident, of course—but the sort of bizarrely horrific accident that seemed to come naturally to Burroughs. One hardly knows, either, how to take his remark, years later, after he had achieved, finally, a substantial if notorious literary success: "I am forced to the appalling conclusion that I never would have become a writer but for Joan's death. . . . I live with the constant threat of possession. . . . I have no choice but to write my way out."[132] As to that, it is undeniable, however, that, in Gary Susman's words, he "pushed the limits of novelistic content and the form of the novel itself" to the point where it has seemed to many less a literary creation than the leftovers of a nightmare. Important leftovers, however. The failed attempts to suppress his *Naked Lunch* in 1966 marked the virtual end of the history of American judicial censorship of literature. At its historic obscenity trial in Boston, Harvard (and MIT and Wellesley and so on) turned out in force to defend Burroughs, including author and alumnus Norman Mailer, poet and instructor John Ciardi, and professor of sociology Paul Hollander.[133] Although the novel is a first-person account of drug rejection that many found hard to credit, Dr. John Barry Sturrock of the Boston City Hospital, a pillar of the Boston establishment, shocked everyone by declaring that, in his experience as a psychiatrist, the book expressed exactly and accurately the experience of using drugs. The rest of Harvard winced and stayed home. But as Gary Susman pointed out, "banned in Boston" was over.[134]

The *Naked Lunch* trial was only the tip of the iceberg, however, of the 1960s, when Harvard became enmeshed in a scandal more than literary, with Burroughs by no means the only star player. In that storied decade of antiwar angst and mind-opening liberation (or, depending on your point of view, the end of civilization as J. Edgar Hoover knew it), Dr. Timothy Leary was appointed director of the Center of Research in Personality in Harvard's Social Relations department. His chief interest was the study of consciousness-expanding drugs; his goal to harness their behavior-modifying properties to improve society. In 1960 he designed a research program with no less than Aldous Huxley, the world's leading proponent of psychedelic experimentation (and author of two books on mescaline, *The Doors of Perception* and *Heaven and Hell*), who happened that year to be a visiting professor at MIT. Leary, planning a symposium for the American Psychological Association's 1961 annual meting in New York, immediately got in touch with Burroughs. Writes Barry Miles:

> This letter from Leary to Burroughs could be said to mark the beginning of the sixties movement. It shows Leary, at the birth of his "psychedelic revolution," seeking an alliance with those fifties renegades, the Beats. . . .
>
> The mutation from Beat to hippie meant a switch from grass to acid, from literature to music, from a small group of writers and artists and jazz musicians to a mass youth movement, from an antipolitical stance to a coalition of anti-war, civil rights, and environmental movements . . . from yippies to radical nuns and priests. . . .
>
> The sixties people were on an audio trip and didn't need much more poetry than John Lennon's lyrics and Bob Dylan's lyrics. Dylan . . . whose early songs reflected his reading of *Howl* and *On the Road*.
>
> At the heart of this . . . generational upheaval was Dr. Leary. . . . There was a time in the sixties when people wore a blue-and-orange button that said "Leary is God." . . .

In 1960, however, Dr. Leary was not yet God, he was a Harvard professor. . . . [135]

A Harvard professor with hallucinogenic drugs to give away, the best-known
today, LSD. And not only Burroughs but Ginsberg, too, were quick to beat
a path to Harvard Yard.

It had been, in fact, at Ginsberg's suggestion, according to Barry Miles,
Ginsberg's biographer, that Leary wrote to Burroughs (his task was to study
and report on the differences between narcotic and psychedelic drugs) as
well as to a whole roster of counterculture luminaries, including Dizzy Gil-
lespie, Willem de Kooning, and Robert Lowell, all of whom agreed to take
all these drugs in aid of a group-therapy project of Leary's at the nearby
state prison in Concord. Thus it was that Ginsberg, too, though his only
known association with Harvard was through Leary's project, became distinctly a part of the gay scene there in the 1960s. Once, in the fall of 1960,
against the rules of his Harvard contract, Leary took his drugs home, and
on one occasion that year, in his Beacon Street house, gave Ginsberg a huge
dose of psilocybin. Stretched out on his bed in a guest room, a record of
Wagner's *Götterdämmerung* thundering through his room, Ginsberg became
sure he was "the creative God." Forthwith, and quite naked, he descended
to the parlor and announced to Leary and Peter Orlovsky that he was the
Messiah. He attempted healings on the spot. Undaunted (they didn't take),
he called Kerouac, announcing to the operator: "This is God. G-O-D. I want
to talk to Kerouac." When he got through, he summoned his friend to
Boston: "Take a plane. . . . The revolution is beginning. Gather all the dark
angels. . . ." It was a great trip. Not since Julia Ward Howe entertained divine
Oscar had Beacon Street been the scene of anything so *outré*.

In another way a better comparison would be to Amy Lowell, toward
whom a backward glance. Humanities scholar Melissa Bradshaw and
women's studies scholar Adrienne Munich, in 2002 the editors of the first
volume of Lowell's poems in decades, note that if "her great progenitors"
were Whitman and Dickinson ("whose voices also went against the grain"),
Lowell's free verse—the work of a "cigar-smoking, Boston Brahmin lesbian
lover"—also very much helped "build the road to Allen Ginsberg, May Sarton, and Sylvia Plath, and beyond."[136]

Ginsberg always entranced the Yard. In 1964, for instance, his biographer
records that

Allen and Peter [Orlovsky, his lover] flew to Boston as guests of Harvard
where Allen was scheduled to give four readings. These were the first
public readings in which he sang as part of his performance. He and
Peter chanted mantras, using Peter's harmonium as accompaniment. . . .
Allen and Peter spent long evenings visiting old friends and drinking in

the Harvard Tavern, and they slept with so many people, male and female, that they were banished from Harvard's Lowell [House] by their hosts, and had to stay with friends for the remainder of their visit. After three weeks of poetry and orgies, they returned to New York.

Ginsberg, as it turned out, intrigued many. In India once, he noted the Dalai Lama's interest in the drug, promising to have "Timothy Leary send him some from Harvard."[137] Ginsberg was more the star of this second act of their generation at Harvard than Burroughs, whose response to the "magic mushroom drug" was less enthusiastic than Ginsberg's. But in the long run it is probably Burroughs's life and work that stand out most, particularly *Naked Lunch*, a cause célèbre that goes right on. Mary McCarthy surprised everyone, for instance, by *liking* the book, comparing *Naked Lunch* to Vladimir Nabokov's *Pale Fire* and *Lolita*, invoking Swift, McCarthy's biographer, Carol Brightman, has written, as Burroughs's "literary ancestor with his own scatological obsessions, but whose chief concern, like Burroughs's, is a fierce repugnance for the hypocrisy of the body politic." *Naked Lunch* was never meant for the general public, McCarthy felt; only for what Brightman called "the downtown literati." Besides, McCarthy liked the book's humor, "peculiarly American, at once broad and sly," she wrote in a very positive review in *The New York Review of Books*. "The surreal side of Burroughs's imagination remind[ed] McCarthy," Brightman wrote, "of a Marx Brothers movie or a Jimmy Durante act; a 'Hell-zapoppin effect of orgies and riots' and metamorphoses, like the Mixmaster in *Naked Lunch* that tries to climb up the puzzled housewife's skirt."[138]

Opinions about Burroughs's books were often almost as extreme as the books themselves. *New Criterion* editor Roger Kimball, even years later, in a joint obituary for Burroughs and Allen Ginsberg, his sometime lover, was still not impressed. "It has been a bad year," he wrote, "for famous drug-abusing literary charlatans."[139] But Barry Miles argues well that the Beats have, in retrospect, mattered a good deal, to homosexuals particularly. The gay movement, Miles writes, "has clear roots in the kind of open-minded comradeship and male bonding found in the early Beats." He cites Ginsberg and Kerouac as one example, Ginsberg and Burroughs as another; then he concludes: "It was a kind of masculine tenderness out of Walt Whitman, virtually unknown in the late forties and fifties"—such Wildean years in gay history?—and it was this Whitmanic discourse that "later became a prototype in the gay community."[140]

Rock musicians have also ensured the Beat legacy. They found Burroughs particularly stimulating: the phrase *heavy metal* was originally Burroughs's; the band Steely Dan was named for a milk-filled dildo in *Naked Lunch*; the work of Patti Smith—she, gloriously, of "Gloria"—reflects Burroughs's influence for rockers. Burroughs, with his violent hallucinatory catalogue of transgressive sexual imagery of control and submission, wasn't just an influence: he was an inspiration. Yet "for all his libertarianism, well-traveled worldliness, and radically innovative art, [Burroughs] remained a conservative (in a libertarian vein) and a stern moralist," insisted Gary Susman in *The Boston Phoenix*. Burroughs's work, he concluded,

> like that of the other Beat revolutionaries, placed him squarely within the American literary tradition. Where the questing Kerouac harked back to the restless Thoreau and the picaresque early Twain, and where the exuberantly breathless Ginsberg echoed the pansexuality of Whitman, Burroughs evoked Emerson's self-reliance (he'd have agreed with Emerson's statement that "nothing is at last sacred but the integrity of your own mind"), Melville's paranoid reading of the world as a system of coded symbols, and the later Twain's grimly satirical pessimism about humanity's future.[141]

Nearly always in coat and tie, Burroughs ended his years far from Harvard Yard, in Lawrence, Kansas; this (by then) member of the American Academy of Arts and Letters slept alone every night in his own home, surrounded (like Gorey) by innumerable cats, but also by a pistol he always kept close at hand. Doubtless he had his reasons. By more than one measure Burroughs was the most evil-speaking and hateful gay man of his generation, at once a monster of self-hatred and a baleful instrument of revenge, who in the view of many only told an ugly truth: "The point of sexual relations between men is nothing that we would call love," he insisted, "but rather what we might call recognition."[142] Politics, repression, rage, prophecy—sex. And the greatest of these may have been rage. "To speak is to lie," Burroughs insisted; "to live is to collaborate."[143] It was a long way from Whitman and Emerson; the Boston Common or Harvard Yard they knew hardly any longer in sight.

6.

"Foxy Grandpa's" Perspective: Transcontinental Homophile

When I first met Prescott Townsend I was a very young man, he was a very old man, proof when I needed proof not only that there was a gay past, but that as a young gay man I had also a future to look forward to.
—Randy Wicker

WHETHER IT WAS Gorey's Harvard Yard "bonfire lynching" or Alsop's Moscow hotel-room entrapment by the K.G.B., or Burroughs's rantings— or, indeed, Matthiessen's suicide—the strains and stresses of the 1950s, that in so many ways unlovely decade, were such that the need for fresh air can be felt even at a distance of fifty or more years later. And whatever it may mean, two of the six original chapters of the pioneering gay advocacy group of those years, the Mattachine Society, named after a medieval fraternity of musicians who wore masks when they performed publicly in order to conceal their identity, were founded by Harvard graduates: Prescott Townsend's Boston Mattachine of 1957 and Franklin Kameny's Washington Mattachine of 1961. Kameny's achievements were greater. But Townsend, much the older of the two (Kameny earned his Harvard degree in 1956; Townsend in 1918), though largely forgotten today, was the prophet. Moreover, as was the case with Lucien Price, Townsend's career spanned, somewhat later than Price's, over half a century—in Townsend's case, from before World War I to the 1970s—and offers, again, a chance for us to consider another Harvard gay life in detail, one as flagrant and notorious as Price's was dignified and discreet. The artist René Ricard, Townsend's protégé originally, used to call the older man "foxy grandpa." Quite a contrast to Price's Stoic perspective, "foxy grandpa's" was no less significant.[1]

Boston Brahmin

IT WAS ONLY very late in his long life that Prescott Townsend might be adjudged "foxy"; in his early years the better word would have been "frisky." Young Prescott, born in 1894, Boston bred and Harvard-plated, grew up boasting, as patrician youngsters were apt to then, of his ancestry. No fewer than twenty-three of his ancestors had come over on the *Mayflower*. That boast, which was made as well in one of his Harvard class reports (and not disputed, so far as I know), is as may be, but it certainly is true that Townsend's third great-great-grandfather signed not only the Declaration of Independence and the Articles of Confederation but also the Constitution of the United States; "the only man," Townsend used to point out, "to be so inconsistent." More immediately, Prescott was the third son of distinctly a Brahmin alliance (like John Wheelwright's—of traders and saints) between the Townsends and the Wendells. His father, Edward Britton Townsend, was the founder and president of an important coal company; his mother, née Kate Wendell, was descended from illustrious "do-gooders." Prescott grew up in the family domiciles in Brookline and the Back Bay, Boston's grandest neighborhoods, attending the famous Church of the Advent, where the All Saints' altar designed by Ralph Adams Cram was a memorial to Prescott's grandmother. After prep school the boys, naturally, were sent to Harvard; after finishing school, the girls—rather progressively—to Bryn Mawr.

Growing up, Boston (even America) was Prescott's in distinctly a personal and proprietorial sense few can claim. It was not only the *Mayflower*, or the Declaration of Independence and the Constitution, that his ancestors had helped to shape. Every generation offered the young man family heroes. On his way each day to the fashionable Volkmann School at the top of Beacon Hill, Prescott could hardly help passing the Ether Memorial in the Boston Public Garden without remembering that one of his great-uncles had been present at the historic first use of ether in 1846 at the Massachusetts General Hospital the monument commemorates; farther along in the garden, depending on his route, was the statue of another ancestor, the great abolitionist Wendell Phillips; continuing up Beacon Street ("street of the sifted few," Henry James called it), young Prescott would have to pass the elegant brick town house of William Prescott, the great nineteenth-century historian, another forebear; even the Bunker Hill Monument, so immense on the Boston skyline in the pre-skyscraper era, was also a family monument: the day would duly come when every year on Bunker Hill Day, the adult Prescott Townsend would take his place in the Bunker Hill Day parade in the role of yet another ancestral worthy, Colonel William Prescott, the hero of that crucial battle of the American Revolution. By then, moreover, it had long since become clear to everyone that Prescott Townsend would more than live up to the revolutionary heritage, at once renowned and reckless, that he was so conscious of inheriting.[2]

His relationship with his parents is also interesting. He spoke of his father, who died in 1910, when Prescott was only fifteen, with some guilt: "Father worked hard and made money," Prescott would later observe in one of his Harvard class reports, "while I got an Oedipus Complex that couldn't be changed." But there is the hint of a somewhat progressive parental attitude in the suggestion young Prescott saw a psychiatrist (more likely than it might seem because Boston was then the spearhead of Freudianism in America; while there in the 1900s Henry James himself sought treatment), and this is reinforced by the assertion in an unpublished manuscript by Adrian Cathcart (a k a John T. Kearney), Townsend's designated biographer, who recounts how Townsend told him that, as a teenager, "as soon as he had realized that his physical affections were directed toward those of his own sex, he informed his parents," who were, he said, "understanding"; only warning him "to be careful."[3] Certainly there is convincing evidence his mother at least was supportive. Joseph McGrath, Townsend's secretary in late life, recalls his employer's devotion to her, and reports that Townsend said more than once he thought she would have been very proud of his progressive politics and social work. On the other hand, his elder brother, Richard, came to be anything but proud; he grew to loathe Prescott and never minded saying so, a more typically (for the time) masculine view that might have reflected more the attitude of Prescott's father.[4]

What stands out from all this—and it is just the sort of thing one would expect from a son of Kate Wendell, herself scion of perhaps the greatest of the abolitionists—is that Prescott Townsend approached college and adulthood very much more open-minded in the matter of sexuality than was the norm. Moreover, a series of precollege summer jobs, part of an extensive trip he made out west at age eighteen, with much hiking and logging and fire fighting, only reinforced his openness generally as a youth to what today we would call the "underclass." Wrote historian Charles Shively many years later in an article about Townsend:

> When he went to work during the summer of 1914 in the logging and mining camps of Idaho and Montana . . . he came in contact with the free-wheeling International Workers of the World (IWW, "Wobblies"), who were organizing unskilled and itinerant workers. Their anarchist politics left a strong imprint on the impressionable youth. . . . IWW reached out to drifters, lumber jacks, and other restless people; they recruited particularly among the "hobos" of the time. The lumber camps and the IWW gave Townsend a quite different view of the world than Harvard. . . . Prescott developed a lifelong interest in street boys and drifters.[5]

When he entered Harvard in the fall of 1914, Prescott seems to have formed a sexual liaison that year with another freshman jock—a polo player—by name of Fred Harvey, the heir to a Kansas City restaurant chain. Fifty years later Townsend had not forgotten Harvey, nor how positively *welcomed* he felt as part of what he conceived as a distinct brotherhood, telling the New York gay activist Randy Wicker in an interview: "I didn't ever feel guilty . . . but I was very frightened . . . I had my first experience at nineteen, but after that I really didn't have any more contacts during the World War. Becoming involved in gay life was a slow process for me because I was so busy going out to dances with girls and working hard on my studies. My brothers before me had been very active with girls socially. Because of this and because I was in the social register, I was always being drawn into things."[6]

He does not seem at the time to have minded. Assigned his freshman year to Gore Hall, one of three splendid new freshman dormitories, their courtyards opening grandly to the Charles River, young Townsend took his meals in Gore's beautiful new vaulted dining hall and played on the dormitory's highly touted freshman tennis team; indeed, though wartime comings and goings would disrupt sports at Harvard in this period, and college records acknowledge no rankings in tennis in Prescott's last year, he claimed in his Harvard fiftieth reunion report that he had been the school's tennis champion. At any rate he was good enough to make Gore's team his first year and, like most jocks, Townsend probably spent more time on the courts than at his studies, about which he is on record only as having mixed feelings about Charles Townsend Copeland—no relation—whose famous open houses he always said that he had much profited by.[7]

Sports, studies, socializing, all the traditional collegiate pastimes, seem, however, to have soon taken a backseat at Harvard in Prescott's time to military training, it being increasingly clear (especially at a Anglophile Harvard) that the U.S. would likely be drawn into the war that by 1915 was raging across Europe. In 1916, as part of the Naval Reserve program at Harvard, Townsend went on a training cruise, and some of his letters home disclose just the contrasts one would expect of a Harvard undergraduate being jump-started into a wartime naval officer. On September 5 of that year, Townsend wrote to his mother: "We had battle practice and drill this morning. Last night I slept under the stars at the foot of the [aft] mast. . . . [We have] been shoveling coal in the bunkers where it was 123 degrees and dust so thick you could not see. . . . Yesterday I tried to organize the handling in a more efficient manner and worked in all the positions both in the Boat and on the beach. Took pictures of the submarines. . . . Looked at a sailboat and went in swimming."

The sailing and swimming side of things, more alluring than organizing boat drills (much less shoveling coal), increased considerably when his ship made port. After one such call at Newport News, Virginia, Townsend reported home more fully as to the other side of his life: "A wonderful dinner and bed at the Auchinclosses. . . . I played tennis a little. . . . Hugh then took us in his Stutz to Bailey's Beach. . . . He was in the class below Jimmy at Groton." Can strawberries and champagne have been far away? For Prescott, an ardent Anglophile all his life, such treats one is sure did not go unappreciated; nor for so idealistic a young man his military duties unfulfilled—in 1917, the year the U.S. entered the war on Britain's side, Prescott followed

suit, leaving Harvard in his junior year and enlisting for active service. Enrolled in 1917 as a chief boatswain mate, he was made an ensign in September
of that year and assigned to a berth aboard the U.S.S. *Illinois,* a battleship
of the Atlantic Fleet. Ultimately he was assigned to the Naval Unit, College
Station, at Texas A&M University, where he became commanding officer.
Quick in, however, Townsend was also quick out—in 1919, as soon as the
armistice was signed. Yet he had served four full years in the reserve and on
active service and merited eleven lines in the published volume recording
Harvard's servicemen in the war.[8] Honorably discharged, he returned to
college for his senior year, graduating as part of the class of 1918 but a year
late, going directly thereafter for graduate study to Harvard Law School.

Like so many people after World War I, Townsend evidently found the
"Roaring Twenties," as they would come to be called, much more alluring
than graduate school. His letters home in 1916 had already disclosed that his
years at Harvard and in the navy had been as formative as his trip out west,
and that he had formed a number of convictions: "I suppose this sounds
very egotistical," he wrote to his mother then, "but I will always try to say
what I think. Most of these people are afraid of the truth. They borrow their
opinions from others and there is no I to their thoughts."[9] Forthwith, his
postwar alumni reports to his classmates announced on the one hand a
newfound agnosticism, but on the other a general resolve to emulate both
Christ and Francis of Assisi in helping people;[10] seriousness of moral purpose,
in other words, had been wedded to a decided independence, somewhat of
a problematic combination for a man of Townsend's sexual orientation. One
wonders why Townsend kept at his studies for a full year. Surely, however,
the progressive crusades of his later life offer a likely clue. Although the law
school in the wake of Justices Brandeis and Felix Frankfurter (who would
so ardently attack the Sacco-Vanzetti verdict) was poised to offer a pulpit
for many progressive causes in the 1920s and '30s, sexual liberation in any
sense was still not one of them by a long shot. Really, Townsend's only
choice, barring surrender to convention, was bohemia, the more distant the
better. At the end of his first year at the law school, he dropped out. At
once he applied for membership in the Harvard Travelers Club, composed
then (it still exists) of those at the beginning of the twentieth century with
the inclination and the means to go adventuring in exotic locales, the farther
from home the better. Townsend was elected in 1921.[11]

Bohemia

HIS FIRST PEREGRINATION, and no easy one, either—Townsend all his
life would be a dedicated outdoorsman—was to the rain forests near the
Rio Blanco in Mexico, where he was, in his own words, "the co-discoverer
of some ancient Taltic [*sic*] stone heads, and had a new species of salamander
named after me."[12] (Again, a Freudian propensity may be found in the nam-

ing of the new species, which was called *Salamandra oedipustownsendentis*). And if that was not exotic enough, Townsend surfaces next in Paris, where in or around 1920 he was planning yet another expedition, this time led by himself, to North Africa.

What exactly landed him in the French capital is not clear (though Paris's bohemia, after all, is always *the* bohemia), but there seems little doubt Townsend fell much under the spell there of André Gide, the French writer many American gays today would not approve of (he was very intolerant, scorned "gender-inappropriate" behavior, and ardently advocated pederasty) but who is still celebrated for having been the first openly homosexual man awarded the Nobel Prize for Literature. Gide's openness, even in the 1920s, was legendary (in 1926 he even came out in print) and that was just the sort of link that would have led the already famous writer and the idealistic young Harvard Law dropout to bond, as they clearly did in Paris, and perhaps even more closely the next year in North Africa. It was there more than a quarter century earlier, in 1895, that a much younger Gide had run into Oscar Wilde and Lord Alfred Douglas, and, at their urging, had his first homosexual sexual experience. Twenty-seven years later, in 1922, Gide and Townsend themselves rendezvoused, or so one may conclude from Townsend's recollection years later (when a Bedouin cloak, or *djellaba*, he cherished appeared to have been stolen) that the cloak had been given him in Algeria by Gide, who, indeed, had it himself, he claimed, from T. E. Lawrence.[13]

Lawrence of Arabia was probably very much in Townsend's mind that year in North Africa as he outfitted his mini caravan of camels and camping gear, with a whole retinue of youths as guides, cooks, and whatever—willing for both work and pleasure, one assumes. (How many gays with the means—Lawrence was not the only one; John Singer Sargent was another—found in this era both adventure and solace in distant and exotic locales?) Indeed, some of Townsend's experiences on this expedition were akin to Lawrence's own: he dined out for years on how at the height of the Rif Rebellion in 1922, determined to make his way and not be bogged down in a war zone, he had nonchalantly braved a brisk exchange of rifle fire between the forces of Abd al-Karim and the Foreign Legion, reducing the startled combatants to an uneasy truce while he passed through, grandly announcing he was an American citizen and as such entitled to safe passage.[14]

Back in Paris, a lesser mentor but closer friend perhaps than the much older Gide was Elliot Paul, only three years Townsend's senior. Paul was a novelist who may also then have been the lover of Townsend, who was perhaps the inspiration for the character of Lancaster Huntington (Primway) in Paul's novel *I'll Hate Myself in the Morning*. A Bostonian too, who in later years became well-known for such books as *The Life and Death of a Spanish Town* (1937), *The Last Time I Saw Paris* (1942), and *Waylaid in Boston* (1953), Paul had served with the U.S. Army in France during World War I, returning to Paris in 1921 as a correspondent for the Associated Press. His first novel,

Indelible, was published in 1922 to considerable acclaim. "[Paul's] role in the literary life of Paris in the 1920's," literary historian David Anderson has written, "was important." And one may assume Townsend went everywhere and met everyone (doubtless including Gide) in the company of Paul, the coeditor with founder Eugene Jolas of *transition*, an avant-garde Paris literary magazine of the 1920s that published some of what would turn out to be the most lively and seminal literature of the twentieth century: not only Gide's work but Ernest Hemingway's and Hart Crane's, as well as an excerpt from James Joyce's then forthcoming *Finnegans Wake*, and art commissioned from Miró and Picasso. Their great champion, Gertrude Stein, was a close friend to Paul. ("I have never seen two persons become friends more quickly than Gertrude and Elliot," novelist Bravig Imbs recalled. "The very first contact was electric." Stein called Paul "a New England Saracen," and it was Paul who wrote for the *Chicago Tribune* the first article on Stein's work to reach a wide public.)[15] It was a formative period in Townsend's life; he was at the heart of the crucible of twentieth-century modernism. Perhaps because of his mother's cancer (she died in 1927) he was back in Boston, however, by the mid-1920s. So was Paul, and the two men were as inseparable in the New England capital as in the French one, both determined, it would seem, to fan the embers of Boston's own Beacon Hill bohemia, which had sustained quite a spirited community (of national importance artistically) in the 1890s but had (with the single and notable exception of Amy Lowell) more or less sputtered out by the 1920s.

The result, "sudden, raucous and boozy . . . with the arts for an indifferent warrant and garret-to-garret hey-hey as a leitmotiv," wrote Lucius Beebe in *Boston and the Boston Legend*, was most evident in the distinctive sociality of a whole series of subterranean cafés (tearooms officially—this was the era of Prohibition in America) with names like the Green Shutters. This last café, the domain of Paul himself, was located on a street so narrow (Cedar Lane Way) one car could barely traverse it in one direction at a time. The café itself was described by Beebe as "a tiny place, seating but thirty patrons, although on special occasions some of the guests preferred to sit on the floor as merely anticipating the time when they would find themselves there anyway," the outcome, he reported, of "heroic portions of gin and vermouth discreetly furnished forth at the Green Shutters in tea cups." Wrote this chronicler of bohemia:

> There were hints of even more exotic practices and prominent Bohemians were apprehended in raids on Negro night clubs in the South End. . . . The studios of Myrtle and Mount Vernon Streets were subjected to frequent [police] raids by embattled [officers] who visioned counterfeiting, cocaine vending and worse wherever a bayberry candle glimmered in the neck of a discarded whiskey bottle. Usually, however, they discovered nothing worse than a temporarily decommissioned playwright or Harvard Latin

instructor under the bed. . . . Psychoanalysis raged through [the] . . . tea-rooms where earnest youths and maidens stared fixedly at each other and exhorted themselves to abandon their uncompensated inferiority fixations. Studio parties turned out to be brawls of Scott Fitzgerald proportions and there was a tidal wave of erotica which surged through the bookshops of Mount Vernon Street.[16]

This was by no means all Townsend's and Paul's doing, but they were, according to Beebe, the key figures in this revived Beacon Hill bohemia. Pointing out rather unkindly that however important he was in Paris, Paul "hail[ed] from one of Boston's drearier suburbs" (Malden—doubtless Townsend's Brahmin status was part of his charm for Paul), Beebe nonetheless acknowledged Paul was "the Hill's most authentic Bohemian," crediting him with having "inaugurated the reign of shiny black suits, broad-brimmed black felt hats, wide Basque belts and Van Dyck beards" that were suddenly everywhere.[17] Townsend himself, meanwhile, in an old brick house he owned at 75 Phillips Street, opened what was, one may be sure, one of the livelier of the new tearooms, the Jolly Roger, and an adjoining ground-floor book-shop named for Paul Revere of all people (Townsend was ever the patriot) and adorned with piratical murals. Possibly, the joke was that the pirates were gay enough. Certainly, Townsend is known in these years to have been a member of a Cornhill poetry-reading club or arts club or gay bar (no one seemed sure even then what it really was; if it was a gay bar, it was one of Boston's first) called the Pen and Pencil, where lecturer and public reader B. Hughes Morris remembers attending entirely respectable public programs of readings.[18] Perhaps, however, it is yet more evidence of why *theatrical* is so often, historically, a synonym for *homosexual* that the principal focus of this 1920s Beacon Hill bohemia was Paul's and Townsend's determination to revive Boston's then languishing little-theater tradition.

One of the country's first, Amy Lowell's Toy Theater, had been started on Lime Street on the Hill in 1912,[19] and it was a somewhat similar institution that Paul and Townsend founded in 1922—the Barn Theatre. It took its name from an antique brick structure, the centerpiece of Joy Court, a picturesque eighteenth- and nineteenth-century cul-de-sac on the Hill's northern slope that Townsend then owned. Soon the Barn Theatre and its artists' colony was surrounded by yet more tearooms—the Brick Oven (which Townsend later admitted was a speakeasy), the Saracen's Head (a memory of Algiers surely), and also Ye Barn Book Shoppe—and an art gallery. The renovations of the old buildings were themselves notable happenings. Townsend also owned an automobile and this made possible, in Beebe's words, "expeditions . . . for purposes of lust and pillage" ranging all over the Boston area, expeditions that involved outraged lumber dealers and stonemasons and such who "witnessed the rape of various matched partitions of their stock in trade which vanished down the road in the hands of persons they usually described

to the police as having donned fancy dress for the purposes of disguise."
Upon one occasion "Elliot Paul put in an appearance with a thousand of
red glazed brick," Beebe recounted. "At another Townsend dragged into
admiring Joy Street behind his car the main steel strut of the proscenium
architectural of the Court Theater, then in process of demolition."[20] It was
all vastly diverting and not unimportant.

> Paul's constant associate was a rangy youth named Prescott Townsend,
> whose strictly accountable background and actual supply of ready cash
> were not particularly held against him even in the most enlightened cir-
> cles. Townsend emerged from Harvard Law School, possessed and wore
> a raccoon skin overcoat that was the envy of Cedar Street, and could talk
> informatively on any given subject for the space it required his auditor
> to consume precisely a quart of gin. The other moving spirit of the
> Boston Stage Society was Catherine Huntington, granddaughter of a
> bishop. . . . She [too] threw in her lot with the esthetes of Cedar Lane
> Way, . . . some of the most curious dervishes ever to whirl and scream
> their ways through the dusty anterooms of art.[21]

Catherine Huntington, Townsend's ally through life in more than the
Barn Theatre, was, indeed, the scion of a bishop—Frederick Dan
Huntington—and in David Felix's *Protest: Sacco-Vanzetti and the Intellectuals*, he nicely encapsulates Huntington by quoting *Time* magazine's profile
of her picketing the State House over that famous issue with poet Edna St.
Vincent Millay, who came from New York for the protest: Huntington, reported *Time*, was "a gentlewoman. While the other arrestees pleaded guilty
silently and paid fines of five dollars, the notables pleaded guilty, made
speeches, and paid ten dollar fines, the Misses Millay and Huntington emphasizing their long American ancestry." Huntington (also homosexual) and
Townsend were to become birds of a feather.[22]

The Barn Experimental Theatre, as it was officially called, opened in 1922
and, like the first-string critics, none of whom were in evidence, Beebe was
inclined to poke much fun at the event, particularly at the opening night
play, *The Clouds*, by Jaraslav Kvapil, "a Hungarian who had been chosen
because nobody on the play committee, far less the Boston public, had ever
heard of him before."[23]

Actually, dramatist Kvapil was Czech, not Hungarian, and not unknown
at all. He was Dvořák's librettist, and had some years previously been offered
the directorship of the Metropolitan Opera in New York. Moreover, Kvapil
was the first Czech director to be accorded worldwide recognition, an exponent of symbolism over realism and of psychological theater à la Stanislavsky. The first in a series of modernist playwrights whose work the Barn
Theatre specialized in, others included Anton Chekhov, August Strindberg,
Jean Cocteau, Gordon Bottomley, André Gide (another memory of North

Africa), and Aleksandr Blok. It is a very avant-garde list that marks the Barn Company as perhaps the best and purest theater—amateur but dedicated and pioneering. Indeed, several plays were advertised as "given for the first time in English" and at least two "for the first time in this country." And although it was, in the trustees' words, "a non-commercial effort . . . to establish a theater in Boston in which we can experiment in new dramatic forms and subjects . . . such as are available in New York at the Provincetown Theater," and entirely amateur, standards were high. The Barn's productions were linked twice, for example, according to surviving playbills of 1923 and 1927 in the Harvard Theatre Collection, to the 47 Workshop of Professor Baker at Harvard, referring to that professor's nationally important course on playwriting. Poet Robert Hillyer, who lived in a mews of Charles Street on Beacon Hill, and who had just been appointed to Harvard's English faculty, was also involved. Set design, moreover, was often a project of a class in that subject at the Vesper George School of Art or the School of Boston's Museum of Fine Arts. Even *The New Yorker* noticed, reporting in 1926 that "sophisticated Bostonians may often be seen sitting on long wooden benches watching performances of Strindberg with expressionist settings, Anatole France, Chekov, and the more modern works of Marcel Achard, Alexander Blok and Jean Cocteau."[24]

In any event, simply by opening, much less sustaining, the Barn Experimental Theatre, Townsend and Paul had achieved much, even if, in the end, it was perhaps more of a footnote than a chapter heading in the history of the American theater. Furthermore, the reference to New York's Provincetown Theater, which folded the same year, 1929, as the Barn Theatre (such institutions were very fragile) points toward Eugene O'Neill, at least one of whose plays the Barn Theatre put on, and links it to a key aspect of its inspiration, the original Provincetown Wharf Theatre.

It is another tale the earliest passages of which were written at Harvard, where O'Neill and Townsend (whether known to each other or not is unclear) both embarked on their studies at the university the same year, 1914. O'Neill's were with the aforesaid George Pierce Baker in his 47 Workshop, sometimes called the crucible of twentieth-century American drama, from which O'Neill, today arguably that century's greatest playwright, found his way within two years to Provincetown, where in 1916 his work was discovered and launched on the world by the Provincetown Players. That loose group of Greenwich Village bohemians included several prominent alumni of the Harvard Dramatic Club who had started to produce original plays in a large fishhouse on Lewis Wharf in P-town. This was transformed into the Wharf Theatre when purchased in 1915 by Mary Heaton Vorse, a successful novelist who is usually credited with "discovering" Provincetown in 1907. (The importance of this was underlined by Ronald Suleski in his 1999 interview with Stephen Watson: "Boston was hidebound and not encouraging to new thinkers [in the 1920s]," Suleski pointed out, adding: "Provincetown was another matter. It had already established its bohemian connection by about 1912 or 1913. Gay people like Charles Demuth and Marsden Hartley were certainly there, not so much seeking a gay mecca as a place where they could find the freedoms of bohemia.")[25]

Exactly when O'Neill's and Townsend's paths crossed is not clear; nor when Townsend began summering in Provincetown in the first place. It was probably in the mid-1920s, by which time the Provincetown Players had all moved back to New York and on to the great if brief success that fueled O'Neill's gathering fame. O'Neill himself, however, went on to summer in P-Town, which continued to claim him; it was to Provincetown that O'Neill eloped to marry his second wife in 1918, and he was living there in the mid-1920s while at work on *The Great God Brown*. So were other members of the original group, Vorse for one, who (it is not hard to believe) found as good use for Townsend's pocketbook in P-town as Elliot Paul and company had on Beacon Hill. Cathcart, in the unpublished manuscript of his Townsend biography, explains:

> Mary Heaton Vorse, the leading light of the Provincetown Players, from the porch of whose house on Commercial Street the first readings of plays that later became full-scale if no-frills productions traditionally are held to have been held, was a long-time acquaintance and collaborator of Prescott. She . . . gave him to know, in no uncertain terms, just how his money could best be spent.
>
> Prescott's angelic nimbus was attained with his putting-up of rescue money for the original production of Eugene O'Neill's "The Great God Brown." Or so he claimed. . . . It is a fact that a mask from that landmark production served as a wall decoration in his bedroom.[26]

Documentation is more sketchy for Townsend's early theatrical years in Provincetown than for his Beacon Hill projects, and only the most episodic glimpses exist of his activities there in the 1920s. Opening a window on both scenes, however, John Cheever, the novelist-to-be we encountered being chased around the Longfellow House by Harry Dana, remembered Townsend in Provincetown very well. The sort of milieu Townsend was a part of (and several reasons why a young artist or writer like Cheever, who already was discovering his homosexuality, was drawn to it) is clear in both Cheever's contemporary and published letters and his biography. Cheever's biographer, Scott Donaldson, for instance, ropes in yet another of our cast of characters here when he writes that Cheever's "orientation was toward the . . . radical element . . . toward Boston's Bohemia . . . [which] was not generally impoverished. One teatime on Beacon Street, Cheever recalled, the aristocratic left-wing poet Jack Wheelwright tossed sandwiches into the fire as unsuitable and caused his pretty Irish maid to cry."[27] It's a story we've already heard. But Wheelwright, though he was indeed a good example of how supportive a place Boston could be for new recruits to art, literature, and bohemia generally, especially before the stock market crash, was actually at the opposite end of the bohemian continuum in the Puritan capital from Townsend. Socially also a patrician, Wheelwright *was* elected to Boston's august Somerset Club. Townsend was not. Wheelwright, as has been noted, was a convinced communist. Townsend, all his life, remained a Republican, in most matters quite moderate. Though he did once visit the Soviet Union, Townsend never even flirted with communism. Indeed, so far as is known, he and Wheelwright were not friends. Nor was Townsend ever likely to have been close to Cheever's other Boston Brahmin gay mentor, Harry Dana, another Marxist. However, Dana was also a professor of drama and a great authority on Soviet theater, and though no membership lists have survived of the Boston Stage Society that ran the Barn Theatre, very likely Dana was a member, the Barn being one of the few places in the U.S. where anything Russian was ever put on. Like Dana, Townsend, too, was likely a supporter of Boston's Trade Union College, radical as he was in social matters.

He may well also have known Dana's friend, Hazel Hawthorne Werner. It was Werner who first took Cheever to Provincetown. Moreover, Cheever's second published story, entitled "Fall River" (1931), dealt with the issue of social discontent after the Fall River, Massachusetts, mill closings of the time. As the story was published in the avant-garde Harvard journal *Hound and Horn,* by proprietor-editor Lincoln Kirstein (of whom more soon), and as Mary Heaton Vorse—the link between O'Neill and Townsend—was herself a labor organizer, one gets the sense that radical social activism (about which Townsend was more radical, in fact, than any of them) was the leitmotiv running through this whole scene. Indeed, it probably accounts for Cheever and Townsend knowing each other in the first place, and why Cheever (in his case only a semi-runaway) was yet another young man that Townsend made it a point to help. We know he was one of Cheever's early patrons because of a letter of 1932 that Cheever wrote to Malcolm Cowley, the editor who ran Cheever's first published story, in 1930, in *The New Republic.* It was written by Cheever from his Beacon Hill rooms. "As soon as I can get enough money together am going away for a week of two. . . . will I be paid for *The New Republic* article? . . . As soon as the music season starts again I will go back to the newspaper for a week or two. Prescott Townsend will very nearly give me his house in Provincetown for a month and Fritz is going to pay for my meals. After having seen Hart Crane I went home and read *The Bridge.* . . . Thanks for a swell time Tuesday night."[28]

What is doubly interesting about this letter is the way Cheever assumes a leading New York editor will know Townsend too, or at least know who he is, though there is no discernable reason why that should be the case. Yet it *was* often the case in reference to Townsend, who by the 1930s, though he had no particular or specific reason to be thought even a minor celebrity, was clearly beginning to be widely known as something of a character, a legend, so to speak, in the making. Certainly that is how Townsend comes across in Cheever's biography, where Townsend's lodgings in Provincetown, which Cheever and his friend Charles Flato rented in the winter of 1932, are described as very picturesque indeed: "a wharf without heat and . . . floorboards wide enough [apart] to see the water [through] at high tide."[29]

Such things wouldn't have bothered Townsend, an outdoorsman who loved to rough it on land or sea. In 1932, for example, he undertook something of the seagoing equivalent of his youthful trip out west by becoming a merchant seaman, signing on the *West Quechee* out of Portland, Oregon.[30] Furthermore, the wide floorboards Cheever complained of may well have been deliberate, for while Townsend would always remain interested in P-Town's theatrical legacy (carried on for years into the 1940s and '50s by his friend Catherine Huntington) his principal creative focus in Provincetown (and in the nearby town of Orleans) shifted over the years to architecture, specifically to an architecture that fascinatingly reflected exactly his outdoorsman aesthetic and also his rather exotic tastes. Charles Shively, so alert to the meaning and importance of Townsend's "hobo" experiences out west as a very young man, also caught best the aesthetic of Townsend's design work in middle age. As an architect, wrote Shively, Townsend used "cast-off materials, bric-a-brac and indigenous or random materials to produce special effects intended to integrate the landscape (urban or Cape Cod . . .) with the surroundings." It was a case of "what anthropologist Lévi-Strauss called 'bricolage,' especially the three structures at 1 Bradford Street, Provincetown: Townsend's own absolutely unique house, assembled from [i.e., surfaced in] driftwood, plastic cast off and other detritus."[31]

Did Townsend realize, I wonder, how apt an architecture of castoffs and other detritus was for his house? Perhaps his many enemies realized only too well how his design symbolized architecturally the thrust of Townsend's social thought and his daily practice of taking in runaways and other gay street youth—themselves "cast off" and considered "detritus" by most of society. Form surely followed function here.

There was, of course, a distinctly problematic aspect to Townsend's social work as he grew older and continued to be drawn to the young—mid- and late teens to early twenties. Asked by activist Randy Wicker in a published interview about his sex life as an older man, Townsend did not dissemble. It had never been difficult to meet his sexual needs, he replied, because "I have a house [in Boston], I have money, I have an automobile. Whether you like to admit it or not, that always is attractive. . . . I also have a house in Provincetown. . . . I'll let [hustlers] work for me and I'll pay them. And, incidentally, I might have some sex sometime. . . . I've never paid for sex directly in my life. . . . That was what made it difficult for the cops to catch me; they couldn't find anyone whom I'd had sex with."[32] Ever the pragmatic Yankee? Yet the line between support and exploitation is a very fine one.

Joseph McGrath, Townsend's secretary, recalls his earliest encounters with Townsend as a young man, and how the older man dined him and took him home for drinks and was, on every occasion, a perfect gentleman. (Doubtless it helped that Townsend drank and even ate very sparingly.) But Townsend's own testimony in the Wicker interview ("I've never paid for sex directly in my life") is an admission, surely, that he constantly paid for it indirectly, and from more than one of his "castoffs."

That he lived such a life in a house he designed from architectural and other castoffs, moreover, discloses patterns and attitudes of mind that would be fascinating to probe. Of course it is tough to do so now. But it is certainly true that Townsend, though he never aspired to practice architecture professionally, took his design work very seriously. In 1938, in his twentieth Harvard class reunion report, he described himself as an "experimental architect";[33] by his forty-fifth report in 1963, he had become just plain "architect."

Townsend had been since boyhood a friend of another and among the most celebrated of Boston's blue bloods, R. Buckminster Fuller, twice thrown out of Harvard but already famous for his geodesic dome. It is noticeable how similar were some of Townsend's ideas to Fuller's, who shared many of Townsend's social concerns. As Townsend explained in one of his Harvard class reports:

> When I spoke at our club luncheon I told how I'd been tilting at windmills of art and architecture and designed [the exterior of the Church of the Holy Spirit] in Orleans. Also aluminum and plastic houses in Provincetown. The Gangway in Provincetown is the final house at Provincetownsend which is my summertime name and address. It was an attempt to make an adequate house reasonably priced. It used the formula of two bedrooms at the right, kitchen and bath in the center, and living room with hanging fireplace to the left. The materials I used were isocyanite and bubbly plastic walls. It also has sliding doors and windows with a laminated roof and driftwood planks for floors and ceilings.[34]

Located beyond the Moors, a landmark P-Town nightspot, "Province-townsend" (to parse the house's name) did have a real gangway at the entry. As to its attractiveness, opinion seems to have been divided between those like Shively who liked its unconventionality, and others who thought it a monster. Townsend's friend, the writer Adrian Cathcart, described it as "surfaced in driftwood . . . [and having] great charm from the outside," saying little about the interior. Critic René Ricard called one of its interiors "beautiful."[35] Adjoining the main house was a barnlike wing, the top floor of which, reached by a forecastle's spiral stair, was called the dormitory. Here was where Townsend sheltered the young street people who came to him, directed by word-of-mouth mostly in P-town's gay bars, one imagines. Perhaps most important was the flat roof, with what Cathcart called its "maze of piping"; Townsend's house was a very early attempt at a solar-heated house.

The lifestyle at Provincetownsend was as bohemian as the architecture. McGrath vividly recalls the first time he took a night's refuge there as a very young man: the huge living room, roaring fire in the hanging central fireplace; a young dancer all but in a state of nature leaping about the fireplace to loud boogie beat; Townsend, clothed as he usually was in a three piece suit, reading the *Times*; ceiling fans all the while twirling. Lowering his paper to stare quizzically at the newcomer, Townsend said, "What have we here?" As this scene illustrates, *bohemian* does not begin to describe Townsend's life at Provincetownsend as the 1930s and '40s merged into the 1950s and '60s. The best one can do perhaps is to quote from *Shock Value*, the autobiography of John Waters, the director of such film comedies—classics now—as *Pink Flamingos* and *Polyester*. Waters, hardly himself very conventional, swam into Townsend's P-Town circle in the summer of 1965, through a girlfriend it would seem. He left in his book rather a fascinating record of the later period of what he called Townsend's "wonderful house":

> I met a girl from Baltimore nicknamed Sigue and moved into her incredible apartment. Sigue's sister Nancy was also there. . . . Nancy later became Mink Stole, one of the most talented members of my film repertory group. . . .
>
> It was like living with a lunatic Swiss Family Robinson. Part of the apartment [in Townsend's house] was made out of a submarine, and trees grew right up through the living room. There was no running water, but it was an incredibly beautiful place. The only real problem was that when it rained, it was like being outside. The only appliance that came with the apartment was a Might Moe heater. It was huge and you poured gas into it and flames shot out. It could dry out a drenched mattress in twenty minutes. There was no rent. You just had to be liked by the incredibly eccentric landlord, Prescott Townsden [*sic*], a notorious seventy-year-old gay liberationist who drove around on a motor scooter and ate nothing but hot dogs. At one time Mink was engaged to him.[36]

Waters actually got that right. Every once in a while Townsend would recall he was not carrying on the family line and propose to someone. It never worked out.

Actually, the trees grew up through a kind of trellis in an interior courtyard, according to McGrath, but as the typo too may indicate, Waters was feeling little pain that P-Town summer. His autobiography, however, documents very clearly that just as the post–World War I Townsend had transformed himself into the complete bohemian—in the 1920s and '30s, whether in Paris, North Africa, Boston, or Provincetown—so did the post–World

War II Townsend evolve into a "seventy-year-old gay liberationist" who was "incredibly eccentric," even "notorious," and even to a film director like Waters, who was once described in *The Boston Globe* as America's "P. T. Barnum of Scatology."

The precipitant of this third and final phase of Townsend's improbable life story? In 1943 he was caught having sex—rumor always had it that it was in one of those deep entryways on Beacon Hill's historic Mount Vernon Street (someone opened his door and presumably called the police)—and this fiercely honest Boston Brahmin queer of bohemian fame, having long since discarded his parents' advice ("be careful"), was not about to back down. Townsend's defining moment had come, and though the police captain, according to Cathcart, was open to a modest bribe, Townsend—though certainly savvy enough to have paid off the cops in the days of his "tearooms"—was in a matter of this sort determined to stand on principle. So he went to jail.[37]

The exact length of Townsend's imprisonment seems beyond recovery today. All that McGrath recalls is that the hard labor his employer was sentenced to (some sort of farmwork) was served at the Suffolk County House of Correction on Deer Island in Boston Harbor, and that Townsend, who had "shipped out" more than once, on tramp steamers as a deckhand, was hardly fazed by it, or by his fellow convicts, who, one imagines, were not dissimilar to the hobos and street types Townsend had always been sympathetic to. Ever the hardheaded Yankee, and (unlike Wilde) with no beloved betrayer to call to task, and ever the optimist anyway ("every knock a boost" was his constant refrain), Townsend was not given either to depression or even to much introspection, and drank very sparingly. No victim he, Townsend made light of it all personally, telling one and all, for example, including his estranged family when he was kicked out of the Social Register, that now he and heiress Barbara Hutton had something in common.[38]

If his psyche remained unbruised, and his strength of character never failed him, his sense of justice, however, remained very much outraged. Admittedly, not one to curse the darkness, he was eager to light the proverbial candle, which—after the manner of his revolutionary and abolitionist ancestors—he eagerly did. In his Harvard class reports after his imprisonment, one sees the two sides of it. Jail he touched on very lightly, in his fortieth report, with patrician condescension—referring pointedly to his *Mayflower* and Revolutionary War ancestry and then to "some amusing and educational bouts with the police." But then he lit a bonfire of a candle. Though he was a Republican, not a Marxist, he *was* a libertarian, and a radical one at that: for the first time, perhaps, in any Harvard alumni class report, in his thirty-fifth report he used the "h" word. "The last phase of my life," he wrote, "has been the fight for social justice. This has also been the most fun. The Demophile Center is one of the three newer organizations in the U.S. dedicated to bringing the problems of the homophile to the attention of the public and aiding in their solution." By the time of his forty-fifth report he was more specific: "I was thrown into jail for refusing to pay $15.00 graft for an act that is not against the law in England, nor in Illinois."[39]

Yankee Homophile

BY COMMON CONSENT the historic breakthrough organization in the history of gays in America, the first enduring American gay rights advocacy group, was the Mattachine Society. It was for Prescott Townsend, who had held all his life to the rigorous, outspoken honesty he had promised to his mother—even in the 1920s, asserted Cathcart, "Prescott was never in the closet"—the last name he would have chosen for the new organization, especially after his arrest and imprisonment, which radicalized him, as we'd say today, from a bohemian into an activist. But the background and circumstances were very different for Harry Hay, a Los Angeles Communist who with a small cohort organized the first Mattachine group in 1951. And Townsend was drawn to such a leftist, secretive group because of its practical activism, its protests, for instance, against the then common practice of police entrapment, protests Townsend naturally identified with. But although Townsend would eventually be in some sense widely accepted as virtually America's first gay activist—his openness and concern with gay street people had been legendary for decades—what influence he exerted over the early days of the Mattachine group was felt more on the East than the West Coast (though he was at the Los Angeles meeting that broke up the original Mattachine in 1953) and did not survive when he was ousted by more moderate, nonconfrontational members, too intimidated, some said, by the intolerance of the McCarthy era.

Townsend, of course, was highly confrontational, and when the two first East Coast Mattachine groups were started—New York's in 1956, Boston's in 1957—there was no doubt where Townsend stood ideologically, which the irrepressible Brahmin made clear, again in his fortieth Harvard class report (unlike the Social Register they couldn't kick him out of that). Trumpeting his own involvement in "two social and educational societies whose members are anonymous: One, Inc. [a magazine] and the Mattachine Society," Townsend was very clear as to his aim: he was "fighting for a better life for millions of Americans," adding, modestly, "I helped start the Boston chapter," which, technically, was true.[40] Two others, Anthony Giattaputo (Harvard class of 1950) and Raymond Mangiafico, were cofounders with him. Townsend, however, was not only the chief founder of one of the first Mattachine groups in the country, he quickly established the Boston Mattachine as the most activist of all the Mattachine groups nationwide, attracting in consequence the same ideological dissension that forced Hay himself out of the Mattachine. By 1959, a New York Mattachine officer was writing Townsend to ask him *not* to commit the Mattachine to a campaign for Massachusetts sodomy-law reform, requesting Townsend to do so only as an individual.[41] When, because of other rifts (for instance, the New York chapter questioned the handling of its dues in 1960 by the national organization), the board of directors voted in 1961 to revoke the charters of the five spin-off Mattachine chapters—Boston, Chicago, New York, Denver, and San Francisco—encouraging them, however, not to disband but to continue on their own, independently, Townsend took immediate advantage of the breakup. His relations with the West Coast moderates had been no better than with their equally timid New York cousins, as he reported in the *Boston Mattachine Newsletter*: "The Chairman was planning a trip to San Francisco to discuss our future relations with the once-National Office of Mattachine but decided to cancel the trip because in two phone calls he made to them, they were unpleasant and even hostile. . . . Bitchery, individual or collective, as manifested by San Francisco," he declared, "can do nothing but give aid and comfort to all those who would like to see us all in Hell."[42] (These included the police, of course; in Denver they raided the homes of Mattachine officers, one of whom went to jail for sixty days for possession of pornography. Townsend was beset on every side.)

In his profile of Townsend years later, Charles Shively detailed some of the issues as he understood them: Townsend, who "opposed [the Mattachine Societies'] desire for respectability," formed his own Demophile Union of Boston," a response as well to the fact that the same ideological tensions that had bedeviled the original Mattachine and then the New York chapter had surfaced in Boston with the more moderate gays eschewing Townsend's leadership. But Townsend never gave up, never could: "While the Boston Mattachine soon collapsed," wrote Shively, "the Demophile Society managed to publish several newsletters, hold meetings."[43] It is a wonder Townsend did not wash his hands of the whole thing; but as he entered old age he found himself living in exciting times, founding his Boston Demophile Union (or Society or Center; it went through several incarnations) at what turned out to be a turning point in the history of the American gay rights movement, a turning point activist historian Stephen Donaldson has focused on:

> 1961 to 1969 saw the evolution of the American homophile movement from a defensive, self-doubting handful of small, struggling groups in California and the Boston-Washington corridor to an assertive, self-confident, nationally organized (if ideologically divided) collection of some three score organizations with substantial allies and a string of major gains. . . .
>
> Landmarks in the evolution were the first public demonstrations organized by the movement in the spring of 1965 at the United Nations in New York in April and at the White House. . . .

The slow pace of the American movement was accelerated in the early and mid-1960's in part under the influence of the black civil rights movement . . . then injected with the tremendous energies that accompanied the opposition to the war in Vietnam. . . . Student uprisings shook the campuses of Columbia and Harvard Universities in 1968 and 1969, and by the late spring of 1969 the country was in a mood of unprecedented mass agitation. It was against this background that the Stonewall Rebellion of June 27–30, 1969, marked the start of a new, radical and even more militant phase of the homosexual movement.[44]

It was in the years just before Stonewall, however, that Townsend was most influential, and it cannot be said too often, in Martin Duberman's words, that for gays "resistance to oppression did not begin in 1969 at Stonewall." It began in the crucial preceding decade. Nor did these developments occur in a vacuum. "Inspired in part by the sit-ins and freedom rides of the black civil rights movement, homophile organizations began to shift their dominant political strategy beginning in the early 1960s," Brett Beemyn and Gregory Conerly have written. "East Coast Chapters of the Mattachine Society led the way in demanding equal rights for lesbigays rather than sympathy and understanding, advocating the use of direct action protest," they continue, noting that "Franklin Kameny of Mattachine-Washington DC, and Randy Wicker of Mattachine-New York emerged as leaders of the more activist homophiles."[45] Noting that both men's goals and strategy "resembled the original vision of the Mattachine Society promoted by founder Harry Hay," Beemyn's and Conerly's focus on Wicker and Kameny, reflecting a similar focus in the work of Martin Duberman, is very important to understanding Townsend's role, for his influence was felt most keenly in the case of Wicker, with whom Townsend early formed a strong alliance.

The older and the younger man at once saw eye to eye. Indeed, Wicker was just the sort of young man Townsend admired: "The first gay man or lesbian who is believed to have come out in the news media was Randy Wicker, a young (relatively more radical) Mattachine Society activist who in 1964 appeared on *The Les Crane Show*, a New York call-in talk show," according to Beemyn and Conerly.

Wicker, who found in Townsend just the two things he most needed— evidence there was both a gay past and a gay future, Townsend at his age disclosing both—also found a brother in arms, and, not surprisingly, the same enemies: "Frustrated by the caution of Curtis Dewees and his lover, Al de Dion, who was then president of the [New York Mattachine] society" (the same Dewees who so dismayed Townsend in 1959), Wicker charged off on his own to do just the things Townsend was always eager to do, but could hardly continue to make effective in the way the handsome, bright, young, and very personable Wicker could. Responding to a gay-negative radio show, Wicker protested so loudly he won coverage in both *The New York Times* and *Newsweek*.[46] Birds of a feather, in Boston and New York, the disheveled old man and the sparkling youth upended the whole attitude. Thus it was, in John Loughery's words, that in 1965 there occurred the historic demonstrations that really heralded Stonewall:

> The Washington action, with ten participants (seven gay men, two lesbians, and a straight woman friend . . .), took place [at the White House] on Saturday, April 17, 1965; its New York counterpart, with twenty-odd participants (including Allen Ginsberg, Peter Orlovsky, and Prescott Townsend from Boston) on Sunday, April 18.[47]

The seventy-one-year-old Townsend at last came into his own: "an organizer, with Randy Wicker and Dick Leitsch, of the first gay rights demonstration," in the words of Cathcart, who added, "I can think of no one more responsible for launching the Gay Rights/Gay Liberation movement than Prescott Townsend. . . . There were no demonstrations, no protest marches for Gay Rights before Prescott; and he was always on the spot for an organized protest no matter whether or not his presence were welcome."[48] (Of why he was, in fact, not always welcome, more soon.) Similarly, five years later, added Cathcart, Townsend, by then seventy-six, drove down to New York with Joe McGrath to take part with a handful of others in a march commemorating the Stonewall Riot of the year before, that being, of course, the first "Christopher Street Liberation Day" on Stonewall I, the first gay pride march anywhere. One of the first two hundred marchers who started that historic walk up Sixth Avenue to Central Park, Townsend saw the crowd finally swell to thousands. Townsend's time was passing, as, indeed, newer and far more radical and confrontational organizations, such as the Gay Liberation Front, took the gay rights movement to new levels of protest.

Townsend, however, had always been ahead of his times, both in theory and in practice. Though focused on gays, Townsend's thinking had always been more wide-ranging. He was once quoted as saying, "The general public wasn't prejudiced against just homosexuals, but against sex per se."[49] And in Townsend's Demophile meetings the discussion was not just about gays but all sorts of "rejected people," a theme reaching back to his trip to the logging camps out west in 1914. And one of his few recorded "sermons" discloses how practical and broad-minded his views were. He wrote: "I emphasize the Menninger Report (*Man Against Himself*) whenever I give a talk to a gay group. . . . Love, Money, Uplift . . . 'Uplift' . . . means sublimating one's masochistic tendencies into art and one's sadistic tendencies into leadership. . . . [Thus] you can channel your aggressive and self-destructive impulses into constructive, life-enriching activities. . . . Older people . . . must sublimate their energies into helping other people. . . . A good first step would be to join Mattachine. . . . Do something, anything, for other people and in doing so you will find happiness."[50]

Similarly, as far back as in the late 1950s, he saw—and so preached in his *Boston Mattachine Newsletter*—that "in most cases of even the best intentioned homosexual partnerships, the effect can be nothing less than a continuous, thorny disaster and a surrender . . . to a way of life which is superficial, hollow, and even vicious." He saw the solution, too: "I believe homosexual partnership must be *worked at* more than any other," he wrote, lamenting that neither church nor state would countenance gay marriage—in 1958! Indeed, Townsend favored not just gay rights, but a woman's right to choose abortion, planned parenthood, and legalized prostitution (as well as the legalization of drugs) because, overall, in Cathcart's words: "What he was after was sexual liberation—freedom on a universal scale without regard to gender or sexual orientation. When he said: 'No two are alike' (referring to the human mind), he meant exactly that." This was his famous "Snowflake Theory." "How difficult it must have been," added Cathcart, "for Prescott, a full-blooded Yankee, a Bostonian and a Harvard man, to resist the compelling urge to categorize."[51] How difficult it still is for us today—when Townsend's view, still controversial, is nonetheless increasingly widespread. Without at all denying the predominance of the two polarities of opposite-sex and same-sex sexuality and our natural preoccupation with them (he never wavered, either, in his emphasis on gay rights), Townsend a half century ago was making room for all sorts of sexualities. No wonder he was so eagerly appreciated on Christopher Street.

Leadership there, however, by no means implied leadership in Harvard Yard. Consider the sad tale of some of Townsend's final appearances there at commencements in 1967 and 1968, just before the Stonewall Rebellion, and the Harvard strike that followed upon the occupation and police action at University Hall in 1969. It was the eve of the cultural shift he'd worked for most of his life. His appearances, however, constituted a two-act comedy, one act each year, and one that would make more Harvard graduates wince today than laugh. As Joseph McGrath tells it, though Townsend had arrived first in 1967 and was thus by tradition entitled to the honor of carrying, at the head of the class of 1918 in the commencement procession, the official stanchion (a tall pole with the class year blazoned on a placard at the top), a number of better-dressed types (class officer types) managed to wrest it from the old man, who seemed bewildered and unbelieving about it all, as well he might, especially when some younger alumni nearby attempted to intervene on Townsend's behalf. They failed that year, but not the next. Determined that on Townsend's fiftieth he should carry the class stanchion (less of a problem that year because at major reunions like the fiftieth any surviving class officers get to carry a much bigger banner elsewhere in the procession), a cohort of younger college alumni under the command of Dennis Milford got to the Yard ridiculously early, claimed the 1918 stanchion, and delivered it at the proper moment to Townsend, who bore it triumphantly into Harvard Yard in the commencement procession.[52] He also carried it home, where it long stood in the corner of the first-floor office and reception room at Lindall Place, his Beacon Hill town house.

Lindall Place

TOWNSEND WAS CLEARLY not welcomed by all to Harvard Yard. But why, one wonders, was he not always welcome, as Cathcart implies, even at these historic first gay rights protests he helped to organize? The answer is that although he would always have made some effort for commencement, Townsend had by then long since ceased to be the dashing figure in the raccoon coat of his youth; indeed, it must be said he made it easier than he need have for his detractors in his last years because of his absolute refusal to take seriously the matter of his dress and hygiene. His fierce independence of the usual conventions, such a strength psychologically—and politically— so refreshing intellectually, became in other entirely social respects a weakness and a failure in what were admittedly small things, but things that undermined his effectiveness. After his first meeting with Townsend in the mid-1960s, Cathcart left this description: "A terrible old man, chop fallen, lanthorn-jawed, beret'd and otherwise clad in the saddest rags I ever saw." Nor did he exaggerate when he added: "I took the extended hand fully expecting fleas to leap off the wrist and thinking 'Where have you been last?' " Though Cathcart is quick to affirm that "despite the comicality of his appearance and certain other of his aspects, Prescott was a highly re- spected and astute political warrior," the image that lingers, that most saw most strongly, was of an apparently homeless derelict, an image Townsend made hardly any effort to counter.[53]

Except perhaps in the movies. When, in the late 1960s, he appeared in an important underground film, virtually as its star, the emphasis on Town- send's thought and life experience and on how impressive he could be when he "preached" had its effect. In 1967 the *National Observer* ran a story about the annual Ann Arbor Film Festival—a national launching pad for under- ground filmmakers, its awards the most prestigious in the field: "The Grand Prize went to Andrew Meyer's black and white 'An Early Clue to the New Direction' . . . [which] hung on a dialogue and plot (of a kind) clearly mov- ing in a new direction." The article also praised "a superb performance by an old man, Prescott Townsend, playing a Boston roué long past his time, who charms a young girl with his reverie and with his 'Snowflake Theory.' "[54] It was Prescott at his best, often brought out by vaguely educational projects, or by collaborations with interlocutors who were apt to be, such was the time and place, equally interesting.

At the Hayes-Bickford Cafeteria in Harvard Square, where she hung out with gay men and some of the Andy Warhol crowd, or at Sharaff's on Beacon Hill or at the weekly poetry-reading sessions of the 1960s at the Charles Street Meeting House across the street, not far from Townsend's house, readings at which he himself read, Townsend invariably shared center stage, for example, with Jessie Whitehead, the daughter of Alfred North Whitehead. Herself by no means a background figure, Jessie, in Cathcart's words, "unfailingly would arrive from Cambridge Sundays and sit in her exotic clothes with a cockatiel [parrot] perched on her fur-draped shoulder and her head wreathed in fumes from a silver-mounted pipe." B. Hughes Morris confirms the scene.[55]

But this was the exotic, the public side of Prescott Townsend's bohemia. At home, a few blocks away on Lindall Place, the scene was much more grimy, though outré enough. Aside from a first-floor, semipublic office and reception room, and his own second-floor study bedroom, his Lindall Place house and the other house backing onto Phillips Street—site of the old Jolly Roger—were filled with an incredible mélange of residents and tenants of all kinds: retired family servants who in "a loony grand-seigneurial way," as Cathcart put it, Townsend supported (though each and every one of them hated the gay men they necessarily kept company with), as well as all sorts of hippies, runaways, deadbeats, students, artists, winos, draft dodgers, and the odd respectable tenant who paid the rent doubtless as much for the floor show as anything else. Furnished in places with wonderful Oriental rugs and eighteenth-century antique furniture and Townsend's magnificent collection of ship models, even pre-Columbian sculpture, the house was also filled with piles of *New York Times*es seemingly in every corner—to open a door was always to raise a small dust cloud—and kitchen arrangements were so chaotic the food odors alone were memorable.

As were the sights sometimes: one of the more respectable of Townsend's tenants, a social worker in her sixties, returning home from the office one rainy night, encountered two young men very much in a state of nature in the hall, midway between sex and shower: unfazed, she stood there, according to one, shaking her umbrella and smiling. "Never mind, boys: I was a missionary once."

Something between some sort of luxurious domicile of ancient Pompeii and a much duskier one in modern New Orleans, the Lindall Place house was, in Cathcart's words, an "unbelievably bizarre and louche household," its leitmotiv, often repeated: "You do not have to have sex with the landlord; but it is better if you do." Some of the wiser of the old hands solved that one, too, appointing one of the better-looking of their number official catamite. One George, of happy memory and no known last name, was responsible, writes Cathcart, for keeping Townsend happy: in other words, "the other tenants would pay him to have sex with Prescott," who as he aged grew more and more randy, it would seem, even resorting at one point to bugging many of the rooms so he could at least listen in. A certain Orwellian air was evident: every rental unit in the adjoining Phillips Street house had not just a microphone in it but a portrait of Prescott!

All of this going on in a setting of what Cathcart called "seedy grandeur" had the effect, as I myself recall it from occasional visits in the 1960s to see McGrath (Townsend's secretary lived on the first floor), of a stage set of sorts, one where you never knew what would happen next. Only that it would be interesting. Perhaps terrifying.[56] And in truth pleasure was not the whole story by any means. Sex wore many masks and held up many mirrors on Lindall Place—the booming subway trains roaring and reverberating past the house on the overhead trestle bridge, a scene right out of Edward Hopper—where the play was as serious as it was fantastic, as much in earnest as madly weird. The ground-floor labyrinth, once a stop on the Underground Railroad in the era of slavery, still had its uses in the era of Vietnam, and Townsend was certainly part of an underground network that smuggled out young men to Canada to avoid the draft. Moreover, for many of the youthful runaways residing there, Prescott's house was a refuge from families that had no use for queers—none at all. Townsend housed and fed them; indeed, according to Cathcart, he put more than one through college. He used to maintain (at minimum cost, of course) his real-estate holding, knowing too that providing shelter and jobs would incite gratitude that made sexual contact more likely.

Yet both Cathcart and McGrath, the former highly critical of Townsend, both independent in judgment, testify that while Townsend might be accused, not entirely in jest, of "slave labor," he was no pedophile. Indeed, his sexual ideal was the blond, fresh-complexioned, blue-eyed Harvard preppy, a type unlikely to turn up homeless at his door, and Townsend was not anyway invariably sexually aggressive. Both, moreover, affirm that Townsend, whatever was in his mind, knew full well how closely monitored he was by the police. Only one source, aside from reports of gossip, Charles Shively, has linked Townsend to the notorious North American Man-Boy Love Association, and alleged guilt-by-association with unnamed friends who were supposedly members of that group hardly impresses.[57] By contrast, two of those Townsend sheltered and mentored, both remarkable men redolent of the back side of the Hill that Townsend in some sense presided over, disclose the truth of the matter much more clearly: the poets René Ricard and Stephen Jonas. René first.

Since the 1970s "America's most controversial arbiter of taste," according to the dust jacket blurb of one of his books (poetry, conjoined with reproductions of his paintings), Ricard has been in various incarnations poet, painter, actor, and art critic, not to forget (this from another dust jacket) "a contemporary Vasari," and in every case of a most unusual sort.[58] He attracts detractors who deeply (and archly) despise him, as well as admirers who obviously utterly delight in him. (The admirers include Robert Creeley, today one of the country's leading poets, and Francesco Clemente, the celebrated Italian painter.) Witness this effusion, which drips with something, from a review of Ricard's 1990 debut as a painter, in *The New Yorker*:

Some observers may have first glimpsed the comet Ricard during the
middle and late sixties, when he appeared as more or less himself (a very
young, bratty, loose-limbed, tightly wired, louche, and infernally charming upstart . . .) in now classic Andy Warhol films, such as "Kitchen,"
with Edie Sedgwick, and "Chelsea Girls," with just about everyone else
in the Factory gang. Others may have sighted him during the seventies
as a *poète maudit*, a period that culminated with the publication, in 1979,
of an impeccably elegant, slim volume of his verses, full of urbane aper-
çus, scabrous longings, cris du coeur, and spleen, and bound in Tiffany-
box blue. And shortly thereafter he "occurred" as an art critic—one
whose style was part guerrilla, part bitch goddess, part publicist, and part
defrocked priest—in time to help ignite the careers of Julian Schnabel,
Keith Haring and Jean-Michel Basquiat.[59]

Having masterfully rendered the conjurer, the reviewer did not entirely neglect the trick—which impresses: "Ricard's handwriting . . . in painted poems
and poetic paintings . . . dispatch[es] acid thoughts in sweet Warholian pas-
tels . . . turning swinish thoughts into haiku-like pearls. The artist behaves
like Caravaggio even as he flirts with Zen; he speaks from the dead, then
hustles a date. . . . Ricard has nothing if not range." Caravaggio? Vasari?
What hath Prescott Townsend wrought?

Ricard, the same reviewer reported, had "already 'done' Boston" by the
time he first appeared in Manhattan, and it seems a witty enough description
of many Bostonians' feelings in the wake of Ricard's picturesque passage
among them under Townsend's auspices, Ricard having been in his youth
nothing if not persistent in his enthusiasms, both sexual and artistic. Indeed,
the Puritan capital in the 1950s and early '60s hardly seems the right time
or place for a youth who seemed to live entirely on his wits and who was
even then, as *The New Yorker* reviewer calls Ricard, "virulently Baude-
lairean." Even "Prescott like[d] René better as a New Yorker,"[60] Cathcart
wrote later, though it would be a mistake to leave the impression *everyone*
in New York liked Ricard. Perhaps his most high-profile feud there was with
Warhol himself, in the course of which Ricard carried performance art to
new levels of acting out, especially when he felt he was being upstaged. ("You
know how horrible René is," Warhol writes of the man he called "the Rex
Reed of the art world," in his published diaries, where Warhol memorializes
Townsend's Beacon Hill as much as his own New York gallery scene with a
glimpse of René in action that not even Frank O'Hara at an Eliot House
cocktail party could have topped: "To the Keith Haring opening. . . . So we
walked into the place and there's René Ricard, and he's screaming, 'Oh my
God! From the sixties to the eighties and I'm *still* seeing you everywhere!'
And I said how could he have said all those things about me in the *Edie*
book and he said that I should have seen it *before* they cut it.")[61]

Townsend, to be sure, would have been amused, but undoubtedly (being big enough and old enough, and entitled to) would have boxed Ricard's ears just the same, it having been Townsend who in the early 1960s carried René Napoleon Ricard, to give him his full name, off to Lindall Place, at the age of fifteen, rescuing the lad from the grimy old mill town of New Bedford. Unlike Elliot Paul (in his case the town was the dreary Malden), or John Cheever (his was Quincy; I rest my case), most of Townsend's cohorts, whether drawn from Boston's inner or outer wastelands (like the Roxbury painter Anthony Senna), did not, alas, score so big in the end. But young Ricard thrived in Townsend's circle. And he never forgot what he owed Townsend for rescuing him from what he called an "intolerable situation," telling Cathcart: "I consider Prescott to have been my patron. He was completely supportive of my ambitions in art. He made it possible for me to inform myself about a number of things I might otherwise not even have known of. . . . Being with him," Ricard declared forthrightly, "I changed my class overnight." To which Cathcart, perhaps taken aback by compliments from a source not always noted for same, and concerned they not be read in consequence as sarcastic, felt bound to add: "All these things are true. Prescott was ever after René to get more painting and drawing done [and] . . . he introduced him to people in the arts."[62] That Townsend, too, was sincere is clear in that nude by Ricard of a mutual friend hung in the place of honor beside the mask from *The Great God Brown* at the head of Townsend's bed in his Lindall Place bedroom. Foxy Grandpa was equally enthusiastic about Ricard's poetry: it was at the Sunday afternoon Charles Street Meeting House series, presided over by Townsend and Jessie Whitehead, Cathcart recalls, that "René gave his first public readings."[63]

How dramatically Ricard's life changed in his early years with Townsend (in whose entourage, however, he was ever the star) can be seen in this anecdote of Cathcart's about a blustery, snowy day in the 1960s when Ricard and Whitehead (complete with cockatiels in the hood of her anorak) dined at a restaurant on Beacon Hill's Charles Street:

> He was one of the most intense people, in his youth, that I have ever known. . . . His restless mind must have been popping all over the place. He had yet to read [Stein's] *Autobiography*. . . . When René had blurted out all he had to say—at least he had not asked Miss Whitehead if she ever had heard of Gertrude Stein—Miss Whitehead fixed him with a cold stare, . . . took a drag on her pipe and began to speak. . . . "I introduced Gertrude Stein to a girl, Alice Toklas [Whitehead had brought Toklas to Stein's to tea]. . . . The following day Gertrude Stein said to me, 'I am rather taken with this Miss Toklas and I think that I shall have her live with me.' . . . I said: 'Well, give it a go, girl, but remember, it can't last forever.' "
>
> In a lifetime of collecting such stories, never have I come across a better example of the Is-my-face-red School.[64]

Now Jessie Whitehead's is not the only version of the Stein-Toklas meeting, but Stein certainly was intimate with the Whiteheads—she described meeting Professor Whitehead as one of three great epiphanies of her life (the other two were Toklas and Picasso). Yet neither Whitehead nor Toklas nor Stein nor Picasso nor anyone else of that world would likely have entered into Ricard's life, of course, but for Prescott Townsend.

Another poet, also gay, also (indeed, much more) subversive, whom Townsend also sheltered in his early years, was Stephen Jonas, whose repute is rising dramatically today, along with his close pal of those days, Jack Spicer. Though some have compared the work of Ricard and Jonas—Robert Creeley, Gerrit Lansing, William Corbett—the two men were very different and never close, only sharing an occasional meal.[65] In the first place, Jonas was, variously, black, Latino, or white, depending on one's own expectations or the poet's projections of the time. He also did a stretch in the army (which one can hardly imagine of the more flamboyant Ricard). Nor was Jonas seen about as part of Townsend's entourage, as Ricard was; Jonas seldom attended Townsend's Thursday evening Demophile Society open houses; Ricard never and Townsend only rarely were noticed at Jonas's weekly salons or "magic evenings" for his friends. Jonas, moreover, was part of a much larger group. In the author's biography printed in one of Ricard's books, for instance, though Jonas is mentioned as an influence, so is John Wieners, a much better known poet.

The life and work of both Jonas and Wieners centered in this period, like the earlier bohemia Townsend and Paul led in the 1920s, on Beacon Hill's back side, indeed in some of the same buildings (the Paul Revere Book Shop was the scene of Demophile discussions in the 1950s), and on Beacon Hill's main drag, Charles Street, much more bohemian then. It was, for instance, at the same Charles Street Meeting House reading series where Ricard debuted that Jonas was introduced (at a reading by Charles Olson in 1954) to Joe Dunn by John Wieners, who himself met Robert Duncan and Robin Blazer—poets all—farther up Charles Street at Scharaff's, the gay restaurant on the corner of Chestnut Street that Townsend and all his circle patronized. "Ever since he walked by the Charles Street Meeting House" that night, declares one critic of the night of the Olson reading (the same night Hurricane Hazel hit Boston in September 1954), and went inside and heard Olson reading, Wieners, then a Harvard librarian, was definitely Olson's "disciple," as were Jonas and Dunn and two other poets they hooked up with within the year to form what Allen Ginsberg called "a mythic Boston poetry gang":[66] Blazer was another Harvard librarian (Townsend was by no means a lonely Harvard presence in this world). And so Jack Spicer, whom Blazer helped to get a job at the Boston Public Library that sustained Spicer for his brief but important Boston stay in 1955–1956.

Enemies as well as friends figured in this circle. Spicer, a brilliant poet but also an alcoholic, was hostile both to Allen Ginsberg (he thought him too populist) and Frank O'Hara (whom he judged superficial). Yet most were involved in Harvard's Poets Theatre during Frank O'Hara's post-Harvard year on Beacon Hill. Wieners, for example, recalls an evocative night and early morning when he, Spicer, and O'Hara went for drinks to the Harvard Gardens, a famous Beacon Hill literary dive (so called because the bar, still there, is located roughly midway on the subway between Harvard Square and Park Street in downtown Boston) and, on their way home, "while I read my poetry in the humid summer evening of Beacon Hill, the both of them wept through the incipient rain and electric-charged air."[67] Indeed, this "gang" of poets may have achieved its high point during what Dunn called "that intense summer" of 1956, when all five—Spicer, Jonas, Blazer, Wieners, and Dunn—were "all living within blocks of each other on the inexpensive side of Beacon Hill," in the words of Jonas's posthumous editor Joseph Torra, "regularly meeting and sharing their work in progress."[68] Few noticed then. One who did was Gerrit Lansing, who wrote in 1968:

> The School of Boston, in poetry, middle of this century, is an occult school, unknown. What literary historian has written of Spicer, Blazer, Wieners, Dunn . . . Jonas? . . .
>
> It is a Boston lingo Jonas tunes up. . . . And behind the meticulous attention to the scene is an awareness of the place of Boston in the twisty course of the Republic. The poet, concerned with economics, alchemy, and history, knows of the occult Gold buried deep under Trinity Church. (Boston State Street Trusts shot up the new nation with money and blood, their only resistance the Southern agrestic nome [a Southern land division] they eventually smashed.)
>
> In [Jonas's] poems in spite of sportive flashes, happy teasing, in the end we are made aware it is a lonely unpaid unhallowed job, this business of auditing the idiomatic junk of hustled streets, shaping it to the purity of song. It is to be a maker in Boston.
>
> > "a hollow
> > victory
> > you celebrate
> > bird singing alone
> > in this cold"
> > (No. x)[69]

These are Townsend's streets of the 1950s and '60s, of course, and that's the same gold under Trinity that built and still helps sustain Harvard, and Townsend and Jonas both knew it. Though one was by birth a Boston Brahmin aristocrat, the other (probably) a Portuguese fisherman's son (or a "mulatto . . . from rural Georgia"; Jonas carefully obscured his origins, which remain mysterious to this day, as does his real name), both the patrician's heir and the seaman's son, finally, were social renegades one is not surprised to find under the same roof; indeed, one could in a sense say of Townsend what poet William Corbett has said of Jonas, by the 1960s the only one of all these counterculture poets remaining continuously in Townsend's orbit on Beacon Hill: Jonas stands, Corbett has said, "for the other Boston, the other side of Beacon Hill from Robert Lowell . . . [and] those worthies who flourish in . . . universities."[70]

That other Boston could be very ugly. It is of Townsend's house as much as of any Jonas lived in on the Hill that Joseph Torra wrote: "Wherever Jonas lived . . . his apartment was inevitably a kind of nexus for various underworld activities. Although Jonas was never a junkie himself [and Townsend never even touched drugs], junkies, prostitutes, thieves, and runaways were common houseguests."[71] Jonas, moreover, though a generous and compassionate friend who had gentle qualities (he was deeply fond of Bach and Mozart), was flawed by a virulent anti-Semitism and deeply, deeply, at odds with American mainstream values. So oppressed was Jonas, for example, by what he called the "grand larceny of modern America" (one of his heroes was Malcolm X) that he hardly left any petty larceny undone. He lived largely on a phony disability check some said he'd rigged while in the army; he once (not at Prescott's) rewired his apartment so the electricity would go on his landlord's bill, and most of his cherished books and records Jonas outright stole from the Boston Public Library. Indeed, he was once convicted and sent to prison for six months for participating in scamming record and book clubs, ordering material later resold for drug money. But prison only seemed to add to the store of experiences that fed his best poems. And though he himself used speed as well as alcohol, suffered repeated bouts of paranoia, and was several times hospitalized for mental problems, poetry and music ever remained the passions of Jonas's life. Indeed, even after the mid-1950s gang of back-of-the-Hill poets had dispersed to all points of the compass, Jonas maintained an ardent transcontinental friendship with Spicer (Jonas is a character—"Washington Jones"—in Spicer's novel *The Tower of Babel*,[72] and both dedicated books to each other), even as Jonas remained, in Torra's words, "the center of an evolving circle of Boston area poets"— younger men whom he mentored—"until his death in 1970."[73]

Although there has always been a certain disconnect between Jonas and the establishment, he was never more like Prescott Townsend than in the fact that he transcended it—being published, for instance, neither in New York nor Boston, but in London, by Ferry Press, which brought out Jonas's first substantial volume of poetry in 1966, followed two years later by his *Excuses for Ear*, work Jonas himself explained this way: "They're swinging & let's hope once & for all the 'jazz poetry' hassle be resolved." (The methodology is in the language, language that "hugs the scene like . . . vowels to necks of consonants"—all this reflecting Jonas's passionate love of music.) Writes Torra: "Jonas is one of the great jazz voices in American poetry; he wrote with an improviser's sensibility. Its spontaneity, starts, stops, inflections are unique. He . . . tuned an idiom to his own jazz ear. . . . Content, meaning, and spelling all came after the fact. . . . He worked his line to make music."[74] A jazz poet, Jonas was also a gay poet, and as he was conventionally masculine—which in the 1950s was rare in someone so completely out and open about his sexuality—that, too, he shared with Townsend. Indeed, the two were on that subject all but brothers in crime. In their biography of Spicer, *Poet Be like God,* Lewis Ellingham and Kevin Killian take special notice, for instance, of the "Newsletter" that Jonas, Wieners, Spicer, Blazer, and Dunn put out in the 1950s, a rag that catches just the gritty, radical spirit of Prescott Townsend's back of the Hill, of Harvard Gardens, twisty brick streets, boozy poetry readings at the Charles Street Meeting House, sleazy old tenements, late-night suppers at Scharaff's, and so on: the newsletter, "a curious blend of acid railery and low camp . . . came with instructions: *Post whatever pages of it poke you in the eye in the most public place you can find—i.e., an art gallery, a bohemian bar, or a lavatory frequented by poets.* It's a very gay text."[75]

Ricard and Jonas, though they may seem to have been two ships who passed in the night (indeed, in opposite directions; Ricard from Boston to New York; Jonas from New York to Boston), are today the tallest trees standing, artistically, of those Prescott Townsend planted in the back of Beacon Hill in the 1950s and '60s, of which Prescott will ever be, as Bob Dylan might have said, some kind of crazy mayor. But it is only Jonas who made the subject, like the locale, his own. Of the Napoleon Club bar, for example, Prescott's favorite trolling ground for Harvard preppies, Jonas wrote: "Even now i find the Napoleon stuffy tho' it has [twice, i think,] / changed hands, frequented by store clerks [more finish than basic / stuff] turnd squires after five & god, yes, the decorators." And of his and Townsend's brick sidewalks, this most subversive of Bostonians showed himself to be, if not a restorer, then a historic preservationist after all: in his Poem XXXIII, written in 1968, Jonas refers to such north slope landmarks as the Barn Theatre, extolling a Boston he associates with Santayana, which was to him "the ass side of the hill," and something else, too, writing, as it would turn out, his truth: "I shall die on the rebel side."[76] He did. Before he died, however, it was Jonas, really, who also immortalized Prescott Townsend's end, which was dramatic enough, a sort of small-scale Götterdämmerung.

All the demons that had beset Prescott throughout his life seemed to gather to do the deed—Townsend, himself, finally, very Lear-like in the face of it all. Was it arson that caused the first fire, when in 1968 Provincetownsend went up in flames? What remained of Townsend's Cape Cod compound, which he was forced to sell, was demolished in aid of a parking lot for the adjoining Moors restaurant. Such a shame. Ricard remembered one room as particularly beautiful—the big room beneath the "dormitory" where Townsend had used "ships-knees as cornice pieces," walls made from the enormous rending-barrel of a broken-up whaler, and a fireplace in the Romanesque style formed of carved brownstone blocks" from the old Boston

Art Club in Copley Square. John Waters, who had summered in a rental apartment of the house just three years earlier, lamented how different was his perspective from that of the locals; Provincetownsend, he thought, was a "wonderful House." But as Charles Shively saw, it was doomed. "Because of his open welcome to the homeless, some believe that 'the Provincetown fathers or their eager sons may have torched the house.' "[77] Three of the Yankee Selectmen of Provincetown did issue "An Appeal to All Decent People," complaining, "We are not getting the support we should in our effort to rid our town of these degenerates."[78] Dazed by now from what must have seemed a never-ending battle, Townsend salvaged what he could and retreated to Lindall Place and Phillips Street. Yet there, too, fire did him in. One house after the other burned down in 1971.[79] Phillips Street was a total loss (it is today a very odd-looking sunken garden, an empty void on the historic streetscape), and at Lindall Place only the exterior brick shell was saved. This time it was Prescott's own fault. Beacon Hill was tolerant enough. But Prescott was never one for having his chimneys swept, and a chimney fire wrote *finis* to it all. Barely escaping with his life, Townsend, nearing eighty, stood outside the house on a winter's night in 1971 and watched the floors collapse in a roaring conflagration that destroyed walls, floors, art, papers, records—everything.

But that was not all. Not only did all three of Townsend's houses burn down within as many years, but at the same time the West End neighborhood all about him facing his Lindall Place house also went up, so to speak, in flames. (Beacon Hill's north slope was always thought of as a part of the West End until all the flatland at the Hill's foot was bulldozed into oblivion in one of the most disastrous urban-renewal projects in American history.) Townsend, truly beset on every side, seemed threatened by more than bulldozers. Jonas saw it clearly enough. In his "Poem XXXIII," the poet refers to "Prescott / (Townsend) about the only remnant of this Boston still above ground, / for as I write, the hammer falls against the best houses / built in North America . . . ," houses Jonas is sure high-rise blocks will be no substitute for.[80]

A few years earlier, in a lucid moment, Townsend had wheezed to Cathcart: "I want three people to write my biography: [Randy] Wicker—to put in the facts; René [Ricard]—to make it racy; and you—to make it properly sardonic."[81] Vintage Prescott. But while some few facts have been rescued here about Townsend and his orbit, "racy" is not the final impression, nor "sardonic." That was not true either of Townsend's bequest of the residue of his estate—he died in a basement apartment with a dirt floor at 50 Garden Street on the north slope in 1973—"to the President and Fellows of Harvard College to be used by the Department of Psychology as part of its general fund to be used in connection with research and study of the homophile and also the study of sexual variants."[82] Nor of the bequest for a lecture series (now run by the Harvard Gay and Lesbian Caucus) given by Jon Perry, a Harvard student once drawn to Townsend's Demophile Center.[83] The Perry lectures are surely also the legacy of gallant old Prescott, in whom both the two archetypes I've posited here seem to have met, though uneasily enough. Whitmanic in his roles of officer, outdoorsman, and adopter of strays, Prescott was Wildean enough in other roles as theatrical patron, exotic traveler, and bohemian designer; above all, in his stubborn determination to go to prison and in his decades-long *De Profundis* of postjail activism and his prophetic defense of the homophile in America.

7.

Finale: Boston, New York, Washington —A Rumor of Angels

So receive me brother...
Or will we leave each other alone...
On the streets of Philadelphia.
                    —Bruce Springsteen

THIS STUDY'S MORE than usually personal and oftentimes near elegiac perspective is one result of the way it focuses at various points on the work's impetus or inspiration: my old Harvard dean and mentor from my undergraduate years, my youthful Harvard best friend and soul mate from my tutorial years, as well as those two figures from my own youth, Lucien Price and Prescott Townsend. It is my perspective, bound somewhat to melancholy and meant here as foil and contrast to this book's necessarily broad, indeed dynamic historical sweep; a sweep in this chapter, finally, almost progressive.

The way Harvard's most important orbit enlarged in the modern period to encompass (somewhere, in our terms, between home and away) all three capitals, of American intellect (Boston), culture and commerce (New York), and politics (Washington), was dynamic enough; still more so the emergence at the same time of a whole new vector in Harvard's gay experience; a third game, as it were, neither primarily "home," nor primarily "away," but a sort of fusion of both fired by an entirely new trajectory of action and study, a whole new landscape of desire where, beginning in the 1960s, nearly all the rules of the road for gays changed utterly.

The idea (that grew out of A. K. Porter's suicide) of a chair to study homosexuality, at Harvard presumably, happened after all—elsewhere—but it was a Harvard-trained scholar, Martin Duberman, who helped found the Gay Academic Union in 1973, and in 1991 the Center for Lesbian and Gay Studies at the City University of New York, the first such program of its kind in the country. So, too, Prescott Townsend's bequest to Harvard (more or less abortive because so little of his fortune survived him) was also realized, not only in some sense through the Perry lectures, but in the work of a great Harvard scholar of psychology, Roger Brown, whose work on sexuality in homosexual old age was pathbreaking. Another and much younger and even more effective activist than Townsend also surfaced: Franklin Kameny, who became the second Harvard graduate to found a big-city Mattachine chapter, in Washington.

Of the background of all these things, Martha Nussbaum has written eloquently in *The New Republic*, where she emphasizes the role of the Harvard medievalist, David Herlihy, onetime president of the American Historical Association, and a founding member of Harvard's Women's Studies Committee, who years earlier had called for

> the establishment of this new discipline in a famous lecture that trans-
> formed the field. He also gave a founding impetus to lesbian and gay
> studies, when he encouraged his doctoral student, John Boswell, to write
> his massive study of homosexuality and the Christian Church. . . . I al-
> ways note with interest the absence of [Herlihy's] distinguished name
> from the conservative attacks on women and gay studies, since he was a
> pioneer in both, and a man universally respected for his learning and
> for his integrity.
>
> What led Herlihy and others to propose radical changes in their own
> professions . . . and to follow them up with political action aimed at
> founding . . . programs to pursue the new studies further? Above all, a
> passion for truth and understanding. . . . That was Herlihy's political
> agenda—radical enough for Harvard in the 1960's. . . . Herlihy was a con-
> servative man, a religious Catholic, dedicated to home and family. But
> in his preference for the openness of reason over exclusionary scholar-
> ship, he was a true radical.[1]

There is indeed a sense in which Herlihy, who was master of Mather House, one of Harvard's residential colleges, emerges in respect to this family of issues as a sort of anti–President Lowell, whose great reform the Houses were. But if Herlihy can be seen as an impetus not only of the new field of gay and lesbian studies but of a new kind of Harvard community (one we'd call today more inclusive, one President Lowell himself could scarcely have imagined), he was the master of a House, not a university president. And it was not to be until Neil Rudenstine became Harvard's president in 1991 that Harvard's gay community was recognized in any concrete way when Rudenstine took the lead in addressing Harvard's Gay and Lesbian Caucus commencement evening at the Faculty Club. In that same year and for the first time at Harvard there occurred a gay and lesbian studies academic conference. The first was at Yale in 1987, attended by a few hundred. By 1991, there were sixteen hundred participants.[2] In the 1970s, as Nessbaum suggests, it was a very different story. I have written elsewhere, for example, of then president Derek Bok's "transformation . . . of Harvard's lackluster School of Public Administration into the dynamic and high-profile Kennedy

School of Government [as] one of the most timely and idealistic responses of Harvard in our time to the needs of contemporary life in America."[3] But Bok, though he did generally support progressive policies with respect to black and women's issues, took no initiatives of lasting import in gender or even in ethnic studies. Harvard's own gay experience only with great difficulty struggled into the light in the 1950s, '60s, and '70s, observable chiefly in the increasingly rebellious profile of gay students, faculty, and alumni.

As we have used the terms here, some were a case of "home," some "away." Boswell was a Bostonian. Another graduate student in history soon to be heard from was Ohioan Charles Shively, who stayed in Boston. Guy Davenport, a budding writer from Duke, was a southerner working on his Ph.D. Raised in Aruba, novelist-to-be Andrew Holleran was an undergraduate in Lowell House. Both settled outside New England after Harvard. In the mid-1950s, Roger Brown came to Harvard from the University of Michigan. Most hailed from New York City. Critic and author Richard Hall was first on the scene in the late 1940s. Like Hall, Andrew Tobias was an undergraduate. Martin Duberman was a graduate student in history who ended up back in New York. He took his doctoral degree in 1957, the year after Kameny took his in astronomy, then departed for Washington. That same year Barney Frank arrived in Cambridge from New Jersey. The way he and Kameny spent their youth and middle age shuttling between Boston, New York, and Washington was typical. So was the fact that the Center for Lesbian and Gay Studies founded by Duberman was at the City University of New York. It was in the same city he had helped to found the Gay Academic Union, the pioneering group of gay scholars in 1973.

Eleven men: in the late 1940s and '50s, Herlihy, Hall, Duberman, Kameny, Frank, Brown; in the 1960s and '70s, Boswell, Shively, Davenport, Tobias, Holleran—the first string, as it were, of this third game. And like the home and away games, several aspects stand out. Recall the four characteristics of the home game: pederasty, aristocracy, secrecy, and guilt. The away game's pattern as it emerged was equally distinctive: politics, repression, rage, and prophecy—and sex. The marks of the third game? Polemic, therapy, insight—and more sex. Heterosexual and homosexual Americans increasingly had that in common.

Dualities

THE MOST RADICAL of these men, Charles Shively, came to Harvard from a working-class Ohio background and immediately bridged academe and the world, becoming a leader of Boston's newly coalescing gay and lesbian community. Described by Dudley Clendinen and Adam Nagourney as "brilliant, eccentric, gently sweet-tempered in person and passionately anarchistic in politics...a Harvard Ph.D. with a coal-miner's taste for up-the-establishment," he came into his own as an activist just after the 1969 Stone-wall Riot, when Shively was prominently identified with the founding of a most unusual newspaper—*Fag Rag*.

For some reason nobody has yet explained, it seemed to be especially Boston's role in the gay movement in America to have sustained perhaps the most radical gay media, not only the *Gay Community News*, which tried to fill the role of the national gay newspaper of record and has been called "the only gay national weekly published continuously since the early 1970s," in Nancy Walker's words, but an even more radical paper, *Fag Rag*.

The need for what might be politely called the gay press was clear very early: Frank Kameny was heard to complain, "When McCarthy was riding high, I was still in graduate school at Harvard. I read the *Boston Herald* every day, I read *The New York Times* every Sunday. I listened to the radio all the time. I read *Time* magazine weekly. Yet I did not learn until some-where around 1958 or 1959 that homosexuality had been a theme of those hearings."[4] That radical as well as more conservative papers were both needed also goes without saying. But for some there was also a need for "the anarchist *Fag Rag*, which [had] . . . an editorial policy oriented toward sex radicalism,"[5] in the words of the highly respected critic—and alumnus of *Fag Rag*—Michael Bronski. So extremist a paper was it that Dudley Clen-dinen and Adam Nagourney could write that if "in some ways, the gay and lesbian community emerging in Boston" in the early 1970s seemed "more advanced that any other in the country," the most conspicuous sign of its stature was that since 1971 "Boston had been home to perhaps the most radical journal of sexual liberation in America—a tabloid called *Fag Rag*," which they describe as celebrating in drawings, prose, and poetry "the un-governed and apparently infinite possibilities of gay male promiscuity."[6]

For many (most?) gays, *Fag Rag* was as appalling as it was to most straights. However, rather in the way Leonard Bernstein's leftist politics and rampaging ego in the 1970s made him vulnerable to the Black Panthers at a (later noto-rious) party in his New York apartment given by his wife despite the Panthers' anti-Zionism,[7] so Prescott Townsend, always in search of the limelight and in his last years especially grateful for any attention at all, accepted the invitation to rather a bizarre birthday party, also in the 1970s, given him by *Fag Rag* de-spite his clear-cut Republican politics. It was a mistake, and one many of his friends regretted almost at once, for ever since Townsend, who was libertarian but not connected in any way with *Fag Rag*, has seemed somehow linked to that paper, described once on the floor of the U.S. Congress as "the most loathsome publication in the English language."[8] Yet Joseph McGrath, Town-send's longtime secretary, is clear that Shively and Townsend, though they knew each other, were not close friends. Nor is there any credible evidence Townsend was an ally in Shively's more extremist activities.[9]

Such publicity, however bad for Townsend, did no harm, of course, to

Fag Rag. Nor did interviews with Gore Vidal, who in 1973 would give a now much quoted and very frank interview to *Fag Rag*, so frank that after its publication Vidal, not entirely tongue in cheek (he was then still a serious political as well as literary figure), opined to the interviewer, John Mitzel, "It's plain that I can never be president now." Vidal later spoke in Boston at an event organized by Mitzel in protest to yet another dimension of the lingering persecutions of those days; indeed, the month before Vidal's speech in 1978 the Boston police had arrested no fewer than 103 men at the landmark Boston Public Library in Copley Square, having first entrapped them. Moreover, as a result of publicity generated by his attendance at Vidal's lecture, bigots forced the resignation of Massachusetts Superior Court Justice Robert N. Bonin. Vidal to Mitzel again: "A fine American story with a happy ending. . . . It looks like anti-fag is now the new McCarthyism."[10]

Shively himself, however, *Fag Rag*'s "philosopher-editor," in Clendinen and Nagourney's words, could upstage anyone, even Vidal. He once testified in Faneuil Hall before the Platform Committee of the Democratic National Committee in a dress—a long dress, and sewn up for him by another *Fag Rag* personality, Larry Anderson, also a Black Panther. Most notably, at the Parkman Bandstand on Boston Common at the finale of a gay pride parade in 1977, Shively appeared in his crimson Harvard doctoral gown and burned his diploma to vigorous and entirely understandable roars of approval (never mind that it may have been a copy). But the hour not only sometimes compels, sometimes it destroys. Shively, his passion too interested, his focus dangerously narrowed, deliberately worked up both himself and the crowd, and completely lost it when he attempted to burn the Bible: time stopped, perhaps, on Boston Common, where unwearied spirits had seen Puritans burn witches but had been spared Nazis burning books, and now endured a devastating recapitulation of both kinds of hate. The result was a near-riot and Shively was restrained, not entirely peacefully.[11] Meanwhile, it proved harder to ignore other views that some attributed to him, such as those about pedophilia since promulgated by the North American Man-Boy Love Association—a vile cause almost universally condemned.

At quite the other end of the spectrum was another high-profile Harvard graduate student of the 1960s, John Boswell, who also had his activist side (he took to the Boston-area lecture circuit in support of gay rights and helped start the first queer dances at Harvard), but whose message, as well as his tactics, was very different from Shively's. Boswell, a Bostonian, came to Harvard from William and Mary and went on after Harvard to Yale, where he ultimately became the A. Whitney Griswold Professor of History. (It was Boswell who would found Yale's Lesbian and Gay Center, now the Research Fund for Lesbian and Gay Studies.) A prodigious scholar as well as an ardent Christian, Boswell would encourage and eventually delight Christians (gay ones particularly) as much as Shively enraged them, especially with the publication of his *Christianity, Social Tolerance, and Homo-*

sexuality. This pathfinding book, which won the American Book Award for History in 1981, advanced an altogether stupendous thesis, Boswell arguing forcefully against what he called "the common idea that religious belief— Christian or other—has been the cause of intolerance in regard to gay people." The result, *The New York Times* would report, "upended medieval scholarship."[12] Writing in the *Book Review*, Stanford historian Paul Robinson called Boswell's book "revolutionary . . . it tells of things heretofore unimagined and sets a standard of excellence that one would have thought impossible in the treatment of an issue so large, uncharted, and vexed." Not the least of Boswell's revelations was to argue that in the late eleventh and early twelfth century there had been "an efflorescence of gay subculture, with a highly developed literature, its own argot and artistic conventions, its own low life, its elaborate responses to critics."

His subtitle was also significant: by insisting upon "Gay People in Western Europe from the Beginning of the Christian Era to the Fourteenth Century," Boswell became a leader among a minority of gay studies scholars (Robert K. Martin, for instance) who in respect to the question of queer identity are called "essentialists," that is, championing the belief that a gay identity in some form has been constant throughout history, though only recently becoming a political as well as a social or sexual identity. Other scholars, the so-called constructionists (for example, Eve Kosofsky Sedgwick), insist that identity is all and that gay in any real sense is a development of the last hundred years or so. Boswell mediated effectively between both extremes, and his formidable scholarship—he read or spoke seventeen languages, including Old Church Slavonic, Old Icelandic, and some classical Armenian, Syriac, and Persian—was such that only one of his footnotes could sometimes spark whole articles in response. Although he did publish on other subjects—his *The Kindness of Strangers: The Abandonment of Children in Western Europe from Late Antiquity to the Renaissance* was widely praised— Boswell's major focus was on gay and lesbian studies and he would famously follow up on his first book in that field with *Same-Sex Unions in Premodern Europe*. Based on his study of the liturgical solemnization of same-sex unions disclosed in more than sixty manuscripts from the eighth to the sixteenth century, Boswell, though he admitted that one could not know if those unions were sexual, nonetheless insisted they were "unmistakably a voluntary, emotional union of two persons," and one that was closely related to heterosexual marriage.

It was a profoundly controversial finale to a brilliant career—Boswell died six months after its publication at only age forty-seven from complications from AIDS. His thesis, moreover, penetrated so far into the mass culture as to have surfaced in the comic strip "Doonesbury," by Garry Trudeau, a strip at least two newspapers withheld from publication. The scholarly consensus seems to be that whether or not Boswell's unions were gay marriages, he had again forced upon scholars many challenging questions, not the least role of the great scholar. As devout a Catholic as Shively was an atheist, Boswell was equally as inflammatory as Shively: but Boswell scored his points the Harvard way—*writing* books, not burning them—and on a much larger stage.[13]

Shively and Boswell, though so unalike in approach, were alike in this: both took their doctorates at Harvard in history, each necessarily concerned with that field's constant process of research and thought, shaping and writing about the past, and the need of any movement concerned with changing the present to keep an eye cocked on its underpinnings. It was something a third historian Harvard would field in this area, Martin Duberman—who, though he earned his doctorate in the decade before Shively and Boswell did, only publicly came out as a gay activist in the early 1970s—became especially noted for.

A Phi Beta Kappa graduate of Yale in 1952 before coming to Harvard in the 1950s, Duberman wrote his first book about the Boston grandee Charles Francis Adams and for it won a Bancroft Prize in 1962. His second book, by which time he had become a tenured professor at Princeton, was about another notable Harvard figure, poet James Russell Lowell, a biography which in 1967 was a National Book Award nominee. But though Duberman's road seemed royal indeed in the 1950s and '60s, as he disclosed in his autobiography, *Cures*, it was plagued by many demons having to do with his struggle with his homosexuality.

He came out at Harvard, yet another of that band of strangers that for most of the twentieth century gave such restless detail to the foreground of the famous view of Harvard's collegiate towers along the ever-cruisy banks of the Charles River. Especially at night. There, along its grassy embankment, leaning over elegant bridges, scouting its paths, lolling (apparently) on the occasional bench, young eyes as quick off the mark as young hormones, one generation after another, they foraged, mostly for sex (always fugitive), usually, too, for answers to a life problem of more complexity then (and certainly a problem no one counseled them about, least of all their friendly professors). Certainly not any of Duberman's professors. Nor any doctor, either. The treatment of one, wrote Duberman, took him "to the brink, not of reconstruction, but of near-negation. It would so thoroughly undermine my ability to accept my own nature," he recalled, "that . . . I would become nearly as homophobic as the culture itself." Indeed, in the 1950s we have a soundtrack thanks to Duberman to the perennial gay dance along the banks of the Charles—indeed to any of the parks he frequented: "I couldn't shake my mother's ancient injunction," he recalled, "*never* to walk through a park alone for fear of the sick people who lingered therein"; to which theme he added: "I had *become* the person my mother had warned me about." Nor did the worry easily dissolve. As late as 1970, the year after Stonewall, when Prescott Townsend, approaching eighty, was tottering bravely up Sixth Avenue in the small core group of maybe two hundred people who started the world's first gay pride parade, Duberman, a vigorous young campus antiwar activist, as the parade triumphantly swelled to thousands, stayed locked up in his Manhattan apartment, "barricaded," he remembered, "by books" and at work on his latest book. But, as he explores in *Cures*, Duberman eventually came to see in retrospect that it was all a necessary prelude to becoming an activist himself, to his taking "some of the anger I vengefully turned inward," as he put it, "and putting it where it belonged—on a repressive culture and on [my therapist] as its representative."[14]

Forced out of Princeton in 1972 (so active in the antiwar movement of those turbulent times that, though tenured, he was penalized as to promotions and salary), Duberman finally triumphed as Distinguished Professor of History at Lehman College at City University of New York. Moreover, his coming out was fructifying in every sense with respect to his creative and scholarly work. Of his next book, *Black Mountain: An Exploration in Community*, he wrote: "My conviction is that when a historian allows more of himself to show—his feelings, fantasies, needs, not merely his skills at information-retrieval, organization and analysis—he is *less* likely to contaminate the data, simply because there is less pretense that he and it are one."[15]

Duberman's positive perspective—an article of faith for many historians of my generation, including me—was not, however, universal. Nor his candidness. Perhaps it was easier then for a homosexual historian to find virtues, professionally, in so volatile a hand of the cards dealt, than, say, for a physicist—at least at Harvard, famously balkanized then, and with few opportunities for a physicist or a historian or anyone else to compare notes, unless it was the men's room of Lamont, Harvard's undergraduate library. An interviewer told Gore Vidal in 1974, when discussing "the cruising scene in Boston," that "the wildest experiences supposedly may be found in university tearooms, especially the notorious Lamont Library at Harvard. The scene there includes passing notes which outline what one is in to." To which Vidal responded that it probably amounted to no more than what the gay poet W. H. Auden used to call "Princeton First Year" (more or less mutual masturbation).[16] More helpfully, years later, Andrew Tobias opined that the complete anonymity of Lamont sex was accounted for "not because young gay men are by nature measurably more disgusting than young straight men, but because they were terrified of being discovered and so couldn't flirt and date and ultimately tryst in a more appealingly romantic way."

The Best Little Boys

TOBIAS, WHO ENTERED Harvard College in 1964, though he came out with glacial slowness, shedding one skin after another very painfully, finally redeemed himself by writing it all down in *The Best Little Boy in the World*. There and in subsequent writings he has left a vivid picture of pre-Stonewall, pre-1969 Harvard. Three of his stories I find particularly interesting,[17] first that of a Winthrop House tutor of this period, John Newmeyer, who lived in the house from 1966 to 1969:

> Our homoerotic world was very like the Oxford of *Brideshead Revisited*, with Tom [Hopkins] as Anthony Blanche constantly egging us on. I was a cautious Charles Ryder; my Sebastian Flyte was Nick Gagarin '70— beautiful, aristocratic, charming, and responsive. It was a time of intense romantic friendships, resonant with youthful laughter and daring and rebellion. These friendships reached sexual consummation only rarely and hesitantly—for me, just four or five times. Late-night knocks on my door, awkward passionate embraces, long intense confessions.

This world made for quite a contrast with that of Bob, another classmate in Winthrop, whose tale was very different: a suicide attempt sophomore year; electro-shock treatments on the advice of a nationally known Harvard psychiatrist; a second suicide attempt; then a third. Yet, remembered Tobias, Bob's tutor was gay, and the tutor after that, too. But they never talked about the subject until long out of Harvard. Still, he'd survived. Nick Gagarin—John Newmeyer's "beautiful, aristocratic, charming, and responsive" Sebastian Flyte figure—did not. He succeeded in killing himself.

Tobias's last story in this Winthrop House gay triptych was that of Nat Butler, who, Tobias remembered, slept night after night a bare thirty feet away, also in torment that *he* was the only one. Of course, writes Tobias, "on one level, I knew there probably were other people like me—regular guys who liked guys—much as we know, mathematically, there is probably other intelligent life in the universe. But how do you make contact?"[18] It was a point made by one of Tobias's stories, Nat's own, in which he recalls that at age three he was given a silver martini shaker by his uncle William Shreve, of Shreve, Crump & Low, the very grand Boston jewelers, a shaker inscribed with the name of Nathaniel Glover Butler, Exeter '64, Harvard '68. Writes Butler:

> Well, I fulfilled all that—Exeter like my father, Harvard like my father (and both my grandfathers and one of my great-grandfathers), and then went into the navy as my father had done, and fought in a war in the South Pacific as my father had done, *and* got admitted to HBS as my father had done—and *still* I hadn't gotten his approval. So I just figured: screw it. I'm going to start doing what I want. The week I started the B-School in '73 was the week I started going to Sporters seven nights a week.

That, of course, was after 1969. That was the year of the Harvard strike, the stunned response of a university radicalized by a violent building takeover by leftist students and their even more violent removal by the police at

President Pusey's behest. It was also the year of the Stonewall Riot at the New York City bar of that name. Vietnam was the catalyst, Tobias declared, changing everything. Not perhaps for Tobias, even in the 1960s still in denial, but certainly for Duberman in the late 1950s when he—so to speak—at least came out at night. As did many. It was all very much like ships passing in the night, except more and more of the ships were showing lights. Barney Frank, for example, who did not experience his first sexual advance until 1968, just the year before Stonewall. It happened late at night, of course, on Boston Common, walking home from City Hall,[19] where by then, in between Harvard degrees, Frank had become the Boston mayor's right-hand man on his way to becoming a United States congressman. His career, beyond our scope here, began in these pre-Stonewall years. Little had Tobias suspected. Not only had his roommate been gay, but so was one of the most popular of Winthrop House's tutors in the early 1960s—Barney Frank.

Tobias himself upset all the cherished stereotypes in 1973, when he came out in print as "John Reid." Already one of the dozen or so most respected financial-advice writers in America, Tobias, as he himself said in 1973, had in prep school and at Harvard "always topped his class, honored his folks, and did well in sports."[20] He was also more to the right than to the left; after his four years in the college, Tobias went on to Harvard Business School, from which he graduated in 1972. Six years later his *The Only Investment Guide You'll Ever Need* was a bestseller.

Stargazer

RIGHT WING, LEFT wing—whatever stereotypes remained, Frank Kameny quickly demolished. The pride and joy of a New York City Jewish family of moderate means but high ambitions, Kameny, born in 1925, was a graduate of Queens College who went directly from his undergraduate years to service in World War II, of which he is a combat veteran: "I fought my way virtually slit trench by slit trench . . . halfway across Germany," Kameny told journalist Charles Kaiser.[21] Returning from active service, Kameny went on to graduate school, where his time was formative. As he told Edmund White: "I went to Harvard where I became active in black civil rights and the American Civil Liberties Union [as a member]. I came out in 1954 when I was twenty-nine. I experienced no guilt. I knew I was right. I regretted I'd wasted fifteen good years but made up for lost time with zest and vigor."[22] Endless hours cruising nightly along the Charles required both, and much early-morning coffee afterward in Harvard Square diners like the Waldorf (Frank O'Hara's favorite) or the Hayes-Bickford (Duberman's choice; Kameny's, too), all the more so if the evening had begun in one or another gay bar (Kameny's favorites, like Duberman's, were the Napoleon and the Casablanca). In the 1970s Kameny talked about this life to Edmund White, whose own thoughts as he "sunned and watched the small sailboats skimming up and down the Charles" with a gay couple in Boston, were actually of San Francisco. "The cities do have their similarities," White wrote. "They are both intimate and sophisticated—and both are very gay." But to White the differences were more remarkable: "Boston is brainy . . . in Cambridge at the subway stop a string quartet . . . entertains waiting passengers with a bit of Alban Berg." But White also saw that "Boston . . . has its own way of suppressing . . . homosexuality. At Harvard . . . undergraduates are too career-oriented to risk compromising their futures," he noted, while "among the graduate students and gay faculty members, the oppression (to the degree it exists) is more subtle."[23] And so, in the 1950s, did Kameny find it, his explorations, like those of his fellows, carefully restricted in consequence to only the most respectable locales. In the interview a perceptive White saw another side of Kameny—"extremely shy, a retiring astronomer whom history forced into leadership"—yet Kameny nonetheless showed White "more feistiness than I've seen in any other gay leader."[24] Thus did White point unerringly to the two sides of Kameny that disclosed very well the two eras he bridged. No bohemian he: Kameny was the most conventional of men, focused utterly on his work, at Harvard and then at Georgetown, where he went to teach after getting his doctorate; no less so thereafter at the U.S. Army Map Service. He was thus all the more rudely shocked when the same fate befell him as we've seen befall Prescott Townsend, class of 1918, decades before: Kameny found himself in trouble with the police, the key episode occurring late one night in Lafayette Park, a traditional gay cruising area across Pennsylvania Avenue from the White House. He was arrested. Later he would be fired. And, like Townsend, Kameny was radicalized.

Kameny then began a long saga of one court battle after another, battles to regain his job, battles predicated on his fundamental belief that no employer (including the U.S. government) had any right to inquire into his private life. A simple enough premise, but Kameny was hardly supported by anyone all the way up to the Supreme Court, which in 1961 declined to hear his case. The result was that, like Townsend before him, Kameny became an activist. And it was in the wake of this event that in 1961 Kameny founded the Washington, D.C., Mattachine, not in the spirit of the timid oldest New York Mattachine establishment but in the more activist spirit that had flared in the Boston chapter in its first years under Townsend when it had been so at odds with both the West Coast and New York branches (without knowing it: Kameny only met Townsend much later in the latter's dotage). Later, when Wicker's activism animated the New York Mattachine, Kameny made common cause with New York. Indeed, Kameny went on to make a very credible run for Congress: "The candidate was *Dr.* Kameny," the PR proclaimed, "a physicist and astronomer, received his Ph.D. from Harvard University. He has taught at Georgetown University and worked in the aerospace industry. He is a combat veteran of World War II." As Dudley Clendinen and Adam Nagourney point out, moreover, Kameny was "completely devoid of any of the feminine mannerisms that the public then associated with homosexuality."²⁵ So, too, was Townsend, but his eccentric "hippie" appearance was very off-putting. Kameny, on the other hand, was no hippie. Of course he lost. But no one expected him to do as well as he did. Moreover, it was just about the only time Kameny did lose. Wrote Clendinen and Nagourney:

> Franklin Kameny had the confidence of an intellectual autocrat, the manner of a snapping turtle, a voice like a foghorn. . . . He cultivated the self-righteous arrogance of a visionary. . . . He was George Patton as gay activist: a brilliant, indomitable man, a general without an army, alone against everyone else. "If society and I differ on something," Kameny said once, "I'm willing to give the matter a second look. If we still differ, then I am right and society is wrong; and society can go its way so long as it does not get in my way. But if it does there's going to be a fight. And I'm not going to be the one who backs down."²⁶

One by one Kameny won his fights. In 1964 he persuaded the Washington chapter of the hitherto not helpful ACLU to challenge the Civil Service Commission's regulations excluding gays from government service, and at its annual convention in 1964 the national ACLU adopted the new policy of its Washington chapter that it was "discriminatory" for the government to refuse to hire people because of their sexual orientation.

Kameny fixated at once, furthermore, on the idea of homosexuality as unhealthy or pathological. In 1966 he also attacked the idea that it was immoral. And by 1968 he was urging gay pride on every opportunity ("Gay is good," his slogan, proceeded clearly from "black is beautiful") and in 1971 led a raucous protest at the annual meeting of the American Psychiatric Association, which still listed homosexuality as a psychological disorder. Homosexuality, so much less a crime because of Alfred Kinsey, and so much less a sin since Boswell's work had been published, ceased also to be a disease largely at the behest of Frank Kameny.²⁷

Nor was that the extent of it. Abolishing crime, sin, and disease was one thing; intellectual respectability of the highest order, of a more literary and artistic sort, verging on—dare one say it—a gay sensibility, was something more. And that was the cause of the now almost totally obscure Richard Hall, Harvard class of 1948, another New Yorker who was successful both as a critic (he would be the first openly gay critic elected to the National Book Critics Circle) and as an author, chiefly of a large number of distinguished short stories, most "unabashedly and almost exclusively gay," in literary historian Claude Summers's words, but dealing with "themes . . . both varied and universal." As a literary historian, moreover, Hall's work was seminal. It was a series of his articles on Henry James that persuaded most critics, including Leon Edel, to acknowledge James's attraction to men. Finally, a *New York Times Book Review* article of 1988 by Hall—"Gay Fiction Comes Home"—really established the gay literary genre in the American mind.[28]

Lest respectability seem entirely to take the edge off the Harvard gay experience, there is always, however, that other figure of late-1950s and early-1960s Harvard Yard, Guy Davenport.

A southerner who after Duke and Harvard (Ph.D., 1961) was a Rhodes scholar at Oxford and professor of English for three decades thereafter at the University of Kentucky at Lexington, Davenport has been teacher, scholar, poet, novelist, essayist, illustrator—a polymath really—and though he has never been popular, his is a really distinctive voice in American letters. His point of view, furthermore, as gay critic Bruce Bawer puts it—is a "flat-out antipathy for the twentieth century . . . more than balanced by an over-whelming enthusiasm for the thinkers and artists who have helped define it," and is allied in Davenport's thinking to his devotion to a nineteenth-century French philosopher, Charles Fourier, who believed that societal harmony requires utter sexual liberation. The results are at once both dazzling and troubling.[29]

A very experimental writer—one sentence can follow another without any connection to time, place, or circumstance, much less logic, yet all seems a kind of verbal fugue that *does* parse—Davenport is a master of allusion and, perhaps more than anything else, he is, if not a historian, literally *writing* history, "History [as] a dream that strays into innocent sleep." Through audacious prose, he seeks, in Walter Sullivan's words, to "establish new connections between old and new, to discover further dimensions in the continuum of human history." Yet there are those who would describe his work simply as pornographic—remember Fourier—which Bawer has faced head-on. Davenport's stories, Bawer writes, have to be understood as set in

> a world that is impossibly lovely, tranquil and timeless. For them, there are no taboos—they feel affection for one another, and sex (whether with man or woman, child or sibling) is their way of expressing it. . . . "Why must we try to figure out why we're hugging anybody" asks [a character]. "Love is love." "Human affinities" says [another] "come from any direction."
>
> In "Apples and Pears" nobody feels hurt or jealous or guilty; nobody's being abused or psychologically damaged. . . . Davenport, magician that he is, *makes* us believe in (and even cherish) this bucolic never-never land.[30]

Yet Bawer (not one to be taken in by so problematic a perspective, however transporting) goes on to say that too often in Davenport's work "affection steals away into the background, leaving nothing behind but sex, sex, sex. At such moments, Davenport . . . is likely to break into detailed descriptions of the male sex organ (for which he has more names . . . than the Eskimos have for snow)."³¹ Bawer also finds Davenport's politics—which are too often injected in his pastoral—disturbing. But he insists, "The perverseness of Davenport's politics in no way negates the value of his work or of his contribution to American literature."

I am reminded of Norman Mailer's first book, *The Naked and the Dead*, wherein he "discovered the unholy trinity—homosexual, reformer, and psychopath—of American male animism," according to Caleb Crain, from whom we learn that Mailer began "to study men intimately" in that book through a cast of characters focused on "the immoral General Cummings (reactionary and homosexual), the overly moral Lieutenant Hearn (reformist and Harvard-educated), and the amoral Staff Sergeant Croft (violent and Texan)." Mailer himself is a graduate of Harvard College, and, like Ernest Hemingway, aggressively unfriendly to things gay and perhaps for the same reason (Mailer is said to have picked a fight with a sailor once who called his poodle "queer"). Thus it makes a certain sense that the Harvard guy of this fictional trio is the overly moral reformer (presumably heterosexual) and the reactionary figure (presumably not Harvard-educated) is the immoral homosexual. There is, to be sure, all the difference in the world between archetypes and stereotypes, but there is a sense in which the one is a reduction of the other and Mailer got it right the first time: many Harvard-educated liberals, overmoral or not, are surely heterosexual; and many reactionaries (wherever they were educated, and whether they are moral *or* immoral) have been, historically, homosexual.³²

A Little Sexual Fizz

AND WHAT OF Roger Brown? Of the first of the 1950s and '60's gay figures to arrive at Harvard nothing has so far been said. Yet his achievement was in many ways the most notable of them all. The John Lindsley Professor of Psychology, Brown was the author of seminal work in three fields—psycholinguistics, social psychology, and cognition. In a long life he accumulated many honors, not least to have been elected to both the American Academy of Arts and Sciences and the National Academy of Sciences. In Paris in 1985 he was awarded the International Prize of the Fyssen Foundation. A great scholar who was also a great teacher (he began his Harvard career as a resident tutor in Kirkland House), Brown was given the Phi Beta Kappa prize for excellence in teaching in 1992. He was, in other words, one of the giants of his field in his generation.³³

When Brown came to Harvard in 1954 from the University of Michigan, he brought not only his doctorate, but his lifelong partner, Albert Gilman. Both were graduate students supported by the GI Bill of Rights, lovers whose union began in a campus men's room and ended on Albert's deathbed four decades and more later. That Brown chose Harvard over Michigan (which matched Harvard's offer when it came), moreover, was because of Albert, the first of many fascinating disclosures in his unconventional autobiography of 1996. (He admits, for example, that on the one hand he chose his students "according to criteria known only to myself, but talent was always the first consideration"—a clear admission it was not the only one—and on the other that he "always kept the sex ratio [between men and women] even on the principle that a little sexual fizz helped sustain the intellectual fizz.")[34] Unconventional? So was most of Brown's memoir, aptly titled *Against My Better Judgment.*

The reviews of Brown's scandalous tell-all book were surprisingly good. Brown's emphasis is not at all on forty years of gay life in Boston (though he does touch briefly on his forays to the Napoleon Club and genteel sherry hours in the Kirkland House Senior Common Room and so on). Rather, he attempts a rigorous, deeply troubling, and surprisingly good study of a gay Harvard professor's life in retirement and old age, an investigation without precedent that staggered many. Indeed, though he asks very pointed questions (is the book an "expression of the chagrin that distinguished gay men must feel—once emerged from the closet—the expression of a need to tell straight friends, after the fact but right in the face, 'what it's really like'?")[35] and insists on sharp truth (in the case of both "the straight and the gay . . . the death of a partner often releases an unrequited sexuality in the survivor"), Jerome Bruner, professor of psychology at New York University, praised Brown's book highly. He called it

> an extraordinary, moving, and "shocking" memoir. There surely has never been one like it. One of the most distinguished and beloved psychologists of his generation, Roger Brown tells of a feverish, five-year personal quest for love, fueled by the grieving loneliness and sexual desire that erupted upon the death of his homosexual lover of 40 years, Al Gilman. Here . . . in naked candor, is the account of a gay 65-year-old in search of young men in their twenties. For sex, for love, for acting out his own unresolved problems? How could they respond to him, he asks, a "dirty old man" (albeit one of the handsomest men of his generation), they in their adventurous, youthful prime?[36]

It would be unfair only to notice what is shocking about Brown's book and not what is wise. A passage I cherish:

> The irony is that, except for the truly dirty old man who is just that and nothing more (if such there be), the one thing he is hoping to buy is true feeling, the innermost self. It is a lonely universe, one of many it seems, and in passing through it one needs close company, a Primary

other. Grant [like Patrick and Skip, below, a prostitute] once asked me what I wanted from him. His ass? I said that would be nice but it was really his soul I wanted. And what use would that be? I would be partnered by you in the infinite time ahead. And to Patrick I once said: "I can't expect you not to fool around. It's your heart I care about." And to Skip: "You're just a boy and highly sexed, but please let me know if you fall in love because that's what matters." And to Albert [Brown's lifelong partner], who once asked me why I wanted to hear a certain piece of music: "To hear it with you. Don't you know that sharing with you is what I care about?" In retrospect I wonder how we all came to be so wise. None of us were students of Plato's discussion of love and the soul, yet we had hit on the right terms concerning what it is the lover truly wants from his beloved.

The game of courtship between sugar daddy and money boy is not basically different from courtship in general. Surely what every true lover wants is the real self of the beloved.[37]

Brown's Harvard colleague, Professor Philip S. Holzman, admitting that Brown was "the author of several acclaimed textbooks and enduring studies of the psychological aspects of language," nonetheless concluded that "Professor Brown, in his self-exposure, may have written his most penetrating psychological study in his depiction of the human condition in late life."[38]

Coming Home

IN 1991 ANDREW Holleran gave a talk about his undergraduate years at Harvard in the 1960s, a talk Roger Brown may have attended, it having been the first Jon Perry lecture. Author in 1978 of the pathbreaking *Dancer from the Dance* (a novel that quickly got beyond the usual post-Stonewall declaration that "gay is good," disclosing very clearly that there is a dark side, too), Holleran, a member of the Violet Quill, along with Edmund White, Felice Picano, and others, admitted to his audience that "the very first novel I ever wrote was about Harvard. . . . I wrote it in a fit of depression, after graduation, when I'd lost all my friends and what seemed to me the only place I'd ever been happy. This novel was set . . . on the terrace overlooking the [Lowell House] courtyard. . . . my sappy attempt to do what Evelyn Waugh did so well in *Brideshead Revisited*." Sappy or no, Holleran could not get the subject of that novel out of his mind. At his twenty-fifth reunion, he admitted, he'd sought out the Lowell court again, where still he could "feel the spell of those evenings in L-14—how happy and romantic I'd been there—and what a dream world we'd lived in, I now realize. At one point I crossed the grass and stood outside the window of my own first room there, looking out onto the courtyard through the fog. I stood there and peered into the window where I'd sat that night, resting my eyes after a night of studying, separated from that moment by twenty-five years of Time, that densest of all mediums through which many things cannot pass."[39] He stood there, remembering how freshman year he'd dated a Wellesley woman. Disturbed that he didn't want to kiss her at evening's end—all the other couples around them, he recalled, "pureed each other's lips"—Holleran went to the Student Health Service, his question a simple one: "Why didn't I want to kiss Debbie?" Student Health, predictably, was brisk: just do it. But he didn't. Instead

> I stopped seeing Debbie altogether. . . . I could hardly bring myself to look up books under the subject "Homosexuality" in the card catalogue at Widener, so frightened was I that someone would see over my shoulder. . . . [Symonds's *A Problem in Modern Ethics*] . . . and a few references in Plato were all I had to comfort myself. . . .
>
> On the walls of the toilet stalls in Lamont Library (it seems like a tale of libraries, after all: that was my Harvard) were written invitations to nude wrestlers. . . . I may have been in love with the beauty of men, but I was not about to be homosexual. . . .
>
> [I] fell into that gloom common to homosexual youths before they have come to terms with themselves: the conviction that I was the only one in the world.[40]

One very early morning though, Holleran recalled, after a long night of studying in his rooms in Lowell House: "I looked through my windows and I saw proof that I was not: a classmate—the house playwright—walking into the foggy courtyard with his arm around another man." It was, Holleran said, "that gray hour when everyone, Harvard itself, was asleep." He remembered thinking of the two men, "They might have been angels."[41]

HOUND AND HORN

Hunting the Sensibility

8.

Yard and River: Between
Pathétique *and* Brideshead

Our journey has advanced—
Our feet were almost come
To that odd Fork in
Being's road—
—Emily Dickinson

THIS STUDY BEGAN with two nineteenth-century visitors to Harvard Yard, fructifying visitors, controversial even then—Walt Whitman and Oscar Wilde—who represent as I see it the two classic gay archetypes: in Whitman's case that of the warrior (and by extension the athlete, the worker, the man's man—in fact, the modern Western bourgeois gay man); in Wilde's case that of the aesthete (by extension the artist, the littérateur, and in some measure the dandy and the bohemian). Now, at book's end, I conclude by focusing in the century following on *two* pairs of figures who further detail both these gay archetypes as they have evolved—not visitors this time but Harvard's own: those two (though very different) aesthetes, Leonard Bernstein and Aaron Copland, respectively undergraduate and Norton Professor (and lovers too, probably); and two warriors if ever there were warriors, though, again, of very different sorts, Virgil Thomson and Lincoln Kirstein, both undergraduates.

Why so heavy an emphasis on music? One might equally study those two gay twentieth-century Harvard architects, the elegant and facile Philip Johnson (surely a kind of aesthete) and the daring and brutalist Paul Rudolph (just as surely representative of the warrior archetype). Their architecture, despite a distinctly masculine sensibility common to both—very hard-edged, even physically risky—shows a differing aesthetic in each case. Or one might mount an analysis of Robert Drake's book of essays on "great books every gay man should read," *The Gay Canon.* Of the thirty-seven of his titles by Americans, no less than eight—or nearly a third—are by Harvard men (seven entirely, one in part).[1] But that's another book. Moreover, by emphasizing music in this book, another pivotal modern homosexual forefather is, so to speak, forced to the surface in the Harvard context, a figure comparable to both Whitman and Wilde, a figure exemplary in his era—whether fairly or not—of almost a third gay archetype (now happily fading)—that of the victim—Pyotr Ilich Tchaikovsky. That composer's presence in Harvard Yard in the late nineteenth century, though never physical, as was the case with both Whitman and Wilde, was hardly less actual.

Harvard and Tchaikovsky

IN OCTOBER 1874 Tchaikovsky, still a young and not yet very well established composer, wrote to Rimsky-Korsakov that their mutual friend, pianist Hans von Bülow, had just telegraphed him to report the acclaim Tchaikovsky's First Piano Concerto had generated at its world premiere in Boston under the auspices of the Harvard Musical Association, and its very progressive conductor, J. B. Lang.[2] Von Bülow had first performed the new work with the orchestra of the influential Harvard alumni group, one of the century's pioneering musical institutions, which sponsored the city's premier symphonic ensemble then. Indeed, Boston's part in launching Tchaikovsky's career worldwide, though hardly unknown, never seems to register very forcefully, for reasons to be now explored here. Certainly it emerges quite clearly from Roland Wiley's summary:

> The fame of [Tchaikovsky's] music began to spread outside Russia . . . during the last half of the 1870's. After a concert in Moscow in Lent of 1874 Hans von Bülow began learning Tchaikovsky's music. . . . He would become an important mentor, playing the solo part at the premiere of The First Piano Concerto in Boston in 1875, conducting the German premiere at Wiesbaden in 1879. . . .
>
> The next milestone after Bülow's recognition was Hans Richter's conducting of Romeo and Juliet in Vienna in November 1876. . . . Paris awaited the International Exhibition of September, 1878. . . .
>
> Tchaikovsky's music had been established in London with a performance of The First Piano Concerto on 11 March 1876. In the United States there had been performances of the first and second string quartets in Boston by January 1876, in the wake of which Bülow reported to Tchaikovsky that in America he was already counted among the five most important contemporary composers.[3]

Tchaikovsky was not easy to please, however, as Herbert Weinstock and Wallace Brockway point out:

> Although Von Bülow had gratefully accepted the dedication . . . Tchaikovsky was depressed because it was not immediately played in Moscow. He was momentarily cheered by a cable from Von Bülow announcing a

magnificent ovation at the world *première* in Boston, but was again plunged into gloom because his finances were so low that to send an answering cable meant spending his last ruble.[4]

Typically, moreover, Tchaikovsky was quickest to see the bad news rather than the good. Elated to learn from von Bülow that the Boston audience had demanded encores of his concerto's finale, Tchaikovsky in his letter to his fellow composer lamented to his friend: "If only that happened here."[5]

It was a characteristic protest in that it could be taken either way—and it is the fact that Tchaikovsky's whole life was somewhat like that and he seems a very different person according to which of the two schools of thought is in the ascendance at any one time. And the composer's homosexuality is central to both schools: those who see his sexuality as a problem that bedeviled him all his life and ultimately caused his suicide, and those annoyed by the gay-negative assumption of that view. In between both, Roland Wiley stakes out somewhat middle ground, noting that while, on the one hand, Tchaikovsky probably "experienced no unbearable guilt over his sexuality," on the other hand, he "took its negative social implication seriously," especially "the threat of allusion to it in the press, and the impact this would have on his family." The prospect, Wiley concludes, made the composer "hyper-sensitive and moody" on the subject.[6]

This judgment accords as well with that of Alexander Poznansky, a leading figure of the school that sees Tchaikovsky as fairly well adjusted sexually, whose conclusions even Anthony Holden, the composer's latest biographer (and formidable proponent of the view that his sexuality was a very great problem for the Russian master), feels it necessary to quote, so authoritative is Poznansky on Tchaikovsky's sexuality:

> "The rigorous moral education [Tchaikovsky] had received from his parents was only enhanced by his highly idealistic view of art and the artist and by his habitual religious reverence." As a result, he considered his homosexuality "natural, and no doubt resented the social stigma it carried," while at the same time he "never related it in his mind to the rest of the ethical standards of the culture to which he belonged."[7]

Further fueling an already ardent and romantic temperament, that resentment, while it seems never to have mounted to full-fledged neurosis, surely lent much of the force one feels in Tchaikovsky's musical expression, so intense as to be sometimes unbearable, of homosexual love. Indeed, he is to be ranked in this respect alongside two figures whom critic Timothy L. Jackson particularly has compared him to, Socrates and Wilde.[8] I would add Whitman, too. Already as a young man making his way in the world, in Holden's words

Tchaikovsky constantly found himself having to deal with unwelcome female advances. Still persuaded by his love of family life that he cherished feminine company, and would surely one day marry, he embarked on a number of flirtations which all went sour with curious abruptness. Why was it that women became "less interesting" . . . on closer acquaintance? Tchaikovsky mused over the problem in letters to his family—not least to his somewhat prurient father, forever egging him on towards marriage—without yet acknowledging the obvious answer.[9]

As a fully self-aware and mature homosexual, he faced also the classic conflict between love and lust, or so many have concluded. But even in so basic a matter as Tchaikovsky's sexual tastes, no real consensus has emerged. He "seems to have shared the world's distaste for the camp behavior of the aunties" of his day, according to Holden, but that author also reports Tchaikovsky had a "penchant for drag costumes" and was known to feminize names when writing to a person he was having an affair with.[10]

One of the few things that is indisputable is the primacy of music in his life. He was a great Francophile, but Mozart was his musical hero. He found joy, too, in his love not only for his family—parents and his brothers—but for his friends and, indeed, for Russia itself, both the literature and landscape of which beguiled and sustained him. So did a succession of lovers. Holden, for example, assigns the role of "wringing from Tchaikovsky the first authentic expression of his true musical voice" not only to his great teacher and mentor, Mily Alexeyevich Balakirev, a leading composer and pedagogue of those days—who suggested, for example, the idea of one of Tchaikovsky's earliest works, the *Romeo and Juliet* overture—but also to Eduard Zak, a young man Tchaikovsky loved so ardently he continued to declare it in his correspondence over a decade after Zak's suicide. Why young Zak was driven to choose Romeo's fate at only age nineteen is not known. Only Tchaikovsky's guilt and sorrow. But Zak, in Holden's words, probably "inspired the sublime love theme in Tchaikovsky's . . . *Romeo and Juliet*,"[11] which was, perhaps, not an unmixed blessing at a time when its composer was so vexed by his sexuality he was urging on at least one other gay man than himself (his brother, Modest) the need to try urgently to overcome it. Musicologist David Brown, the author of the definitive four-volume study of Tchaikovsky's life and work, has called *Romeo and Juliet* "a memorial masterpiece which is likely to remain unsurpassed as an expression of young and tragic love."[12]

The complexities of Tchaikovsky's life and work are well illustrated by the context of his Fourth Symphony, dedicated to a person who loved (indeed, supported) him but would never agree to meet him, and who would, years later, dump Tchaikovsky without notice and without appeal. This person was at the symphony's premiere, but the dedicatee's presence was as covert as the composer's dedication. "To my best friend," Tchaikovsky wrote on the score. And it hardly clarifies matters to report that not only did Tchaikovsky never meet his best friend but, although he was famously homosexual, that person was a woman: Nadezhda von Meck.

An unusual and exotic situation? Consider the case, a continent away and half century later, of the Anglo-American poet W. H. Auden and his significant other, Chester Kallman. Auden chiefly figured in Harvard's gay experience in distinctly an underground capacity, through a highly informal but vital and largely homosexual literary network centered on Eliot House. In F. O. Matthiessen's Senior Common Room there, already touched on in Chapter 3, then tutor Harry Levin is on record as recalling that in the 1930s T. S. Eliot himself much dwelled on Auden's genius, while another Eliot House tutor of that era, Theodore Spencer, is known until his death to have been Auden's private critic and censor, to whom Auden sent all his manuscripts. The poet was also a presence in Eliot House's Junior Common Room (among students, that is, as much as professors and tutors), particularly in the circle of Leonard Bernstein, of whom more soon, whose admiration for Auden was such that in the first decade of his career the poet's *The Age of Anxiety,* which won a Pulitzer in 1948, inspired Bernstein's symphony of the same name. A few times Auden surfaced publicly at Harvard: in 1939, when, according to I. A. Richards, he lectured there, and again in 1946, when he read a poem in Cambridge commissioned by the college's Phi Beta Kappa chapter.[13]

There may, however, have been a reason for Auden's low profile in Harvard Yard, disreputable enough and only rumor, but which all but mandates his name arising in this book. He is perhaps the most outrageous example of a "genre" of "victim's tales" I've tended to avoid here because so wearying—tales of people rejected by Harvard for this or that because of suspicions about their sexuality—suspicions often only too warranted, alas, but, as often happens, quite unwarranted, always a convenient enough excuse to allay disappointment, and hardly ever possible to document, anyone guilty of such a thing being naturally apt to take great care to hide any evidence of the deed. Thus only two such examples find a place in this book: Leonard Bernstein's rejection as music director of the Boston Symphony Orchestra and—Auden's failure to attain the Charles Eliot Norton professorship at Harvard at about the same time. Both are rumors that make so much sense, *not* to believe them is the greatest difficulty.

Certainly Auden was conspicuous in just the way Bernstein was for his sexuality, and at a time when most homosexuals took care not to be; the very repressed Newton Arvin, for instance, whom Auden replaced at Smith College (instead of Harvard?) in 1953, the year Arvin taught at Harvard, where he was being considered as a replacement after Matthiessen's suicide. (Auden, in fact, sublet Arvin's apartment at Smith.) If that was the year (during which Nathan Pusey became Harvard's president) Auden was reportedly passed over for the prized professorship, Smith certainly solved the problem that Pusey—highly conservative, despite his opposition to McCarthyism and his modernist architectural tastes—might have had with Auden. Certainly, his sexuality was less a problem at a women's college like Smith, to which, for whatever reason, Arvin also returned at year's end. Certainly, too, Auden is rumored to have sustained other such losses because of his homosexuality—for example, a projected *Time* magazine cover.[14]

Auden's life situation was as complicated as Tchaikovsky's had been three generations earlier. Indeed, Auden once wrote that Kallman was to him "emotionally a mother, physically a father and intellectually a son,"[15] never mind, of course, that Kallman had also been Auden's lover (briefly) and best friend (lifelong), all the while conducting their own independent love life with others (on one occasion in Auden's case with a woman). That this independence was at the younger man's insistence and to Auden's dismay was not, moreover, the disaster one might predict for one of the greatest twentieth-century poets, who no less than Lincoln Kirstein ranked in the company of Stravinsky and Picasso. The Anglo-American gay poet of the mid-twentieth century, like the Russian composer of the late nineteenth, apparently thrived on it all. One of Auden's biographers, Humphrey Carpenter, points out that at a lecture on Shakespeare's sonnets in 1946, Auden asserted:

> The artist is not likely to be content with a relationship in which love is returned with equal force; he wants instead to undergo the experience of unrequited love, in order to test his personality and strengthen it. Ultimately, Auden declared the artist *is* strong, and can benefit from this situation. . . . That he himself did so is suggested by the fact that in the five years after the crisis [with Kallman, when the younger man made plain his need for an independent love life, Auden] wrote three long poems which are the most ambitious and sustained work he had yet tackled, and which to some extent, all grew out of what had happened between him and Chester . . . [who] provided a vital stimulus to [Auden's] emotions and imagination.[16]

One of these poems was *The Age of Anxiety*, which not only inspired Bernstein's symphony but a ballet by another famously gay artist, choreographer Jerome Robbins—a progression that suggests a homosexual, artistic, and musical continuum hardly less intriguing than the more literary Eliot House network already touched on here; another place, perhaps to hunt the gay sensibility.

Auden's next work, furthermore, after *The Age of Anxiety*, was a collaboration with Kallman—the "mother," "father," "son," best friend, sometime lover, and now collaborator—on the libretto of Stravinsky's *The Rake's Progress*, of which one of Auden's biographers, Humphrey Carpenter, wrote: "To be united with Chester artistically [was] a kind of enactment of marriage for Auden, and a substitute for physical relations."[17] Certainly it was a better substitute than the one used by Tchaikovsky and von Meck, who engineered a marriage between *his* niece and *her* son; a ceremony, of course, Mme. von Meck did not attend.[18] Nor, finally, are such complexities unknown to the present day, as a glance at this book's acknowledgments will confirm. Welcome to gay life, nineteenth, twentieth, or twenty-first century.

Tchaikovsky, by no means unique, was, however, more moody and impulsive: in the year he composed the Fourth he married a woman of whom he knew little more than that she was besotted with him. The marriage was a disaster.[19] But, declares Holden, the music was not: "All the frustrations of Tchaikovsky's endemic homosexuality and bottled-up emotions . . . are let loose in [the Fourth Symphony]—the first and perhaps least important work in a line of masterpieces *in this vein* [emphasis added] which included the *Manfred* Symphony and the last two symphonies [nos. 5 and 6], the symphonic ballad, *The Voyevoda,* and *The Queen of Spades.*"[20] Insofar as the Fourth Symphony is concerned, Tchaikovsky himself described it in a letter to von Meck significantly more positively, as "express[ing] . . . phase[s] of depression" but relieved by the occasional daydream. And the form that daydream took, that relief, in Tchaikovsky's imagination, I find very significant—call this sensitivity or bias as you will; I suspect a gay scholar may be more alert to its significance: "Some blissful, radiant human image hurries by and beckons you away" is the way he put it.[21] Women as well as men may be blissful and radiant, but I know what was on Tchaikovsky's mind.

Into which we have hardly gone further than did the highly introspective composer himself, who wrote to a critic of the day: "I should not wish to write symphonic works which express nothing, which consist only of empty experiments with chords, rhythms and modulations. Of course my symphony is programmatic, but its program is such that it cannot be expressed in words. . . . Shouldn't a symphony . . . express all those things for which there are no words, but which the soul wishes to express, and which need to be expressed?"[22]

Even in Boston, even at Harvard—especially at Harvard!—not only youth, but youth especially, would seem to have agreed with Tchaikovsky in its desire for more emotionally direct music. Remember, thanks to von Bülow, the First Piano Concerto was not the only premiere of an early work of Tchaikovsky offered in Boston in the 1870s. In 1876 the composer had yet another report from America from his friend and mentor:

> He heard from von Bülow about the warm reception accorded the First String Quartet in Boston, where interest in his work had grown since the success of the first Piano Concerto. . . . Tchaikovsky was also gaining a following in Vienna. Even Liszt was impressed. . . .
>
> Heartened by success abroad, if still regarding himself as a prophet with honour in his own country, [Tchaikovsky redoubled his work schedule].[23]

Soon not only Boston and Vienna were swooning, but Moscow and St. Petersburg after all: Tolstoy was seen to be moved to tears by the *andante* of the First String Quartet.[24] Indeed, as Holden charts, the next decade very much consolidated Tchaikovsky's career: "The early 1880's . . . would propel him toward an international celebrity . . . [as] after its triumphant premiere in Boston von Bülow had played his First Piano concerto with great success"[25]—chiefly in the Old World, of course, but as Tchaikovsky's fame waxed worldwide, it by no means waned in Harvard's orbit.[26]

The Puritan Capital

AS MUSICOLOGIST ELLEN Knight has written, "the Gilded Age was a golden age for music in Boston. . . . an era of great, even brilliant activity,"[27] and though Tchaikovsky is only one of a dozen composers whose work she cites as stimulating "a new spirit" in the New England capital, the significance of Tchaikovsky's role has hardly been fully addressed.

The underlying reasons for this new spirit are easily discerned. It was an era dominated in America by two Boston composers, George Whitefield Chadwick of the New England Conservatory of Music, incorporated in 1870, and John Knowles Paine of Harvard, who, when he was appointed professor of music in 1875, was the first such in any American university. That professorship, a cherished goal of the Harvard Musical Association, was as great an achievement as the H.M.A Orchestra that the year before had premiered Tchaikovsky's First Piano Concerto. Greater still was the establishment in 1881 by Harvard's great benefactor, Henry Lee Higginson, of the Boston Symphony Orchestra (for which J. B. Lang, the conductor of the Tchaikovsky premiere, performed it twice as soloist in the 1880s continuing Boston's love affair with the Russian master. And significantly elevating it), for this is the orchestra of which one hundred years later critic Richard Dyer would write of its "glorious history": "Several works that are now part of the furniture of every civilized mind were written for [it]. . . . It ranks on the exalted level where every institution is unique."[28] Indeed, by its very first anniversary so large perhaps was the vacuum in America it made bold to fill, it had already established itself as pre-eminent nationally; by the end of its first decade it was also important internationally, not least because new as well as old music was regularly heard, none more potent than that of Tchaikovsky.

The orchestra's first conductor, Sir George Henschel, knew the Russian master well, and was responsible for the BSO's first performances of the composer in the early and mid-1880s. Even more important, the orchestra's conductor at the end of the 1880s, "adulated in words by the public like a matinee idol," was Arthur Nikisch ("the idol of his day," Harold Schonberg called him), of near hypnotic presence and "the most impressive and influential conductor of his day," according to Elliott W. Galkin. Trained under no less than Liszt, Verdi, Brahms, Bruckner, and Wagner, Nikisch was credited by Hugo Leichtentritt not only with making the BSO into "one of the foremost [orchestras] in the world,"[29] but with having been "more responsible than any other conductor for the world celebrity of Tchaikovsky."[30] It was "Nikisch who, after the cool reception of Tchaikovsky's Symphony no. 5 under the composer's direction in St. Petersburg in 1888, vindicated it triumphantly," according to Galkin, "in the same city."[31] (Tchaikovsky himself was enthralled with Nikisch, opining once, "[He] does not seem to conduct, but to exercise some mysterious spell.")[32] In Boston the next year, 1889, Nikisch's efforts hardly abated, especially on his numerous American tours. He performed work by Tchaikovsky every year of his Boston tenure, including the Fourth Symphony in 1890 and again in 1892; that year, too, he conducted the Boston premiere of the Fifth Symphony, as he did in 1893 of the First Violin Concerto. Indeed, in the 1890s, Boston heard Tchaikovsky's works with greater and greater frequency, including the American premiere by the Boston Pops orchestra of the *Nutcracker* Suite.[33]

If Nikisch's championing of Tchaikovsky was unambiguous evidence that Boston's ongoing welcome since his earliest days only grew more intense in the 1890s, another less welcoming constituency may have been developing, as might be seen in the fact that when in 1891—during the tenure in Boston of Nikisch, his greatest champion worldwide—Tchaikovsky, in America as the star of the dedication of New York's Carnegie Hall, conducted Victor Herbert's Boston Festival Orchestra—an ensemble "embrac[ing]," according to musicologist Edward Waters, "many musicians from the Boston Symphony"—both in Philadelphia and Baltimore, but not in Boston, which Tchaikovsky bypassed.[34] Interestingly, when the Harvard Musical Association dedicated a new clubhouse two years later, in 1893, the guest of honor was Dvořák, in Boston to conduct his requiem. A good friend of Franz Kneisel (he of the famous Kneisel Quartet, who performed at the dedication and would, for example, in 1894 perform the world premiere of Dvořák's String Quartet no. 12 in F ("the American"), Dvořák, who is also known to have read Longfellow constantly while composing the *New World* Symphony, admittedly had his own links to Boston.[35] And had Tchaikovsky been in America in November 1893, rather than May 1891, the Harvard Musical Association would perhaps have invited him to its dedication. But the reason why the Russian composer didn't go to Boston and the Czech composer did remains mysterious. Dvořák, of course, had the reputation of being not only respectable, but devout. Was Tchaikovsky "banned in Boston," shunned by influential puritans who had perhaps grown more influential since Oscar Wilde, albeit controversially, had been accepted in 1882? A decade, at least in Wilde's case, seems to have made some difference. In 1893, when *Lady Windermere's Fan* opened in Boston in its American premiere, Wilde, though his agent thought he should go to America to attend, refused to revisit a city he had previously seemed to delight in, and where his American publisher, moreover, Copeland & Day, was based. The year of Tchaikovsky's death, perhaps by suicide, was 1893; two years later came Wilde's own arrest and imprisonment—two huge international homosexual scandals.

A central question, indeed, is how much homosexuality in Tchaikovsky's case, any more than in Wilde's, really registered in Harvard's milieu. All those epicene Wildean 1890s posters of the Hasty Pudding Club, like Edward Penfield's murals of those languid athletes in the Randolph Hall breakfast room, pose the same question.[36] It was an era, after all, when *The New York Times* would report Wilde's trial at great length without even once actually noting what he did. Presumably *The Times* could be entirely sure, however, enough would be understood, that no one would be in any doubt—as indeed no one was.[37] In the same way, the New York society rag, *Town Topics*, could be sure of the titillation that their gossip about Timothée Adamowski would cause. The first conductor of the Boston Pops and the first violinist of the BSO—the soloist in 1893 at the Boston premiere of Tchaikovsky's violin concerto (dedicated, recall, to another violinist!)—Adamowski was highlighted by the New York scandal sheet: "The blond Adonis among the violinists of the Boston Symphony," *Town Topics* cooed but very pointedly, was "the gay young bachelor, smiled on by all women, but conquered by none."[38]

The furor caused in Boston in 1894 by Tchaikovsky's Sixth Symphony, the year after its world premiere in Russia, and the death of its composer within days of the first performance, shines a very bright light, moreover, on the question of just what registered in Harvard's immediate milieu.

Boston generally, and Harvard particularly, took its music very seriously, and composers from Wagner to Dvořák stimulated much debate in this period. The BSO's second conductor, William Gericke, reported that "during the first performance of Brahms's no. 3 the audience left the hall in hundreds, and, still more at the first performance of Anton Bruckner's Symphony no. 7 (1887); so that during the last movement we were more people on the stage than in the audience."[39] But in the case of Tchaikovsky's Sixth, the nature of the debate was not only remarkably fervid but surprisingly specific, informed it would seem by the history of the symphony itself.

Pathétique: *Symphony Hall to Harvard Yard*

THE SUBJECT OF Tchaikovsky's final masterwork—which as recently as in the wake of September 11, 2001, critics have reminded us is in the same league as Homer's tales of Troy and Picasso's *Guernica,* as well as the great works of Sophocles and Shakespeare in countering grave tragedy with grave beauty—is "homosexual tragedy."[40] These are Havelock Ellis's words, and they are of special importance because what sparked the Sixth Symphony— its program, indeed, its pulse—was the composer's relationship with Vladimir (Bob) Davidov, Tchaikovsky's favorite nephew since childhood.

It was a relationship the composer rejoiced in on the one hand but was anxious about on the other. Although pedophilia can, of course, be either heterosexual or homosexual, the highly scrupulous Tchaikovsky—who was *not* at all given to the homosexual version of the sort of heterosexual scandals Wagner, for instance, seemed to court in the same period—probably internalized the lamentable tendency to impute pedophilia more often to homosexuals, probably because of some confusion with pederasty. Very much a family man, needful of both giving and receiving affection, and childless as well as partnerless, Tchaikovsky could easily be accused of *over*-scrupulosity; but whether he was really in danger of ever acting improperly with his young nephew, or whether, instead, he was reading too much into his affection for Davidov, we can never probably know. But Tchaikovsky had himself become sexually aware in his early teens, and by the time his young nephew reached that age, Tchaikovsky's concern about the situation was revealed in his 1884 summer diary, which is divided between the sort of angst that suggests guilt and the sort of joy in his favorite nephew's development and growth that suggests paternal love. To confound his sexuality with his family is, as we've seen, a characteristic of Tchaikovsky's, and it is only to be expected that his guilt over being homosexual in the first place seemed in his mind to carry over and "infect" his feelings for his nephew. Certainly the composer's letters to his brother, Modest, who was also gay, and a teacher, are filled with warnings of the dangers of such situations.[41]

Significantly, Tchaikovsky's deep love for his nephew survived Bob's puberty, which seems not to be the norm in pedophilia. "Furthermore, there are certainly indications that Bob returned the composer's love." And as he developed into a vigorous young man, any problem, of course, disappeared. Bearing in mind that most accept now that sexual orientation, whether genetic or environmental, is precognitive (discovered, as it were, not chosen), it is surely important that as he grew up, Bob Davidoff discovered his own homosexuality, and was, by the time Tchaikovsky wrote the Sixth Symphony and dedicated it to him, twenty-one years old. An officer, and by then part of a small cohort of like-minded twenty-somethings, admirers of the composer, with whom Tchaikovsky regularly socialized and caroused, Bob Davidoff took the lead in this group, which called itself the "Fourth Suite." (Tchaikovsky only wrote three.)

If any suspicion of pedophilia passed away, however, the usual difficulties—much worse difficulties for the emotionally needy Tchaikovsky—bedeviled his and Davidov's adult relationship, which evolved into a kind of intimate romantic friendship. Most important, perhaps, was the age disparity between a fifty-three-year-old and a twenty-one-year-old, a disparity that may be explained by recourse to Rutgers anthropologist Helen Fisher's model of romantic love. According to Fisher, it typically has three aspects—lust, attraction, and attachment—and whatever order Tchaikovsky progressed through them in, it is clear, by all accounts, that in at least two of the three aspects of romantic love Davidov returned the composer's affections. But Tchaikovsky was typically no less intense in any one of these three aspects of romantic love than in any other, and for whatever reason there developed, in Holden's words, "a growing crisis of confidence about Bob, the result of which are the sublime agonies of the *Pathétique*,"[42] the telling name the composer gave to his greatest work, detailing what had become the great love of his life.

The issues on either side are long past assessing. David Brown is harsh in his judgment of Davidov, who had, he feels, "grown into a restless and moody young man who did not reciprocate in any matching degree his uncle's devotion."[43] This situation, in us all, in our youth, can lead to a certain boorishness. On the other hand, this is a heavy burden to place on anyone, much less a young man, and Holden's view is scarcely fairer, either to Tchaikovsky or to Davidov, who as he grew older became, according to Holden, "more than merely an object of adoration. He was an obsession"[44] for Tchaikovsky. Really, it seems much simpler than that. Tchaikovsky was in love. And if it was not requited physically (necessarily, given their ages), it probably was in other ways. After all, from Plato to Dante to Simone Weil to Iris Murdoch to Carson McCullers, thinkers have endlessly asserted that though love is a joint experience, even when both people are of the same generation, there is always one who is more the lover, the other the beloved; and that it is the lover, not the beloved, who is most vulnerable, especially if the beloved is younger: youthful beauty "de-centers" the lover, placing the beholder at more risk by far. Tchaikovsky, though he knew what it was like to be the beloved, was—all his life—overwhelmingly the lover. Never more so than with Davidov.[45]

It was not the usual prescription for fulfillment on either side. Whether or not the composer of the *Pathétique* killed himself or died of cholera, its dedicatee certainly did commit suicide in later years, after Tchaikovsky's death. Although Tchaikovsky's and Davidov's adult relationship had certainly its lighthearted side—uncle and nephew cruising in St. Petersburg's Zoological Gardens, a popular homosexual rendezvous, for example—the stress of Tchaikovsky's death (tragic whether through illness or suicide) seems to have traumatized Davidov. He used the royalties the composer had left him to establish, with Modest Tchaikovsky, the Tchaikovsky Museum, which still exists at his country estate, and he gave up his military career to dedicate himself to it. But at only age thirty-four, in 1906, Davidov lost a long battle against depression and shot himself.

But for the *Pathétique* itself, the prescription was triumphant. Tchaikovsky, fiercely proud of it, loved it, he said, above all his other works, and boasted that there was "much that is new in this symphony where form is concerned, one point being that the finale will not be a loud allegro, but the reverse, a most unhurried adagio."[46] Unhurried, indeed—the Sixth is the bleakest in all of Western music of the first rank, so much so that for years it has been widely interpreted as Tchaikovsky's "death wish." Surely, how-

ever, this is the meaning a startled respectability has given this great symphony, in the face of the once-unacceptable fact that what the Sixth really
speaks to, like Plato's *Symposium,* was for long necessarily obscured; not
only homosexual love, but the truth of one of Oscar Wilde's keenest admonitions: "Pleasures may turn a heart to stone, riches may make it callous,
but sorrows cannot break it. Hearts live by being wounded."⁴⁷ Thus the
Pathétique, pronounced by musicologist David Brown "the most truly original symphony since Beethoven's Ninth," and "one of the greatest and most
original instrumental achievements of the century."⁴⁸

What could the Puritan capital, in fact, know of such things? Let us
string together an anecdote here and a review there. For instance, Sir
George Henschel, the first conductor of the Boston Symphony, happened
to entertain Tchaikovsky in his London home a few months before the
Pathétique's world premiere in Russia and Tchaikovsky's death a week
later. Henschel is known to have been worried by how depressed Tchaikovsky seemed. Though no longer at the helm in Boston, Henschel had
many close friends there, including Henry Lee Higginson himself, and it
would be surprising if he hadn't shared that intelligence with Higginson at
a time when there loomed large the Boston premiere of the Sixth by the
Boston Symphony Orchestra, its conductor, Nikisch, Tchaikovsky's biggest
champion, who would himself become legendary for what Bruno Walter
would call an "overpowering rendering of Tchaikovsky's *Pathétique.*"⁴⁹ Nikisch surely scheduled the premiere, though an unrelated misunderstanding having led him to return to Europe, the Boston premiere was
conducted by his successor, Emil Paur. He, in turn, would perform the
Sixth again and again, every year thereafter until 1898, when he conducted
it twice. (Indeed, until 1906, when Carl Muck became director, a conductor who according to Earle Johnson "detested" the Sixth, it was performed
by the BSO virtually every year.⁵⁰) Moreover, in the reviews of the
premiere, at least two of the critics, whether from Henschel or some other
source (rumor was widespread), used the word *suicide,* shocking in Boston
in 1894. In such an atmosphere, full of speculation about whether or not
Tchaikovsky had killed himself, it is hardly reaching very far to conclude
more than one Harvard professor at his daily *Boston Evening Transcript*
thought he knew very well why.

Similarly among undergraduates in Harvard Yard. The *Pathétique* he
heard surely more than once at Symphony Hall certainly arises, for instance,
in the autobiography of Daniel Gregory Mason, later a well-known American
composer and in the 1890s a student in Harvard College, who in his own reminiscences of the 1890s quotes the words of his classmate, Charles Flandrau—
he of the very Wildean *Harvard Episodes:*

> In the college rooms of Daniel Gregory Mason some of us frequently sat
> up most of the night listening to Mason and his roommate [Pierre La

Rose] play Grieg and Brahms, Chopin, Bizet, Tchaikovsky . . . until a light repast of hot dogs, scrambled eggs and beer was indicated [and it was time to return to one's own room] in the steel blue Massachusetts dawn. . . . [51]

Let us dwell a bit on the Yard in Mason's students days. Mason himself described his rooms as at the back of Matthews Hall overlooking (to the left) Harvard Square and (to the right) Massachusetts Hall, then lecture halls and encumbered by now long-since removed fire escapes that Mason recalled "at certain hours would be black with students retiring from Charles Eliot Norton's course in fine arts on the upper floor." He remembered, too, his man of the moment, a Whitmanic figure, it would seem, caught in a Wildean discourse: William Vaughn Moody, "whose deep liquid blue eyes" Mason never forgot, "seemed to look through appearances into essences." Pipe-smoking and studious—"from time to time [he] dropped brief comments, often hardly more than resonant ejaculations, somehow more liberating, more refreshing than volumes of the carefully manicured epigrams current in our set," Mason recalled. "To talk with him, to bathe one's spirit, after struggles for cleverness, in his rich silences, was like coming home to truth and beauty."[52] People talked like that then, and Mason was clearly remembering being in love with Moody, a proctor in Grays Hall, the dormitory diagonally across the Yard from Matthews, an arrangement conducive to intimacy, and to long walks and talks, in which congenial youths discover each other, as Mason also remembered years later:

> In winter there was hot rum toddy over my open coal fire, or walks in the bleak sunsets across Harvard Bridge . . . to dine at Marliave's, where, as [a friend] said, "one played at being abroad," or to hear the Boston Symphony concert and discuss it afterwards over beer and Welsh rabbits. . . . As spring came there were mint juleps in Boston, or boating at Riverside, or long afternoon trudges; and in the evenings there were magical walks up Brattle Street, fragrant with lilacs, or the Fresh Pond, ghostly in mist and moonlight. And always there was the fascination of Moody's imagination-releasing figures of speech, his fertile silences, his irresponsible humor, comical slang, and shouting gusto of laughter, his deep, contagious sense of the infinite mystery and richness of life. . . . In all the years of interesting life that separate me now from my senior year I have found nothing else quite so formative as those magical walks with Moody up lilac-scented Brattle Street.[53]

This landscape of the gay life of Harvard Yard in the 1890s—in every sense of the word *gay*—did include other types. There was Mason's fellow student, Neddie Hill—"athletics and all forms of sport, so boring to me, filled him with enthusiasm"—with whom Mason wrote the music for "Granada," a Hasty Pudding Club theatrical he found a pleasant antidote to

Professor Paine on Western music. There were also professors to be attentive to; among them the nearby Mr. Norton, responsible, Mason recalled, for "extending my sensitiveness to beauty from music and literature to the plastic arts of painting, sculpture and architecture." And there was Santayana: Mason took Philosophy Eight, "Aesthetics," his senior year, sitting about "a long table in a room in Sever Hall [focusing finally on Santayana's own thought] as it was crystallized a year or so later in his book, *The Sense of Beauty*." William James, too, impressed Mason with "his handsome person, easy geniality, and brilliant talk. . . . He could make psychology seem as natural as small talk. He almost gossiped about it."[54]

Above all, however, in Mason's life in Harvard Yard, there was music; and the *Pathétique* not only arises, it conspicuously trumps everything else in Mason's memories of his undergraduate years. "There was," he would write, "that feverishly exciting but terrifying *Pathétique*, in which Tchaikovsky had put into music all the sense of metaphysical mystery and dread, of horror, even, that haunted us in our more serious moods, and that seemed to be always lying in wait for us when we were tempted for the moment to fancy life comprehensible."[55] "Feverishly exciting," "terrifying," "dread," "horror," "haunted"—these are words many scholars, rightly or wrongly, have used about Tchaikovsky himself, who does often seem, like Mason, to sense it all "lying in wait." It is an echo, if not of exact truth, then of an era's perception. I think of critics Wallace Brockway and Herbert Weinstock, who in a volume published many years later (1939) felt bound to acknowledge what they called the Sixth Symphony's "gross sentimentality" and "unhealthy self-pity," but they added that it was useless to fret over either, much less over its "over-fervid emotionalism" (I almost said "feverish excitement"); better, they argue, to emphasize the *Pathétique*'s "strength and beauty." "Pointless," they conclude, "to prate of vulgar tears, willfulness, bombast, and morbidity, when the ocean is coming straight at you."[56]

Mason *understood*. So, apparently, did another Bostonian—the American composer Henry Hadley, an obscure figure now, but once highly regarded (his conducting posts included San Francisco and Seattle), born and raised in Somerville and a student and lifelong disciple of Chadwick. Hadley's experience offers another of those few and fugitive clues that are all we have to depend on from this so discreet era. According to Nicholas E. Tawa, Hadley was so overwhelmed, indeed distraught, the first time he heard the *Pathétique* that he "left the auditorium in such a state of agitation, in spite of a blind[ing] snowstorm, he did not realize he had forgotten his hat." That there could well have been a homosexual dimension to the experience in Hadley's reading of it seems likely, moreover. Research on his life, though too narrow to yield more than speculation, and episodic at that, does disclose what may be telltale clues: Hadley is known to have set work by Amy Lowell, Paul Verlaine, and even Oscar Wilde himself—in the last case, *Salomé*, a tone poem of 1905–1906 (premiered by the Boston Symphony in 1907) that was undertaken *after* Wilde's tragedy. Hadley was thus being conspicuous, even provocative, in his identification with Wilde, against whom numberless sermons were preached in Boston in the years after his scandal broke. (Like Santayana, whose *Lucifer* is yet unprobed, so is Hadley's tone poem of the same name.)[57]

Yet a third focus, on a conspicuous conflict about the *Pathétique* that broke out between two of Boston's leading critics, Philip Hale and William Foster Apthorp (a former Yale man, then later a Harvard man), yields the most significant evidence of all that just by listening to the Sixth so closely and identifying with it so ardently Mason, for example, told us much more, perhaps, than he thought.

The opinion of Hale, who judged the *Pathétique* to be "an amazing human document" (it "shakes the soul," he wrote), could not have diverged more sharply from that of his colleague; so much so Hale later wrote, in print, about how he "well remember[ed] the sensation [Tchaikovsky's] Sixth Symphony made in Boston when Mr. Paur brought it out, when the late William Foster Apthorp described the music as 'obscene.'" It was, Hale remarked, "a singular word to apply to it." Singular, indeed, and that word was followed by many more of that ilk, according to Hale, "indignant denunciatory letters . . . sent to the *Evening Transcript* . . . by persons who, as Charles Reade once said of letter writers to the newspapers, had no other waste-pipe for their intellect."[58]

Is "homosexual music" finally named? The word, of course, had not yet come fully into widespread general use. Nor by the 1930s, when Hale's reviews were published, had "gay"—though *Town Topics*' description of Boston's first violinist as such surely anticipates later usage. But Apthorp, if he did not speak of homosexual music, certainly spoke of "obscene" music, just as Mason had described the *Pathétique* as "feverishly exciting" music. And I submit that, beyond the obvious sexual resonance, any doubt that "gay music" is exactly what was meant in Boston in 1893 in our sense of the term today is documented by Hale's use (on top of Apthorp's own "obscene") of the phrase "things we think and dare not say." Note scholar Eve Kosofsky Sedgwick's findings:

> Sexuality between men had, throughout the Judeo-Christian tradition, been famous among those who knew about it at all precisely for having no name—"unspeakable," "unmentionable," "not to be named among Christian men," are among the terms. . . . Of course, its very namelessness, its secrecy, was a form of social control.[59]

In fact, Hale's words—"things we think and dare not say"—in connection with the controversy surrounding the *Pathétique*'s Boston premiere of 1894 are rooted in exactly the same ancient discourse as were Lord Alfred Douglas's of a year later when, in 1894, in his poem "Two Loves" he famously declaimed about "the love that dare not speak its name."[60]

Indeed, when Hale wrote of the way the "wild gaiety" of the Sixth was overborne by a lamentation such as to "shake the soul," he almost seemed a modernist about the homosexual sensibility of the *Pathétique*: "Tchaikovsky narrowly escapes the reproach of vulgarity," he wrote, "but the earnestness, the sincerity of the speech makes its way."[61] Furthermore, Hale added, touching on just the modernism that is so key a theme of this chapter, "the very modernity of Tchaikovsky, his closeness to us as *spokesman* [emphasis added] of the things we think and *dare not say* [again, my emphasis], these qualities may war against his lasting fame; but in our day and generation he is the supreme interpreter by music of elemental and emotional thought.... We are under his mighty spell." When faith returned, Hale went on to sermonize, Tchaikovsky might fade.[62] But until then modernist doubt would have its hero.

But faith, at least as Hale knew it, had not yet returned when a half century later there was Harvard's own Leonard Bernstein, himself gay, and if not quite cast to be America's own Tchaikovsky as a composer, certainly his ardent admirer and interpreter (of the *Pathétique* particularly, as we shall see), and by no means dissimilar to the Russian master as both man and musician, not least in his torments about his own sexuality. The half century in Harvard Yard between the late-nineteenth-century era of Tchaikovsky and his admirers and the mid-twentieth-century era of Bernstein is, so to speak, the middle movement of this last chapter. And its most conspicuous theme is best heard at just the intersection of Harvard and homosexuality we are staking out here, at first more like a campsite than a landmark, a place called modernism.

Modernism

CRITIC MARGOT PETERS has written, of London, but of Anglo-American culture generally in the 1890s, that it was an era of "icon-smashing vitality, of modernism." And among the evidence she cites—some of it clear enough, such as socialism and the New Drama; some just emerging from underground, like "Uranian love," as homosexuality was widely called then—she makes a point of noting "the early twentieth-century rechristening of aestheticism and Decadence as 'Modernism,'" a factor Richard Ellmann also focuses on, observing that by the 1890s "aesthete [was] almost a euphemism for homosexual."[63]

Nowhere more so than in Harvard Yard, where evidence of this surfaces, not only in student memories of the time (those already referred to here of Daniel Gregory Mason, for instance, who specifically recalled that "in those days the decadence we knew ultimately as ultramodernism was just beginning")[64] but also in the correspondence of Harvard president Charles Eliot, who wrote in 1896 to Thomas Wentworth Higginson—he, significantly, of the tussle in Boston in 1882 over Oscar Wilde and Julia Ward Howe—that aestheticism seemed to him "one of the most discouraging phenomena of the last twenty years." That Eliot also made the connection (however discreetly) between aestheticism and homosexuality is suggested, furthermore, by his wariness toward Santayana, whom he called "abnormal,"[65] another code word for *homosexual*. He felt a similar wariness, we know, toward Ralph Adams Cram. In fact, Eliot distrusted Santayana (and Cram, and doubtless others) as much as Thomas Wentworth Higginson disliked Wilde—and for the same reason.

That Boston, and Harvard particularly, was a trigger of the most controversial modernism in America may surprise. Consider, first, however, the situation overall. At the start of the American century, when (as we noted in Chapter 7) New York and Washington were coalescing into the nation's preeminent commercial, cultural, and political capitals, Boston, long supposed to be the American Athens, was trying to consolidate its resources so as to assert itself as the country's intellectual capital. It was Boston's role that was most problematic. The idealism of the "city on a hill," Emerson declared, "fated to lead the civilization of North America,"[66] had stalled somewhat in the post–Civil War era. Oliver Wendell Holmes Jr., for example, very much disillusioned, observed at war's end, according to historian Louis Menand, that finally he saw that Boston was not the measure of all things. Yet what Holmes Jr. hardly saw was that he himself would be a luminary of a new, greater Boston, the role of which in the national life Menand has detailed brilliantly in *The Metaphysical Club*.

Its title derives from an obscure club that met for only a few months in Old Cambridge in 1872, its leaders three Bostonians—Holmes, William James, and Charles Sanders Peirce—the last a brother of the Harvard Graduate School of Arts and Sciences' founding dean of Chapter 1, James Mills Peirce, the secret homosexual polemicist. These three leaders of the Metaphysical Club, and their disciple, John Dewey, Menand calls "the first modern thinkers in the United States."[67] Of these three, consider William James and his brother Henry. A pioneer of the New Psychology, and the author of "the two texts that defined the field for most American and many European scholars," in Robert Crunden's words, William James "revolutionized thinking about consciousness," when he concluded that it was "a stream of thought, of consciousness." That, in turn, led him to a study of spiritualism, a questionable interest at Harvard but in tune with the Boston tradition of skepticism and rational inquiry. Forthwith, "brother Henry," writes Crunden, "devoted *The Bostonians* to an acerbic examination of the subject." Moreover, he adds, "even as William James was only beginning to put into words the scientific version of the stream-of-consciousness, his younger brother had embodied it in [*The Portrait of a Lady*]. Not Proust, not Joyce, but Henry James deserves chief credit for this extraordinary innovation in literature." The two Jameses, in fact, were key precursors of modernism. Though not full-fledged modernists (William, writes Crunden, "mentioned sexuality in one paragraph on animal behavior and promptly, even nervously, launched into one of his ethical sermonettes . . . [about] his peculiarly Bostonian inhibitions"),[68] the effect of their work on modernism was immediate and crucial. For instance, William's theory of emotions: that there is no criterion to distinguish between spiritual and bodily feeling, and that bodily action must be interposed between mental states to understand them. Which is to say we are not insulted, feel angry, and then hit someone; the bodily change of the striking follows directly on being insulted and it is our feeling of that bodily change which *is* the emotion of feeling angry. According to Crunden, when that was "conveyed to Ernest Hemingway by Gertrude Stein such notions changed the way Americans thought, talked, and wrote." Similarly with Henry: "American modernists knew instantly that he had supplied them with the precedents they needed to put mental realities into art."[69]

One of the reasons we miss this and other evidence of Harvard's role in the rise of modernism is because it was largely overlooked by Van Wyck Brooks in those famous tomes we have all looked to for years (overmuch, I'm afraid) as authoritative. Brooks's work, admittedly brilliant, is also deeply flawed, especially the sequel to his Pulitzer Prize–winning *The Flowering of New England, 1815–1865*, a sequel not nearly so good: *New England: Indian Summer 1865–1915*. Title and dates say it all, recording the steady decline of Boston at century's end from its status as the American Athens, a decline heralded by Harvard's own decline in the mid-nineteenth century after President Kirkland's early-nineteenth-century university aspirations for Harvard proved premature.

Yet Brooks hardly takes sufficient account at all of Harvard's recovery and, indeed, renaissance, after 1870, under Eliot, who revived Kirkland's vision triumphantly; or of its subsequent rise to preeminence, spearheading (along with the new MIT, the reconstituted Harvard Medical School, the Boston Symphony, the Museum of Fine Arts, and other such institutions) what became in many ways a new Augustan age in Boston. Which in turn reflected much Brooks ignored. The influence of Tchaikovsky never arises in either book, for instance, while that of Tolstoy comes up in both volumes, a dozen or more times in the second of the two. Did fewer Bostonians hear (or play—it was the age of the parlor grand or upright piano) Tchaikovsky than read Tolstoy? Not in Harvard Yard, if Mason is to be believed. But Brooks was a literary historian, and failed to see that cultural and intellectual centers, though they do indeed rise and fall in stature, do not usually do so in unison—certainly not in all fields at the same time. By the mid-1880s, though Boston's energy by then was almost entirely spent as a literary center, it was, as we've seen, already an important center in America for the "new music." Leaving aside other fields, the fact is that as a cultural and intellectual center Boston either waxed or waned in the decades to either side of

1900, according to whether or not you consider literature or music. And by the 1920s, though no new Emerson or Hawthorne or Dickinson had surfaced, Bostonians were more than ready for the genius who did surface in their midst, a man who would be the foremost human face of modernism in Boston, and among the foremost in the Western world, but in music, not literature—Serge Koussevitzky.

Who he? So do the years pass. Humphrey Burton, in his biography of Bernstein, called Koussevitzky unequivocally "the most influential conductor of the twentieth century." Wrote critic Richard Dyer in 1981:

> The conductor who is still the one most associated with the Boston Symphony Orchestra is Serge Koussevitzky, whose quarter-century tenure defined the orchestra as the greatest in the world and whose commitment to the cause of new music is cited with reverence by older generations. [He was also the founder of the] Berkshire Music Center [at Tanglewood], one of the great music schools of the world. . . . [In 1981] nearly 20 percent of the musicians in the country's major orchestras—and an astonishing 40 percent of all the principal players—have been students there. Koussevitzky himself presented more than one hundred and twenty-five world premieres. . . . Stravinsky's *Symphony of Psalms* [was] a Koussevitzky commission.[70]

IN PARIS BEFORE coming to Boston, Koussevitzky had led premieres of works by Ravel, Scriabin, and Honegger. He was an intimate both of Stravinsky and Prokofiev. (And Nikisch was his teacher; in return for having his debts paid at cards, Nikisch trained Koussevitzky as a conductor.)[71] "The groundbreaking music of American composers," *New York Times* critic David Mermelstein has written, was "ultimately absorbed into the canon largely through the efforts of one man, Serge Koussevitzky, the first major maestro to make 'modern' American music a priority. . . . [He] blazed a trail"[72]—somewhat in the same way, actually, as Isabella Stewart Gardner. Koussevitzky, in fact, succeeded Gardner as the cause célèbre, indeed, monstre sacré, of the New England capital; indeed, according to Moses Smith, before coming to America, he "had set his mind on the Boston Symphony Orchestra, which his idol, Nikisch, had conducted in the [18]90's." Not surprisingly, his conducting, especially of Tchaikovsky, was compared to Nikisch's.[73]

Just as Gardner as tastemaker held sway in the wake of her "master," Charles Eliot Norton, and in parallel with those two presiding geniuses of Boston in the Gilded Age, H. H. Richardson and Frederick Law Olmsted, Koussevitzky, too, had to share the stage in Harvard's immediate orbit. In his case he reigned with Ralph Adams Cram and, after the late 1930s, Walter Gropius, as well as Edward Hopper and Eugene O'Neill (in O'Neill's case the principal carrier of the New England tradition of puritan angst in the twentieth century), though in the last two cases at some remove, as both Hopper and O'Neill were essentially New Yorkers. O'Neill's work in the 1930s was as likely as not to be "banned in Boston." In the same era, however, the "icon-smashing" music of Stravinsky was as likely as not to be premiered, even commissioned, in the New England capital. Neither Koussevitzky nor Stravinsky was gay. But Virgil Thomson was. Thus to Harvard Yard in the 1920s, as in the 1890s, a place where "aestheticism" (by then entirely rechristened "modernism") kept very happy company with "Uranian love" (by then also rechristened "homosexuality").

Thomson was one of the five composers of what Anthony Tommasini has called the "commando squad,"[74] five composers whose work "invaded the established musical order in America." The others were Walter Piston, Roger Sessions, Roy Harris, and Aaron Copland. They were not, to be sure, the very first American composers who could be called "modernist." Indeed, no more than modernism in music was altogether a tale of homosexuals was it entirely a tale of Harvard or Koussevitzky. That maestro completely ignored, for instance, the genius of the 1900s on his left wing, the pioneering Yale-educated composer, Charles Ives.[75] It is also true that even revolutions wear out, their edge dulled, but in their day the commando squad was radical enough; and four of the five men were associated with Harvard; two were homosexual. That almost half the group was gay, by the way, was not exceptional; it was common knowledge amongst musicians of this period that the Composers' League so abounded with gays in the 1920s that it was dubbed by many the Homintern.

Virgil Thomson's experience of Harvard Yard in the 1920s has much in common with Emerson's and Gay's experience; the continuities of the Yard have always included the darting glances of young men's fancies.[76] Still more was Thomson's Yard comparable to Ned and Tom's of Civil War days (Thomson, goaded by a speech by Theodore Roosevelt about "sexless" pacifists, was determined "to get into the fighting," in his biographer's words,[77] in the First World War); and most of all was it similar to Daniel Gregory Mason's Yard of the 1890s, with its intense crushes and late nights and long walks. In fact, Thomson's Yard can as easily be projected forward into Frank O'Hara's and John Ashbery's in the 1950s or Andrew Holleran's in the 1970s, or, indeed mine of the same decade. Thomson, for example, compassed in some ways both the gay archetypes. He was somewhat effeminate—composer Ned Rorem recalled his "swishy voice." But he was also a fighter born, his "foppish side," as Tommasini puts it, "offset by his pugnaciousness."[78] Yet what was quite unlike Emerson or Gay or Ned or Tom or Mason and Moody and their cohort was that whether or not Thomson was aware of any discontinuity between his own gender identification and others' perception of him, he arrived at Harvard not only clear about his sexuality in his own mind, but fully conscious of what a huge problem it was. "I didn't want to be queer. No! No! No!" he later recalled. And who could blame him? "In those days," he recalled, "if you got caught around Harvard you got kicked out. And the same way with the instructors!"[79]

Predictably, therefore, Thomson passed much of his earliest time in college deep in unrequited love. The object of his love, or lust, was Briggs Buchanan, another undergraduate who fulfilled his father's every fear (he being a self-made millionaire) that his son would become involved with the "wrong" people at Harvard. Thomson, when not playing the organ at Boston's King's Chapel, devoted most of his free time to Buchanan, who at eighteen was eight years Thomson's junior and looking for a mentor. Thomson obliged, taking Briggs on "walking tours of the Boston museums and the architecture on Commonwealth Avenue." But as to anything more physical, Briggs proved illusive, writing to his new friend: "The light I seek is in sight. The necessity for a natural means of expression I clearly see. . . . The equally pressing need for sex expression is not yet clear, however, nor the means. I wonder—, but there is nothing I can say. I must wait, but wait with open eyes, my desires in view." That summer, from the depths of his family's place in suburban Denville, New Jersey, Buchanan seemed more interested—but at a safe distance: "What a heaven," he recalled Harvard being: "[Here] I have . . . no Atlas Cafe to go to, no Liberal Club, no movies, only a damned monotonous lake to look at in the suburbs with suburban people and their . . . suburban minds. . . . I long to escape."[80] Not exactly to Thomson, however. For whatever reason—because he was even more determined than Thomson to obscure his sexual orientation or just not in love with him or, perhaps, just scared—Briggs Buchanan seems never to have allowed Thomson to bring things to a head. "Briggs wanted Virgil to be his mentor, not his lover," Tommasini suggests. And one is not surprised to learn after graduation Briggs made a successful and happy heterosexual marriage, blessed with two sons, and became altogether a devoted heterosexual family man. One is not surprised, either, to learn Thomson became a fixture in the life of Briggs's family, into which after a decent interregnum he was integrated, after the fashion of the day. The situation, like the context, never came up: that Thomson was a "homosexual," Tommasini writes, "was perfectly understood, but never discussed."[81]

For the rest of it, the post-Freudian world, much less innocent than the 1890s, denied much and repressed more, but with great style—especially along the Gold Coast, so called because all Harvard's fashionable clubs and posh student apartment houses were there, centered on Mt. Auburn Street— and this was very much the backdrop for Thomson's undergraduate years. Although he rowed skulls and played tennis occasionally, he was more of a "clubby" than a "jock," finding his niche at the Liberal Club, where he met some lifelong friends. They included many gays; among them Henry-Russell Hitchcock, who would become one of the country's leading architectural historians, Lincoln Kirstein, and, most important of all, in 1922, Maurice

Grosser, a fellow undergraduate, the closest thing to a life partner Thomson would ever have. Grosser, in Ned Rorem's words, was "arguably the brains behind Virgil's brains."[82]

A painter, Grosser was born in Alabama in 1903 of German Jewish immigrant parents confused by their son's passion for books and math and daydreaming. In consequence they sent him to a very tough high school for troublesome boys. Grosser was that, though anything but a slow learner, especially at Harvard (where he majored in math—graduating with honors). At the same time he was drawn at once to the surrounding bohemian life; he attended the Old Howard burlesque theater, for example, quite regularly, and frequented ethnic cafés and even took rather risqué life-drawing classes at the Boston School of Architecture as well as art history classes in the fine arts department at the Fogg. In fact, he makes an interesting contrast with Thomson, a corrective for those whose history comes in each era neatly packaged, because Grosser was obviously noticeably less vexed about his sexual orientation than Thomson. Indeed, years later, as the gay liberationist movement developed in the 1970s, when the two had been linked for decades, it was even more noticeable that while Thomson often tipped into "hostility to openly gay people . . . Grosser was thrilled by the new openness and activism," according to Tommasini, who points out that Grosser "lived openly as a gay man decades before Stonewall." Furthermore, while for Thomson sexual encounters (though he engaged in them) were always heavy with guilt and humiliation, his friend actually "enjoyed sexual adventures, encounters with strangers," Tommasini writes, even at Harvard.

Although a 1920s version of Tuckernuck was lacking, other opportunities beckoned. The summer of his junior year Grosser had passed some time with a classmate at the Cape Cod "Love Farm," as the newspapers called it, of the young Harvard graduate Charles Garland. There Grosser experimented with heterosexual sex with an older woman, passed her on to his friend, who liked it better, and ended up living with both, a summer threesome in the older woman's Buzzards Bay estate. Grosser was experimenting again. Handsome, muscular, and very confident, Grosser was always open to events, which he easily mastered, though invariably gentle and courteous in mien. This Cape Cod affair, for instance, had been intended as but a prelude to "a merchant marine adventure with . . . a tough and sturdy young man"—the one he fixed up with the older woman. Typical, too, of Grosser was the way he took to motorcycles. Grosser, once called "a courtly Southern gentleman with a jolt of 'Jewish nervousness,'" possessed so much "solidity of strength and character . . . [and was so] gentle, dependable, wise [and] nonjudgmental" that he was, in Tommasini's words, enormously steadying for Thomson.[83]

Although their relationship only became physically sexual in the somewhat more freewheeling atmosphere of Paris in the 1920s, where both found themselves after graduation, the romance between Thomson and Grosser blossomed at Harvard immediately after they met. Much as he had with Briggs Buchanan, Thomson "took Maurice gallery hopping on Newbury Street," and "it was in Virgil's company," Tommasini writes, that "Maurice saw his first Cezanne," an experience no more sophisticated, I'm sure, than their relationship, which would always be a very open one, in an era when heterosexual marriages of that sort were not unknown, either.

In later years, both took up with much younger men. Thomson and Grosser's relationship, always primary, was not exclusive, never monogamous. The object of Thomson's affection years later, when nearly sixty, was a strikingly handsome twenty-eight-year-old from West Virginia who served in the Army Air Corps in World War II and then studied art history at Ohio State, and who was attracted to older men. In Grosser's case, he fell in love at seventy with a thirty-three-year-old Vietnam War veteran, Paul Sanfaçon, a rebellious, rambunctious, and irreverent young man, but also articulate, well traveled, and a brilliant anthropologist, a lecturer at New York's American Museum of Natural History. (It was Sanfaçon who once pointed out that the trees Maurice painted, with their intertwining branches, always reminded him of "what it was like to have sex with Maurice, who enveloped you in his limbs.")[84]

At Harvard Thomson consolidated and defined his passionate interest in music. He was deeply involved with the Harvard Glee Club, whose new director, Archibald T. Davison, became Koussevitzky's perennial collaborator, making the glee club virtually the Boston Symphony chorus, and much influenced by his adviser, Edward Burlingame Hill, the closest thing to a modernist then in sight on Harvard's music faculty, where he taught "Modern French Music: D'Indy, Fauré Debussy" in the teeth of conservative faculty disdain. A critic and composer as well, he was much influenced by Ravel. Hill's own music in the early 1930s would include his *Jazz Studies for Two Pianos*, and in his writings he allowed himself considerable "excitement about Stravinsky and respect for Schoenberg." Hill's other students included Randall Thompson, Elliott Carter, and Walter Piston himself. Thomson was Hill's teaching assistant.

But it was less in his field of concentration, and more broadly in his general studies and in the Harvard intellectual scene overall, that Thomson found his most formative experiences and influences, the key one probably being S. Foster Damon, then a Harvard graduate student (later he taught at Brown). Bostonian, Damon graduated from Harvard College with the class of 1914 on the eve of World War I, when T. S. Eliot himself was just quitting the Yard and embarking on the voyage that soon enough would yield *The Waste Land*. I wonder if young Thomson, reading it (doubtless in a dorm room decorated, like Eliot's old room, with posters of paintings by Picasso), had any inkling he was about to become a key part of all this—indeed, a collaborator of one of Picasso's closest friends, very much a part of the Harvard network, a network that in the twentieth century was increasingly not only modernist in sympathy but international in scope. At its heart was Gertrude Stein. A graduate of Radcliffe College, Stein was as much of a Harvard student as a woman could be in the 1890s, and by Thomson's day was well on her way to becoming modernism's reigning high priest. Thomson's new friend Damon was a keen acolyte.

Distinctly an intellectual maverick—scholar, teacher, and composer— Damon was the founder and editor of the *Harvard Musical Review,* where he took the lead in constantly calling attention to the music of such avant-garde figures as Schoenberg, Strindberg, Sibelius, and Erik Satie, the music of the last of whom influenced Thomson particularly. Damon was also the first biographer of the Boston modernist poet Amy Lowell, and it seems not entirely a coincidence that one of Thomson's first compositions, written at Harvard in his junior year, was a setting of Lowell's "Vernal Equinox." It has been called "a striking choral work," and in it Thomson links Lowell with Oscar Wilde in its quotation of the psalm *De Profundis,* which had been the title of Wilde's anguished letter from prison.

Damon's own sexual orientation can only be surmised. He was one of a number of figures (it was distinctly a pattern) who enjoyed usually childless marriages with sisters of well-known gay ex- or would-be lovers; in Damon's case with the sister of poet John Wheelwright. But Damon's influence bridged many circles, as Richard Kennedy, the biographer of E. E. Cummings, discloses in touching on Damon's relationship with that very heterosexual poet. Of Damon, Kennedy wrote:

> A handsome, blond-haired enthusiast of the arts . . . [he was a leader of the] Harvard aesthetes. . . . He introduced [Cummings] to Debussy, to Stravinsky, and to the delightful satiric piano sketches of Erik Satie. . . . He took him to the Armory Show in 1913 when it traveled to Boston, and Cummings was ecstatic over the sculptures of Brancusi. He took him to New York after a Harvard-Yale boatrace. . . . He owned a rare copy of Gertrude Stein's *Tender Buttons,* which delighted and bewildered Cummings. . . . He took Cummings out drinking for the first time in his life [in downtown Boston at] Jake Wirth's sawdust-strewn restaurant on Stuart Street [and Cummings] ended the evening, much to Damon's mirthful scorn, hanging over a bridge and puking into the Charles River. . . . [85]

What a wonderful window all this opens on the role of the Harvard tutor (even, or perhaps most of all, when only a graduate student), ever eager to guide developing undergraduates. Damon's "rare copy of Gertrude Stein's *Tender Buttons,*" one of the treasures of his library in his rooms above the Western Club in Harvard Square, was almost certainly the volume Damon shared just a few years later with Thomson, who entered Harvard three years after Cummings left. And just as it sparked Cummings (in whose work even at Harvard his biographer saw "surprises in the images [that] go beyond . . .

the Imagist school into the wrenching world of Cubism: The crossover of senses and associations [for example, in the line] the screech of dissonant flowers"),[86] so, too, was Stein's book influential, profoundly so, in what would be, years later, perhaps Thomson's best work. Setting Amy Lowell was only a beginning. In Tommasini's words, "*Tender Buttons* not only led to a meeting with [Stein, who was to be Thomson's] most important collaborator, but gave him a vision for an entirely fresh way to write music."[87]

Heady days—Thomson's 1920s and '30s—his circle very much in the vanguard of modernism's gathering force in America. In 1931, for instance, one of Thomson's friends, another undergraduate, recorded his experience of Harvard's intellectual life in that period. Remembered more than sixty years later, it shows how intimately that milieu was a part of the lives of modernism's founding fathers and mothers, including Stravinsky himself. Like the story of Damon introducing first Cummings, then Thomson, to the work of Gertrude Stein in his Harvard Square rooms, here another window opens into the lives of now obscure, largely forgotten figures who disclose the nature of the influences undergraduates felt then:

> In a fine Federal house on Chestnut Street, Beacon Hill, lived Edward Motley Pickman, with his wife, Hester. He was of the clan of John Lothrop Motley ... [and] was at work on a recondite study of early Christian theology. . . . Jack Wheelwright told me . . . that, for him, knowing Ted and Hester Pickman were at-home on Chestnut Street made Boston preferable to London, Paris, Florence, or New York. . . . Edward Pickman was a personage of stalwart delight, erudition, and glow. . . . A movement proposing him to head Harvard gathered force at President Lowell's retirement. . . . Igor and Vera Stravinsky were married at the Pickmans' Bedford farm.[88]

Koussevitzky, of course, was Stravinsky's publicist. Stein was Picasso's— tireless—promoter. Thomson's lot, ultimately, was to become Stein's. And, inevitably, hers became his—which was fortunate because Thomson was the member of the "commando squad" Koussevitzky least took to. *Promoter*, admittedly, may not be the exact word for what Thomson did for Stein; what do you call the person who turns your literary work (not a libretto) into an opera? More fundamentally, how does one do such a thing at all with so prickly a personality as Stein? Yet Thomson's role as much the younger of the two and ever Stein's admirer was always clear. So much so that there was more than a little reason for optimism when the idea of Thomson transforming a text by Stein into an opera first arose after his graduation, when he gravitated quite naturally to Paris and to Stein's puce-colored salon at 27 rue de Fleurus, the salon so famous in Western art history, and so famously hung (to the ceiling) with Stein's accumulation of Picasso and other moderns, not least the master's iconic if slightly skewed image of Stein herself. Yet Harvard no less than Paris mattered in all this. Not only Damon and Stein, Thomson's mentor and inspirer-collaborator, respectively, but also Thomson's patron hailed from the Harvard milieu, for if Damon was godfather to the idea, the angel who made it all possible was "Jessie" Lassell. Her daughter Hildegard and her cousin Philip (gay, attractive, "a playboy of wondrous charm" in Thomson's words; in other words probably an instigator) had early become interested in Thomson's work when during his Harvard days he played the organ as his part-time job in their church in the Boston suburb of Whitinsville. There the Lassells lived in baronial splendor.[89] Furthermore, although Stein and Thomson, their generations at Harvard more than two decades apart, did not meet until Paris, it was their mutual experiences of Harvard, Thomson felt, that generated the affinity and finally made the idea of their collaboration practicable. "We had both enjoyed Harvard," Thomson explained, adding somewhat wittily (and surely hinting at another experience common to them both): "We got on like a couple of Harvard boys."

Other affinities emerged. An early effort of Thomson's to set Stein's very short poem called "Susie Asado" had been a great success. It was published along with nine other songs by other moderns—Sessions, Copland, also Marc Blitzstein (who himself set a poem by Cummings; it was a very hermetic world). Of all these songs, Tommasini feels, "None is more daring and, in its way, more modern than 'Susie Asado.'" The "meanings . . . are certainly abstract," Tommasini writes, "though activated by Thomson's setting, they don't seem to be absent." Thomson himself explained at the time:

My theory was that if a text is set correctly for the sound of it, the meaning will take care of itself. And the Stein texts, for prosodizing in this way, were manna. With meanings already abstracted, or absent, or so multiplied that choice among them was impossible, there was no temptation toward tonal illustration, say of birdie babbling by the brook or heavy heavy hangs the heart. You could make a setting for sound and syntax only, then add, if needed, an accompaniment equally functional.[90]

IT WAS CLEAR Thomson had "revealed a genuine affinity for Gertrude's words" (crafted into a libretto by Grosser). Indeed, Stein herself would write in *The Autobiography of Alice B. Toklas* that she "delighted in listening to her words framed by his music." As well she might. Thomson certainly took Stein's work seriously enough. In approaching *Four Saints in Three Acts*—a full-scale opera, after all, not a short song—he adopted a new technique: "Seated at his piano, he would read the words aloud, over and over, until musical rhythms, contours, and shapes suggested themselves. He wanted music that was straightforward and water clear, music that would not just support but launch every nuance of Stein's words."[91] Thomson, clearly, was at the height of his creative powers, his mind wonderfully open to all sorts of things, and ranging questingly across many boundaries. The result, Ned Rorem judged, was "as American as baseball."[92]

To be sure, not everyone—even the commando squad's students—*liked* Thomson and Stein's new opera. At a one-man version put on by Thomson in Boston in 1929 Elliott Carter, a leading student of Walter Piston and later a considerable figure in Harvard music, was not impressed: "People thought the music not very interesting musically, though the Stein text was interesting."[93] However, as one Harvard network had generated the idea and then the backing, so did another, and a hardly less gay one, launch the opera itself, a circle of college friends this time. Kirk Askew, Henry-Russell Hitchcock, and "Chick" Austin were responsible for pulling off the world premiere of *Four Saints in Three Acts* in 1934 at the Wadsworth Athenaeum in Hartford, Connecticut,[94] of which Austin had been named director through another Harvard circle—the Fogg Art Museum circle, the New York chapter of which was the laboratory for most of the project's development, Thomson having like the others been drawn to the nation's cultural capital in the 1920s. Not that he had entirely shifted his focus from Paris. As one friend wrote, for all of them "Harlem was far more an arrondissement of Paris than a battleground of Greater New York." Tommasini explains that for Thomson, and for the Askew circle generally, the possibility of illicit pleasure was one of Harlem's attractions: "It was where men could find men to have sex with. . . . At the Askew salon, or anywhere in mixed company, one did not speak of this. But in Harlem, with . . . a homosexual subculture that was more visible and less tormented, it was not difficult to procure men."[95]

Thomson, thus motivated, found himself sparked creatively as well, most notably by one of these postmidnight excursions in early January 1933, when he was much intrigued by the Gershwin and Arlen songs as sung by Jimmy Daniels, a black singer then in his early twenties. Thomson often seemed sexually drawn to black men, but whether or not that was the case with Daniels, what struck Thomson most, according to Tommasini, was "the naturalness of Daniel's diction: the words just came out clearly, as if he were speaking them, yet with no loss to the lyricism of the vocal line." Thomson turned to Russell Hitchcock, his fellow traveler that night as on so many others, and said: "You know, I think I'm going to cast my opera entirely with Negro singers." Daniels's effect on Thomson was, in Tommasini's words, "not a matter of conscious enunciat[ing]. . . . Words and voice were one." Thomson, of course, had jumped immediately to the conclusion Daniels's skill and artistry derived specifically from his racial background; a sort of "blacks-got-rhythm" and don't-over-intellectualize-everything attitude that confirms how often Thomson was given to stereotyping (and not just blacks). Still, we see and use artistically what we need to, perhaps, and as Tommasini points out, "Thomson's decision to employ an all-black cast in his opera had another dimension relating to Mabel Dodge Luhan's prediction . . . that *Four Saints in Three Acts* 'would destroy opera the way Picasso has destroyed old painting.' "[96] The comparison is not far-fetched: Stein wrote, many have thought, what Picasso painted. Using an all-black cast in an opera not about a black subject was another way of flouting convention, of audaciously proclaiming that opera as it had been known was dated, and that *Four Saints in Three Acts*, with its hermetic text and after-the-fact scenario, would be just the needed energizer. That it was. No less than Toscanini, Gershwin, Cecil Beaton, and Dorothy Parker showed up at the Broadway opening. And if *The Times* critic, Olin Downes, was dismissive, the *Boston Evening Transcript* critic, H. T. Parker, who had given Thomson his start in journalism, loved it. So did Chicago, where the production later traveled. Altogether, it was, in Tommasini's words, "the avant-garde succès de scandale of the day."[97] And pop culture followed soon enough. The very next year, at the world premiere in Boston in 1935 of Gershwin's *Porgy and Bess* (a brilliant, event, attended by both Irving Berlin and Cole Porter), it was observed by all concerned that Gershwin had appropriated *Four Saints'* all-black choir *and* its conductor, Alexander Smallens.[98]

An outstanding example of gay artistic collaboration, *Four Saints in Three Acts* can be singled out in other ways. Thomson, who had no Tchaikovskian desire to express his inner conflicts, at least consciously, disdained really any thought of that kind of gay sensibility in his music. But *Four Saints* may be said to have achieved another kind of gay sensibility to the extent he was successful (as Stein thought he was) in interpreting Stein's speech in musical form. Stein's work, indeed, suggests to me, as others,[99] she tried to develop something of a literary parallel to the discontinuous Cubist view of the world, obviously apt to Stein's need to, however discreetly, disclose her lesbianism. There is a triple-layered effect here: painting, prose, music.

This, too, was rooted in the Harvard experience.[100] Stein's student articles in *The Harvard Psychological Review*, written very much under the influence of her teacher William James, are obviously not much read. But they "represented the beginning of her lifelong interest in character typology," according to Corinne Blackmer, and Stein herself wrote in *The Autobiography of Alice B. Toklas* that one of those early articles represented the beginning of the "method of writing to be afterwards developed in *Three Lives* [Stein's first mature work, published in 1909]."[101]

One other work of Thomson's compels attention in this connection: his much later opera, *Byron*, reminiscent of a project by Tchaikovsky himself— his *Manfred* symphony of 1885—also focused on the life of the British poet, already notorious in Tchaikovsky's day for his bisexuality, specifically his affair with his half sister, who had a child with him. Byron's infraction was compounded by the fact that he was apparently with equal passion a lover of young men. Thus it was that between Tchaikovsky's increasingly revelatory Fourth and Fifth symphonies his *Manfred* Symphony has come to seem a sort of meditation by Tchaikovsky on his sexuality.

The way all this would *not* be repressed is fascinating, is it not? Thomson, no disciple of Tchaikovsky, nor his particular admirer, was nonetheless very much like that Russian master not only in his sexuality but in the way he exorcised his angst about it. The differences *Byron* highlights are equally fascinating. Thomson, in the mid-twentieth century, could not help being more open and less judgmental than Tchaikovsky about the whole nature of queer sexuality. The Metropolitan Opera commissioned *Byron*, but rejected it. Sir Rudolf Bing, its director, found *Byron* very offensive; not, because of its scandalous subject or content, nor even for its gay aspect, but because he found Thomson's *attitude* beyond enduring. As Tommasini puts it: rather than "characteriz[e Byron's] lechery through tortured chromaticism and dissonance," what Bing judged to be Thomson's blithely cavalier musical treatment seemed nonjudgmental and thus too permissive and approving for Bing.[102] And this despite the fact that Thomson, when not lifted up, as it were, by his creative and artistic urges, stereotyped and put down gays just as he did Jews and blacks, an attitude which even in his artistic work could be problematic. Speaking of Thomson's famously all-black choir in *Four Saints*, Tommasini observes the two sides of the thing: "To his credit, Thomson gave black artists an unprecedented opportunity to topple stereotypes and portray Spanish saints in what would be an elegant and historic production. However, the fact of their color was used to sully, in a sense, the rarefied white world of opera."

It is not the first time here we have encountered the sort of madly mixed motives of a man who was an aesthetic progressive (Thomson was certainly avant-garde in his admiration for Gertrude Stein and Erik Satie) but a political conservative, if not reactionary. Even when he was the hugely powerful chief music critic of the *New York Herald Tribune* in the 1940s and early '50s, Thomson was very reluctant to defend a fellow composer from charges by a Republican congressman that his left-wing sympathies made it inappropriate to perform his music on a state occasion. The music was *A Lincoln Portrait*, the composer Aaron Copland.[103]

If Virgil Thomson's career, beyond its own value, illuminates how Harvard's homosexual experience has historically enabled patterns of mentoring and patronage and artistic collaboration, Copland, the greatest luminary of the Harvard-Koussevitzky circle, brings us back full circle to the homosexual aspect in the actual creative process in the first place—not again to Tchaikovsky's work, not to the work of a foreign master whose influence was felt at Harvard, but to the work of a modern master, "the father of American music," in Ned Rorem's words, at least after 1925: Aaron Copland. ("Aaron," Rorem wrote in 2001, "was the king, and still is.")[104] In another way so does a lesser composer but a uniquely brilliant figure in modern musical history bring us back along the same arc to the same creative place—Leonard Bernstein—who himself strongly identified with Tchaikovsky, as we will see, thus closing the circle all the more tightly.

Many a strand of the web both of "commando squad" and "homitern" linked all these gay composers, happily and unhappily, professionally and personally. Copland, according to Ned Rorem, owed a lot to Thomson musically. "The greatest masters are not the greatest innovators," Rorem contends, and just as Bernstein would do better what Marc Blitzstein did first, so Copland, Rorem concluded, "borrowed (and glorified)" from Thomson.[105] Personally, while Copland and Bernstein were close friends, possibly lovers, Copland and Thomson were never more than respectful but wary colleagues; Copland confessed once he "never really felt personally comfortable with Virgil, what with his airs, his cigarette holder, and his effeminate mannerisms."[106]

The fact is Copland was a very moderate sort of person, much less conspicuously gay, for example, than Thomson. Though he did not make a great deal of it, Copland, however, in no sense soft-pedaled the fact that he was queer. Indeed, he used to complain that Bernstein, married to a woman and as often seen with women as men, was a "P.H."—"phony homosexual,"[107] a reflection of an attitude shaped importantly by his reading, not only of Freud (Copland actually psychoanalyzed himself) and Havelock Ellis—whose long historical peregrination through the history of homosexuality from Plato to Michelangelo to Whitman much engaged Copland—but of Whitman and also Gide, of whose books *Corydon* was the most influential, arguing for the social good of homosexual mentoring of young men. If Copland was, as biographer Howard Pollack reports, "extraordinarily relaxed about his sexuality," it was because his reading buttressed his own lifelong conviction that, as he once said, "God made me the way I am."

In the gay landscape of his day, which Pollack maps very well—"effeminate homosexuals ('fairies'), more conventionally masculine homosexuals ('queers'), and essentially heterosexual men who engaged in homosexual sex ('trade')—Copland identified in the second group."[108] He did not, however, Pollack notes, "seek out sailors and other 'trade,' as did a number of his friends." Rather, he was attracted to bright, young musicians and artists, also "queers." Indeed, Copland was the model of today's well-adjusted, middle-class American gay in a way Auden and Thomson and Bernstein never were. And this despite the fact he did not succeed in forming a stable, lifelong marriage: "Over the years," Pollack notes, "the gap in age between Copland and his boyfriends naturally widened; by the 1950s, he was sometimes more than thirty years older than they." Yet Copland was so well adjusted, he usually negotiated these shoals well enough with partners for the most part equally levelheaded in this respect, one of whom said once: "I helped him stay young and he helped me to mature."[109]

According to the dancer Erik Johns, one of Copland's lovers and collaborators, these relationships involved "the classic Greek thing with an older man adoring and mentoring a younger guy." And Pollack adds, "Copland believed that, in love relationships, every man was either a father or a son. . . . Even in his professional relationships with composers, he often guided and supported troubled young men. A similar impulse animated his love life; indeed, the line was often a thin one." This was all the more possible because of Copland's basic good nature and sterling character. He grew to be a man many people actually revered. Though some of his friends thought him serious to a fault, he was shy, warm, fun-loving, and invariably loyal, a caring and dependable friend and in his love life "sexually candid and uninhibited . . . a gentle, sensitive lover," while at the same time very sophisticated and knowing. Entirely monogamous, only rarely promiscuous, he was, even in middle age, "old and wise enough," in the words of one contemporary, "to know that's what what kids did," and though he didn't want to know the specifics, he was generally understanding of his partners' need for very open, nonexclusive relationships, in which Copland, the older man, might be the primary but not the sole lover.[110]

Although his private and public lives were not entirely seamless—he preferred in press and radio interviews and such to describe himself as "a bachelor"—for his era "Copland lived a relatively open homosexual life." Pollack again: "He never tried to 'pass,' nor did he ever seriously entertain the idea of a marriage of convenience, a commonplace among homosexuals of his time"; Copland "became one of the earliest homosexual composers of prominence to cohabitate with his romantic partners."[111]

The most important of these was Victor Kraft, a violinist whom Copland met when he was thirty-two and Kraft sixteen and his student. Kraft, though a child prodigy, went on to give up the violin and become a well-known photographer, covering the Spanish Civil War as a photojournalist; he ultimately saw his work appear in such publications as *The New York Times* and *Life* magazine. He was beautiful, with penetrating blue eyes, well built, and he possessed a deep and almost musical voice. Copland's relationship with Kraft eventually became rather troubled, though Copland never failed of loyalty, nor, perhaps, in his way, did Kraft. Though he wanted to be like Copland, unambiguously gay and monogamous, Kraft's friends said he was drawn not just to men but equally strongly to women, in midlife marrying several, by one of whom he had a son. In classic fashion, Kraft at one point found Copland a house nearby his and his wife's (where the composer obligingly took up residence) and called on Copland to be the godfather of Kraft's child, who was mentally handicapped, and to whom Copland left one of the largest bequests in his will. Copland and Kraft's friendship through all this never faltered, though Copland was sorely tried more than once and ultimately had other relationships, in succession, that offered the composer himself more support.

How much did Copland's homosexuality play into his music? A striking parallel with Tchaikovsky at once arises in my mind. That master (whose work Copland did not overly like, by the way, calling it "neurotic") once shared with Mme. von Meck the relationship or dynamic between his joy and his angst in composing the Fourth Symphony, observing that the depression brought on by the angst was relieved and enlightened by an occasional daydream: wrote Tchaikovsky, "Some blissful, radiant, human image hurries by and beckons you away." Spanning centuries, and linking nineteenth-century St. Petersburg and twentieth-century Boston, Copland, in his breezy, masculine American way, said much the same thing once, at Tanglewood, when he was observed to catch the eye of a handsome young man: "There goes," he quipped, "my Fourth Symphony." So, too, Ned Rorem is on record, indeed, as saying he'd seen Copland "struck dumb by the beauty of a passing human being."[112]

Copland and Kraft were friends, too, of Benjamin Britten and Peter Pears, another gay couple, and it was Copland—to switch gears here again from motivation and inspiration to patronage and collaboration—who introduced Britten to Koussevitzky, who commissioned Britten's opera, *Peter Grimes*; similarly, another of Copland's lovers, Erik Johns, did the libretto for *The Tender Land*, Copland's own opera. It was, moreover, a work with a famously homosexual subtext: "No one can stop the way I feel," one character sings. "No one can ever tell me I can't love." That was bold, from a man of known leftist sympathies generally who was also a Jew. That it was even acceptable then is a measure of Copland's stature. His innocence, Ned Rorem has written, was a "sophisticated innocence."[113]

The contrast with Thomson particularly is striking. Thomson was by no means so admired. With reason, it would seem. Privately, he was known to belittle Copland in a way that verged on anti-Semitism. He remarked, for instance, that "musically, [Copland] knows how to make five cents perform the services of a dollar." Was it also Thomson, one wonders, who observed, "Aaron Copland's musical ideas are like pennies shrewdly invested, rather than pearls advantageously set"? That observation was certainly unambiguously anti-Jewish.[114] On the other hand, there is a sense in which Thomson, in his usual negative way, was on to something, for more positive-sounding instances can be found of others who heard a Jewish sensibility in Copland's work, in their case not with disdain but respect. I love critic Paul Rosenfeld's observation, for example, that listening to Copland's music seemed to him like hearing something "fine Hebraic, harsh and solemn, like the sentences of brooding rabbis."[115] And Copland himself, though he dismissed "the Eastern European thing" and even "the Jewish national aspect" (presumably Zionism) as not at all influential in his music, by no means disputed that there was a Jewish aspect in the first place. It was an aspect he was at one and the same time wary of (the "Jewish melos" easily led, he once told a student, to "a worn romanticism") and also sometimes inspired by. For example, he observed that in addition to "the need to find a musical language that would have an American quality, I had also a—shall we say

Hebraic—idea of the grandiose, of the dramatic and the tragic, which was expressed to a certain extent in the Organ Symphony, and very much in the Symphonic Ode."[116] Whatever critics heard, moreover, Copland in his composing, as in life generally, did not use such words as *grandiose* and *tragic* at all loosely, but made very fine distinctions indeed—for example, between characteristics that seemed to him German as opposed to Jewish: contrasting Jewish "grandiosity" with German "bombast," the Jews' "deep sense of the tragedy of all life" with the Germans' general "pessimism." Even his Jewish detractors were similarly persnickety, faulting the composer on the basis of some pretty fine distinctions of their own, similar to discussion among gays as between the Wildean and Whitmanic archetypes. Lazare Saminsky, for example, complained that Copland was more "Judaic" than "Hebraic" in his sensibility. (There was Jewishness all right, but the "wrong" kind!) What Saminsky and his co-religionists heard was not the echoes they craved of the ancient Jewish tradition—of the shofar and the temple chant of David dancing before the Ark—but echoes instead of the European Jewish ghetto, and much too much of what they judged "assimilationism," with Western culture as a whole, American particularly. Indeed, it is for the American sensibility of his music that Copland is famous. His genius that way also ran a risk.[117]

Now we are plainly dealing with stereotypes here, this play clearly coming from the same corner of the ballpark as the one that suggests a gay man who is not effeminate is trying to prove something about himself by covering up his "true nature" and "trying" to be manly, never mind if the poor guy's captain of the football team. What is the standard phrase in the personals? "Masculine-appearing"—as if one was playing a role, as, indeed, it must seem to those (gay and straight alike) who expect the stereotypical Wildean figure—Thomson in this case. Poor Copland. To many he must have seemed too good to be true. Of a leftist homosexual Brooklyn Jew, mainstream society also had (has, even now) certain expectations. Thus critics have been known to point out how problematic it was for some that a Jew could compose as Copland did in the "white-bread-of-the-prairie idiom." The only way Richard Taruskin can explain it is to imply . . . that Copland "cashed in on nationalism." It's a little like saying, as a member of Boston's St. Botolph Club did in a letter to me once, that I write about "perverted" sex because it sells books.[118]

An American sensibility? Certainly. A Jewish sensibility? Probably. A gay sensibility? It is the emerging question here, is it not? Sufficient now to invoke Pollack's observation that throughout his career, Copland had to contend with accusations, often uttered covertly, that he was the leader of a Jewish or homosexual or leftist "cabal," or all three. It is more important, however, to notice his biographer's assertion that "Copland's identity as a homosexual included conventional notions of gender attributes," out of which the composer constructed "the concept of a restrained and humane 'manliness.' " Very Whitmanic.[119]

Actually, more than a Jewish or a gay or an American sensibility, at first many of his contemporaries heard in Copland's work a New York sensibility. This seems to have faded, however, since Bernstein's *West Side Story*, after which milestone the genius of Copland as a composer has increasingly been seen as more universally American—encompassing as it does, after all, the prairie as well as the skyscraper—while Bernstein, in the wake of his famous New York musical, is the composer who has come to all but own in the musical imagination the New World capital. All of which is the more interesting because Bernstein, who always seemed a New Yorker born, was actually a native Bostonian, a graduate both of Boston Latin School and Harvard College; Copland, who was far from attending either, was the actual New Yorker, born and bred there. But Copland was also the real Bostonian, nurtured above all by the intellectual and moral support of the Harvard/Koussevitzky circle.

It is often forgotten that "the press," in Richard Dyer's words, "were as hostile to Copland and company as their predecessors had been toward Tchaikovsky and Brahms," and how unique Koussevitzky was in creating a "Boston audience [that] was sympathetic to his advocacy [and] his zeal in presenting unknown compositions to audiences ... the serious attention he gave to rehearsing [them] seeming to convince listeners."[120] George Gershwin himself—more than Copland, perhaps, an exemplar of the New York sensibility—when he turned from Broadway to more classical music, had to seek out Koussevitzky. He quite failed to interest the New York Philharmonic in his *Second Rhapsody*; it was not until several years after Gershwin's death that Toscanini conducted Gershwin's work, and with no great conviction either, according to Gershwin biographer Charles Schwartz: "Toscanini's interpretation was anything but definitive. ... He had little experience—and even less inclination—in conducting contemporary music of Gershwin's kind." The result was dismal. Schwartz notes, "[T]he Boston Symphony's rendition of the Second Rhapsody was another matter. Koussevitzky had long been a champion of contemporary music ... and was wholly sympathetic. ... He and his orchestra went all out for Gershwin [who himself was the soloist] and did well by the Second Rhapsody ... in its world premiere in Boston."[121]

Episodic in his interest in Gershwin, Koussevitzky was "unshakable," in David Mermelstein's words, "in his allegiance to Copland." But "despite Copland's residence in Manhattan, the New York Philharmonic (in pre-Bernstein days) gave surprisingly few performances of his music," according to Pollack. Boston, however, adopted Copland completely, and he responded warmly. "Just as every ten-year-old American boy dreams of being president some day," Copland wrote, "so every twenty-nine-year-old American composer dreams of being played by Koussevitzky."[122] Installed by that conductor as head of the composition department of the Boston Symphony's Tanglewood Music School, a post he held for a quarter century, and chosen by

Harvard as the first American musician (and the second in the world, after Stravinsky) to hold the Charles Eliot Norton professorship, America's most eminent lectureship in the arts, Copland directed that after his death his ashes be scattered at Tanglewood, where the memorial music he requested was led by the Harvard Glee Club.

New York

THOUGH HE, TOO, in his younger years, was a protégé of Koussevitzky's and would be prominently associated with Tanglewood, Leonard Bernstein had a very different story. Nonetheless, Lenny certainly profited enormously from his years at Harvard, which he entered in 1935. Certainly he was affected by the full force of the old Boston musical tradition, which promptly and utterly he rejected. Under Arthur Tillman Merritt, his tutor in Eliot House, Bernstein wrote his senior thesis on "The Absorption of Race Elements into American Music," a thesis in which he made a point of attacking George Chadwick and the Boston classicists, America's founding school of composers in the late nineteenth century. Newly interesting today for their perhaps tentative but pioneering work, to a young man in the 1930s they were still a living—or, rather, strangling—tradition in American music which Bernstein instinctively disliked. He castigated them for being too much dependent on specific American ethnic strains—Indian or African, for instance—in their Americanism. Instead, he praised the very different Americanism of the modernist composers of his day, such as Copland and Harris and Sessions; their music, he thought, relied not on folk material, but on a new Americanness.

In classic Harvard fashion, however, it was the overall liberal arts curriculum and, above all, his extracurricular activities that seemed to matter most to Bernstein. Because he was Jewish he was not eligible for the college's social clubs. (That this bothered him somewhat may be suggested by the fact that he self-consciously broadened his A's at Harvard and insisted upon the aristocratic *styne*, not the democratic Yiddish *steen*, in the pronunciation of his name.) Yet he was a lively, indeed magnetic, young man, short (5'8") but broad-shouldered and quite handsome, a good athlete (squash, swimming, rowed a skiff, high jump), and a gifted musician. He tried out for the *Harvard Advocate*, the leading college literary journal, of which he became music editor, and where his criticism was pronounced by his biographer much livelier than his class essays.[123] Even more important were three key mentors—mentors not only musical, but sexual.

The first to appear, in January 1937, Bernstein's sophomore year, was Dimitri Mitropoulos. A figure almost larger than life, Mitropoulos caused a sensation as guest conductor during this period in Boston; Bernstein was overwhelmed. Lenny, in his own words, "went bananas," and at a subsequent meeting—some said at a Harvard gay party the young man crashed—Mitropoulos was so charmed he invited Bernstein to a week of his rehearsals at Symphony Hall. Although it involved dumping his midyear exams, young Bernstein proved more than willing, for reasons he alluded to in a sketchy but transparent short story he subsequently wrote for one of his courses. In it he named his chief protagonist Eros Mavro and recounted an episode we know actually happened at the Café Amalfi, a legendary bohemian restaurant of those days behind Symphony Hall, where in the course of lunch with Bernstein and another friend (who corroborated the story) the famous conductor affixed an oyster to the end of a fork which he put into the younger man's mouth, Bernstein all the while seductively cooperating. In fact, it has never been clear who seduced whom that day. But Meryle Secrest puts it well when she points out the likely liberating effect on young Bernstein, who by all indications was struggling with his sexuality, of meeting "a famous man, powerfully handsome and magnetic, with the physique of a Greek god [Mitropoulos was an avid mountain climber], for whom such relationships were acceptable, normal and natural. To see someone so at ease with his feelings and making no secret of them, who was (after all) from a strongly religious background," must have been memorable for Bernstein, the more so as he seems to have been as smitten as Mitropoulos, though the latter was forty years old.[124]

Then (in Bernstein's senior year) there was Marc Blitzstein, and in this case there is no doubt who was the pursuer. The composer of the militantly pro-labor musical *The Cradle Will Rock*, the opening of which in New York had all but caused a riot, Blitzstein came to Boston to see the Harvard production of the controversial show Bernstein with his usual chutzpah had resolved to put on. "I met his plane at East Boston [now Logan International Airport]. It was still rather daring to fly then! . . . He attended our dress rehearsal that morning and then we walked, all afternoon," Bernstein fondly remembered, "by the Charles River. . . . That image leaps up in my mind," he added years later. "Marc lying on the banks of the Charles, talking, bequeathing to me his knowledge, insight, warmth." Humphrey Burton put it bluntly:

> Blitzstein's visit bowled Bernstein over. Blitzstein played the piano at the cast party in a Harvard Square restaurant after the show, singing songs from the new musical he was writing. . . . He had a witty, sardonic, almost hypnotic presence. . . . His single-mindedness was an object lesson for Bernstein. Here was a man who had made a firm choice. . . . He had decided to become a professional composer. . . .
>
> The tremors within Bernstein occasioned by Marc Blitzstein's homosexuality must have gone deeper still. . . . The older man's ruthless honesty about himself would not have gone unremarked. Could [Bernstein] achieve a similar self-awareness and find peace within himself?[125]

Fortuitously, surely, the third "visitor" of Bernstein's Harvard years, whose effect was perhaps most decisive of all, was Aaron Copland himself.

Although he was raised in upper-middle-class suburban Boston, the son of prosperous parents, Bernstein's upbringing was actually quite limited, especially culturally. It was not until Boston Latin School that he discovered, as he later put it, "that people could buy a ticket and go to hear Rachmaninoff play a recital in Symphony Hall. How amazing. I mean, to think how provincial one was and how restricted one was in the ghetto created by my father around me."[126] In time-honored fashion the cocoon burst at Harvard. Bernstein again: "If you really want to know the beginning, . . . there was this librarian of Eliot House, . . . I. Bernard Cohen," Bernstein once told Vivian Perlis, Copland's first biographer. "He became a very good friend of mine. . . . He introduced me to Picasso and to Gertrude Stein . . . [and] 'Modernism.' . . . Joyce was still banned," Bernstein recalled. "I read *Ulysses*— I. B. got me a copy. . . . He had a great love for music and poetry, and he was my kind of guy—I mean he was a mentor."[127] One could as well be in Foster Damon's rooms overlooking Harvard Square with Virgil Thomson or E. E. Cummings decades earlier.

Cohen and Bernstein took advantage as a matter of course (and in Bernstein's case with the zeal of a convert) of Boston's music life, and one concert in particular Bernstein never forgot: the Boston tryout of a dancer who encouraged them to attend her forthcoming New York debut, which Cohen duly arranged for himself and the largely penniless Bernstein to attend. Bernstein's recollection:

> It was just wonderful. . . . We had seen this in Boston, so we were the ones who could say, "Oh," to our neighbors . . . "wait until you see this one, this is the killer." . . . For everybody else in the front row of that balcony it was news. . . . On my right sat this unknown person . . . of a charm not to be described. . . . It was Aaron Copland. . . . I was blown away. . . . I pictured [him] as a sort of patriarch, a Moses-like or Walt Whitman-like figure, with a beard. . . . I was shocked to meet this young-looking, smiling, giggling fellow whose birthday it happened to be. And he invited everybody in the row . . . [including Virgil Thomson and Victor Kraft back to his loft.] . . . And it was my real introduction to New York.[128]

Whether or not they slept with each other, they became lifelong intimates: "Aaron and I had a personal relationship, of course, that was very strong," Bernstein has written. "He came to Boston . . . and he stayed in the guest quarters at Eliot House, which I arranged. Whenever he came to Boston, we saw each other, and the few times I came to New York."[129]

Most notably, Copland came to the New England capital for the Harvard Classical Club's production of Aristophanes' *The Birds* in 1939. Bernstein had composed incidental music for this effort, recalled by one and all as a wild ride indeed, there being deliberate and highly memorable aspects of the production inspired by the notorious strip shows of Boston's legendary Old Howard burlesque theater, much frequented by Bernstein and his cohort (for research purposes, of course) during this period. Whatever Copland thought of Bernstein's music is not known. But Harold Shapero remembered that "Lenny conducted with such flair that Aaron quickly realized his young friend was a born orchestral conductor." "Copland," according to Shapero, "arranged meetings with Koussevitzky, who immediately accepted Lenny for his conducting class. . . . Lenny's conducting career was launched."[130]

Whether or not it was quite that simple (though Burton agrees Copland was the decisive force in Bernstein's decision), the importance of Copland to Bernstein can hardly be exaggerated, as a letter extant from the early 1940s documents: "I've never felt about anyone before as I do about you," Bernstein wrote to Copland: "This is not a love letter, but I'm quite mad about you."[131] The letter was written at Tanglewood, with which Bernstein, a graduate student in 1939–1941 at the Curtis Institute of Music in Philadelphia, began his long and crucial association in 1940. That year he was Koussevitzky's student and also Copland's, and in the year following, 1941, he made his professional conducting debut, conducting the Boston Pops. The year after that he had become Koussevitzky's own assistant. His trajectory seemed clear.

Yet Bernstein did not succeed Koussevitzky. The man who did, Charles Münch, in Joan Peyser's words, came to town for his vetting in 1949 "describing a new Honegger work as 'horizontal music,' rather stern and unsentimental. He was talking the language of the Boston sensibility,"[132] continues Peyser, and there is no doubt the BSO was more interested in the patrician Münch, born to white-tie, than in democratizing Lenny, so fond of T-shirts. But all indications are that race and sexuality trumped everything else.

How anti-Semitic was Boston in this period? Virgil Thomson's attitude toward Copland in this respect has already arisen here; so, too, the anti-Italian prejudice of which the Sacco-Vanzetti case became an internationally known example. And it hardly surprises that Thomson was also dismissive toward Walter Piston, the Harvard professor and American composer of considerable renown then, but who Thomson thought was "embarrassed by his Italian heritage (the original family name was Pistone)" and who, Thomson felt, "took on Boston Brahmin airs."[133] Actually, Irving Fine, a Jewish professor at Harvard and later at Brandeis who was trained at Harvard under Piston, could have testified that Piston took on only the most admirable such airs: in 1945, Piston, according to musicologist Nicholas Tawa, "resign[ed] from the Harvard Musical Association when an individual opposed Fine's application [i.e., election for membership], owing to his being Jewish."[134] The fact that Piston, Harvard's foremost music teacher of the era (three years later, in 1948, Koussevitzky premiered the symphony for which Piston won a Pulitzer Prize), was reported to feel so abused for being so treated by the venerable Harvard Musical Association is startling evidence of the virulence of Boston's anti-Semitism in the years just before Bernstein's rendezvous with the search committee of the Boston Symphony.

Indeed, Koussevitzky himself is quite baldly described by two otherwise admiring critics as a leading example (Mahler, of course, is foremost) of "Jewish-born conductors [who] converted [to Christianity] for professional reasons,"[135] and though it is sometimes suggested Koussevitzky reaffirmed his Jewishness toward the end of his life in Boston, his funeral occurred at Beacon Hill's Episcopal Church of the Advent.

It is in this context that one must consider the whole matter of Bernstein's marriage, and, indeed, Koussevitzky's urgent advice to his young protégé that (as Bernstein himself confided at the time in letters) he should "marry immediately,"[136] this on top of his urging Bernstein to change his obviously Jewish surname. Although Copland was perhaps harsh to speak privately (to Paul Moore) of Bernstein's marriage as "window dressing," or a form of camouflage,[137] Burton can put no better face on the whole matter than to write that while Bernstein never would give way as to his name, his "decision to get married surely had a relevance, however subconscious, to the drama of Koussevitzky's succession. . . . Bernstein's feelings for Felicia [Montealegre Cohn] were not fabricated or dissembled; he was not that kind of man. But their engagement announcement was made less than a month after the couple had begun spending time in each other's exclusive company." That was the first engagement, announced at the end of 1946, barely a month before newspaper reports in January 1947 hinted Bernstein would succeed Koussevitzky. By September reports appeared that the engagement was off, and six months later that Münch, not Bernstein, had won the Boston post. Then, five years later, in August 1951 (Koussevitzky having died that January), the second engagement was announced—by Koussevitzky's widow—culminating in Bernstein's marriage within a month. Another of Bernstein's biographers, Joan Peyser, minced no words: "Bernstein was still trying to build a career that would make him acceptable as Koussevitzky's successor in Boston." In that he failed. But ultimately he did marry Felicia. Peyser again, devastatingly:

Bernstein was married in Koussevitzky's white suit and wore Koussevitzky's shoes. In his book *Findings*, a photograph of him smiling politely, with his arm around the waist of his beaming bride accompanies a poem he stopped writing when, he notes in introductory words to the poem, he realized he had become a "very well behaviorized chimpanzee." It was like a caption.

The marriage may have made Bernstein's future career possible. Besides what it did to help him "ingest" Koussevitzky, it was also a signal . . . of his willingness to compromise. . . . Bernstein certainly came to regard Felicia with some of the tenderness and attachment he felt for the women in his family. But how much passion, how much calculation lay behind the decision to marry is open to question. . . .

It appears Bernstein tried to be faithful to his wife, but even in the first year of marriage he invited [John] Mehegan to participate in a jazz festival [Bernstein was running] at Brandeis.[138]

Mehegan, a jazz pianist and a graduate of Juilliard, who later taught there and at Yale, was the composer of the incidental music for Tennessee Williams's *A Streetcar Named Desire*; very sharp, very independent, masterful, politically leftist, quite funny, too. And though married to a woman, he was hardly the man to repulse Bernstein, with whom a long and intimate relationship ensued.[139] One wonders what the new Mrs. Bernstein thought. Certainly a kind of pattern was emerging, the troublesome aspects of which were obscured by Bernstein's appointment to direct the New York Philharmonic—a much better fit than Boston—and by his subsequent celebrity career as conductor, teacher, and composer, he being in critic James Oestreich's words, "America's first native-born conducting superstar."[140]

It was a career easily criticized—as Bernstein himself was wont to do; there were many more gala opening nights than composing stretches in Martha's Vineyard. But though he did not succeed Koussevitzky, Bernstein more than fulfilled his master's dearest dreams, for throughout his career Bernstein "brought to [modern] American music," David Mermelstein has written, "the wider audiences sought by his mentor, Serge Koussevitsky."[141] Bernstein was the first American, moreover, to lead a major American orchestra. And as for the disappointments, his and others, David Denby has well written that "Bernstein (who could have been after all, plausibly, a pianist, conductor, teacher [Socratic or Talmudic], composer [pop or classic] or actor, so gifted was he) seemed almost

sensually overendowed, like a second-rate movie star of the forties. Here was a man without modesty or reserve, and at times he was hard to take: his shoulder-shaking boogie-woogie at the piano, complete with sympathetic groans, could shame the label off a bottle of bourbon. Yet the critics who thought Bernstein merely vain missed the special, self-punishing nature of his ambition; they underestimated how much he put himself at risk, how many things he held himself responsible for. Bernstein tried to pull everything together—serious music and popular music, youngsters and grownups, tragedy and comedy. He wanted America to become a mature musical culture—one that boasted both symphonic masterpieces and a thriving popular music enriched by the masterpieces.

He believed in the universal language of art. . . . Vanity was only a small part of the story.[142]

It was probably inevitable that he "disappointed and exasperated" so many; "if I knew what I wanted to say," he told a friend a day or two before his death, "I wouldn't be sitting here now."[143]

Bernstein's is a mixed record. Martin Bernheimer was not wrong, surely, to complain in Bernstein's music of a "discomforting tendency toward sugar-coating and melodic kitsch, toward bombast and bathos."[144] But critical opinion—the latest edition of the authoritative *Grove Dictionary* expands Bernstein's entry from one to five pages[145]—is moving in Bernstein's favor in the 2000s: tonality has not died; is, in fact, newly fashionable; and the worlds of classical music and musical theater no longer seem so disparate. Thus there is new respect for a work once widely condescended to, *West Side Story*, which so well joined Bernstein's feeling for popular culture with his classical training in the service of the social causes so dear to him. Indeed, *West Side Story*, the premiere of which took place in Washington in August 1957, is at once the glory and the problem of Leonard Bernstein—a serious work, surely, but not (by certain standards) serious music. It is on the one hand just a musical; on the other, it is in its way unique, indeed, unrivaled in the history of American music. It also is at the center of any discussion of Bernstein's own contribution to the matter of a gay musical sensibility.

Historically, of course, Bernstein is fair game for all sides in this debate. Because he was homosexual, but at the same time cherished his family— not only his children but his wife, too—his friends, relatives, and colleagues all contended then and now from their rather rigid positions about Bernstein's "true nature." On the one hand, Harold Shapero would carry on about Bernstein's very Tchaikovsky-like "struggle with homosexuality," a struggle full of good and bad and right and wrong. On the other, Arthur Laurents thought it no more complicated than "a gay man who got married," hardly unusual then. Bernstein, Laurents thought, "wasn't conflicted about it at all," and Laurents added that Bernstein's marriage had "nothing to do with pretending to be heterosexual or anything like that." Instead, leaving aside the matter of career, Stephen Sondheim emphasized the matter of family: "The *idea* of family" was, Sondheim asserted, "deeply rooted" in Bernstein. A point of view obviously sensible; Bernstein's was an era when there was no possibility at all of homosexual marriage or of a gay man or woman having a family.[146]

West Side Story is also an important landmark of an issue developing throughout this study. A collaboration made in heaven ("the continual flow between us was an enormous excitement," Jerome Robbins recalled),[147] it was the work not only of Bernstein, but of director-choreographer Robbins, author Arthur Laurents, and lyricist Stephen Sondheim with Bernstein, who composed the music[148]—which is to say of four gay men. Also four Jews. It was a debate even then. There was, all claimed, *no* gay sensibility. "There is one sensibility all four of us share which . . . really *does* inform the work," Laurents reported. "We're all Jews."[149] Period. "Our Jewishness as the source of passion against prejudice" was Laurent's argument. Sondheim was of like mind.[150] A generational perspective surely. What was important to these men *was* what *was* important. End of debate. In the short run, that is. In the long run, journalist Charles Kaiser, author of *The Gay Metropolis*, takes perhaps the deeper view, seeing the tremendous achievement of *West Side Story* in perspective, deriving from

> the similarities between the experiences of Jews and homosexuals in New York City: two oppressed minority groups who have struggled mightily, and very successfully, to travel out of invisibility. . . .
>
> Regardless of whether the collaborators' portrayal of prejudice was shaped more by their gayness or their Jewishness, together they had created the most vibrant musical portrait of twentieth-century Manhattan . . . an achievement that remains unrivaled. . . . The show has been performed tens of thousands of times in almost every major city of the world.[151]

Recall *New York Times* drama critic Brooks Atkinson's judgment of *West Side Story*, so full of "wildness, ecstasy and anguish," he insisted, "the subject is not beautiful. But," he added, "what *West Side Story* draws out of it is beautiful. For it has a searching point of view."[152] One is reminded of Weinstock's and Brockway's view of Tchaikovsky's *Pathétique*. Perhaps what Copland found, so much more quietly and thoughtfully in twentieth-century America, was Bernstein's vocation to conceive of more sensuously.

In the fall of 1972, by then full of honors, Leonard Bernstein was back at Harvard, installed in handsome rooms in his old stomping ground, Eliot House, overlooking the river where in his youth he had rowed his skiff and walked with Marc Blitzstein. For two years, on and off, his life was dominated by the prodigious effort of having succeeded Stravinsky, Copland, and Hindemith as the Charles Eliot Norton Professor.[153] A ringing defense of tonality in music, Bernstein's lectures were dedicated by him when published in book form to a young man whom he had met in San Francisco in 1971: Tom Cothran, then the music director of a California radio station. Cothran was sharp, eager, bright, and cute, and Bernstein fell deeply in love; he was fifty-three, Cothran twenty-four. For the first time Bernstein experienced a deep and, as it turned out, sustained homosexual love. Though, happily, there was lust, too, this was different. Writes Burton: "During the twenty years of his marriage . . . [Bernstein] had had homosexual encounters, but he had never entered into a loving relationship with a man"—a man, Burton adds, who was "the only person who might have filled the void left by Felicia" when she died. The first acknowledgment of the Norton lectures is to Cothran "whose musical sensibilities and poetic insights fertilized my every idea."[154] Many doubtless bridled. As usual Bernstein felt too much, just as (many believed) Tchaikovsky had. Unlike Tchaikovsky, however, Bernstein also said too much. And as was the case with that master, there was a terrible price to be paid. Nor, significantly, did this seem to surprise Bernstein.

It was a world away and then some, and in another sense no very different world at all, when, on tour in Russia in 1988, he made a pilgrimage to the tomb of Tchaikovsky. He had stayed up all night in St. Petersburg— Leningrad it then was—so as to be able to visit not only Tchaikovsky's grave, but Pushkin's, too. Gay and Jewish and white and American, Bernstein certainly was. But he was also Russian. Like Tchaikovsky. Like Koussevitzky. And there was a kind of "apostolic succession," too; in Russia as a boy of sixteen, Koussevitzky, something of a child prodigy on the double bass long before becoming a conductor, had been presented to Tchaikovsky, who had actually accompanied the young man on the piano in his own First String Quartet, the one premiered to such raves in Boston in 1876. Then Koussevitzky had paid the card-playing debts (in return for private lessons) of Arthur Nikisch, later the conductor of the Boston Symphony Orchestra famous for being Tchaikovsky's champion. All his own life, Koussevitzky, as Nikisch had been, was especially prized for his interpretations of Tchaikovsky's works—particularly "the peculiarly affecting quality of his highly personal reading of the *Pathétique*"—giving rise, Moses Smith has written, virtually to "a cult." (That this was particularly true of Tchaikovsky's Fifth Symphony I know very well, for my mother must have been one of the cult's charter members. The recording previously referred to here as a "coming-out" soundtrack was the Fifth Symphony, no other, and it was conducted by—who else?—Koussevitzky. I remember to this day the deep burgundy cover of the 78 RPM album, with its depiction of a handsome Russian officer in a sky-blue tunic slashed with white.) Bernstein knew, Humphrey Burton has written, that "he was part of a great line that stretched back through Koussevitsky to Nikisch."[155] In fact, after conducting Tchaikovsky's Fifth in London once, Bernstein proudly wrote Koussevitzky some older concertgoers had said it was "better than Nikisch." Bernstein was clearly very proud.[156]

"Lenny, baby," of course, also, on another occasion, made a joke of the subject. It was Bernstein's way. On one occasion at Tanglewood he shocked even his rather jaded cohort by singing very loudly and more than once, to one of Tchaikovsky's melodies in the Fifth, "Ev'rybody out of the closet!"[157] But, under the surface, it was all a deadly serious business to him. Hence his pilgrimage to Tchaikovsky's grave. Indeed, the deepest link between Bernstein and Koussevitzky, who was not gay, nor American, nor Jewish religiously, may have been nationality. Reflecting once as to why Koussevitzky became his "surrogate father," Bernstein said not only that Koussevitzky "had no children of his own and I had a father whom I loved very much but who was not for this music thing at all," but he also added: "There was something about [Koussevitzky] being Russian that was terribly moving and close to me."[158] Indeed, Bernstein identified very closely with Tchaikovsky himself. According to biographer Joan Peyser, Bernstein actually took a screen test to play Tchaikovsky in a proposed Hal Wallis movie, and similarly, on another occasion, put himself in Hollywood's way. "Each time he was drawn to a role, it was one he perceived as an extension of himself, a fantasy he had of himself at the time," Peyser writes. "In his youth the part had been George Gershwin"—read Jewish—while "after he met Felicia [Bernstein's wife], it was Tchaikovsky, a homosexual composer protected by his beautiful patroness, Baroness von Meck"—read gay.[159] Or was the association Bernstein made with Tchaikovsky's wife, rather than with Tchaikovsky's patron, von Meck? Bernstein's marriage was certainly complicated enough to sustain either interpretation. It was not the catastrophe Tchaikovsky's was, but the very proof of that—Leonard and Felicia's three children—in the end landed Leonard Bernstein in situations even Tchaikovsky had been spared.[160]

Worst of all, perhaps, was what ensued when Bernstein's daughter Jamie, herself Harvard-bound at eighteen, reported to her mother how "deeply shocked" she was to have heard through friends at Tanglewood "ugly rumors" (this was fully a half century ago) about her father's homosexual past, as she put it. Summoned home to talk, she and her father had what can only be described as a bonding experience from hell. After dinner "father and daughter walked up to his studio. They sat side by side on the swing out on the porch," Burton recounts, and Leonard Bernstein told his daughter that "everything she'd heard was a lie. Her father's denial left [Jamie] confused," but, she said later, it was "all I had to go on for years." It went on and on: the denial, the lying, the ambivalence. Husband and wife kept the "secret" of Bernstein's sexuality so well from their children that when the bubble burst and the crisis exploded in everyone's face the other daughter, Nina, learned of her parents' breakup "read[ing] about it over someone's shoulder on a bus on her way to school. She had been told almost nothing, she complained later; she never was."[161]

The Bernsteins split over Tom Cothran. Felicia Bernstein gave something very close to an ultimatum that her husband must not spend so much time with Cothran, to whom she became unpleasant as his threat became more explicit. When Bernstein demurred and confronted his wife, the scene became in every sense Tchaikovsky-like, and Bernstein "never forgot the curse she uttered when he told her he was leaving her for Cothran." Pointing her finger at him in fury, she hissed: "You're going to die a bitter and lonely old man." To all of which Cothran, "a wonderful, twinkly, bright, endearing person," who rejoiced as well in "a lively, well-stocked mind"—these are the judgments of contemporaries—must have been more than an easier alternative. He had been an English major at Berkeley before he dropped out and was as fluent in music as in literature and philosophy. "Very cute, goofy, and quick on the trigger," in the words of Jamie Bernstein. She also recalled Cothran was enough of a self-starter that he bought "an ancient VW for a hundred dollars and rebuilt the engine himself."[162] Exhilarating. But also guilt-making. Bernstein would always care deeply for his wife; falling in love with Cothran did not change that. Nor did his and Cothran's perhaps intense feelings for each other make them compatible "live-ins"; the middle-aged maestro soon missed home and devoted wifely attentions hardly to be expected from Cothran. The young man, moreover, Burton speculates, also probably tired of frequent "guiltbergers," as Bernstein himself called his guilty outbursts. Soon enough Bernstein sought out his wife again, only to have their reconciliation overwhelmed by her diagnosis of lung cancer. Felicia Bernstein's early death devastated him, as would Cothran's from AIDS. Leonard Bernstein brought much that was his own to his reading of Tchaikovsky's *Pathétique*.

That reading, indeed, could be quite a provocation. Witness this part of a 1986 review in the *Los Angeles Times* by Martin Bernheimer of Bernstein's performance of what that critic called a particularly "pathetic *Pathétique*":

> The trite Tchaikovsky rituals . . . were bathed in torrents of blood, sweat and tears. Emoting above and beyond any call, Bernstein acted out a series of virtuosic charades. . . . As always the audience adored the Lennie show. The protagonist looked picturesquely spent, ecstatic, . . . as if he and his symphonic cohorts had somehow succeeded in scaling at least three Mount Everests. The exquisite ardor of the moment could be expressed only in an ever-increasing orgy of hugs and kisses. I left before the maestro embraced the stagehands.[163]

The last line surely is not the only deliberate slap evident here. In other paragraphs "flamboyant" is used more than once; the conductor is said to be "acting" and (in another place) a "charade"; the embraces at performance's end—never mind their same-sex aspect—are described as an "orgy of hugs and kisses"; worst of all, and certainly most telling, Bernstein's nickname, Lenny, is rendered in its feminine form—Lennie. Well, I wasn't there. For the concert, that is. I've encountered the rest of it—blatant homophobia—too many times to call it anything else.

There was another perspective. Indeed, many noticed, in David Denby's words in *The New Yorker*, that again and again in his later years "Bernstein went to the edge. He would slow music down until it threatened to lose its shape, and then, emphasizing the grandeur and sense of victory embedded in a piece, pull things together at the brink of dissolution."[164] It was a response Tchaikovsky (Mahler, too) was always likely to evoke. Denby writes of Mahler performances by Bernstein that were "harrowing"; Burton of Tchaikovsky performances that were "searingly intense." Indeed, the latter quotes a memory of Bernstein coming off the podium after the *Pathétique* once "white of face and seemingly in a trance: 'I have been on the brink,' he murmured." And it was noted that his tempi told the story: they became so intense that night they "seemed to be becoming slow to the point of stasis." It was evidence that Burton was correct to think Bernstein "came to identify as closely with Tchaikovsky as he did with Mahler."[165]

Indeed, one wonders if Bernstein knew of Solomon Volkov's report that at the Sixth's premiere in St. Petersburg in 1893, at the symphony's end, when "Tchaikovsky slowly lowered the baton," there was in the audience "dead silence." Indeed, instead of applause, stifled sobs came from various parts of the hall. The audience was stunned and Tchaikovsky stood there, silent, motionless, his head bowed."[166] Fast-forward to another world, on a road west of Boston, when Harry Kraut of the Boston Symphony found himself one night in Bernstein's car as the composer drove home from Tanglewood, he all the while getting increasingly excited about Tom Cothran, whom he'd recently met and with whom he was clearly falling ever more and more deeply in love. Though Bernstein was getting more and more "excited," Kraut remembered that "the car went slower and slower, until it stopped moving altogether, right in the middle of Route Seven."[167]

Not just his attraction to Cothran, but Bernstein's sexual orientation generally seems to have influenced more than his behavior; it importantly shaped his work as a composer. I think Marc Blitzstein gave voice to this conclusion in his observation about Bernstein's "Serenade / After Plato's *Symposium*": "[It] haunts me all the time," avowed Blitzstein. But the composer's relationship with Cothran seems in this respect to have been particularly fructifying. Consider Bernstein's exquisite setting of Walt Whitman's "To What You Said," a part of *Songfest*, a work of twelve songs for voice and orchestra, each a literary fragment celebrating some aspect of diversity, a work that was a collaboration between Bernstein and Cothran, who chose the poems together while the two of them were living together in the late summer of 1976. (Bernstein had separated from Felicia, she devastated and abandoned in Martha's Vineyard, Massachusetts, he guilty but nonetheless frolicking with Cothran in Carmel, California.) Indeed, whatever clarity and insight Bernstein felt at his self-realization of himself as a homosexual man (and it had involved the cruel desertion of his wife) that late summer in Carmel, Tchaikovsky-like "the pain seemed to spark [Bernstein's] creativity: in the space of a week in September he wrote four songs destined for his *Songfest* cycle," according to Burton, who declared of the Whitman setting that even his wife "could hardly have remained unmoved by the beauty of Bernstein's setting of the Walt Whitman poem. . . . The words express with uncloying simplicity the tender feeling that one man can have for another; the meltingly beautiful melody [is] first heard on a solo cello and then hummed by the other five soloists as the baritone intones the poem to a descant."[168]

Finally, then, a gay sensibility after all, though what many would have put first I have come to last. So many sensibilities. "It's the best we've got," Bernstein said once of Copland's music. It may still be. Ned Rorem has called Copland "the father of American music." And yet I wonder if the posterity of these two famous friends and lovers will accept—I hope so—that while Copland's achievement is the more lasting, it was Bernstein's to pronounce the blessing.

The text of Whitman's, "a recently discovered poem about the poet's homosexual secret . . . never published in his lifetime,"[169] according to Jack Gottlieb, sung at the world premiere performance in Washington by bass Donald Gramm, is a fitting close here, very much an American *Pathétique*.

> To what you said, passionately clasping my hand,
> 　　　this is my answer:
> Though you have strayed hither, for my sake, you
> 　　　can never belong to me, nor I to you,
> Behold the customary loves and friendships—the
> 　　　cold guards,
> I am that rough and simple person
> I am he who kisses his comrade lightly on the lips
> 　　　at parting, and I am one who is kissed in return,
> I introduce that new American salute
> Behold love choked, correct, polite, always suspicious
> Behold the received models of the parlors—What are
> 　　　they to me?
> What to those young men that travel with me?

Picking Up the Torch

IF LEONARD BERNSTEIN and Aaron Coplan were arguably different kinds of aesthete, Lincoln Kirstein, even more than Virgil Thomson, was surely the warrior; none fiercer.

The son of a partner of Filene's Department Store in Boston (and perhaps the namesake of its founder, Lincoln Filene, celebrated in retail lore as the inventor of "the world-famous bargain basement"), young Lincoln was the son of one of Boston's leading Jewish families. Only the family of U.S. Supreme Court justice Louis Brandeis among the city's Jews rivaled the Kirsteins in the Puritan capital in the early years of the twentieth century, where young Kirstein grew up surrounded in equal measure by love, culture, wealth, and privilege. His family's Back Bay town house was on Commonwealth Avenue, not far from the model for its artistic decor, Isabella Stewart Gardner's Fenway Court. It was not far, either, from the august precincts of the Boston Public Library in Copley Square, of which young Kirstein's father would become in the 1920s president of the board of trustees and the collaborator in respect of the library's art with no less than John Singer Sargent, who himself mentored Lincoln Kirstein as a boy more than once. Even closer to the Kirstein manse were Symphony Hall and Jordan Hall and the Boston Opera House, sacred places in American music history, places where even as a boy Kirstein plotted rendezvous with the likes of Nijinsky, Caruso, and Pavlova. Here youth first considered art, then love.

Easier to catch the first in memory than the second. But Kirstein came close, remembering years later how he was drawn to the "half-shot young men," he began to spy aimlessly walking on Commonwealth Avenue each day across from the Kirsteins' town house. About this Kirstein did not just dream, as the young Nabokov might have: "Somewhere between twelve and thirteen," when he was "precociously keen," his family "all safely asleep," Kirstein later recalled, "I dreamed of appointments to keep" and early one morning "got up and got dressed in the dark," and slipped out the front door onto Commonwealth Avenue's broad, grassy mall. "Block after block through the light dew" he shadowed one such young man around, at once curious and wary, anxious and pining: "If only two fellows could talk." But, of course, they never did; not even the brief dialogue John Cheever would remember—at a later period in his life—on a similar Back Bay peregrination, already recorded here.

Kirstein charted his own erotic landscape well enough those early mornings on Commonwealth Avenue, street so apparently proper and pure, Kirstein, however, "drawn, hot, aching, and wild"; but hardly seen by the other man, to whom, he muses, he must have seemed "half a man" or "half a child." Harsh even then, Kirstein described himself as "damp in teenage erotics of fear" as he beat his pre-dawn path up the mall: "A-B-C spells love," he wrote (the intersecting street names are alphabetical), wondering, "mayn't I magic his blindness to see?" And so on, ringing—perhaps only John Betjeman has done it better—the bell changes of youth's sexual arousal: "My prowls in a tom-kitten youth," Kirstein called these early-morning walks, in which, he insisted, he pursued "some vague personal truth." And this despite his father's warnings against "living dangerously." He was not to take such risks, the young man remembered the elder Kirstein saying; "nor discover how or why I was born," youth protested, stubbornly.[170] A dewy morning on Commonwealth Avenue, up which a few hours later his father's Rolls-Royce—the first, it was said, in the Back Bay—would carry his father off downtown. What a scene, and how deliciously Proustian.

Kirstein soon enough exchanged Commonwealth Avenue for Harvard Yard, where he arrived in 1925. Here, too, he contrived another erotic landscape, where just as inevitably many of those he made friends with there, tutors and mentors of all kinds, have been met before in these pages: most important, S. Foster Damon, who had introduced E. E. Cummings to Gertrude Stein's work. Indeed, so great was Damon's influence that decades later Kirstein still made a point of haranguing Harvard for banishing his old tutor to "provincial exile" in Providence, Rhode Island, when, after Harvard had denied Damon tenure, that distinguished scholar of William Blake (as he would become) took up a career at Brown. The nature of Damon's influence on Kirstein? Consider young Lincoln's declaration: "Blake's beautiful painting of *Glad Day*, a blazingly brilliant nude youth seen against the full spectrum of a rainbow, was my current personification of Melville's Jack Chase and Billy Budd, and of Walt Whitman's comrades."[171] Wrote Kirstein:

> When I was a freshman at Harvard, Foster Damon, my tutor, gave me *White-Jacket* and *Israel Potter* to read. The reputation of *Moby-Dick* was at the crest of its recognition. The manuscript of *Billy Budd* lay in Widener Library. I paid a classmate to transcribe Melville's virtually illegible handwriting, since Damon told me that the recently published Constable "complete" edition was full of errors.[172]

Kirstein's whole undergraduate experience at Harvard was like that; and when he wasn't hanging out with Foster Damon, he was keeping hardly less stimulating company with the poet we've encountered so often before here, John Wheelwright, of whom there is still more to learn, through Kirstein's eyes this time, who saw in the poet an authentic Puritan, combining extremes of High Episcopal liturgy, proto-Trotskyite metaphysic and post-Ruskinian taste, . . . both monk and dandy, a sort of "Anglican Trotskyite" who convinced young Kirstein that "life was not a career but a service."[173] It was advice Kirstein never forgot: Over fifty years after Wheelwright's death, Kirstein wrote admiringly of this now obscure figure and marvelous poet:

> After Harvard he had educated himself in Paris and Florence. Now he lived in Boston with his sister, in a suite of red-and-black Pompeiian chambers on upper Beacon Street. . . . Jack Wheelwright was "Wheels." . . . He might deliver a lay-sermon at the Church of the Advent. . . . On the next night, Jack, clad in dinner jacket and black-tie, would address a gang of Socialist-Labor Party protesters in Roxbury or Somerville. Afterward, he would ride the subway to a debutante's coming out ball. . . . For me, Jack was a character relayed from *The Princess Casamassina* . . . He proved Brattle Street and Beacon Street could boast of much, including T. S. Eliot, e. e. cummings, and himself. Through Jack, I inhabited a vivid landscape. . . . [174]

More specifically, it was Wheelwright's "attachment to the odd orthodoxy of the Cowley Fathers that brought [Kirstein] closer, at least in thought, to T. S. Eliot, who more than any one person was responsible," Kirstein wrote, "in my mind for the pattern of what a magazine might be. . . . [Eliot's] magazine, *The Criterion*, was indeed for me and many of my generation 'a standard of judging.' . . . I was fifteen years old when an older friend . . . gave me a copy, volume L, number 7. . . . Its contents included . . . a longish poem entitled *The Waste Land*." Out of all this came Kirstein's own little magazine—*Hound and Horn*.

One of the secret pleasures of the collegiate neighborhood of Old Cambridge—which not for nothing is often called Boston's Left Bank (as often, Boston's conscience)—is the way one generation comes and goes, but never *really* goes, not in terms of the national—often the international—culture, which it continually tweaks and troubles, and often shapes pretty decisively, all the while by some sort of bush telegraph never losing touch with or letting up the pressure on newer generations of Harvard types, themselves coming and going, disheveled youth seen perhaps only at a reunion bash at Locke Ober's or an *Advocate* reading, in passing, when the newly or nearly great return to Boston to canoodle; but always *addressed*, never lost sight of, in everything thought or written, whenever it may be, begetting—thank God—riposte and rebellion as often as admiration or discipleship. Thus whole new movements and cycles of movements and writings and revelations, all in a sort of endless pattern of wind and surf (the Gold Coast *as coast*), of intellect and conviction, nonsense and genius—that is really the pulse on which hangs *everything*. T. S. Eliot's *Criterion* for example, had a number of ancestors in those "little magazines" of the 1890s (for the Harvard ones, most notably *The Mahogany Tree* and *Knight Errant*, see Chapter 1); there were indeed personal links between the generations—Bruce Rogers, for instance, one of the Beacon Hill bohemian cohort that produced *Knight Errant* in the 1890s, designed the typography of *Hound and Horn* in the 1920s.

Why a new magazine? *The Harvard Advocate* repelled Kirstein (as well as *Hound and Horn*'s cofounder, Kirstein's Gore Hall housemate Varian Fry) as vigorously as *Criterion* inspired. Their overtures rejected, Kirstein and Fry, in the grand Harvard tradition of giving your own party, not crashing another's (founding the Delphic Club, for instance, has always been thought to have been J. P. Morgan's riposte to his rejection by the august Porcellian Club), decided on a new magazine, its house gods Stein, Joyce, Stravinsky, and Picasso. Kirstein was frank: "I was an adventurer and *Hound and Horn* was my passport."[175]

As it turned out, his most important adventures at Harvard, however, were to be with the two presiding geniuses of the Fogg Art Museum, director Edward Waldo Forbes, a Boston Brahmin of the highest rank, a grandson of Ralph Waldo Emerson; and Paul Sachs, scion of New York's prestigious Goldman, Sachs investment house, whose "museum course" was famous the world over. "Between them," recalled Kirstein, "they guaranteed the Fogg's future [budget] personally," and it was to this quarter that Kirstein and his friends, artistic as well as literary, directed vigorous complaint: "The Boston

Museum of Fine Arts lagged behind New York and Chicago institutions in showing contemporary art,"[176] they charged, and according to Sybil Gordon Kantor, Sachs met the protest by "challeng[ing] them to create a gallery themselves."[177] He would not give them space at the Fogg; but he did offer moral and logistical support.

It was, again, a case of start your own club. Added Kantor, however:

> Closer to the truth was the fact that Denman Ross, who was associated with both the Boston Museum of Fine Arts and the Fogg as a teacher, trustee, and generous donor, had a significant influence, and he was vehemently opposed to modern art. . . . John Walker, reminiscing about Ross, claimed that he was as determined as Hitler to prevent the dissemination of what he considered decadent art.

Ross, though a friend of Isabella Stewart Gardner and much more than a regionalist of traditional tastes, seems in old age to have ossified in the face of the modernist challenge, to which he reacted almost violently. The effect of his conservatism is felt even now among twenty-first-century followers of the so-called Boston School of painting. But the genteel tradition, as Santayana christened this whole even then rather stale approach, was dominant in Kirstein's student days and it is no wonder that Kirstein, for all his love of Isabella Stewart Gardner's Fenway Court and Ralph Adams Cram's stained glass (Kirstein, at Sargent's suggestion, did an apprenticeship with Cram's glassmaker Charles Connick), joined with his friends, in Kantor's words, "in rebel[ling] against the tradition of gentility at Harvard in the 1920's—a tradition that derived in a straight line from the Norton-Ruskin-Berenson nineteenth-century dictum of good taste."[178]

Yet other aspects of the Boston Brahmin tradition, Kantor notices, however conservative, were more appealing: "Harvard students were traditionally encouraged to broaden their horizons with the implicit message that America had not yet caught up with the cultural opportunities found in Europe," for example, and it was just that exposure to Europe that led Kirstein and his friends, once back in Boston, to confront so forcefully Harvard's conservators of tradition. In 1929 Kirstein and his fellow modernists started the Harvard Society for Contemporary Art (at a dinner given by Sachs at Shady Hill, Charles Eliot Norton's old house north of Harvard Yard), their goal, in the words of a later Fogg Museum director, John Coolidge, "to pick up the torch lit by the Armory Show of 1913 and to introduce younger Americans to the arts of the early twentieth century and of our own time."[179]

The day-to-day leadership, as well as the driving force in terms of long-term vision, was Kirstein's, aided and abetted by a group of three friends entitled to be thought of as cofounders: the precocious scion of a famous New York German-Jewish banking family, Eddie Warburg; a young woman, highly gifted and scholarly, ambitious too, Agnes Mongan, the daughter of an Irish-Catholic Boston surgeon; and the high-society son of a rich Pittsburgh businessman, John Walker III, most of whom were to be found most days in earnest conference with Kirstein at lunch in Schrafft's restaurant in Harvard Square, plotting how to launch the new society. As its home they took rooms—207 and 208 (the walls of which they painted white, the ceilings silver)—at 1400 Massachusetts Avenue, in the heart of the square, above the Harvard Cooperative Society.[180]

Kirstein's tactics and strategy could hardly have been bettered. In the first place, he and his friends enlisted the aid of the small group of serious modernist collectors in America in a position to lend their holdings, offering what was in intellectual terms a prime location on the American rialto for exposure and polemic. Then, too, Kirstein, though his purpose was to pick up the Armory Show torch, by no means forgot Bostonians' shocked response when that show had traveled from New York to Boston in 1913. Thus Kirstein counted not only on the support of the Fogg Art Museum and Boston's Museum of Fine Arts (which were thereby relieved of the uncomfortable obligation of adding *any* modernist works to their collections while still being seen to be open to it), but also on the likely *lack* of support of the famously conservative Boston critics, whose hostility would all the more effectively publicize the Harvard Society's heresies. Indeed, key to the society's success was the overall Boston cultural and intellectual climate: however adventuresome musically, in literary and artistic terms in this period quite hidebound. A letter by a Harvard graduate student, Alfred Barr, published on page one of *The Harvard Crimson* in 1926, later widely reprinted, entitled "Boston Is Modern Art Pauper"[181] put the matter baldly enough.

Sure enough: the society's first show, entitled *Americans*, which opened in February 1929, was startling, an exhibition of American art that showed, in Kantor's words, "the first wave of modernist artists in America."[182] Kirstein recalled years later that "not one of these artists" in the show (which included the work of Edward Hopper, Georgia O'Keeffe, Charles Demuth, George Bellows, John Sloan, Arthur B. Davies) "had been shown at Boston's Art Club, or the Museum of Fine Arts."[183] That not only in itself thrilled Kirstein, but heralded just the critical reaction he sought: "The [*Boston*] *Evening Transcript* did satisfyingly attack Edward Hopper," Kirstein recalled, and while the somewhat more liberal *Herald* and *Globe* actually applauded, even they rose up in wrath to attack the society's second show, *The School of Paris*[184]—which featured works by Braque, de Chirico, Miró, Man Ray, Modigliani, and Brancusi, complementing a Fogg show that Barr called "the first exhibition of Modern French painting since the Armory Show of 1913."[185] Located as they were in a metropolitan, rather than a provincial, city and at a great university, not a small college, the society's shows, moreover, attracted huge crowds—in the case of its second exhibition some thirty-five hundred in three weeks—and the third show of 1929 was particularly popular because it was a one-man show of a prominent Boston artist of the 1900s, Maurice

Prendergast, who had been more or less kept afloat then by only one major Boston collector, Sarah Sears, and had ultimately moved to New York. Walter Pack, who did the catalogue, recognized Prendergast as "the first American artist to appreciate Cezanne and build on him."[186]

The modernist gods themselves gathered around. Both T. S. Eliot and Igor Stravinsky were in residence at Harvard, for example, in the 1930s as, sequentially, Norton Professor. Stravinsky, meanwhile, was a friend of Wheelwright's close friend, historian Edward Motley Pickman, and his wife, Hester (whose Beacon Hill house was such a refuge for Wheelwright and company; the Stravinskys, recall, were married at the Pickmans' country house outside Boston that year, and it was Hester Pickman who translated Rilke for *Hound and Horn*). Indeed, among the giants only Picasso was not personally in evidence. But such were those heady days that Eddie Warburg all but repaired the omission by buying himself an important early blue-period painting his senior year at Harvard—which Sachs promptly exhibited at the Fogg.[187] Another soon-to-be modernist master also very much at hand was Alexander Calder, who came up from New York, wrote Kirstein, and "gave us the public premiere of his *Circus*, now enshrined in the Whitney Museum."[188] Again "the Boston critics lambasted its presentation at Harvard." (The whole experience was deliciously of the sort Kirstein loved. While staying in Warburg's Holworthy Hall rooms, where Calder had assembled his sculpture, the artist, sitting on the toilet in Warburg's bathroom, noticed the cork plug of a disused gas fixture, which reminded him—alert of eye as always—of a nipple. Forthwith the gas outlet became the left breast of a large and voluptuous nude, which Calder chalked on the bathroom wall, a nude soon famous all over Harvard. Writes Nicholas Fox Weber: "It was the first time that many of America's future leaders saw an actual piece of contemporary art."[189])

The battle was joined, as we saw with Prendergast, intimately as well as globally; also contemporaneously; not all the shows, nor all the lending collectors either, were European, or even New Yorkers! There was one Bostonian with an important collection of modern art, John Spaulding.[190] His treasure, and that of another collector from Washington and a third from Chicago, were resources Kirstein had access to. Indeed, the first one-person Boston show of one of that city's leading contemporary artists, the still shamefully neglected Margaret Sargent, took place in the Harvard Society's first year.[191] Even more of a hit was an exhibition of the work of another scion of Boston's first families, Buckminster Fuller, he of the Dymaxion House and (later) the geodesic dome. Sargent's husband was a Harvard man. So was Fuller. So, too, was Philip Johnson, an undergraduate then who would return to Harvard in the 1940s and as a student in the design school would design a brilliant house for himself on Ash Street, near Harvard Yard, which distinctly foretold his later and more famous Glass House. It was very different from Fuller's Dymaxion House, which Johnson hated, but Fuller's house in its boldness and originality nonetheless bowled Johnson over.

These circles were certainly not all gay. But right from the beginning there was in all Kirstein's projects not only the factor of his own homosexuality, but much broader gay themes. The first issue of *Hound and Horn* was heavy with gay contributors, including Newton Arvin, Henry-Russell Hitchcock, and Virgil Thomson's lover, painter Maurice Grosser. A reproduction of a portrait by Grosser of John Wheelwright also appeared in *Hound and Horn*, as well as another illustration from a very homoerotic painting by the same artist: *Narcisse Noir*, depicting a scantily clad young black man. And for the magazine's logo the designer Rockwell Kent drew a very homoerotic sketch of a muscular nude—almost certainly Kirstein himself—on horseback (Pegasus), being restrained by another man—also nude.[192] Moreover, it went very deep: The name *Hound and Horn* derived from Brahms's "Hunting Horn" trio Kirstein recalled he and Varian Fry first heard (on a viola, rather than a horn) at a musical soirée at Elmwood—the stately home of Mrs. Arthur Kingsley Porter. Such intersections.[193]

There were many others. Professor Alfred North Whitehead, to whom Lucien Price (Chapter 4) was friend and Boswell, and whose daughter, Jessie, was co-guru of bohemian Charles Street on Beacon Hill with Prescott Townsend (Chapter 6), was Philip Johnson's first great hero at Harvard. His second was H.-R. Hitchcock (already noted here as later Newton Arvin's faculty colleague at Smith—that's Chapter 5), who had come to Harvard in 1921 as an ardent disciple of—Professor Porter (Chapter 3). Hitchcock and Johnson became friends after Johnson read an article by Hitchcock published by Kirstein in *Hound and Horn*—"The Decline of Architecture," one of several he wrote at this time (another, which Johnson particularly liked, was on J. J. P. Oud in *The Arts*), which very blatantly heralded the work Hitchcock and Johnson would famously do, within only a few years, defining the new International Style that they in fact christened. Indeed it was actually in *Hound and Horn*—in "Four Harvard Architects" in September 1928—that Hitchcock first used the term *international style*. "Architecture should be devoid of elements introduced for the sake of ornament alone; to the engineering solution of a building problem nothing should be added." Stunned, Philip Johnson had a "Saint Paul experience" that led him ineluctably to architecture.[194] No gridlock at these intersections.

Barr, the author of that 1926 *Harvard Crimson* attack on Boston's conservatism, was a key figure in this scene. "Barr himself," Sybil Kantor has written, "aggressively seeking outlets for the establishment of modernism in the United States, had the opportunity to present [in 1927] the first course in modern art in America (if not in the world) at Wellesley College,"[195] a course that included much architecture (field trips to modernist buildings like Cambridge's Necco Factory and the Back Bay's Motor Mart garage) and missed hardly anything, from films (Fritz Lang's *Metropolis*) and dance (the Ballet Russe) to recitals of music by the likes of George Antheil, Debussy, and Stravinsky, and naturally emphasized the work of Picasso and Matisse.[196]

Meanwhile, Kirstein's efforts on behalf of the Harvard Society for Contemporary Art, far from abating, became even more controversial. In 1932, Kirstein abandoned all restraint and hurled insult in the face of President Abbott Lawrence Lowell, Harvard's great champion of the Jewish quota and validater of Sacco and Vanzetti's execution: that year, in the fall, Kirstein exhibited twenty-three gouaches at the Society's Harvard Square gallery, all by Ben Shahn entitled *The Passion of Sacco and Vanzetti*.[197] Not surprisingly, all the posters advertising the show were removed from Harvard's notice boards. It was not quite being "banned in Boston," but the event was surely meant to burn every bridge in sight from both sides.

The Harvard Thing

"MAKE NO MISTAKE, the Museum of Modern Art began at Harvard,"[198] Munroe Wheeler once asserted, while Kantor reports that Abby Rockefeller, visiting the Fogg on the eve of the museum's founding, told Sachs she wanted to copy in New York "*en gros* what [the Harvard Society] was doing."[199] Sachs, meanwhile, was quick to take control; his account being that he accepted to be a trustee only on the condition, according to Kantor, he be given the right to name the first director. He chose Alfred Barr. And as late as 1950, so keen was the Fogg's continuing interest, that Meredith Clausen, in her biography of Pietro Belluschi, could refer to "Boston, which was then [after Walter Gropius's reign at Harvard] the architectural capital of the country, with even MOMA in New York in effect being run from there."[200] Indeed, the original Harvard Society, while it lasted, Kantor observes, "was always one step ahead of the Museum of Modern Art, showing work never before seen in America," including the first Bauhaus exhibition. In fact, Calder's first one-man show at MOMA was not until nearly fifteen years after his Harvard show, and many of MOMA's earliest and most successful shows were reprises of those conceived by the Harvard Society. At MOMA, moreover, "the values being promulgated were more established than the Harvard Society's in Boston," Nicholas Fox Weber has written. In New York "the congratulations were more readily forthcoming. . . . [That wasn't] what the Harvard boys wanted. The Modern had opened with Seurat and Van Gogh; [the Harvard Society] had charged forward with the likes of Bucky Fuller, Calder, and Brancusi. Nothing could get them to compromise. They were ardent about what they showed."[201]

Meanwhile, Kirstein could not get out of town fast enough. "I wanted to repudiate Harvard, I wanted to repudiate Boston,"[202] he later wrote; this from a man who would carry to as high a summit as anyone in twentieth-century American culture the banner of the "city on a hill," as Boston's founder,

John Winthrop, famously called the new settlement in 1630 in his shipboard sermon before he led the first settlers ashore. The discontinuity is striking and astonishing; and probing it illuminates a theme building throughout this book, as between "home" and "away," a theme disclosed most vividly in Kirstein's own description of his youthful perspective of Boston. Of the Brahmin aristocracy that dominated it he wrote: "Centered on Boston's Beacon Hill, their reign reached to suburbs studded by . . . Adams, Cabot, Emerson, Forbes, Hallowell, Holmes, Lowell, Shaw, Sturgis . . . [and] enclaves north and west of Beacon Hill or Brattle Street—Pride's Crossing, Manchester, Annisquam, Nahant, Milton, Concord, Lexington, and south to Cape Cod and Naushon Island," all places filled, he continued, with "role models at whom I marveled."[203] Not surprisingly, Justice Brandeis more or less had the same feelings as a youth, particularly of Harvard president Charles Eliot, one of his mentors, and there is no doubt Boston was a school for such as they in the late nineteenth and early twentieth century. Thus, Kirstein would declare in his old age, in his memoirs, that his "identification with a society of living and thinking New England dynastic actors gave a security and assurance prompting freedom of action, a sense of inevitability of possibility achieved which I do not think any other locus in America then offered. Wide worlds were open." It was, this Boston, his most formative life experience, its effect utterly liberating, deeply energizing. Note that his key word was *possibility*: "What was magical about Harvard," Kirstein would later write, "was its whiff of limitless possibility."[204]

If Kirstein was right to think his first act could only have happened in Boston, however, under Harvard's venerable umbrella, he soon enough saw that this great civilization—Emerson's, and Thoreau's and Channing's and William Lloyd Garrison's and Henry Adams's and Charles Eliot's and Henry Lee Higginson's and Justice Brandeis's and Amy Lowell's and John Singer Sargent's (and Kirstein's, too, really)—was more and more slipping into eclipse (for only a few generations, it would now appear from a twenty-first-century perspective of Boston's history, but doubtless with every appearance of permanent decline to young Kirstein). Boston was becoming, for him, I suggest, no place for act two. In the 1980s he would write:

> All through this period I was very much preoccupied with Charles Eliot Norton's beautiful estate, where Paul Sachs ruled the roost, and Gerry's Landing, where his partner, Edward Emerson Forbes, gave splendid parties. More glamorous was a house on Beacon Hill where the heirs of Henry Adams and Mrs. Jack Gardner continued their elevated taste and life of the mind. It was the ghost of Henry Adams that presided over *Hound & Horn* . . . and my own attachment to a vanished Boston.[205]

Ghosts, however, Kirstein knew, can only do so much. Especially when their living heirs seem exhausted, unthinking, even hostile. Surely Kirstein felt what Leonard Bernstein would later put very well indeed when he wrote as an undergraduate in *The Harvard Advocate*: "Boston, you must remember, is not a city to be trifled with. If it chooses to sleep it can be very nasty when forcefully wakened. . . . Its resistance to change . . . is phenomenal."[206] There were very few Belle Gardners or Sergei Koussevitzkys who could withstand the attack and endure, much less triumph.

The forces of reaction were so strong in the early twentieth century, I have concluded, because of the preoccupation that sapped much of Bostonians' energies and led eventually to its near strangulation; a situation especially dangerous, moreover, to young Kirstein: the ruinous struggle deeply civicly invested and high-achieving but instinctively clannish and stubborn natives, Boston's Brahmin aristocracy, with much exploited and almost deliberately downtrodden newly arrived immigrants who were deeply resentful. As the Brahmins felt more and more besieged by the great numbers of immigrants, they grew more and more defensive and bigoted; the immigrants, meanwhile, seemed almost to hoard up lovingly their accumulating resentments against their oppressors. This was vexing in many big cities in America, but because of Boston's legacy as the Puritan "city on a hill," as what Oliver Wendell Holmes Sr. called "Liberty's 'virgin home,' its Bethlehem,"[207] and just because the American Athens, as it was so often called, in many ways did live up to its legacy in the nineteenth century, so the never-ending futility of the long ethnic wars was in Boston most acutely disillusioning. Each side—like Thoreau and Emerson—set impossibly high standards for the other, while often bringing out the worst in each other as their expectations were hardly ever met. In the end, only when both sides were swamped after World War II by Boston's increasingly diverse colleges and universities did Boston begin to regain its balance and vitality.

In Kirstein's era what brought all this to a head, of course, was the Sacco-Vanzetti trial, which I think historian H. A. Crosby Forbes is right to think, as he has many times told me, marked the loss of nerve of Boston Brahmins so decisively their role as ruling class was fatally compromised. Certainly it is the clearest continuity of purpose in Kirstein's youth. In *Mosaic*, a half century later, he brings the matter up twice in widely separated references, both startling. In one place Kirstein baldly notes that the chauffeur who drove his father's Rolls-Royce was the "son of the anarchist executed on the opinion of A. Lawrence Lowell, Harvard's president," an indication too of how intimate was Kirstein's link with this protest.[208] The other reference discloses that among the first actions of Kirstein once he moved—fled, really—to Manhattan was one that mirrored his last in Boston: "I bought for the Museum of Modern Art [Ben Shahn's] painting of a Bronx River Bridge, and when in 1932 I organized a mural show from which decorators of Rockefeller Center were to be chosen, he contributed an inflammatory panel of the President of Harvard gloating over the open coffins of Sacco and Vanzetti."[209] Enough said. No one tore down the posters in Manhattan.

The effect of what Brahmins and immigrants warred over, furthermore, was hardly the worst of it for someone like Kirstein. What the Brahmins and most of the immigrants did agree upon was itself problematic, particularly with the Irish, the most numerous and most politically active immigrant group. Each side encouraged the other in a rigid Puritan moralism that began to shade into an increasingly conservative, even philistine, attitude to cultural matters generally and the arts especially. Soon the image of the "Athens of America" was superseded by that of "Banned in Boston." The *Bacchante* controversy of 1895 heralded this: that statue, a gift of Charles McKim for the magnificent new Boston Public Library, was rejected because the joyous—or was it libertine?—nude woman holds both innocent babe and grapes, hardly less provoking than a wineglass. The statue today raises not an eyebrow; then it caused a furor. Boston's Jews, usually progressive both in politics and the arts, were naturally apt to feel somewhat stranded in such a landscape, even at Harvard; though the liberal tradition would come to dominate the law school, the university as a whole was long dominated by conservatives, as the Sacco-Vanzetti scandal showed only too clearly.[210]

Not all affinities in that era between natives and immigrants in Boston ended up so disastrously. When Harvard hired Walter Gropius in the late 1930s the Bauhaus founder and modernist architecture pioneer gave Boston's progressive circles new life as he built on the affinities of the Bauhaus and Puritan aesthetics a movement that would transform American architecture. But that would all flower in a reviving post–World War II Boston, as the Brahmin-immigrant war subsided. Growing up in Boston in the 1910s and '20s, Kirstein certainly felt the hostility of that war in the era of Mayor James Curley at its climax; and surely not less but more as he became sexually self-aware, knowing as he did that the judgment of the time about homosexuality was one of those areas about which both sides, united in their moralism, would be equally condemnatory—and Kirstein doubly vulnerable as a Jew. (Cheever, after all, confronted by a policeman on Commonwealth Avenue, might have been Kirstein.)

So alone and isolated on all counts did young Kirstein feel that he would later write he had not just "no dynasty," but "I had no family."[211] And, absurdly, it was true. It was not just that the Brahmin Boston he loved was losing its nerve and vanishing; even in that Boston, *especially* in that Boston, he could see no place for himself. His was one of the great Jewish families of America; only the Brandeises enjoyed greater stature. And Kirstein was hardly at all overtly discriminated against; at Harvard he had made his way into the highest reaches of intellectual, cultural, and social life. But—in the nicest possible way—it must have been *by his friends* that he was made to feel this way. In the bigoted, narrow Boston Brahmin sense, he *didn't* have a family.

There was a story told about his father, elected (shamefacedly—how could they not elect him, so eminent and public-spirited a citizen-benefactor was Louis Kirstein) to Boston's august Somerset Club. "His refusal [to accept their invitation], he thought, caused less surprise than relief," said his son. Only a few noticed that if the Brahmins had risen above their prejudice to elect Kirstein, in not wanting to in any way seem to take advantage and force himself on anyone, Louis Kirstein showed himself at least as much a Brahmin, in the best sense, as they: he saved his friends a lot of trouble. Stories repeated a hundred years later about Joseph Kennedy Sr. lose a lot of force in retrospect because he later became so morally problematic and was ultimately widely disliked, even despised. But stories about Louis Kirstein keep their force because he was universally admired.

By his son, too; though Lincoln Kirstein did once refer to his father as "one of Boston's housebroken, token aliens," he never forgot his counsel: "My father taught me . . . that the duty, despair, and destiny of Jews was to survive and proceed. Why, or for what," the younger Kirstein wrote, "he left for me to discover."[212]

One might well in that respect ask why Kirstein did not seek out and make common cause after graduation with other like-minded Bostonians; for example, the Harvard group of modernist-leaning architect Nathaniel Saltonstall, touched on previously here. The year the Harvard Society for Contemporary Art finally ran out of steam, 1936, Saltonstall and some friends (including two of the founders of the Harvard Society, Paul Sachs and Agnes Mongan) started the Boston Museum of Modern Art (with a benefit by a Harvard student, Leonard Bernstein, at the Saltonstalls' Beacon Street town house, Bernstein's first public performance) in association with the then six-year-old New York MOMA. The Boston effort, like the Harvard Society for Contemporary Art a noncollecting undertaking, was at first most closely related, however, to the Fogg Art Museum: "The relationship between Harvard art museums and [the Boston MOMA] began with its very first exhibition, a Gauguin show, in May 1936. Organized for the new museum by the Wildenstein Gallery, it was held at the Fogg," Caroline A. Jones has written in *Modern Art at Harvard.* "Other exhibitions were held at the Germanic [now the Busch-Reisinger] Museum," Jones continued, and once the Boston MOMA had its own facility (rented rooms at 14 Newbury Street), exhibitions were shared, including the "pioneering exhibition of Edvard Munch" organized by James Sachs Plaut, Boston's first director (another graduate of the Fogg Museum course of Paul Sachs, his uncle).[213]

Indeed, Boston's new museum became best known, according to critic David Ross, for its "seminal attitude" toward expressionism generally and its "unique advocacy of German and Northern European modernism" particularly, thus reflecting Kirstein's eclectic taste far more than did New York's MOMA under Barr, who made that museum into a temple of abstract art overall, and the School of Paris especially, disdaining all realism or figurative art of any kind, including expressionism, which Barr thought regressive. When in 1948 this conflict came to a head—Plaut insisting "everything produced in our own times" was modern, not just abstract art—Boston dropped "Modern Art" from its name and became the Institute of *Contemporary* Art, an institution for years hobbled by the same Boston conservatism Kirstein protested—but distinctly a survivor—now the oldest noncollecting contemporary arts institution in the country, what Elisabeth Sussman calls an "often controversial renegade offspring of the MOMA" in New York and, from the beginning, always as welcoming to representational as to abstract art. In this, of course, it reflects exactly the nomenclature—as well, of course, as the noncollecting aspect—of the original Harvard Society for *Contemporary* Art,[214] in connection with which it was Kirstein himself, as he reiterated in his memoirs, who had argued for *contemporary* and not *modern* in the society's name.[215]

Whatever kept him and Saltonstall from hooking up was not the basic question, however. By the time Kirstein graduated in 1932, the fierceness of his anger—of almost biblical, prophetic dimensions—was very evident; the real question was whether Kirstein, finally, could deal with his love/hate relationship with Boston at all, especially so long as his father was still so eminent a presence in the old Puritan capital.

For Boston itself, whose cultural riches remain such that few notice how much poorer culturally it still is because of young Kirstein's departure, the loss has only grown more apparent through the years. Kirstein was neither the first nor the last Bostonian to give thanks for New York and move there. But his departure was critical in that it foretold a decline in Boston outside academe of Jewish influence. And because Jews responded historically more to progressive Brahmin intellectualism, whereas the Irish responded at first more to repressive Brahmin moralism, the loss of the Jewish weight on one side of the scale would prove especially problematic, tending to tilt the emphasis in Boston, for example, from the intellectual life and the arts to politics and sports, good things in themselves, of course, but fatal in the way secondary things always are when made primary and central to identity. Emerson's and Brandeis's Boston does indeed survive outside the academy in (Ted) Kennedy's Boston, and in Yo-Yo Ma's, and John Updike's, and the late Stephen Jay Gould's. But in popular imagery, today's highest vocation of the "city on a hill" (to be, as British philosopher Alfred North Whitehead once put it, the capital city, not just of American, but of Western learning)[216] seems too often to pale before rather embarrassing shouts of "Beat the Yankees." Boston's loss of Babe Ruth was a great shame, no doubt. The loss of Lincoln Kirstein was a far greater loss, speaking as it did to Boston's soul, its primary identity.

Thus, historically, in the twentieth century there would come to be two Bostons: the Boston that (in the 1920s) *hired* Roland Hayes as a soloist with the Boston Symphony—the first time an African-American artist appeared in such a role with a major American orchestra[217]—and (in the 1940s) the Boston that rejected Jackie Robinson, the Red Sox being the last team to racially integrate in the major leagues.

Which Boston was it that would tear down (and not replace) its opera house—which Kirstein always remembered fondly: "My first brush with the dance as an autonomous, spectacular activity," Kirstein wrote in 1994, "was in 1916 when Diaghilev's Ballets Russes appeared in Boston's Opera House." As a matter of fact, Kirstein, age nine, was "not permitted to attend," having noisily disgraced himself at the opera house the year before during Puccini's *La Bohème*; Nijinsky was to make his Boston debut and Mrs. Kirstein was concerned lest her son become nettled by "exposure to high emotive display" and the legendary "violence of Nijinsky's performance." What the Kirsteins were up against is clear, however, in the bald reportage of Diaghilev's biographer, Richard Buckle, reportage that caught exactly the two Bostons:

> The tour began at Boston, which, with its neighboring university of Harvard, was the intellectual capital of the United States. It had an opera house . . . and one of the ablest music critics, H. T. Parker, to write about the Ballet. Diaghilev took special trouble over the lighting. [But] Mayor Curley gave instructions to Chief of Police Casey that the Russians were to show no bare flesh except their toes.[218]

To be sure, Buckle admits that Nijinsky's *Faune* was about "sexual orgy and masturbation," controversial everywhere. But although the star's wife, in her biography of her husband, emphasized that they "had many friends in Boston" and that the legendary Nijinsky "enjoyed most evenings in the company of [John Singer] Sargent, who at the time was painting the library in the city, and [with] George Copeland, the pianist, who played Debussy for him,"[219] it seems clear the Nijinskys no less than the Kirsteins (themselves Sargent's good friends) were making the best of a bad situation, one which distinctly pitted Boston's philistines against Boston's sophisticates. By the time young Kirstein was allowed a comparable treat—to see the legendary Pavlova in 1920—the Boston Opera Company was already defunct (Kirstein saw Pavlova at Symphony Hall) and by the time he wrote of all this the city's splendid opera house (the design of his friend John Wheelwright's father's firm) had itself been reduced to rubble, replaced by a parking lot. Significantly the same fate, whenever it has threatened Fenway Park, has been beaten back fiercely.

Who in Boston before World War I would have predicted the opera house's demise? Or the ballpark's triumph? Or that Boston would become the sort of place where it was a case of either/or in the first place? Of course Boston had long been wary of opera and ballet, and the contrast with the Boston Symphony is significant; no one will ever tear Symphony Hall down; in Boston, moreover, baseball is to sports what symphony is to music. But Lincoln Kirstein had different values and a keen critical eye. I suspect by the 1920s, however generally, he would indeed have bet on Fenway Park, not the Boston Opera House, though years later, when Kirstein was closely involved (with Philip Johnson) in the design of Lincoln Center—New York too would tear down its historic opera house, but replace it with one far grander—Kirstein's model for artistic embellishment (thwarted; New York isn't paradise) was modeled on the Boston Public Library. Kirstein never forgot his Boston, having learned it, as it were, the hard way; indeed, its loss cost him something, I believe; though it cost Boston more when in 1932 he departed. "I wanted," he told Nicholas Jenkins bluntly, "to repudiate Harvard, I wanted to repudiate Boston."[220] And so he did.

Moreover, he did so in what looks for all the world a lot like what used to be called "homosexual panic." And though he blurred any focus on that aspect of his life in *Mosaic*, his is really the last sort of life that can be understood without discussion of his sexuality. The reason he so baffled and bewildered one person after another was surely that Kirstein—our last protagonist in this study of the Harvard gay experience—was an unusual fusion of *both* the Wildean and the Whitmanic archetypes at a level of genius or nearly. An aesthete of aesthetes, what Christopher Isherwood nonetheless saw in Kirstein as a young man was "a mad clipper ship captain out of Melville; his hair cropped like a convict's . . . his eyes . . . examining you through a microscope."[221]

A formidable captain. Gaston Lachaise did a number of nude drawings as well as a sculpture of the tall (6'2"), muscled Kirstein, who also posed for several of Lachaise's large bas-relief plaques at Rockefeller Center, and in each what Jenkins calls Kirstein's "commanding physical presence" was inescapable. Commanding and dangerous, this aesthete was no stranger to fisticuffs, as is well conveyed in Pavel Tchelitchev's tripartite portrait, which captures so many different aspects of Kirstein's character: the baseballer in an athletic jacket keeps good company with the business executive in his three-piece suit, and both with the naked Kirstein—who has put on boxing gloves. I am reminded of the frustrations of the hero of Brian Malloy's novel *The Year of Ice*, where Kevin, in love with a classmate, struggles to let it out. Writes reviewer Suzanne Berne:

> The only way Kevin can express his feelings, however, is by tackling his beloved during football games, then slapping the side of his head. "I do this for two reason," Kevin confides. "First, 'cause if I smack him, nobody will guess that I want to pick him up in my arms and kiss him really hard, right on the lips. And, second, he's got to be reminded that I'm tougher than he is."[222]

Kirstein, for all his sophistication, was I think a lot like that. Even in *Mosaic* (his last pass, as an old man, at his Harvard years), he was alternately hiding and in your face insofar as his sexuality was concerned. Yet a close reading of the book discloses the skeleton of virtually another Harvard gay novel, one no less characteristic of the 1920s scene at Harvard than was *Two College Friends* of the Civil War era or *Harvard Episodes* or *The Cult of the Purple Rose* of the fin-de-siècle. Indeed, Kirstein's tale is a kind of variation on a theme of *Brideshead Revisited*, the first part of which is something very close to the great Oxford gay novel of its era, which was also Kirstein's era at Harvard.

The Beautiful Trap

BRIDESHEAD IS TOO much about life in general, its themes universal and transcendent, to be called any kind of gay novel; it is, in fact, more about art and religion than sexuality. Taking a grand but despoiled family seat (called Brideshead in the book; Castle Howard was the setting in the magnificent PBS dramatization of the novel) as a symbol of religious and aristocratic decline into atheistic and vulgar philistinism, *Brideshead*'s author, Evelyn Waugh (yes, a right-wing snob, but perhaps of the best kind), sought in his masterpiece to rescue some understanding of patrician standards for posterity at a time, during World War II, when all trace of them seemed dead or dying. To do so he set himself the task, as he put it, of delineating "the operation of divine grace on a group of diverse but closely connected characters," men and women either upheld by those aristocratic and religious standards or perhaps, according to your point of view, bedeviled by them. A eulogy, as it turned out, a bit premature, Waugh's thesis in *Brideshead* is nonetheless intransigent: Humankind's most splendid achievements, relationships aside, can amount, finally, only to vanity; that there is "no abiding city" beyond the hope of religion, even in the art which expresses that hope.

It is the largest possible subject, of course, about which opinions will always vary. Indeed, Waugh's point of view, darkly conservative Roman Catholic in its theology and to us today also rather Old World in its sexuality, is not mine, though I have more sympathy with his (equally outdated) social theory. But, like so many admirers, I read and reread *Brideshead* because in it homosexuality is treated quite constructively yet realistically in this large context. No other literary work of its stature of the last century (except, perhaps, Proust's *A la recherche du temps perdu*, to which *Brideshead Revisited* has been compared) treats—as Waugh does, brilliantly—homosexual love as so natural and normal in both the long and the short run. And no novel deals with it so idyllically and yet so unromantically, and as so healthy and significant a part of the largest possible human discourse, though no less ruinous—or, indeed, less redemptive—in its possibilities than heterosexual love. That discourse can seem to a gay person today at times hostile. But Waugh's novel could not in actuality be more gay-positive, as we would now say, above all in the way *Brideshead* compasses both opposite-sex and same-sex love, if anything somewhat privileging the gay variant, in its most overarching (and most positive) theme, which critic Frank Kermode saw as Waugh's insistence that "to know and love one other human being is the root of all wisdom."[223]

I could not agree more about that basic thesis or that it is central to Waugh's own; indeed it is central as well to this study of the Harvard gay experience. I would only add how necessary it is today to make the distinction between "know and love" and "in love with." Waugh's subject, supremely, is the former. However, that said, it is not the least interesting aspect of *Brideshead Revisited* that while it by no means focuses on sexual appetites or worldly luxuries generally—certainly not on what today we'd call the gay lifestyle—the book does not ignore sexual appetites. In fact, Waugh very much affirms their benefit, as Kermode also sees: "Sex is also an agent, though a devious one, of grace," Kermode writes. He adds, more generally, that to be at "paradisial Brideshead"—"Brideshead before the Fall"—was "for various reasons, and not only for its luxuries, to be very near heaven." An astonishing comparison, it is not only Kermode's—it is Waugh's, similar to another comparison even more remarkable, also Waugh's: *Brideshead*, finally, is not least about youth, the languors of which Waugh insists in his book are in some sense comparable to the Beatific Vision itself.[224] And those languors, as they appear in the pages of *Brideshead*, are very gay indeed.

Certainly neither Lord Sebastian Flyte, the svelte, worldly, charming, tennis-playing, wine-loving sybarite "renowned for his beauty,"[225] and Charles Ryder, curious, handsome, slower, but steadier-seeming, as plucky but more levelheaded than Sebastian, are celebrated by Waugh, each of them, as most vital and intense friends and lovers, deeply invested in the other. Nor, when their idyll hits the rocks, does it do so for any of the stereotypical reasons or yield any of the conventional outcomes. Their lives, to be sure, both unravel. Charles goes on to become a minor painter (emphasis on the minor) and to marry and divorce, and then falls in love with one of Sebastian's sisters only for both to be thwarted, in much the same way as he and Sebastian were. Sebastian, meanwhile, increasingly an exile, living somewhere in North Africa, turns into a rootless, dissipated alcoholic. He suffers greatly and it is indeed because he, more than anyone, has been in his youth psychologically maimed; but this is not in any way imputed to his sexuality, but to his aristocratic—and very devout—mother, a highly dysfunctional lady, as we would say today (a devout "femme fatale" Sebastian calls her), whom no one—not even the steady Charles—can hope to rein in. (Himself devout as well as conservative, Evelyn Waugh was, however, no fool.)

Nor does Sebastian's suffering ever defeat him: he is, when last heard of, ever-loving and ever-loved—in fact, very holy—the disgrace of his downfall is not seen at all as his but as the result of how badly his family has treated him. Truly, in a very real sense, everything Sebastian touches in *Brideshead Revisited* turns to gold; at least every person profits very much by the experience of knowing him, including Charles, whose soul Sebastian, then Julia, saves. *Brideshead Revisited* is the graduate course; thus not for everyone. And something very similar can be said of Lincoln Kirstein and his story—and from the beginning, even before sexuality comes into it at all, for sons of wealthy and civic-minded Jews at Harvard were situated entirely comparably in the 1920s socially to aristocratic Roman Catholics like Sebastian at Oxford.[226]

Curiously, not a lot has ever been made of the Harvard connections, both literary and historical, that arise in Oxford-oriented *Brideshead*; several of them, as one might expect, are more or less gay-tinged. Two examples come to mind. There is the episode (admittedly more Waugh than Harvard in its gay coloration) where Anthony Blanche, an outrageously effeminate friend of Sebastian's, declaims *The Waste Land* (thereby disclosing, by the way, at least a whiff of a contemporary homosexual perception of the poem) from the balcony of Sebastian's rooms in Christ Church during the luxurious lunch at which Charles and he embark on their affair in earnest.[227] Then, too, the inn at Thame, near Oxford, where Blanche tries to turn Charles against Sebastian one night at dinner, was once a very real inn Waugh knew well, the Spreadeagle, whose picturesque proprietor, John Fothergill (a protégé of Oscar Wilde's best friend, Robert Ross), was set up in business by Ned Warren, the Harvard aesthete to which Boston's Museum of Fine Arts owes so much of its classical collection.[228]

Lincoln Kirstein in the 1920s—in the same decade as Waugh set down Charles and Sebastian at Oxford in his novel (written in 1944)—mostly played Charles Ryder's part at Harvard: "I went full of curiosity," Charles wrote of that first lunch with Sebastian, on the strength of whose quick response he would find in his host all he so truly sought beyond that "low door in the wall" which Charles was sure somewhere at Oxford opened on an "enclosed and enchanted garden." Recalled Kirstein in this vein at Harvard: "I cast myself as an adventurer, though I was one without much of a passport."

As Charles made good a similar lack with Sebastian, however, so did Lincoln Kirstein with one of his own classmates. And though in Kirstein's case there was also *Hound and Horn* and the Harvard Society for Contemporary Art to help him gain "tentative admittance to a map of Xanadu," the low door to the garden one imagines as hardly less enclosed or enchanted in Kirstein's mind than Ryder's was opened in Kirstein's case at Harvard by Francis Cabot Lowell.[229]

August name, handsome lad (Frank to his friends): young Lowell was of those Boston Lowells who we are told by ancient rhyme talked only with Cabots, who themselves talked only with God. Nephew to poet Amy Lowell, also to astronomer Percival Lowell (discoverer of the "canals" of Mars) and as well to Guy Lowell, architect of Boston's Museum of Fine Arts, Frank Lowell, above all, was nephew to Harvard's president, Abbott Lawrence Lowell.

When Kirstein and Lowell first meet, like Charles and Sebastian in *Brideshead*, it is in circumstances tellingly, even annoyingly, physical, if vaguely erotic. Whereas Sebastian throws up through the open window of Charles's ground-floor room at Oxford, but most dashingly outfitted in full evening dress, in Kirstein and Lowell's case they are in line at an infirmary, waiting half naked for a physical, but at an age when such a fleshly experience of the right person can be exciting. Certainly Kirstein remembered it so:

> impatient and bored . . . I turned around and glanced at the broad, bare chest, and then the face, of [Frank Lowell]. A youth of arresting stance, close-cropped fair hair and a big chin, he exuded a wide breadth of ruddy, muscular command. We exchanged tritenesses. . . . Then a few moments later I heard him ask if I'd chosen a roommate for the coming year. . . . With a surge of pure, animal attraction I heard myself (with some other person's voice) say: "I've got a place. Would you like to look at it?" He faced me, hard, for seconds, and said, "Sure."[230]

Although the two hit it off, from the first Kirstein sounds more like Charles than Frank Lowell does Sebastian. In fact, Kirstein seemed almost sometimes to play both parts. Even then his was a psyche intricate enough to carry it off. Lowell's seems more straightforward, not surprisingly; it was he who seemed to take to heart the advice to Charles of cousin Jasper in *Brideshead*: perhaps the bit about avoiding Anglo-Catholics because they were all sodomites (substitute Jews in Kirstein's case); certainly the warning that if Charles didn't watch out, his second year at Oxford would be all used up trying to live down (and shed) the friends made in his first year. At the end of sophomore year, it was Lowell who dumped Kirstein.[231]

Such youthful abandonments are always traumatic; think Edward Gorey, dismayed when at junior year's end he was dropped by Frank O'Hara. Kirstein blamed himself in his autobiography—alluding plausibly enough to his frequent borrowings of Lowell's clothes and his tipsy late hours (his roommate, wrote Kirstein, was "a steady, single-minded puritan: no nonsense or waste motion"). Carefully, almost too carefully, he absolved Lowell absolutely of any suspicion of bigotry; indeed, Lowell himself, he knew, was "by no means enchanted with the social landscape into which he'd been born."[232] All of which—for one cannot but see how protective of Lowell Kirstein was—makes more likely my own surmise that Lowell's dumping marked, in fact, the end of some sort of affair.

Am I too wildly speculating? Certainly Kirstein signals unmistakably his lust of Lowell ("a surge of pure animal attraction" leaves very little to even the post-Victorian imagination), and Lowell, in first bringing up the matter of becoming roommates in such a situation, seems to have played his part. And if only a year together seems to suggest the relationship soon seemed somehow storm-tossed or star-crossed—even unwise in the first place ("I heard myself [with some other person's voice]")—an even sharper intimation that the depths of *Brideshead* are found here, too, comes immediately in Kirstein's subsequent account of his increasingly complicated relations with Frank Lowell's family.

In *Brideshead*, Sebastian does everything he can to keep Charles away from his family—baldly admitting he is afraid they will charm Charles and seduce him away.[233] But it is to no avail; and Kirstein seems to suggest this very thing happened in his case when he writes: "[By] the time we parted, I'd been bounteously adopted by [Frank's] father, mother, and two sisters." Adopted? Perhaps *suborned* would have been Frank Lowell's word. If so, it was Sebastian's part Lowell played that time, or so it seems when Kirstein frankly writes that the Lowell family "bestowed on me the unadulterated balm which I had failed to purloin from Frank."[234]

None of them were unworthy, it must be said, these Boston aristocrats, of comparison with the lordly Flytes of Brideshead, whether Lord or Lady Marchmain or Sebastian's brother or sisters: the father, Fred Lowell, was a good-enough painter that Kirstein offered him a one-man show sponsored by the Harvard Society for Contemporary Art; the mother Kirstein described as "an exquisitely aging, *carte de visite* replica of Louisa May Alcott or Emily Dickinson"; while Frank's sisters ring even deeper bells as Kirstein describes them: enter Lady Julia and Lady Cordelia, Sebastian's sisters, the first of whom Charles calls really Sebastian's all-but-identical twin, stage left;[235] stage right: enter Alice and Marianna Lowell, of the first of whom Kirstein writes, "she might have been Frank's twin." Shades of Charles Ryder, whose glorious revels in 1920s Oxford had nothing on Lincoln Kirstein's romps through Harvard during the same decade: "Thus," Kirstein recalled, "I came to bask in a most delectable season. I no longer lacked a passport; by the middle of that year [rooming with Frank Lowell] my name was listed with the mother of every debutante in Boston for coming-out balls. . . ."[236]

As was also the case with Ryder's story in *Brideshead*, in Kirstein's, too, "town" (Boston's Back Bay and Old Cambridge neighborhoods instead of London's St. James's quarter and collegiate Oxford) was only the half of it: "country" (for Kirstein, instead of Brideshead, the Lowells' estate west of Boston, set amid the then rural suburbs of Concord and Lexington) was almost more important. Kirstein became intimately familiar with the Lowells' "large, hip-roofed castle of comfort, shingled in the [Eighteen-] Eighties," the amenities of which ranged from "a wide inglenook clad with Morris and De Morgan tiles" and "clipper-ship models under bell-glass, marine mementoes of whale bone or narwhal tusks made by Salem 1812 prisoners of war" to "delicious light Swiss suppers of cheese fondues, melon balls, raw spinach, walnuts, and cocoa."[237] Lincoln Kirstein lived in the Lowell castle a life he would describe as an old man as no less idyllic than the one Waugh portrayed Sebastian and Charles enjoying at Brideshead before setting out for Venice.[238] Wrote Kirstein:

> In heedless bewitchment I dreamed of marrying Alice or Marianna: preferably both. Thereby, I'd become Frankie's brother (skip the "in-law" . . .). I'd learned to ride . . . and, by dint of practice . . . I advanced

to elementary exercises in classic dressage.... We rode daylong ... across field and pasture, through heavy woods. We dismounted on the edge of Walden Pond to toss stones into a cairn already heaping to Thoreau's memory. In Lexington there was a cottage upon whose small window panes Nathaniel Hawthorne had scratched both his and his wife's names. In its parlor ... Jack Ames ... gave us tea, while the horses cropped grass on a front lawn which had not been mown since Hawthorne's day. . . .

The quatrain of my Harvard years reads as an Edenic golden age.[239]

The shift in focus (but only the immediate focus) from Frank to his sisters comes earlier in Kirstein's story than Charles Ryder's shift in *Brideshead* from Sebastian to his sisters, Julia and Cordelia, the first of whom (the twin) Charles all but marries. But the storylines—in each case of life thwarted—are practically identical at this point, first at Harvard and then in Concord and Lexington for Kirstein, at Oxford and at Brideshead for Ryder, and, finally, for Kirstein not Venice, as for Ryder, and then World War II, but New York and Paris the decade after graduation. When Ryder describes himself at book's end in *Brideshead* as "homeless, childless, middle-aged and loveless," he is hardly very much ahead of Kirstein after his graduation from Harvard.

For Kirstein as for Ryder, moreover, there was the same lingering aftertaste, the same warm, ebullient summer turned to harshest winter; the same idyllic happiness seemingly paid for over and over again in some kind of (however sybaritic or otherwise successful, on the surface) exile from what mattered most, it hardly mattered whether homosexual or heterosexual. There was, too, the same redemption or nearly—in Charles's case through Catholicism, in Kirstein's through the arts, dance particularly. And Kirstein's self-judgment in the end is as harsh as Charles's, harsher because it is Sebastian who sends a heartsick Charles away, saying he is "no help"; Kirstein, on the other hand, though equally heartsick, wrenches free himself. "Even while I savored every gilded moment up to the hilt," Kirstein recalled, "I came to dread the 'life' I'd been living as a fictive veneer upon which I had no claim"—it is the invariable lament of the outsider, whether unsuitable in sexual orientation or racial heritage or social standing—"and I was eventually driven to mean-spirited, total repudiation of it. After I came to Manhattan in 1931, I never saw Concord or Lexington again." Insisted Kirstein: "I wanted to put a finish to Harvard and Boston."[240] Significantly, his attack on President Lowell in exhibiting *The Passion of Sacco and Vanzetti* at Harvard was equally insulting to Frank Lowell, President Lowell's nephew. That year, 1932, Lincoln Kirstein departed from Boston, and from the Lowells, for good.

If he was spared Charles Ryder's return to a despoiled Brideshead, Kirstein also had his shock years afterward—the Lowells themselves, as a family, encountered once more in his life, and one of the sisters after that. It was in a New York theater lobby during the intermission of an opera Kirstein was producing, as much a chance reunion as Charles's revisiting Brideshead. But the deeper comparison is really with Charles's surprised encounter at his gallery opening (a decade after their last meeting) with Anthony Blanche, whose postmortem about Charles in a London gay bar afterward is utterly devastating. So was Kirstein's on himself, as he described his running into the Lowells:

> We stood in the theater lobby with little to say. How to justify or explain churlish guilt, with my overmastering compulsion to be rid of it all?
>
> I'd been hypnotized by a false position, which I'd not dared define and had coolly tossed away. . . . I wrenched myself loose from a beautiful trap. Twenty years on I tried to apologize to Marianna. . . . Trying to evade a gush of shame and sorrow, I quit the dinner table, compounding my ferocious sadness with trivial discourtesy.[241]

L'Envoi

NOT ONLY LINCOLN Kirstein but his circle generally seems to have made it a point after graduating from Harvard to get no closer to New England's capital than Hartford, Connecticut—as far away from Boston as one could get and still be in New England. *Four Saints in Three Acts* received its world premiere there in 1934, at that city's Athenaeum, on to which Chick Austin also added a modernist version of Harvard's Fogg Art Museum courtyard, and it was there that Kirstein himself first thought to launch the ballet he was determined America would have, its home, like McKim's *Bacchante*, in New York, where Kirstein's most enduring accomplishment may be to have founded the New York City Ballet, soon enough among the world's greatest dance companies. This is not the place to detail his career; sufficient to quote Nicholas Jenkins's observation that Kirstein went on to become "a massive presence in American culture."[242]

As had been the case with the Harvard Society for Contemporary Art, it was not just New York's Museum of Modern Art that reflected Kirstein's insistence that contemporary art in America should be *American* art. So, too, was this evident in dance. Thus *Alma Mater*, for instance, the first public performance of the American Ballet (significant name), trained by the genius Kirstein brought to America to accomplish his goal, George Balanchine. The subject hadn't changed. Its chief protagonist was a sort of punch-drunk halfback, its costumes were designed by John Held, sometime illustrator of the Yale/Princeton game program. *Alma Mater* was a tongue-in-cheek ode to the rah-rah stadium set, "a ballet," a *Newsweek* photo caption explained, "in which Harvard satirizes Yale."[243]

Or was one Harvard perhaps satirizing another Harvard? Every school has its rah-rah types. They come, so to speak, in all types and sizes, including intellectuals. What is it that Boston Latin School students famously chant at football games? "Pursue them! Pursue them! Make them relinquish the ball!"[244] Leonard Bernstein, a Latin School graduate, certainly knew that cheer. So probably did another, George Santayana, and Isabella Stewart Gardner, too, fixtures all in Harvard football history, where the cast of characters just in this book has included people both in the stands and on the team. Indeed, who is satirizing whom—in Harvard stadium or anywhere else within our purview here (satirizing or admiring or blaming or aping or taking inspiration from or making fun of or just plain needing)—is a most subtle business, as I hope by now has become clear.

What does stand out more clearly in this book's finale, in which I have deliberately cast first Bernstein and then Kirstein in the lead, is that (both being so much men of their era and thus as adept at denial as *all* the makers, for instance, of *West Side Story*), it is a nice question which was more of a problem for either man, being a Jew or being a homosexual. Certainly in the case of each man *both* their ethnicity and their sexuality troubled their native Boston—ever by inheritance the Puritan capital, however cosmopolitan (who was it who called John Fitzgerald Kennedy an Irish Brahmin?)—just as Harvard, however diverse, is ever the Puritan boast ("till the stock of the Puritans die").[245] Certainly, too, both their ethnic and sexual "disabilities" in Boston seemed almost assets in New York; the two men are only the last of many we've met here who document that; though the point has never perhaps been more dramatically made than in the way the New York Philharmonic, graceful herald of that city's more diverse and opportunistic boast, sought Bernstein as eagerly as the Boston Symphony—"aristocrat of orchestras"—rejected him. New York, though it has, historically, loved Yale and Princeton more, seems hardly to have loved Harvard less.

Which leads to another, larger, question. If, indeed, there is a Harvard sensibility, or a Boston sensibility, or a Jewish or an American or a Southern or a New York or a medieval or modern sensibility, or a leftist or rightist or a warrior or an aesthete sensibility—are there not also sexual, as there are ethnic and vocational and period and regional and gender, sensibilities? Is there not a gay sensibility?

For me at book's end the question has now become a hypothesis—of course there is a gay sensibility, likely more than one. Don't ask, don't tell is *not* an adult response to anything. To be sure, all this is another book. Yet this hypothesis seems to me the climax of this book, raised exactly in venerable Harvard Yard, where we have found in Harvard's own gay experience, historically, so many instances of such a sensibility helping to shape American culture so largely.

Wherefore Harvard? Do not forget the Whitmanic musings about the swaying elms of its ancient yard, scribbled by the chief protagonist of *Two*

College Friends, on a Civil War battlefield. Or too quickly scant the Wildean purple lamp lit in the same yard in the fin-de-siècle, still spoken of nearly a hundred years later. Think of Andrew Holleran's foggy early morning in Lowell House court, and why that court was the scene of his projected sequel to *Brideshead Revisited*. (Of course, 1960s Brideshead/Harvard was very much a middle-class experience; Kirstein's 1920s Brideshead/Harvard was comparable to Waugh's Oxford. The mansion belonging to Kirstein's parents on Boston's Commonwealth Avenue was as grand as Marchmain House in London.)

Think, finally, as he went in search of Sebastian Flyte, how many Charles Ryder spoke for at Harvard as much as at Oxford (and do not forget Tchaikovsky or Bernstein or most of all Copland): "I went," Ryder declared, "full of curiosity, and the faint, unrecognized apprehension that here, at last, I should find that low door in the wall, which others, I knew, had found before me, which opened on an enclosed and enchanted garden, which was somewhere, not overlooked by any window, in the heart of that grey city."[246]

Or, instead, consider a rural New England landscape where stands a landmark, now a memorial, designed by one Harvard friend for another, both gay, both important shapers of American culture: Philip Johnson's evocation of (tribute to? commentary on?) Lincoln Kirstein on his Connecticut estate. Near to the Glass House, so happy a passage in the life of American architecture, whatever it be to Johnson, the Kirstein Tower is an abstract congregation of concrete cubes, which Johnson describes as "a staircase that goes nowhere." What does that mean? Why are the steps "very, very high"? Says its designer: "You're up in the air with no support, no nothing." The interviewers, Hilary Lewis and John O'Connor, recall Johnson referring in connection with the Kirstein Tower to his concept of "safe danger," a concept that with reference to another work of his provoked Johnson to ask: "And the whole question of safe danger in my plans . . . is that sexual or not? Probably."[247]

Two other critics, Stover Jenkins and David Mohney, also note Johnson's observation that "danger can make one appreciate architecture to a much greater degree," and that this clearly informs their own description of the tower: "Those with the fortitude to make it to the tower's top can read an inscription honoring Lincoln Kirstein on a small plaque embedded in the highest brick."[248] Fortitude? Danger? What does it mean that Johnson built this tower? Or that Kirstein himself—although he was alive and able when Johnson designed it in 1985—never climbed it, not at least by 1994, the date of the Johnson interview about it. Only Johnson himself has climbed it. Why? And why does he insist one climb it to read the inscription? Did he make an exception for Kirstein? The inscription has never been published. Who says that at the turn of the twentieth and the twenty-first centuries the gay subculture has lost that beguiling habit of revealing to conceal and concealing to reveal? Not at Harvard.

Acknowledgments

TEN YEARS AGO, in 1992, I began work in earnest on *Boston Bohemia,* volume one of my biography of Ralph Adams Cram, the first of my books of particular relevance to the field of Gay and Lesbian studies. Although I have persevered as well in architectural history—my study of the life and work of Isabella Stewart Gardner, *The Art of Scandal,* appeared in 1997; a second volume bound in with the first of *Built in Boston* followed in 1999; while my *Harvard University: An Architectural Tour* came out just last year— the perceptive reader will find in *The Crimson Letter,* not certainly the second volume of the Cram study (which is yet to come), but very much a companion volume to *Boston Bohemia;* Boston and Harvard being forever two sides of the same thing, it was, I suppose, only to be expected.

There is, however, a kind of underground history to all this, first mooted by Peter Gomes, Harvard's Plummer Professor, when he observed in a review of *Boston Bohemia* that while it had received good notices in a wide variety of learned and popular media throughout the country, and was one of five finalists for the PEN/Winship Prize for Best New England book of the Year, no Boston media (including *The Boston Globe*) had reviewed it (with the single exception, later, of Christopher Lydon on NPR). Gomes went on to opine—I thought then melodramatically—that particularly in the old Boston ruling-class enclaves of State Street bankers and Social Register dowagers my work, if it continued to explore sexuality as much as architecture, would increasingly threaten such circles, however unreasonably, and end up, not "banned" (even in Boston, especially in Boston, that's no longer done), but "ignored"—ignored to death, of course, being the hope.

Although Professor Gomes has not seen the manuscript of *The Crimson Letter,* given the way I always emphasize in my acknowledgments those people and institutions to be credited with having a significant impact on the creative process, he must be my first acknowledgment here. As one of the first black professors at Harvard and one of the first gay Republicans anywhere, he was not being melodramatic at all; just confirming the counsel to me about the same time of Prudence Steiner, a leader in Harvard Hillel, to whom goes my second thank-you note, who counseled me in a dispute with a certain dean (over the vetoing of a Harvard gay history walking tour I'd proposed) that one had to keep close watch the better you got, especially on those who as you rose in prominence found you more threatening and would thus themselves be more dangerous.

Never mind. Boston is to New York, it's often been said, as London is to Paris, and it's hard to cast oneself as the victim when, far from having been hurt by the *Globe,* my next book ended up featured in brilliant color on the front cover of *The New York Times Book Review.* That was the Gardner biography and, similarly, though I've never been asked to speak even once at the Gardner Museum—even when my biography of its founder was lauded as a *Times* Notable Book of the Year—I am content to have been asked to talk instead about Gardner at the Phillips Collection in Washington. I even somewhat enjoy the irony in feeling forced to resign from the Harvard Club of Boston in the year between the publication of my two books about Harvard. Nor do I mind probably as much as I should that the Boston Public Library still refuses to publish (though they have duly paid for it) my evidently too inclusive guide to that landmark. Or, indeed, that the Gardner Museum grows, not less, but more narrow-minded, refusing now even to sell my biography of its founder. I've gotten used to it. And I don't expect reading *The Crimson Letter* will change their minds, either.

Behold, the next acknowledgment: Michael Denneny, senior editor in 1997 of St. Martin's Press. Himself a legend, the father of gay publishing in this country, Michael was unswayed by a certain Boston publisher's aversion to my work—turned down the Gardner book flat, later a bestseller—and Michael made sure *The Crimson Letter* would happen against considerable odds, financial as well as ideological.

There *is* always another side to it—even in Boston, where the Gardner Museum staff, by the way, just directs inquiries for my book at their bookstore to the Museum of Fine Arts' shop down the street, which does a brisk business in selling it. Nor can the powers that be at the Gardner entirely suppress me there, either, thanks to Harvard's Freshman Dean's Office, which asks me every year to lead a group of incoming freshmen on a tour of the Gardner. It's even got to the point that the Boston Athenaeum recently asked me to lecture, not on architecture, but on Gay and Lesbian studies: "The Saint Botolph Club Visits Trinity Church; or, John Singer Sargent Has a Date with Phillips Brooks" was a success, thanks initially to the courage of its first proposer, Crystal Flores, and the later support of Richard Wendorf and Stephen Nonack. (That's *Bishop* Brooks, by the way—and another club I felt forced to resign from.)

On the subject of my (increasingly notorious, I fear) Gardner Museum talks for freshmen, which touch prominently, of course, on the Harvard gay experience in Isabella Stewart Gardner's day, I am happy to be able to report (as the Gardner Museum will surely not be to hear) that it was one of my student interlocutors at one of those talks, Amit R. Paley, who broke the story in 2002 in *The Harvard Crimson* of an important and hitherto un-known (to me at least) slice of Harvard history, the story of President Abbott Lawrence Lowell's encouragement of a quite secret "court" of administrators who in 1920 mounted quite a brutal persecution of homosexuals at Harvard. Paley's article disclosed two related student suicides in the 1920s, either of which makes for a telling comparison with the faculty suicide discussed here (of one of Harvard's greatest luminaries, A. K. Porter) in the next decade. It would be easy to exaggerate my role as any sort of spark of such incendiary journalism; but one could hardly exaggerate the importance of Paley's and *The Crimson's* role in exposing such a scandal, indisputably Harvard's own.

The journalist's, of course, in the well-worn phrase, is the first draft of his-tory; the historian, whose job it is to construct the final draft, even if one of several, must wait for the dust to settle. Paley's material is raw material indeed, still unsifted, and a bit naïve. As Harvard professor Warren Goldfarb said to me, it would be interesting to delve into cases in the years since the 1920s, as people continued to be expelled for being gay in our own lifetimes (and still are in the armed forces). The *Crimson* article was a brilliant job of investigative reporting, but it tells us nothing new, nor is it by itself more than a dramatic footnote. (It's a basis, I think, for a better play than for a historical work.)

The times do continue to change, do they not? In fact, as I look back on the decade since *Boston Bohemia* first raised the subject of gay Harvard, it has clearly been a decade less of harassment (for me certainly) than of gathering strength and support, which began, after all, with the decision of Bruce Wilcox and the University of Massachusetts Press to publish *Boston Bohemia* in the first place, despite the attacks on it by one of the readers of the manuscript. But for that decision of ten years ago *The Crimson Letter* would never have happened at all. Thereby, moreover, hangs yet another tale, a more personal one but hardly less important.

Emerson, though he is ever the individualist, writing that "the condition high friendship demands is ability to do without it. . . . we must be our own before we can be another's," asserts in his great essay on friendship (being also ever the realist) that "we walk alone in the world. Friends such as we desire are dreams and fables." Yet he adds at once: "But a sublime hope cheers ever the faithful heart, that elsewhere . . . souls are now acting, en-during, and daring, which can love us, and which we can love."

Such a community of souls must always come to mind, of course, at any book's end, when one begins to add up all the debts that have accumulated during its research and writing; but in the case at decade's end of *The Crim-son Letter* these debts are especially keenly felt. And require me to be very clear in my terms, *friendship* being a word often I think ill understood.

Two elements of friendship are identified by Emerson, each sovereign:

One is truth. . . . Every man alone is sincere. At the entrance of a second person, hypocrisy begins. . . . but a friend . . . exercises not my ingenuity, but me. . . . The other element of friendship is tenderness. We are holden to men by every sort of tie, by blood, by pride, by fear, by hope, by lucre, by lust, by hate, by admiration . . . but we can scarce believe that so much character can subsist in another as to draw us by love.

What a wonderful evocation of the ideal exchange in a friendship—truth and tenderness—and one which Emerson gets quickly to the root of when he describes its acting out in "conversation, which is the practice and consummation of friendship."

Consummation? It is a word more frequently used of lovers' sex than friends' talk. Yet how significant that Emerson only deepens the comparison when he brings to my mind that old truism—"two's company, three's a crowd"—not about romance, but about friendship, the context in which he finds the "law *of one to one* preemptory for conversation. . . . three cannot take part in a conversation of the most sincere and searching sort." Arguing that the "freedom of great conversation . . . requires the absolute running together of two souls into one," and that there are, really, no "great conversationalists" except with the right person ("it is affinity that determines which two shall converse"), Emerson—a member of many Boston dining clubs—frowns as much, in the context of close friendship, on the conversational threesome or foursome or whatever as most of us would on the sexual threesome or any form of orgy.

A digression: Our own day-to-day experience is surely telling in these respects. In our youth especially, when the single person, gay or straight, as much out of curiosity as hormones, is so much more likely to set aside the constraints of morality in such matters, how many sexual partners—chosen, of course, mostly for their looks—have we cheerfully romped in bed with only to endure thereafter a tedious breakfast? Then in middle age, when our choice of partner if we are still single will hopefully have something more to do with personality than looks alone, breakfast, so to speak, becomes dinner; and it's dinner that's the revel, not the sexual grappling thereafter, which is now what is apt to be found tedious, more and more documenting Gore Vidal's controversial truism that we do not always have sex with the person we're in bed with, but, instead, often with another partner in our imagination (not as creepy as it sounds, by the way: Vidal's point being that sophisticated people ought to be able to enjoy sharing knowledge of each other's imaginary—usually younger—partner; in their after-talk at least, if not in their foreplay).

Still, it is a bit grim sounding. Not quite the ideal. Yet how to avoid it all? Douglass's Law: in youth, skip breakfast—be honest, be blunt; don't (after your romp in the sack) linger even for coffee. Take off. It may even be kinder in the long run. After early middle age, on the other hand, skip the sex; be blunt still; after dinner go home alone, concentrate on Santayana's advice to cultivate a "chastity of the mind," no less vital than that of the body, hope for sweet dreams—and another dinner.

Another digression. Douglass's law, of course, signals unmistakably that the author of *The Crimson Letter* is a decade older now than the author of *Boston Bohemia*; in high middle age at fifty-something, and, indeed, peering over its stout ramparts to late middle age. Moreover, the fact is not that youth hasn't always wanted breakfast, too, or middle age sex (old age, too, probably) but that youth is as seldom up to conversation as middle age to sex. The body—however hard you work at it, or medicate it—does not improve as one ages; the mind can; as Oscar Wilde said so well: "the body is born young and grows old. . . . life's tragedy." But he saw too that "the soul is born old, but grows young. That is the comedy of life."

Comedy and tragedy, Wilde's wit discloses at once why conversation, unlike sex, has no ruses (however benign) like the erotic ones Vidal highlights to fall back on. Nor, frankly, needs: this substitution of friends for lovers in mid-life marks no decline. Emerson again:

> Love, which is the essence of God, is not for levity, but for the total worth of man. . . . Happy the house that shelters a friend! . . . He who offers himself a candidate for that covenant, comes up, like an Olympian, to the great games, where the first-born of the world are the competitors. He proposes himself for contests where Time, Want, Danger, are in the lists, and he alone is victor who has truth enough in his constitution to preserve the delicacy of his beauty from the wear and tear of all these. The gifts of fortune may be present or absent, but all the speed in that contest depends on intrinsic nobleness, and the contempt of trifles.

Contests? While certainly professedly Socratic, I would put less emphasis on that aspect than Emerson does; the reason I am the self-appointed secretary of all my regular lunches and dinners with friends is that they are an effective counter to a scholar's necessary (and hardly always welcome) solitude. But the fact is that this long riff on friendship as I understand it— what Emerson calls "high friendship"—is by way of explaining the meaning of the chief acknowledgments of this book, which all the others herald: the important interlocutors of my daily life, my "regulars" at one encounter after another, usually quite long (and liquid) meals.

Such things can wax or wane, of course; circumstances (nearly always arising out of family life or geography) can close down many valued possibilities; it was Elizabeth Bowen, the Anglo-Irish writer whom Charles McGrath has likened to a darker Jane Austen, who observed, "the heart may think it knows better: the senses know that absence blots people out. We have really no absent friends." I think of Jamie Hardigg, and Kurt and Mary Jane Sligar. There is, however, a hard core I have found myself depending on during the difficult two years of writing this book, to whom I shall always be especially grateful: Joe McGrath, one of my oldest friends (and, indeed, an important participant in some of the historical events chronicled in *The*

Crimson Letter); Peter Kadzis, who read the manuscript with the keen eye of both editor and friend—in which order I would not like to say; and Michael DeLacey, who is always, thank God, as critical as he is sympathetic; Michael's description of friendship, for example, is one I cherish—"when you see through someone but still quite like the view." Weekly or nearly, at lunch or dinner, I benefit greatly from knowing these men, to whom my smartest salute.

I've also benefited from less frequent but still fairly regular talk with Crosby Forbes, Tim O'Donnell, B. Hughes Morris, Archie Epps, Smoki Bacon and her husband, Dick Concannon, Jeff Mills, Jon Shaw, Dennis Sheehan, Michael Klineschmidt, Carl Scovel, Bruce Jenneker, Bill Fowler, and Richard Newman, the last two of whom also read the manuscript and favored me with their criticism, for which I am grateful. I think it fair to say Bill leans to the right and Richard to the left, and both have always made so much sense to me I hardly like to reach any view in the absence of either of theirs.

THE ONLY OTHER person who has read any part of all of my manuscript—which is to say the parts of it in which he arises—is the man to whom *The Crimson Letter* is dedicated, alas anonymously, the necessary explanation for which brings us back to Emerson, who in this department too is a good guide, as when in the essay on friendship he writes of "unrequited love," which, like the word *consummation*, is now more often used for erotic love than for friendship love. That has, of course, its sexual aspect (what doesn't?), but seems today—when sex more often validates love instead of the other way around—so much less important. After all, does not sex always trump conversation?

Not in my experience. Though it is hard to imagine that anyone could place a higher priority on sex than I did in my twenties, it was not until my forties that the most important relationship thus far in my life yielded the most intimate experience of another person I've ever had—not sex, but a college diary, lent to me to read by a young friend going away to graduate school. Furthermore, remembering reading it today, I am reminded of many long talks and late nights and early mornings with another friend years earlier.

I am talking about the two men—one of whom arises first in the prologue, and both in Chapter 7—the older dean and mentor of my undergraduate days at Harvard and the younger friend and soul mate of my later tutorial days (Harvard 1950, 1972, 1990) as well as of the subject of Chapter 4, Lucien Price, Harvard 1913—quite a continuum. Add to these men Harrison Hale Schaff, the honorary (live-in and very hands-on) uncle of my teenage years (a Williams man), and my mother and my maternal grandmother, Geraldine and Margaret Shand Groves, who sought Schaff's (as he Price's) aid in raising me, and we have now arrived at the most fundamental acknowledgments of what it will by now have become clear to the reader has been an intensely personal book to write.

This perspective of mine, as I admit at the start of Chapter 7, is "somewhat bound to melancholy." In part this is for obvious reasons: not just the dean, but all my youthful mentors (among whom Frank Moloney, Walter Whitehill, George Ursul, Elliott Perkins, and David McCord must also be named) are now gone. But (full disclosure) so is the younger soul mate.

Never my lover, but hardly less important as my most intimate friend ever, as he is still my chief muse, Will (the name we've agreed I should use; he is not a public figure and values his privacy) has come to somewhat different conclusions than I have about the meaning of love, friendship, and mutual respect for each other's feelings. Though our feelings have not I think really changed— we love each other, but are not "in love," a crucial distinction—we don't ever see each other quite deliberately. He continues—our go-between tells me—to thrive on my books, but pointedly ignores their dedication to him, which, in turn, I now make anonymous—as I have with *The Crimson Letter*—lest I seem annoying. Yes, the situation has its stubborn, pathetic side. Yet while it is not my place to say anything of Will's work, of my own I can certainly say that, in its much more modest way (than the *Pathétique*, say, or *The Age of Anxiety*), one does what one can with one's art and not just for oneself.

Meanwhile, I have nothing but good to say of a situation Emerson— who had (see Chapter 1) his own problems with Thoreau—also addressed: while he admitted it could "hardly be said without a sort of treachery to the relation[ship]," one thing Emerson, no more I, could leave unsaid is that though "it is thought a disgrace to love unrequited," as he wrote in his essay on friendship, "the great will see that true love cannot be unrequited." Amen.

SUPPORTERS, BEST FRIENDS, advisers, dedicatee, parents, and mentors—to these must now be added a man I can only call best of patrons, whose importance it is hard to exaggerate, and who is now a good friend, too: Rawson Wood. He and his wife, Bessie—she gone now, but never, I think, to be forgotten—and Rawson's second wife, Marcia, have enabled my work for years now, relieving me of many worries. My old and much valued (and much missed) colleague, Professor Margaret Henderson Floyd of Tufts, used to say in the 1970s that my mother (who did all my typing then as well as paid so many of my bills) was the secret to my productivity. Today it is Rawson. Interestingly, as an editor of *The Harvard Crimson* some seventy years ago, Rawson wrote many editorials, not on anything like Harvard's gay experience (never touched on then) but certainly on Sacco and Vanzetti and President Lowell, a subject that arises frequently in *The Crimson Letter*.

It may seem to the reader a bit of a plot to report that Rawson is also a Harvard man (class of 1930, surely crossing paths more than once, though unknowing, with my father, class of 1932). I must add that my agent is, too—best of agents—Upton Birnie Brady, class of 1950.

The team in New York that has put this book together has also proved exemplary, chiefly the skillful support in so many ways of Associate Editor Julia Pastore.

Finally, deepest thanks to my editor, Tim Bent, a Cornell man, I'm glad to say (though with a Harvard doctorate), whose imaginative response to my ideas and analysis has sparked a critical dialogue that has added a great deal to *The Crimson Letter*. (The—brilliant—title of the book is Tim's, by the way; the fact that I have possessed the original jacket art for years just shows how fated such things really are, and how like minds, however un-knowingly, do conspire.)

In this as in so much, Emerson's "sublime hope" has thus, in my experience of the decade *The Crimson Letter* is the culmination of, more than been fulfilled, not least in these unique contributions to the creative process, contributions that have yielded this book. For the rest of it, my more narrowly professional courtesies will be found with my scholarly debts in the source notes, my invariable custom, though this time I've grouped them together at the head of the notes where they may be, perhaps, easier to locate. The immediate impetus for *The Crimson Letter* was a speech given by me at the annual Harvard Gay and Lesbian Caucus commencement dinner at the Harvard Faculty Club in 1997 and conversation thereafter with caucus organizers Warren Goldfarb, Robert Mack, Mitchell Adams, and Kevin Smith, to whom grateful acknowledgment is made.

Finally, my usual prayer at book's end, Henry Adams's, according to Robert Mane's excellent study, *Henry Adams on the Road to Chartres*: "To me, accuracy is relative. I care very little whether my details are exact, if only my *ensemble* is in scale."

P. D. S-T.

November 2000
Hotel Vendôme—Boston Public Library—
Boston Athenaeum—Café Iruña

Notes

The following have materially aided my research:

Louis Caldarella, Janice Chadbourne (Boston Public Library), William Coes, Lina Coffey (Boston Athenaeum), Kenneth Conant, William Corbett, Robert Creeley, Thomas Crooks, James Cuno (Fogg Art Museum), Jan Davinitz (Boston Public Library), Peter Drummey (Massachusetts Historical Society), Lee Eisman (Harvard Musical Association), Trevor Fairbrother, Antoinette Fern (Houghton Library), Burt Hanson, Harley Holden (Harvard University Archives), Patrick Horrigan, Anita Israel (Longfellow National Historic Site), Franklin Kameny, Robert Kiley (Adams House, Harvard University), Gerrit Lansing, Richard Lilly, Victoria Macy (Adams House, Harvard University), Marion Mainwaring, Joseph McGrath, Maureen Melton (Museum of Fine Arts, Boston), James E. Miller Jr., Owen Miller (Boston Public Library), Joan Navarse, Richard Newman, Stephen Nonack (Boston Athenaeum), Aaron Paul (Harvard University Art Museums), Eldridge Pendleton (Society of St. John the Evangelist Archives), Joseph Torra, Robert Twombly, Paul Varnell, George Abbott White, Randy Wicker, Karen Wilkin, Frederick Wilson (Houghton Library), and Richard Wunder.

1: THE WARRIOR ARCHETYPE: *Walt Whitman's Harvard*

1. Justin Kaplan, *Walt Whitman, a Life* (New York: Simon and Schuster, 1980), 249.
2. Robert K. Martin, *The Homosexual Tradition in American Poetry* (Austin: University of Texas Press, 1979), 35.
3. *Leaves of Grass* evolved through seven versions, 1855, 1856, 1860, 1867, 1871, 1876, and 1881; the two that are discussed here are those of 1860 and 1881, for which see Jerome Loving, *Walt Whitman* (Berkeley: University of California Press, 1999), 238–250, 414–420.
4. Walt Whitman, *Specimen Days*, quoted in *State of Mind*, ed. R. N. Linscott (New York: Farrar, Straus, 1948), 178.
5. Kaplan, *Walt Whitman*, 248.
6. Kaplan, *Walt Whitman*, 249. See also Robert D. Richardson, Jr., *Emerson: The Mind on Fire: A Biography* (Berkeley: University of California Press, 1995), 529.
7. Felice Picano, "Effeminacy in Pre-Stonewall America," *Harvard Gay and Lesbian Review* (fall 1998), 41, 42.
8. For the Gay Olympics, see Brian Pronger, "Gay Games," *Encyclopedia of Homosexuality*, ed. Wayne R. Dynes (New York: Garland, 1990), 453–454.
9. Paul Moor, "Remembering Lenny," *Harvard Gay and Lesbian Review* (summer 1994), 18.
10. R. W. Emerson, *Representative Men* (Cambridge: Belknap Press of Harvard University Press, 1996), 50.

11. Henry Wiencek, "Yale and the Price of Slavery," *New York Times* (8 August 2001), sec. A, p. 27.
12. Robert K. Martin, "American Literature: Nineteenth Century," *The Gay and Lesbian Literary Heritage*, ed. Claude J. Summers (New York: Henry Holt, 1995), 27.
13. Richardson, *Emerson*, 9.
14. Kaplan, *Walt Whitman*, 248.
15. Richardson, *Emerson*, 9.
16. Graham Robb, "Bosom Buddies," *New York Times Book Review* (3 June 2001), 18. For Emerson's Hafez translations, see R. W. Emerson, *Poems* (Boston: James Munroe, 1847). Also Richardson, *Emerson*, 423–427.
17. Ralph Waldo Emerson, "Love," *Essays* (New York: Vintage, 1990).
18. Hafez, quoted in Richardson, *Emerson*.
19. R. W. Emerson, *The Journals and Miscellaneous Notebooks of Ralph Waldo Emerson*, ed. William H. Gilman, et al. (Cambridge: Harvard University Press, 1960–1982). See also Martin, *The Homosexual Tradition*, 74.
20. Emerson, quoted in Caleb Crain, *American Sympathy: Men, Friendship, and Literature in the New Nation* (New Haven: Yale University Press, 2001), 159.
21. *Journals of Emerson*, 74.
22. Emerson, quoted in Crain, *American Sympathy*, 159.
23. Ibid., 170.
24. Richardson, *Emerson*, 34.
25. Crain, *American Sympathy*, 159–160.
26. Ibid., 151–152.
27. Jonathan Ned Katz, *Love Stories: Sex Between Men Before Homosexuality* (Chicago: University of Chicago Press, 2001).
28. Crain, *American Sympathy*, 153.
29. Richardson, *Emerson*, 285, 463. See also Marylynne Diggs, "Henry Thoreau," *The Gay and Lesbian Literary Heritage*, 701.
30. Crain, *American Sympathy*, 267.
31. Richard Ellmann, *Oscar Wilde* (New York: Random House, 1987), 181; Richardson, *Emerson*, 419.
32. Crain, *American Sympathy*, 222, 216, 211.
33. Allen, *The New Walt Whitman Handbook*, (New York: New York University Press, 1975). 3.
34. Ibid., 256.
35. Richardson, *Emerson*, 527–528, 530.
36. Ibid., 527.
37. The page of the Athenaeum Register from March 1860 is illustrated in The History Project, *Improper Bostonians: Lesbian and Gay History from the Puritans to Playland* (Boston: Beacon Press, 1998), 50.
38. Kaplan, *Walt Whitman*, 27, 26.
39. Richardson, *Emerson*, 528.
40. Whitman, quoted in Clifton Joseph Furness, "Walt Whitman Looks at Boston," *New England Quarterly* (July 1928), 353–370.
41. For Trowbridge, see Kaplan, *Walt Whitman*, 254–255; for O'Connor, ibid., 34–35.
42. Jerome Loving, *Walt Whitman: The Song of Himself* (Berkeley: University of California Press, 1999), 239. See also Kaplan, *Walt Whitman*, 35.
43. Charles T. Sempers, "Walt Whitman and His Philosophy," *Harvard Monthly* (January 1888), 162; William Sloane Kennedy, *Reminiscences of Walt Whitman* (London: Alexander Gardner, 1896). See also Loving, *Walt Whitman*, 446, 458.
44. Loving, *Walt Whitman*, 404, 406.
45. Ibid., 416. See also Kaplan, *Walt Whitman*, 20.
46. Andrew Delbanco, "Barbaric Yawp," *New York Times Book Review* (22 August 1999), 5.
47. Kennedy, *Reminiscences*, passim.
48. Loving, *Whitman*, 305–306.

49. Sheldon M. Novick, *Henry James: The Young Master* (New York: Random House, 1996), 135; *Walt Whitman: Selected Poems, 1855–1892,* ed. Gary Schmidgall (New York: St. Martin's Press, 1999), 469–471.

50. Kaplan, *Walt Whitman,* 311.

51. Leon Edel, *Henry James* (New York: Harper and Row, 1985), 599.

52. Novick, *Henry James* 311; Kaplan, *Walt Whitman,* 311.

53. Douglass Shand-Tucci, *Harvard University: An Architectural Tour* (New York: Princeton Architectural Press, 2001), 88.

54. James, quoted in Ariel Swartley, "Henry James' Boston," *Boston Globe Magazine* (12 August 1984), 10–45.

55. Novick, *James,* 109–110. See also the same author's "Outing Henry James," *Boston Book Review* (December 1998), 28, 29.

56. Christopher Lane, "Enigmas of Love," *Gay and Lesbian Review Worldwide* (spring 2000), 43.

57. Ibid., 44.

58. Ibid.

59. The film most relevant in the context of this study is *The Bostonians.*

60. For Whitman's interest in opera and theater, however, see Kaplan, *Whitman,* 78–79, 175–179, 213, 308, 366.

61. Robert K. Martin, "Walt Whitman," *The Gay and Lesbian Literary Heritage,* 737.

62. Walter Pater, *Plato and Platonism: A Series of Lectures* (London: Macmillan, 1893), 222.

63. Gore Vidal, "Christopher Isherwood's Kind," *United States* (New York: Random House, 1993), 395.

64. Robert K. Martin, *Hero, Captain and Stranger: Male Friendship, Social Critique, and Literary Form in the Sea Novels of Herman Melville* (Chapel Hill: University of North Carolina Press, 1986), 49.

65. Martin, "Whitman," *The Gay and Lesbian Literary Heritage,* 737, 740.

66. Delbanco, "Barbaric Yawp," 15.

67. Gregory W. Bredbeck, "Edward Carpenter," *The Gay and Lesbian Literary Heritage,* 144.

68. See Joseph Harry and William B. DeVall, *The Social Organization of Gay Males* (New York: Praeger, 1978).

69. O'Connor, quoted in Allen, *The New Walt Whitman Handbook,* 3.

70. Ibid., 3.

71. Ibid, 4.

72. Ibid., 42–43.

73. For *Joseph and His Friend,* see Roger Austen, *Playing the Game: The Homosexual Novel in America* (Indianapolis: Bobbs-Merrill, 1977), 9–11.

74. Fred W. Loring, *Two College Friends* (Boston: Loring, 1871).

75. Peter Gay, *The Tender Passion* (New York: Oxford University Press, 1986), 212.

76. A. L. Rowse, *Homosexuals in History* (New York: Macmillan, 1977), 337. Rowse, *Homosexuals in History: A Study of Ambivalence in Society, Literature, and the Arts* (New York: Macmillan, 1977), 21–22.

77. Patricia O'Toole, *The Five of Hearts: An Intimate Portrait of Henry Adams and His Friends, 1880–1918* (New York: Crown, 1990), 200.

78. E. M. Forster, *Maurice* (New York: Norton, 1971), 151.

79. Martin, *The Homosexual Tradition,* 112.

80. Fred W. Loring, *The Boston Dip and Other Verses* (Boston: Loring, 1871). For an overall discussion, see Douglass Shand-Tucci, "A Gay Civil War Novel Surfaces," *The Best of the Harvard Gay and Lesbian Review,* ed. Richard Schneider Jr. (Philadelphia: Temple University Press, 1997), 109–117.

81. For William W. Chamberlain, see Harvard College Class of 1870 report of 1911; for Fred W. Loring, see the same class's report of 1880, both published in Cambridge by Harvard University.

82. The dedication to Chamberlain takes the form of a letter that prefaces the book.

83. For Thomas R. Sullivan, see Douglass Shand-Tucci, *Boston Bohemia* (Amherst: University of Massachusetts Press, 1995), 209–213.

84. Fred Kaplan, *Gore Vidal: A Biography* (New York: Doubleday, 1999), 642–643.

85. John Boswell, *Christianity, Social Tolerance, and Homosexuality* (Chicago: University of Chicago Press, 1980), 24, 25.

86. For William Lawrence, see Shand-Tucci, *Boston Bohemia*, 165, 271–272.

87. Jonathan Gathorne-Hardy, *The Old School Tie* (New York: Viking, 1977), 166.

88. Ibid.

89. For Henry Adams's Hasty Pudding Club minutes, see Douglass Shand-Tucci, *The Art of Scandal: The Life and Times of Isabella Stewart Gardner* (New York: HarperCollins, 1997), 84–86.

90. Alice Stone Blackwell, quoted in Jonathan Ned Katz, *Gay/Lesbian Almanac: A New Documentary* (New York: Harper and Row, 1983), 176–177.

91. For a discussion of Achilles and Patroclus in the gay context, see Shand-Tucci, *Boston Bohemia*, 154, 156.

92. Andrew S. Brown, *Oxford Classical Dictionary*, eds. Simon Hornblower and Antony Spawforth (Oxford: Oxford University Press, 1996), 7.

93. David M. Halperin, *Oxford Classical Dictionary*, 721.

94. David M. Sacks, "Homosexuality," *A Dictionary of the Ancient Greek World* (New York: Oxford University Press, 1995), 115.

95. Vidal, "Isherwood," *United States,* 394.

96. Sacks, "Homosexuality," *A Dictionary of the Ancient Greek World,* 117.

97. For the Sacred Band in the Victorian public-school context, see Gathorne-Hardy, *The Old School Tie,* 166.

98. C. J. Tuplin, "Sacred Band," *Oxford Classical Dictionary,* 1343.

99. *Cambridge Illustrated History of Ancient Greece*, ed. Paul Cartledge (Cambridge, U.K.: Cambridge University Press, 1998), 189.

100. Tuplin, "Sacred Band," *Oxford Classical Dictionary,* 1343.

101. John F. Lazenby, "Leuctra," *Oxford Classical Dictionary,* 858.

102. Ibid., 315; Sacks, *A Dictionary of the Ancient Greek World,* 56.

103. Linda Dowling, *Hellenism and Homosexuality in Victorian Oxford* (Ithaca, N.Y.: Cornell University Press, 1994), xiv.

104. Ibid., 70, 130.

105. Ibid., 33.

106. G. Edward White, *Justice Oliver Wendell Holmes: Law and the Inner Self* (New York: Oxford University Press, 1993), 43.

107. Dowling, *Hellenism*, 80. See also ibid., 27, 142.

108. Ibid., 82.

109. Symonds, quoted in Dowling, *Hellinism*, 87.

110. Ronald Story, *The Forging of the Aristocracy: Harvard and the Boston Upper Class, 1800–1870* (Middletown, Conn.: Wesleyan University Press, 1980), 114.

111. James Gifford, *Dayneford's Library: American Homosexual Writing, 1900–1913* (Amherst: University of Massachusetts Press, 1995), 6.

112. Ibid.

113. Stephen Hardy, *How Boston Played: Sport, Recreation, and Community, 1865–1915* (Boston: Northeastern University Press, 1982), 7. Higginson's "Saints and Their Bodies" appeared in the March 1858 *Atlantic.*

114. Bainbridge Bunting, *Harvard: An Architectural History* (Cambridge: Belknap Press of Harvard University Press, 1985), 96–98.

115. Hardy, *How Boston Played*, 53.

116. Higginson, quoted in Kim Townsend, *Manhood at Harvard: William James and Others* (New York: Norton, 1996), 278.

117. For Stoddard, see Roger Austen, *Genteel Pagan: The Double Life of Charles Warren*

Stoddard, ed. John W. Crowley (Amherst: University of Massachusetts Press, 1991).

118. Higginson, quoted in Tilden G. Edelstein, *Strange Enthusiasm: A Life of Thomas Wentworth Higginson* (New York: Atheneum, 1970), 211.

119. Eve Kosofsky Sedgwick, *Between Men: English Literature and Male Homosocial Desire* (New York: Columbia University Press, 1985), 29, 207.

120. Townsend, *Manhood at Harvard*, 17.

121. Eve Kosofsky Sedgwick, *Epistemology of the Closet* (Berkeley: University of California Press, 1990), 49.

122. Michel Foucault, quoted in David F. Greenberg, *The Construction of Homosexuality* (Chicago: University of Chicago Press, 1988), 487.

123. Townsend, *Manhood at Harvard*, 43.

124. George Santayana, "Philosophy on the Bleachers," *Harvard Monthly* (July 1894), 181–190. For the Santayana–William James relationship, see Townsend, *Manhood at Harvard*, 148.

125. Townsend, *Manhood at Harvard*, 146. See also John McCormick, *George Santayana* (New York: Paragon, 1988), 97.

126. Townsend, *Manhood at Harvard*, 190.

127. Ibid, 164.

128. Ibid., 147.

129. Ibid., 148.

130. Ibid., 149.

131. Sedgwick, *Between Men*, 28, 206.

132. Stoddard, quoted in Austen, *Genteel Pagan*, xxviii.

133. Ibid., 88.

134. Ibid., 152.

135. Burton Kline, "Agassiz's Right-Hand Man," *Boston Evening Transcript*, 5 June, 1912, 28.

136. Ibid., 21.

137. Curtis Prout, "William Sturgis Bigelow," *Harvard Magazine* (September–October 1997), 50.

138. T. R. Sullivan to I. S. Gardner (16 May 1892), Isabella Stewart Gardner Museum Archives, Boston.

139. John Crowley, quoted in Austen, *Genteel Pagan*, xxxix.

140. Xavier Mayne [pseudonym of Edward I. Stevenson], *The Intersexes: A History of Similisexualism as a Problem in Social Life*, quoted in Katz, *Gay/Lesbian Almanac*, 330, 405.

141. Gifford, *Dayneford's Library*, 113.

142. Ibid., 114.

143. For Owen Wister, see Gifford, *Dayneford's Library*, 101–103.

144. Harvey Mansfield, "The Partial Eclipse of Manliness," *Times Literary Supplement* (July 17, 1998), 14–15.

145. For the London Steelers, see [Boston] *Bay Windows* (8 July 1999), 7.

146. Peter Cassels, "A Brave Athlete," [Boston] *Bay Windows* (30 March–5 April 2000), 1, 4–5.

147. Michael Joseph Gross, "Gay Blades," *Boston Magazine* (April 1999), 62.

148. Robert Lipsyte, "The Emasculation of Sports," *New York Times Magazine* (2 April 1995), 50–57.

149. James Kincaid, "With Brave Young Dead," *New York Times Book Review* (16 August 1992), 14.

150. Perry Miller, *Nature's Nation* (Cambridge: Belknap Press of Harvard University Press, 1987), 3.

151. John Leland, "Silence Ending," *New York Times* (May 6, 2000), sec. A, p. 14.

152. John D'Emilio, *Sexual Politics, Sexual Communities* (Chicago: University of Chicago Press, 1983), 158.

153. Robert Lipsyte, "A Major League Player's Life," *New York Times* (6 September 1999).
154. Owen Wister, *The Virginian* (New York: Penguin, 1988). See also Gifford, *Dayneford's Library*, 103; Townsend, *Manhood at Harvard*, 269, 274.
155. Townsend, *Manhood at Harvard*, 273.
156. Ibid., 172.
157. James H. Jones, *Alfred C. Kinsey: A Public/Private Life* (New York: Norton, 1997), 50–51.
158. Vidal, "Theodore Roosevelt, an American Sissy," *United States*, 733.
159. Evelyn Waugh, *A Little Learning* (Boston: Little, Brown, 1964), 160.
160. John M. Clum, "Dramatic Literature: Modern Drama," *The Gay and Lesbian Literary Heritage*, 200.
161. Earl Miner, "Love Poetry," *The New Princeton Encyclopedia of Poetry and Poetics* (Princeton, N.J.: Princeton University Press, 1993), 710.
162. Jones, *Alfred C. Kinsey*, 54–59.
163. Bruce Bawer, "The Poet Out and About," *Washington Post Book World* (31 August 1997), 3.
164. Ibid.
165. Gary Schmidgall, *Walt Whitman: A Gay Life* (New York: Dutton, 1997), 113–114, 313.
166. Richard Hall, *Essays on Gay Literature*, ed. Stuart Kellogg (New York: Harrington Park Press, 1985), 86.
167. Douglass Shand-Tucci, *Harvard University: An Architectural Tour* (New York: Princeton Architectural Press, 2001), 293.
168. Linda Dowling, *Hellenism and Homosexuality in Victorian Oxford* (Ithica, N.Y. Cornell University Press, 1984), 143.

2: THE AESTHETE ARCHETYPE: *Oscar Wilde's Harvard*

1. Linda Dowling, *Hellenism and Homosexuality in Victorian Oxford* (Ithaca, N.Y.: Cornell University Press, 1994), 1–4.
2. Jerome Loving, *Walt Whitman: The Song of Himself* (Berkeley: University of California Press, 1999), 166–167.
3. Paul Berman, "Aria of Myself," *New Republic* (8 December 2000), 4.
4. Christopher Hitchens, "Bosie," *New York Review of Books* (21 November 2000), 26.
5. Richard Ellmann, *Oscar Wilde* (New York: Random House, 1988), 44.
6. Wilde, quoted in Ellmann, *Oscar Wilde,* 170.
7. Gregory Woods, *A History of Gay Literature: The Male Tradition* (New Haven: Yale University Press, 1998), 177.
8. Claude J. Summers, "Oscar Wilde," *The Gay and Lesbian Literary Heritage*, ed. Claude J. Summers (New York: Henry Holt, 1995), 743–744.
9. Ibid., 747.
10. Ellmann, *Oscar Wilde*, 471.
11. Woods, *A History of Gay Literature*, 176.
12. Ellmann, *Oscar Wilde*, 181.
13. Wilde, quoting Emerson, in Ellmann, *Oscar Wilde*, 508.
14. Oscar Wilde, *Correspondence: The Complete Letters of Oscar Wilde*, eds. Merlin Holland and Rupert Hart-Davis (New York: Henry Holt, 2000), 175. See also Davis Coakley, *Oscar Wilde* (Dublin: Town House, 1994), 167, 184.
15. Wilde, *Correspondence*, 33.
16. Robert Ross to Luce & Co, 11 February 1909, in *Bibliography of Oscar Wilde*, ed. Stuart Mason (Boston: Milford House, 1941), 492–493.
17. Ellmann, *Oscar Wilde*, 183, 200–201.
18. J. B. O'Reilly to T. R. Sullivan, undated, ca. 1882, St. Botolph Club Archive, Massachusetts Historical Society.
19. Ellmann, *Oscar Wilde*, 171.

20. Wilde, *Correspondence*, 126, 132, 134, 137.

21. Wilde, quoted in Ellmann, *Oscar Wilde*, 182–183.

22. For Evert Wendell, see the 1901 and 1932 class reports of the Harvard College Class of 1882 and Owen Wister's *Harvard Graduates' Magazine* obituary of 1918, Evert Wendell File, Harvard University Archives.

23. Richard D. Mohr, *Gay Ideas: Outing and Other Controversies* (Boston: Beacon Press, 1992), 213.

24. Peter Gay, *The Tender Passion* (New York: Oxford University Press, 1984), 265.

25. Ibid., 269.

26. Eve Kosofsky Sedgwick, *Epistemology of the Closet* (Berkeley: University of California Press, 1990), 168.

27. 1901 Report, Harvard College Class of 1882, Evert Wendell File, Harvard University Archives.

28. For the *Transcript*'s pronouncement of a triumph, see Ellmann, *Oscar Wilde*, 185; for the *London Daily News* report, ibid., 176; for Wilde's report of his being entertained in Boston, see Wilde to Mrs. George Lewis (12 February 1882), *Correspondence*, 136–137; for his return lectures, see Wilde to Col. W. F. Morse (early March 1882), *Correspondence*, 146; for the fracas at Yale, see Davis Coakley; for Julia Ward Howe's account, see Laura E. Richards and Maud Howe Elliott, *Julia Ward Howe, 1819–1910* (Dunwoody, Ga.: Norman S. Bera, 1970), 72.

29. Wilde, *Correspondence*, 226. See also Douglass Shand-Tucci, *The Art of Scandal* (New York: HarperCollins, 1997), 42–60.

30. Richards and Elliott, *Julia Ward Howe*, 70. For Higginson's article, see "Unmanly Manhood," *Women's Journal* (February 4, 1982).

31. Ellmann, *Oscar Wilde*, 161, 183–184.

32. Howe, quoted in Ellmann, *Oscar Wilde*, 183–184, 203.

33. Ibid., 184.

34. Mary Warner Blanchard, *Oscar Wilde's America: Counterculture in the Gilded Age* (New Haven: Yale University Press, 1998), 29.

35. Ibid.

36. Carson McCullers, *Ballad of the Sad Café* (New York: Bantam, 1971), 24–25.

37. Higginson, quoted in Blanchard, *Oscar Wilde's America*, 29.

38. James W. Tuttleton, *Thomas Wentworth Higginson* (Boston: Twayne, 1978), 82.

39. Tilden G. Edelstein, *Strange Enthusiasm* (New York: Atheneum, 1970), 299.

40. Anna M. Wells, *Dear Preceptor: The Life and Times of Thomas Wenworth Higginson* (Boston: Houghton Mifflin, 1963), 49.

41. Edelstein, *Strange Enthusiasm*, 81.

42. Tuttleton, 83.

43. Edelstein, *Strange Enthusiasm*, 313.

44. Blanchard, *Oscar Wilde's America*, 29.

45. Ibid., 30. The letter (28 February 1882) is reproduced in Wilde, *Correspondence*, 142–143.

46. Ellmann, *Oscar Wilde*, 183.

47. Wilde, *Correspondence*, 176.

48. Ellmann, *Oscar Wilde*, 151–152.

49. Wilde, quoted in Ellmann, *Oscar Wilde*, 170.

50. Ellmann, *Oscar Wilde*, 181.

51. Ibid., 152.

52. Mary Blanchard, "Near the Coast of Bohemia" (unpublished paper, Rutgers University, Department of History, 1992), 32–33.

53. Martin Green, *The Mount Vernon Street Warrens: A Boston Story* (New York: Scribner's, 1989), 160.

54. Charles M. Flandrau, *Harvard Episodes* (Boston: Copeland and Day, 1897), 61, 73, 75, 205.

55. *Harvard Graduates' Magazine* 5 (September 1905), at the Boston Public Library.

56. George Santayana, *The Middle Span* (New York: Scribner's, 1945), 29.

57. A collection of these posters lines the club's staircase to the bar and former dining room. As of writing, the building is closed for restoration.

58. Douglass Shand-Tucci, *Boston Bohemia* (Amherst: University of Massachusetts Press, 1995), 492 n. 110, 233, 235.

59. Shand-Tucci, *Harvard University* 125–126.

60. Santayana, quoted in Shand-Tucci, *Harvard University*, 126. For Santayana's similar involvement at the Tavern Club, see Roger Austen, *Genteel Pagan: The Double Life of Charles Warren Stoddard* (Amherst: University of Massachusetts Press, 1991), 126–127, and George Santayana, *Persons and Places: The Background of My Life* (New York: Scribner's, 1944), 71.

61. Xavier Mayne, *The Intersexes,* quoted in Jonathan Ned Katz, *Gay/Lesbian Almanac* (New York: Harper and Row, 1983), 329.

62. Albert Parry, *Garrets and Pretenders: A History of Bohemianism in America* (New York: Dover reprint, 1960), 138.

63. Francis Watson, quoted in Mark De Wolfe Howe, *A Partial (and Not Impartial) Semi-Centennial History of the Tavern Club, 1833–1934* (Boston: The Club, 1934), 8–9.

64. Owen Wister, quoted in Howe, *History of the Tavern Club,* 14–15, 23, 24.

65. Austen, *Genteel Pagan,* 126. See also John McCormick, *George Santayana: A Biography* (New York: Paragon, 1987), 119.

66. Joseph Chamberlain, "American Cities in Fiction—I: Boston," *The Chap-Book* (15 April 1898), 434. See also Frances Carruth, *Fictional Rambles in & about Boston* (New York: McClure, Phillips, 1902), 131.

67. Doris Birmingham, "Boston's St. Botolph Club," *Archives of American Art* (summer 1992), 26, 31.

68. Austen, *Genteel Pagan,* 127.

69. T. Dwight to I. S. Gardner (18 September 1892 and 15 December 1908), Gardner Museum Archives.

70. Susan Sinclair, senior archivist at the Gardner museum, interview by the author, December 1996.

71. Morris Carter, *Isabella Stewart Gardner and Fenway Court* (Boston: Houghton Mifflin, 1925), 4.

72. Shirley Everton Johnson, *The Cult of the Purple Rose* (Boston: Gorham Press, 1902). For *The Importance of Being Earnest,* see Karl Beckson, *London in the 1890's* (New York: Norton, 1992), 52–55. For a more mainstream view of *The Cult of the Purple Rose,* see Kim Townsend, *Manhood at Harvard: William James and Others* (New York: Norton, 1996), 143.

73. Johnson, *The Cult of the Purple Rose,* 60–61.

74. Ibid., 57–58.

75. Lincoln Kirstein, *Mosaic: Memoirs* (New York: Farrar, Straus & Giroux, 1994), 86. See also Douglass Shand-Tucci, *Boston Bohemia,* 70–72, 170–172, 333–335, 424 n. 25.

76. F. G. Hall, et al., *Harvard Celebrities: A Book of Caricatures & Decorative Drawings* (Cambridge: Harvard University Press, 1901), 24.

77. Daniel Gregory Mason, "At Harvard in the Nineties," *New England Quarterly* (March 1936), 43–47, 58. See also Shand-Tucci, *Boston Bohemia,* 171–172, and Chapter 10 of this volume.

78. Arlo Bates, *The Pagans* (New York: Henry Holt, 1884), 23; Shand-Tucci, *Boston Bohemia,* 380.

79. Ralph Adams Cram, *My Life in Architecture* (Boston: Little, Brown, 1934), 91, 92–93.

80. Nancy Finlay, *Artists of the Book in Boston, 1890–1910* (Cambridge: Houghton Library, 1985), x, 11.

81. Gelett Burgess, "The Bohemians of Boston," *Enfant Terrible* (April 1898), n.p.

82. Estelle Jussim, *Slave to Beauty: The Eccentric Life and Controversial Career of F. Holland Day* (Boston: Godine, 1981), 46, 269, 285.

83. Donald Stephens, *Bliss Carman* (New York: Twayne, 1966), 26–27, 31. See also Alan

H. MacDonald, *Richard Hovey, Man & Craftsman* (Durham, N.C.: Duke University Press, 1957). Both Carman and Hovey figure importantly in Shand-Tucci, *Boston Bohemia*, passim.

84. For a discussion of Carman's 1914 Harvard Phi Beta Kappa poem, see Shand-Tucci, *Boston Bohemia*, 410–414.

85. Charles Wentworth, quoted in Shand-Tucci, *Boston Bohemia*, 147, 150, 509 n. 73.

86. Nicholas Kilmer, *Thomas Buford Meteyard, 1865–1928: Paintings and Watercolors* (New York: Berry Hill Galleries, 1989), 28–30.

87. Wilde, *Correspondence*, 150. See also Kilmer, *Meteyard*, 6.

88. Kilmer, *Meteyard*, 8, 10. See also Elizabeth Robins, *Both Sides of the Curtain* (London: Heineman, 1940), 201.

89. Wilde, *Correspondence*, 302, 394.

90. Shand-Tucci, *Boston Bohemia*, 331.

91. Marion Mainwaring, *Mysteries of Paris: The Quest for Morton Fullerton*, quoted in Hermione Lee, "Gatzby of the Boulevards," *London Review of Books* (8 March 2001). See also Kilmer, *Meteyard*, 8.

92. Ellmann, *Oscar Wilde*, 179.

93. Shand-Tucci, *Boston Bohemia*, 331.

94. Ibid., 341.

95. Ibid., 331, 333.

96. Henry G. Fairbanks, *Louise Imogen Guiney* (New York: Twayne, 1973), 56; Jussim, *Slave to Beauty*, 7.

97. Gelett Burgess, "Where Is Bohemia," *The Romance of the Commonplace* (San Francisco: Elder & Shepard, 1902), 128–132.

98. Austen, *Genteel Pagan*, 138.

99. Green, *The Mount Vernon Street Warrens*; H. David Sox, *Bachelors of Art: Edward Perry Warren & the Lewes House Brotherhood* (London: Fourth Estate, 1991), 13–14. See also Shand-Tucci, *Boston Bohemia*, 219–222. Wilde's letters make no mention of such a meeting, but Warren was a friend of Robert Ross, Wilde's first lover and best friend, and several young men of Wilde's circle lived at Lewes House.

100. Charles C. Calhoun, "An Acorn in the Forest," *Bowdoin Magazine* (September 1987), 5, 11.

101. Aaron J. Paul, *Fragments of Antiquity* (Cambridge: Harvard University Art Museum, 1997), 7–21.

102. Green, *The Mount Vernon Street Warrens*, 73.

103. Calhoun, "Acorn," 4.

104. Ibid.

105. Green, *Warrens*, 236. See also Humphrey Carpenter, *The Brideshead Generation: Evelyn Waugh and His Friends* (Boston: Houghton Mifflin, 1990), 113–115.

106. "Acorn," 6. See also Walter Muir Whitehill, *Museum of Fine Arts, Boston: A Centennial History* (Cambridge: Belknap Press, 1970), I, 42.

3: HOME: *Old Cambridge, Beacon Hill, Back Bay, North Shore*

1. Lucius Beebe, *Boston and the Boston Legend* (New York: Appleton, 1936), 305–315; The History Project, *Improper Bostonians: Lesbian and Gay History from the Puritans to Playland* (Boston: Beacon Press, 1998), 160–183.

2. Douglass Shand-Tucci, *Harvard University: An Architectural Tour* (New York: Princeton Architectural Press, 2001), 75.

3. Jean Stein, *Edie, An American Biography*, ed. George Plimpton (New York: Knopf, 1982), 124–125.

4. Ibid., 124–125.

5. Ibid., 126–127.

6. Ibid., 129–130.

7. Hilton Als, "Friends of Dorothy," *New Yorker* (24 April 1995), 89–90, 94.

8. Ibid., 98.
9. Paul Varnell, typescript of untitled, unpaginated article dated 1999.
10. Louis Menand, *The Metaphysical Club* (New York: Farrar, Straus & Giroux, 2001), 347.
11. Edwin A. Robinson, "Perry, Thomas Sargent," *Dictionary of American Biography*, (New York: Scribner's, 1934) VII, 493–494; Ernest Samuels, *Bernard Berenson: The Making of a Connoisseur* (Cambridge: Belknap Press, 1979), 34–35, 50, 162.
12. Hubert Kennedy, "Fierce and Quixotic Ally," *Harvard Magazine* (November–December 1982), 62–63.
13. James Mills Peirce, quoted in Kennedy, "Fierce and Quixotic Ally," 63.
14. Ibid., 64.
15. Ibid., 63.
16. See Linda Dowling, *Hellenism and Homosexuality in Victorian Oxford* (Ithaca, N.Y.: Cornell University Press, 1994), passim.
17. Jonathan Ned Katz, *Gay American History* (New York: Crowell, 1976), 376. Katz first disclosed Peirce's homosexuality in this work.
18. Symonds, quoted in Kennedy, "Fierce and Quixotic Ally," 64.
19. Jonathan Ned Katz, *Love Stories* (Chicago: University of Chicago Press, 2001), 314.
20. Ibid., 313.
21. Bert Hansen, "Has the Laboratory Been a Closet? Gay and Lesbian Lives in the History of Science and Medicine," unpublished lecture, Wesleyan University (25 April 1996).
22. Allan Bloom, *Love and Friendship* (New York: Simon and Schuster, 1993), 431, 546.
23. Christina Nehring, "The Higher Yearning," *Harper's* (September 2001), 71–72.
24. Ibid., 70, 71, 72.
25. Ibid., 72.
26. Raymond Clark Archibald, "Peirce, James Mills," *Dictionary of American Biography* II: 397–398.
27. Ibid., 405.
28. Jung, quoted in Robert H. Hopcke, *Jung, Jungians and Homosexuality* (Boston: Shambhala, 1991), 27.
29. Shand-Tucci, *Harvard University*, 251–254.
30. Frank D. Ashburn, *Peabody of Groton, a Portrait* (Cambridge: Riverside Press, 1967), 155–156.
31. Douglass Shand-Tucci, *The Art of Scandal: The Life and Times of Isabella Stewart Gardner* (New York: HarperCollins, 1997), 82–84.
32. Douglass Shand-Tucci, *Boston Bohemia* (Amherst: University of Massachusetts Press, 1995), 163–165, 232, 237.
33. Harvard College Class of 1928, *Fiftieth Anniversary Report* (Cambridge: The University, 1978), 560; *Twenty-fifth Anniversary Report* (1953), 540. Saltonstall's entries are characteristically short.
34. William McBrien, *Cole Porter: A Biography* (New York: Vintage, 1998), 186. See also *Dissent* (Boston: Northeastern University Press, 1985), 12–15.
35. Jean Gould, *Amy: The World of Amy Lowell and the Imagist Movement* (New York: Dodd, Mead, 1975), 180; C. David Heymann, *American Aristocracy: The Lives and Times of James Russell, Amy, and Robert Lowell* (New York: Dodd, Mead, 1980), 224.
36. Stephen Watson, *Strange Bedfellows: The First American Avant-Garde* (New York: Abbeville Press, 1991), 28; Van Wyck Brooks, *New England Indian Summer, 1865–1915* (New York: Dutton, 1940), 533.
37. My research on Lowell's little theater period is ongoing. It ultimately had issue in the Toy Theater on Beacon Hill and then the Copley Theatre in the Back Bay, for which see my forthcoming *The Passions of Copley Square*.
38. John Malcolm Brinnin, *The Third Rose: Gertrude Stein and Her World* (Boston: Little, Brown, 1959), 56–77.
39. Gould, *Amy*, 75–95.

40. Van Wyck Brooks, *New England: Indian Summer* (New York: Dutton, 1940), 525.
41. Robert M. Crunden, *American Salons: Encounters with European Modernism* (New York: Oxford University Press, 1993), 235.
42. Douglass Shand-Tucci, *The Passions of Copley Square* (forthcoming).
43. Gould, *Amy*, 259, 302.
44. Ibid., 119, 259. For "Gestures of the Dead," see *Collected Poems of John Wheelwright* (New York: New Directions, 1971), 50.
45. For Sacco and Vanzetti, see Spence Burton in this chapter, and Lincoln Kirstein in Chapter 8.
46. Amy Lowell, quoted in Gould, *Amy*, 191.
47. Winnfield Scott, quoted in Gould, *Amy,* 195.
48. Robert Lowell, "91 Revere Street," *Collected Prose*, ed. Robert Giroux (New York: Farrar, Straus & Giroux, 1987), 336–337.
49. Ibid., 338.
50. Austin Warren, introduction, *Collected Wheelwright*, xiv.
51. Ibid., xiii.
52. Alan M. Wald, "Erasing . . . Boston's Forgotten Marxist Poets," *New Boston Review* (January–February 1981), 20–21.
53. *Rollo's Journey to Cambridge,* first published in 1879, was still in print in 1926. An excerpt was included in William Bentick-Smith, *The Harvard Book* (Cambridge: Harvard University Press, 1982).
54. Barrett Wendell, quoted in Alan M. Wald, *The Revolutionary Imagination: The Poetry and Politics of John Wheelwright and Sherry Mangan* (Chapel Hill: University of North Carolina Press, 1983), 39–40, 42, 44, 47, 253 n. 22. For the Lampoon Castle, see Shand-Tucci, *Harvard University*, 108.
55. Ibid., 47, 59–60, 129–130.
56. The driver of the car is described as "drunken."
57. "Boston Public Library," *Collected Wheelwright*. See also Austin Warren, introduction to *Collected Wheelwright*, xv.
58. Austin Warren, introduction to *Collected Wheelwright*, xv.
59. *Time* magazine, quoted in Wald, *Imagination*, 24, 38, 93.
60. Donald L. Kemmerer, "Andrew, A. Piatt," *Dictionary of American Biography* (New York: Scribner's 1968), Supplement Two, 15–16. See also Arlen J. Hansen, *Gentlemen Volunteers: The Story of the American Ambulance Drivers in the Great War, August 1914–September 1918* (New York: Arcade, 1996); Joseph E. Garland, "The American Field Service," *Eastern Point* (Dublin, N.H.: William L. Bauhaus, 1971), 294–298.
61. Garland, *Eastern Point*, 282–284; Garland, *The North Shore* (Beverly, Mass.: Commonwealth, 1998), 310.
62. Garland, *The North Shore*, 214, 308.
63. *Beauport Chronicle*, eds. E. Parker Hayden Jr. and Andrew L. Gray (Boston: Society for the Preservation of New England Antiquities, 1991), v; Garland, *The North Shore*, 210.
64. *Beauport Chronicle*, 88–89.
65. Ibid., 76–77, 88–89.
66. Garland, *The North Shore*, 310; *Beauport Chronicle*, 111–112.
67. Nancy Curtis and Richard Nylander, Introduction, *Beauport* (Boston: Godine, 1990), 7, 11.
68. Garland, *The North Shore*, 209; *Beauport Chronicle*, 109; Louise Hall Tharp, *Mrs. Jack: A Biography of Isabella Stewart Gardner* (Boston: Little, Brown, 1965), 277–278.
69. Garland, *Eastern Point*, 316.
70. Garland, *The North Shore*, 311.
71. Copeland appeared on *Time*'s cover on 17 January 1927.
72. J. Donald Adams, *Copey of Harvard: A Biography of Charles Townsend Copeland* (Boston: Houghton Mifflin, 1960), 2.
73. Granville Hicks, *John Reed* (New York: Benjamin Bloom, 1968), 37.

74. Brook Atkinson, quoted in Shand-Tucci, *Harvard Guide*, 181–182.

75. Ibid., 72.

76. Conrad Aiken, quoted in Adams, *Copey of Harvard*, 84.

77. Adams, *Copey of Harvard*, 153–155.

78. Ibid., 196–201.

79. Ibid., 72, 79, 100, 103–105.

80. Walter Lippman, quoted in Adams, *Copey of Harvard*, 101.

81. Adams, *Copey of Harvard*, 2.

82. M. C. Ross, "Porter, Arthur Kingsley," *Dictionary of American Biography* (New York: Scribner's, 1944), Supplement One 660.

83. Walter Muir Whitehill, "Arthur Kingsley Porter," *Analecta Biographica*: A *Handful of New England Portraits* (Brattleboro, Vt.: Stephen Greene Press, 1969), 16.

84. Ross, "Porter," 601.

85. Whitehill, "Porter," 17.

86. John Coolidge, "Harvard's Teaching of Architecture and the Fine Arts, 1928–1985," *Architectural Education in Boston*, ed. M. H. Floyd (Boston: Boston Architectural Center, 1989), 60.

87. Ross, "Porter," 601.

88. Whitehill, "Porter," 21.

89. Alan Priest, *The Sculpture of Joseph Coletti* (New York: Macmillan, 1968), 135, 163.

90. Ibid., viii, xii.

91. St. George's was designed by Ralph Adams Cram, for whom Coletti did his earliest sculptural work. Cram, like Sargent, ranks as Coletti's major patron in his youth.

92. A. Kingsley Porter, *Beyond Architecture* (Boston: Marshall Jones, 1918), 76–77.

93. Phyllis Grosskurth, *Havelock Ellis*: A *Biography* (New York: Knopf, 1980), 418–419.

94. Richard Norton Smith, *The Harvard Century: The Making of a University to a Nation* (Cambridge: Harvard University Press, 1986), 85.

95. H. W. L. Dana, "The Mad Tea Party," undated typescript, Longfellow National Historic Site Archives (LNHSA), U.S. Park Service. The event occurred on 11 June 1936. See also the typescript "Re Henry Dana conference with Mr. E. M. Parker, April 22, 1936."

96. John Loughery, *The Other Side of Silence: Men's Lives and Gay Identities*: A *Twentieth-Century History* (New York: Henry Holt, 1998), 108.

97. Richard S. Kennedy, *Dreams in the Mirror*: A *Biography of E. E. Cummings* (New York: Liveright, 1980), 310, 505 n. 13.

98. "1933 Report," Harvard College Class of 1903, Harvard University Archives.

99. "1920 Report," Harvard College Class of 1903, Harvard University Archives.

100. The codicil is dated October 1915, LNHSA, U.S. Park Service.

101. "1920 Report," Harvard College Class of 1903, Harvard University Archives.

102. "1938 Report," Harvard College Class of 1903, Harvard University Archives.

103. *Boston Herald* (5 April 1935), 110.

104. Interview with Anita Israel, archivist at the Longfellow Historic Site, Cambridge, Mass., June 2002.

105. Robert Creeley, telephone interview by the author, March 2002.

106. John Loughery, "The Wisdom of the Aunties," *Harvard Gay and Lesbian Review* (fall 1999), 39–40.

107. Ibid., 41.

108. Ibid., 40.

109. See Bernard F. Dick, *The Hellenism of Mary Renault* (Carbondale: Southern Illinois University Press, 1972), 33, 50.

110. Dick, *Mary Renault*, 104.

111. Ibid., 111.

112. Ibid., 33, 36.

113. The names of Dana's correspondents appear on the correspondence, which is open to the public, LNHSA, U.S. Park Service.

114. Dana's undergraduate journals are dated only by month and day. These entries are dated 21 March. LNHSA, U.S Park Service.

115. M. Fullerton to H. Dana (20 March 1911), LNHSA, U.S. Park Service.

116. K. Young to H. Dana: 23 May, year unknown; 1 September and 13 September 1908; 16 July and 30 August 1910; 3 January 1911, LNHSA, U.S. Park Service.

117. Dana diary, 26 January 1902, LNHSA, U.S. Park Service.

118. E. Dana to H. Dana, 17 March 1936, LNHSA, U.S. Park Service.

119. R. A. Cram to Edward Mueller, 1939–1941, Cram Collection, Boston Public Library.

120. Harvard College Class of 1915, *Twenty-fifth Anniversary Report* (Cambridge: The University, 1940); typescript, Society of St. John the Evangelist Archives, Cambridge, Massachusetts.

121. The conventual church of SS. Mary and John was built by Burton in his brother's memory.

122. S. Burton to H. Dana, 23 September 1910, LNHSA, U.S. Park Service.

123. S. Burton to H. Dana, 14 Oct. 1910, typescript, St. John the Evangelist Archives.

124. For a fuller discussion of this circle, see Douglass Shand-Tucci, "Gothic Modernist," unpublished manuscript of volume 2 of *Ralph Adams Cram, Life and Architecture*, Massachusetts Historical Society. Mitchell lived almost next door to the Cowley Monastery at The Strathcona, 993 Memorial Drive. Letters in his papers (to N. Saltonstall, 20 March 1940; to Elizabeth Zaddo, 23 March 1939; to G. S. Sykes, 28 July 1936; to S. Burton, April 1940; to K. Banner, 1 Dec. 1941; and to Lucy Taggart 3 Aug. 1943) document Mitchell's friendships with a gay circle that included Nathaniel Saltonstall. John Wheelwright, and Spence Burton.

125. Eldridge Pendleton, typescript re: portraits, Society of St. John the Evangelist Archives.

126. "Sacco-Vanzetti Watchers Find Refuge in Church," *Boston Globe*, undated clipping; untitled, *Church Times*, undated clipping; untitled clipping, *Time* (5 September 1927), Society of St. John the Evangelist Archives.

127. Rose Macaulay, *Letters to a Friend from Rose Macaulay, 1950–1952*, ed. Constance Babbington Smith (New York: Athenaeum, 1962), 298.

128. Richard P. Wunder, telephone interview by the author, July 2002.

129. William L. MacDonald, "Whittemore, Thomas," *Dictionary of American Biography* (New York: Scribner's, 1974), Supplement Four, 890–891.

130. Douglass Shand-Tucci, *The Art of Scandal*, 271–273.

131. Lincoln Kirstein, *Mosaic*, 165.

132. Robin Karson, *Fletcher Steele, Landscape Architect: An Account of the Gardenmaker's Life, 1885–1971* (New York: Abrams, 1989), 121. See also Shand-Tucci, "Gothic Modernist," MHS Archives.

133. Malcom Freiberg, "Stewart, Mitchell" (Massachusetts Historical Society Proceedings, 72), 261. See also Harvard College Class of 1915, *Fiftieth Anniversary Report*, Cambridge: The University, 1965), 355.

134. S. Mitchell to A. Soons, 10 July 1940; J. Dos Passos to A. Poore, undated; Mitchell Papers, Boston Athenaeum. See also Melvin Landsberg, *John Dos Passos' Correspondence with Arthur K. McComb* (Winot: University Press of Colorado, 1991), 244–245.

135. S. Mitchell to R. Hillyer, 17 October 1924, Mitchell Papers, Boston Athenaeum.

136. Loughery, "The Wisdom of the Aunties," 40–41.

137. Louis Leonard Tucker, *The Massachusetts Historical Society: A Bicentennial History, 1791–1991* (Boston: The Society, distributed by Northeastern University Press, 1991), 335.

138. S. Mitchell to R. Beatty, 23 January 1944, Mitchell Papers, Boston Athenaeum.

139. *Improper Bostonians*, compiled by the History Project (Boston: Beacon Press, 1998), 123–125.

140. Tucker, *The Massachusetts Historical Society*, 335.

141. S. Mitchell to S. Burton, 1 April 1940, Mitchell Papers, Boston Athenaeum.

142. Kennedy, *Dreams*, 82.

143. Ibid., 193.

144. Stewart Mitchell journals, Mitchell Papers, Boston Athenaeum: I:46 (Pankhurst); 90 (Wilson); 116 (Caruso); 140 (subway); 237 (Armory Show); 251 (martini); 125 (Old Howard); 285 (rowing); 241 (Olympics); 33 (abnormal); 180 (Bliss Carman); 239 (suicidal); 210 (sex); 232 (effeminate); 169 (masturbation); 178 (Burton); II: 47 (Pavlova); 67 (Sargent murals); 77 (Fenway Court); 159 (Bergson); 181 (Squantum air meet); 154 (Astarte); 18, 33 (Marliave's); 86 (fraternity); 187 (wrestling); 169 (hermaphrodite); 34 (Wilde); 44 (*Phaedrus*); 149 (Symonds); 55 (Tchaikovsky); 66 ("Hound of Heaven"); 94 (Swinburne); 97 (*Lady Windermere's Fan*); 156 (Tristan); IV: 159 (see *inversion*).

145. Mitchell to R. Beatty, 23 January 1944; C. Wright to S. Mitchell to S. Mitchell, 3 May 1943; Mitchell Papers, Boston Athenaeum.

146. Lynne Waldeland, *John Cheever* (Boston: Twayne, 1979), 19; Scott Donaldson, *John Cheever: A Biography* (New York: Random House, 1988), 46, 50.

147. Gore Vidal, *Palimpsest: A Memoir* (New York: Random House, 1995), 115.

148. John Cheever, "The President of the Argentine," *Atlantic* (April 1976), 43–45.

149. Carmine Esposito, "Cheever, John," *Gay and Lesbian Literary Heritage*, 160.

150. Dana's photographs are in the LNHSA, U.S. Park Service; Mitchell's in the Mitchell Papers, Boston Athenaeum.

151. The most sympathetic full-length treatment is found in May Sarton, *Faithful Are the Wounds* (New York: Rinehart, 1955).

152. *Rat and the Devil*, ed. Louis K. Hyde (Hamden, Conn.: Archon, 1978), 12.

153. Donald E. Pease, "F. O. Matthiessen," *Dictionary of Literary Biography* (Detroit: Gale, 1988), No. 68: 139.

154. There is now a Matthiessen Memorial at Eliot House: his old tutorial study, stocked with his library, marked by a stately slate and gilt roundel by the British sculptor John Skelton.

155. Harry Levin, *Matty at Eliot House* (Cambridge: The House, 1982), 4. See also *Rat and the Devil*, 152–153.

156. Levin, *Matty*, 14; *Rat and the Devil*, 223.

157. Pease, "Matthiessen," 143.

158. *Rat and the Devil*, 4.

159. David Bergman, *Gaity Transfigured: Gay Self-Representation in American Literature* (Madison: University of Wisconsin Press, 1991), 94; *Rat and the Devil*, 8.

160. *Rat and the Devil*, 47; Bergman, "Matthiessen," 57, 87–88.

161. Bergman, "Matthiessen," 89–90.

162. Ibid., 91.

163. Ibid., 94, 96.

164. Ibid., 97.

165. Ibid., 98.

166. Ibid., 100–101.

167. Levin, *Matty*, 12–13, 15.

168. Hyde, *Rat and the Devil*, 3, 200.

169. Levin, *Matty*, 14; see also Bernard Carman, "The Persecution of F. O. Matthiessen," *Harvard Magazine* (May–June, 2000), 99; May Sarton, *Faithful Are the Wounds*.

4: A STOIC'S PERSPECTIVE: *Ohio Hellenist*

1. Michael Berthold writes of this kind of marginality in his "Newton Arvin," *Dictionary of Literary Biography* (Detroit: Gale, 1988), no. 100: 12–13.

2. Louis M. Lyons, *Newspaper Story: One Hundred Years of the Boston Globe* (Cambridge: Belknap Press of Harvard University Press, 1971), 178.

3. W. Raymond McClure, *Prometheus: A Memoir of Lucien Price, January 6, 1883–March 30, 1964* (Boston: privately printed, 1965), 2, 44–47.

4. Ibid., 1.

5. Ibid., 5, 44–47; Lyons, *Newspaper Story*, 178. *The Agamemnon* was performed in Greek in Harvard's stadium in 1906.

6. Lyons, *Newspaper Story*, 175; McClure, *Prometheus*, 5.

7. Ibid., 178.

8. Ibid., 176–176.

9. McClure, *Prometheus*, 8; Lyons, *Newspaper Story*, 225; Harvard College Class of 1903 *Twenty-fifth Anniversary Report* (The University, 1928), 200. Lyons notes that whereas the *Globe* was editorially silent, the Boston media generally was not: the *Atlantic*, the *Transcript*, and the *Herald* (which won a Pulitzer for one Sacco-Vanzetti editorial), all took an active role editorially. A protégé of Price's at the *Globe*, however, Gardner Jackson, attracted to the *Globe* by Price (who hired him), was, according to Lyons, a "vital force" on the Sacco-Vanzetti defense committee; so much so he left the *Globe*. One assumes the Taylors were very anti-Sacco-Vanzetti.

10. Samuel Eliot Morison, quoted in McClure, *Prometheus*, 33.

11. McClure, *Prometheus*, 9, 13, 21.

12. Price, quoted in McClure, *Prometheus*, 18, 19, 21.

13. McClure, *Prometheus*, 51.

14. Ibid., 12, 21, 34, 35.

15. Finley, quoted in McClure, *Prometheus*, 34, 35.

16. *Western Reserve Alumni Bulletin* (fall 1964), unpaginated clipping (reprint from the *Atlantic*, May 1927) of Price's "Hardscrabble Hellas."

17. Ted Shawn, quoted in McClure, *Prometheus*, 34; Julia L. Foulkes, *Modern Bodies* (Chapel Hill: University of North Carolina—Greensboro, 2002), 79, 86–88, 93. Price's letters to Shawn are in the Harvard Theatre Collection.

18. McClure, *Prometheus*, 15.

19. Ibid., 55.

20. Bernard F. Dick, *The Hellenism of Mary Renault* (Carbondale: Southern Illinois University Press, 1972), 8–9.

21. McClure, *Prometheus*, 44–47.

22. Ibid., 26, 30, 44.

23. Lucien Price, *Immortal Youth: A Study in the Will to Create* (Boston: McGrath Sherrill Press, 1919).

24. Price, *Immortal Youth*, 5, 10.

25. Ibid., 18.

26. Ibid., 12–14, 31.

27. Dick, *The Hellenism of Mary Renault*, 35.

28. A. L. Rowse, *Homosexuals in History: A Study of Ambivalence in Society, Literature and the Arts* (New York: Macmillan, 1977), 337.

29. Price, *Immortal Youth*, 45.

30. Lucien Price, *Litany for All Souls* (Boston: Beacon Press, 1945), 60.

31. Ibid., 8–9, 13.

32. Ibid., 29.

33. Ibid., 37, 42.

34. Ibid., 44.

35. Ibid., 14–15, 18, 32–33, 69.

36. McClure, *Prometheus*, 8–11, 10, 44. See also Lucien Price, *Dialogues of Alfred North Whitehead* (Boston: Little, Brown, 1954).

37. McClure, *Prometheus*, 44–47.

38. J. Robin Baitz, interview with David Hare, *New York Times* (26 April 1998), 41.

39. John le Carré, *Tinker, Tailor, Soldier, Spy* (New York: Knopf, 1974), 331–332, 342, 346.

40. Baitz, interview with David Hare, 41.

41. Eduart T. Salmon, "love and friendship," *Oxford Classical Dictionary* eds. A. Spawforth and S. Hornblower (Oxford: Oxford University Press, 1996), 885.

42. McClure, *Prometheus*, 37–38.

43. William Cobb, trans. *The Symposium and the Phaedrus: Plato's Erotic Dialogues* (Albany: State University of New York Press, 1993).

44. Gore Vidal, *Palimpsest* (New York: Penguin, 1995), 122; Larry Kramer, "The Sadness of Gore Vidal," *Gore Vidal*, ed. Donald Weise (San Francisco: Cleis Press, 1999), 259.

45. Fred Kaplan, *Gore Vidal* (New York: Anchor, 1999), 546.

46. Vidal, quoted in Kaplan, *Gore Vidal*, 546.

47. Price, quoted in McClure, *Prometheus*, 48.

48. Kaplan, *Gore Vidal*, 546.

49. I remember Price saying this, but I cannot date the remark; nor do I know if he ever said anything similar in writing.

50. Robert F. Kiernan, *Gore Vidal* (New York: Ungar, 1982), 51–52.

51. Kaplan, *Gore Vidal*, 546.

52. McClure, *Prometheus*, 57.

53. Vidal, *Palimpsest*, 386.

54. McClure, *Prometheus*, 47–51.

55. M. Morgan Holmes, "Lucian," *Gay and Lesbian Literary Heritage*, 456.

56. McClure, *Prometheus*, 50, 35, 49.

57. Ibid., 50.

58. Ibid., 35.

59. Ibid., 71.

60. Dick, *The Hellenism of Mary Renault*, 110.

5: AWAY: *Left Bank, Red Square, Harlem, Greenwich Village*

1. William L. MacDonald, "Whittemore, Thomas," *Dictionary of American Biography* (New York: Scribner's, 1974), Supplement Four, 890–891.

2. James E. Miller Jr., *T. S. Eliot's Personal Waste Land: Exorcism of the Demons* (University Park: Pennsylvania State University Press, 1977), 1–16. For the articles referred to, see John Peter, "A New Interpretation of *The Waste Land*," *Essays in Criticism* 2 (July 1952), 242–266, and the same author's "Postscript" (with a reprint of the original article), *Essays in Criticism* 19 (April 1969), 165–166.

3. Ibid., 12–13, 128.

4. Ibid., 106, 164.

5. Ibid., 372 n. 1.

6. T. S Eliot, "A Commentary," *The Criterion* (April 1934), 452.

7. *The Letters of T. S. Eliot*, ed. Valerie Eliot (London: Faber & Faber, 1988), xvii.

8. Miller, *T. S. Eliot's Personal Waste Land*, 15–16.

9. Ibid., 49.

10. Ibid., x, 10.

11. T. S. Eliot, *Letters*, 25, 27, 30, 31, 271; Peter Ackroyd, *T. S. Eliot* (New York: Simon and Schuster, 1984), 38.

12. Ackroyd, *Eliot*, 38.

13. T. S. Eliot, *Letters*, 21, 32.

14. Ibid., 34–35.

15. Alexander Chancellor, "De-lightful, De-licious, De-ceitful," *New York Times Book Review* (29 November 1998), 9.

16. Cole Porter, quoted in William McBrien, *Cole Porter* (New York: Vintage, 1998), 50, 51.

17. Alan Rich, quoted in McBrien, *Cole Porter*, 50, 55–56, 75–76.

18. McBrien, *Cole Porter*, 186, 225–226, 290, 352.

19. Ibid., 154–155, 248–250, 251, 253.

20. Chancellor, 9.

21. Bruce Nugent, *Gay Rebel of the Harlem Renaissance*, ed. Thomas H. Wirth (Durham, N.C.: Duke University Press, 2002), 10–11.

22. *Alain LeRoy Locke Bibliography* (Howard University: Interim edition, undated), 1–2.

23. Jeffrey C. Stewart, "Alain LeRoy Locke at Oxford," *Journal of Blacks in Higher Education* 31 (spring 2001): 112, 117.
24. *Alain Locke: Reflections on a Modern Renaissance Man,* ed. Russell J. Linnemann (Baton Rouge: Louisiana State University, 1982), 31.
25. Locke, quoted in Henry Louis Gates Jr., and Cornel West, *The African-American Century: How Black Americans Have Shaped Our Country* (New York: Simon & Schuster, 2000), 238.
26. Darwin Turner, "Cullen, Countee" *Dictionary of American Biography* (New York: Scribner's 1974), Supplement Four, 200–201.
27. Gates and West, *African-American Century,* 238.
28. I do not know if Baldwin ever put this quote in print; it was relayed to me by Richard Newman.
29. Van Wyck Brooks, quoted in Barry Werth, *The Scarlet Professor: Newton Arvin: A Literary Life Shattered by Scandal* (New York: Doubleday, 2001), 14–21, 141.
30. Ibid., 40–41, 56; Michael Berthold, "Newton Arvin," *Dictionary of Literary Biography* (Detroit: Gale, 1988) no. 100: 12–13.
31. Ibid., 165; Gerald Clarke, *Capote: A Biography* (New York: Simon & Schuster, 1988), 111.
32. Werth, *The Scarlet Professor,* 35, 299.
33. Barry Werth, "The Scarlet Professor," *New Yorker* (5 October 1998), 36.
34. Michael Berthold, "Newton Arvin," *Dictionary of Literary Biography,* 14–15.
35. Werth, *The Scarlet Professor,* 76; Berthold, "Arvin," 18.
36. Werth, *The Scarlet Professor* 3, 102, 109–110.
37. Truman Capote, quoted in Werth, *The Scarlet Professor,* 102–103.
38. Werth, "The Scarlet Professor," *New Yorker,* 60–61; Werth, *The Scarlet Professor,* 105.
39. Werth, *The Scarlet Professor,* 143, 155, 228; Werth, "The Scarlet Professor," *New Yorker,* 67.
40. Robert W. Merry, *Taking on the World: Joseph and Stewart Alsop—Guardians of the American Century* (New York: Penguin, 1996), 361.
41. George Stephanopoulos, "Glory," *New York Times Book Review* (30 Dec. 2001), 17.
42. Merry, *Taking on the World,* xx, 55.
43. Berlin, quoted in Merry, *Taking on the World,* 360, 361.
44. Merry, *Taking on the World,* 361–363.
45. Ibid., 204, 320, 329, 330, 363.
46. Gore Vidal, *Sexually Speaking,* ed. Donald Weise (San Francisco: Cleis Press, 1999), 207.
47. Gore Vidal, *United States: Essays* (New York: Random House, 1993), 345.
48. Ibid., 344.
49. John Loughery, *The Other Side of Silence: Men's Lives and Gay Identities—A 20th-Century History* (New York: Henry Holt, 1998), 187.
50. Vidal, *United States,* 343.
51. Mark A. Graves, "Burns, John Horne," *The Gay and Lesbian Literary Heritage,* ed. Claude J. Summers (New York: Henry Holt, 1995), 119–120.
52. Vidal, *United States,* 343.
53. Ibid., 345–346.
54. James H. Jones, *Alfred C. Kinsey* (New York: Norton, 1997), 140–141.
55. Ibid., 163, 167, 169, 170, 171.
56. Ibid., 530–531.
57. Ibid., xvii, 4, 772.
58. Richard Rhodes, "Father of the Sexual Revolution," *New York Times Book Review* (2 Nov. 1997), 10–11.
59. Robert Rosenstone, quoted in Shand-Tucci, *Harvard,* 129.
60. Peter Davison, *The Fading Smile: Poets in Boston, 1955–1960, from Robert Frost to Robert Lowell to Sylvia Plath* (New York: Knopf, 1994), 11.

61. Ibid., 11, 12.
62. Brad Gooch, *City Poet: The Life and Times of Frank O'Hara* (New York: Knopf, 1993), 318.
63. Ibid., 318–319.
64. Sybil Gordon Kantor, *Alfred H. Barr, Jr., and the Intellectual Origins of the Museum of Modern Art* (Cambridge: MIT Press, 2002), 4.
65. Meredith L. Clausen, *Pieto Belluschi* (Cambridge: MIT Press, 1994), 223.
66. David Lehman, *The Last Avant-Garde: The Making of the New York School of Poets* (New York: Anchor, 1999), 50.
67. Gooch, *City Poet*, 31, 47.
68. Ibid., 48.
69. O'Hara, quoted in Gooch, *City Poet*, 64, 66.
70. Gooch, *City Poet*, 87.
71. Ibid., 101–102.
72. Lehman, *The Last Avant-Garde*, 49.
73. Gooch, *City Poet*, 100.
74. Lehman, *The Last Avant-Garde*, 92.
75. Ibid., 53.
76. Gooch, *City Poet*, 138.
77. Ibid., 122–123.
78. Koch, quoted in Lehman, *The Last Avant-Garde*, 50–51.
79. English, quoted in Gooch, *City Poet*, 123, 135.
80. Ibid., 163. The Silver Dollar is called The Gulch in O'Hara's novel. See also Gooch, *City Poet*, 153, for "Memorial Day, 1950," which Ashbery thought highly of, in which the Silver Dollar figures. "The 4th of July" remains unpublished.
81. Gooch, *City Poet*, 115, 121; Lehman, *The Last Avant-Garde*, 53.
82. Gooch, *City Poet*, 134.
83. Gooch, *City Poet*, 130; Lehman, *The Last Avant-Garde*, 54.
84. Ciardi, quoted in Gooch, *City Poet*, 127.
85. Lehman, *The Last Avant-Garde*, 336.
86. Gooch, *City Poet*, 127.
87. Lehman, *The Last Avant-Garde*, 137.
88. O'Hara, quoted in Gooch, *City Poet*, 157, 281.
89. Ibid., 218.
90. Gooch, *City Poet*, 270.
91. Ibid., 214.
92. Ibid., 205.
93. For O'Hara's work at MOMA, see Gooch, *City Poet*, 257–260.
94. O'Hara, quoted in Gooch, *City Poet*, 204.
95. Typically O'Hara, though gay, loved Scollay Square's Old Howard burlesque theater, which he always associated with his close friend, the poet Bunny Lang, who, though the Social Register daughter of the onetime organist of Kings Chapel in Boston, once did a famous gig there as a chorus girl.
96. Gooch, *City Poet*, 194–195.
97. Lehman, *The Last Avant-Garde*, 165, 166, 167.
98. Lehman, *The Last Avant-Garde*, 165; Gooch, *City Poet*, 221, 250–251.
99. Gooch, *City Poet*, 435.
100. Ibid., 9.
101. Ibid., 331, 336.
102. Ibid., 349, 364.
103. Ibid., 330, 362.
104. Ibid., 254.
105. Edward Gorey, *The Listing Attic* (New York/Boston: Duell, Sloan, and Pearce/Little, Brown, 1953).

106. Gorey, quoted in Karen Wilkin, *Ascending Peculiarity: Edward Gorey on Edward Gorey* (New York: Harcourt, 2001), 110, 123.
107. Gooch, *City Poet*, 115, 116, 133.
108. Gorey, quoted in Wilkin, *Ascending Peculiarity*, 102, 103.
109. Ibid., 102, 118, 119, 148, 149.
110. Ibid., x, xii, 96, 98.
111. Ibid., 96, 98, 115.
112. Dyer, quoted in Wilkin, *Ascending Peculiarity*, 116.
113. Lehman, *Avant-Garde*, 7; Gooch, *City Poet*, 115.
114. Lehman, *The Last Avant-Garde*, 13.
115. Ashbery, quoted in Gooch, *City Poet*, 115.
116. Ibid.
117. Lehman, *The Last Avant-Garde*, 6–7.
118. The lecture was published: John Ashbery, *Other Traditions* (Cambridge: Harvard University Press, 2000).
119. Ibid., 80, 84.
120. Ibid., 5, 84.
121. Gregory Woods, *A History of Gay Literature: The Male Tradition* (New Haven: Yale University Press, 1998), 387.
122. Vendler, quoted in Lehman, *The Last Avant-Garde*, 157.
123. Ashbery, *Traditions*, 159 n. 24.
124. Karen Wilkin, "Mr. Earbrass Jots Down a Few Visual Notes: The World of Edward Gorey," in Clifford Ross and Karen Wilkin, *The Word of Edward Gorey* (New York: Abrams, 1996), 81; Gooch, *City Poet*, 139.
125. David Lehman, "The Avant-Garde," *Boston Sunday Globe* (21 July 1996), sec. N, p. 16.
126. See Carmine Esposito, "Kerouac, Jack," and Scott McLemee, "Ginsberg, Allen," both in *The Gay and Lesbian Literary Heritage*, ed. Claude J. Summers (New York: Henry Holt, 1995), 331, 420–421.
127. Ted Morgan, *Literary Outlaw* (New York: Holt, 1988), 57–58.
128. Ibid., 57–58.
129. Ibid., 63, 65.
130. The theme of rejection is pervasive in Burroughs's life.
131. William S. Burroughs, *Junkie* (New York: Penguin, 1977).
132. Gary Susman, "The Last Beat," *Boston Phoenix* (5 August 1997), 5.
133. Ibid., 6.
134. Ibid., 5; interview John Sturrock, M.D., July 1999.
135. Barry Miles, *Ginsberg* (New York: Simon & Schuster, 1989), 346.
136. Miles, *Ginsberg*, 276–279. Miles sets this scene very generally—"at Leary's comfortable house on Beacon Street in Boston" (pp. 276–279); in his own memoir, *Flashbacks*, Leary is more specific, locating these events in "a three-story mansion on a hill . . . [with] 185 stone steps up to the front door" (pp. 36, 46–50) in Newton Center, a Boston suburban neighborhood through which Beacon Street continues from the intown Back Boy neighborhood. See also *Selected Poetry of Amy Lowell*, eds. Melissa Bradshaw, and Adrienne Munich (New Brunswick, N.J.: Rutgers University Press, 2002), xxxiii, xxxvi, xxxvii.
137. Miles, *Ginsberg*, 305, 339–340.
138. Carol Brightman, *Writing Dangerously* (New York: Clarkson-Potter, 1992), 474–475, 478–479, 480.
139. Roger Kimball, Ginsberg/Burroughs obituary, *Wall Street Journal* (August 1997), 17.
140. Miles, *Ginsberg*, 532.
141. Susman, "Beat," 4.
142. *Conversations with William S. Burroughs*, ed. Allen Hibbaw (Jackson: University of Mississippi, 1979), 134.
143. Susman, "Beat," 5.

6: "FOXY GRANDPA'S" PERSPECTIVE: *Transcontinental Homophile*

1. Adrian Cathcart, "Queer for Justice," unpublished manuscript, collection of Joseph McGrath, 125. Another copy of the manuscript, which I have not seen, is in the collection of the Boston Athenaeum. So discursive, opinionated, and episodic as to be unpublishable, it is nonetheless reliable when the author recalls the subject of Townsend. For Cathcart (aka John Keatney), see Stephen Nonack's report in the reference department, *Boston Athenaeum: Reports for 2000* (Boston: The Athenaeum, 2000), 91–92.
2. Ibid., 36, 39, 40.
3. Harvard College Class of 1918, *Fortieth Anniversary Report* (Cambridge: The University, 1958), 212. 1958), 211; Cathcart, "Queer," 36.
4. Joseph McGrath, interview by the author, June–July, 2001.
5. Charles Shively, "Prescott Townsend," *Gay Pioneers*, typescript identified only by date (1 October 2000), in the collection of Joseph McGrath, 2–3.
6. Cathcart, "Queer," 118; Randy Wicker, "Boston's Bohemian Blueblood," *Gay*; undated loose copy, collection of Joseph McGrath, 9.
7. *Harvard College Class of 1918, Fiftieth Report* (Cambridge: The University, 1968), 614. See also Freshman Register, Harvard University Archives; Cathcart, "Queer," 12, 78.
8. Cathcart, "Queer," appendix.
9. Townsend, quoted in Cathcart, "Queer," appendix.
10. Harvard College Class of 1918, *Fortieth Anniversary Report* (Cambridge: The University, 1958), 212.
11. Harvard College Class of 1918, Thirtieth Anniversary Report (Cambridge: The University, 1948), 304.
12. Harvard College Class of 1918, *Fortieth Anniversary Report* (Cambridge: The University, 1958), 211.
13. Cathcart, "Queer," 33, 136.
14. Ibid., 34, 35.
15. John Malcolm Brinnin, *The Third Rose: Gertrude Stein and Her World* (Boston: Little, Brown, 1959), 289; Lucius Beebe, *Boston and the Boston Legend* (New York: Appleton-Century, 1936), 303, 305, 314.
16. Beebe, *Boston Legend*, 306.
17. Ibid.
18. B. Hughes Morris, interview by the author, January–October 2001.
19. Jean Gould, *Amy* (New York: Dodd, Mead, 1975), 95. See also Douglass Shand-Tucci, "Gothic Modernist," unpublished manuscript (Volume 2 of *Ralph Adams Cram: Life and Architecture*). The manuscript is on deposit in the Archives of the Massachusetts Historical Society and available to be read without restriction.
20. Beebe, *Boston Legend*, 308; Cathcart, "Queer," 27; map of Barn complex, Harvard Theatre Collection.
21. Beebe, *Boston Legend*, 306–307; Cathcart, "Queer," 90–93. In a program for the 1924–1925 season, Townsend and Huntington are listed as two of eight trustees of the Boston Stage Society; the others: Lawrence J. Bottom, Sally White, and William Bard Johnstone, Creighton Hill, Irene Cushing, and Raymon McCully). Advertisements note seven businesses in the Barn complex: The Saracen's Head (a tearoom), the Barn Book Shop, Kendall Northrop (interior decorating), Sally White (gowns and costumes), Josef Woitowicz (photgrapher to Harvard, Radcliffe, and Wellesley College dramatic clubs), William Wilson (dance instruction), and the Barn Print Shop.
22. File of miscellaneous clippings about the Sacco-Vanzetti protest, in which both Huntington and Millay arise, Huntington Papers, Harvard Theatre Collection, Houghton Library.
23. Beebe, *Boston Legend*, 309.
24. For Jaroslav Kvapil's life and work, see entries under Kvapil in *The New Grove Dictionary of Opera*, ed. Stanley Sadie (London: Routledge, 1994) and *Enciclopedia dello*

Spettacolo, ed. Silvio d'Amico (Rome: Casa Editrice Le Maschere, 1959). For Baker, see "Edward Massey," loose clipping (marked *Post,* March 27). Other such include "Negro spirituals" (marked *Globe,* 1/19/25) and "Remodeled Stable" (p. 3, 1923, otherwise unidentified). All in Huntington Papers, Harvard Theatre Collection. Membership secretary to B. F. Dow, 16 June 1926. See also "The Boston Stage Society," loose clipping marked "*New Yorker,* 1926, 18." Huntington Papers, Harvard Theatre Collection.

25. The history of theater in Provincetown is confusing: the first Wharf Theatre of 1915, now world renowned, was a wreck by the mid-twenties; the Wharf Players Theatre which succeeded it in 1923 was destroyed in a 1939 storm; the Boston-based New England Repertory Company of Huntington replaced it the next year, in 1940, and was called the Provincetown Playhouse on the Wharf, quite a significant theater in its own right, having mounted premieres by both Tennessee Williams and Edward Albee. It was sold in 1973, however, and did not survive a 1977 fire. For the Watson/Suleski interview, see *The Harvard Gay and Lesbian Review* (spring 1999), 41.

26. Cathcart, "Queer," 29.

27. Scott Donaldson, *John Cheever* (New York: Random House, 1988), 45–46

28. *The Letters of John Cheever* ed. Benjamn Cheever (New York: Simon and Schuster, 1986), 29.

29. Donaldson, *Cheever,* 50.

30. Cathcart, "Queer," 26.

31. Shively, "Townsend," 9.

32. Wicker, "Blueblood," 9; see also Cathcart, "Queer," 125.

33. *Harvard College Class of 1918, Twentieth Report* (Cambridge: The University, 1938), 147.

34. *Harvard College Class of 1918, Forty-Fifth Report* (Cambridge: The University, 1963), 193.

35. Ricard, quoted in Cathcart, "Queer," 111, 194.

36. John Waters, *Shock Value* (New York: Thunder's Mouth, 1995), 48.

37. Cathcart, "Queer," 168–169. History Project, *Improper Bostonians* (Boston: Beacon, 1998) cites a report of Townsend's arrest and trial as appearing in the *Mid-town Journal* (29 Jan. 1943), n.p.

38. Ibid., 2, 19; Joseph McGrath, interview by the author, June 2001.

39. Harvard College Class of 1918, *Forty-Fifth Anniversary Report* (Cambridge: The University, 1963), 193.

40. Harvard College Class of 1918, *Fortieth Anniversary Report* (Cambridge: The University, 1958), 212; *Fiftieth Anniversary Report* (1968), 614.

41. John D'Emilio, *Sexual Politics, Sexual Communities* (Chicago: University of Chicago Press, 1983), 83; *Improper Bostonians,* 196.

42. A complete file of the *Boston Mattachine Newsletter* is in the Boston Athenaeum.

43. Shively, "Townsend," 11.

44. Stephen Donaldson, "Homosexual Movement," *Encyclopedia of Homosexuality,* ed. Wayne R. Dynes (New York: Garland, 1990), 840, 842, 843.

45. Brett Beemyn, and Gregory Conerly, "Chronology," *St. James Press Gay and Lesbian Almanac,* ed. Neil Schlager (Detroit: St. James, 1998), 6; see also Martin Duberman, *Stonewall* (New York: Penguin, 1993), 99, 100, 106–109.

46. Beemyn and Conerly, "Chronology," 96; John D'Emilio, *Sexual Politics, Sexual Communities,* 158–159. Footage by Townsend of the event was included in the Andrew Meyer film "An Early Clue to the New Direction."

47. John Loughery, *The Other Side of Silence* (New York: Henry Holt, 1998), 267–270.

48. Cathcart, "Queer," 167, 176.

49. Townsend, quoted in Wicker, "Blueblood," 10; Cathcart, "Queer," 176.

50. Townsend, quoted in Wicker, "Blueblood," 9, 13.

51. *Boston Mattachine Newsletter,* passim, Boston Athenaeum. This point of view, and Townsend's "Snowflake" theory particularly, is discussed in Cathcart, "Queer."

52. Cathcart, "Queer," 145–148; Joseph McGrath, interview by the author, June 2001.

53. Ibid., 55; I myself can document the truth of Cathcart's anecdote.
54. Douglas M. Davis, "Out of a Midwestern Showcase," *National Observer* (20 March 1967), 17.
55. Cathcart, "Queer," 85–86; B. Hughes Morris, interview by the author, May 2000.
56. Cathcart, "Queer," 52, 58, 63, 119; interview Joseph McGrath; my own reminiscences.
57. Shively, "Townsend," 13; Cathcart, "Queer," 122, 149.
58. *Francesco Clemente: A Portrait*, Photography by Luca Babini, essay by René Ricard (New York: Aperture, 1999), dust jacket blurb. See also Reva Wolf, *Andy Warhol* (Chicago: University of Chicago Press, 1997), 121–122; René Ricard, *Trusty Sacophagus Co* (New York: Inanout Press, 1990), bib notes.
59. "Art," *New Yorker* (14 May 1990); see also Janet Malcolm, "A Girl of the Zeitgeist," *New Yorker* (20 October 1986), 60.
60. Cathcart, "Queer," 257.
61. *The Andy Warhol Diaries*, ed. Pat Hackett (New York: Warner, 1989), 484, 551.
62. Cathcart, "Queer," 64.
63. Ibid., 87.
64. Ibid., 87–88.
65. Ibid., 45, 185. Interviews, Messrs. Creeley, Lansing, Corbett.
66. Stephen Jonas, *Selected Poems*, ed. Joseph Torra (Hoboken, N.J.: Talisman House, 1994), 3; Allen Ginsberg, back cover; Cathcart, "Queer," 84.
67. Brad Gooch, *City Poet* (New York: Knopf, 1993), 279.
68. Torra, introduction to Jonas's *Selected Poems*, 4.
69. Gerrit Lansing, introduction to Part One, Jonas's *Selected Poems*, 20.
70. William Corbett, back cover of Jonas's *Selected Poems*.
71. Torra, introduction to Jonas's *Selected Poems*, 6.
72. Ibid., 3.
73. Ibid., 1.
74. Ibid., 8.
75. Lewis Ellingham and Kevin Killian, unpublished manuscript, quoted by Torra, introduction to Jonas's *Selected Poems*, 4.
76. Torra, *Jonas*, 237, 238, 239.
77. Shively, "Townsend," 9–19.
78. Cathcart, "Queer," appendix.
79. 15 Lindall Place has a new interior; 75 Phillips Street was torn down.
80. Jonas, "Poem XXXIII," *Selected Poems*, 237, 238.
81. Cathcart, "Queer," 2.
82. Ibid., 232.
83. I knew Perry at Lindall Place and later at Eliot House. He was a close friend of Joe McGrath.

7: FINALE: *Boston, New York, Washington—A Rumor of Angels*

1. Martha Nussbaum, "Why Gay Studies? The Softness of Reason: A Classical Case for Gay Studies," *New Republic* (13 July 1992), 26–33.
2. Ethan Bronner, "Study of Sex," *New York Times* (28 December 1997), 1, 14.
3. Douglass Shand-Tucci, *Harvard University: An Architectural Tour* (New York: Princeton Architectural Press, 2001).
4. Dudley Clendinen and Adam Nagourney, *Out for Good* (New York: Simon and Schuster, 1999), 125; Nancy Walker, "The Iconoclast"; Frank Kameny, "The Very Mad Scientist," 97; *Making History: The Struggle for Gay and Lesbian Equal Rights, 1945–1990*, ed. Eric Marcus (New York: HarperCollins, 1992), 293–304, 93–103.
5. Michael Bronski, *Culture Clash: The Making of Gay Sensibility* (Boston: South End Press, 1984), 151.
6. Clendinen and Nagourney, *Out for Good*, 125.
7. Humphrey Burton, *Leonard Bernstein* (New York: Doubleday, 1994), 94.

8. Clendinen and Nagourney, *Out for Good*, 313.

9. Joseph McGrath, interview by the author, April 2002.

10. Fred Kaplan, *Gore Vidal* (New York: Random House, 1999), 726–727.

11. Clendinen and Nagourney, *Out for Good*, 126, 312–316.

12. David W. Dunlap, "John Boswell . . . ," *New York Times* (25 December 1994), 44.

13. Ibid., 44. Boswell also had his activist side and lectured while at Harvard for the Gay Speakers Bureau.

14. Martin Duberman, *Cures: A Gay Man's Odyssey* (New York: Penguin, 1991), 163; Paul Russell "Martin Duberman," *The Gay 100* (New York: Citadel Press, 1995), 293.

15. Ibid., 294.

16. Gore Vidal, *Sexually Speaking* (San Francisco: Cleis Press, 1999), 230.

17. Andrew Tobias, "Gay Like Me," *Harvard Magazine* (January–February 1998), 53, 54, 56.

18. Ibid., 53.

19. Clendinen and Nagourney, *Out for Good*, 129.

20. Tobias, quoted in David Brudnoy, "On the Tobias Phenomenon," *Bay Windows* (27 November 1998), 45.

21. Charles Kaiser, *The Gay Metropolis, 1940–1996* (Boston: Houghton Mifflin, 1997), 138.

22. Kameny, quoted in Edmund White, *States of Desire: Travels in Gay America* (New York: E. P. Dutton, 1980), 350.

23. Ibid., 297, 300.

24. Ibid., 328.

25. Clendinen and Nagourney, *Out for Good*, 114, 117.

26. Kameny, quoted in Clendinen and Nagourney, *Out for Good*, 113–114.

27. Clendinen and Nagourney, *Out for Good*, 199–217.

28. Claude J. Summers, "Hall, Richard," *The Gay and Lesbian Literary Heritage*, ed. Claude J. Summers (New York: Henry Holt, 1995), 356.

29. Bruce Bawer, *Diminishing Fictions: Essays on the Modern American Novel and Its Critics* (St. Paul: Graywolf, 1988), 241.

30. Ibid., 243.

31. Ibid., 244.

32. Caleb Crain, "Stormin' Norman," *The New York Time Book Review* (19 December 1999), 7.

33. Thomas E. Crooks interview, January 1998.

34. Roger Brown, *Against My Better Judgment: An Intimate Memoir of an Eminent Gay Psychologist* (New York: Haworth Press, 1996), 180.

35. Ibid., 72–73.

36. Jerome Bruner, pre-publication review pamphlet (Haworth Press), unpaginated.

37. Brown, *Against My Better Judgment*, 252–253.

38. Philip S. Holzman, pre-publication pamphlet (Haworth Press), undated, unpaginated.

39. Andrew Holleran, "My Harvard," *The Best of the Harvard Gay and Lesbian Review*, ed. Richard Schneider, Jr. (Philadelphia: Temple University Press, 1997), 4, 18. The article originally appeared in the Winter 1994 number.

40. Andrew Holleran, "My Harvard," *Our Harvard*, ed. Jeffrey L. Lant (New York: Taplinger, 1982), 251, 252. The first version of Holleran's article which in its final and different form appeared in *The Harvard Gay and Lesbian Review* in 1994.

41. Ibid., 253. Holleran, Roman Catholic, dropped the reference to angels twelve years later in the final version.

8: YARD AND RIVER: BETWEEN *PATHÉTIQUE* AND *BRIDESHEAD*

1. Robert Drake, *The Gay Canon: Great Books Every Gay Man Should Read* (New York: Anchor, 1998).

2. Anthony Holden, *Tchaikovsky* (New York: Viking, 1995), 100.

3. Roland John Wiley, "Tchaikovsky, Pyotr Ilych," *The New Grove Dictionary of Music and Musicians*, ed. Stanley Sadie (London: Macmillan, 2001), 161–162.

4. Herbert Weinstock and Wallace Brockway, *Men of Music* (New York: Simon and Schuster, 1939), 510.

5. Holden, *Tchaikovsky*, 100.

6. Wiley, "Tchaikovsky," 147.

7. Holden, *Tchaikovsky*, 82.

8. Timothy L. Jackson, *Tchaikovsky Symphony no. 6 (Pathétique)* (Cambridge, U.K.: Cambridge University Press, 1999), 14.

9. Holden, *Tchaikovsky*, 55.

10. Ibid., 81, 82.

11. Ibid., 73.

12. David Brown, *Tchaikovsky* (London: Gollancz, 4 volumes: 1978, 1982, 1986, 1991), II: 195.

13. Humphrey Carpenter, *W. H. Auden: A Biography* (Boston: Houghton Mifflin, 1981), 137, 141, 341, 347–348.

14. Peter Kadziz, interview by the author, April 2001 and June 2002. See also Gore Vidal, *Palimpsest* (New York: Penguin, 1995), 92.

15. Carpenter, *W. H. Auden*, 262.

16. Ibid., 316–317.

17. Ibid., 353.

18. Holden, *Tchaikovsky*, 230–232.

19. Ibid., 121–150.

20. Ibid., 171.

21. Brown, *Tchaikovsky*, I: 164.

22. Ibid., II: 163.

23. Holden, *Tchaikovsky*, 104–105.

24. Ibid., 78.

25. Ibid., 206.

26. The best discussion of Tchaikovsky's career in this period is in Holden, *Tchaikovsky*, 98–117.

27. Ellen Knight, *Charles Martin Loeffler: A Life Apart in American Music* (Chicago: University of Illinois Press, 1993), 86.

28. Richard Dyer, "A Critic Looks at a Century of Music," *Boston Globe Magazine* (18 October 1981), 10.

29. Elliott W. Galkin, *A History of Orchestral Conducting: In Theory and Practice* (New York: Pendragon Press, 1988), 639, 647, 739.

30. Ibid., 643.

31. Ibid.

32. Wiley, "Tchaikovsky," 919.

33. H. Earle Johnson, *Symphony Hall, Boston* (Boston: Little, Brown, 1950), 56. For the BSO's Tchaikovsky performances, see 390–392.

34. Holden, *Tchaikovsky*, 304.

35. *The Harvard Musical Association* (Boston: Harvard Musical Association, 1992), 9–13.

36. For a discussion of the relationship of such terms as *aesthete* or *decadent* to homosexuality, see Douglass Shand-Tucci, *Boston Bohemia* (Amherst: University of Massachusetts Press, 1994), 182, 240.

37. Jonathan Ned Katz, *Gay/Lesbian Almanac* (New York: Harper & Row, 1983), 258–265.

38. "Saunterings," *Town Topics* (12 November 1896), 10.

39. Mark A. De Wolfe Howe, *The Boston Symphony Orchestra, 1881–1931* (Boston: Houghton Mifflin, 1931), 63.

40. Weinstock and Brockway, *Men of Music*, 527.

41. Holden, *Tchaikovsky*, 114.

42. Ibid., 131.

43. Brown, *Tchaikovsky*, IV: 471.

44. Holden, *Tchaikovsky*, 309.

45. See Carson McCullers, *The Ballad of the Sad Café* (New York: Bantam, 1971), 26.
46. Tchaikovsky, quoted in Holden, *Tchaikovsky*, 332.
47. A reproduction of Wilde's holograph, otherwise unattributed, was sent to me by Mr. Louis Caldarella.
48. Brown, *Tchaikovsky*, IV: 458.
49. Galkin, *Orchestral Conducting*, 643; Holden, *Tchaikovsky*, 339.
50. Johnson, *Symphony Hall*, 49.
51. Daniel Gregory Mason, "At Harvard in the Nineties," *New England Quarterly* (March 1936), 46.
52. Ibid., 43, 47–48.
53. Ibid., 48–49.
54. Ibid., 65, 67, 58.
55. Ibid., 48.
56. Weinstock and Brockway, *Men of Music*, 528.
57. Nicholas E. Tawa, *From Psalm to Symphony* (Boston: Northeastern University Press, 2001), 263, 264. For the effect of Wilde's death in Boston, see Shand-Tucci, *Boston Bohemia*, 423–425. See also the discussions in this study of H. H. Schaff's and Amy Lowell's post–Wilde scandal work.
58. [Philip Hale], *Great Concert Music*, ed. John N. Burk (New York: Garden City Publishing Co., 1935), 350.
59. Eve Kosofsky Sedgwick, *Between Men: English Literature and Male Homosocial Desire* (New York: Columbia University Press, 1985), 94.
60. Douglas Murray, *Bosie: A Biography of Lord Alfred Douglas* (New York: Hyperion, 2000), 35–36.
61. Hale, *Great Concert Music*, 351.
62. Ibid., 350.
63. Shand-Tucci, *Boston Bohemia*, 457.
64. Mason, "Harvard," 66.
65. John McCormick, *George Santayana: A Biography* (New York: Paragon, 1987), 97.
66. Shaun O'Connell, *Imagining Boston: A Literary Landscape* (Boston: Beacon Press, 1990), 37.
67. Louis Menand, *The Metaphyiscal Club* (New York: Farrar, Straus & Giroux, 2001), xi.
68. Robert M. Crunden, *American Salons: Encounters with European Modernism, 1885–1917* (New York: Oxford University Press, 1993), 41, 43, 44, 47.
69. Ibid., 43, 56.
70. Humphrey Burton, *Leonard Bernstein* (New York: Doubleday, 1994), 74; Dyer, "Critic," 12.
71. Galkin, *Orchestral Conducting*, 723. See also Moses Smith, *Koussevitzky* (New York: Allen, Towne & Heath, 1947), 32.
72. David Mermelstein, "A Battle for the New American Music," *New York Times* (9 May 1999), 20.
73. Smith, *Koussevitzky*, 38, 50, 119, 160.
74. Anthony Tommasini, *Virgil Thomson: Composer on the Aisle* (New York: Norton, 1997), 270–271.
75. Hugo Leichtentritt, *Serge Koussevitzky, the Boston Symphony Orchestra and the New American Music* (Cambridge: Harvard University Press, 1946), 155.
76. For the infatuation of Emerson and Martin Gay, see chapter 1, 15–20.
77. Tommasini, *Virgil Thomson*, 56.
78. Ibid., 354, 371.
79. Ibid., 69.
80. Ibid., 109, 110.
81. Ibid., 110, 111, 120.
82. Ibid., 88, 107; Ned Rorem, *A Ned Rorem Reader* (New Haven: Yale University Press, 2001), 226.
83. Tommasini, *Virgil Thomson*, 144–147, 149, 537, 539.

84. Ibid., 146, 509, 511.
85. Richard S. Kennedy, *Dreams in the Mirror: A Biography of E. E. Cummings* (New York: Liveright, 1980), 78–79.
86. Ibid., 99.
87. Tommasini, *Virgil Thomson*, 82.
88. Lincoln Kirstein, *Mosaic: Memoirs* (New York: Farrar, Straus & Giroux, 1994), 109, 112.
89. Tommasini, *Virgil Thomson*, 165.
90. Ibid., 135, 136–137.
91. Ibid., 159, 168.
92. Rorem, *A Ned Rorem Reader*, 227.
93. Tommasini, *Virgil Thomson*, 201.
94. Ibid., 236–239.
95. Ibid., 225.
96. Ibid., 37, 226–227.
97. Ibid., 37.
98. Ibid., 265.
99. The critic Corinne Blackmer particularly comes to mind.
100. John Ashbery, *Other Traditions* (Cambridge: Harvard University Press, 200), 78.
101. Gertrude Stein, *The Autobiography of Alice B. Toklas* (New York: Avon, 1977), 105. See also John M. Brinnin, *The Third Rose* (Reading, Mass.: Addison-Wesley, 1987), 29.
102. Tommasini, *Virgil Thomson*, 491–492.
103. Ibid., 227, 425–427.
104. Rorem, *A Ned Rorem Reader*, 231, 237.
105. Ibid., 205.
106. Copland, quoted in Tommasini, *Virgil Thomson*, 349.
107. Joan Peyser, *Bernstein* (New York: Morrow, 1987), 54.
108. Howard Pollack, *Aaron Copland: The Life and Work of an Uncommon Man* (Chicago: University of Illinois Press, 2000), 235. See also Tommasini, *Virgil Thomson*, 71.
109. Pollack, *Aaron Copland*, 235, 248.
110. Ibid., 236.
111. Ibid., 238.
112. Ibid., 526: Rorem, *A Ned Rorem Reader*, 236.
113. Pollack, *Aaron Copland*, 469–478.
114. Ibid., 520.
115. Rosenfeld, quoted in ibid., 521.
116. Pollack, *Copland,* 523, 524.
117. Taruskin, quoted in ibid., 589.
118. Richard Taruskin, quoted in Pollack, *Copland,* 531. The original article appeared in *The New York Times* of 22 August 1993. As for the letter from a St. Botolph Club member, I prefer not to identify the writer but the letter is part of a file in my papers, open to the public at the Massachusetts Historical Society.
119. Pollack, *Aaron Copland*, 524, 554.
120. Dyer, "Critic," 11.
121. Charles Schwartz, *Gershwin* (Cambridge: Da Capo, 1990).
122. Pollack, *Aaron Copland*, 123.
123. Burton, *Bernstein*, 18, 34, 35, 44, 47–48, 50–51.
124. Ibid., 36–37; Meryle Secrest, *Leonard Bernstein: A Life* (New York: Alfred A. Knopf, 1994), 48, 51.
125. Burton, *Leonard Bernstein*, 53–54.
126. Bernstein, in Vivian Perlis, "An Interview with Vivian Perlis," *Leonard Bernstein: The Harvard Years*, ed. Claudia Swan (New York: Eos Orchestra, 1999), 21.
127. Ibid., 19.
128. Ibid., 21–23.

129. Perlis, "Interview," 23; Joan Peyser, *Bernstein: A Biography* (New York: Morrow, 1987), 13, 96.
130. Harold Shapero, "Lenny at Harvard," *Leonard Bernstein: The Harvard Years*, 52; Burton, *Bernstein*, 59.
131. Burton, *Leonard Bernstein*, 82.
132. Peyser, *Bernstein*, 156.
133. Tommasini, *Virgil Thomson*, 270.
134. Nicholas E. Tawa, *From Psalm to Symphony* (Boston: Northeastern University Press, 2001), 372. Fine was not blackballed after all. The year Piston resigned, 1945, Fine was elected. He remained a member, however, for only five years (although he taught in the Boston area all of his life), and Piston, a member since 1928, never rejoined the HMA after his resignation, although he, too, continued teaching in the Boston area and remained professionally but not socially involved with the HMA.
135. Galkin, *Orchestral Conducting*, 625.
136. Burton, *Leonard Bernstein*, 156.
137. Paul Moore, "Remembering Lenny," *Harvard Gay and Lesbian Review* (summer and fall issues, 1994), 17.
138. Burton, *Leonard Bernstein*, 158; Peyser, *Bernstein*, 197, 198.
139. Burton, *Leonard Bernstein*, 167.
140. James R. Oestreich, "The Maestro Defies Convention Even in Death," *New York Times* (17 December 2000), 38.
141. David Mermelstein, "Measuring a Maestro," *New Yorker* (17 August 1990), 42–43.
142. David Denby, "The Trouble with Lenny," *New Yorker* (17 August 1990), 42–43.
143. Burton, *Leonard Bernstein*, 530.
144. Martin Bernheimer, "Perpetual Promise," *Opera News* (July 2000), 30.
145. "Bernstein, Leonard," *The New Grove Dictionary of Music and Musicians*, ed. Stanley Sadie (New York: Grove, 2001), vol. 2, 445–449.
146. Charles Kaiser, *The Gay Metropolis, 1940–1996* (New York: Harcourt Brace, 1997), 89.
147. Ibid., 91.
148. Ibid., 89–94.
149. Ibid., 93.
150. Ibid., 93.
151. Ibid., 93–94.
152. Burton, *Leonard Bernstein*, 276.
153. Ibid., 410–415.
154. Ibid., 196, 405, 421, 489; Galkin, *Orchestral Conducting*, 723, 346.
155. Smith, *Koussevitzky*, 346, 1L; Burton, *Leonard Bernstein*, 196.
156. Burton, *Leonard Bernstein*, 150.
157. Ibid., 473.
158. Peyser, *Bernstein*, 79.
159. Burton, *Leonard Bernstein*, 140, 142; Peyser, *Bernstein* 145–146, 311.
160. Burton's description of Bernstein's private life is the best.
161. Burton, *Leonard Bernstein*, 399, 437.
162. Ibid., 405, 431, 436, 439, 447.
163. Bernheimer, "Promise," 30–31; Burton, *Leonard Bernstein*, 439.
164. Denby, "Lenny," *New Yorker*, 42–53.
165. Burton, *Leonard Bernstein*, 505.
166. Solomon Volkov, *St. Petersburg* (New York: Simon and Schuster, 1995), 115.
167. Burton, *Leonard Bernstein*, 405.
168. Ibid., 437, 443, 444.
169. Burton, *Leonard Bernstein*, 444.
170. *By With To and From: A Lincoln Kirstein Reader*, ed. Nicholas Jenkins (New York: Farrar, Straus & Giroux, 1991), 17–19.

171. Lincoln Kirstein, *Mosaic: Memoir* (New York: Farrar, Straus & Giroux, 1994), 38, 188.
172. *By With To and From,* 248.
173. *By With To and From,* 21, 25, 42.
174. Kirstein, *Mosaic,* 86–88.
175. *By With To and From,* 21, 25.
176. Kirstein, *Mosaic.*
177. Sybil Gordon Kantor, *Alfred H. Barr, Jr., and the Intellectual Origins of the Museum of Modern Art* (Cambridge: MIT Press, 2002), 200.
178. Ibid., 126, 200.
179. Ibid., 124, 126; John Coolidge, "Harvard's Teaching of Architecture and the Fine Arts, 1928–1985," *Architectural Education in Boston,* ed. M. H. Floyd (Boston: Boston Architectural Center, 1989), 60.
180. The society's executive committee consisted of Kirstein. Walker, and Warburg, but "early on Agnes Mongan became part of this inner circle that held daily meetings at Schrafft's restaurant in Harvard Square during the winter of 1928–1929. While Walker only attended once in a while, Mongan was a constant presence" (Kantor, *Barr,* 199).
181. Alfred H. Barr Jr., "Boston Is Modern Art Pauper," *The Harvard Crimson* (30 October 1926), 1.
182. Kantor, Barr, 202.
183. Kirstein, *Mosaic,* 174.
184. Ibid., 174.
185. Kantor, *Barr,* 204.
186. Ibid., 206.
187. Kirstein, *Mosaic,* 170.
188. Ibid., 175.
189. Nicholas Fox Weber, *Patron Saints* (New Haven: Yale University Press, 1992), 94. Calder's first one-man show at MOMA didn't occur until nearly fifteen years later. Kantor judges that "including Calder in this early history of modernism was perhaps the single most important contribution of the society."
190. Ibid., 94.
191. Ibid., 57.
192. Kirstein nowhere identifies himself with either figure in the logo, so far as I know; nor does anyone else. It is wholly my surmise.
193. Kirstein, *Mosaic,* 104.
194. Henry-Russell Hitchcock, "The Architectural Work of J. J. P. Oud," *Arts* (13 February 1928), 97; Kantor, *Barr,* 194, 259; Franz Schulze, *Philip Johnson* (New York: Knopf, 1994).
195. Kantor, *Barr,* 93.
196. Fox Weber, *Patron Saints,* 15.
197. Ibid., 123.
198. Kantor, *Barr,* 97.
199. Ibid., 97.
200. Meredith L. Clausen, *Pietro Belluschi* (Cambridge: MIT Press, 1994), 223.
201. Kantor, *Barr,* 207; Fox Weber, *Patron Saints,* 112.
202. Kirstein, quoted in Nicholas Jenkins, "The Great Impresario," *New Yorker* (13 April 1998), 56.
203. Kirstein, *Mosaic,* 95.
204. Ibid., 92.
205. *By With To and From,* 38.
206. Bernstein, quoted in Tawa, *From Psalm to Symphony,* 354.
207. Sally M. Promey, *Painting Religion in Public: John Singer Sargent's Triumph of Religion at the Boston Public Library* (Princeton: Princeton University Press, 1999), 151.
208. Kirstein, *Mosaic,* 49.

209. Ibid., 183.
210. Shand-Tucci, *Boston Bohemia*, 216, 217, 227–228, 240, 435, 440, 491–492 n. 2. See the Library seal controversy (also referred to by Kirstein), 214–216.
211. *By With To and From*, xiv. For obvious reasons Kirstein did not formulate his view in print quite the same way. Indeed, more than once he implied no dynasty was a gift of independence from his father. That may be, but Young Kirstein found it a mixed blessing in the face of how attractive the mature Boston Brahmin (not the collegiate version) was to him. His attitude makes a nice comparison to Justice Brandeis, for which see Douglass Shand-Tucci, *Harvard University*, 109–110, 139.
212. Kirstein, *Mosaic*, 19, 20; Jenkins, "The Great Impresario," 50.
213. Fox Weber, *Saints*, 236; Caroline A. Jones, *Modern Art at Harvard* (New York: Abbeville Press, 1985), 48.
214. Elisabeth Sussman, "Taking a Risk"; Reinhold Heller, "The Expressionist Challenge"; *Dissent* (Boston: Institute of Contemporary Art, 1985), 5–6, 9–53.
215. Kirstein, *Mosaic*, 172.
216. Walter Muir Whitehill, *Boston in the Age of John Fitzgerald Kennedy* (Norman: University of Oklahoma Press, 1966), xii: "In so far as the world of learning today possesses a capital city, Boston with its neighboring institutions approximates to the position that Paris occupies in the Middle Ages."
217. Richard Dyer, "Now Playing, the Centennial," *Boston Globe Magazine* (8 Oct. 2001), 14. Hayes appeared with the Boston Symphony Orchestra in 1923.
218. Kirstein, *Mosaic*, 211; Richard Buckle, *Diaghilev* (New York: Athenaeum, 1979), 302–303.
219. Romola Nijinsky, *Nijinsky and the Last Years of Nijinsky* (New York: Simon and Schuster, 1980), 349.
220. Jenkins, "The Great Impresario," 56.
221. Ibid., 53.
222. Suzanne Berne, "A Boy's Life," *New York Times Book Review* (13 Aug. 2002), 13.
223. Frank Kermode, "Introduction," *Brideshead Revisited* (New York: Knopf, 1993), xiii, xviii.
224. Kermode, Ibid., xv, xvi, xviii; Waugh, *Brideshead*, 69.
225. Kermode, Ibid., xvii.
226. Kirstein, significantly, knew something of a Roman Catholic variant on the Flytes. Hester Pickman was the daughter of Margaret Chanler, a devout Roman Catholic; the Chanlers in the country had mass celebrated every Sunday by a priest sent to their home, "an Irishman from a neighboring parish. Mrs. Chanler forgave us both; for his accent and my heresy."
227. Waugh, *Brideshead*, 27–28.
228. Humphrey Carpenter, *The Brideshead Generation* (Boston: Houghton Mifflin, 1998), 114–115.
229. Kirstein, *Mosaic*, 95.
230. Ibid., 96.
231. Ibid., 97.
232. Ibid., 97.
233. Waugh, *Brideshead*, 32. See also 29–30.
234. Kirstein, *Mosaic*, 97.
235. Waugh, *Brideshead*, 65–66, 274.
236. Kirstein, *Mosaic*, 97, 98.
237. Ibid., 98–99.
238. Waugh, *Brideshead*, 67, 69–70.
239. Kirstein, *Mosaic*, 98–99.
240. Waugh, *Brideshead*, 314; Kirstein, *Mosaic*, 184.
241. Kirstein, *Mosaic*, 100.
242. Jenkins, "The Great Impresario," 48.
243. Fox Weber, *Patron Saints*, 258.

244. Peter Kadzis, interview June 2002.
245. Samuel Gilman's "Fair Harvard," was first sung in 1936 at Harvard's Tricentennial. See Samuel Eliot Morison, *Three Centuries of Harvard* (Cambridge: Harvard University Press, 1936), 268.
246. Waugh, *Brideshead*, 26.
247. Hilary Lewis and John O'Connor, *Philip Johnson: The Architect in His Own Words* (New York: Rizzoli, 1994), 45.
248. Stover Jenkins and David Mohney, *The Houses of Philip Johnson* (New York: Abbeville Press, 2001), 259.

Notes for the Illustrations

1. The illustration is from the Caproni catalogue of 1901. It is not known exactly when this Boston firm created a cast of this Hermes, but Wilde certainly did not give Harvard the original and would likely have arranged the purchase in Boston.
2. The illustration, apparently no longer extant, was in the Tavern Club archives as late as 1934 when M. A. De Wolfe Howe's *A Partial (and Not Impartial) Semi-Centennial History of the Tavern Club* was published. I photographed the Sturgis sketch and a nude photograph of the painter Dennis Miller Bunker through the courtesy of Mr. Al Walker, the Boston art dealer.
3. The topmost horizontal panel of *Saint Kavin* shows the Visionists at table in what is probably a parody of the Last Supper.
4. According to Mr. Tom Vince of Western Reserve Academy, 115 College Street, Hudson, Ohio, not just *Prometheus* but all memory of it has vanished.
5. I am told by the photographer that Philip Johnson has since painted the Kirstein tower yellow. It was previously gray.
6. In *Mosaic*, Kirstein inadvertently misleads, perhaps to assuage his sense of loss, when he reports as it turned out Nijinsky, for emotional reasons, did not dance in Boston in 1916, his understudy, Alexander Gavrilov, appearing instead. However, according to Olive Holmes in *Motion Arrested* (Middletown, Conn.: Wesleyan University Press, 1982), which reproduces reviews of and an interview with Nijinsky by the legendary *Boston Transcript* critic, H. T. Parker, though Nijinsky missed the first part of the ballet's 1916 American tour in January-February, he did not miss the second part in November, and while Gavrilov and also Adolph Bolm substituted for him in Boston in *Petrouchka* and *Le Spectre de la Rose* because of an ankle injury, Nijinsky did dance at the Boston Opera House himself that November in his famous role in *L'Après-Midi d'un Faune.* He also appeared in Boston in *Les Sylphides* and, most important, in *Till Eulenspiegel,* a new ballet he had choreographed over the summer of 1916 at a remote hotel on the Maine coast, in which he showed himself at the height of his creative power. Indeed, this was the ballet Kirstein must most have lamented missing over the years. It was not done again in the United States until 1951 in New York. See Holmes, *Motion,* 124–139.
7. For a complete discussion of Hadzi's *Omphalos,* see Douglass Shand-Tucci, *Harvard University: An Architectural Tour* (New York: Princeton Architectural Press, 2001), 65–66.

Acknowledgments for the Illustrations

BOSTON ATHENAEUM: Philip Johnson House, Cambridge, Massachusetts; Silver Dollar Bar, Downtown Boston.

BOSTON PUBLIC LIBRARY, Fine Arts Department: *Hermes* of Praxiteles (*P. P. Caproni Catalogue,* 1901).

BERTRAM GROSVENOR GOODHUE, *A Book of Architectural and Decorative Drawings* (New York: Architectural Book Publishing Company, 1914): Cram, Goodhue, and Ferguson, design for proposed First Church, Cambridge.

HARVARD UNIVERSITY, Provost's University Cultural Properties Survey, Fogg Art Museum: Randolph Hall murals.

Harvard University Handbook (Cambridge: Harvard University Press, 1936): Weld Boat House and Charlesbank Harvard; Mount Auburn Street Gold Coast.

MASSACHUSETTS HISTORICAL SOCIETY (photographs by author): Harvard Yard; Weeks Bridge; Signet Society; Eliot House; Lindall Place, Beacon Hill; Omphalos.

W. RAYMOND McCLURE, *Prometheus: Lucien Price* (Boston: Privately printed, 1965): Arthur Spear, *Prometheus.*

RICHARD PAYNE, photographer, Houston, Texas: Kirstein Tower, Philip Johnson estate, Connecticut.

Collection of the author: Boston Common; title page of Santayana's *Sonnets*; cover of *Songs from Vagabondia*; F. S. Sturgis sketch; *Saturday Evening Post* cover; *Saint Kavin* cover; Longfellow House; Commonwealth Avenue; Boston Opera House.

Collection of GEORGE ABBOTT WHITE: F. O. Matthiessen. (Used by permission.)

Collection of RANDY WICKER: Provincetownsend interior. (Used by permission.)

Index